Essentials of Criminal Procedure

Essentials of Criminal Procedure

DAVID C. BRODY
Professor of Criminal Justice
Washington State University

CAROLINA ACADEMIC PRESS
Durham, North Carolina

Library of Congress cataloging-in-publication data
is available at catalog.loc.gov

ISBN 978-1-5310-3445-0
eISBN 978-1-5310-3446-7

Carolina Academic Press
700 Kent Street
Durham, North Carolina 27701
(919) 489-7486
www.cap-press.com

Dedicated to Stella, Buddy, Kelly, Garth, Pete, Joey, and Mookie.

Thank you for your love and support over the years.

Contents

Preface

Criminal procedure is the linchpin of the criminal justice system. The operation and management of criminal justice institutions, the acts performed and decisions made by street-level criminal justice professionals, and the policies enacted by policymakers must fit within the strictures of criminal procedure law. In broad terms, criminal procedure law defines the power of the government and rights of the citizenry related to law enforcement officials' investigation of crimes, the prosecution of accused offenders, and pretrial, trial, and postconviction judicial proceedings. The foundational principles, which are the primary focus of this book, are embedded in the United States Constitution and interpreted by the Supreme Court. This book aims to expose criminal justice students not only to the law of criminal procedure but also to the role it plays across the criminal justice system, as well as the impact and importance it has on the real world.

The primary goals of this book are to help students understand criminal procedure law and develop their critical and analytical thinking skills. To achieve this goal, I diverge from the traditional textbook and casebook styles of presentation. Instead, I use a hybrid method of presentation that uses three distinct components.

The first component is the traditional case-study method. I present a select number of important Supreme Court opinions that establish the law. Cases are edited significantly to make the key facts, issues, and holdings accessible to undergraduate students. Cases are not, however, edited to the point where they fail to present sufficient facts and legal reasoning so that students may understand the logic and basis for the holding. I believe this method of case editing challenges students without being overwhelming.

The second component is the use of explanatory text to clarify constitutional principles and enhance student understanding of the cases and concepts presented. Beyond being explanatory, the post-case text presents students with additional case law, as well as theoretical and practical discussion questions for class discussion or individual work. I believe this method of presentation refrains from spoon-feeding students the law but expands their understanding of the law by considering additional case law and presenting theoretical questions.

The third component I use is the presentation of real-world and fictional hypothetical scenarios that illustrate the types of situations criminal justice professionals face regularly. These items are presented throughout the text in two ways. The first is through the multiple "You Be the Judge" scenarios in each chapter, which present the students with the facts from actual cases and have them apply the law they are learning to those facts to answer directed questions.

The second tool specifically designed to foster critical thinking is the presentation of hypothetical fact scenarios and associated questions at the end of each chapter. These scenarios require students to possess a firm understanding of the law and be able to apply it to the facts by using critical thinking. Answers to both styles of questions are presented in the text's instructor's manual.

Throughout this book, I have included a number of features designed to promote student learning. These include:

- Chapter learning objectives
- Tables that summarize or illustrate specific legal standards
- "You Be the Judge" scenarios
- Key terms linked to a glossary
- End-of-chapter Review Questions
- End-of-chapter hypothetical scenarios and questions
- Links to Supreme Court Oral Arguments for cases presented

While instructors should find enough in these pages to give students a comprehensive introduction to criminal procedure law, as with all texts prepared for undergraduate students, this book does not attempt to cover all aspects of criminal procedure law. Instead, I hope the materials whet student appetites for learning more about the relationship between law and the criminal justice system while enhancing their critical thinking skills. At the same time, I hope it provides instructors with a foundation to build upon and the flexibility to teach this fascinating subject in the manner and depth they desire.

David Brody

Pullman, Washington

Essentials of Criminal Procedure

CHAPTER 1

The Law of Criminal Procedure: Of Means and Ends

LEARNING OBJECTIVES

After reading this chapter, students should be able to:

- Understand the importance of Criminal Procedure Law
- Explain the goals and objectives of criminal procedure law
- Understand the challenges associated with "Means-Ends" situations and reconcile various goals of the criminal justice system
- Understand the value judgments and interests associated with the crime control and due process perspectives
- Learn how to effectively brief a case
- Explain the conflict between public safety and individual liberties

The Challenges and Goals of Criminal Procedure Law

The police and the government in the United States wield tremendous power, but like the sword held by Lady Justice, this power is double-edged and can cut both ways. This power is used to protect the innocent, secure individual liberties, and convict those who have violated the law and are dangerous to society. However, this power can also be used tyrannically to harass the innocent, abuse vocal dissidents, and suppress the marginalized. Criminal procedure law attempts to ensure the state can investigate, arrest, and convict the guilty, but that innocent Americans can live their lives free and without fear of unnecessary government intervention or control. However, this is a delicate, complicated balancing act with many different thoughts, theories, and philosophies about where the lines should be drawn. It frequently falls on the United States Supreme Court to be the final arbiter by interpreting the Constitution and drawing these lines.

Procedural issues dominate the daily administration of criminal justice. **Criminal procedure law** (hereafter, criminal procedure) comprises the legal rules and principles that regulate the administration of criminal justice. In other words, the laws and regulations the government must abide by when it suspects, arrests, or convicts someone of a crime. This body of law traditionally is understood as governing (1) police work, including the detection and investigation of crimes, and arrest decisions; (2) the pretrial decisions of magistrates, prosecutors, grand juries, and judges, involving such matters as bail, the preliminary review, screening of charges, and filing formal criminal charges; (3) the adjudication of charges through guilty pleas and trials; (4) the sentencing process; and (5) appeals and post-conviction review of criminal convictions and sentences. This book focuses on the law governing police practices, pretrial decisions, and adjudication. These issues form the core of criminal procedure. Concentrating on them allows us to give them the attention their significance and complexity demand.

Few areas of the law are as captivating as criminal procedure. Although many state and federal rules of criminal procedure are defined by statute, the principles animating these rules ultimately spring from the United States Constitution and related state constitutional provisions. The courts, especially the United States Supreme Court, determine the scope and limits of these constitutional principles as they decide cases involving murder, rape, armed robbery, drug offenses, and other serious crimes. Through their case decisions, the courts put the law into action.

Goals and Objectives of Criminal Procedure

Criminal procedure has several goals and objectives. First, accuracy in the criminal justice process is paramount. Reliable fact-finding is essential if the criminal justice system is to ensure the guilty are punished and the innocent remain free. The "verdict" rendered by a judge or jury at the conclusion of a trial is an announcement that literally means "speak the truth."

The United States holds freedom as sacrosanct, and getting the correct verdict is paramount. Requiring the government to go through several steps and court proceedings before convicting someone of a crime ensures that innocent people are not wrongfully convicted. Despite the extensive procedural protections afforded to citizens before conviction, wrongful convictions still happen in the United States. Research suggests that 1–3% of incarcerated people are wrongfully convicted (Zalman, et al. 2008). If no procedural protections were afforded to citizens, it is not difficult to imagine how many more people would be wrongfully convicted.

A further goal of criminal procedure is to ensure the criminal justice system is viewed as legitimate. **Legitimacy** is the belief that legal authorities should be obeyed and that individuals should defer to their judgments (Tyler & Huo, 2002). When the public views the criminal justice system and its representatives favorably and legitimately, people are more likely to comply with the law and contact the police when they need assistance. In contrast, when people think the criminal justice system is unfair, it gives them a negative perception of the criminal justice system and its representatives, such as the police. When people view the criminal justice system negatively, they are less likely to obey the law, cooperate with the police, or reach out to the police when they see a crime or need assistance. Criminal procedure promotes fairness and legitimacy of the justice system by setting laws and rules that the government must abide by when it convicts someone of a crime. Being treated fairly by the government and according to established rules and procedures should not be underestimated or underappreciated. Citizens of several countries worldwide would appreciate being afforded such protections and rights. These protections and rights protect citizens from an overarching or overzealous government and arbitrary action.

Take, for example, the case of Jason Rezaian—a dual citizen of the United States and Iran. Rezaian is a native of San Francisco and the Tehran correspondent for the *Washington Post*. On the evening of July 22, 2014, the Iranian government raided the home of Rezaian and his wife. Rezaian, his wife, and other associates were arrested (Warrick & Morello, 2014). Two weeks after the arrest, the State Department of the United States had no information on the whereabouts of Rezaian (Gearan, 2014). After five months of detention, Rezaian's family still did not know why he was being held.

He was held in solitary confinement in deplorable conditions that threatened his physical and psychological health. He experienced persistent eye infections that threatened to disable him permanently. He also had inflammation in his groin, making it difficult to stand. Despite all of this, Rezaian said one of the most challenging aspects was the almost complete isolation and uncertainty of when he would be released. He was not allowed to confer with an attorney for several months. The judge assigned to his case was notorious for being biased, hard-nosed, and handing out only the harshest punishments available, including death. A member of Human Rights Watch said that past defendants who appeared before the judge had not been allowed to present any defense on their behalf (Morello, 2015). Fortunately, citizens of the United States have constitutional rights and limits placed on the police to protect them from such arbitrary government action, which helps give legitimacy to the criminal justice system and its actors.

Related to fairness and legitimacy is the goal of **equality**. Equality is being treated fairly under the law according to established rules or norms. This concept is personified by the iconic blindfolded Lady Justice that adorns many courthouses, and most famously, the United States Supreme Court. Additionally, the phrase "Equal Justice Under Law" is engraved on the front entrance to the United States Supreme Court. Equality means that all citizens will be treated fairly and equally before the law regardless of a person's race, gender, sexual orientation, education, socioeconomic status, or a host of other factors. Irrespective of a person's standing in society or the egregious nature of the alleged crime they have committed, everyone is afforded the same procedural opportunities to prove their innocence in a court of law.

Another goal of criminal procedure is achieving **finality** by ending contested criminal cases. Finality not only benefits the government but also the defendant. Defendants are the beneficiaries of rules designed to produce a final resolution of criminal matters. For example, double-jeopardy principles prevent the retrial of a defendant acquitted of a crime, even if compelling evidence of guilt surfaces after the trial's completion. Statutes of limitation and speedy-trial provisions may prohibit suspected offenders from ever being brought to trial when unjustifiable delays occur in filing or prosecuting criminal charges.

In contrast, finality interests also may be asserted by the government or invoked by the courts to the defendant's detriment. Thus, for example, appellate courts may refuse to consider defendants' claims of error that were not preserved by a timely objection during trial, when immediate corrective action could have been taken. Similarly, federal courts may decline to review issues in state cases that were not presented on appeal to the state courts or that were not raised at the first opportunity in the federal courts through a petition for a writ of **habeas corpus**.

A federal statute, 28 U.S.C. §2254(a), authorizes the federal courts to "entertain an application for a writ of habeas corpus on behalf of a person in custody under the judgment of a state court only on the ground that he is in custody in violation of the Constitution or laws or treaties of the United States." The Supreme Court and Congress have imposed significant restrictions in recent years on the availability of federal habeas corpus review of criminal convictions and sentences. Respect for the finality of state court judgments has been a significant reason for these limitations. Curtailing repeated reviews of criminal convictions and sentences is further justified in the name of preserving scarce judicial resources and by the belief that justice is best served when an offender ultimately is required to accept the legitimacy of their punishment.

Individual Liberties v. Public Safety

Individual citizens and communities suffer profoundly at the hands of criminals. Society as a whole is injured when criminal acts disrupt people's lives, undermine moral values, and inspire fear and insecurity. It is debilitating to a community if crime is allowed to flourish. At the same time, individuals accused of committing crimes have much at stake. Tremendous stigma, social disapproval, and disruption of the person's life accompany a criminal accusation or conviction. Once convicted, offenders face fines, probationary supervision, prison, or even possibly execution at the hands of the government. Some individuals accused of committing a crime have valid defenses in the form of an excuse or justification, such as self-defense, or they may not have been involved at all in the crime they have been accused of committing. Not only do the guilty and the accused have an interest in ensuring that criminal laws are administered fairly, but law-abiding citizens do as well. Each criminal case decided by the courts potentially involves issues and questions much bigger than the facts and circumstances of the specific case. These cases provide a forum for resolving the perpetual tensions involved in preserving individual liberties and ensuring public safety.

However, ascertaining the truth about suspected crimes cannot be the only function of the criminal justice process. For example, few people would condone using the rack or other forms of torture to coerce confessions from suspected criminals, or citizens being strip-searched at the whim of a police officer, or enthusiastically entertain a police search in their home in the dead of night. Undoubtedly, such activities would prove highly effective police practices, improve crime control, and be effective at discriminating the guilty from the innocent. Yet they illustrate that limits must be placed on fact-finding efforts, regardless of their effectiveness, even if those limits sometimes impede an otherwise commendable search for the truth. Safeguarding individual freedoms, checking abuses of power by law enforcement, and preserving basic fairness in government-citizen interactions are also important goals of criminal procedure.

Crime Control v. Due Process

One of the principal challenges confronting criminal procedure is reconciling the diverse objectives of the criminal justice system. It must do so amidst many operating constraints while being mindful of the unique facts and circumstances of individual cases. This reconciliation process requires identifying the rights and interests at stake in each case, assigning appropriate weight to the respective interests, and then balancing or prioritizing those interests to arrive at a decision on the case issues. Even if not recognized formally, these ingredients are implicit in most court decisions involving constitutional criminal procedure issues.

Herbert Packer, a renowned American legal scholar, profoundly influenced criminal justice theory by articulating two key models: the **Crime Control Model** and the **Due Process Model**. Introduced in his 1968 book *The Limits of the Criminal Sanction*, these frameworks offer competing ideals regarding the nature and purpose of the criminal justice process. Packer's models are not strict blueprints for practice but conceptual tools designed to highlight the tensions and values underlying criminal justice. Understanding these models is essential for anyone studying law, criminology, or public policy because they underscore enduring debates about security, liberty, efficiency, fairness, and the role of government.

The Crime Control Model

The Crime Control Model prioritizes the repression of criminal conduct as the most important function of the criminal justice system. According to Packer, the ability of the state to maintain public order and social stability depends on efficient, swift, and decisive action against crime. The emphasis is on **efficiency**, **speed**, and **finality**. The Crime Control Model has five key features.

1. Presumption of Guilt
   The model operates on a pragmatic belief that if someone is arrested and charged, there is a strong likelihood they are guilty. Therefore, the criminal process should work like an assembly line, quickly moving cases toward conviction.
2. Efficiency and Speed
   The system should prioritize high rates of apprehension and conviction with minimal delays. Prolonged trials and appeals are seen as hindrances rather than safeguards.
3. Focus on Law Enforcement
   Police and prosecutors play central roles. Their professional judgment is trusted to screen out weak cases early and push strong ones forward with minimal interference.
4. Limited Protections for the Accused
   Procedural safeguards, such as the right to silence or exclusionary rules against improperly obtained evidence, are viewed skeptically if they obstruct the goal of reducing crime.
5. Finality
   Once a verdict is reached, it should be treated as final to preserve efficiency and respect for the system.

Proponents of crime control argue that without strong, efficient law enforcement, crime can spread, undermining public trust and endangering freedoms. They justify the model's restriction of individual rights by arguing that there are four theoretical bases that support its dominant role in the criminal justice system.

One of the primary goals of the Crime Control Model is to deter criminal behavior. By swiftly and efficiently prosecuting offenders, this model sends a clear message that crime will not be tolerated and that perpetrators will be held accountable for their actions. This, in turn, creates a disincentive for individuals to engage in criminal activity, as the perceived risk of punishment outweighs the potential benefits.

The Crime Control Model recognizes society's need for justice and seeks to provide a sense of closure for victims and their families. It acknowledges that punishment is a necessary response to wrongdoing, demonstrating that criminal behavior will not be overlooked and that justice will be served. Moreover, the criminal justice system will focus on punishment, not rehabilitation.

The central focus of punishment under the Crime Control Model is incapacitation. Incapacitation aims to reduce the overall level of crime by isolating offenders and restricting their ability to engage in further criminal activity. It emphasizes removing dangerous individuals from society, thereby protecting the public from further harm. This is particularly crucial in cases involving violent or repeat offenders, as their continued presence in the community poses an ongoing threat to public safety.

The lynchpin driving the Crime Control Model is its focus on efficiently allocating resources. Limited resources within local government and especially the criminal justice system necessitate an efficient approach to prosecuting criminal cases. The crime control model seeks to make the most of these resources by streamlining the process and prioritizing the pursuit of convictions over lengthy trials and appeals. This ensures that the system can handle a higher volume of cases, allowing for a more effective response to criminal activity.

The Due Process Model

The Due Process Model is rooted in the belief that the protection of individual rights and liberties is of paramount importance within the criminal justice system. This model emphasizes the need for a fair and impartial process that safeguards the accused against potential abuses of power. Several key justifications underscore the significance of the Due Process Model.

1. Presumption of innocence

   A fundamental tenet of the due process model is the presumption of innocence until proven guilty beyond a reasonable doubt. This principle ensures that the prosecution has the burden of proof, protecting individuals from wrongful convictions and arbitrary punishment.

2. Protection of civil liberties

   Due process safeguards constitutional rights, such as the right to a fair trial, legal representation, and freedom from unreasonable search and seizure. By prioritizing these liberties, the model seeks to prevent government overreach and ensure that justice is served in a manner consistent with democratic principles.

3. Fairness and equality

   The Due Process Model strives to guarantee that all individuals are treated fairly and equitably by the criminal justice system, regardless of their social status, race, or financial resources. This includes providing access to legal representation and ensuring that the legal process is transparent and impartial.

4. Accuracy and reliability

   A thorough and meticulous legal process, which involves careful examination of evidence and multiple opportunities for appeal, helps to minimize the risk of wrongful convictions and enhances the overall accuracy and reliability of the criminal justice system.

5. Promotion of trust in the justice system

   The due process model fosters public trust and confidence in the criminal justice system by demonstrating a commitment to fairness, transparency, and the protection of individual rights.

Comparing the Two Models

The due process and crime control models serve as crucial counterbalances. Both models are focused on important concepts needed in the criminal justice system. Not surprisingly, rather than operating at one extreme or the other, the American criminal justice system finds a balance between crime control and due process. Box 1.1 presents a simple comparison between the two models.

Box 1.1 Comparison of the Crime Control Model and the Due Process Model

Feature	Crime Control Model	Due Process Model
Focus	Efficiency in repressing crime	Protection of individual rights
Presumption	Guilt	Innocence
System Metaphors	Assembly line	Obstacle course
View of Police	Trustworthy and Professional	Potentially abusive & fallible
Priority	Social order	Procedural justice

Packer explores the Means/Ends conundrum facing a society that seeks to provide public safety while protecting individual liberties from an academic and theoretical perspective. The next article provides a dramatic illustration of the difficulty in balancing the different perspectives. As you read *The Dirty Harry Problem* and hopefully watch the movie Dirty Harry, which it is based on, consider the values at stake and how you might act if faced with the situation Dirty Harry faces. Prior to reading the article, we suggest you view the scene from the film, which can be accessed on YouTube: https://www.youtube.com/watch?v=buNwwAximcE

Carl B. Klockars, *The Dirty Harry Problem*

Klockars, C. B. (1980). The Dirty Harry problem. *The Annals of the American Academy of Political and Social Science, 452*(1), 33–47.

The Dirty Harry problem draws its name from the 1971 Warner Brothers film Dirty Harry and its chief protagonist, antihero Inspector Harry "Dirty Harry" Callahan. The film features a number of events that dramatize the Dirty Harry problem in different ways, but the one which does so most explicitly and most completely places Harry in the following situation. A 14-year-old girl has been kidnapped and is being held captive by a psychopathic killer. The killer, "Scorpio," who has already struck twice, demands $200,000 ransom to release the girl, who is buried with just enough oxygen to keep her alive for a few hours. Harry gets the job of delivering the ransom and, after enormous exertion, finally meets Scorpio. At their meeting Scorpio decides to renege on his bargain, let the girl die, and kill Harry. Harry manages to stab Scorpio in the leg before he does so, but not before Scorpio seriously wounds Harry's partner, an inexperienced, idealistic, slightly ethnic, former sociology major.

Scorpio escapes, but Harry manages to track him down through the clinic where he was treated for his wounded leg. After learning that Scorpio lives on the grounds of a nearby football stadium, Harry breaks into his apartment, finds guns and other evidence of his guilt, and finally confronts Scorpio on the 50-yard line, where Harry shoots him in the leg as he is trying to escape. Standing over Scorpio, Harry demands to know where the girl is buried. Scorpio refuses to disclose her location, demanding his rights to a lawyer. As the camera draws back from the scene Harry stands on Scorpio's bullet-mangled leg to torture a confession of the girl's location from him.

As it turns out, the girl is already dead and Scorpio must be set free. Neither the gun found in the illegal search, nor the confession Harry extorted, nor any of its fruits—including the girl's body—would be admissible in court.

The Dirty Harry problem asks when and to what extent does the morally good end warrant or justify an ethically, politically, or legally dangerous means to its achievement? In itself, this question assumes the possibility of a genuine moral dilemma and posits its existence in a means-ends arrangement which may be expressed schematically as follows:

Figure 1.1 The Dirty Harry Problem

	MEANS: Morally Good (+)	MEANS: Morally Dirty (−)
ENDS: Morally good (+)	A + +	B − + The Dirty Harry Problem
ENDS: Morally dirty (−)	C + −	D − −

It is important to specify clearly the terms of the Dirty Harry problem not only to show that it must involve the juxtaposition of good ends and dirty means, but also to show what must be proven to demonstrate that a Dirty Harry problem exists. If one could show, for example, that box B is always empirically empty or that in any given case the terms of the situation are better read in some other means-ends arrangement, Dirty Harry problems vanish. At this first level, however, I suspect that no one could exclude the core scene of Dirty Harry from the class of Dirty Harry problems. There is no question that saving the life of an innocent victim of kidnapping is a "good" thing nor that grinding the bullet-mangled leg of Scorpio to extort a confession from him is "dirty."

There is, in addition, a second level of criteria of an empirical and epistemological nature that must be met before a Dirty Harry problem actually comes into being. They involve the connection between the dirty act and the good end. Principally, what must be known and, importantly, known before the dirty act is committed, is that it will result in the achievement of the good end. In any absolute sense this is, of course, impossible to know, in that no acts are ever completely certain in their consequences. Thus the question is always a matter of probabilities. But it is helpful to break those probabilities into classes which attach to various subcategories of the overall question. In the given case, this level of problem would seem to require that three questions be satisfied, though not all with the same level of certainty.

In *Dirty Harry*, the first question is, Is Scorpio able to provide the information Dirty Harry seeks? It is an epistemological question about which, in *Dirty Harry*, we are absolutely certain.

Second, we must know there are means, dirty means and nothing other than dirty means, which are likely to achieve the good end. One can, of course, never be sure that one is aware of or has considered all possible alternatives, but in Dirty Harry there would appear to be no reason for Scorpio in his rational self-interest to confess to the girl's location without being coerced to do so.

The third question which must be satisfied at this empirical and epistemological level concedes that dirty means are the only method which will be effective, but asks whether or not, in the end, they will be in vain. We know in Dirty Harry that they were, and Harry himself, at the time of the ransom demand, admits he believes that the girl is already dead. Does not this possibility or likelihood that the girl is dead destroy the justification for Harry's dirty act? Although it surely would if Harry knew for certain that the girl was dead, I do not think it does insofar as even a small probability of her being saved exists. The reason is that the good to be achieved is so unquestionably good and so passionately felt that even a small possibility of its achievement demands that it be tried. For example, were we to ask, If it were your daughter would you want Harry to do what he did? It would be this passionate sense of unquestionable good that we are trying to dramatize.

Once we have satisfied ourselves that a Dirty Harry problem is conceptually possible and that, in fact, we can specify one set of concrete circumstances in which it exists, one might think that the most difficult question of all is, What ought to be done? I do not think it is. I suspect that there are very few people who would not want Harry to do something dirty in the situation specified. I know I would want him to do what he did, and what is more, I would want anyone who policed for me to be prepared to do so as well. Put differently, I want to have as police officers men and women of moral courage and sensitivity.

But to those who would want exactly that, the Dirty Harry problem poses its most irksome conclusion. Namely, that one cannot, at least in the specific case at hand, have a policeman who is both just and innocent. The troublesome issue in the Dirty Harry problem is not whether under some utilitarian calculus a right choice can be made, but that the choice must always be between at least two wrongs. And in choosing to do either wrong, the policeman inevitably taints or tarnishes himself.

Dirty Harry problems arise quite often. For policemen, real, everyday policemen, Dirty Harry problems are part of their job and thus considerably more than rare or artificial dramatic exceptions.

Although the exclusionary rule is the manifest target of Dirty Harry, it more than anything else, makes Dirty Harry problems a reality in everyday policing. It is the great virtue of exclusionary rules—applying in various forms to stops, searches, seizures, and interrogations—that they hit directly upon the intolerable, though often, I think, moral desire of police to punish. These rules make the very simple point to police that the more they wish to see a felon punished, the more they are advised to be scrupulous in their treatment of him. Put differently, the best thing Harry could have done for Scorpio was to step on his leg, extort his confession, and break into his apartment.

If Dirty Harry problems can be shown to exist in their technical dimensions—as genuine means-ends problems where only dirty means will work—the question of the magnitude and urgency of the ends that the dirty means may be employed to achieve must still be confronted. Specifically, it must be shown that the ends of dirty means are so desirable that the failure to achieve them would cast the person who is in a position to do so in moral disrepute.

The two most widely acknowledged ends of policing are peacekeeping and law enforcement.

An interpretation of law enforcement which is compatible with empirical studies of police behavior (as peacekeeping is) and police talk in America (which peacekeeping generally is not) is an understanding of the ends of law enforcement as punishment. There are, of course, many theories of punishment, but the police seem inclined toward the simplest: the belief that certain people who have committed certain acts deserve to be punished for them. What can one say of the compelling and unquestionable character of this retributive ambition as an end of policing and policemen?

The alternative the Dirty Harry problem leads us to is ensuring that the craftsman regards his dirty means as dirty by applying the same retributive principles of punishment to his wrongful acts that he is quite willing to apply to others! It is, in fact, only when his wrongful acts are punished that he will come to see them as wrongful and will appreciate the genuine moral—rather than technical or occupational—choice he makes in resorting to them.

If under such conditions our craftsman police officer is still willing to risk the employment of dirty means to achieve what he understands to be unquestionably good ends, he will not only know that he has behaved justly, but that in doing so he must run the risk of becoming genuinely guilty as well.

In urging the punishment of policemen who resort to dirty means to achieve some unquestionably good and morally compelling end, we recognize that we create a Dirty Harry problem for ourselves and for those we urge to effect such punishments. It is a fitting end, one which teaches once again that the danger in Dirty Harry problems is never in their resolution, but in thinking that one has found a resolution with which one can truly live in peace.

FURTHER CASE LAW, REFLECTIONS, AND QUESTIONS

1. Is it possible to reconcile Professor Klockars' conclusions about Inspector Callahan's (Dirty Harry) torturing Scorpio to attempt to learn the whereabouts of the girl Scorpio had kidnapped—"I know I would want him to do what he did"—with his "urging the punishment of policemen who resort to dirty means to achieve some unquestionably good and morally compelling end"?
2. Do you think Inspector Callahan's tactics were justified under the circumstances? Does your answer to this question dictate what should be done with evidence uncovered due to these tactics? That is, if Harry justifiably broke into Scorpio's apartment and stood on Scorpio's "bullet-mangled leg" to find the kidnapped child, does it necessarily follow that the resulting evidence should be admitted at a later trial? Conversely, even if Harry was wrong in his actions, is it inevitable that the evidence must be excluded at a later trial? What ends and means of criminal procedure are in conflict in this particular Dirty Harry problem?
3. Professor Klockars suggests that Dirty Harry problems often occur in everyday police work. The vast majority of such dilemmas doubtlessly are resolved without ever coming to the attention of the courts. Nevertheless, some means-ends problems eventually are considered judicially, allowing judgment to be rendered dispassionately and long after the questionable law enforcement practices took place.

Judicial Opinions: How Criminal Procedure Law Is Made

The law of criminal procedure is primarily established through judicial opinions written by appellate courts that interpret the Constitution and Bill of Rights. In this book, we will examine how the United States Supreme Court has interpreted these documents.

Consider the following example. The Bill of Rights provides that a person charged with a criminal offense has the right to be determined guilty by a jury. While this may seem straightforward enough, in reality, it is not. Ask yourself, what should be considered a crime? Obviously, acts such as murder, robbery, and assault constitute crimes. But what about speeding, shoplifting, littering, or trespassing? Should a person receive a jury trial for each of these offenses?

Most people would reason that such minor offenses should not require a jury trial. However, where do we draw the line? What if the shoplifting charge involved a ring worth $100? $2,000? So, where do we draw the line? As we will see later in this book, the Supreme Court has interpreted where we draw the line and, accordingly, what the 6th Amendment means. The rules, logic, and reasoning in these judicial opinions make up the law of criminal procedure. It is these judicial opinions that we will primarily study throughout this book.

Briefing a Case

There are many different ways to learn and understand the law. The case method is primarily utilized in our text and most law schools. The case method uses court decisions to exemplify and learn principles of the law. Studying case opinions helps reveal the law as a principled and dynamic process. Legal rules are in constant evolution. They are refined in response to changing values, social conditions, and unique factual circumstances. It is important to appreciate the origins and history of the rules of law to help understand their current form and their appropriate application. Carefully studying judicial opinions helps illuminate the legal principles that control case decisions. Although knowledge of legal rules is valuable, the analytical skills associated with identifying the premises of judicial decisions, extracting general principles from the rules announced in cases, and testing the application of these principles in different fact situations are much more reliable measures of a student's understanding of the law.

While the payoffs from studying judicial decisions are considerable, a significant investment is required. Reading case law is significantly more time-consuming and challenging than reading summaries or narrative accounts of case decisions. This is especially true of the first few encounters with judicial opinions. However, this is an excellent and valuable skill for students of the law and practitioners in the criminal justice system. One tested method to help understand and extract meaning from a case decision is "briefing" a case.

A **case brief** is simply a structured summary of a case decision, generally presented in the majority opinion of the court. It is prepared to enhance analysis of a court's reasoning, as a reference for class discussion, and as an aid for reviewing course materials in preparation for examinations. A brief can, and doubtlessly should be an individualized tool for analysis, reference, and review. However, some basic features should be included. A brief should begin with the case's name and its complete citation. It is important to know which court decided the case and the year of its decision. The full citation contains this information and will enable you to look up the case in the library or on the internet and read it in its entirety if you later wish to do so. It is also recommended that you record the page in this book where the case you are briefing begins for easy reference between your notes and the text.

The critical components of a case brief are:

1. facts
2. issue(s)
3. holding
4. rationale

Of course, the facts of the case must be gleaned from the opinion. The **facts** reported in the opinion are generally a significantly condensed version of what happened and sometimes might bear a faint resemblance to what actually happened. This filtering process continues as a case progresses through different appellate courts and additional layers of judicial review. Nevertheless, these are the only facts at your disposal, and you must rely on them as you read and prepare to brief the case. Since your job is to summarize the case, you should not mechanically report all of the facts supplied in the court's narrative but rather focus on the relevant facts. Facts are relevant only to the extent that they relate to the issue and, ultimately, the holding in a case. Thus, you should be selective in the facts or historical events you record.

The judicial history of a case is usually included as part of the facts. This history reports where the case originated and how it arrived in the court responsible for the opinion you are briefing. For example, you might note that the defendant—commonly abbreviated as "D" or "Δ"(the Greek letter delta)—was convicted of murder in a specific state trial court, that their conviction was affirmed on appeal by the state court of appeals and by the state supreme court, and that the U.S. Supreme Court then granted ***certiorari*** (exercised its discretionary authority to review the case). We discuss the typical progression of a criminal case through the state and federal court systems in greater detail in Chapter 2.

The **issue** is the legal question presented to the court for decision. Cases occasionally involve more than a single legal issue. Courts sometimes state the issue they are deciding on early in an opinion and do so quite clearly. At other times, courts seem unwilling or unable to pinpoint the questions they are deciding, and you will have to frame case issues as you understand them. You should state the issue concisely and accurately. Be mindful that how a court defines an issue can be crucial to the resolution of a case. There may be times when you take exception to how a court states an issue, and you should note your disagreement.

The statement of the issue in your brief should capture the crux of the controversy confronting the court and should always be written in the form of a question. It should be sufficiently comprehensive to inform a listener about the case. A question framed along the lines of, "Should the confession be admissible?" or, "Should the police have secured a warrant?" is inadequate.

Consider the greater understanding of a case conveyed by issues stated in the following terms: "Does the federal Constitution require the states to appoint legal counsel for a person charged with a felony who is too poor to hire a lawyer?" "Would the capital punishment of an offender who was only 16 years old at the time he committed murder amount to cruel and unusual punishment, in violation of the Eighth Amendment to the U.S. Constitution?"

Stating the issue presented in a case accurately and with the proper degree of precision—neither hopelessly general nor detailed and convoluted to the point of incomprehensibility—can be a true art. This skill is perhaps the most important step in understanding the case, so you should be prepared to devote the necessary thought and effort to define the precise question before the court.

The **holding** of a case can usually be stated in the form of a complete response to the issue you have identified. For example, "The cruel-and-unusual-punishments clause of the Eighth Amendment has been interpreted to prohibit the execution of offenders who were just 16 years old when they committed a capital crime" is a statement of a case holding that resolves the issue we posed above. The holding reveals what the court decided in the case and corresponds to the general rule that can be extracted from the case decision. The rule then becomes **precedent**, or the basis of future decisions in like cases. The doctrine of precedent, or ***stare decisis***, plays a central role in the evolution of case law. Lawyers and judges examine the similarities and differences between cases to help determine whether the rule announced in a previous decision governs the resolution of a case that later comes before a court.

The **rationale** is the explanation of how a court arrived at its holding. To justify their rulings, courts typically rely on precedent, the text of constitutions and statutes, history, logic, policy implications, value preferences, empirical evidence, case facts, and other analytical devices. You may not always agree with or be persuaded by the rationale offered to support a court's holding. Indeed, the regularity with which **concurring** and **dissenting** opinions are written should convince you that there is ample room for disagreement with the prevailing rationale in case decisions. Thus, you should think critically about the reasons offered in support of a court's decision as you outline them and make a note of any questions that occur to you. Concurring and dissenting opinions can be quite helpful in suggesting possible flaws or weaknesses in the majority opinion's rationale.

The Law in Action

The first case we will examine is *Brown v. Mississippi,* which bears more than a passing similarity to Inspector Callahan's fictional interaction with Scorpio. *Brown v. Mississippi* was decided by the U.S. Supreme Court in 1936. These facts are quoted from a dissenting opinion written by a judge on the Mississippi Supreme Court. The state supreme court had approved admitting the defendants' confessions into evidence and had affirmed their convictions and death sentences. Think about how the Supreme Court reached its decision and what standard it laid out for other courts to apply in the future.

So far, we have examined the problem of balancing the criminal justice system's competing aims from theoretical and illustrative perspectives. We now turn to how the Supreme Court has examined these concerns.

Consider the following cases—*Brown v. Mississippi* and *Rochin v. California*—the first of which bears more than a passing similarity to Inspector Callahan's fictional interaction with Scorpio. *Brown v. Mississippi* was decided by the U.S. Supreme Court in 1936. These facts are quoted from a dissenting opinion written by a judge on the Mississippi Supreme Court. The state supreme court had approved admitting the defendants' confessions into evidence and had affirmed their convictions and death sentences.

Brown v. Mississippi

297 U.S. 278 (1936)

Mr. Chief Justice Hughes delivered the opinion of the Court.

The question in this case is whether convictions, which rest solely upon confessions shown to have been extorted by officers of the State by brutality and violence, are consistent with the **due process** of law required by the Fourteenth Amendment of the Constitution of the United States.

Petitioners were indicted for the murder of one Raymond Stewart, whose death occurred on March 30, 1934. They were indicted on April 4, 1934, and were then arraigned and pleaded not guilty. Counsel were appointed by the court to defend them. Trial was begun the next morning and was concluded on the following day, when they were found guilty and sentenced to death.

Aside from the confessions, there was no evidence sufficient to warrant the submission of the case to the jury. After a preliminary inquiry, testimony as to the confessions was received over the objection of defendants' counsel. Defendants then testified that the confessions were false and had been procured by physical torture. The case went to the jury with instructions, upon the request of defendants' counsel, that if the jury had reasonable doubt as to the confessions having resulted from coercion, and that they were not true, they were not to be considered as evidence. On their appeal to the Supreme Court of the State, defendants assigned as error the inadmissibility of the confessions.

The judgment was affirmed. We [subsequently] granted a writ of certiorari.

There is no dispute as to the facts upon this point and as they are clearly and adequately stated in the dissenting opinion of [Mississippi Supreme Court] Judge Griffith (with whom Judge Anderson concurred)—showing both the extreme brutality of the measures to extort the confessions and the participation of the state authorities—we quote this part of his opinion in full, as follows

"The crime with which these defendants, all ignorant negroes, are charged, was discovered about one o'clock p.m. on Friday, March 30, 1934. On that night one Dial, a deputy sheriff, accompanied by others, came to the home of Ellington, one of the defendants, and requested him to accompany them to the house of the deceased, and there a number of white men were gathered, who began to accuse the defendant of the crime. Upon his denial they seized him, and with the participation of the deputy they hanged him by a rope to the limb of a tree, and having let him down, they hung him again, and when he was let down the second time, and he still protested his innocence, he was tied to a tree and whipped, and still declining to accede to the demands that he confess, he was finally released and he returned with some difficulty to his home, suffering intense pain and agony. The record of the testimony shows that the signs of the rope on his neck were plainly visible during the so-called trial. A day or two thereafter the said deputy, accompanied by another, returned to the home of the said defendant and arrested him, and departed with the prisoner towards the jail in an adjoining county, but went by a route which led into the State of Alabama; and while on the way, in that State, the deputy stopped and again severely whipped the defendant, declaring that he would continue the whipping until he confessed, and the defendant then agreed to confess to such a statement as the deputy would dictate, and he did so, after which he was delivered to jail.

"The other two defendants, Ed Brown and Henry Shields, were also arrested and taken to the same jail. On Sunday night, April 1, 1934, the same deputy, accompanied by a number of white men, one of whom was also an officer, and by the jailer, came to the jail, and the two last named defendants were made to strip and they were laid over chairs and their backs were cut to pieces with a leather strap with buckles on it, and they were likewise made by the said deputy definitely to understand that the whipping would be continued unless and until they confessed, and not only confessed, but confessed in every matter of detail as demanded by those present; and in this manner the defendants confessed the crime, and as the whippings progressed and were repeated, they changed or adjusted their confession in all particulars of detail so as to conform to the demands of their torturers. When the confessions had been obtained in the exact form and contents as desired by the mob, they left with the parting admonition and warning that, if the defendants changed their story at any time in any respect from that last stated, the perpetrators of the outrage would administer the same or equally effective treatment.

"Further details of the brutal treatment to which these helpless prisoners were subjected need not be pursued. It is sufficient to say that in pertinent respects the transcript reads more like pages torn from some medieval account, than a record made within the confines of a modern civilization which aspires to an enlightened constitutional government.

"All this having been accomplished, on the next day, that is, on Monday, April 2, when the defendants had been given time to recuperate somewhat from the tortures to which they had been subjected, the two sheriffs, one of the county where the crime was committed, and the other of the county of the jail in which the prisoners were confined, came to the jail, accompanied by eight other persons, some of them deputies, there to hear the free and voluntary confession of these miserable and abject defendants. The sheriff of the county of the crime admitted that he had heard of the whipping but averred that he had no personal knowledge of it. He admitted that one of the defendants, when brought before him to confess, was limping and did not sit down, and that this particular defendant then and there stated that he had been strapped so severely that he could not sit down, and as already stated, the signs of the rope on the neck of another of the defendants were plainly visible to all. Nevertheless the solemn farce of hearing the free and voluntary confessions was gone through with, and these two sheriffs and one other person then present were the three witnesses used in court to establish the so-called confessions, which were received by the court and admitted in evidence over the objections of the defendants duly entered of record as each of the said three witnesses delivered their alleged testimony. There was thus enough before the court when these confessions were first offered to make known to the court that they were not, beyond all reasonable doubt, free and voluntary; and the failure of the court then to exclude the confessions is sufficient to reverse the judgment, under every rule of procedure that has heretofore been prescribed, and hence it was not necessary subsequently to renew the objections by motion or otherwise.

"The spurious confessions having been obtained—and the farce last mentioned having been gone through with on Monday, April 2d—the court, then in session, on the following day, Tuesday, April 3, 1934, ordered the grand jury to reassemble on the succeeding day, April 4, 1934, at nine o'clock, and on the morning of the day last mentioned the grand jury returned an indictment against the defendants for murder. Late that afternoon the defendants were brought from the jail in the adjoining county and arraigned, when one or more of them offered to plead guilty, which the court declined to accept, and, upon inquiry whether they had or desired counsel, they stated that they had none, and did not suppose that counsel could be of any assistance to them. The court thereupon appointed counsel, and set the case for trial for the following morning at nine o'clock, and the defendants were returned to the jail in the adjoining county about thirty miles away.

"The defendants were brought to the courthouse of the county on the following morning, April 5th, and the so-called trial was opened, and was concluded on the next day, April 6, 1934, and resulted in a pretended conviction with death sentences. The evidence upon which the conviction was obtained was the so-called confessions. Without this evidence a peremptory instruction to find for the defendants would have been inescapable. The defendants were put on the stand, and by their testimony the facts and the details thereof as to the manner by which the confessions were extorted from them were fully developed, and it is further disclosed by the record that the same deputy, Dial, under whose guiding hand and active participation the tortures to coerce the confessions were administered, was actively in the performance of the supposed duties of a court deputy in the courthouse and in the presence of the prisoners during what is denominated, in complimentary terms, the trial of these defendants. This deputy was put on the stand by the state in rebuttal, and admitted the whippings. It is interesting to note that in his testimony with reference to the whipping of the defendant Ellington, and in response to the inquiry as to how severely he was whipped, the deputy stated, 'Not too much for a negro; not as much as I would have done if it were left to me.' Two others who had participated in these whippings were introduced and admitted it—not a single witness was introduced who denied it. The facts are not only undisputed, they are admitted, and admitted to have been done by officers of the state, in conjunction with other participants, and all this was definitely well known to everybody connected with the trial, and during the trial, including the state's prosecuting attorney and the trial judge presiding."

....

The State is free to regulate the procedure of its courts in accordance with its own conceptions of policy, unless in so doing it "offends some principle of justice so rooted in the traditions and conscience of our people as to be ranked as fundamental." *Snyder v. Massachusetts*, 291 U.S. 97, 105 (1934). The State may abolish trial by jury. It may dispense with indictment by a grand jury and substitute **complaint** or **information.** But the freedom of the State in establishing its policy is the freedom of constitutional government and is limited by the requirement of due process of law. Because a State may dispense with a jury trial, it does not follow that it may substitute trial by ordeal. The rack and torture chamber may not be substituted for the witness stand. The State may not permit an accused to be hurried to conviction under mob domination—where the whole proceeding is but a mask—without supplying corrective process. The State may not deny to the accused the aid of counsel. Nor may a State, through the action of its officers, contrive a conviction through the pretense of a trial which in truth is "but used as a means of depriving a defendant of liberty through a deliberate deception of court and jury by the presentation of testimony known to be perjured." And the trial equally is a mere pretense where the state authorities have contrived a conviction resting solely upon confessions obtained by violence. The **due process clause** requires "that state action, whether through one agency or another, shall be consistent with the fundamental principles of liberty and justice which lie at the base of all our civil and political institutions." It would be difficult to conceive of methods more revolting to the sense of justice than those taken to procure the confessions of these petitioners, and the use of the confessions thus obtained as the basis for conviction and sentence was a clear denial of due process.

In the instant case, the trial court was fully advised by the undisputed evidence of the way in which the confessions had been procured. The trial court knew that there was no other evidence upon which conviction and sentence could be based. Yet it proceeded to permit conviction and to pronounce a sentence. The conviction and sentence were void for want of the essential elements of due process, and the proceeding thus vitiated could be challenged in any appropriate manner. It was challenged before the Supreme Court of the State by the express invocation of the Fourteenth

Amendment. That court entertained the challenge, considered the federal question thus presented, but declined to enforce petitioners' constitutional right. The court thus denied a federal right fully established and specially set up and claimed and the judgment must be Reversed.

FURTHER CASE LAW, REFLECTIONS, AND QUESTIONS

1. What action would you take if you were a federal court judge confronted with the facts in *Brown v. Mississippi*? Should it matter that a state court had already reviewed the defendants' claims and found no constitutional error?
2. What new concern arises concerning the defendants' confessions in Brown v. Mississippi that were not an issue in the hypothetical Dirty Harry problem? Would your resolution of the issues presented in Brown be any different if, after having been subjected to the deputy sheriff's course of conduct, the defendants had led the deputy to a hidden grave in which the murder victim was buried?
3. What principles of justice are "so rooted in the traditions and conscience of our people as to be ranked as fundamental"?
4. Based on the decision in *Brown*, what do you think would happen in the prosecution of Scorpio?
5. How would you state the rule that the Court established in *Brown*?

Box 1.2: Briefing a Case

Brown v. Mississippi, 297 U.S. 278 (1936)

Facts. The Petitioners were indicted for a murder that occurred on March 30, 1934. The Petitioners were indicted on April 4, 1934, arraigned thereafter, and pled not guilty. Counsel were appointed by the court to defend them. The trial began the next morning and was concluded on the following day. The Petitioners were found guilty after a trial solely based on their confessions. During the trial, the Petitioners testified that the confessions were untrue and procured after physical torture. The Petitioners appealed to the Supreme Court of Mississippi, arguing that their Fourteenth Amendment rights were violated. The Supreme Court of Mississippi affirmed the trial court's judgment.

Petitioners filed a motion in the Mississippi Supreme Court for a new trial on the grounds that all the evidence against them was obtained by coercion and brutality known to the court and the district attorney, and that petitioners had been denied the benefit of counsel or opportunity to confer with counsel in a reasonable manner. The state supreme court again ruled against the Petitioners. Petitioners were granted a writ of certiorari.

Issue. Do convictions that rest solely upon confessions shown to have been extorted by officers of the state by brutality and violence, violate the due process of law required by the Fourteenth Amendment of the Constitution?

Holding. Yes, the due process clause was violated.

Rationale. The due process clause requires that state action be consistent with the fundamental principles of liberty and justice that lie at the base of all our civil and political institutions. While states may regulate the procedure of their courts in accordance with their own conceptions of policy, they may not if it offends some principle of justice so rooted in the traditions and conscience of our people as to be ranked as fundamental.

The actions by the police and courts in the present case were such that "[i]t would be difficult to conceive of methods more revolting to the sense of justice than those taken to procure the confessions of these petitioners, and the use of the confessions thus obtained as the basis for conviction and sentence was a clear denial of due process."

The egregious police actions to coerce confessions out of the defendants in *Brown v. Mississippi*, coupled with the clear racial overtones, are enough to shock and disturb any reasonable person in the twenty-first century. Such actions are undoubtedly a stain on the history of police in America, but are fortunately a relic primarily left in the past. If the police went too far in *Brown v. Mississippi*, what about the police taking a suspected seller of illegal drugs to the hospital to have his stomach pumped after observing the suspect swallow what appeared to be drugs? Should such methods be disapproved? Would it matter if the police were in a position to observe the suspect swallow the substance only after they had illegally entered his home?

Unlike *Brown v. Mississippi*, this issue is not primarily a relic of the past. Instead, the police conduct similar searches frequently by obtaining a search warrant or possessing an exception to the search warrant requirement and conducting forced blood draws on people suspected of driving under the influence.

Rochin v. California

342 U.S. 165 (1952)

MR. JUSTICE FRANKFURTER delivered the opinion of the Court.

Having "some information that [the petitioner here] was selling narcotics," three deputy sheriffs of the County of Los Angeles, on the morning of July 1, 1949, made for the two-story dwelling house in which Rochin lived with his mother, common-law wife, brothers, and sisters. Finding the outside door open, they entered and then forced open the door to Rochin's room on the second floor. Inside they found petitioner sitting partly dressed on the side of the bed, upon which his wife was lying. On a "nightstand" beside the bed the deputies spied two capsules. When asked "Whose stuff is this?" Rochin seized the capsules and put them in his mouth. A struggle ensued, in the course of which the three officers "jumped upon him" and attempted to extract the capsules. The force they applied proved unavailing against Rochin's resistance. He was handcuffed and taken to a hospital. At the direction of one of the officers, a doctor forced an emetic solution through a tube into Rochin's stomach against his will. This "stomach pumping" produced vomiting. In the vomited matter were found two capsules which proved to contain morphine.

Rochin was brought to trial before a California Superior Court, sitting without a jury, on the charge of possessing "a preparation of morphine" in violation of the California Health and Safety Code. Rochin was convicted and sentenced to sixty days' imprisonment. The chief evidence against him was the two capsules. They were admitted over petitioner's objection, although the means of obtaining them was frankly set forth in the testimony by one of the deputies, substantially as here narrated.

On appeal, the District Court of Appeal affirmed the conviction, despite the finding that the officers "were guilty of unlawfully breaking into and entering defendant's room and were guilty of unlawfully assaulting and battering defendant while in the room," and "were guilty of unlawfully assaulting, battering, torturing and falsely imprisoning the defendant at the alleged hospital."

This Court granted certiorari, because a serious question is raised as to the limitations which the Due Process Clause of the Fourteenth Amendment imposes on the conduct of criminal proceedings by the States.

. . . .

The vague contours of the Due Process Clause do not leave judges at large. We may not draw on our merely personal and private notions and disregard the limits that bind judges in their judicial function. Even though the concept of due process of law is not final and fixed, these limits are derived from considerations that are fused in the whole nature of our judicial process. These are considerations deeply rooted in reason and in the compelling traditions of the legal profession. The Due Process Clause places upon this Court the duty of exercising a judgment, within the narrow confines of judicial power in reviewing State convictions, upon interests of society pushing in opposite directions.

The faculties of the Due Process Clause may be indefinite and vague, but the mode of their ascertainment is not self-willed. In each case "due process of law" requires an evaluation based on a disinterested inquiry pursued in the spirit of science, on a balanced order of facts exactly and fairly stated, on the detached consideration of conflicting claims, on a judgment not *ad hoc* and episodic but duly mindful of reconciling the needs both of continuity and of change in a progressive society.

Applying these general considerations to the circumstances of the present case, we are compelled to conclude that the proceedings by which this conviction was obtained do more than offend some fastidious squeamishness or private sentimentalism about combatting crime too energetically. This is conduct that shocks the conscience. Illegally breaking into the privacy of the petitioner, the struggle to open his mouth and remove what was there, the forcible extraction of his stomach's contents—this course of proceeding by agents of government to obtain evidence is bound to offend even hardened sensibilities. They are methods too close to the rack and the screw to permit constitutional differentiation.

It has long since ceased to be true that due process of law is heedless of the means by which otherwise relevant and credible evidence is obtained. This was not true even before the series of recent cases enforced the constitutional principle that the States may not base convictions upon confessions, however much verified, obtained by coercion. These decisions are not arbitrary exceptions to the comprehensive right of States to fashion their own rules of evidence for criminal trials. They are not sports in our constitutional law but applications of a general principle. They are only instances of the general requirement that States in their prosecutions respect certain decencies of civilized conduct. Due process of law, as a historic and generative principle, precludes defining, and thereby confining, these standards of conduct more precisely than to say that convictions cannot be brought about by methods that offend "a sense of justice." See Mr. Chief Justice Hughes, speaking for a unanimous Court in *Brown v. Mississippi*, 297 U.S. 278, 285–286. It would be a stultification of the responsibility which the course of constitutional history has cast upon this Court to hold that in order to convict a man the police cannot extract by force what is in his mind but can extract what is in his stomach.

To attempt in this case to distinguish what lawyers call "real evidence" from verbal evidence is to ignore the reasons for excluding coerced confessions. Use of involuntary verbal confessions in State criminal trials is constitutionally obnoxious not only because of their unreliability. They are inadmissible under the Due Process Clause even though statements contained in them may be independently established as true. Coerced confessions offend the community's sense of fair play and decency. So here, to sanction the brutal conduct which naturally enough was condemned by the court whose judgment is before us, would be to afford brutality the cloak of law. Nothing would be more calculated to discredit law and thereby to brutalize the temper of a society.

On the facts of this case the conviction of the petitioner has been obtained by methods that offend the Due Process Clause. The judgment below must be Reversed.

FURTHER CASE LAW, REFLECTIONS, AND QUESTIONS

1. If the clarity of rules and the related ability of the police and courts to follow and apply those rules are legitimate concerns of the law of criminal procedure, how successful is Justice Frankfurter's explanation that the police conduct in *Rochin* "shocks the conscience"? What sort of guidance does a "shock-the-conscience" test provide for future cases? Whose conscience? How far must conduct go before it becomes shocking? Because the sheriff's deputies escorted Rochin to a hospital for procedures supervised by a physician, precisely what did the Court find shocking to the conscience in this case?
2. Note that the Court relied on the Fourteenth Amendment's due process clause to invalidate the convictions in both *Brown v. Mississippi* and *Rochin v. California*. "Due process of law" is an inherently imprecise standard. You may have wondered why, in *Brown*, the justices did not base their decision on the more specific prohibition against compelled self-incrimination found within the Fifth Amendment, or in Rochin, why the Court did not invoke the Fourth Amendment's protection against unreasonable searches and seizures. The answers primarily lie in the dates these cases were decided (1936 and 1952, respectively) and the Court's position at those times on whether rights specified in the Fifth Amendment, the Fourth Amendment, and elsewhere in the Bill of Rights directly applied to criminal proceedings in the state courts. We elaborate on this issue in Chapter 2.
3. Justice Frankfurter acknowledged elsewhere in *Rochin* that giving meaning to a concept such as due process of law "is a function of the process of judgment, [and] the judgment is bound to fall differently at different times and differently at the same time through different judges." Nevertheless, he insisted that:

> the vague contours of the Due Process Clause do not leave judges at large. We may not draw on our merely personal and private notions and disregard the limits that bind judges in their judicial function. Even though the concept of due process of law is not final and fixed, these limits are derived from considerations that are fused in the whole nature of our judicial process. These are considerations deeply rooted in reason and in the compelling traditions of the legal profession. 342 U.S., at 170–71 72.

When standards are so imprecise, is there any doubt that, try as they might to avoid it, the general life experiences and values that inform judges' reasoning will influence the decisions in cases? Isn't this inevitable? Is it altogether bad?

Conclusion

The issues introduced in this chapter illustrate many of the fundamental tensions inherent in criminal procedure law. Few other areas of law require the resolution of such dramatically opposed interests, with such compelling consequences to both individual citizens and organized society. The operating rules of criminal procedure law must prioritize and often resolve conflicts between deeply significant constitutional and policy objectives. These rules must be effective in the uncompromising context of the investigation and trial of criminal cases in which individuals and entire communities may have suffered grievous wrongs. As Justice Frankfurter once observed, "It is a fair summary of history to say that the safeguards of liberty have frequently been forged in controversies involving not very nice people." *United States v. Rabinowitz*, 336 U.S. 56, 69 (1950) (dissenting opinion).

One of the objectives of criminal procedure law is to promote reliable fact-finding or the ascertainment of the truth. This goal must occasionally be tempered to protect the individual liberties Americans cherish, including rights to be free from overreaching police, prosecutorial, and judicial action. Respecting the sovereignty of the states within this country's federal governmental system and helping to resolve cases finally and efficiently are additional ends of the law of criminal procedure. Assigning those interests weight and then balancing the competing interests is largely the courts' task through their interpretation and application of statutes and constitutional principles.

We have stressed in this chapter that the study of criminal procedure law appropriately focuses on the reasoning and analysis employed by the courts in justifying their decisions. It is far more important to understand how and why a court decided a case as it did than to simply be able to recite the case holding. We strongly urge that you "brief" cases during your studies to promote your understanding of the reasoning used by the courts and your ability to apply relevant legal principles in different contexts. There is no better tool for critically analyzing judicial rationale than the briefing process.

Value judgments often influence the resolution of criminal procedure issues. Professor Packer's description of the "crime control" and "due process" models of criminal procedure is a helpful summary of the dominant competing values in this area of law. You undoubtedly will notice the clash between the crime control and due-process schools of thought in the cases that lie ahead. Indeed, justifying preferences for the principles represented by these different models, in the context of deciding individual cases, is perhaps the principal recurring challenge in criminal procedure law.

KEY TERMS

case brief
caselaw
concurring opinion
crime control perspective
criminal procedure law
dissenting opinion
due process clause
due process perspective
facts
habeas corpus
holding
indictment
information
issue
majority opinion
precedent
rationale
stare decisis
writ of certiorari

REVIEW QUESTIONS

1. Is the law stable and constant, or is it a more dynamic process? If it is more dynamic and changing, name several factors that influence this change.
2. What are the goals and objectives of criminal procedure? Which goal or objective do you think is the most important?
3. What are the main challenges associated with the application of criminal procedure?
4. What do scholars mean when they refer to the "Dirty Harry Problem?"
5. What two contrasting principles are the bases for the development of criminal procedure?
6. Of the two criminal justice models presented by Herbert Packer, which model seeks to maintain individual liberties? How does this model attempt to do so?
7. Considering the "crime control" and "due process" perspectives, which perspective do you think aligns the best with a conservative political ideology? What about a more liberal political ideology?
8. What is the purpose of a case brief? What are a brief's key components?
9. What is precedent? Why is it important in the establishment of criminal procedure law?
10. How do *Brown v. Mississippi* and *Rochin v. California* relate to each other?

REFERENCES

Gearan, A. (2014, August 5). U.S. has no information on jailed Post reporter. Retrieved from Washington Post. https://www.washingtonpost.com/world/national-security/us-has-no-information-on-jailed-post-reporter/2014/08/05/e0e17e52-1ce7-11e4-9b6c-12e30cbe86a3_story.html

Klockars, C. B. (1980). The Dirty Harry problem. *The Annals of the American Academy of Political and Social Science, 452*(1), 33-47.

Packer, H. (1968). *The limits of the criminal sanction.* Stanford University Press.

Tyler, T. R., & Huo, Y. J. (2002). *Trust in the law: Encouraging public cooperation with the police and courts.* Russell Sage Foundation.

Warrick, J. & Morello, C. (2014, December 10). Detention taking 'devastating toll' on Post reporter locked up in Iran. *Washington Post.* Retrieved from https://www.washingtonpost.com/national/detention-taking-devastating-toll-on-post-reporter-detained-in-iran/2014/12/10/bf4036a8-8015-11e4-9f38-95a187e4c1f7_story.html

Zalman, M., Smith, B., & Kiger, A. (2008). Officials' estimates of the incidence of "actual innocence" convictions. *Justice Quarterly, 25*(1), 72-100.

CHAPTER 2

Building Blocks for the Study of Criminal Procedure

LEARNING OBJECTIVES

After reading this chapter, students should be able to:

- Understand federalism and the relationship between state and federal court systems
- Know which amendments in the Bill of Rights and the United States Constitution regulate and influence criminal procedure
- Comprehend the debate concerning the Incorporation Doctrine and how the Incorporation Doctrine changed criminal procedure at the state level
- Explain the importance of the Supremacy Clause
- Comprehend the process by which a criminal case moves through the criminal justice system and what happens at each of the individual stages in the court process
- Understand the system of case reporters where judicial opinions are published for the federal and state systems

Introduction

This chapter lays the groundwork for examining criminal procedure by presenting fundamental principles and key components of the judicial system. It begins by exploring core concepts, including federalism, the Bill of Rights, incorporation, the **Supremacy Clause**, and the influence of state constitutions on criminal procedure. Additionally, it delves into historical debates surrounding these topics to provide context for their development and current applications.

Next, the chapter offers a detailed overview of the typical adjudication process for a felony charge in a state court, tracing the steps from arrest to appeal. This procedural outline is followed by examining the structure and organization of the federal court system, highlighting the various levels of courts and their respective roles.

To facilitate a deeper understanding of the judicial system, the chapter also discusses the mechanics of federal and state court citations and provides guidance on locating court cases. This practical knowledge equips readers with essential tools for navigating and comprehending the legal landscape.

While this chapter diverges from the case study method utilized elsewhere in the book, it sets the stage for subsequent case analyses by establishing foundational concepts and frameworks. Although readers may be familiar with some topics, others may be new or warrant additional explanation. As these subjects will reemerge in later discussions, this chapter serves as an introduction to prepare readers for more comprehensive explorations of criminal procedure issues.

On Courts and Constitutions: State and Federal Relationships

One distinguishing feature of the American government is **federalism**, the division of power between the states and the national government. Following the much-impassioned debate, the framers of the United States Constitution defined the proper relationship between the state and federal governments and their respective spheres of authority. The Constitution enumerates and thus limits the power of the federal government's legislative, executive, and judicial branches. The Tenth Amendment to the Constitution, which was ratified in 1791, three years after the Constitution was adopted, provides that powers not delegated to the federal government by that founding charter are reserved to the states. The Tenth Amendment was adopted as part of a compromise between the Federalists—who favored a strong national government and urged that the United States Constitution be ratified by the original 13 states—and the Antifederalists—who distrusted the idea of a strong national sovereign and opposed ratification of the Constitution for that reason.

State and federal governments have distinct powers in some matters; in others, their authority overlaps, which can be confusing and cumbersome. The states have control over the criminal laws they adopt and over deciding how violators of those laws should be punished. The overwhelming number of crimes committed in this country are offenses against states and are prosecuted and disposed of in the state courts and state criminal justice systems. Beyond state crimes, the federal government, through Congress, has defined certain conduct as crimes against the national sovereign, and those offenses are punished according to federal law.

Federalism is also efficient because of the division of labor and the ability to afford more control to local governments. This system not only ensures a more effective distribution of responsibilities but also empowers localities to address the specific needs of their communities. Additionally, federalism safeguards minority rights by decentralizing power and allowing for diverse approaches to policy across the country.

However, the balance of power between federal and state governments remains a point of contention, as critics argue that the federal government often oversteps its bounds. Contentious issues such as abortion, marijuana laws, and the response to the Coronavirus pandemic have reignited debates surrounding states' rights and the proper scope of federal authority.

Despite these complexities, state and local agencies—including law enforcement, courts, and corrections facilities—are obligated to uphold the United States Constitution as the foundation of the law. While states may build upon these constitutional principles, they cannot erode or diminish the rights and protections guaranteed to citizens. As such, federalism serves as a dynamic framework that enables both unity and diversity, requiring continuous negotiation and adaptation to maintain the balance between centralized and localized governance.

The Bill of Rights and Its Application to the States

The United States Constitution was ratified in 1788 after an extensive debate between Federalists, who favored its adoption, and Antifederalists, who objected to several new constitutional features. Federalists, including Alexander Hamilton, John Jay, and James Madison, who collaborated on the essays that make up the famous *Federalist Papers*, perceived the need for a strong national government. They cited numerous deficiencies in the Articles of Confederation, which were the nation's governing charter before 1788. For example, under the Articles of Confederation, the federal government had no authority to levy taxes, regulate interstate commerce, or preempt the states from coining money. Leadership in the executive branch was diffused among a series of special committees, and no federal judiciary had been created. For their part, Antifederalists such as Patrick Henry, Luther Martin, and George Mason feared that the creation of a powerful central government would compromise state sovereignty. Although this concern was motivated mainly by economic interests, the prospect of concentrating too much power in the national government also stirred memories of King George's tyrannical reign and was cited as a threat to individual liberties.

To appease the Antifederalists and bolster their case for ratification, the Federalists extended a promise that immediately upon adoption of the Constitution, the First Congress would prepare and submit to the states a series of amendments that would specifically limit the powers of the new federal government. Such assurances were made in several state conventions in which the Constitution's ratification was debated. The crucial point for our purposes is that the proposed amendments to the Constitution would limit the *federal* government; certainly, the Antifederalists and others contemplating this action had no desire to see the state governments subjected to additional regulation.

True to this plan, Congress approved a dozen amendments to the newly ratified Constitution in 1789 and then forwarded them to the state legislatures for their consideration. The required approval of three-fourths of the state legislatures was secured for 10 amendments by 1791. These original amendments to the Constitution are collectively known as the **Bill of Rights**. Several of them limited the new government's power over individuals in ways directly relevant to criminal procedure law. (Select amendments to the United States Constitution are reprinted in the Appendix.) In light of the government's extraordinary authority to punish people by fine, imprisonment, and even execution, and the related risk that this authority would be abused, it is understandable that the Bill of Rights devoted much attention to protecting individual liberties in enforcing criminal laws. Nevertheless, it merits emphasis that the Bill of Rights protections originally were enacted as limitations on the federal government's power and that they were not meant to apply against the states or influence the enforcement of state criminal laws (*Barron v. The Mayor and City Council of Baltimore*, 32 U.S. 7 Pet. 243 [1833]).

The adoption of the Fourteenth Amendment in 1868 represented a significant departure from the design of the first ten amendments. The Fourteenth Amendment, in part, directly addresses state governments. It provides that:

> No State shall make or enforce any law which shall abridge the privileges and immunities of citizens of the United States; nor shall any State deprive any person of life, liberty, or property, without due process of law; nor deny to any person within its **jurisdiction** the equal protection of the laws.

Controversy brewed for several generations about the nature of the relationship between the Fourteenth Amendment and the specific rights guaranteed in the Bill of Rights. Questions mainly focused on the meaning of the **due process clause** in this context. When the Fourteenth Amendment promised that no "State [shall] deprive any person of life, liberty, or property, without due process of law," was this a shorthand way of saying that the states must recognize the same rights in their criminal proceedings as the ones spelled out in the Bill of Rights? In other words, must the states respect protections against unreasonable searches and seizures (as in the Fourth Amendment), against compelled self-incrimination, double jeopardy, the right to indictment by a grand jury (Fifth Amendment), and the right to a speedy and public trial by jury, a notice of the accusation, confrontation, compulsory process, and the assistance of counsel (Sixth Amendment), and the rights to bail and freedom from excessive fines and cruel and unusual punishments (Eighth Amendment), or else violate an individual's rights to due process of law?

The Incorporation Debate

Applying specific provisions in the Bill of Rights to the states via the 14th Amendment involves what is referred to as incorporation. While all agreed that some rights should be applied to the states, the specific rights and the basis for their incorporation were hotly debated. Beginning in the late 1800s, courts and legal scholars debated on what theoretical basis rights should be incorporated. These debates have centered around three doctrines.

Fundamental Fairness

The **fundamental fairness doctrine** was first adopted by the Supreme Court in *Hurtado v. California*, 110 U.S. 516 (1884). The *Hurtado* court held that provisions of the Bill of Rights did not apply to the states so long as state procedures fell within the limits of those fundamental principles of liberty and justice that were embodied in the Fourteenth Amendment. 110 U.S. at 535. Over time, the Court found that governmental actions that "shock the conscience," "offended civilized sensibilities," or went beyond a community's social sense of "fair play" or "decency" would give rise to **incorporation** of the rights involved in the particular case. See *Rochin v. California*, 342 U.S. 165 (1952). The standards required courts to evaluate the applicability of specific rights on a case-by-case basis and inhibited predictability.

Total Incorporation

Under the **total incorporation** doctrine, any right mentioned in the Bill of Rights should be applied to the state. Simply put, under the principle of total incorporation, the states and the federal government have the same obligations to honor the rights and liberties of their citizens.

Selective Incorporation

The **selective incorporation** paradigm of absorption by the Fourteenth Amendment says that the states are obligated to grant only those rights and liberties included in the Bill of Rights that are fundamental principles of liberty. This doctrine favors incorporating specific protections provided for in the Bill of Rights that would be considered independently from each other. Rights enumerated in the Bill of Rights would apply to the states if they were found to apply "those fundamental principles of liberty and justice which lie at the base of all our civil and political institutions."

The "incorporation versus fundamental fairness" controversy came to a head in the 1960s in a series of criminal procedure cases decided during Earl Warren's tenure as Chief Justice of the Supreme Court. In what has been hailed by some as a "due-process revolution" that dramatically reshaped the federal-state landscape in criminal procedure law, the Warren Court selectively incorporated most of the Bill of Rights guarantees through the Fourteenth Amendment's due-process clause by ruling that they must be observed in state proceedings. Eschewing both the total incorporation and the fundamental fairness philosophies, a majority of the justices examined the specific criminal procedure rights in the first 10 amendments to determine whether each should apply to the states. If a right was incorporated, it applied in state cases according to the same rules ("jot for jot") as it did in federal cases. Justice White's opinion for the Court in *Duncan v. Louisiana*, 391 U.S. 145 (1968), held that the Sixth Amendment right to trial by jury applies to the states through the Fourteenth Amendment's due-process clause. We reproduce the portion of this opinion that explains the standard used by the Court when it selectively incorporates Bill of Rights protections via the Fourteenth Amendment.

Duncan v. Louisiana

391 U.S. 145 (1968)

MR. JUSTICE WHITE delivered the opinion of the Court.

The Fourteenth Amendment denies the states the power to "deprive any person of life, liberty, or property, without due process of law." In resolving conflicting claims concerning the meaning of this spacious language, the Court has looked increasingly to the Bill of Rights for guidance; many of the rights guaranteed by the first eight Amendments to the Constitution have been held to be protected against state action by the Due Process Clause of the Fourteenth Amendment. That clause now protects the right to compensation for property taken by the state; the rights of speech, press, and religion covered by the First Amendment; the Fourth Amendment rights to be free from unreasonable searches and seizures and to have excluded from criminal trials any evidence illegally seized; the right guaranteed by the Fifth Amendment to be free of compelled self-incrimination; and the Sixth Amendment rights to counsel, to a speedy and public trial, to confrontation of opposing witnesses, and to compulsory process for obtaining witnesses.

The test for determining whether a right extended by the Fifth and Sixth Amendments with respect to federal criminal proceedings is also protected against state action by the Fourteenth Amendment has been phrased in a variety of ways in the opinions of this Court. The question has been asked whether a right is among those "fundamental principles of liberty and justice which lie at the base of all our civil and political institutions,' " *Powell v. State of Alabama*, 287 U.S. 45, 67 (1932); whether it is "basic in our system of jurisprudence," *In re Oliver*, 333 U.S. 257, 273 (1948); and whether it is "a fundamental right, essential to a fair trial," *Gideon v. Wainwright*, 372 U.S. 335, 343–344 (1963). The claim before us is that the right to trial by jury guaranteed by the Sixth Amendment meets these tests. The position of Louisiana, on the other hand, is that the Constitution imposes upon the states no duty to give a jury trial in any criminal case, regardless of the seriousness of the crime or the size of the punishment which may be imposed. Because we believe that trial by jury in criminal cases is fundamental to the American scheme of justice, we hold that the Fourteenth Amendment guarantees a right of jury trial in all criminal cases which—were they to be tried in a federal court—would come within the Sixth Amendment's guarantee. Since we consider the appeal before us to be such a case, we hold that the Constitution was violated when appellant's demand for jury trial was refused.

FURTHER CASE LAW, REFLECTIONS, AND QUESTIONS

1. Can you imagine a system of justice that could fairly be administered without using a body of citizens (i.e., a trial jury) to listen to the evidence and decide whether a defendant is guilty of criminal charges? Would such a system resemble how criminal justice is administered in the United States? Which of these questions was of principal interest to the Court in *Duncan*?
2. Justice Harlan wrote a lengthy dissenting opinion in *Duncan.* It was a spirited refutation of selective incorporation and a defense of the position "that 'due process of law' requires only that criminal trials be fundamentally fair." In his view, "The Bill of Rights is not necessarily irrelevant to the search for guidance in interpreting the Fourteenth Amendment, but the reason for and nature of its relevance must be articulated." He argued that the Court's task:

   > [I]s to start with the words "liberty" and "due process of law" and attempt to define them in a way that accords with American traditions and our system of government. This approach, involving a much more discriminating process of adjudication than does "incorporation," is, albeit difficult, the one that was followed throughout the nineteenth and most of the present century. It entails a "gradual process of judicial inclusion and exclusion," seeking, with due recognition of constitutional tolerance for state experimentation and disparity, to ascertain those "immutable principles of justice which inhere in the very idea of free government which no member of the Union may disregard."

   Do standards such as these strike you as being more subjective—that is, determined according to the predilections of individual judges—or objective—that is, ascertainable by reference to external, neutral principles? Do they provide meaningful guidance to the police, prosecutors, and other courts? Is their generality and flexibility more of an asset or a liability to constitutional adjudication?

The controversy surrounding the incorporation of Bill of Rights protections through the Fourteenth Amendment to apply in state criminal proceedings marked a tremendously significant chapter in the development of constitutional criminal procedure. Through the cases cited in Justice White's opinion in *Duncan v. Louisiana* and others, the Supreme Court proceeded to "federalize" state criminal procedure rules by selectively incorporating Bill of Rights guarantees. Today, with only a few exceptions, the same rights relating to criminal procedure spelled out in the first ten amendments must also be observed in the state courts. While concluding that the Second Amendment's right "to keep and bear Arms" is binding on the states as well as on the federal government, Justice Alito's majority opinion for the Court in *McDonald v. City of Chicago*, 561 U.S. 742, (2010) included a lengthy discussion of the incorporation debate and the history of the relationship between the Bill of Rights and the Fourteenth Amendment's Due Process Clause.

Although most of the rights in the Bill of Rights have been incorporated via the Fourteenth Amendment and made applicable to state court proceedings, not all of them have. For example, one exception to the general rule that the states must observe the Bill of Rights protections in their criminal cases involves the right to indictment by a grand jury. Although the Fifth Amendment provides for indictment by a grand jury in "capital or otherwise infamous crime[s]," (i.e., felonies), and such a procedure must be followed in federal criminal prosecutions, the Supreme Court has ruled that the states need not use grand jury indictments to begin felony prosecutions (See, *Hurtado v. California*, 110 U.S. 516, [1884]). Additionally, incorporation is not just a relic of history. The Eighth Amendment's prohibition against excessive fines was recently incorporated and made applicable to state court proceedings in *Timbs v. Indiana*, 586 U.S. 146 (2019). Furthermore, there are still rights yet to be looked at by the Court. For example, the justices have not decided whether the Third Amendment's prohibition against quartering soldiers applies to state proceedings via the Fourteenth Amendment.

In the wake of the "due-process revolution" produced by Warren Court decisions during the 1960s, state and federal rules of constitutional criminal procedure increasingly became synonymous (see Box 2.1). As the Supreme Court established rights that both federal and state criminal justice officials were constitutionally required to observe, the states generally were forced to respond by affording defendants greater protections to satisfy these threshold expectations. There is no question that criminal procedure law has been fundamentally transformed due to the Supreme Court's selective incorporation of Bill of Rights protections to the states. However, federal constitutional standards have not entirely displaced state sources of law in criminal procedure issues.

Box 2.1 Rights Incorporated by the Fourteenth Amendment

Amendment	Right	Important Case
First	Freedom of Speech	*Fiske v. Kansas* (1927)
Second	Right to bear arms	*McDonald v. Chicago* (2010)
Fourth	Unreasonable Search and Seizure	*Wolf v. Colorado* (1949)
	Exclusionary Rule	*Mapp v. Ohio* (1961)
Fifth	Self-Incrimination	*Malloy v. Hogan* (1964)
	Double Jeopardy	*Benton v. Maryland* (1969)
Sixth	Right to Counsel	*Gideon v. Wainwright* (1963)
	Confront Witnesses	*Pointer v. Texas* (1965)
	Speedy Trial	*Klopfer v. North Carolina* (1967)
	Compulsory Process	*Washington v. Texas* (1967)
	Public Trial	*In re Oliver* (1948)
	Impartial Jury	*Duncan v. Louisiana* (1968)
Eighth	Cruel and Unusual Punishment	*Robinson v. California* (1962)
	Excessive Fines	*Timbs v. Indiana* (2019)

State Constitutions and Criminal Procedure

Referring to himself and the other members of the Supreme Court, Justice Jackson once remarked that "we are not final because we are infallible, but we are infallible only because we are final" (*Brown v. Allen*, 344 U.S. 443, [1953]). This observation accurately summarizes the Supreme Court's authority in interpreting the United States Constitution. Under the Constitution's **supremacy clause**, the state courts must honor the Supreme Court's federal constitutional decisions even if they disagree with them. State judges are not at liberty either to diminish the scope of federal constitutional protections defined by the Supreme Court or to rule that the Supreme Court misinterpreted the federal Constitution by not going far enough to protect individual rights.

Supreme Court rulings interpreting the Bill of Rights, the Fourteenth Amendment, and other federal constitutional provisions determine whether the government's conduct squares with minimally acceptable constitutional standards. In other words, the Supreme Court sets the floor, not the ceiling, of individual rights. Even though they cannot cut back on federal constitutional safeguards, the states are perfectly free to enact statutes that give individuals greater rights and afford more rights to their citizens. Enhanced protections for individual liberties can also be provided through another source: state constitutions. State courts can rely on a state statute or constitutional provision to extend (but not diminish) a criminal defendant's rights beyond what the federal Constitution requires. When it takes such action, its state law ruling is insulated from further review by the United States Supreme Court.

The State and Federal Court Systems

The State Court Process

To the consternation of criminal justice students, the criminal adjudication process can be complex and convoluted. States vary in how they structure their criminal court process. Further complicating the process of studying is that states sometimes use different names for the same proceeding. While reading the general description below (we will cover these processes in greater detail throughout the book), it should not be forgotten that each state has slight nuances that may be lost in the explanation below. The process will also be more streamlined and different for someone charged with a misdemeanor offense. The court process discussed below is the average or typical state court process for someone accused of a felony in a state court.

Arrest, Booking, and Initial Appearance

A suspect is booked into the county jail immediately following an arrest, whether based on an arrest warrant or probable cause. When the police book a suspected offender, they record the suspect's name and address, the offense for which the suspect was arrested, and the date and time of the **booking**. The suspect is fingerprinted and photographed. These record-keeping procedures are usually completed at the county jail or occasionally at the police station. They are performed routinely and do not determine whether or with what offense a suspect will be formally charged later.

After booking, a complaint is filed with a magistrate, accusing the suspect of a crime. A **complaint** is a brief statement of the specific charges against the suspect. It must be supported by the sworn statement of a complainant affirming that the allegations in the complaint are accurate to the best of the complainant's knowledge. The complainant need not be the victim or a witness to the alleged crime; the arresting police officer, who may have no direct knowledge of the facts supporting the complaint, often serves as the complainant. The complaint serves as the pending charges against the suspect until formal charges are brought through either an information or an indictment. Once the complaint has been filed, the suspect officially becomes a defendant.

A defendant in custody following an arrest has the right to a prompt judicial determination that probable cause supports their continued detention. This proceeding, which ordinarily is required within 48 hours of arrest, is most commonly referred to as the first or initial appearance, or by other names in different states.

The **initial appearance** on the complaint is a brief, nonadversarial proceeding. Magistrates, who are court officials but are not necessarily lawyers, and are not judges, preside at first appearances in many jurisdictions. At this proceeding, the defendant appears before the magistrate in person or over video conference from the local jail. The most important part of the initial appearance is the magistrate making a judicial determination of probable cause to ensure the police had the requisite justification for arresting the person. Although this is frequently *pro forma* (as a matter of form), it is an essential check on government power. It is important that someone, an objective magistrate not engaged in the competitive task of ferreting out crime, ensures the police have the right to arrest the defendant. In addition, the magistrate is responsible for informing the defendant of the charges made in the complaint and advising them of certain rights, including the right to representation by counsel, the right to appointment of counsel if indigent, and the right to remain silent. An inquiry into indigency is also made so the magistrate can determine whether the accused qualifies for court-appointed counsel. More often than not, the magistrate will also consider **bail** at this hearing and decide if the person should be released on their own recognizance, based on a set bail amount, or held pending trial. In some jurisdictions, a separate bail hearing will be held.

The next step in a state felony prosecution is a judicial determination of probable cause to go forward to trial, which occurs via a preliminary hearing, a grand jury proceeding, or possibly both, depending on the state. The **preliminary hearing** is an adversarial proceeding where the prosecution must present sufficient evidence to convince a judge that there is probable cause to believe the accused committed the crime alleged in the complaint. A preliminary hearing is typically held between several days and a few weeks after the initial appearance. The defense rarely presents evidence at a preliminary hearing and will primarily only cross-examine witnesses. The judge's job is not to decide guilt or innocence in this proceeding. Instead, the judge determines whether probable cause exists to support the charges to go forward to trial. The defense is not obligated to present anything, and it would likely be disadvantageous to do so. This hearing allows the defense to examine some witnesses and evidence the prosecution will use if and when the case is scheduled for trial. If the judge concludes that there is probable cause to believe that the defendant committed the charged crime, and this threshold showing is seldom satisfied, the defendant is bound over for further proceedings. Frequently, the defense will voluntarily waive the preliminary hearing.

Another way to determine if there is probable cause to go forward to trial, which is required in many states, is a grand jury proceeding. A **grand jury** indictment is a formal charge reflecting the judgment of at least a majority of the citizens serving on the grand jury that there is probable cause to believe that the accused committed the crime. Grand juries commonly number up to 23 people. However, they have the authority to require additional witnesses to appear. Where the preliminary hearing is adversarial, the grand jury is considered an informal "secret" proceeding where only the prosecution, grand jurors, and any possible witnesses who have been called are present. Historically, the grand jury was considered necessary because decisions are made by an independent panel of regular citizens, not government officials. The grand jury is designed to serve as a check on government power, overzealous prosecution, and protection against biases that prosecutors or judges might harbor. When a grand jury returns a true bill of indictment before the preliminary hearing is scheduled, such action preempts the need for a preliminary hearing. Bypassing the preliminary hearing can be advantageous to the prosecution because it does not have to present witnesses or other evidence in a public, adversarial proceeding and thus reveal information about its case.

Additionally, some states do not use grand juries. Instead, a prosecutor's **information** serves as the formal charging instrument for felony trials. To check prosecutorial charging powers, a preliminary hearing and a judicial determination of probable cause are usually mandatory when a prosecutor's information is the exclusive charging instrument unless the defendant waives the proceeding.

Arraignment

After being bound over from the preliminary hearing or the issuance of a true bill on the indictment from a grand jury, the next hearing is the **arraignment**. The indictment or information replaces the complaint as the formal charging instrument at this stage. In this context, an arraignment is a summary proceeding at which the defendant appears in court, is advised of the official charges filed, and is asked to enter a plea of guilty or not guilty to the charges. It is common for defendants to waive their right to appear at the arraignment and for their attorneys to enter a not-guilty plea on their behalf. A not-guilty plea entered at the arraignment can later be switched to a plea of guilty. The judge will schedule a trial date at the arraignment, presuming a plea of not guilty. However, it is assumed most cases will never reach trial and that the defendant will eventually agree to a plea bargain.

Plea Negotiations and Pretrial Motions

Once a defendant is formally arraigned, the case typically gets transferred to a trial court. For a felony, this would be a **court of general jurisdiction**. At this point, the parties will participate in discovery, which involves disclosing information and evidence collected by the parties. After reviewing the materials disclosed during discovery and conducting witness interviews, the parties will enter into plea negotiations. Assuming this does not lead to a plea bargain, the parties will file **pretrial motions**. These include motions to suppress unlawfully seized evidence from being used at trial, motions to bar irrelevant witnesses from testifying, and similar motions that set the stage for the trial.

The Criminal Trial

Although most cases in the United States are adjudicated via a plea bargain, a small number of cases make it to trial. A criminal trial is the perfect personification of our adversarial system in action, with the prosecution and defense presenting their respective sides. Ideally, the jury can ferret out the truth or at least a just decision after this process. The principal job of the trial courts is to determine whether a criminal defendant is guilty as charged and, if so, to impose a sentence. At a felony trial, a jury hears testimony, considers evidence, and renders a verdict of guilty or not guilty. For a person to be found guilty of a crime, the jury must unanimously find that the prosecution proved beyond a reasonable doubt that the defendant committed the crime.

Sentencing

Presuming the jury finds the defendant guilty, or if there is no trial and the defendant pleads guilty, a sentencing hearing follows. It is up to the judge to impose a sentence on the defendant. However, if the guilty plea was the result of a plea bargain, there is a heavy influence from the prosecution concerning the sentence that the judge must approve. Before sentencing, the judge is provided a presentence investigation report about the defendant that informs them about their history and information about, for example, psychological and medical or financial issues that may influence sentencing. A judge's decision concerning the sentence or punishment imposed might also be constrained by the type of sentencing used in the state or legislation in a state concerning certain crimes or sentences for repeat offenders. For example, some states use sentencing guidelines. There are also three-strikes laws and mandatory minimums.

Appeals, Discretionary Review, and Post-conviction Motions

A defendant convicted of a crime has the right to at least one **appeal** to a higher court. This involves asking a higher court to review the record of the lower court proceedings for errors in the application of the law. This does not involve relitigating facts that the jury has decided, but on legal matters decided by the judge. In most states, this will be an appeal to an intermediate court, typically called a Court of Appeals, while in the federal system, appeals are heard by a Circuit Court of Appeals. Above these courts sit state supreme courts and the United States Supreme Court. A defendant does not have a right to have their case heard by these higher courts. The standard method of asking a higher court to consider a case following the initial appeal is by a petition for a writ of certiorari, or a petition for **discretionary review**. A state supreme court usually will review a court of appeals' decision in a criminal case only if it determines that the issues are novel or of such general importance that they merit consideration.

Following a state supreme court's adverse action on appeal or on writ of certiorari, a criminal defendant has three options to seek further judicial review of their conviction and sentence: (1) file a motion for post-conviction relief in the trial court; (2) petition the United States Supreme Court to issue its writ of certiorari and consider the case; or (3) file a petition for a writ of habeas corpus in a U.S. District Court, asking that court to review federal constitutional issues presented in the case.

A state postconviction motion typically raises claims that could not have been presented on appeal. This happens when the record reviewed by the appeals court lacks information necessary for the resolution. The most common claims of this nature involve allegations that defense counsel provided ineffective representation; that prosecutorial misconduct, such as the failure to disclose exculpatory evidence or the use of perjured testimony, tainted the trial; or that newly discovered evidence supporting the defendant's innocence surfaced after the completion of the trial. When confronted with such claims, the trial-level court will preside over an evidentiary hearing where necessary and rule on the defendant's motion for a new trial. Then, based on the record developed at this hearing, either the defendant or the state is in a position to appeal an adverse ruling to the appropriate state appeals court. Until a defendant has "exhausted state remedies" by raising challenges to a conviction or sentence in the state courts, the federal courts will not consider these issues. Such a policy is designed to allow state judges the first chance to rule on legal issues arising in the state courts, which is consistent with principles of Federalism and also helps spare the federal courts from being overwhelmed. Because a defendant generally is required to join all case-related issues in a single federal habeas corpus petition, state post-conviction claims generally are pursued before federal habeas corpus relief is sought.

A state defendant's other post-appeal options for challenging their conviction or sentence—filing a petition for a writ of certiorari in the United States Supreme Court and filing a petition for a writ of habeas corpus—involve the federal court system.

The Federal Court System

The federal courts are organized much like state court systems. Federal crimes are prosecuted in federal trial courts, the U.S. District Courts. If a defendant is convicted, they can appeal to an intermediate appellate court, the United States Court of Appeals, in the appropriate federal circuit. The United States Supreme Court is at the top of the federal court system. Virtually all of the Supreme Court's docket is determined by the justices' discretionary decisions to hear cases on petitions for writ of certiorari. The Court will hear a case if four of the nine members of the Supreme Court vote to grant "cert." Each year, the Supreme Court receives thousands (recently, more than 8,000) certiorari petitions, yet the justices typically decide about 100 cases, give or take a few.

The pretrial process in the federal system—from arrest to booking, the filing of a complaint, a magistrate's determination of probable cause to support an arrestee's detention, the suspect's first appearance before a magistrate, the preliminary hearing, indictment by a grand jury (which is required in federal felony cases), arraignment, and pretrial motions—also closely resembles typical state criminal justice procedures.

Ninety-four U.S. District Courts are scattered throughout the United States and U.S. territories. At least one federal district court exists in each state and the District of Columbia. Two or more U.S. district courts serve larger and more heavily populated states. Such states are subdivided into the Northern, Southern, Eastern, Western, and/or Middle Districts, and the district courts conduct their business accordingly. One or more (sometimes many more) judges are assigned to each U.S. district court; well over 600 fully active judges staff the 94 courts. Even when two or more judges have been appointed to the same court, U.S. district court judges almost always decide cases individually, rather than using multi-judge panels.

In addition to presiding over federal criminal trials, U.S. District Court judges perform other functions, including the important job of ruling on the federal habeas corpus petitions filed by state prisoners. A federal statute, 28 U.S.C. §2254, authorizes state prisoners to petition a federal district court for habeas corpus relief on the ground that their conviction or sentence was obtained or imposed in violation of the United States Constitution. A federal court's review is limited to federal constitutional issues, so questions that turn solely on the proper interpretation or application of state law cannot be considered.

U.S. Circuit Courts of Appeal decide appeals from U.S. District Court rulings. The 50 states and federal territories are divided into 11 geographic regions or circuits. One U.S. Court of Appeals presides over each of these circuits. Another U.S. Court of Appeals, the Federal Circuit Court of Appeals, is assigned to the District of Columbia, owing to the large volume of federal business conducted in the nation's capital. The Federal Circuit Court of Appeals has also been designated to decide appeals in patent, copyright, trademark, and other specialized cases. Figure 2.2 shows how these federal circuits are distributed across the country.

The U.S. courts of appeals decide appeals only from the U.S. district courts within their respective circuits. Thus, the First Circuit Court of Appeals resolves appeals from the federal district courts that sit in Maine, New Hampshire, and Massachusetts; the Second Circuit Court of Appeals hears appeals from the U.S. district courts in Vermont, New York, and Connecticut; and so on. (See Figure 2.1.) The authority of the U.S. courts of appeals does not extend beyond their geographic boundaries. For example, while all of the federal district courts in Maine, New Hampshire, and Massachusetts must abide by the rulings of the First Circuit Court of Appeals, no other district court in the country is required to do so. The different U.S. courts of appeals occasionally disagree about the proper interpretation of the law, and these disagreements may not be resolved until the Supreme Court announces a rule that binds all of the federal courts.

Figure 2.1 Geographic Boundaries of Federal Circuit Courts of Appeal

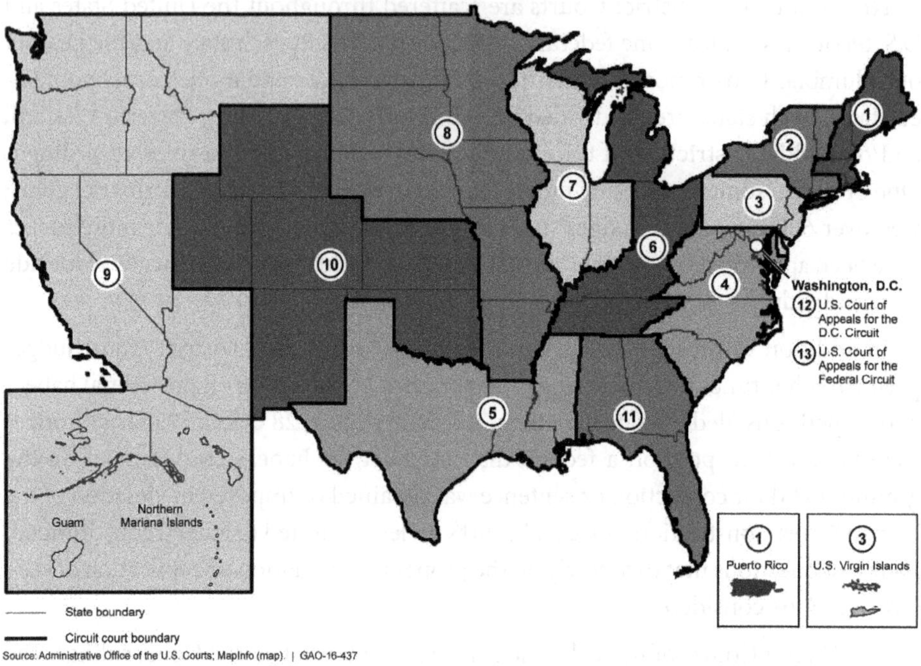

Cases appealed to the U.S. courts of appeals are initially considered by three-judge panels. Most of these courts have between 10 and 15 fully active (non-senior) judges, although the First Circuit has fewer (about 6) and the Ninth Circuit includes significantly more (about 29) active judges. The party who loses the appeal can ask all judges on the court to sit ***en banc*** ("in the bench") and reconsider the decision of a three-judge panel. Such *en banc* hearings are rare and granted only in controversial cases.

The U.S. Supreme Court is the court of last resort in the federal system and on all issues of federal law. Nine justices serve on the Supreme Court, one of whom is appointed by the president as the chief justice. As we have discussed, it is quite rare for the Supreme Court to hear cases on appeal; the justices almost always choose the cases they will decide by considering petitions for a writ of certiorari.

Once a case reaches the Supreme Court, lawyers for the **petitioner** and **respondent** are required to file briefs and present oral arguments to the justices. In this context, a brief is the written argument and collection of authorities submitted to a court concerning a legal question.

Case Citations: Finding the Law

As we have previously discussed, the term cases generally refers to Federal and state appellate court opinions in studying criminal procedure. The judicial decisions presented in this book were originally published in volumes called case reporters. Information contained in case citations enables you to locate unedited case opinions in a library, in a computer database, or on the internet if you ever want to read a case in its entirety. In addition, you must be familiar with case reporters and citation format to conduct legal research.

In general, case citations include

- the case name,
- the volume and page number of the case reporter in which the case is found,
- a court designation, and
- the year the case was handed down.

In the citation for UNITED STATES V. BLACKBURN, *940 F.2d 107* (4th Cir. 1991):

- The text in SMALL CAPS is the case name, identifying the parties to the appellate case.
- *The text in italics* is the reporter (book) citation. In this case, F.2d refers to the Federal Reporter, Second Series. This citation shows that the case is a United States Court of Appeals opinion since only those courts' opinions are in this reporter.
- The text in **bold** is the Court identifier and the year of the decision. This case is from the 4th Circuit Court of Appeals and was decided in 1991.

Federal Case Citations

Federal case reporters are court-specific. Therefore, all United States Supreme Court opinions, all United States Court of Appeals opinions, and any published United States District Court opinions are located in their own reporters.

United States Supreme Court Opinions

United States Supreme Court opinions can be found in three different reporters. The "official" reporter of the United States Supreme Court is the United States Reports (U.S.). In addition, two "unofficial" reporters are published by private vendors. The first is the Supreme Court Reporter (S.Ct.) and the second is United States Supreme Court Decisions, Lawyers' Edition (L.Ed.), and United States Supreme Court Decisions, Lawyers' Edition, 2nd (L.Ed.2nd). In this text, we only use the citation for the official reporter.

Powell v. State of Alabama, 287 U.S. 45, 53 S. Ct. 55, 77 L.Ed. 158 (1932)

This case can be found in volume 287 of the United States Reports on page 45. It can also be found at volume 53 of the Supreme Court Reporter, at page 55, and 77 of the United States Supreme Court Decisions, Lawyers' Edition, at page 158. The case was decided in 1932.

Federal Appellate Court Opinions

United States Court of Appeals decisions are found in the Federal Reporter series (F., F.2d, F.3d, and F. 4th). The parenthetical at the end of the citation includes a circuit court of appeals identification. See the example below:

United States v. de la Jara, 973 F.2d 746 (9th Cir. 1992)

This case is found on page 746 of volume 973 of the Federal Reporter, 2nd series. The 9th Circuit Court of Appeals decided it in 1992.

United States District Court Opinions

Generally, any published United States District Court opinions will be found in the Federal Supplement (F.Supp.) and Federal Supplement, 2nd (F.Supp.2nd). The specific district court is identified in the parenthetical at the end of the citation, as is the year it was decided.

United States v. Copeland, 369 F. Supp.2d 275 (E.D.N.Y. 2005)

This case is found in volume 369 of the Federal Supplement at page 275. It was decided by the United States District Court for the Eastern District of New York in 2005.

State Case Citations

Almost all the opinions published in state case reporters are written by appellate court judges. State trial court opinions generally are not published in case reporters.

Published state court opinions are included in the case reporters that make up the West Group's National Reporter System. The West Group is a division of the Thomson Reuters Company, one of the country's largest publishers of law books and other legal materials.

The West Group created the geographic regions into which the states have been grouped solely for their publication purposes. Those regional groupings are not analogous to the federal judicial circuits, in which each U.S. district court within a circuit is bound by a court of appeals' rulings from that same circuit. In other words, even though state court opinions from Alabama, Florida, Louisiana, and Mississippi are published in the Southern Reporter, 3d Series, this does not mean that Alabama appellate court opinions have any special significance to the courts in the other states.

State court case citations follow the same pattern as federal case citations, e.g., *State v. Mangold*, 414 A.2d 1312 (N.J. 1980). This is a 1980 decision of the New Jersey Supreme Court, found in volume 414 of the Atlantic Reporter (second series) on page 1312.

Conclusion

In this chapter, we have deviated from the customary format of succeeding chapters, in which we emphasize the case method of study and emphasize analyzing judicial decisions. We have made this departure to provide important background information to the ensuing cases and materials.

We introduced the structure and procedural steps involved in state and federal criminal prosecutions. This review examined the pretrial, trial, and postconviction stages of both the state and federal judicial systems.

We also discussed the origins of the Bill of Rights, or the first ten amendments to the U.S. Constitution. We emphasized the original understanding that those constitutional amendments were designed to limit the federal government's authority, not the states. The subsequent enactment of the Fourteenth Amendment, with its stipulation that "nor shall any *State* deprive any person of life, liberty, or property, without due process of law," eventually would work dramatic changes in criminal procedure law. Through a series of cases decided in the 1960s, the Warren Court "selectively incorporated" most of the criminal procedure safeguards contained in the Bill of Rights and made them applicable to the states by operation of the Fourteenth Amendment's due-process clause. Consequently, these fundamental constitutional rights must now be observed in state criminal proceedings.

With this foundation laid, we are ready to explore the law related to search and seizure.

KEY TERMS

appeal	incorporation
arraignment	information
bail	initial appearance
Bill of Rights	jurisdiction
booking	magistrate
complaint	petitioner
court of general jurisdiction	preliminary hearing
discretionary review	pretrial motions
due process Clause	respondent
en banc	selective incorporation
federalism	supremacy clause
fundamental fairness doctrine	total incorporation
grand jury	

REVIEW QUESTIONS

1. What are some reasons that a criminal procedure issue, like the legality of a search, might be resolved differently on state constitutional grounds than under the federal Constitution?
2. What are the differences between total incorporation and selective incorporation?
3. What is the importance of the Fourteenth Amendment in its relation to individual freedoms?
4. What was the main reason for the development of the Bill of Rights?
5. What is your opinion on incorporation? Do you think questions of criminal procedure should have primarily been left up to individual states and that by incorporating much of the Bill of Rights, the federal government usurped states' rights? Or do you think this was a necessary approach to criminal procedure in the United States and that the advantages outweigh the negatives?
6. What is the general structure of the adjudication process for someone charged with a felony in state court? Please name and give a general overview of the main proceedings throughout the process.
7. How many justices must vote to grant certiorari for the Supreme Court to hear a case? How many cases does the Supreme Court hear per year? How many do they get requested to hear?
8. What information can you glean from a case citation?
9. What rights have been incorporated by the Fourteenth Amendment?
10. What is the standard a right must meet to be incorporated?

CHAPTER 3

Introduction to the Law of Search and Seizure

LEARNING OBJECTIVES

After reading this chapter, students should be able to:

- Critically analyze the Fourth Amendment and issues linked to it.
- Realize the significance of the Fourth Amendment to the criminal justice system.
- Know that the Fourth Amendment doesn't ban all searches and seizures, only "unreasonable" ones.
- Comprehend the importance of the term Reasonable Expectation of Privacy in search and seizure law.
- Understand the different constitutional protections associated with open fields, curtilages, and abandoned property.
- Provide examples illustrating the difference between objective and subjective expectation of privacy.
- Understand the purpose behind the exclusionary rule.
- Understand the exceptions to the exclusionary rule.
- Comprehend what fruit of the poisonous tree is and how it relates to the exclusionary rule.
- Understand that the Fourth Amendment applies only to government actions, not actions of private individuals.

Introduction

> The right of the people to be secure in their persons, houses, papers, and effects, against unreasonable searches and seizures, shall not be violated, and no Warrants shall issue, but upon probable cause, supported by Oath or affirmation, and particularly describing the place to be searched, and the persons or things to be seized.
>
> United States Constitution, Fourth Amendment

The Framers of the Fourth Amendment used just 53 words to enshrine in the Bill of Rights the rights of individuals to be free from unreasonable government searches and seizures. Its first clause protects people's rights to "be secure" in their "persons, houses, papers and effects" against "unreasonable searches and seizures." The amendment's second clause prohibits warrants from being issued unless they are based on "probable cause" and supported by the applicant's "Oath or affirmation." It additionally requires that warrants "particularly" describe "the place to be searched, and the persons or things to be seized."

Despite its brevity, the Fourth Amendment has been the subject of extensive Supreme Court interpretations and scholarly analyses, as the legal community endeavors to delineate its scope and application. This has led to a complex web of rules, exceptions, and caveats regarding search and seizure law. What is so highly evocative about these 53 words? By the end of this chapter, you will be in a much better position to answer this question.

In the following pages, we will examine a host of issues related to the Fourth Amendment and the law of search and seizure. Thus, we will consider the interests that the Fourth Amendment was designed to safeguard by exploring the definitions of a "search" and a "seizure" and asking what makes a search or a seizure "unreasonable." We will investigate the relationship between the Fourth Amendment's first clause—which prohibits unreasonable searches and seizures—and its second clause, which governs the warrant process. Should it be presumed that a search or seizure conducted without the prior authorization of a warrant is "unreasonable"? If so, would exceptional circumstances make a warrantless search or seizure reasonable? What did the Framers mean by the "probable cause" requirement that is a part of the warrant clause? Must all searches and seizures at least be supported by "probable cause" if they are to be reasonable?

Ideally, citizens of the United States can trust the police never to violate the Constitution; however, this is not the case. Note that the Fourth Amendment fails to explain what should happen if a search or seizure is conducted unconstitutionally. In other words, if the police illegally search or seize someone, what should be the consequence of this unconstitutional action? What should be the remedy? Should the police be punished? Should an illegally seized person be released, or should unlawfully seized evidence, such as a murder weapon, drugs, or a confession, be ruled inadmissible at trial? Should the evidence be able to be used at other proceedings, such as a preliminary hearing?

By prohibiting unreasonable searches and seizures and through its regulation of the warrant process, the Fourth Amendment places important limits on law enforcement officers' efforts to detect and investigate crimes. Imagine a society that imposed no restrictions on the police authority to search people's homes or their persons or arrest them on suspicion of a crime. Permitting warrantless home searches at 3:00 a.m., allowing indiscriminate searches of people and their purses, backpacks, and other belongings, and granting the police unlimited authority to arrest and detain citizens almost certainly would help law enforcement officials uncover evidence of criminal wrongdoing and apprehend people who commit crimes. However, such benefits would come at a cost to individual liberties and privacy that most Americans would be unwilling to bear.

By the same token, if the Constitution placed too stringent restrictions on investigating individuals suspected of committing crimes, the police would be unable to carry out law enforcement functions necessary to protect society and its law-abiding citizens. The Framers of the Fourth Amendment appreciated the need for legitimate law enforcement activity. Accordingly, they did not ban all searches and seizures, only "unreasonable" ones. They specifically approved of searches and seizures conducted under warrants based on probable cause that particularly describe what or who is to be searched or seized.

The Fourth Amendment requires balancing individual citizens' freedoms and right to privacy versus the legitimate needs of the police to enforce the law. In other words, this personifies the delicate balancing act between individual rights versus public safety and security discussed in Chapter 1. Working out the appropriate balancing of interests in search and seizure cases is not always easy, especially since the stakes for both individuals and the government tend to be high. It is frequently up to the United States Supreme Court to decide where the compromise between these two competing interests should lie. As a result, search and seizure law is both intriguing and challenging. We begin by considering the particular interests protected by the Fourth Amendment.

Katz and the Reasonable Expectation of Privacy

Charles Katz was a well-known sports betting handicapper whose illegal activities had come to the attention of the FBI. In February of 1965, as part of their investigation into interstate sports betting, the FBI placed a listening and recording device outside a public telephone booth near his home, from which Katz routinely relayed wagering information to bookmakers. After hearing Katz's side of conversations with bookmakers during which he made incriminating statements, the FBI arrested Katz, who was subsequently charged with eight counts of transmitting wagering information over a telephone between states.

At trial, Katz's lawyer asked the court to suppress the recordings as evidence on the grounds that the FBI agents placed a listening device on the phone booth without a search warrant, violating the Fourth Amendment; therefore, the evidence should be inadmissible at trial. The trial court judge denied the motion and ruled that the recordings were admissible. Katz was subsequently found guilty on all charges.

Katz appealed his conviction to the U.S. Court of Appeals for the Ninth Circuit, arguing that the recordings could not be used as evidence against him. A three-judge panel of the Ninth Circuit affirmed Katz's conviction. The court found that because the listening device nor the FBI agents physically penetrated the telephone booth, no Fourth Amendment search occurred. As such, the FBI did not need a search warrant to place the device. Katz then appealed to the U.S. Supreme Court, which granted certiorari.

In a landmark decision, *Katz v. United States*, 389 US 347 (1967), a seven-member majority of the Supreme Court overturned the conviction. In abandoning the **trespass doctrine**, which required a physical trespass to occur for the Fourth Amendment to be implicated, the majority opinion stated that the Fourth Amendment protects people, not places. Accordingly, the Court held that physical trespass is unnecessary for the Fourth Amendment to be implicated. Rather, the key to understanding whether a search has occurred revolved around the right to privacy.

The Court found that when Katz entered the booth and closed the door behind him, he reasonably believed it to be his private space. The fact that he could be seen through the booth's glass door or that it was located in a public place did not matter because Katz clearly expected that his conversation was private. In other words, he had a **reasonable expectation of privacy**.

Justice Harlan summarized how the majority opinion should be interpreted in his concurring opinion. In so doing, he laid out a two-pronged formula that should be used to determine if a **search** took place. This is called the *Katz* test. The first part of the *Katz* test asks whether a person exhibited an actual (**subjective**) **expectation of privacy**. That is to say, did the person believe his actions were private? The second part of the test asks whether the person's expectation was one that society would recognize as reasonable (**objective expectation of privacy**). In other words, if the Fourth Amendment permitted this form of surveillance, would this infringe too much on privacy according to the average American? This second test is referred to as the objective component of the test.

Applying this test to the facts presented in *Katz*, the Court held that by shutting the phone booth door before speaking on the phone, Katz clearly considered his conversation private. Moreover, this expectation was one that society would find reasonable and consistent with the goals of living in a free and open society. Accordingly, the actions of the FBI constituted a search and violated the Fourth Amendment.

The importance of the *Katz* test in the law of search and seizure cannot be overstated. If a person does not have a reasonable expectation of privacy, "a search" has not occurred, and the Fourth Amendment has not been implicated. It is only in situations where there is a reasonable expectation of privacy that the Fourth Amendment protects a person. According to the Katz Test, the court will consider some interrelated factors when determining if a person has a reasonable expectation of privacy. First, where did the search occur? For example, the home is afforded the most stringent constitutional protections, while a public park would have limited protections. Second, to what extent did the person attempt to secure their privacy? A conversation between two people on a public sidewalk will be treated differently from one in a private office.

The following section and cases present examples considered by the Supreme Court that illustrate this standard and the interrelated factors.

Abandoned Property

To what extent should "assumption of risk" determine whether an individual has a recognizable privacy interest under the Fourth Amendment? Pay particular attention to this theme in *California v. Greenwood* and in the cases that follow. Does leaving an item on a public street eliminate any expectation of privacy the property owner may have possessed? At first glance, *Greenwood* may seem unlikely to implicate fundamental constitutional freedoms, but it involves principles close to the heart of the Fourth Amendment. The case addresses whether the police's inspection of garbage deposited by the occupant of a dwelling at his curbside is a "search" within the meaning of the Fourth Amendment. As you read it, consider whether you agree with Justice White's reasonable expectation of privacy analysis, or that of Justice Brennan's dissenting opinion.

California v. Greenwood

486 U.S. 35 (1988)

Justice White delivered the opinion of the Court.

The issue here is whether the Fourth Amendment prohibits the warrantless search and seizure of garbage left for collection outside the curtilage of a home. We conclude, in accordance with the vast majority of lower courts that have addressed the issue, that it does not.

I

In early 1984, Investigator Jenny Stracner of the Laguna Beach Police Department received information indicating that respondent Greenwood might be engaged in narcotics trafficking.

Stracner sought to investigate this information by conducting a surveillance of Greenwood's home. She observed several vehicles make brief stops at the house during the late-night and early-morning hours, and she followed a truck from the house to a residence that had previously been under investigation as a narcotics trafficking location.

On April 6, 1984, Stracner asked the neighborhood's regular trash collector to pick up the plastic garbage bags that Greenwood had left on the curb in front of his house and to turn the bags over to her without mixing their contents with garbage from other houses. The trash collector cleaned his truck bin of other refuse, collected the garbage bags from the street in front of Greenwood's house, and turned the bags over to Stracner. The officer searched through the rubbish and found items indicative of narcotics use. She recited the information that she had gleaned from the trash search in an affidavit in support of a warrant to search Greenwood's home.

Police officers encountered both respondents at the house later that day when they arrived to execute the warrant. The police discovered quantities of cocaine and hashish during their search of the house. Respondents were arrested on felony narcotics charges. They subsequently posted bail.

The police continued to receive reports of many late-night visitors to the Greenwood house. On May 4, Investigator Robert Rahaeuser obtained Greenwood's garbage from the regular trash collector in the same manner as had Stracner. The garbage again contained evidence of narcotics use. Rahaeuser secured another search warrant for Greenwood's home based on the information from the second trash search. The police found more narcotics and evidence of narcotics trafficking when they executed the warrant. Greenwood was again arrested.

The Superior Court dismissed the charges against respondents on the authority of *People v. Krivda*, 486 P2d 1262 (1971), which held that warrantless trash searches violate the Fourth Amendment and the California Constitution. The court found that the police would not have had probable cause to search the Greenwood home without the evidence obtained from the trash searches. The Court of Appeal affirmed.

The warrantless search and seizure of the garbage bags left at the curb outside the Greenwood house would violate the Fourth Amendment only if respondents manifested a subjective expectation of privacy in their garbage that society accepts as objectively reasonable. Respondents do not disagree with this standard.

They assert, however, that they had, and exhibited, an expectation of privacy with respect to the trash that was searched by the police: The trash, which was placed on the street for collection at a fixed time, was contained in opaque plastic bags, which the garbage collector was expected to pick up, mingle with the trash of others, and deposit at the garbage dump. The trash was only temporarily on the street, and there was little likelihood that it would be inspected by anyone.

It may well be that respondents did not expect that the contents of their garbage bags would become known to the police or other members of the public. An expectation of privacy does not give rise to Fourth Amendment protection, however, unless society is prepared to accept that expectation as objectively reasonable.

Here, we conclude that respondents exposed their garbage to the public sufficiently to defeat their claim to Fourth Amendment protection. It is common knowledge that plastic garbage bags left on or at the side of a public street are readily accessible to animals, children, scavengers, snoops, and other members of the public. Moreover, respondents placed their refuse at the curb for the express purpose of conveying it to a third party, the trash collector, who might himself have sorted through respondents' trash or permitted others, such as the police, to do so. Accordingly, having deposited their garbage "in an area particularly suited for public inspection and, in a manner of speaking, public consumption, for the express purpose of having strangers take it," *United States v. Reicherter*, 647 F2d 397, 399 (CA 3 1981), respondents could have had no reasonable expectation of privacy in the inculpatory items that they discarded.

Furthermore, as we have held, the police cannot reasonably be expected to avert their eyes from evidence of criminal activity that could have been observed by any member of the public. Hence, "[w]hat a person knowingly exposes to the public, even in his own home or office, is not a subject of Fourth Amendment protection." *Katz v. United States, supra,* at 351.

The judgment of the California Court of Appeals is therefore reversed .

JUSTICE BRENNAN, with whom JUSTICE MARSHALL joins, dissenting.

Scrutiny of another's trash is contrary to commonly accepted notions of civilized behavior. I suspect, therefore, that members of our society will be shocked to learn that the Court, the ultimate guarantor of liberty, deems unreasonable our expectation that the aspects of our private lives that are concealed safely in a trash bag will not become public.

Respondents deserve no less protection just because Greenwood used the bags to discard rather than to transport his personal effects. Their contents are not inherently any less private, and Greenwood's decision to discard them, at least in the manner in which he did, does not diminish his expectation of privacy.

A trash bag, like [other] containers, "is a common repository for one's personal effects" and, even more than many of them, is "therefore inevitably associated with the expectation of privacy." *See California v. Rooney*, 483 US 307, 320–21, n 3 (1987) (White, J., dissenting) (Renowned archaeologist Emil Haury once said, "If you want to know what is really going on in a community, look at its garbage.") A single bag of trash testifies eloquently to the eating, reading, and recreational habits of the person who produced it. A search of trash, like a search of the bedroom, can relate intimate details about sexual practices, health, and personal hygiene. Like rifling through desk drawers or intercepting phone calls, rummaging through trash can divulge the target's financial and professional status, political affiliations and inclinations, private thoughts, personal relationships, and romantic interests. It cannot be doubted that a sealed trash bag harbors telling evidence of the "intimate activity associated with the 'sanctity of a man's home and the privacies of life,' " which the Fourth Amendment is designed to protect.

In evaluating the reasonableness of Greenwood's expectation that his sealed trash bags would not be invaded, the Court has held that we must look to "understandings that are recognized and permitted by society." Most of us, I believe, would be incensed to discover a meddler—whether a neighbor, a reporter, or a detective—scrutinizing our sealed trash containers to discover some detail of our personal lives. That was, quite naturally, the reaction to the sole incident on which the Court bases its conclusion that "snoops" and the like defeat the expectation of privacy in trash.

That is not to deny that isolated intrusions into opaque, sealed trash containers occur. When, acting on their own, "animals, children, scavengers, snoops, [or] other members of the general public," actually rummage through a bag of trash and expose its contents to plain view, "police cannot reasonably be expected to avert their eyes from evidence of criminal activity that could have been observed by any member of the public."

Had Greenwood flaunted his intimate activity by strewing his trash all over the curb for all to see, or had some nongovernmental intruder invaded his privacy and done the same, I could accept the Court's conclusion that an expectation of privacy would have been unreasonable. Similarly, had police searching the city dump run across incriminating evidence that, despite commingling with the trash of others, still retained its identity as Greenwood's, we would have a different case. But all that Greenwood "exposed to the public," were the exteriors of several opaque, sealed containers.

The mere *possibility* that unwelcome meddlers might open and rummage through the containers does not negate the expectation of privacy in its contents any more than the possibility of a burglary negates an expectation of privacy in the home; or the possibility of a private intrusion negates an expectation of privacy in an unopened package; or the possibility that an operator will listen in on a telephone conversation negates an expectation of privacy in the words spoken on the telephone.

Nor is it dispositive that "respondents placed their refuse at the curb for the express purpose of conveying it to a third party, who might himself have sorted through respondents' trash or permitted others, such as police, to do so." In the first place, Greenwood can hardly be faulted for leaving trash on his curb when a county ordinance commanded him to do so. More importantly, even the voluntary relinquishment of possession or control over an effect does not necessarily amount to a relinquishment of a privacy expectation in it. Were it otherwise, a letter or package would lose all Fourth Amendment protection when placed in a mailbox or other depository with the "express purpose" of entrusting it to the postal officer or a private carrier; those bailees are just as likely as trash collectors (and certainly have greater incentive) to "sor[t] through" the personal effects entrusted to them, "or permi[t] others, such as police to do so." Yet, it has been clear for at least 110 years that the possibility of such an intrusion does not justify a warrantless search by police in the first instance.

FURTHER CASE LAW, REFLECTIONS, AND QUESTIONS

1. Notice how the two opinions in *Greenwood* apply the same standard of law and facts but reach different outcomes. How is this possible?
2. A handful of states—Hawaii, New Hampshire, New Jersey, New Mexico, Oregon, and Washington—have rejected *Greenwood* and have interpreted their state constitutions to protect citizens from warrantless police inspections of their garbage and **abandoned property**. Do you see anything these states have in common? See if you can determine if your state has taken up a case about the possibility of rejecting *Greenwood* on state Constitutional grounds.

Box 3.1 You Be the Judge

The IRS suspected Alan Scott of involvement in a scheme to defraud the United States by filing false income tax returns. IRS agents systematically seized and combed through garbage bags left for collection by Scott in front of his house. Their search revealed numerous shredded documents reduced to 5/32-inch strips. IRS agents pieced together these documents and discovered they contained incriminating evidence. The agents then used this evidence to establish probable cause to request various search warrants. The search warrants were issued and executed, and the searches garnered additional evidence used to indict Scott on 47 counts of tax fraud. Scott moved to suppress the reconstructed documents and the evidence seized pursuant to the search warrants, arguing that he had manifested an objectively reasonable expectation of privacy in the shredded remnants, which the Fourth Amendment protected.

Do you agree with Scott that he maintained a reasonable expectation of privacy over the shredded documents? See *United States v. Scott*, 975 F.2d 927 (1st Cir. 1992).

False Friends

Many of the essential principles from *Katz* and other related search cases—reasonable expectation of privacy, assumption of risk, and knowing exposure—are quite evident in the so-called "false friend" cases. For example, imagine joining a club at your university and becoming good friends with Jim. After going to a few club meetings, you invite Jim back to your apartment for a few drinks. Unbeknownst to you, Jim is actually an undercover police officer undercover to fight the drug problem at your school. While at your apartment, you decide to take out some "party favors," and you do a few lines of cocaine. Jim obviously does not join you, and he quickly leaves. Later, based upon the evidence gathered by Jim while in your apartment, the police execute a search warrant on your apartment. Did Jim violate your Fourth Amendment rights? In other words, did you have a reasonable expectation of privacy, and was this an illegal search conducted by the police?

The U.S. Supreme Court, prior to *Katz*, ruled on a similar case and based their decision on the assumption of risk. In *Hoffa v. United States*, 385 U.S. 293 (1967), the Court ruled when Hoffa invited an undercover police informant into his hotel room, this was not a search within the meaning of the Fourth Amendment. When Hoffa invited someone into his hotel room and volunteered information, he assumed the risk the person he spoke to could be a police officer or an informant. In the words of the Court, the Fourth Amendment does not protect ". . . a wrongdoer's misplaced belief that a person to whom he voluntarily confides his wrongdoing will not reveal it."

Hoffa was decided before *Katz*. The U.S. Supreme Court ruled on a similar case, *United States v. White*, 401 U.S. 745 (1971), post-*Katz*, affirmed the ruling in Hoffa, and did so in the language of *Katz* and under the terms of a reasonable expectation of privacy. However, *White* also extended the question from *Hoffa* further. What if, for example, a person invites an undercover police officer or informant into their home, and the person is "wired" and records or transmits the information to the police? According to the Court in *White*, *Katz* and a reasonable expectation of privacy left the ruling in Hoffa undisturbed and unaffected. Furthermore, the fact that the undercover informant in White was wired and transmitted the conversations to the police via radio transmission is a distinction without a difference under the Fourth Amendment assumption of risk analysis from *Hoffa*, and the ruling is the same. No Fourth Amendment search took place in either case.

In the "false friend" and "wired false friend" cases of Hoffa and White, we learn about the assumption of risk and Justice Stewart's concept of "knowing "exposure" from Katz. When a person invites an individual into their home or another constitutionally protected area and volunteers information to that person, they have assumed the risk that the person might be a police officer or an informant. This is a risk that the person takes by talking to another person and knowingly exposing information, and a Fourth Amendment search has not occurred. Just because the person might not have consented to volunteer the information if they knew the person was a police officer or an informant does not implicate the Fourth Amendment or make this a search in any way.

Homes, Curtilage and Open Fields

Recall that the Fourth Amendment explicitly states that people have a right to be secure in their homes. The Supreme Court has strictly enforced this doctrine in applying the reasonable expectation of privacy analyses. We can all agree that a person has a reasonable expectation of privacy within her home. That begs the question, however, what is meant by a "home"? Is it the physical structure of the house? The house and the yard? The house and all surrounding property adjacent to the home, regardless of its size?

The Supreme Court has held that a person's house and the "curtilage" are protected by the Fourth Amendment. The curtilage is the area immediately surrounding a dwelling that "harbors the 'intimate activity associated with the sanctity of a man's home and the privacies of life,' *United States v. Dunn*, 480 U.S. 294 (1987). Identifying the specific boundaries of a curtilage can be difficult. Four factors cited by the Court in Dunn to determine whether an area should be considered a curtilage include,

1. The distance from the house to the place alleged to be curtilage;
2. Whether the area asserted to be curtilage is within a fence or other enclosure surrounding the home;
3. Whether the area is used to conduct domestic activities; and
4. The steps taken by the resident to protect the area from observation by passersby.

An area adjacent to a dwelling that is not considered a curtilage is considered an "open field." Under the open fields doctrine, the area beyond the curtilage does not fall under Fourth Amendment protection, even if the open field is located on private property. In other words, a warrantless search conducted in an area beyond the curtilage does not violate the Constitution. Remember, as Justice Harlan said in *Katz*, the Fourth Amendment "protects people, not places." As a result of this, whether an area is considered curtilage or open fields can have important consequences.

In the following case, the Court clarified the extent to which the open fields doctrine is valid post-*Katz* and also considered the impact of a homeowner's putting up signage and fencing on the expectation of privacy analysis.

Oliver v. United States

466 U.S. 170 (1984)

JUSTICE POWELL delivered the opinion of the Court.

The "open fields" doctrine, first enunciated by this Court in *Hester v. United States*, 265 US 57 (1924), permits police officers to enter and search a field without a warrant. We granted certiorari in these cases to clarify confusion that has arisen as to the continued vitality of the doctrine.

I

[Case] No. 82-15. Acting on reports that marihuana was being raised on the farm of petitioner Oliver, two narcotics agents of the Kentucky State Police went to the farm to investigate. Arriving at the farm, they drove past petitioner's house to a locked gate with a "No Trespassing" sign. A footpath led around one side of the gate. The agents walked around the gate and along the road for several hundred yards, passing a barn and a parked camper. At that point, someone standing in front of the camper shouted: "No hunting is allowed, come back up here." The officers shouted back that they were Kentucky State Police officers, but found no one when they returned to the camper. The officers resumed their investigation of the farm and found a field of marihuana over a mile from petitioner's home.

Petitioner was arrested and indicted for "manufactur[ing]" a "controlled substance." 21 USC §841(a)(1). After a pretrial hearing, the District Court suppressed evidence of the discovery of the marihuana field. Applying *Katz v. United States*, 389 US 347 (1967), the court found that petitioner had a reasonable expectation that the field would remain private because petitioner "had done all that could be expected of him to assert his privacy in the area of farm that was searched." He had posted "No Trespassing" signs at regular intervals and had locked the gate at the entrance to the center of the farm. Further, the court noted that the field itself is highly secluded: it is bounded on all sides by woods, fences, and embankments and cannot be seen from any point of public access. The court concluded that this was not an "open" field that invited casual intrusion.

The Court of Appeals for the Sixth Circuit, sitting *en banc*, reversed the District Court.

[Case] No. 82-1273. After receiving an anonymous tip that marihuana was being grown in the woods behind respondent Thornton's residence, two police officers entered the woods by a path between this residence and a neighboring house. They followed a footpath through the woods until they reached two marihuana patches fenced with chicken wire. Later, the officers determined that the patches were on the property of respondent, obtained a warrant to search the property, and seized the marihuana. On the basis of this evidence, respondent was arrested and indicted.

The trial court granted respondent's motion to suppress the fruits of the second search. The warrant for this search was premised on information that the police had obtained during their previous warrantless search, that the court found to be unreasonable. "No Trespassing" signs and the secluded location of the marihuana patches evinced a reasonable expectation of privacy. Therefore, the court held, the open fields doctrine did not apply. The Maine Supreme Judicial Court affirmed.

II

The rule announced in *Hester v. United States* was founded upon the explicit language of the Fourth Amendment. That Amendment indicates with some precision the places and things encompassed by its protections. As Justice Holmes explained for the Court in his characteristically laconic style: "[T]he special protection accorded by the Fourth Amendment to the people in their 'persons, houses, papers, and effects,' is not extended to the open fields. The distinction between the latter and the house is as old as the common law." *Hester v. United States*, 265 US, at 59.

Nor are the open fields "effects" within the meaning of the Fourth Amendment. In this respect, it is suggestive that James Madison's proposed draft of what became the Fourth Amendment preserves "[t]he rights of the people to be secured in their persons, their houses, their papers, and their other property, from all unreasonable searches and seizures."

Although Congress' revisions of Madison's proposal broadened the scope of the Amendment in some respects, the term "effects" is less inclusive than "property" and cannot be said to encompass open fields. We conclude, as did the Court in deciding *Hester v. United States*, that the government's intrusion upon the open fields is not one of those "unreasonable searches" proscribed by the text of the Fourth Amendment.

III

This interpretation of the Fourth Amendment's language is consistent with the understanding of the right to privacy expressed in our Fourth Amendment jurisprudence. Since *Katz v. United States*, the touchstone of [Fourth] Amendment analysis has been the question whether a person has a "constitutionally protected reasonable expectation of privacy." The Amendment does not protect the merely subjective expectation of privacy, but only those "expectation[s] that society is prepared to recognize as 'reasonable.'"

No single factor determines whether an individual legitimately may claim under the Fourth Amendment that a place should be free of government intrusion not authorized by warrant. In assessing the degree to which a search infringes upon individual privacy, the Court has given weight to such factors as the intention of the Framers of the Fourth Amendment, the uses to which the individual has put a location, and our societal understanding that certain areas deserve the most scrupulous protection from government invasion. These factors are equally relevant to determining whether the government's intrusion upon open fields without a warrant or probable cause violates reasonable expectations of privacy and is therefore a search proscribed by the Amendment.

In this light, the rule of *Hester v. United States*, that we reaffirm today, may be understood as providing that an individual may not legitimately demand privacy for activities conducted out of doors in fields, except in the area immediately surrounding the home. This rule is true to the conception of the right to privacy embodied in the Fourth Amendment. The Amendment reflects the recognition of the Founders that certain enclaves should be free from arbitrary government interference. For example, the Court since the enactment of the Fourth Amendment has stressed "the overriding respect for the sanctity of the home that has been embedded in our traditions since the origins of the Republic."

In contrast, open fields do not provide the setting for those intimate activities that the amendment is intended to shelter from government interference or surveillance. There is no societal interest in protecting the privacy of those activities, such as the cultivation of crops, that occur in open fields. Moreover, as a practical matter these lands usually are accessible to the public and the police in ways that a home, an office, or commercial structure would not be. It is not generally true that fences or "No Trespassing" signs effectively bar the public from viewing open fields in rural areas. And both petitioner Oliver and respondent Thornton concede that the public and police lawfully may survey lands from the air. For these reasons, the asserted expectation of privacy in open fields is not an expectation that "society recognizes as reasonable."

We conclude, from the text of the Fourth Amendment and from the historical and contemporary understanding of its purposes, that an individual has no legitimate expectation that open fields will remain free from warrantless intrusion by government officers.

B

Petitioner Oliver and respondent Thornton contend, to the contrary, that the circumstances of a search sometimes may indicate that reasonable expectations of privacy were violated; and that courts therefore should analyze these circumstances on a case-by-case basis. The language of the Fourth Amendment itself answers their contention.

Nor would a case-by-case approach provide a workable accommodation between the needs of law enforcement and the interests protected by the Fourth Amendment. Under this approach, police officers would have to guess before every search whether landowners had erected fences sufficiently high, posted a sufficient number of warning signs, or located contraband in an area sufficiently secluded to establish a right of privacy. The lawfulness of a search would turn on "'[a] highly sophisticated set of rules, qualified by all sorts of ifs, ands, and buts and requiring the drawing of subtle nuances and hairline distinctions.'" This Court repeatedly has acknowledged the difficulties created for courts, police, and citizens by an ad hoc, case-by-case definition of Fourth Amendment standards to be applied in differing factual circumstances. The ad hoc approach not only makes it difficult for the policeman to discern the scope of his authority, it also creates a danger that constitutional rights will be arbitrarily and inequitably enforced.

IV

In any event, while the factors that petitioner Oliver and respondent Thornton urge the courts to consider may be relevant to Fourth Amendment analysis in some contexts, these factors cannot be decisive on the question whether the search of an open field is subject to the Amendment. Initially, we reject the suggestion that steps taken to protect privacy establish that expectations of privacy in an open field are legitimate. It is true, of course, that petitioner Oliver and respondent Thornton, in order to conceal their criminal activities, planted the marihuana upon secluded land and erected fences and "No Trespassing" signs around the property. And it may be that because of such precautions, few members of the public stumbled upon the marihuana crops seized by the police. Neither of these suppositions demonstrates, however, that the expectation of privacy was legitimate in the sense required by the Fourth Amendment. The test of legitimacy is not whether the individual chooses to conceal assertedly "private" activity. Rather, the correct inquiry is whether the government's intrusion infringes upon the personal and societal values protected by the Fourth Amendment. As we have explained, we find no basis for concluding that a police inspection of open fields accomplishes such an infringement.

Nor is the government's intrusion upon an open field a "search" in the constitutional sense because that intrusion is a trespass at common law. The existence of a property right is but one element in determining whether expectations of privacy are legitimate. "The premise that property interests control the right of the Government to search and seize has been discredited." *Katz*, 389 US, at 353. Even a property interest in premises may not be sufficient to establish a legitimate expectation of privacy with respect to particular items located on the premises or activity conducted thereon.

The common law may guide consideration of what areas are protected by the Fourth Amendment by defining areas whose invasion by others is wrongful. The law of trespass, however, forbids intrusions upon land that the Fourth Amendment would not proscribe. For trespass law extends to instances where the exercise of the right to exclude vindicates no legitimate privacy interest. Thus, in the case of open fields, the general rights of property protected by the common law of trespass have little or no relevance to the applicability of the Fourth Amendment.

V

We conclude that the open fields doctrine, as enunciated in *Hester*, is consistent with the plain language of the Fourth Amendment and its historical purposes. Moreover, Justice Holmes' interpretation of the Amendment in Hester accords with the "reasonable expectation of privacy" analysis developed in subsequent decisions of this Court. We therefore affirm *Oliver v. United States*; *Maine v. Thornton* is reversed and remanded for further proceedings not inconsistent with this opinion.

FURTHER CASE LAW, REFLECTIONS, AND QUESTIONS

1. Oliver and Thornton posted "No Trespassing" signs on their property. Oliver had blocked the entry road to his farm with a locked gate. Each man's marijuana garden was on a secluded plot of land. Criminal trespass laws were in effect in each of their states. How does the Court justify its conclusion that "an individual has no legitimate expectation that open fields will remain free from warrantless intrusion by government officers"?
2. What, precisely, are "open fields"? In a section of the opinion not presented, the Court cautions that "an open field need be neither 'open' nor a 'field' as those terms are used in common speech."
3. In your opinion, does the Court's ruling in Oliver v. United States adequately strike a balance between individual privacy rights and the needs of law enforcement to investigate and prevent crime, or does it lean too heavily in favor of one side? What alternative approaches or legal frameworks might better address the tension between privacy and public safety in contemporary society?

Aerial Surveillance, Technology, and the Reasonable Expectation of Privacy

When law enforcement officers enter a home or step onto a home's curtilage, it is clear that their actions implicate a person's reasonable expectation of privacy. Such steps must therefore follow the strictures of the Fourth Amendment. A different problem is present when law enforcement searches a home or property adjacent to a house using aerial surveillance or technological enhancements to observe areas not readily on public display. For example, what if the police pointed an extremely sensitive microphone at your home and listened to your conversation in your living room from the comfort of their patrol car across the street? In evaluating whether these steps violate the Fourth Amendment, the Supreme Court continued to use the two-part reasonable expectation of privacy Katz Test.

Aerial Surveillance

In considering whether aerial surveillance violates a person's reasonable expectation of privacy, courts will consider a variety of items. Variables such as the type of aircraft, the altitude from which the observations were made, and the steps taken by the property owner to maintain their privacy are factors that are used in this assessment. Consider the following cases.

Acting on a tip that the respondent in *California v. Ciraolo*, 476 U.S. 207 (1986) was growing marijuana in his backyard, two Santa Clara police officers secured an airplane and flew at an altitude of 1,000 feet over Ciraolo's property to investigate. Ciraolo's backyard was surrounded by two fences—one 6 feet tall and the other 10 feet tall—and thus could not be observed from ground level. The police officers did not obtain a search warrant before flying the plane over Ciraolo's property. They were able to identify several 8-foot-to-10-foot-high marijuana plants growing within the fenced area of the backyard and took several aerial photographs with a standard 35-mm camera. Armed with this information, the officers later obtained and executed a search warrant, seizing 73 marijuana plants from Ciraolo's backyard. Ciraolo moved to suppress—that is, to prohibit the evidence from being used at trial to help prove his guilt—the marijuana plants, claiming that the police had "searched" his premises when they peered into his backyard from the vantage point of the airplane. He argued that the "search" was unlawful because a warrant had not authorized it. The trial court denied this motion, the marijuana plants were admitted into evidence, and Ciraolo was convicted of cultivating the illegal substance. On appeal, however, the California Court of Appeals agreed with Ciraolo's contention and reversed his conviction. The U.S. Supreme Court reversed (5–4), through an opinion written by Chief Justice Burger.

The majority opinion conceded that Ciraolo had "clearly met the test of manifesting his own subjective intent and desire to maintain privacy as to his unlawful agricultural pursuits." Yet it concluded that Ciraolo's claim that his backyard had been illegally "searched" must fail because Ciraolo did not qualify under the second part of the Katz inquiry: "Is society willing to recognize that [subjective] expectation [of privacy] as reasonable?" The Chief Justice reasoned that:

> [T]he observations by Officers Shultz and Rodriquez in this case took place within public navigable airspace in a physically nonintrusive man-

> ner; from this point, they were able to observe plants readily discernible to the naked eye as marijuana. That the observation from aircraft was directed at identifying the plants and the officers were trained to recognize marijuana is irrelevant. Such observation is precisely what a judicial officer needs to provide a basis for a warrant. Any member of the public flying in this airspace who glanced down could have seen everything that these officers observed. On this record, we readily conclude that respondent's expectation that his garden was protected from such observation is unreasonable and is not an expectation that society is prepared to honor.

Just three years after deciding *Ciraolo*, the Court considered a similar question in Florida v. Riley, 488 U.S. 445 (1989): "Whether surveillance of the interior of a partially covered greenhouse in a residential backyard from the vantage point of a helicopter located 400 feet above the greenhouse constitutes a 'search' for which a warrant is required under the Fourth Amendment." Imagine a police helicopter hovering over a residence at an altitude of 400 feet to allow law enforcement officers to peer down and inspect the homeowner's property. Should this activity be characterized as a "search"? The answer to this question is crucial to whether the police can conduct helicopter surveillances without first obtaining judicial authorization (i.e., a search warrant). The Supreme Court, through a **plurality opinion** authored by Justice White and joined by three other justices, relied on *Ciraolo* to conclude that the helicopter-assisted inspection of the property did not violate a reasonable expectation of privacy and hence did not constitute a "search" within the meaning of the Fourth Amendment. The Court stressed that property owners must anticipate that property may be observed from the air.

Since Riley was decided in 1989, technology has expanded exponentially. Individual citizens, let alone law enforcement agencies, own and regularly use flying drones and high-definition cameras that can provide clear pictures of areas that were not observable thirty years ago. Does the analysis used in Riley and Ciraolo leave the door open for increased surveillance using new technologies? To date, the Supreme Court has not addressed when and how the use of drones for surveillance violates expectations of privacy.

Searches using Technological and Sensory Enhancements

Privacy issues arise with particular urgency in a society in which rapid technological advances have dramatically compromised citizens' ability to insulate themselves from surveillance. Some have questioned whether traditional legal doctrine remains adequate to safeguard individual privacy in light of the new technology. Is the *Katz* Test too antiquated to afford privacy protections to citizens in a society steeped in cell phones, social media, GPS, and Apple?

As we have already seen, the Supreme Court has upheld using visual and audible enhancements obtained through technology. In the following case, the U.S. Supreme Court considered whether law enforcement's use of a technological innovation in the form of a thermal imaging device violated an individual's Fourth Amendment rights because it infringed on a "reasonable expectation of privacy."

Kyllo v. United States

533 U.S. 27 (2001)

JUSTICE SCALIA delivered the opinion of the Court.

This case presents the question whether the use of a thermal-imaging device aimed at a private home from a public street to detect relative amounts of heat within the home constitutes a "search" within the meaning of the Fourth Amendment.

I

In 1991 Agent William Elliott of the United States Department of the Interior came to suspect that marijuana was being grown in the home belonging to petitioner Danny Kyllo, part of a triplex on Rhododendron Drive in Florence, Oregon. Indoor marijuana growth typically requires high-intensity lamps. In order to determine whether an amount of heat was emanating from petitioner's home consistent with the use of such lamps, at 3:20 a.m. on January 16, 1992, Agent Elliott and Dan Haas used an Agema Thermovision 210 thermal imager to scan the triplex. Thermal imagers detect infrared radiation, which virtually all objects emit but which is not visible to the naked eye. The imager converts radiation into images based on relative warmth—black is cool, white is hot, shades of gray connote relative differences; in that respect, it operates somewhat like a video camera showing heat images. The scan of Kyllo's home took only a few minutes and was performed from the passenger seat of Agent Elliott's vehicle across the street from the front of the house and also from the street in back of the house. The scan showed that the roof over the garage and a side wall of petitioner's home were relatively hot compared to the rest of the home and substantially warmer than neighboring homes in the triplex. Agent Elliott concluded that petitioner was using halide lights to grow marijuana in his house, which indeed he was. Based on tips from informants, utility bills, and the thermal imaging, a Federal Magistrate Judge issued a warrant authorizing a search of petitioner's home, and the agents found an indoor growing operation involving more than 100 plants. Petitioner was indicted on one count of manufacturing marijuana. He unsuccessfully moved to suppress the evidence seized from his home and then entered a conditional guilty plea.

The Court of Appeals held that petitioner had shown no subjective expectation of privacy because he had made no attempt to conceal the heat escaping from his home, and even if he had, there was no objectively reasonable expectation of privacy because the imager "did not expose any intimate details of Kyllo's life," only "amorphous 'hot spots' on the roof and exterior wall." We granted certiorari.

II

"At the very core" of the Fourth Amendment "stands the right of a man to retreat into his own home and there be free from unreasonable governmental intrusion." *Silverman v. United States*, 365 U.S. 505 (1961). With few exceptions, the question whether a warrantless search of a home is reasonable and hence constitutional must be answered no.

On the other hand, the antecedent question of whether or not a Fourth Amendment "search" has occurred is not so simple under our precedent.

The present case involves officers on a public street engaged in more than naked-eye surveillance of a home. We have previously reserved judgment as to how much technological enhancement of ordinary perception from such a vantage point, if any, is too much. While we upheld enhanced aerial photography of an industrial complex [before] we noted that we found "it important that this is *not* an area immediately adjacent to a private home, where privacy expectations are most heightened."

III

It would be foolish to contend that the degree of privacy secured to citizens by the Fourth Amendment has been entirely unaffected by the advance of technology. The question we confront today is what limits there are upon this power of technology to shrink the realm of guaranteed privacy.

The *Katz* test—whether the individual has an expectation of privacy that society is prepared to recognize as reasonable—has often been criticized as circular, and hence subjective and unpredictable. While it may be difficult to refine *Katz* when the search of areas such as telephone booths, automobiles, or even the curtilage and uncovered portions of residences are at issue, in the case of the search of the interior of homes—the prototypical and hence most commonly litigated area of protected privacy—there is a ready criterion, with roots deep in the common law, of the minimal expectation of privacy that *exists*, and that is acknowledged to be *reasonable*. To withdraw protection of this minimum expectation would be to permit police technology to erode the privacy guaranteed by the Fourth Amendment. We think that obtaining by sense-enhancing technology any information regarding the interior of the home that could not otherwise have been obtained without physical "intrusion into a constitutionally protected area," constitutes a search—at least where (as here) the technology in question is not in general public use. This assures preservation of that degree of privacy against government that existed when the Fourth Amendment was adopted. On the basis of this criterion, the information obtained by the thermal imager in this case was the product of a search.

The government maintains, however, that the thermal imaging must be upheld because it detected "only heat radiating from the external surface of the house." The dissent makes this its leading point, contending that there is a fundamental difference between what it calls "off-the-wall" observations and "through-the-wall surveillance." But just as a thermal imager captures only heat emanating from a house, so also a powerful directional microphone picks up only sound emanating from a house—and a satellite capable of scanning from many miles away would pick up only visible light emanating from a house. We rejected such a mechanical interpretation of the Fourth Amendment in *Katz,* where the eavesdropping device picked up only sound waves that reached the exterior of the phone booth. Reversing that approach would leave the homeowner at the mercy of advancing technology—including imaging technology that could discern all human activity in the home. While the technology used in the present case was relatively crude, the rule we adopt must take account of more sophisticated systems that are already in use or in development.

The government also contends that the thermal imaging was constitutional because it did not "detect private activities occurring in private areas." It points out that in *Dow Chemical* we observed that the enhanced aerial photography did not reveal any "intimate details." *Dow Chemical,* however, involved enhanced aerial photography of an industrial complex, which does not share the Fourth Amendment sanctity of the home. The Fourth Amendment's protection of the home has never been tied to measurement of the quality or quantity of information obtained. In the home, our cases show, all details are intimate details, because the entire area is held safe from prying government eyes.

Limiting the prohibition of thermal imaging to "intimate details" would not only be wrong in principle; it would be impractical in application, failing to provide "a workable accommodation between the needs of law enforcement and the interests protected by the Fourth Amendment." To begin with, there is no necessary connection between the sophistication of the surveillance equipment and the "intimacy" of the details that it observes which means that one cannot say (and the police cannot be assured) that use of the relatively crude equipment at issue here will always be lawful. The Agema Thermovision 210 might disclose, for example, at what hour each night the lady of the house takes her daily sauna and bath—a detail that many would consider "intimate"; and a much more sophisticated system might detect nothing more intimate than the fact that someone left a closet light on. We could not, in other words, develop a rule approving only that through-the-wall surveillance which identifies objects no smaller than 36 by 36 inches, but would have to develop a jurisprudence specifying which home activities are "intimate" and which are not. And even when (if ever) that jurisprudence were fully developed, no police officer would be able to know in advance whether his through-the-wall surveillance picks up "intimate" details—and thus would be unable to know in advance whether it is constitutional.

We have said that the Fourth Amendment draws "a firm line at the entrance to the house." That line, we think, must be not only firm but also bright—which requires clear specification of those methods of surveillance that require a warrant. While it is certainly possible to conclude from the videotape of the thermal imaging that occurred in this case that no "significant" compromise of the homeowner's privacy has occurred, we must take the long view, from the original meaning of the Fourth Amendment forward.

Where, as here, the government uses a device that is not in general public use, to explore details of the home that would previously have been unknowable without physical intrusion, the surveillance is a "search" and is presumptively unreasonable without a warrant.

The judgment of the Court of Appeals is reversed; the case is remanded for further proceedings consistent with this opinion.

FURTHER CASE LAW, REFLECTIONS, AND QUESTIONS

1. If Agent Elliot, standing on a sidewalk outside of Kyllo's home, had been able to place his hand near the house's exterior wall and feel the warmth radiating from it, would he have "searched" the home? What if, wanting a more sensitive measure than his own hand, he held a thermometer next to the wall and recorded the temperature; would such conduct amount to a "search"? What, if anything, is different about using a hand, a thermometer, or a thermal-imaging device to detect whether heat is emanating from the wall of a house?

2. Does a thermal-imaging device directly provide information about a house's interior, or does it instead simply provide information that allows reasonable inferences about what may be transpiring within the house? Is using a thermal-imaging device to measure escaping heat any different from observing smoke coming from a chimney or, as Justice Stevens suggests, observing patterns of melting snow on a rooftop? Of what significance, if any, is the "through the wall" versus "off the wall" distinction?

3. How critical is it that the technology used in Kyllo was directed at the home? What if the thermal-imaging device had been trained on a business establishment instead of a home? What if the police had a device—similar to the metal detectors wands used at airports and other locations—that was sensitive at some distance to dense metal objects, and aimed the device at people in an effort to detect concealed handguns? What result would you expect under Kyllo?

4. One crucial factor for the majority was that the use of thermal imaging devices

was "not in general use." Kyllo was decided more than 20 years ago, and thermal imaging devices are much more common today. Do you think the Court will ever reject the Kyllo holding, based upon the more widespread use of technology, such as thermal imaging devices?

Tracking Devices

Courts have had occasion to consider the constitutionality of using other sensory enhancement devices by law enforcement. In *United States v. Jones*, 565 U.S. 400 (2012), the Supreme Court considered whether the Fourth Amendment was violated when police placed a GPS tracking device to Jones' car to facilitate monitoring its location from afar for nearly a month. The Supreme Court found that putting a GPS device on a car for the purposes of tracking a person's movements requires a search warrant. While all nine justices agreed that the police acted unconstitutionally, there was disagreement regarding the specific doctrine utilized. Justice Scalia, writing for himself and three other Justices, found that the physical intrusion necessary to place the GPS device on the car constituted a search under the Fourth Amendment. Justice Alito, representing the view of four Justices, wrote that placing the device on the car was not necessarily unconstitutional; however, using it to track a person's movements for twenty-eight days violated an individual's reasonable expectation of privacy. Justice Sotomayor, writing for herself, found that placing a tracking device on a car and monitoring the car's movements, regardless of how long a period the car was tracked, violated a person's reasonable expectation of privacy.

In *Grady v. North Carolina*, 575 U.S. 306 (2015), the Supreme Court considered the constitutionality of a North Carolina statute that required recidivist sex offenders to wear a satellite-based monitoring device on their ankle for the rest of their lives. In a per curiam opinion, the Court held that placing a satellite-based monitoring device on a recidivist sex offender constituted a search within the scope of the Fourth Amendment. The Court based its decision on the fact that attaching the ankle monitor to Grady involved physically intruding on his body without consent for purposes of obtaining information concerning his movements. The Court sent the case back to the trial court to determine if the search was reasonable under the circumstances.

Other technologies have had mixed results. In *Carpenter v. United States*, 585 U.S. 296 (2018), the Supreme Court held that a search warrant is required to obtain cell site location information regarding an individual's cell phone use. Courts have generally found that using night vision goggles does not violate the Constitution so long as a police officer is in a place they have a right to be, *United States v. Vela*, 486 F. Supp. 2d 587 (WD Tex. 2005). As new technologies emerge, courts will face increasing challenges in determining where to draw the line on a person's expectation of privacy.

The Exclusionary Rule

Origins and Evolution of the Exclusionary Rule

The **Exclusionary Rule** is a judicially created prophylactic rule designed to safeguard the Fourth Amendment and other rights and ensure evidence obtained in violation of the Constitution is inadmissible at trial to prove guilt. Remember from the discussion above that the Fourth Amendment does not state what should happen when the government violates the Fourth Amendment. Common sense dictates that the police follow the law and the Constitution on their own accord; however, history shows this is not the case. Until the implementation of the Exclusionary Rule, the police could violate the Fourth Amendment, and there were few, if any, consequences. As the Court said, without the Exclusionary Rule, the Fourth Amendment ". . . is reduced to 'a form of words.'" *Silverthorne Lumber Company v. United States,* 251 U.S. 385, 390 (1920). As with many things with the U.S. Supreme Court, the development of the Exclusionary Rule was slow and processional and in response to the social conditions at the time. Despite implementing the Exclusionary Rule, some argue that it has been significantly narrowed in recent years and does not afford the same protections as originally intended by the U.S. Supreme Court. This history of the Exclusionary Rule begins in 1911 with the federal case of *Weeks.*

In 1911, federal and state law enforcement officers made a warrantless entry into the Kansas City home of Fremont Weeks, in violation of Weeks's Fourth Amendment rights. They seized numerous pieces of evidence, including Weeks's personal papers, and some of the evidence was used to support Weeks's conviction in federal court for using U.S. mail to transport illegal lottery coupons. The U.S. Supreme Court reversed the conviction. In a unanimous opinion written by Justice Day, the Court ruled that the evidence seized in violation of Weeks's Fourth Amendment rights should not have been admitted at his trial. *Weeks v. United States,* 232 U.S. 383 (1914). Justice Day wrote:

> The effect of the 4th Amendment is to put the courts of the United States and Federal officials, in the exercise of their power and authority, under limitations and restraints as to the exercise of such power and authority, and to forever secure the people, their persons, houses, papers, and effects, against all unreasonable searches and seizures under the guise of law. This protection reaches all alike, whether accused of crime or not, and the duty of giving to it force and effect is obligatory upon all entrusted under our Federal system with the enforcement of the laws. The tendency of those who execute the criminal laws of the country to obtain conviction by means of unlawful seizures should find no sanction in the judgments of the courts, which are charged at all times with the support of the Constitution, and to which people of all conditions have a right to appeal for the maintenance of such fundamental rights.

> The efforts of the courts and their officials to bring the guilty to punishment, praiseworthy as they are, are not to be aided by the sacrifice of those great principles established by years of endeavor and suffering which have resulted in their embodiment in the fundamental law of the land.
>
> [T]he 4th Amendment was intended to secure the citizen in person and property against unlawful invasion of the sanctity of his home by officers of the law, acting under legislative or judicial sanction. This protection is equally extended to the action of the government and officers of the law acting under it. To sanction such proceedings would be to affirm by judicial decision a manifest neglect, if not an open defiance, of the prohibitions of the Constitution, intended for the protection of the people against such unauthorized action.

Make special note of the fact that *Weeks* involved a Fourth Amendment violation committed by federal law enforcement officers and the use of illegally seized evidence in a *federal* criminal trial.

Recall from our discussion in Chapter Two that the protections of the U.S. Constitution's Bill of Rights—including the Fourth Amendment—applied initially only against federal authorities and not against state officials. The "incorporation" of specific Bill of Rights guarantees to the states, by operation of the Fourteenth Amendment's due-process clause, was delayed for nearly half a century after the *Weeks* decision.

Following *Weeks,* while a number of states maintained or enacted an exclusionary rule on their own, a majority of states declined to exclude unlawfully seized evidence from state criminal trials. In *Wolf v. Colorado*, 338 U.S. 25 (1949), the Supreme Court held that states did not have to exclude evidence obtained in violation of the Fourth Amendment from trial. Instead, the Court found that states could utilize other means or methods to protect individuals' Fourth Amendment rights. At the time, the Court was more deferential to "states' rights" and gave individual states the option of how they wanted to protect and enforce the Fourth Amendment. In the following case, which was decided twelve years after *Wolf*, the Supreme Court reconsidered whether states were required to exclude improperly seized evidence from trial.

Mapp v. Ohio

367 U.S. 643 (1961)

MR. JUSTICE CLARK delivered the opinion of the Court.

On May 23, 1957, three Cleveland police officers arrived at appellant's residence in that city pursuant to information that "a person [was] hiding out in the home, who was wanted for questioning in connection with a recent bombing, and that there was a large amount of policy paraphernalia being hidden in the home." Miss Mapp and her daughter by a former marriage lived on the top floor of the two-family dwelling.

Upon their arrival at that house, the officers knocked on the door and demanded entrance but appellant, after telephoning her attorney, refused to admit them without a search warrant. They advised their headquarters of the situation and undertook a surveillance of the house.

The officers again sought entrance some three hours later when four or more additional officers arrived on the scene. When Miss Mapp did not come to the door immediately, at least one of the several doors to the house was forcibly opened and the policemen gained admittance. Meanwhile Miss Mapp's attorney arrived, but the officers, having secured their own entry, and continuing in their defiance of the law, would permit him neither to see Miss Mapp nor to enter the house. It appears that Miss Mapp was halfway down the stairs from the upper floor to the front door when the officers, in this highhanded manner, broke into the hall. She demanded to see the search warrant. A paper, claimed to be a warrant, was held up by one of the officers. She grabbed the "warrant" and placed it in her bosom. A struggle ensued in which the officers recovered the piece of paper and as a result of which they handcuffed appellant because she had been "belligerent" in resisting their official rescue of the "warrant" from her person. Running roughshod over appellant, a policeman "grabbed" her, "twisted [her] hand," and she "yelled [and] pleaded with him" because "it was hurting." Appellant, in handcuffs, was then forcibly taken upstairs to her bedroom where the officers searched a dresser, a chest of drawers, a closet and some suitcases. They also looked into a photo album and through personal papers belonging to the appellant. The search spread to the rest of the second floor including the child's bedroom, the living room, the kitchen and a dinette. The basement of the building and a trunk found therein were also searched. The obscene materials for possession of which she was ultimately convicted were discovered in the course of that widespread search.

At the trial no search warrant was produced by the prosecution, nor was the failure to produce one explained or accounted for.

The State says that even if the search were made without authority, or otherwise unreasonably, it is not prevented from using the constitutionally seized evidence at trial, citing *Wolf v. Colorado*, 338 US 25 (1949), in which this Court did indeed hold "that in a prosecution in a State court for a State crime the Fourteenth Amendment does not forbid the admission of evidence obtained by an unreasonable search and seizure." On this appeal, it is urged once again that we review that holding.

I

[I]n the year 1914, in the Weeks Case, this Court "for the first time" held that "in a federal prosecution the Fourth Amendment barred the use of evidence secured through an illegal search and seizure." *Wolf v. Colorado* (338 US at 28). This Court has ever since required of federal law officers a strict adherence to that command which this Court has held to be a clear, specific, and constitutionally required—even if judicially implied—deterrent safeguard without insistence upon which the Fourth Amendment would have been reduced to "a form of words." Holmes, J., *Silverthorne Lumber Co. v. United States*, 251 US 385, 392 (1920).

There are in the cases of this Court some passing references to the Weeks rule as being one of evidence. But the plain and unequivocal language of Weeks—and its later paraphrase in Wolf—to the effect that the Weeks rule is of constitutional origin, remains entirely undisturbed.

II

In 1949, 35 years after Weeks was announced, this Court, in *Wolf v. Colorado* again for the first time, discussed the effect of the Fourth Amendment upon the States through the operation of the Due Process Clause of the Fourteenth Amendment. It said: "[W]e have no hesitation in saying that were a State affirmatively to sanction such police incursion into privacy it would run counter to the guaranty of the Fourteenth Amendment."

Nevertheless, after declaring that the "security of one's privacy against arbitrary intrusion by the police" is "implicit in 'the concept of ordered liberty' and as such enforceable against the States through the Due Process Clause," and announcing that it "stoutly adhere[d]" to the Weeks decision, the Court decided that the Weeks exclusionary rule would not then be imposed upon the States as "an essential ingredient of the right."

The Court's reasons for not considering essential to the right to privacy, as a curb imposed upon the States by the Due Process Clause, that which decades before had been posited as part and parcel of the Fourth Amendment's limitation upon federal encroachment of individual privacy, were bottomed on factual considerations. While they are not basically relevant to a decision that the exclusionary rule is an essential ingredient of the Fourth Amendment as the right it embodies is vouchsafed against the states by the Due Process Clause, we will consider the current validity of the factual grounds upon which Wolf was based.

The Court in Wolf first stated that "[t]he contrariety of views of the States" on the adoption of the exclusionary rule of Weeks was "particularly impressive" and, in this connection, that it could not "brush aside the experience of States which deem the incidence of such conduct by the police too slight to call for a deterrent remedy by overriding the [States'] relevant rules of evidence." While in 1949, prior to the Wolf Case, almost two-thirds of the States were opposed to the use of the exclusionary rule, now, despite the Wolf Case, more than half of those since passing upon it, by their own legislative or judicial decision, have wholly or partly adopted or adhered to the Weeks rule.

[T]he second basis elaborated in Wolf in support of its failure to enforce the exclusionary doctrine against the States was that "other means of protection" have been afforded "the right to privacy." The experience of California that such other remedies have been worthless and futile is buttressed by the experience of other States. The obvious futility of relegating the Fourth Amendment to the protection of other remedies has, moreover, been recognized by this Court since Wolf.

III

Today we once again examine Wolf's constitutional documentation of the right to privacy free from unreasonable state intrusion, and, after its dozen years on our books, are led by it to close the only courtroom door remaining open to evidence secured by official lawlessness in flagrant abuse of that basic right, reserved to all persons as a specific guarantee against that very same unlawful conduct. We hold that all evidence obtained by searches and seizures in violation of the Constitution is, by that same authority, inadmissible in a state court.

IV

Since the Fourth Amendment's right of privacy has been declared enforceable against the States through the Due Process Clause of the Fourteenth, it is enforceable against them by the same sanction of exclusion as is used against the federal government. Were it otherwise, then just as without the Weeks rule the assurance against unreasonable federal searches and seizures would be "a form of words," valueless and undeserving of mention in a perpetual charter of inestimable human liberties, so too, without that rule the freedom from state invasions of privacy would be so ephemeral and so neatly severed from its conceptual nexus with the freedom from all brutish means of coercing evidence as not to merit this Court's high regard as a freedom "implicit in the concept of ordered liberty." Therefore, in extending the substantive protections of due process to all constitutionally unreasonable searches—state or federal—it was logically and constitutionally necessary that the exclusion doctrine—an essential part of the right to privacy—be also insisted upon as an essential ingredient of the right newly recognized by the Wolf Case. In short, the admission of the new constitutional right by Wolf could not consistently tolerate denial of its most important constitutional privilege, namely, the exclusion of the evidence which an accused had been forced to give by reason of the unlawful seizure. To hold otherwise is to grant the right but in reality to withhold its privilege and enjoyment. Only last year the Court itself recognized that the purpose of the exclusionary rule "is to deter—to compel respect for the constitutional guaranty in the only effectively available way—by removing the incentive to disregard it." *Elkins v. United States*, 364 U.S. 206 (1960).

V

Moreover, our holding that the exclusionary rule is an essential part of both the Fourth and Fourteenth Amendments is not only the logical dictate of prior cases, but it also makes very good sense. There is no war between the Constitution and common sense. Presently, a federal prosecutor may make no use of evidence illegally seized, but a State's attorney across the street may, although he supposedly is operating under the enforceable prohibitions of the same Amendment. Thus the State, by admitting evidence unlawfully seized, serves to encourage disobedience to the Federal Constitution which it is bound to uphold.

There are those who say, as did Justice (then Judge) Cardozo, that under our constitutional exclusionary doctrine "[t]he criminal is to go free because the constable has blundered." *People v. Defore*, 242 NY, at 21, 150 NE, at 587. In some cases this will undoubtedly be the result. But, as was said in *Elkins*, "There is another consideration—the imperative of judicial integrity." 364 US, at 222. The criminal goes free, if he must, but it is the law that sets him free. Nothing can destroy a government more quickly than its failure to observe its own laws, or worse, its disregard of the charter of its own existence.

The ignoble shortcut to conviction left open to the state tends to destroy the entire system of constitutional restraints on which the liberties of the people rest. Having once recognized that the right to privacy embodied in the Fourth Amendment is enforceable against the States, and that the right to be secure against rude invasions of privacy by state officers is, therefore, constitutional in origin, we can no longer permit that right to remain an empty promise. Because it is enforceable in the same manner and to like effect as other basic rights secured by the Due Process Clause, we can no longer permit it to be revocable at the whim of any police officer who, in the name of law enforcement itself, chooses to suspend its enjoyment. Our decision, founded on reason and truth, gives to the individual no more than that which the Constitution guarantees him, to the police officer no less than that to which honest law enforcement is entitled, and, to the courts, that judicial integrity so necessary in the true administration of justice.

Reversed and remanded.

MR. JUSTICE HARLAN, whom MR. JUSTICE FRANKFURTER and MR. JUSTICE WHITTAKER join, dissenting.

I would not impose upon the States this federal exclusionary remedy. The reasons given by the majority for now suddenly turning its back on Wolf seem to be notably unconvincing.

First, it is said that "the factual grounds upon which Wolf was based" have since changed, in that more States now follow the Weeks exclusionary rule than was so at the time Wolf was decided. While that is true, a recent survey indicates that at present one-half of the States still adhere to the common-law non-exclusionary rule, and one, Maryland, retains the rule as to felonies.

But in any case surely all this is beside the point, as the majority itself indeed seems to recognize. Our concern here, as it was in Wolf, is not with the desirability of that rule but only with the question whether the States are Constitutionally free to follow it or not as they may themselves determine, and the relevance of the disparity of views among the States on this point lies simply in the fact that the judgment involved is a debatable one.

For us the question remains, as it has always been, one of state power, not one of passing judgment on the wisdom of one state course or another.

Further, we are told that imposition of the Weeks rule on the States makes "very good sense," in that it will promote recognition by state and federal officials of their "mutual obligation to respect the same fundamental criteria" in their approach to law enforcement and will avoid " 'needless conflict between state and federal courts.'"

An approach which regards the issue as one of achieving procedural symmetry or of serving administrative convenience surely disfigures the boundaries of this Court's functions in relation to the state and federal courts. Our role in promulgating the Weeks rule and its extensions was quite a different one than it is here. There, in implementing the Fourth Amendment, we occupied the position of a tribunal having the ultimate responsibility for developing the standards and procedures of judicial administration within the judicial system over which it presides. Here we review state procedures whose measure is to be taken not against the specific substantive commands of the Fourth Amendment but under the flexible contours of the Due Process Clause. I do not believe that the Fourteenth Amendment empowers this Court to mold state remedies effectuating the right to freedom from "arbitrary intrusion by the police" to suit its own notions of how things should be done.

FURTHER CASE LAW, REFLECTIONS, AND QUESTIONS

1. *Mapp* was among the earliest of the Warren Court decisions marking the "due-process revolution." Indeed, the undercurrent of state-federal relations and the proper role of the federal Constitution in governing state rules of criminal procedure is evident in Justice Harlan's dissenting opinion in *Mapp* and largely accounts for the different outcomes in *Wolf* and *Mapp*. In *Ker v. California*, 374 U.S. 23 (1963), the justices expressly held that the Fourth Amendment's prohibition against unreasonable searches and seizures is enforceable against the states through the Fourteenth Amendment's due process clause.

2. What is the apparent source of authority for the exclusionary rule, as identified in Justice Clark's majority opinion in *Mapp*? That is, does the exclusionary remedy appear to be part and parcel of the constitutional right to be free from unreasonable searches and seizures? Or is it a judicially designed safeguard created to protect that right without being directly mandated by the Constitution? What are the expressed rationales, or justifications, for the exclusionary rule?

3. In *Mapp*, the court quotes Justice Cardozo, "The criminal is to go free because the constable has blundered." What does Justice Cardozo mean by this? How often do you think a criminal goes free because of the Exclusionary Rule?

The Standing Requirement

Generally, a party requesting relief from a court must allege that he or she has personally suffered an injury that the court can redress. The "injury in fact" requirement means that the party must "'show that he personally suffered some actual or threatened injury as a result of the putatively illegal conduct' of the [other party]." *Valley Forge Christian College v. Americans United for Separation of Church and State*, 454 U.S. 464, 472 (1982). This concept is known as "standing." The standing requirement helps to ensure that the courts resolve actual controversies between parties, as opposed to rendering abstract policy or advisory decisions.

The **standing** requirement also applies in criminal cases. A criminal defendant can hope to prevail on a claim involving a denial of constitutional rights only if his or her personal rights are at issue. In other words, the rights in the Fourth Amendment cannot be vicariously asserted. In the context of search and seizure law, he or she must show that he or she had a reasonable expectation of privacy regarding the area searched, not someone else. The case of *Rawlings v. Kentucky*, 448 U.S. 98 (1980), illustrates this concept.

In *Rawlings*, the defendant had placed his illegal drugs in a friend's purse. Police searched the purse in the defendant's presence, and he admitted ownership of the narcotics. After he was charged with illegal possession of the drugs, he moved to suppress the evidence obtained from the purse. The state court ruled that he lacked standing to object to the search of his friend's (Cox) purse, and the U.S. Supreme Court agreed.

> At the time petitioner dumped thousands of dollars worth of illegal drugs into Cox's purse, he had known her for only a few days. According to Cox's uncontested testimony, petitioner had never sought or received access to her purse prior to that sudden bailment. Nor did petitioner have any right to exclude other persons from access to Cox's purse. Moreover, even assuming that petitioner's version of the bailment is correct and that Cox did consent to the transfer of possession, the precipitous nature of the transaction hardly supports a reasonable inference that petitioner took normal precautions to maintain his privacy. In addition to all the foregoing facts, the record also contains a frank admission by petitioner that he had no subjective expectation that Cox's purpose would remain free from governmental intrusion.

> Petitioner contends nevertheless that, because he claimed ownership of the drugs in Cox's purse, he should be entitled to challenge the search regardless of his expectation of privacy. We disagree. While petitioner's ownership of the drugs is undoubtedly one fact to be considered in this case, *Rakas v. Illinois* 439 U.S. 128 (1978) emphatically rejected the notion that "arcane" concepts of property law ought to control the ability to claim the protections of the Fourth Amendment.
>
> Had petitioner placed his drugs in plain view, he would still have owned them, but he could not claim any legitimate expectation of privacy. Prior to *Rakas*, petitioner might have been given "standing" in such a case to challenge a "search" that netted those drugs but probably would have lost his claim on the merits. After *Rakas*, the two inquiries merge into one: whether governmental officials violated any legitimate expectation of privacy held by petitioner.
>
> In sum, we find no reason to overturn the lower court's conclusion that petitioner had no legitimate expectation of privacy in Cox's purse at the time of the search. *Rawlings v. Kentucky*, 448 U. S. at 105.

Following the Court's decisions in *Rawlings* and *Rakas*, mere ownership of an item does not give a defendant standing to object to the search during which the item was seized. Rather, standing centers around whether a person has a legitimate expectation of privacy over the area searched.

Justification for the Exclusionary Rule

Under the exclusionary rule, evidence obtained from unconstitutional police conduct is precluded from being used at trial. This is so regardless of the defendant's guilt, innocence, or the probative value of the excluded evidence. Sometimes, this leads to charges being dismissed. Why would the Court mandate such extreme measures?

There are three primary arguments made to justify the use of the exclusionary rule:

- Deterring police misconduct
- Providing a mechanism to protect individual rights
- Maintenance of judicial integrity

As you will see throughout the remainder of this chapter, the Supreme Court has repeatedly emphasized that the primary purpose of the exclusionary rule is to deter police misconduct. Under this viewpoint, if excluding evidence from trial will not have a deterrent effect on the actions of law enforcement agents, the application of the exclusionary rule is questionable. As we will see shortly, this has led to the Court establishing a number of exceptions to the exclusionary rule.

A second justification for the exclusionary rule is that it is necessary to protect individual rights effectively. Without the exclusionary rule, the Fourth Amendment would be meaningless in a practical sense. The exclusionary rule provides the only remedy that mitigates the harm caused to a defendant from constitutional violations. Absent the exclusion of evidence, courts could not ensure that an individual's rights are protected.

A third justification for the exclusionary rule is that it is necessary to preserve the court's integrity. How can a court operating under the authority of the Constitution perform its duties without the ability to reject evidence obtained unconstitutionally? Allowing convictions based on constitutional violations diminishes the moral standing of the court, and if not checked, could severely damage the integrity and legitimacy of the justice system. By excluding illegally seized evidence, a court can maintain its moral integrity and instill confidence in the public that citizens' rights will be protected.

As will be evident in the remainder of the chapter, as the country entered into a law-and-order mindset, the Court became less willing to allow defendants to go free because the police made a mistake. Along this vein, the Court took a closer look at how deterrence might operate in justifying the exclusion of evidence and began a trend that continues to this day under which courts increasingly focus on whether excluding evidence obtained under specific factual scenarios serves a deterrent purpose. Under this framework, the exclusionary rule began to be curtailed, and exceptions to the exclusionary rule began to dominate Fourth Amendment law.

Exceptions to the Exclusionary Rule

Beginning in the mid-1970s, the Supreme Court decided a number of cases limiting the application of the exclusionary rule. Several themes emerged from these cases: that the exclusionary rule is not a personal constitutional right but a judicially created remedy; that its purpose is to deter the police from unlawful searches and seizures and not to promote "judicial integrity"; and that the presumed deterrence benefits of the rule must be carefully assessed in different contexts to determine whether they are worth the costs to the truth-finding function of a criminal trial. As we examine the exceptions to the exclusionary rule, be on the lookout for these themes.

Good Faith Exception

Recall that the exclusionary rule centers on deterring police from violating the Fourth Amendment. Given this fact, prosecutors long argued that excluding evidence obtained by an officer who had no ill intentions and acted in good faith would serve no deterrent purpose. The acceptance of this argument led to the good-faith exception to the exclusionary rule. The **good-faith exception** allows prosecutors to use evidence obtained from a search based on an unlawful search warrant if law enforcement officers reasonably believed the warrant to be lawful. Since its establishment in

1984, the good-faith exception has expanded to other situations as the Supreme Court began limiting the use of the exclusionary rule.

In *United States v. Leon*, 468 U.S. 897 (1984), police applied to a judge for a search warrant of Leon's home based on the evidence from their surveillance. A judge issued the warrant, and the police recovered large quantities of illegal drugs. Leon was subsequently indicted on multiple narcotics offenses. Subsequently, the District Court granted a motion to suppress the evidence seized because the warrant was improperly issued, finding that the police lacked probable cause. The Court of Appeals affirmed the suppression order.

The Supreme Court reversed. It held that when a police officer obtains a facially valid warrant from a judge and acts as it allows, excluding the evidence would serve no deterrent purpose. Under the rule established by Leon, which is known as the good-faith exception, if the officer searched and relied on the warrant with objectively reasonable good faith, the exclusionary rule does not apply. This requires that (a) the police reasonably believe the search warrant affidavit provides probable cause for the search; (b) the warrant is facially valid and includes specifics regarding the pace to be searched and the items to be searched for, and (c) the warrant was issued by a "neutral and detached" judge and not simply rubber-stamped. According to the Leon Court, these requirements ensured that the police were acting in good faith.

The Court also applied the good-faith exception in a companion case to *Leon—Massachusetts v. Sheppard*, 468 U.S. 981 (1984). In *Sheppard,* a police detective applied for a warrant to search the defendant's home for evidence of a murder. Because it was Sunday, the detective applied for the warrant at a judge's home. Although the judge told the detective that the warrant he signed would authorize a search for evidence of a murder, the written warrant erroneously permitted a search only for evidence of controlled substances. On executing the search warrant, the detective and other officers seized evidence of the murder. The evidence was suppressed by the state court because, to the extent the warrant was intended to authorize a search for evidence of a homicide, it failed to "particularly describ[e]" the items to be seized. The U.S. Supreme Court reversed. It ruled that because "there was an objectively reasonable basis for the officers' mistaken belief" that "the warrant authorized the search that they conducted," the evidence was admissible by application of the good-faith exception to the exclusionary rule. "We refuse to rule that an officer is required to disbelieve a judge who has just advised him, by word and by action, that the warrant he possesses authorizes him to conduct the search he has requested." *Id.* at 489–90.

What about a situation where police relied on a statute that was later found to be unconstitutional? In *Illinois v. Krull,* 480 U.S. 340 (1987), the police entered a place of business and found incriminating evidence in reliance on a state statute that authorized the warrantless inspection of the premises and records of various companies engaged in the sale of motor vehicles and vehicular parts. The statute was subsequently found to be unconstitutional. The Court "granted certiorari to consider whether a good-faith exception to the Fourth Amendment exclusionary rule applies when an officer's reliance on the constitutionality of a statute is objectively reasonable, but the statute is subsequently declared unconstitutional." Justice Blackmun authored the majority opinion in a 5–4 decision that answered that question in the affirmative.

> The application of the exclusionary rule to suppress evidence obtained by an officer acting in objectively reasonable reliance on a statute would have as little deterrent effect on the officer's actions as would the exclusion of evidence when an officer acts in objectively reasonable reliance on a warrant. Unless a statute is clearly unconstitutional, an officer cannot be expected to question the judgment of the legislature that passed the law. If the statute is subsequently declared unconstitutional, excluding evidence obtained pursuant to it prior to such a judicial declaration will not deter future Fourth Amendment violations by an officer who has simply fulfilled his responsibility to enforce the statute as written. *Id.* at 349–50.

It is important to remember that the good-faith exception only applies in specific circumstances. Just because an officer believes their actions are legal and correct does not mean that the good-faith exception will apply. Instead, the officer must have an objective good faith belief that they are relying on a facially valid warrant or reliance on other "good" information, such as a statute, precedents, or as considered in the following case, a government database.

Herring v. United States

555 U.S. 135 (2009)

CHIEF JUSTICE ROBERTS delivered the opinion of the Court.

On July 7, 2004, Investigator Mark Anderson learned that Bennie Dean Herring had driven to the Coffee County Sheriff's Department to retrieve something from his impounded truck. Herring was no stranger to law enforcement, and Anderson asked the county's warrant clerk, Sandy Pope, to check for any outstanding warrants for Herring's arrest. When she found none, Anderson asked Pope to check with Sharon Morgan, her counterpart in neighboring Dale County. After checking Dale County's computer database, Morgan replied that there was an active arrest warrant for Herring's failure to appear on a felony charge. Pope relayed the information to Anderson and asked Morgan to fax over a copy of the warrant as confirmation. Anderson and a deputy followed Herring as he left the impound lot, pulled him over, and arrested him. A search incident to the arrest revealed methamphetamine in Herring's pocket, and a pistol (which as a felon he could not possess) in his vehicle.

There had, however, been a mistake about the warrant. The Dale County sheriff's computer records are supposed to correspond to actual arrest warrants, which the office also maintains. But when Morgan went to the files to retrieve the actual warrant to fax to Pope, Morgan was unable to find it. She called a court clerk and learned that the warrant had been recalled five months earlier. Normally when a warrant is recalled the court clerk's office or a judge's chambers calls Morgan, who enters the information in the sheriff's computer database and disposes of the physical copy. For whatever reason, the information about the recall of the warrant for Herring did not appear in the database. Morgan immediately called Pope to alert her to the mix-up, and Pope contacted Anderson over a secure radio. This all unfolded in 10 to 15 minutes, but Herring had already been arrested and found with the gun and drugs, just a few hundred yards from the sheriff's office.

Herring was indicted in the District Court for the Middle District of Alabama for illegally possessing the gun and drugs. He moved to suppress the evidence on the ground that his initial arrest had been illegal because the warrant had been rescinded. The Magistrate Judge recommended denying the motion because the arresting officers had acted in a good-faith belief that the warrant was still outstanding. Thus, even if there were a Fourth Amendment violation, there was "no reason to believe that application of the exclusionary rule here would deter the occurrence of any future mistakes." The District Court adopted the Magistrate Judge's recommendation, and the Court of Appeals for the Eleventh Circuit affirmed.

II

When a probable-cause determination was based on reasonable but mistaken assumptions, the person subjected to a search or seizure has not necessarily been the victim of a constitutional violation. The very phrase "probable cause" confirms that the Fourth Amendment does not demand all possible precision. And whether the error can be traced to a mistake by a state actor or some other source may bear on the analysis. For purposes of deciding this case, however, we accept the parties' assumption that there was a Fourth Amendment violation. The issue is whether the exclusionary rule should be applied.

A

The Coffee County officers did nothing improper. Indeed, the error was noticed so quickly because Coffee County requested a faxed confirmation of the warrant.

The Eleventh Circuit concluded, however, that somebody in Dale County should have updated the computer database to reflect the recall of the arrest warrant. The court also concluded that this error was negligent, but did not find it to be reckless or deliberate. That fact is crucial to our holding that this error is not enough by itself to require "the extreme sanction of exclusion."

B

1. The fact that a Fourth Amendment violation occurred—i.e., that a search or arrest was unreasonable—does not necessarily mean that the exclusionary rule applies. Indeed, exclusion "has always been our last resort, not our first impulse," and our precedents establish important principles that constrain application of the exclusionary rule.

First, the exclusionary rule is not an individual right and applies only where it "'result[s] in appreciable deterrence.'" *United States v. Leon*, 468 U.S. 897, 909 (1984). We have repeatedly rejected the argument that exclusion is a necessary consequence of a Fourth Amendment violation. Instead we have focused on the efficacy of the rule in deterring Fourth Amendment violations in the future.

In addition, the benefits of deterrence must outweigh the costs. "We have never suggested that the exclusionary rule must apply in every circumstance in which it might provide marginal deterrence." "[T]o the extent that application of the exclusionary rule could provide some incremental deterrent, that possible benefit must be weighed against [its] substantial social costs." The principal cost of applying the rule is, of course, letting guilty and possibly dangerous defendants go free—something that "offends basic concepts of the criminal justice system." "[T]he rule's costly toll upon truth-seeking and law enforcement objectives presents a high obstacle for those urging [its] application."

These principles are reflected in the holding of *Leon*: When police act under a warrant that is invalid for lack of probable cause, the exclusionary rule does not apply if the police acted "in objectively reasonable reliance" on the subsequently invalidated search warrant. We (perhaps confusingly) called this objectively reasonable reliance "good faith."

The extent to which the exclusionary rule is justified by these deterrence principles varies with the culpability of the law enforcement conduct. As we said in *Leon*, "an assessment of the flagrancy of the police misconduct constitutes an important step in the calculus" of applying the exclusionary rule.

Indeed, the abuses that gave rise to the exclusionary rule featured intentional conduct that was patently unconstitutional. In *Weeks*, a foundational exclusionary rule case, the officers had broken into the defendant's home (using a key shown to them by a neighbor), confiscated incriminating papers, then returned again with a U.S. Marshal to confiscate even more. Not only did they have no search warrant, which the Court held was required, but they could not have gotten one had they tried. They were so lacking in sworn and particularized information that "not even an order of court would have justified such procedure."

Equally flagrant conduct was at issue in *Mapp v. Ohio*, 367 U.S. 643 (1961), which extended the exclusionary rule to the States. Officers forced open a door to Ms. Mapp's house, kept her lawyer from entering, brandished what the court concluded was a false warrant, then forced her into handcuffs and canvassed the house for obscenity. An error that arises from nonrecurring and attenuated negligence is thus far removed from the core concerns that led us to adopt the rule in the first place.

3. To trigger the exclusionary rule, police conduct must be sufficiently deliberate that exclusion can meaningfully deter it, and sufficiently culpable that such deterrence is worth the price paid by the justice system. As laid out in our cases, the exclusionary rule serves to deter deliberate, reckless, or grossly negligent conduct, or in some circumstances recurring or systemic negligence. The error in this case does not rise to that level.

The pertinent analysis of deterrence and culpability is objective, not an "inquiry into the subjective awareness of arresting officers." We have already held that "our good-faith inquiry is confined to the objectively ascertainable question whether a reasonably well-trained officer would have known that the search was illegal" in light of "all of the circumstances." These circumstances frequently include a particular officer's knowledge and experience, but that does not make the test any more subjective than the one for probable cause, which looks to an officer's knowledge and experience, but not his subjective intent.

4. We do not suggest that all recordkeeping errors by the police are immune from the exclusionary rule. In this case, however, the conduct at issue was not so objectively culpable as to require exclusion. In *Leon* we held that "the marginal or nonexistent benefits produced by suppressing evidence obtained in objectively reasonable reliance on a subsequently invalidated search warrant cannot justify the substantial costs of exclusion." The same is true when evidence is obtained in objectively reasonable reliance on a subsequently recalled warrant.

If the police have been shown to be reckless in maintaining a warrant system, or to have knowingly made false entries to lay the groundwork for future false arrests, exclusion would certainly be justified under our cases should such misconduct cause a Fourth Amendment violation. Petitioner's fears that our decision will cause police departments to deliberately keep their officers ignorant are thus unfounded.

Petitioner's claim that police negligence automatically triggers suppression cannot be squared with the principles underlying the exclusionary rule, as they have been explained in our cases. In light of our repeated holdings that the deterrent effect of suppression must be substantial and outweigh any harm to the justice system, we conclude that when police mistakes are the result of negligence such as that described here, rather than systemic error or reckless disregard of constitutional requirements, any marginal deterrence does not "pay its way." In such a case, the criminal should not "go free because the constable has blundered."

The judgment of the Court of Appeals for the Eleventh Circuit is affirmed.

FURTHER CASE LAW, REFLECTIONS, AND QUESTIONS

1. How should a "negligent" error be distinguished from one made "recklessly"? Which is the better characterization of the error made in Herring's case?
2. When would errors in a database fairly be characterized as "systemic"? And how would an individual, such as Herring, whose information was erroneously retained in a database, be able to make a showing of "systemic" error?
3. What implications, if any, does the Court's analysis in Herring have for the exclusionary rule's application in other types of cases involving police errors other than faultily maintained databases? For example, can you imagine a police officer "negligently" but erroneously concluding that probable cause exists to support an arrest, or "negligently" but erroneously expanding the scope of a search beyond reasonable limits, so that the exclusionary rule would not be triggered?
4. As you have no doubt observed, it is the deterrent effect of excluding evidence that is the key to cases involving good faith errors by police. Do you see a problem with this?

Box 3.2: You Be the Judge

Steve, a police officer, pulled Evan's car over to cite him for a traffic violation. Officer Steve then ran a computer check, which indicated that an outstanding warrant existed for Evan's arrest. The officer accordingly placed Evan under arrest, and a subsequent search of Evan and his car produced marijuana. Later, it was determined that the computer report of the outstanding arrest warrant for Evan was erroneous. A court had quashed (invalidated) the warrant over two weeks earlier. However, due to an oversight by a court clerk, the computer records were not corrected. Nonetheless, Evan was charged with possession of marijuana. Should the marijuana seized be excluded from Evan's trial?

See *Arizona v. Evans*, 514 U.S. 1 (1995)

Impeachment

The exclusionary rule generally precludes illegally obtained evidence from being used at trial during the prosecution's case in chief; the presentation of evidence by the prosecution to prove guilt. One exception to this rule is that the prosecution can use unconstitutionally seized evidence to impeach the testimony of a defendant who testifies in his or her own defense. Specifically, such evidence can be used to impeach a defendant's credibility. In other words, this evidence can be used to question the truthfulness or veracity of a defendant's testimony during cross-examination. Absent this exception, defendants would be free to testify untruthfully in circumstances where the only evidence available to contradict the testimony has been precluded from being presented at the trial.

Consider a situation where police improperly seize stolen merchandise for use in a defendant's robbery trial. The evidence that was seized from the defendant's home without a warrant in violation of the Fourth Amendment included the defendant's fingerprints and DNA. At trial, the defendant testified that he or she had never seen the stolen items, let alone touched them. In light of the fingerprints and DNA left on the evidence, this testimony is patently untrue. This is clearly a lie. Under the **impeachment exception**, the prosecution could confront the defendant with the evidence during cross-examination. While the jury would be instructed not to consider this evidence as proof that a crime was committed, the jury could consider whether the defendant's testimony was truthful.

This is an important exception to prevent testimony that the court, prosecutor, and defense know to be false. While this exception makes otherwise excluded evidence admissible at trial for this limited purpose, it should be noted that it only applies to the defendant's testimony. Excluded evidence cannot be used to impeach the testimony of other witnesses.

Collateral Proceedings

The exclusionary rule does not apply to collateral proceedings. Although this is technically not an exception to the exclusionary rule, because it is just when the exclusionary rule does not apply, it can easily be thought of as one. **Collateral proceedings** are hearings not directly related to a defendant's trial, particularly the prosecution's case-in-chief. Such proceedings include bail hearings, grand jury proceedings, preliminary hearings, immigration hearings, sentencing, and parole or probation revocation hearings. There are several reasons behind this rule. First, these proceedings are premised on the consideration of all facts available, and there is no determination of guilt. Excluding evidence from the presiding judge would limit his or her ability to make an informed decision on the specific matter under consideration. A second basis for their admission at collateral proceedings is that their exclusion would not significantly deter police from committing constitutional violations. As police know that evidence found to be illegally obtained will be excluded from being presented to a jury at trial, excluding it from pre-or post-trial proceedings does not add to any deterrent effect. As such, the value of accurate fact-finding in collateral proceedings outweighs any deterrent impact their exclusion would have.

Fruit of the Poisonous Tree

As we have seen, the exclusionary rule is designed to deter the police from violating people's Fourth Amendment rights. In the most straightforward form and application of the rule, the police obtain direct evidence in violation of the Fourth Amendment. For example, the police illegally search someone without the requisite justification and obtain evidence implicating that person in a crime. However, what happens if the police obtain secondary or **derivative evidence** from an unconstitutional search? In other words, what happens if the police obtain evidence *indirectly* from an unconstitutional search? Application of the exclusionary rule prohibits evidence directly resulting from an illegal search or seizure from being used to prove guilt in a criminal trial and to secondary, or derivative, evidence that is the fruit of the poisonous tree. The "**fruit of the poisonous tree**" is the colorful metaphor describing the relationship between a constitutional violation and the related discovery of evidence. If the evidence—the "fruit" is a direct product of the illegality—the "poisonous tree," then it is tainted by the constitutional violation and should not be used in a trial. Does it follow that evidence seized following a violation of a suspect's constitutional rights can never be admitted at a criminal trial? Must that evidence be suppressed at least if it can be shown that the police would not have discovered it, but for" the constitutional violation?

Consider the following example. Police illegally searched Bob's apartment, suspecting it is being used as part of a drug-smuggling operation. While no drugs were found, police did find a notebook that contained the notation, "Pick up drugs from Locker 22 at the City Bus Station on Monday. If the police use the information from the notebook to obtain a search warrant for Locker 22, should the drugs found in the locker be admissible at a subsequent trial? The logical and correct answer is no. Although the drugs were not seized during an illegal search, the information used to obtain the search warrant was derived from an unconstitutional search of Bob's apartment. The drugs would be the fruit of the poisonous tree.

While this rule makes logical sense, it can be complicated in application. Although seemingly straightforward, according to the Court, there are situations when it would be inappropriate to exclude evidence derived tangentially from an illegal search. The Court has adopted three doctrines to limit the situations under which evidence will be excluded from trial as being the fruit of the poisonous tree.

Attenuation (Purging the Taint)

The primary exception to the fruit of the poisonous tree doctrine involves attenuation or ***purging the taint***. Attenuation, which means a reduction in size or effect, exists when the causal link or connection between the illegal police conduct and the seized evidence is weak. Consider the example above. The connection between the search of Bob's apartment and the seizure of the drugs is quite close and very strong. However, what if, rather than finding drugs in the locker, the police found a package addressed to Jim? After seizing the package, the police go to Jim's home to ask him about drugs. Jim tells them he knows nothing about drugs, but tells them his neighbor, Beth, deals drugs frequently. Police go to Beth's home and find a large amount of heroin in her entryway. Police seize the heroin and use it to charge Beth. Should the heroin be precluded from Beth's trial as being the fruit of the poisonous tree? Courts would say no. There are too many intervening circumstances between Bob's apartment and Beth's home. These intervening events are examples of circumstances "purging the taint" of the illegal search. As the connection between the drugs and the search of Bob's apartment is **attenuated**, the taint would be purged, and the evidence would not be considered the fruit of the poisonous tree.

In *Brown v. Illinois,* 422 U.S. 590 (1975) and *Hudson v. Michigan,* 547 U.S. 586 (2006), the Court outlined several attenuation factors to determine if the purged taint exception applies: temporal proximity, intervening events, intervening acts of free will, and severity of the violation. In the following case, *Utah v. Strieff*, 579 U.S. 232 (2016), the Supreme Court applied the *Brown* factors to a *Terry* stop.

Utah v. Strieff

579 U.S. 232 (2016)

JUSTICE THOMAS delivered the opinion of the Court.

To enforce the Fourth Amendment's prohibition against "unreasonable searches and seizures," this Court has at times required courts to exclude evidence obtained by unconstitutional police conduct. But the Court has also held that, even when there is a Fourth Amendment violation, this exclusionary rule does not apply when the costs of exclusion outweigh its deterrent benefits. In some cases, for example, the link between the unconstitutional conduct and the discovery of the evidence is too attenuated to justify suppression. The question in this case is whether this attenuation doctrine applies when an officer makes an unconstitutional investigatory stop; learns during that stop that the suspect is subject to a valid arrest warrant; and proceeds to arrest the suspect and seize incriminating evidence during a search incident to that arrest. We hold that the evidence the officer seized as part of the search incident to arrest is admissible because the officer's discovery of the arrest warrant attenuated the connection between the unlawful stop and the evidence seized incident to arrest.

I

This case began with an anonymous tip. In December 2006, someone called the South Salt Lake City police's drug-tip line to report "narcotics activity" at a particular residence. App. 15. Narcotics detective Douglas Fackrell investigated the tip. Over the course of about a week, Officer Fackrell conducted intermittent surveillance of the home. He observed visitors who left a few minutes after arriving at the house.

These visits were sufficiently frequent to raise his suspicion that the occupants were dealing drugs.

One of those visitors was respondent Edward Strieff. Officer Fackrell observed Strieff exit the house and walk toward a nearby convenience store. In the store's parking lot, Officer Fackrell detained Strieff, identified himself, and asked Strieff what he was doing at the residence.

As part of the stop, Officer Fackrell requested Strieff's identification, and Strieff produced his Utah identification card. Officer Fackrell relayed Strieff's information to a police dispatcher, who reported that Strieff had an outstanding arrest warrant for a traffic violation. Officer Fackrell then arrested Strieff pursuant to that warrant. When Officer Fackrell searched Strieff incident to the arrest, he discovered a baggie of methamphetamine and drug paraphernalia.

The State charged Strieff with unlawful possession of methamphetamine and drug paraphernalia. Strieff moved to suppress the evidence, arguing that the evidence was inadmissible because it was derived from an unlawful investigatory stop. At the suppression hearing, the prosecutor conceded that Officer Fackrell lacked reasonable suspicion for the stop but argued that the evidence should not be suppressed because the existence of a valid arrest warrant attenuated the connection between the unlawful stop and the discovery of the contraband.

II

In the 20th century the exclusionary rule—the rule that often requires trial courts to exclude unlawfully seized evidence in a criminal trial—became the principal judicial remedy to deter Fourth Amendment violations.

Under the Court's precedents, the exclusionary rule encompasses both the "primary evidence obtained as a direct result of an illegal search or seizure" and, relevant here, "evidence later discovered and found to be derivative of an illegality, the so-called fruit of the poisonous tree. But the significant costs of this rule have led us to deem it applicable only where its deterrence benefits outweigh its substantial social costs. Suppression of evidence has always been our last resort, not our first impulse.

We have accordingly recognized several exceptions to the rule. Three of these exceptions involve the causal relationship between the unconstitutional act and the discovery of evidence. First, the independent source doctrine allows trial courts to admit evidence obtained in an unlawful search if officers independently acquired it from a separate, independent source. Second, the inevitable discovery doctrine allows for the admission of evidence that would have been discovered even without the unconstitutional source. Third, and at issue here, is the attenuation doctrine: Evidence is admissible when the connection between unconstitutional police conduct and the evidence is remote or has been interrupted by some intervening circumstance so that the interest protected by the constitutional guarantee that has been violated would not be served by suppression of the evidence obtained.

Turning to the application of the attenuation doctrine to this case, we first address a threshold question: whether this doctrine applies at all to a case like this, where the intervening circumstance that the State relies on is the discovery of a valid, pre-existing, and untainted arrest warrant. The three factors articulated in *Brown v. Illinois*, 422 U.S. 590 (1975), guide our analysis. First, we look to the "temporal proximity" between the unconstitutional conduct and the discovery of evidence to determine how closely the discovery of evidence followed the unconstitutional search. *Id.*, at 603. Second, we consider "the presence of intervening circumstances." *Id.*, at 603–604. Third, and "particularly" significant, we examine "the purpose and flagrancy of the official misconduct." *Id.*, at 604. In evaluating these factors, we assume without deciding (because the State conceded the point) that Officer Fackrell lacked reasonable suspicion to initially stop Strieff.

The first factor, temporal proximity between the initially unlawful stop and the search, favors suppressing the evidence. Our precedents have declined to find that this factor favors attenuation unless "substantial time" elapses between an unlawful act and when the evidence is obtained. Here, however, Officer Fackrell discovered drug contraband on Strieff's person only minutes after the illegal stop. As the Court explained in *Brown*, such a short time interval counsels in favor of suppression; there, we found that the confession should be suppressed, relying in part on the "less than two hours" that separated the unconstitutional arrest and the confession.

In contrast, the second factor, the presence of intervening circumstances, strongly favors the State. In this case, the warrant was valid, it predated Officer Fackrell's investigation, and it was entirely unconnected with the stop. And once Officer Fackrell discovered the warrant, he had an obligation to arrest Strieff. A warrant is a judicial mandate to an officer to conduct a search or make an arrest, and the officer has a sworn duty to carry out its provisions. Officer Fackrell's arrest of Strieff, thus, was a ministerial act that was independently compelled by the pre-existing warrant. And once Officer Fackrell was authorized to arrest Strieff, it was undisputedly lawful to search Strieff as an incident of his arrest to protect Officer Fackrell's safety.

Finally, the third factor, "the purpose and flagrancy of the official misconduct," *Brown*, supra, at 604, also strongly favors the State. The exclusionary rule exists to deter police misconduct. The third factor of the attenuation doctrine reflects that rationale by favoring exclusion only when the police misconduct is most in need of deterrence—that is, when it is purposeful or flagrant.

Officer Fackrell was at most negligent. In stopping Strieff, Officer Fackrell made two good-faith mistakes. First, he had not observed what time Strieff entered the suspected drug house, so he did not know how long Strieff had been there. Officer Fackrell thus lacked a sufficient basis to conclude that Strieff was a short-term visitor who may have been consummating a drug transaction. Second, because he lacked confirmation that

Strieff was a short-term visitor, Officer Fackrell should have asked Strieff whether he would speak with him, instead of demanding that Strieff do so. Officer Fackrell's stated purpose was to "find out what was going on [in] the house." Nothing prevented him from approaching Strieff simply to ask. But these errors in judgment hardly rise to a purposeful or flagrant violation of Strieff's Fourth Amendment rights.

While Officer Fackrell's decision to initiate the stop was mistaken, his conduct thereafter was lawful. The officer's decision to run the warrant check was a negligibly burdensome precaution for officer safety. And Officer Fackrell's actual search of Strieff was a lawful search incident to arrest. Moreover, there is no indication that this unlawful stop was part of any systemic or recurrent police misconduct. To the contrary, all the evidence suggests that the stop was an isolated instance of negligence that occurred in connection with a bona fide investigation of a suspected drug house. Officer Fackrell saw Strieff leave a suspected drug house. And his suspicion about the house was based on an anonymous tip and his personal observations.

Applying these factors, we hold that the evidence discovered on Strieff's person was admissible because the unlawful stop was sufficiently attenuated by the pre-existing arrest warrant. Although the illegal stop was close in time to Strieff's arrest, that consideration is outweighed by two factors supporting the State. The outstanding arrest warrant for Strieff's arrest is a critical intervening circumstance that is wholly independent of the illegal stop. The discovery of that warrant broke the causal chain between the unconstitutional stop and the discovery of evidence by compelling Officer Fackrell to arrest Strieff. And it is especially significant that there is no evidence that Officer Fackrell's illegal stop reflected flagrantly unlawful police misconduct.

We hold that the evidence Officer Fackrell seized as part of his search incident to arrest is admissible because his discovery of the arrest warrant attenuated the connection between the unlawful stop and the evidence seized from Strieff incident to arrest. The judgment of the Utah Supreme Court, accordingly, is reversed.

FURTHER CASE LAW, REFLECTIONS, AND QUESTIONS

1. What implications does this have for incentivizing police to conduct suspicionless stops on known criminals? In dissent, Justice Sotomayor noted that the majority opinion took away any deterrent value provided by the exclusionary rule for improper stops such as those that occurred in *Strieff*. Is she correct?

2. What do you think the impact of *Utah v. Strieff* has had on police practices and procedures? How has this decision influenced law enforcement strategies concerning stops, searches, and the admissibility of evidence in subsequent legal proceedings?

The Independent Source and Inevitable Discovery Doctrines

So far, we have seen evidence that is discovered during an illegal search, as well as evidence that is the fruit of an illegal search, may not be used by the prosecution to prove a defendant's guilt at trial. Two other related exceptions to the fruit of the poisonous tree involve the discovery of evidence connected to an illegal search or interrogation if the prosecution can show it would have been discovered absent the unlawful police conduct. The **inevitable discovery doctrine** provides that evidence seized as part of an unconstitutional search or interrogation is admissible at trial if the government can prove that the evidence would have been inevitably discovered by lawful means regardless of the illegal police actions. The **independent source doctrine** provides that evidence seized as part of an unconstitutional search or interrogation is admissible at trial if the government can prove it would have been discovered by lawful means that are entirely independent of the illegal police activity. The following case, *Nix v. Williams*, discusses both doctrines and illustrates the difficulty in distinguishing one from another.

Nix v. Williams

467 U.S. 431 (1984)

CHIEF JUSTICE BURGER delivered the opinion of the Court.

In 1969, the respondent Williams was convicted of the first-degree murder of 10-year-old Pamela Powers. That conviction was reversed because a police detective had gained an admission from Williams concerning the whereabouts of the victim's body in violation of Williams' right to the assistance of counsel, guaranteed under the Sixth and Fourteenth Amendments. *Brewer v. Williams*, 430 U.S. 387 (1977). Williams was retried for the murder in 1977.

At Williams' second trial in 1977 in the Iowa court, the prosecution did not offer Williams' statements into evidence, nor did it seek to show that Williams had directed the police to the child's body. However, evidence of the condition of her body as it was found, articles and photographs of her clothing, and the results of postmortem medical and chemical tests on the body were admitted. The trial court concluded that the state had proved by a preponderance of the evidence that, if the search had not been suspended and Williams had not led the police to the victim, her body would have been discovered "within a short time" in essentially the same condition as it was actually found.

The challenged evidence was admitted and the jury again found Williams guilty of first-degree murder; he was sentenced to life in prison. On appeal, the Supreme Court of Iowa again affirmed. That court held that there was in fact a "hypothetical independent source" exception to the Exclusionary Rule.

In 1980 Williams renewed his attack on the state-court conviction by seeking a writ of habeas corpus in the United States District Court for the Southern District of Iowa. The District Court conducted its own independent review of the evidence and concluded, as had the state courts, that the body would inevitably have been found by the searchers in essentially the same condition it was in when Williams led police to its discovery. The District Court denied Williams' petition. The Court of Appeals for the Eighth Circuit reversed.

II

The Iowa Supreme Court correctly stated that the "vast majority" of all courts, both state and federal, recognize an inevitable discovery exception to the Exclusionary Rule. We are now urged to adopt and apply the so-called ultimate or inevitable discovery exception to the Exclusionary Rule.

Williams contends that evidence of the body's location and condition is "fruit of the poisonous tree," i.e., the "fruit" or product of Detective Leaming's [improper interrogation.]. He contends that admitting the challenged evidence violated the Sixth Amendment whether it would have been inevitably discovered or not. Williams also contends that, if the inevitable discovery doctrine is constitutionally permissible, it must include a threshold showing of police good faith.

The core rationale consistently advanced by this Court for extending the Exclusionary Rule to evidence that is the fruit of unlawful police conduct has been that this admittedly drastic and socially costly course is needed to deter police from violations of constitutional and statutory protections. This Court has accepted the argument that the way to ensure such protections is to exclude evidence seized as a result of such violations notwithstanding the high social cost of letting persons obviously guilty go unpunished for their crimes. On this rationale, the prosecution is not to be put in a better position than it would have been in if no illegality had transpired.

By contrast, the derivative evidence analysis ensures that the prosecution is not put in a worse position simply because of some earlier police error or misconduct. The independent source doctrine allows admission of evidence that has been discovered by means wholly independent of any constitutional violation. That doctrine, although closely related to the inevitable discovery doctrine, does not apply here; Williams' statements to Leaming indeed led police to the child's body, but that is not the whole story. The independent source doctrine teaches us that the interest of society in deterring unlawful police conduct and the public interest in having juries receive all probative evidence of a crime are properly balanced by putting the police in the same, not a worse, position than they would have been in if no police error or misconduct had occurred.

When the challenged evidence has an independent source, exclusion of such evidence would put the police in a worse position than they would have been in absent any error or violation. There is a functional similarity between these two doctrines in that exclusion of evidence that would inevitably have been discovered would also put the government in a worse position, because the police would have obtained that evidence if no misconduct had taken place. Thus, while the independent source exception would not justify admission of evidence in this case, its rationale is wholly consistent with and justifies our adoption of the ultimate or inevitable discovery exception to the Exclusionary Rule.

It is clear that the cases implementing the Exclusionary Rule "begin with the premise that the challenged evidence is *in some sense* the product of illegal governmental activity." *United States v. Crews*, 445 US 463 (1980) (emphasis added). Of course, this does not end the inquiry. If the prosecution can establish by a preponderance of the evidence that the information ultimately or inevitably would have been discovered by lawful means—here the volunteers' search—then the deterrence rationale has so little basis that the evidence should be received. Anything less would reject logic, experience, and common sense.

The requirement that the prosecution must prove the absence of bad faith, imposed here by the Court of Appeals, would place courts in the position of withholding from juries relevant and undoubted truth that would have been available to police absent any unlawful police activity. Of course, that view would put the police in a worse position than they would have been in if no unlawful conduct had transpired. And, of equal importance, it wholly fails to take into account the enormous societal cost of excluding truth in the search for truth in the administration of justice. Nothing in this Court's prior holdings supports any such formalistic, pointless, and punitive approach.

Significant disincentives to obtaining evidence illegally—including the possibility of departmental discipline and civil liability—also lessen the likelihood that the ultimate or inevitable discovery exception will promote police misconduct. In these circumstances, the societal costs of the Exclusionary Rule far outweigh any possible benefits to deterrence that a good-faith requirement might produce.

C

[T]hree courts independently reviewing the evidence have found that the body of the child inevitably would have been found by the searchers. Williams challenges these findings, asserting that the record contains only the "post hoc rationalization" that the search efforts would have proceeded two and one-half miles into Polk County where Williams had led police to the body.

When that challenge was made at the suppression hearing preceding Williams' second trial, the prosecution offered the testimony of Agent Ruxlow of the Iowa Bureau of Criminal Investigation. Ruxlow had organized and directed some 200 volunteers who were searching for the child's body.

The searchers were instructed "to check all the roads, the ditches, any culverts. If they came upon any abandoned farm buildings, they were instructed to go onto the property and search those abandoned farm buildings or any other places where a small child could be secreted." Ruxlow testified that he marked off highway maps of Poweshiek and Jasper Counties in grid fashion, divided the volunteers into teams of four to six persons, and assigned each team to search specific grid areas. Ruxlow also testified that, if the search had not been suspended because of Williams' promised cooperation, it would have continued into Polk County, using the same grid system. Although he had previously marked off into grids only the highway maps of Poweshiek and Jasper Counties, Ruxlow had obtained a map of Polk County, which he said he would have marked off in the same manner had it been necessary for the search to continue.

The search had commenced at approximately 10 a.m. and moved westward through Poweshiek County into Jasper County. At approximately 3 p.m., after Williams had volunteered to cooperate with the police, Officer Leaming, who was in the police car with Williams, sent word to Ruxlow and the other Special Agent directing the search to meet him at the Grinnell truck stop and the search was suspended at that time. Ruxlow also stated that he was "under the impression that there was a possibility" that Williams would lead them to the child's body at that time. The search was not resumed once it was learned that Williams had led the police to the body, which was found two and one-half miles from where the search had stopped in what would have been the easternmost grid to be searched in Polk County. There was testimony that it would have taken an additional three to five hours to discover the body if the search had continued; the body was found near a culvert, one of the kinds of places the teams had been specifically directed to search.

On this record it is clear that the search parties were approaching the actual location of the body and we are satisfied, along with three courts earlier, that the volunteer search teams would have resumed the search had Williams not earlier led the police to the body and the body inevitably would have been found.

The judgment of the Court of Appeals is reversed, and the case is remanded for further proceedings consistent with this opinion.

JUSTICE BRENNAN, with whom JUSTICE MARSHALL joins, dissenting.

[T]he Court concludes that unconstitutionally obtained evidence may be admitted at trial if it inevitably would have been discovered in the same condition by an independent line of investigation that was already being pursued when the constitutional violation occurred. I agree that in these circumstances the "inevitable discovery" exception to the exclusionary rule is consistent with the requirements of the Constitution.

In its zealous efforts to emasculate the exclusionary rule, however, the Court loses sight of the crucial difference between the "inevitable discovery" doctrine and the "independent source" exception from which it is derived. When properly applied, the "independent source" exception allows the prosecution to use evidence only if it was, in fact, obtained by fully lawful means. It therefore does no violence to the constitutional protections that the exclusionary rule is meant to enforce. The "inevitable discovery" exception is likewise compatible with the Constitution, though it differs in one key respect from its next of kin: specifically, the evidence sought to be introduced at trial has not actually been obtained from an independent source, but rather would have been discovered as a matter of course if independent investigations were allowed to proceed.

In my view, this distinction should require that the government satisfy a heightened burden of proof before it is allowed to use such evidence. The inevitable discovery exception necessarily implicates a hypothetical finding that differs in kind from the factual finding that precedes application of the independent source rule. To ensure that this hypothetical finding is narrowly confined to circumstances that are functionally equivalent to an independent source, and to fully protect the fundamental rights served by the exclusionary rule, I would require clear and convincing evidence before concluding that the government had met its burden of proof on this issue. Increasing the burden of proof serves to impress the fact-finder with the importance of the decision and thereby reduces the risk that illegally obtained evidence will be admitted.

Because the lower courts did not impose such a requirement, I would remand this case for application of this heightened burden of proof by the lower courts in the first instance.

FURTHER CASE LAW, REFLECTIONS, AND QUESTIONS

1. What if the search party in Nix v. Williams had not been 200-strong and had not approached to within two and one-half miles of where the body was discovered when the search was called off? What if only a dozen people had been looking for the body and had been more than 10 miles from it, but headed in its general direction when the search was terminated? What is the significance of the disagreement between the majority and dissenting opinions regarding the burden of proof required to justify the conclusion that the body inevitably would have been discovered?

2. The Court of Appeals had ruled that the state must prove that the original constitutional violation was not committed in bad faith to benefit from the inevitable-discovery rule. How does such a requirement relate to the purposes of the exclusionary rule? Why does Chief Justice Burger's opinion for the Supreme Court reject this requirement?

3. What if no search party had actively been searching for the body, but testimony had been offered that a search party would have been formed the next day and that the search would have proceeded county by county pursuant to the gridded-map system described in the majority opinion? Under those circumstances, would the application of the inevitable-discovery rule be justified?

Box 3.3 You Be the Judge

Later that same evening, the agents arrested Segura in the lobby of the apartment building, took him to the apartment, knocked on the door, and, when Colon opened it, unconstitutionally entered the apartment without requesting or receiving permission. The agents observed, in plain view, various pieces of drug paraphernalia. Colon was then arrested, and he and Segura were taken into custody. Two agents remained in the apartment awaiting the warrant, but because of "administrative delay," the search warrant was not issued until some 19 hours after the initial entry into the apartment.

Before trial, both men filed a motion to suppress all evidence seized based on the illegal entry into the apartment. Assuming that the initial entry into the apartment was unconstitutional, should the evidence seized pursuant to the subsequent search warrant be suppressed? Do either the independent source rule or the inevitable discovery rule apply? Why/why not? What information from the chapter can you use to support your answer?

See *Segura v. United States*, 468 U.S. 796 (1984).

Box 3.4 You Be the Judge

On December 6, 2002, Amtrak Police Officer Romano searched Amtrak's reservation computer to determine whether any of the passengers scheduled to depart Chicago's Union Station on that date had purchased their tickets under suspicious circumstances. He discovered that Mr. Jim's ticket purchase fit a drug-courier profile. Jim arrived at the platform twenty minutes before the train's scheduled departure time. Upon learning of Jim's arrival, Officer Romano and a second officer approached Jim's compartment, identified themselves, and showed Mr. Jim their badges. At the officers' request, Jim gave them his identification and ticket and told them he was traveling to Seattle to visit a girlfriend. The officers asked Jim whether he was carrying any drugs, weapons, or large sums of money. They noticed that Jim was sweating when he replied that he was not carrying any of those items. When the officers inquired about the backpack and briefcase in his compartment, Jim stated that the bags were his, that he had packed them himself, and that no one had given him anything to carry. Jim allowed the officers to search the backpack; they found nothing incriminating. Jim denied the officers' request to search the briefcase. Officer Romano then took the briefcase from the compartment and asked Jim if he had a key to the briefcase. Mr. Jim said he did not. He explained that he had used a knife to open it. He then told Officer Romano that the briefcase contained $50,000.

The officers then asked Romano to accompany them to the Amtrak police office, and Jim complied. Officer Romano used a pocketknife to open the briefcase and discovered that it contained bundles of money totaling over $100,000. He then quickly shut the briefcase. A police dispatcher was called, and it was requested that a police dog (the "canine unit") be brought to the office to conduct a sniff search of the briefcase. Later, the canine unit arrived at the office and alerted to the briefcase, indicating that it contained drugs or money contaminated with drugs. The currency was removed from the briefcase, sealed into evidence bags, and sent to a bank to be counted.

Assume that opening the briefcase with a pocketknife violated Jim's rights. Can the money found in the briefcase still be admissible in court under an independent source or inevitable discovery rationale? See *United States v. Marrocco*, 578 F.3d 627 (7th Cir. 2009).

Conclusion

For a violation of the Fourth Amendment to be found, two things must be considered and found to be present. First, there must have been a search. Second, the search must be found to be unreasonable. In this chapter, we considered the necessary factors that make a government exploration a search.

For a search to have taken place for Fourth Amendment purposes, the person against whom the search is directed must have a reasonable expectation of privacy over the area and items being searched. This requires the presence of an actual expectation of privacy in the mind of the subject of the search, as well as an expectation of privacy that society deems reasonable. Absent both parts of a reasonable expectation of privacy, a search for Fourth Amendment purposes has not occurred.

A person loses their expectation of privacy when they reveal an area or item to the general public. As we have seen, when an item is abandoned by a person, any privacy right the person had in the item is abandoned. Similarly, when a conversation is easily overheard in a public setting, the words spoken are no longer within a zone of privacy. If a building, field, yard, lot, or other item is in an open field, it no longer involves a reasonable expectation of privacy.

Even an object inside a home or within a curtilage that is observable from a place where law enforcement officers have a right to be is no longer protected against a "search." This includes items that have been exposed to the public so that they can be observed via overflights by drones or aircraft.

Once it is determined that a search by the government or law enforcement has taken place, and it is determined that a crime has occurred, the question becomes how the evidence seized or observed in the search can be used in a subsequent prosecution. The Fourth Amendment is silent on an appropriate remedy for a violation. The Supreme Court has created a judicial rule that unconstitutionally obtained evidence must be excluded from the trial of the person who has standing to object to its seizure. Over time, the Supreme Court has adopted several "exceptions" to this rule of exclusion. These include exceptions based on the good faith of law enforcement officers in committing the illegal search, the nature of the judicial proceeding in which the evidence is used, and the requirement that there be a direct linkage between the unlawful act and the discovery of the evidence, and the possibility that the evidence would have been inevitably discovered without the search or retrieved based on information from an independent source. Should any of these exceptions be found to be present, the evidence seized in violation of the Fourth Amendment is not subject to the exclusionary rule.

Understanding what constitutes a search and what sanctions could be imposed if an illegal search is performed is just the first step in understanding criminal procedure related to the Fourth Amendment. In fact, this chapter is the first of five chapters in this book dealing with the topic. The next four chapters deal with the second broad question regarding the constitutionality of a search: Was the search reasonable?

KEY TERMS

abandoned property
attenuated
collateral proceedings
curtilage
derivative evidence
exclusionary rule
expectation of privacy
fruit of the poisonous tree
good-faith exception
impeachment exception
independent source
inevitable discovery
objective expectation of privacy
open fields doctrine
plurality opinion
expectation of privacy
search
standing
subjective expectation of privacy
trespass doctrine

REVIEW QUESTIONS

1. What is a reasonable expectation of privacy? Is it important to distinguish between an objective and a subjective expectation of privacy? Why or why not?
2. What element made the difference in the result in the Katz and Greenwood cases? In other words, what did Katz have that Greenwood did not? What sort of precedent was formed by the ruling in Greenwood?
3. What items are required to be present for the good faith exception to the search warrant requirement to apply?
4. How has the Supreme Court dealt with search and seizure law given the advances in technology?
5. What is the difference between curtilage and an open field? Does the Constitution protect both areas? Why or why not?
6. What is the primary purpose of the exclusionary rule? Does the rule achieve this goal?
7. What type of evidence can be called "fruit of the poisonous tree?" Is this type of evidence ever admitted in court?
8. In what ways is the fruit of the poisonous tree doctrine limited?
9. What is the inevitable discovery doctrine? Does it violate the Fourth Amendment? Why or why not?
10. How do the independent source and inevitable discovery doctrines differ?

APPLYING THE LAW

Below are five hypothetical fact scenarios. To practice your understanding of the law that you learned in this chapter and your ability to apply it, answer each question posed by applying that law to the hypothetical scenarios. Your answers should be supported by relevant case law and judicially created rules and tests.

1. Todd, a gang leader, was staying at the Davenport Hotel. The FBI was tipped off that he would be meeting with one of his fellow gang members and that they would be talking about the disappearance of a rival gang leader. To corroborate the tip, the FBI arranged with the hotel manager to let them use the room next to Todd. Placing a listening device that they purchased at Walmart on the common wall, the agents overheard Todd make incriminating statements indicating his involvement in the murder of the missing gang leader. Relying on this information, the FBI arrested Todd. Todd has moved to suppress the evidence concerning the contents of his conversation.

   How should the court decide Todd's motion?

2. Tyler has a marijuana growing operation in his backyard. A 10-foot wooden fence surrounds his yard. His main grow area is just behind his back deck, where he frequently drinks, smokes, barbeques, and hangs out with friends. Unfortunately for Tyler, a neighbor has called and tipped off the police about his growing operation. While the police do not have enough probable cause to get a warrant to seize the plants, they investigate the alleged growing operation.

   In the situations below, determine if a search has occurred according to the Fourth Amendment. If a search according to the Fourth Amendment has occurred, was it legal?

   a. An officer climbs a nearby telephone pole on the street with preinstalled pole steps used by maintenance workers, looks into Tyler's backyard, and sees the plants.

   b. The police notice a large gap under the fence, where it looks like a dog has dug a hole for access. They crawl under the fence, enter Tyler's backyard, and see the plants.

   c. The police contact the neighbor who called about the plants. The neighbor lives a few houses away and says you can see the marijuana plants from her third-story deck. She invites the officers in, and they go out onto her balcony and use binoculars to see the plants in Tyler's backyard.

   d. One officer pulls a drone out of his trunk, flies it over Tyler's backyard, and sees the marijuana plants.

   e. An officer with an old pair of AirPods throws both AirPods over the fence and near Tyler's back porch. He sits in his patrol car across the street and uses the function on his iPhone to listen to Tyler's conversations on his back porch.

3. Phil worked as a maintenance person for an apartment building. One day, while fixing Dawn's dishwasher, he snooped through her apartment. In a dresser drawer, he found a hand grenade. Terrified, he called his sister Patty, who worked for the FBI. Patty told him to carefully pick up the grenade and deliver it to her office. Dawn was subsequently charged with illegal possession of a hand grenade.

   May Dawn invoke the Fourth Amendment to seek suppression of the grenade at trial?

4. Last Friday, the residents at College Hill apartments had a huge party. Sadly, Lisa overdosed at the party and died. All the partygoers and apartment residents denied knowledge of the circumstances surrounding the organization of the party or Lisa's death. As part of their investigation, police searched (without a warrant) through a community dumpster in an alley behind the apartment building. Inside the dumpster, they found a hypodermic needle and a stack of party invitations. They checked these items for fingerprints and found Nick's fingerprints on the needle and Paul's prints on most of the invitations. While Paul is a resident of

the apartment building, Nick is not. The police arrest Nick and Paul for their role in the tragic events.

Their attorneys each file a motion to suppress the evidence against their clients under the Fourth Amendment. Were Paul's and/or Nick's rights violated? What evidence, if any, should be suppressed?

5. Police Officer Sarah responds to a noise complaint at an apartment complex. Upon arriving at the scene, she hears loud music and arguing from Apartment 2B. Without a warrant or consent, Sarah illegally enters the apartment to investigate and discovers a small quantity of illegal drugs on the living room table. She then arrests the occupant, John, for drug possession.

   After John's arrest, Sarah learns from a neighbor that John had been bragging about a large drug stash hidden in his apartment. Based on this information, Officer Sarah applies for and obtains a search warrant for John's apartment. During the search, she discovers a substantial amount of drugs hidden in a closet. John is subsequently charged with drug possession and intent to distribute.

   John's defense attorney files a motion to suppress the evidence of the drugs found in the closet, arguing that Officer Sarah's initial entry into the apartment was unlawful because it violated John's Fourth Amendment rights. In response, the prosecution contends that the evidence should be admissible under the inevitable discovery doctrine, asserting that Officer Sarah would have eventually obtained a warrant based on the neighbor's tip, leading to the discovery of the drugs in the closet.

   How should the court rule?

ORAL ARGUMENTS

California v. Greenwood, http://www.oyez.org/cases/1980-1989/1987/1987_86_684/argument

Herring v. United States, http://www.oyez.org/cases/2000-2009/2008/2008_07_513/argument

Katz v. United States, http://www.oyez.org/cases/1960-1969/1967/1967_35/argument

Kyllo v. United States, http://www.oyez.org/cases/2000-2009/2000/2000_99_8508/argument

Mapp v. Ohio, http://www.oyez.org/cases/1960-1969/1960/1960_236/argument

Nix v. Williams, http://www.oyez.org/cases/1980-1989/1983/1983_82_1651/argument

Oliver v. United States, http://www.oyez.org/cases/1980-1989/1983/1983_82_15/argument

Utah v. Strieff, https://www.oyez.org/cases/2015/14-1373

CHAPTER 4

Search and Arrest Warrants

LEARNING OBJECTIVES

After reading this chapter, students should be able to:

- Critically analyze the Fourth Amendment and issues linked to it.
- Describe the legal requirements to obtain a search or arrest warrant
- Know how probable cause for a warrant is determined and what it means to particularly describe the place to be searched or the person or things to be seized
- Understand the two prongs of the Aguilar-Spinelli test and how it evolved into the Gates test
- Describe the limited circumstances when a facially sufficient affidavit used to obtain a warrant can be challenged after the fact
- Comprehend the rule and nuances associated with executing arrest and search warrants
- Describe the exceptions to the "knock and announce" rule and the level of justification needed for one of the exceptions to apply

Introduction

The ability of the police to conduct searches, seizures, and arrests is limited by the Fourth Amendment, which states:

> The right of the people to be secure in their persons, houses, papers, and effects, against unreasonable searches and seizures, shall not be violated,

> and no Warrants shall issue, but upon probable cause, supported by Oath or affirmation, and particularly describing the place to be searched, and the persons or things to be seized.

The first clause of the Amendment is known as the reasonableness clause. It requires that searches, seizures, and arrests be reasonable. A constitutionally valid search may be conducted by police with or without a warrant, so long as police follow the dictates laid out by the Supreme Court to ensure its reasonableness. We examine the mandates involved with warrantless searches in Chapter 6. This chapter considers the substantive and procedural requirements for obtaining and executing a search or arrest warrant.

The first portion of this chapter examines what is necessary for police to obtain a warrant. In the second section, we consider the constitutional limitations imposed by the Supreme Court concerning how a warrant can be executed. Once again, as you read the materials, keep in mind the balance the Constitution and the Supreme Court have tried to achieve in implementing the Fourth Amendment and search and seizure law.

Required Elements of a Search Warrant

A person's home is their castle. Requiring a search warrant before the government can enter a person's home is paramount to individual liberty. In a constitutional democratic republic, such as the United States, no one is okay with a police officer being able to enter a home based on a hunch or just because they want to. Furthermore, specific criteria for a valid search warrant authorizing a search must be laid out and enforced. The author of the Fourth Amendment, James Madison, explicitly included some requirements for a **search or arrest warrant** to be considered valid.

1. A neutral and detached magistrate must issue it.
2. A warrant application must be made under oath or affirmation.
3. It must be based on probable cause; and
4. It must describe the place to be searched and the items to be searched for with particularity.

Neutral Detached Magistrate

Shadwick v. City of Tampa

407 U.S. 345 (1972)

MR. JUSTICE POWELL delivered the opinion of the Court.

The charter of Tampa, Florida, authorizes the issuance of certain arrest warrants by clerks of the Tampa Municipal Court. The sole question in this case is whether these clerks qualify as neutral and detached magistrates for purposes of the Fourth Amendment. We hold that they do.

Appellant was arrested for impaired driving on a warrant issued by a clerk of the municipal court. He moved the court to quash the warrant on the ground that it was issued by a nonjudicial officer in violation of the Fourth and Fourteenth Amendments. When the motion was denied, he initiated proceedings in the Florida courts by means of that State's writ of common-law certiorari. The state proceedings culminated in the holding of the Florida Supreme Court that the clerk and deputy clerks of the municipal court of the City of Tampa are neutral and detached 'magistrates' ... for the purpose of issuing arrest warrants within the requirements of the United States Constitution. ...

I

A clerk of the municipal court is appointed by the city clerk from a classified list of civil servants and assigned to work in the municipal court. The statute does not specify the qualifications necessary for this job, but no law degree or special legal training is required. The clerk's duties are to receive traffic fines, prepare the court's dockets and records, fill out commitment papers and perform other routine clerical tasks. Apparently he may issue subpoenas. He may not, however, sit as a judge, and he may not issue a search warrant or even a felony or misdemeanor arrest warrant for violations of state laws. The only warrants he may issue are for the arrest of those charged with having breached municipal ordinances of the city of Tampa.

Appellant, contending that the Fourth Amendment requires that warrants be issued by "judicial officers," argues that even this limited warrant authority is constitutionally invalid. He reasons that warrant applications of whatever nature cannot be assured the discerning, independent review compelled by the Fourth Amendment when the review is performed by less than a judicial officer. It is less than clear, however, as to who would qualify as a "judicial officer" under appellant's theory. There is some suggestion in appellant's brief that a judicial officer must be a lawyer or the municipal court judge himself. A more complete portrayal of appellant's position would be that the Tampa clerks are disqualified as judicial officers not merely because they are not lawyers or judges, but because they lack the institutional independence associated with the judiciary in that they are members of the civil service, appointed by the city clerk, "an executive official," and enjoy no statutorily specified tenure in office.

II

Past decisions of the Court have mentioned review by a "judicial officer" prior to issuance of a warrant. In some cases the term "judicial officer" appears to have been used interchangeably with that of "magistrate." In others, it was intended simply to underscore the now accepted fact that someone independent of the police and prosecution must determine probable cause. The very term "judicial officer" implies, of course, some connection with the judicial branch. But it has never been held that only a lawyer or judge could grant a warrant, regardless of the court system or the type of warrant involved.

The Court frequently has employed the term "magistrate" to denote those who may issue warrants. *Coolidge* v. *New Hampshire*, 403 U.S. 443, 449-453 (1971). Historically, a magistrate has been defined broadly as a public civil officer, possessing such power, legislative, executive, or judicial, as the government appointing him may ordain, or, in a narrower sense "an inferior judicial officer, such as a justice of the peace. More recent definitions have not much changed.

An examination of the Court's decisions reveals that the terms "magistrate" and "judicial officer" have been used interchangeably. Little attempt was made to define either term, to distinguish the one from the other, or to advance one as the definitive Fourth Amendment requirement. We find no commandment in either term, however, that all warrant authority must reside exclusively in a lawyer or judge. Such a requirement would have been incongruous when even within the federal system warrants were until recently widely issued by nonlawyers.

To attempt to extract further significance from the above terminology would be both unnecessary and futile. The substance of the Constitution's warrant requirements does not turn on the labeling of the issuing party. The warrant traditionally has represented an independent assurance that a search and arrest will not proceed without probable cause to believe that a crime has been committed and that the person or place named in the warrant is involved in the crime. Thus, an issuing magistrate must meet two tests. He must be neutral and detached, and he must be capable of determining whether probable cause exists for the requested arrest or search. This Court long has insisted that inferences of probable cause be drawn by a neutral and detached magistrate instead of being judged by the officer engaged in the often competitive enterprise of ferreting out crime. In *Coolidge* v. *New Hampshire*, *supra*, the Court last Term voided a search warrant issued by the state attorney general "who was actively in charge of the investigation and later was to be chief prosecutor at the trial." *Id.*, at 450. If, on the other hand, detachment and capacity do conjoin, the magistrate has satisfied the Fourth Amendment's purpose.

III

The requisite detachment is present in the case at hand. Whatever else neutrality and detachment might entail, it is clear that they require severance and disengagement from activities of law enforcement. There has been no showing whatever here of partiality, or affiliation of these clerks with prosecutors or police. The record shows no connection with any law enforcement activity or authority which would distort the independent judgment the Fourth Amendment requires. Appellant himself expressly refused to allege anything to that effect. The municipal court clerk is assigned not to the police or prosecutor but to the municipal court judge for whom he does much of his work. In this sense, he may well be termed a "judicial officer." While a statutorily specified term of office and appointment by someone other than "an executive authority" might be desirable, the absence of such features is hardly disqualifying. Judges themselves take office under differing circumstances. Some are appointed, but many are elected by legislative bodies or by the people. Many enjoy but limited terms and are subject to re-appointment or re-election. Most depend for their salary level upon the legislative branch. We will not elevate requirements for the independence of a municipal clerk to a level higher than that prevailing with respect to many judges. The clerk's neutrality has not been impeached: he is removed from prosecutor or police and works within the judicial branch subject to the supervision of the municipal court judge.

Appellant likewise has failed to demonstrate that these clerks lack capacity to determine probable cause. The clerk's authority extends only to the issuance of arrest warrants for breach of municipal ordinances. We presume from the nature of the clerk's position that he would be able to deduce from the facts on an affidavit before him whether there was probable cause to believe a citizen guilty of impaired driving, breach of peace, drunkenness, trespass, or the multiple other common offenses covered by a municipal code. There has been no showing that this is too difficult a task for a clerk to accomplish. Our legal system has long entrusted nonlawyers to evaluate more complex and significant factual data than that in the case at hand. Grand juries daily determine probable cause prior to rendering indictments, and trial juries assess whether guilt is proved beyond a reasonable doubt. The significance and responsibility of these lay judgments betray any belief that the Tampa clerks could not determine probable cause for arrest. We decide today only that clerks of the municipal court may constitutionally issue the warrants in question. . . . Nor need we determine whether a State may lodge warrant authority in someone entirely outside the sphere of the judicial branch. Many persons may not qualify as the kind of "public civil officers" we have come to associate with the term "magistrate." Had the Tampa clerk been entirely divorced from a judicial position, this case would have presented different considerations. Here, however, the clerk is an employee of the judicial branch of the city of Tampa, disassociated from the role of law enforcement. On the record in this case, the independent status of the clerk cannot be questioned.

What we do reject today is any *per se* invalidation of a state or local warrant system on the ground that the issuing magistrate is not a lawyer or judge. Communities may have sound reasons for delegating the responsibility of issuing warrants to competent personnel other than judges or lawyers.

We affirm the judgment of the Florida Supreme Court.

Affirmed.

FURTHER CASE LAW, REFLECTIONS, AND QUESTIONS

1. What are the potential implications of allowing non-judges to issue warrants?
2. The Court's decision in Shadwick emphasized the need for "neutral and detached" magistrates. What might be some factors that could compromise a magistrate's neutrality and detachment?
3. The Court occasionally has been asked to decide whether the person issuing a search warrant qualifies as a "neutral and detached" judicial officer. For example, the justices have concluded that search warrants approved under the following circumstances failed the requirement for a "neutral and detached" judicial officer:

    - A search warrant signed by the state attorney general, who later served as the chief prosecutor in the defendant's trial. *Coolidge v. New Hampshire*, 403 U.S. 443 (1971).
    - A search warrant approved by an unsalaried justice of the peace, who was paid a $5 fee on issuing a warrant but received nothing if he denied a warrant application. *Connally v. Georgia*, 429 U.S. 245 (1977).
    - A search warrant issued by a magistrate authorizing the seizure of "obscene" items when the magistrate accompanied the police to the bookstore in question and actively assisted in the search for incriminating materials. Under these circumstances, the magistrate had failed to maintain detached neutrality: He was not acting as a judicial officer but as an adjunct law-enforcement officer. *Lo-Ji Sales, Inc. v. New York*, 442 U.S. 319 (1979).

It is important that a magistrate reviewing an **affidavit** and signing off on a warrant not be a "rubber stamp" for the police. Signing a search warrant has critical implications. The requirement to have a neutral and detached magistrate acts as an essential check on government power and protection for the citizenry. One study found that the average time to review a warrant application was two minutes and forty-eight seconds (Duizend, et al., 1986). The same study also found that less than 10% of applications were rejected.

Box 4.1 You Be the Judge

Rich is charged with possession of stolen property. The property was seized pursuant to a search warrant for his parents' house. The warrant, which contained ample probable cause, was signed by county court magistrate Bill. In addition to being a magistrate, Bill works part-time as a deputy sheriff. Bill had nothing to do with the case against Rich in his work as a deputy. Nonetheless, Rich filed a motion in court to have the evidence seized pursuant to the warrant excluded from trial as it violated the Fourth Amendment.

As a judge, would you grant Rich's motion? Why or why not?

See *People v. Payne*, 424 Mich. 475, 381 N.W.2d 391 (1985).

Oath or Affirmation

The Fourth Amendment requires that a search warrant be issued based on the facts submitted in a search warrant application made under oath or affirmation. The oath or affirmation requirement is typically met by specifying the facts that give rise to probable cause in a police officer's affidavit attached to the warrant application. Due to the need to obtain a warrant promptly, warrant applications may also be submitted in person or telephonically so long as they are made under oath or affirmation. Regardless of how they are submitted, the facts stated in the warrant application will be considered by the judicial officer authorized to issue warrants.

This leaves open the question when, if ever, should the veracity and accuracy of the affidavit be explored.

Franks v. Delaware

438 U.S. 154 (1978)

MR. JUSTICE BLACKMUN delivered the opinion of the Court.

This case presents an important and longstanding issue of Fourth Amendment law. Does a defendant in a criminal proceeding ever have the right, under the Fourth and Fourteenth Amendments, subsequent to the *ex parte* issuance of a search warrant, to challenge the truthfulness of factual statements made in an affidavit supporting the warrant?

I

The controversy over the veracity of the search warrant affidavit in this case arose in connection with petitioner Jerome Franks' state conviction for rape, kidnaping, and burglary. On Friday, March 5, 1976, Mrs. Cynthia Bailey told police in Dover, Del., that she had been confronted in her home earlier that morning by a man with a knife, and that he had sexually assaulted her. She described her assailant's age, race, height, build, and facial hair, and gave a detailed description of his clothing as consisting of a white thermal undershirt, black pants with a silver or gold buckle, a brown leather three-quarter-length coat, and a dark knit cap that he wore pulled down around his eyes.

That same day, petitioner Franks coincidentally was taken into custody for an assault involving a 15-year-old girl, Brenda B., six days earlier. After his formal arrest, and while awaiting a bail hearing in Family Court, petitioner allegedly stated to Robert McClements, the youth officer accompanying him, that he was surprised the bail hearing was "about Brenda B. I know her. I thought you said Bailey. I don't know her." At the time of this statement, the police allegedly had not yet recited to petitioner his rights under *Miranda v. Arizona.*

On the following Monday, March 8, Officer McClements happened to mention the courthouse incident to a detective, Ronald R. Brooks, who was working on the Bailey case. On March 9, Detective Brooks and Detective Larry D. Gray submitted a sworn affidavit to a Justice of the Peace in Dover, in support of a warrant to search petitioner's apartment. In paragraph 8 of the affidavit's "probable cause page," mention was made of petitioner's statement to McClements. In paragraph 10, it was noted that the description of the assailant given to the police by Mrs. Bailey included the above-mentioned clothing. Finally, the affidavit also described the attempt made by police to confirm that petitioner's typical outfit matched that of the assailant. Paragraph 15 recited: "On Tuesday, 3/9/76, your affiant contacted Mr. James Williams and Mr. Wesley Lucas of the Delaware Youth Center where Jerome Franks is employed and did have personal conversation with both these people."

Paragraphs 16 and 17 respectively stated: "Mr. James Williams revealed to your affiant that the normal dress of Jerome Franks does consist of a white knit thermal undershirt and a brown leather jacket," and "Mr. Wesley Lucas revealed to your affiant that in addition to the thermal undershirt and jacket, Jerome Franks often wears a dark green knit hat."

The warrant was issued on the basis of this affidavit. Pursuant to the warrant, police searched petitioner's apartment and found a white thermal undershirt, a knit hat, dark pants, and a leather jacket, and, on petitioner's kitchen table, a single-blade knife. All these ultimately were introduced in evidence at trial.

Prior to the trial, however, petitioner's counsel filed a written motion to suppress the clothing and the knife found in the search; this motion alleged that the warrant, on its face, did not show probable cause, and that the search and seizure were in violation of the Fourth and Fourteenth Amendments. At the hearing on the motion to suppress, defense counsel orally amended the challenge to include an attack on the veracity of the warrant affidavit; he also specifically requested the right to call as witnesses Detective Brooks, Wesley Lucas of the Youth Center, and James D. Morrison, formerly of the Youth Center. Counsel asserted that Lucas and Morrison would testify that neither had been personally interviewed by the warrant affiants, and that, although they might have talked to another police officer, any information given by them to that officer was "somewhat different" from what was recited in the affidavit. Defense counsel charged that the misstatements were included in the affidavit not inadvertently, but in "bad faith." Counsel also sought permission to call Officer McClements and petitioner as witnesses, to seek to establish that petitioner's courthouse statement to police had been obtained in violation of petitioner's Miranda rights, and that the search warrant was thereby tainted as the fruit of an illegally obtained confession.

The trial court sustained the State's objection to petitioner's proposed evidence. The motion to suppress was denied, and the clothing and knife were admitted as evidence at the ensuing trial. Petitioner was convicted. In a written motion for judgment of acquittal and/or new trial, petitioner repeated his objection to the admission of the evidence, stating that he "should have been allowed to impeach the Affidavit used in the Search Warrant to show purposeful misrepresentation of information contained therein."

The motion was denied, and petitioner was sentenced to two consecutive terms of 25 years each and an additional consecutive life sentence.

III

Whether the Fourth and Fourteenth Amendments, and the derivative exclusionary rule made applicable to the States under *Mapp v. Ohio,* 367 U.S. 643 (1961), ever mandate that a defendant be permitted to attack the veracity of a warrant affidavit after the warrant has been issued and executed, is a question that encounters conflicting values. The bulwark of Fourth Amendment protection, of course, is the Warrant Clause, requiring that, absent certain exceptions, police obtain a warrant from a neutral and disinterested magistrate before embarking upon a search. In deciding today that, in certain circumstances, a challenge to a warrant's veracity must be permitted, we derive our ground from language of the Warrant Clause itself, which surely takes the affiant's good faith as its premise: "[N]o Warrants shall issue, but upon probable cause, supported by Oath or affirmation. . . ." Judge Frankel, in *United States v. Halsey,* 257 F. Supp. 1002, 1005 (SDNY 1966), put the matter simply:

> [W]hen the Fourth Amendment demands a factual showing sufficient to comprise 'probable cause,' the obvious assumption is that there will be a '*truthful* showing' (emphasis in original). This does not mean 'truthful' in the sense that every fact recited in the warrant affidavit is necessarily correct, for probable cause may be founded upon hearsay and upon information received from informants, as well as upon information within the affiant's own knowledge that sometimes must be garnered hastily. But surely it is to be 'truthful' in the sense that the information put forth is

> believed or appropriately accepted by the affiant as true. It is established law, that a warrant affidavit must set forth particular facts and circumstances underlying the existence of probable cause, so as to allow the magistrate to make an independent evaluation of the matter. If an informant's tip is the source of information, the affidavit must recite 'some of the underlying circumstances from which the informant concluded' that relevant evidence might be discovered, and "some of the underlying circumstances from which the officer concluded that the informant, whose identity need not be disclosed, . . . was 'credible,' or his information reliable.

Because it is the magistrate who must determine independently whether there is probable cause, it would be an unthinkable imposition upon his authority if a warrant affidavit, revealed after the fact to contain a deliberately or recklessly false statement, were to stand beyond impeachment.

In saying this, however, one must give cognizance to competing values that lead us to impose limitations. They perhaps can best be addressed by noting the arguments of respondent and others against allowing veracity challenges. The arguments are several.

First, respondent argues that the exclusionary rule, created in *Weeks v. United States,* personal constitutional right, but only a judicially created remedy extended where its benefit as a deterrent promises to outweigh the societal cost of its use; that the Court has declined to apply the exclusionary rule when illegally seized evidence is used to impeach the credibility of a defendant's testimony, is used in a grand jury proceeding, or is used in a civil trial, and that the Court similarly has restricted application of the Fourth Amendment exclusionary rule in federal habeas corpus review of a state conviction. Respondent argues that applying the exclusionary rule to another situation — the deterrence of deliberate or reckless untruthfulness in a warrant affidavit — is not justified for many of the same reasons that led to the above restrictions; interfering with a criminal conviction in order to deter official misconduct is a burden too great to impose on society.

Second, respondent argues that a citizen's privacy interests are adequately protected by a requirement that applicants for a warrant submit a sworn affidavit and by the magistrate's independent determination of sufficiency based on the face of the affidavit. Applying the exclusionary rule to attacks upon veracity would weed out a minimal number of perjurious government statements, says respondent, but would overlap unnecessarily with existing penalties against perjury, including criminal prosecutions, departmental discipline for misconduct, contempt of court, and civil actions.

Third, it is argued that the magistrate already is equipped to conduct a fairly vigorous inquiry into the accuracy of the factual affidavit supporting a warrant application. He may question the affiant, or summon other persons to give testimony at the warrant proceeding. The incremental gain from a post-search adversary proceeding, it is said, would not be great.

Fourth, it is argued that it would unwisely diminish the solemnity and moment of the magistrate's proceeding to make his inquiry into probable cause reviewable in regard to veracity. The less final, and less deference paid to, the magistrate's determination of veracity, the less initiative will he use in that task.

Fifth, it is argued that permitting a post-search evidentiary hearing on issues of veracity would confuse the pressing issue of guilt or innocence with the collateral question as to whether there had been official misconduct in the drafting of the affidavit.

Sixth and finally, it is argued that a post-search veracity challenge is inappropriate because the accuracy of an affidavit, in large part, is beyond the control of the affiant. An affidavit may properly be based on hearsay, on fleeting observations, and on tips received from unnamed informants whose identity often will be properly protected from revelation under *McCray v. Illinois,* 386 U.S. 300 (1967).

None of these considerations is trivial. Indeed, because of them, the rule announced today has a limited scope, both in regard to when exclusion of the seized evidence is mandated and when a hearing on allegations of misstatements must be accorded. But neither do the considerations cited by respondent and others have a fully controlling weight; we conclude that they are insufficient to justify an *absolute* ban on post-search impeachment of veracity. On this side of the balance, also, there are pressing considerations:

First, a ban on impeachment of veracity could denude the probable cause requirement of all real meaning. The requirement that a warrant not issue "but upon probable cause, supported by Oath or affirmation," would be reduced to a nullity if a police officer was able to use deliberately falsified allegations to demonstrate probable cause, and, having misled the magistrate, then was able to remain confident that the ploy was worthwhile.

Second, the hearing before the magistrate not always will suffice to discourage lawless or reckless misconduct. The pre-search proceeding is necessarily *ex parte,* since the subject of the search cannot be tipped off to the application for a warrant, lest he destroy or remove evidence. The usual reliance of our legal system on adversary proceedings itself should be an indication that an *ex parte* inquiry is likely to be less vigorous. The magistrate has no acquaintance with the information that may contradict the good faith and reasonable basis of the affiant's allegations. The pre-search proceeding will frequently be marked by haste, because of the understandable desire to act before the evidence disappears; this urgency will not always permit the magistrate to make an extended independent examination of the affiant or other witnesses.

Third, the alternative sanctions of a perjury prosecution, administrative discipline, contempt, or a civil suit are not likely to fill the gap. *Mapp v. Ohio* implicitly rejected the adequacy of these alternatives. Mr. Justice Douglas noted this in his concurrence in *Mapp* where he quoted from *Wolf v. Colorado*, 338 U.S. 25, 42 (1949):"self-scrutiny is a lofty ideal, but its exaltation reaches new heights if we expect a District Attorney to prosecute himself or his associates for well meaning violations of the search and seizure clause during a raid the District Attorney or his associates have ordered."

Fourth, allowing an evidentiary hearing, after a suitable preliminary proffer of material falsity, would not diminish the importance and solemnity of the warrant-issuing process. It is the *ex parte* nature of the initial hearing, rather than the magistrate's capacity, that is the reason for the review. A magistrate's determination is presently subject to review before trial as to *sufficiency* without any undue interference with the dignity of the magistrate's function. Our reluctance today to extend the rule of exclusion beyond instances of deliberate misstatements, and those of reckless disregard, leaves a broad field where the magistrate is the sole protection of a citizen's Fourth Amendment rights, namely, in instances where police have been merely negligent in checking or recording the facts relevant to a probable cause determination.

Fifth, the claim that a post-search hearing will confuse the issue of the defendant's guilt with the issue of the State's possible misbehavior is footless. The hearing will not be in the presence of the jury. An issue extraneous to guilt already is examined in any probable cause determination or review of probable cause. The requirement of a substantial preliminary showing should suffice to prevent the misuse of a veracity hearing for purposes of discovery or obstruction. And because we are faced today with only the question of the integrity of the affiant's representations as to his own activities, we need not decide, and we in no way predetermine, the difficult question whether a reviewing court must ever require the revelation of the identity of an informant once a substantial preliminary showing of falsity has been made. *McCray v. Illinois,* 386 U.S. 300 (1967), the Court's earlier disquisition in this area, concluded only that the Due Process Clause of the Fourteenth Amendment did not require the State to expose an informant's identity routinely, upon a defendant's mere demand, when there was ample evidence in the probable cause hearing to show that the informant was reliable and his information credible.

Sixth and finally, as to the argument that the exclusionary rule should not be extended to a "new" area, we cannot regard any such extension really to be at issue here.

IV

In sum, and to repeat with some embellishment what we stated at the beginning of this opinion: there is, of course, a presumption of validity with respect to the affidavit supporting the search warrant. To mandate an evidentiary hearing, the challenger's attack must be more than conclusory, and must be supported by more than a mere desire to cross-examine. There must be allegations of deliberate falsehood or of reckless disregard for the truth, and those allegations must be accompanied by an offer of proof. They should point out specifically the portion of the warrant affidavit that is claimed to be false; and they should be accompanied by a statement of supporting reasons. Affidavits or sworn or otherwise reliable statements of witnesses should be furnished, or their absence satisfactorily explained. Allegations of negligence or innocent mistake are insufficient. The deliberate falsity or reckless disregard whose impeachment is permitted today is only that of the affiant, not of any nongovernmental informant. Finally, if these requirements are met, and if, when material that is the subject of the alleged falsity or reckless disregard is set to one side, there remains sufficient content in the warrant affidavit to support a finding of probable cause, no hearing is required. On the other hand, if the remaining content is insufficient, the defendant is entitled, under the Fourth and Fourteenth Amendments, to his hearing. Whether he will prevail at that hearing is, of course, another issue.

Because of Delaware's absolute rule, its courts did not have occasion to consider the proffer put forward by petitioner Franks. Since the framing of suitable rules to govern proffers is a matter properly left to the States, we decline ourselves to pass on petitioner's proffer. The judgment of the Supreme Court of Delaware is reversed, and the case is remanded for further proceedings not inconsistent with this opinion.

It is so ordered.

FURTHER CASE LAW, REFLECTIONS, AND QUESTIONS

1. What impact might the *Franks* decision have on law enforcement practices? How might police departments ensure that warrant affidavits are accurate and truthful?
2. The Court's decision in *Franks* requires defendants to make a "substantial preliminary showing" of deliberate or reckless falsehood in a warrant affidavit before challenging its veracity. What factors might a court consider in determining whether this threshold has been met?
3. Compare the Supreme Court's reasoning in *Franks v. Delaware* with its earlier decision in *Shadwick v. City of Tampa*. How do these cases collectively shape the contours of Fourth Amendment protections?

Probable Cause to Search

Similarities exist in how probable cause is substantiated for an arrest or search. In both arenas, there are two central questions: what constitutes probable cause and what evidence may be used to establish it. The following case addresses both inquiries.

Draper v. United States

358 U.S. 307 (1959)

MR. JUSTICE WHITTAKER delivered the opinion of the Court.

Petitioner was convicted of knowingly concealing and transporting narcotic drugs in Denver, Colorado. His conviction was based in part on the use in evidence against him of two "envelopes containing [865 grains of] heroin" and a hypodermic syringe that had been taken from his person, following his arrest, by the arresting officer. Before the trial, he moved to suppress that evidence as having been secured through an unlawful search and seizure. After hearing, the District Court found that the arresting officer had probable cause to arrest petitioner without a warrant and that the subsequent search and seizure were therefore incident to a lawful arrest and overruled the motion to suppress.

The evidence offered at the hearing on the motion to suppress established that one Marsh, a federal narcotic agent with 29 years' experience, was stationed at Denver; that one Hereford had been engaged as a "special employee" of the Bureau of Narcotics at Denver for about six months, and from time to time gave information to Marsh regarding violations of the narcotics laws, for which Hereford was paid small sums of money, and that Marsh had always found the information given by Hereford to be accurate and reliable. On September 3, 1956, Hereford told Marsh that James Draper (petitioner) recently had taken up abode at a stated address in Denver and "was peddling narcotics to several addicts" in that city. Four days later, on September 7, Hereford told Marsh "that Draper had gone to Chicago the day before [September 6] by train [and] that he was going to bring back three ounces of heroin [and] that he would return to Denver either on the morning of the 8th of September or the morning of the 9th of September also by train." Hereford also gave Marsh a detailed physical description of Draper and of the clothing he was wearing, and said that he would be carrying "a tan zipper bag," and that he habitually "walked real fast."

On the morning of September 8, Marsh and a Denver police officer went to the Denver Union Station and kept watch over all incoming trains from Chicago, but they did not see anyone fitting the description that Hereford had given. Repeating the process on the morning of September 9, they saw a person, having the exact physical attributes and wearing the precise clothing described by Hereford, alight from an incoming Chicago train and start walking "fast" toward the exit. He was carrying a tan zipper bag in his right hand and the left was thrust in his raincoat pocket. Marsh, accompanied by the police officer, overtook, stopped, and arrested him. They then searched him and found the two "envelopes containing heroin" clutched in his left hand in his raincoat pocket and found the syringe in the tan zipper bag. Marsh then took him (petitioner) into custody. Hereford died four days after the arrest and therefore did not testify at the hearing on the motion.

The crucial question for us then is whether knowledge of the related facts and circumstances gave Marsh "probable cause" within the meaning of the Fourth Amendment to believe that petitioner had committed or was committing a violation of the narcotic laws. If it did, the arrest, though without a warrant, was lawful and the subsequent search of petitioner's person and the seizure of the found heroin were validly made incident to a lawful arrest, and therefore the motion to suppress was properly overruled and the heroin was competently received in evidence at the trial.

Petitioner contends (1) that the information given by Hereford to Marsh was "hearsay" and, because hearsay is not legally competent evidence in a criminal trial, could not legally have been considered, but should have been put out of mind, by Marsh in assessing whether he had "probable cause" to arrest petitioner without a warrant, and (2) that, even if hearsay could lawfully have been considered, Marsh's information should be held insufficient to show "probable cause" to believe that petitioner had violated or was violating the narcotic laws and to justify his arrest without a warrant.

[We disagree] Nor can we agree with petitioner's contention that Marsh's information was insufficient to show probable cause to believe that petitioner had violated or was violating the narcotic laws and to justify his arrest without a warrant. The information given to narcotic agent Marsh by "special employee" Hereford may have been hearsay to Marsh, but coming from one employed for that purpose and whose information had always been found accurate and reliable, it is clear that Marsh would have been derelict in his duties had he not pursued it. And when, in pursuing that information, he saw a man, having the exact physical attributes and wearing the precise clothing and carrying the tan zipper bag that Hereford had described, alight from one of the very trains from the very place stated by Hereford and start to walk at a "fast" pace toward the station exit, Marsh had personally verified every facet of the information given him by Hereford except whether petitioner had accomplished his mission and had the three ounces of heroin on his person or in his bag. And surely, with every other bit of Hereford's information being thus personally verified, Marsh had "reasonable grounds" to believe that the remaining unverified bit of Hereford's information — that Draper would have the heroin with him — was likewise true.

In dealing with probable cause as the very name implies, we deal with probabilities. These are not technical; they are the factual and practical considerations of everyday life on which reasonable and prudent men, not legal technicians, act. Probable cause exists where "the facts and circumstances within [the arresting officers'] knowledge and of which they had reasonably trustworthy information [are] sufficient in themselves to warrant a man of reasonable caution in the belief that" an offense has been or is being committed.

We believe that, under the facts and circumstances here, Marsh had probable cause to believe that petitioner was committing a violation of the laws of the United

States relating to narcotic drugs at the time he arrested him. The arrest was therefore lawful, and the subsequent search and seizure, having been made incident to that lawful arrest, were likewise valid. It follows that petitioner's motion to suppress was properly denied and that the seized heroin was competent evidence lawfully received at the trial.

Affirmed.

FURTHER CASE LAW, REFLECTIONS, AND QUESTIONS

1. The Court in *Draper* defines "probable cause." Does the definition help clarify the meaning of probable cause? Does *Draper* at least clarify that the *type* and the *amount* of evidence necessary to establish probable cause differ from the proof expected in trials?
2. Note that probable cause is measured against an objective standard. Although a police officer might initially decide to make an arrest without a warrant, a judge will determine whether probable cause existed. In some cases, probable cause can be based on the officer's direct observation of criminal activity. In other cases, an informant's report or a tip might provide the exclusive basis for probable cause. In other situations, probable cause may be based on some combination of an informant's tip and a police investigation. *Draper* falls into this last category of cases.
3. It is important to remember that probable cause is an initial foundation for arrest decisions. Once this standard is satisfied, the police have the authority to make an arrest, but they usually also have the discretion to decline to do so.

In the arrest and search warrant context, the magistrate (or judge) must arrive at an *independent* judgment that there is probable cause to believe that a seizable item is located in the place to be searched or that a named person committed a specific criminal act. The magistrate cannot blindly rely on conclusions or inferences drawn by police officers. Accordingly, the officers who apply for a warrant must detail the underlying facts so that the magistrate can determine whether probable cause exists.

A classic set of facts in which the information supplied by the police was ruled insufficient for the magistrate to reach an independent determination about probable cause was presented in *Aguilar v. Texas*, 373 U.S. 108 (1964). There, a justice of the peace had issued a search warrant based on an application submitted by police officers which read, in relevant part, "Affiants have received reliable information from a credible person and do believe that heroin, marijuana, barbiturates and other narcotics and narcotic paraphernalia are being kept at the above-described premises for the purpose of sale and use contrary to the provisions of the law."

For just a moment, put yourself in the shoes of the justice of the peace who has been asked to approve the search warrant in *Aguilar*. Assume that the police who filled out the affidavit (the **affiants**) gave you no more information than is reported above. Remember the cardinal rule in this area: you, as the judicial officer, must be provided with sufficient underlying facts to arrive at an independent judgment about whether probable cause exists. Does the affidavit permit you to make this decision based on your evaluation of the facts, or do you find yourself dependent on conclusions or inferences drawn by the police? For example, precisely what "information" did the police receive, and what supports the judgment that it is "reliable?" You may recall from *Draper v. United States* that probable cause may be based on hearsay. Accordingly, the police can report what they heard their informant say, and the informant need not appear before the magistrate during the warrant application process. Nevertheless, what did the police offer in *Aguilar* to substantiate their claim that a "credible" person supplied their information?

The Supreme Court ruled that the search warrant in *Aguilar* was issued improperly. Rather than making an independent assessment of the facts necessary to supply probable cause, the justice of the peace had served "merely as a rubber stamp for the police." The justices concluded that:

> [A]lthough an affidavit [in support of an application for a search warrant] may be based on hearsay information and need not reflect the direct personal observation of the affiant the magistrate must be informed of some of the underlying circumstances from which the informant concluded that the narcotics were where he claimed they were, and some of the underlying circumstances from which the officer concluded that the informant was "credible" or his information "reliable." 378 U.S., at 114–115 (cites omitted).

This passage identifies two crucial components of probable-cause decisions that depend on informants' tips. The first relates to the informant's ***basis of knowledge*** ("the underlying circumstances from which the informant concluded that the narcotics were where he claimed they were"). The second concerns the informant's ***veracity*** (credibility) or ***reliability*** ("the underlying circumstances from which the officer concluded that the informant was 'credible' or his information 'reliable'").

Five years after deciding *Aguilar*, the Court elaborated on the probable-cause requirements for a search warrant in *Spinelli v. United States*, 393 U.S. 410 (1969). The justices ruled in *Spinelli* that information supplied by an informant, even though inadequate by itself to justify issuing a search warrant, might help establish probable cause when the police independently gather information corroborating all or part of the informant's tip.

In *Spinelli*, the FBI had been "informed by a confidential, reliable informant that William Spinelli was operating a handbook and accepting wagers by means of the telephones which have been assigned" specified phone numbers. FBI agents then sought to verify facts supplied by the informant since the tip alone was clearly inadequate under *Aguilar* to provide probable cause for a search warrant for Spinelli's apartment. They did so by confirming that Spinelli indeed operated telephones with the identified phone numbers and by tracking Spinelli's movements over a five-day period. They communicated this additional information to the magistrate when they applied for the search warrant. The Court confirmed that a magistrate properly considers independent corroboration of an informant's tip by law enforcement agents for determining whether probable cause exists to issue a search warrant, but ruled that under the facts of Spinelli's case, the corroborative information remained insufficient to provide probable cause.

How might the corroboration of an informant's tip by the police help provide probable cause for a search warrant under *Aguilar* and *Spinelli*? Might the magistrate get a better indication that the informant was a credible source if some of the information they had supplied to the police panned out as accurate? Might the magistrate reasonably conclude that, if details provided by the informant in some respects checked out as correct, it would be more likely that the informant was privy to knowledge important for issuing a warrant?

Aguilar and *Spinelli* reigned for the next several years as the principal cases governing probable cause in the search warrant context. The "two-pronged ***Aguilar-Spinelli*** **test**" for probable cause was widely understood as requiring that the informant's basis of knowledge and veracity or reliability must *independently* meet a threshold of sufficiency before an informant's tip could be used to help establish probable cause. This requirement occasionally infringed on the ability of police to obtain search warrants when it was apparent that probable cause existed. For example, consider a case where very detailed, specific information about where stolen goods were held was given to police by an anonymous source. Even if the police verified the accuracy of the information before applying for a search warrant, the warrant request would be denied because there was no independent information to support the informant's reliability. Similarly, if a gang member who had provided accurate information to police on dozens of occasions told police that a gang was stockpiling weapons in a specific warehouse, but provided no details beyond that, once again, a warrant would not be issued. In other words, requiring that each prong of the *Aguilar-Spinelli* test be met independently of each other was frequently too high of a bar to reach.

Box 4.2 Summary of *Aguilar-Spinelli* Two-Pronged Test

	Veracity	Basis-of-Knowledge
Question	Why should the magistrate or police believe the informant?	How did the informant acquire the information in question?
Concern	The credibility of the informant	The reliability of the information
Established	By demonstrating previous reliability of information obtained from the informant and showing a record of truthful tips	Demonstrating personal first-hand knowledge of the information
Example	Naming and stating the number of previous tips that have led to successful prosecutions or if the informant implicates themself in a crime, which suggests the information is reliable	The informant knows the suspect is selling drugs from their home because they observed the crime or bought drugs from the home
Corroboration	If both prongs cannot be met independently of each other, this may be overcome if the police corroborate and verify some of the information and facts provided by the informant	

Realizing the absurdity of such results, the Supreme Court modified the *Aguilar-Spinelli* test in *Illinois v. Gates*. As you read *Gates*, consider how the Supreme Court modified the test and whether you think this modification was necessary in light of the facts.

Illinois v. Gates

462 U.S. 213 (1983)

MR. JUSTICE REHNQUIST delivered the opinion of the Court.

Bloomingdale, Ill., is a suburb of Chicago located in DuPage County. On May 3, 1978, the Bloomingdale Police Department received by mail an anonymous handwritten letter which read as follows:

> This letter is to inform you that you have a couple in your town who strictly make their living on selling drugs. They are Sue and Lance Gates, they live on Greenway, off Bloomingdale Rd. in the condominiums. Most of their buys are done in Florida. Sue, his wife, drives their car to Florida, where she leaves it to be loaded up with drugs, then Lance flys down and

> drives it back. Sue flys back after she drops the car off in Florida. On May 3rd she is driving down there again and Lance will be flying down in a few days to drive it back. At the time Lance drives the car back he has the trunk loaded with over $100,000.00 in drugs. Presently they have over $100,000.00 worth of drugs in their basement.
>
> They brag about the fact they never have to work and make their entire living on pushers. I guarantee if you watch them carefully you will make a big catch. They are friends with some big drug dealers, who visit their house often.

The letter was referred by the Chief of Police of the Bloomingdale Police Department to Detective Mader, who decided to pursue the tip. Mader learned, from the office of the Illinois Secretary of State, that an Illinois driver's license had been issued to one Lance Gates, residing at a stated address in Bloomingdale. He contacted a confidential informant, whose examination of certain financial records revealed a more recent address for the Gates, and he also learned from a police officer assigned to O'Hare Airport that "L. Gates" had made a reservation on Eastern Airlines flight 245 to West Palm Beach, Fla., scheduled to depart from Chicago on May 5 at 4:15 p.m.

Mader then made arrangements with an agent of the Drug Enforcement Administration for surveillance of the May 5 Eastern Airlines flight. The agent later reported to Mader that Gates had boarded the flight, and that federal agents in Florida had observed him arrive in West Palm Beach and take a taxi to the nearby Holiday Inn. They also reported that Gates went to a room registered to one Susan Gates and that, at 7:00 a.m. the next morning, Gates and an unidentified woman left the motel in a Mercury bearing Illinois license plates and drove northbound on an interstate frequently used by travelers to the Chicago area. In addition, the DEA agent informed Mader that the license plate number on the Mercury registered to a Hornet station wagon owned by Gates. The agent also advised Mader that the driving time between West Palm Beach and Bloomingdale was approximately 22 to 24 hours.

Mader signed an affidavit setting forth the foregoing facts, and submitted it to a judge of the Circuit Court of DuPage County, together with a copy of the anonymous letter. The judge of that court thereupon issued a search warrant for the Gates' residence and for their automobile.

At 5:15 a.m. on March 7th, only 36 hours after he had flown out of Chicago, Lance Gates, and his wife, returned to their home in Bloomingdale, driving the car in which they had left West Palm Beach some 22 hours earlier. The Bloomingdale police were awaiting them, searched the trunk of the Mercury, and uncovered approximately 350 pounds of marijuana. A search of the Gates' home revealed marijuana, weapons, and other contraband. The Illinois Circuit Court ordered suppression of all these items, on the ground that the affidavit submitted to the Circuit Judge failed to support the necessary determination of probable cause to believe that the Gates' automobile and home contained the contraband in question. This decision was affirmed in turn by the Illinois Appellate Court and by a divided vote of the Supreme Court of Illinois.

The Illinois Supreme Court concluded — and we are inclined to agree — that, standing alone, the anonymous letter sent to the Bloomingdale Police Department would not provide the basis for a magistrate's determination that there was probable cause to believe contraband would be found in the Gates' car and home. The letter provides virtually nothing from which one might conclude that its author is either honest or his information reliable; likewise, the letter gives absolutely no indication of the basis for the writer's predictions regarding the Gates' criminal activities. Something more was required, then, before a magistrate could conclude that there was probable cause to believe that contraband would be found in the Gates' home and car.

The Illinois Supreme Court also properly recognized that Detective Mader's affidavit might be capable of supplementing the anonymous letter with information sufficient to permit a determination of probable cause. In holding that the affidavit in fact did not contain sufficient additional information to sustain a determination of probable cause, the Illinois court applied a "two-pronged test," derived from our decision in *Spinelli v United States*, 393 US 410 (1969). The Illinois Supreme Court, like some others, apparently understood *Spinelli* as requiring that the anonymous letter satisfy each of two independent requirements before it could be relied on. According to this view, the letter, as supplemented by Mader's affidavit, first had to adequately reveal the "basis of knowledge" of the letter writer — the particular means by which he came by the information given in his report. Second, it had to provide facts sufficiently establishing either the "veracity" of the affiant's informant, or, alternatively, the "reliability" of the informant's report in this particular case.

We agree with the Illinois Supreme Court that an informant's "veracity," "reliability" and "basis of knowledge" are all highly relevant in determining the value of his report. We do not agree, however, that these elements should be understood as entirely separate and independent requirements to be rigidly exacted in every case, which the opinion of the Supreme Court of Illinois would imply. Rather, as detailed below, they should be understood simply as closely intertwined issues that may usefully illuminate the commonsense, practical question whether there is "probable cause" to believe that contraband or evidence is located in a particular place.

This **totality of the circumstances** approach is far more consistent with our prior treatment of probable cause than is any rigid demand that specific "tests" be satisfied by every informant's tip. Perhaps the central teaching of our decisions bearing on the probable cause standard is that it is a "practical, nontechnical conception.

As these comments illustrate, probable cause is a fluid concept — turning on the assessment of probabilities in particular factual contexts — not readily, or even usefully, reduced to a neat set of legal rules. Informants' tips doubtless come in many shapes and sizes from many different types of persons. Rigid legal rules are ill-suited to an area of such diversity. "One simple rule will not cover every situation."

Moreover, the "two-pronged test" directs analysis into two largely independent channels — the informant's "veracity" or "reliability" and his "basis of knowledge." There are persuasive arguments against according these two elements such independent status. Instead, they are better understood as relevant considerations in the totality of circumstances analysis that traditionally has guided probable cause determinations: a deficiency in one may be compensated for, in determining the overall reliability of a tip, by a strong showing as to the other, or by some other indicia of reliability.

If, for example, a particular informant is known for the unusual reliability of his predictions of certain types of criminal activities in a locality, his failure, in a particular case, to thoroughly set forth the basis of his knowledge surely should not serve as an absolute bar to a finding of probable cause based on his tip. Likewise, if an unquestionably honest citizen comes forward with a report of criminal activity — which if fabricated would subject him to criminal liability — we have found rigorous scrutiny of the basis of his knowledge unnecessary. Conversely, even if we entertain some doubt as to an informant's motives, his explicit and detailed description of alleged wrongdoing, along with a statement that the event was observed first-hand, entitles his tip to greater weight than might otherwise be the case. Unlike a totality of circumstances analysis, which permits a balanced assessment of the relative weights of all the various indicia of reliability (and unreliability) attending an informant's tip, the "two-pronged test" has encouraged an excessively technical dissection of informants' tips, with undue attention being focused on issues that cannot sensibly be divorced from the other facts presented to the magistrate.

We also have recognized that affidavits are normally drafted by nonlawyers in the midst and haste of a criminal investigation. Technical requirements of elaborate specificity once exacted under common law pleading have no proper place in this area. Likewise, search and arrest warrants long have been issued by persons who are neither lawyers nor judges, and who certainly do not remain abreast of each judicial refinement of the nature of "probable cause." The rigorous inquiry into the *Spinelli* prongs and the complex superstructure of evidentiary and analytical rules that some have seen implicit in our *Spinelli* decision, cannot be reconciled with the fact that many warrants are quite properly issued on the basis of nontechnical, commonsense judgments of laymen applying a standard less demanding than those used in more formal legal proceedings. Likewise, given the informal, often hurried context in which it must be applied, the "built-in subtleties" of the "two-pronged test" are particularly unlikely to assist magistrates in determining probable cause.

We conclude that it is wiser to abandon the "two-pronged test" established by our decisions in *Aguilar* and *Spinelli*. In its place we reaffirm the totality of the circumstances analysis that traditionally has informed probable cause determinations. The task of the issuing magistrate is simply to make a practical, commonsense decision whether, given all the circumstances set forth in the affidavit before him, including the "veracity" and "basis of knowledge" of persons supplying hearsay information, there is a fair probability that contraband or evidence of a crime will be found in a particular place. And the duty of a reviewing court is simply to ensure that the magistrate had a "substantial basis for conclud[ing]" that probable cause existed. We are convinced that this flexible, easily applied standard will better achieve the accommodation of public and private interests that the Fourth Amendment requires than does the approach that has developed from *Aguilar* and *Spinelli*.

Our earlier cases illustrate the limits beyond which a magistrate may not venture in issuing a warrant. Sufficient information must be presented to the magistrate to allow that official to determine probable cause; his action cannot be a mere ratification of the bare conclusions of others. In order to ensure that such an abdication of the magistrate's duty does not occur, courts must continue to conscientiously review the sufficiency of affidavits on which warrants are issued. But when we move beyond the "bare bones" affidavits present in cases such as *Aguilar*, this area simply does not lend itself to a prescribed set of rules, like that which had developed from *Spinelli*. Instead, the flexible, commonsense standard better serves the purpose of the Fourth Amendment's probable cause requirement.

Our decisions applying the totality of circumstances analysis outlined above have consistently recognized the value of corroboration of details of an informant's tip by independent police work.

Our decision in *Draper v United States*, 358 US 307 (1959) is the classic case on the value of corroborative efforts of police officials.

The showing of probable cause in the present case was fully as compelling as that in *Draper*. Even standing alone, the facts obtained through the independent investigation of Mader and the DEA at least suggested that the Gates were involved in drug trafficking. In addition to being a popular vacation site, Florida is well-known as a source of narcotics and other illegal drugs. Lance Gates' flight to Palm Beach, his brief, overnight stay in a motel, and apparent immediate return north to Chicago in the family car, conveniently awaiting him in West Palm Beach, is as suggestive of a pre-arranged drug run, as it is of an ordinary vacation trip.

In addition, the magistrate could rely on the anonymous letter, which had been corroborated in major part by Mader's efforts — just as had occurred in *Draper*. The Supreme Court of Illinois reasoned that *Draper* involved an informant who had given reliable information on previous occasions, while the honesty and reliability of the anonymous informant in this case were unknown to the Bloomingdale police. While this distinction might be an apt one at the time the police department received the anonymous letter, it became far less significant after Mader's independent investigative work occurred. The corroboration of the letter's predictions that the Gates' car would be in Florida, that Lance Gates would fly to Florida in the next day or so, and that he would drive the car north toward Bloomingdale all indicated, albeit not with certainty, that the informant's other assertions also were true.

Finally, the anonymous letter contained a range of details relating not just to easily obtained facts and conditions existing at the time of the tip, but to future actions of third parties ordinarily not easily predicted. The letter writer's accurate information as to the travel plans of each of the Gates was of a character likely obtained only from the Gates themselves, or from someone familiar with their not entirely ordinary travel plans. If the informant had access to accurate information of this type a magistrate could properly conclude that it was not unlikely that he also had access to reliable information of the Gates' alleged illegal activities. Of course, the Gates' travel plans might have been learned from a talkative neighbor or travel agent; under the "two-pronged test" developed from *Spinelli*, the character of the details in the anonymous letter might well not permit a sufficiently clear inference regarding the letter writer's "basis of knowledge." But, as discussed previously, probable cause does not demand the certainty we associate with formal trials. It is enough that there was a fair probability that the writer of the anonymous letter had obtained his entire story either from the Gates or someone they trusted. And corroboration of major portions of the letter's predictions provides just this probability. It is apparent, therefore, that the judge issuing the warrant had a substantial basis for concluding that probable cause to search the Gates' home and car existed. The judgment of the Supreme Court of Illinois therefore must be reversed.

FURTHER CASE LAW, REFLECTIONS, AND QUESTIONS

1. In separate opinions, Justices White and Brennan argued that the "practical, commonsense decision" the Court in *Gates* encourages magistrates to make regarding whether "there is a fair probability that contraband or evidence of a crime will be found in a particular place" provides insufficient guidance to police and magistrates alike, and thus undermines the interests protected by the Fourth Amendment's probable cause requirement. Do you agree? Or do you agree with the majority that the *Aguilar-Spinelli* test was too rigid, excessively technical, and perhaps damaging to the government's ability "to provide for the security of the individual and of his property?" How do these differing views suggest a clash of the "due process" and "crime control" models of criminal procedure described by Packer in Chapter 1?

2. The totality of circumstances approach allows a flexible standard to be employed by a court to determine the presence of probable cause. In *Florida v. Harris*, 568

U.S. 237 (2013), the United States Supreme Court overturned a Florida Supreme Court decision that imposed strict rules for determining whether dog sniffs were sufficiently reliable to provide probable cause. The facts of *Harris* were not disputed. Patrol officer Wheetley pulled over respondent Clayton Harris for a routine traffic stop. Observing Harris's nervousness and an open beer can, Wheetley asked to search Harris's truck. When Harris refused, Wheetley had Aldo, a trained drug detection dog, conduct a sniff test. That search turned up nothing Aldo was trained to detect, but did reveal pseudoephedrine and other ingredients for manufacturing methamphetamine. Harris was arrested and charged with illegal possession of those ingredients. Wheetley testified about his and Aldo's extensive training in drug detection at a suppression hearing before trial. Harris's attorney contested the reliability of Aldo's certification and performance in the field, particularly in the stop of Harris's truck. The trial court denied the motion to suppress, but the Florida Supreme Court reversed. It held that a wide array of evidence was necessary to establish probable cause, including field-performance records showing how many times the dog has falsely alerted. Absent such records, the State could not sufficiently prove the dog's reliability in drug detection to show probable cause.

A unanimous U.S. Supreme Court reversed. Citing *Gates*, the Court held that in testing whether an officer has probable cause to conduct a search, all that is required is the kind of "fair probability" on which reasonable and prudent people act. This calls for a court to consider whether all the facts surrounding the alert, viewed through the lens of common sense, would make a reasonably prudent person think that a search would reveal contraband or evidence of a crime.

3. The Court affirmed that it did away with the *Aguilar-Spinelli* test and replaced it with the *Gates* totality of the circumstances test *in Massachusetts v. Upton*, 466 U.S. 727 (1984). Although the Court did away with the *Aguilar-Spinelli* test, magistrates can still consider the reliability, validity, and basis of knowledge to determine if there is probable cause. In other words, considering these three factors can help them clarify and reflect whether there is probable cause based on the totality of the circumstances. Additionally, based on state constitutional grounds, five states still require the use of the *Aguilar-Spinelli* test: Alaska, Massachusetts, New Mexico, New York, and Washington State. Remember, state courts can grant more protections to citizens in their states, above and beyond what the United States Constitution requires, but they cannot take rights away.

4. **Anticipatory warrants.** An anticipatory warrant is a warrant based upon an affidavit showing probable cause that at some future time specific evidence of a crime will be located at a particular place. In *United States v. Grubbs,* 547 U.S. 90 (2006), postal inspectors learned that Grubbs had ordered a videotape containing child pornography delivered to his home through the mail. They applied to a

> federal Magistrate Judge for a warrant to search Grubbs' home, with the provision that execution of the warrant "will not occur unless and until the parcel [believed to contain the pornography] has been received . . . and has physically been taken into the residence."

Anticipatory warrants require a judge to find (1) that it is *now probable* that (2) contraband, evidence of a crime, or a fugitive *will be* on the described premises (3) when the warrant is executed. The probability determination for an anticipatory warrant also looks at the likelihood that the condition will occur, and therefore that the listed object of seizure will be on the described premises. In other words, two prerequisites of probability must be satisfied. It must be true not only that *if* the triggering condition occurs "there is a fair probability that evidence of a crime will be found in a particular place," but also that there is probable cause to believe the triggering condition *will occur*. In *Grubbs*, the delivery of the videotape to Grubbs' residence would establish probable cause for the search. In addition, the affidavit established probable cause to believe the triggering condition would be satisfied.

Although rarely used, anticipatory warrants are a useful and efficient means for law enforcement to obtain a warrant for contraband expected to be at a future location without waiting for its actual arrival.

The Particularity Requirement

The Fourth Amendment requires that warrants "shall issue particularly describing the place to be searched and the person or things to be seized." Regarding describing the place to be searched, courts have found that a street address — and in multi-unit buildings, an apartment number — is sufficiently specific. So long as the warrant describes the specific address and unit to be searched, the warrant need not specify where the evidence is believed to be located in the building.

The general rule regarding the **particularity requirement** for a specific description of the place to be searched is that it "is enough if the description is such that the officer with a search warrant can, with reasonable effort, ascertain and identify the place intended." *Steele v. United States*, 267 U.S. 498, 503 (1925). Problems arise when the place as described in the search warrant is imprecise and subject to interpretation. The Supreme Court addressed this issue in the case of *Maryland v. Garrison*, 480 U.S. 79 (1987).

In *Garrison*, Baltimore, police officers obtained a warrant to search one Lawrence McWebb and "the premises known as 2036 Park Avenue third floor apartment" for marijuana and related paraphernalia. When they applied for the warrant, the police reasonably believed that only one apartment was on the premises described in the warrant. In fact, the third floor was divided into two apartments, one occupied by McWebb and one by Garrison. Before the officers executing the warrant became aware that they were in a separate apartment occupied by the respondent, they had discovered drugs that eventually were used to convict Garrison of a crime. Garrison appealed his conviction, arguing that the place to be searched as described in the search warrant was overbroad, and anything found in his apartment should be held inadmissible.

In an opinion written by Justice Stevens, the Supreme Court (6–3) upheld the warrant and the ensuing search. The Court held that police acted in good faith and searched in an authorized location.

> Plainly, if the officers had known, or even if they should have known, that there were two separate dwelling units on the third floor of 2036 Park Avenue, they would have been obligated to exclude respondent's apartment from the scope of the requested warrant. But we must judge the constitutionality of their conduct in light of the information available to them at the time they acted.
>
> [T]he validity of the search of respondent's apartment pursuant to a warrant authorizing the search of the entire third floor depends on whether the officers' failure to realize the overbreadth of the warrant was objectively understandable and reasonable. Here it unquestionably was. The objective facts available to the officers at the time suggested no distinction between McWebb's apartment and the third-floor premises. *Maryland v. Garrison,* 480 U.S. at 89

The second component of the particularity requirement involves the items to be seized. The particularity requirement for items sought to be seized pursuant to a search warrant serves several purposes. First, it supports the probable cause requirement. If the police cannot describe specifically what they are looking for, they are unlikely to have probable cause to search for the item and are more likely to be on a fishing expedition. Second, it limits the legitimate scope of searches. If police are searching only for stolen televisions, they may not look in dresser drawers or other places too small to hold them. In other words, the size of the objects sought delineates the scope of the search. Additionally, the search must end once the items designated in a search warrant are found.

To prevent unduly expansive searches, the United States Supreme Court has found overly broad and general descriptions of items to be searched for to violate the particularity requirement. Warrants containing vocabulary such as "evidence of criminality" or contraband, or broad types of items, such as jewelry, electronics, or clothing, are unacceptable. Additionally, rather than listing a category of items, of which there may be many different varieties, the warrant must say as specifically as possible, for example, the specific type of jewelry, the kind of electronics, and the particular item of clothing, for a warrant to be acceptable.

In the following case, the Supreme Court considered the basis for requiring enforcement of the particularity requirement.

Groh v. Ramirez

540 U.S. 551 (2004)

JUSTICE STEVENS delivered the opinion of the Court.

Respondents, Joseph Ramirez and members of his family, live on a large ranch in Butte-Silver Bow County, Montana. Petitioner, Jeff Groh, has been a Special Agent for the Bureau of Alcohol, Tobacco, and Firearms (ATF) since 1989. In February 1997, a concerned citizen informed petitioner that on a number of visits to respondents' ranch the visitor had seen a large stock of weaponry, including an automatic rifle, grenades, a grenade launcher, and a rocket launcher. Based on that information, petitioner prepared and signed an application for a warrant to search the ranch. The application stated that the search was for "any automatic firearms or parts to automatic weapons, destructive devices to include but not limited to grenades, grenade launchers, rocket launchers, and any and all receipts pertaining to the purchase or manufacture of automatic weapons or explosive devices or launchers." Petitioner supported the application with a detailed affidavit, which he also prepared and executed, that set forth the basis for his belief that the listed items were concealed on the ranch. Petitioner then presented these documents to a Magistrate, along with a warrant form that petitioner also had completed. The Magistrate signed the warrant form.

Although the application particularly described the place to be searched and the contraband petitioner expected to find, the warrant itself was less specific; it failed to identify any of the items that petitioner intended to seize. The warrant did not incorporate by reference the itemized list contained in the application. It did, however, recite that the Magistrate was satisfied the affidavit established probable cause to believe that contraband was concealed on the premises, and that sufficient grounds existed for the warrant's issuance.

The day after the Magistrate issued the warrant, petitioner led a team of law enforcement officers, including both federal agents and members of the local sheriff's department, in the search of respondents' premises. The search uncovered no illegal weapons or explosives. When the officers left, petitioner gave Mrs. Ramirez a copy of the search warrant, but not a copy of the application, which had been sealed. The following day, in response to a request from respondents' attorney, petitioner faxed the attorney a copy of the page of the application that listed the items to be seized. No charges were filed against the Ramirezes.

Respondents sued petitioner and the other officers under *Bivens* v. *Six Unknown Fed. Narcotics Agents*, 403 U.S. 388 (1971), and Rev. Stat. §1979, 42 U.S.C. §1983 raising eight claims, including violation of the Fourth Amendment. The District Court entered summary judgment for all defendants. The court found no Fourth Amendment violation. The Court of Appeals held that the warrant was invalid because it did not "describe with particularity the place to be searched and the items to be seized."

II

The warrant was plainly invalid. The Fourth Amendment states unambiguously that "no Warrants shall issue, but upon probable cause, supported by Oath or affirmation, and *particularly describing* the place to be searched, and the persons or things to be seized." (Emphasis added.) The warrant in this case complied with the first three of these requirements: It was based on probable cause and supported by a sworn affidavit, and it described particularly the place of the search. On the fourth requirement, however, the warrant failed altogether. Indeed, petitioner concedes that "the warrant. . . was deficient in particularity because it provided no description of the type of evidence sought."

The fact that the *application* adequately described the "things to be seized" does not save the *warrant* from its facial invalidity. The Fourth Amendment by its terms requires particularity in the warrant, not in the supporting documents. And for good reason. The presence of a search warrant serves a high function, and that high function is not necessarily vindicated when some other document, somewhere, says something about the objects of the search, but the contents of that document are neither known to the person whose home is being searched nor available for her inspection. We do not say that the Fourth Amendment forbids a warrant from cross-referencing other documents. Indeed, most Courts of Appeals have held that a court may construe a warrant with reference to a supporting application or affidavit if the warrant uses appropriate words of incorporation, and if the supporting document accompanies the warrant. But in this case the warrant did not incorporate other documents by reference, nor did either the affidavit or the application (which had been placed under seal) accompany the warrant. Hence, we need not further explore the matter of incorporation.

Petitioner argues that even though the warrant was invalid, the search nevertheless was "reasonable" within the meaning of the Fourth Amendment. He notes that a Magistrate authorized the search on the basis of adequate evidence of probable cause, that petitioner orally described to respondents the items to be seized, and that the search did not exceed the limits intended by the Magistrate and described by petitioner. Thus, petitioner maintains, his search of respondents' ranch was functionally equivalent to a search authorized by a valid warrant.

We disagree. This warrant did not simply omit a few items from a list of many to be seized, or misdescribe a few of several items. Nor did it make what fairly could be characterized as a mere technical mistake or typographical error. Rather, in the space set aside for a description of the items to be seized, the warrant stated that the items consisted of a "single dwelling residence. . . blue in color." In other words, the warrant did not describe the items to be seized *at all*. In this respect the warrant was so obviously deficient that we must regard the search as "warrantless" within the meaning of our case law. Because the right of a man to retreat into his own home and there be free from unreasonable governmental intrusion stands at the very core' of the Fourth Amendment, our cases have firmly established the basic principle of Fourth Amendment law that searches and seizures inside a home without a warrant are presumptively unreasonable. Thus, absent exigent circumstances, a warrantless entry to search for weapons or contraband is unconstitutional even when a felony has been committed and there is probable cause to believe that incriminating evidence will be found within.

Petitioner asks us to hold that a search conducted pursuant to a warrant lacking particularity should be exempt from the presumption of unreasonableness if the goals served by the particularity requirement are otherwise satisfied. He maintains that the search in this case satisfied those goals–which he says are "to prevent general searches, to prevent the seizure of one thing under a warrant describing another, and to prevent warrants from being issued on vague or dubious information," because the scope of the search did not exceed the limits set forth in the application. But unless the particular items described in the affidavit are also set forth in the warrant itself (or at least incorporated by reference, and the affidavit present at the search), there can be no written assurance that the Magistrate actually found probable cause to search for, and to seize, every item mentioned in the affidavit. In this case, for example, it is at least theoretically possible that the Magistrate was satisfied that the search for weapons and explosives was justified by the showing in the affidavit, but not convinced that any evidentiary basis existed for rummaging through respondents' files and papers for receipts pertaining to the purchase or manufacture of such items. Or, conceivably, the Magistrate might have believed that some of the weapons mentioned in the affidavit could have been lawfully possessed and therefore should not be seized. The mere fact that the Magistrate issued a warrant does not necessarily establish that he agreed that the scope of the search should be as broad as the affiant's request. Even though petitioner acted with restraint in conducting the search, the inescapable fact is that this restraint was imposed by the agents themselves, not by a judicial officer.

We have long held, moreover, that the purpose of the particularity requirement is not limited to the prevention of general searches. A particular warrant also "assures the individual whose property is searched or seized of the lawful authority of the executing officer, his need to search, and the limits of his power to search."

It is incumbent on the officer executing a search warrant to ensure the search is lawfully authorized and lawfully conducted. Because petitioner did not have in his possession a warrant particularly describing the things he intended to seize, proceeding with the search was clearly "unreasonable" under the Fourth Amendment. The Court of Appeals correctly held that the search was unconstitutional.

FURTHER CASE LAW, REFLECTIONS, AND QUESTIONS

1. Why did the Court find that the warrant was facially invalid, and what does this mean for future law enforcement procedures?
2. If the police found weapons during the search, do you think they would have been admissible at trial despite the Court's finding the search violated the Fourth Amendment? Remember *United States v. Leon* as you consider the question.
3. In a dissenting opinion, Justice Thomas argued that even though the warrant was defective, the search should be considered constitutional so long as it was reasonable. Do you agree with this sentiment?
4. The requirements for a search warrant are summarized in Box 4.4.

Box 4.3 You Be the Judge

An investigation into fraudulent real estate settlement activities showed that Andresen, while acting as a settlement attorney, had defrauded the purchaser of certain realty (Lot 13T). The investigators obtained warrants to search the petitioner's offices. The warrants listed specific items pertaining to Lot 13T to be seized, "together with other fruits, instrumentalities and evidence of a crime at this time unknown." In the ensuing search, several incriminating documents were seized. *Andresen* was then charged with the crime of false pretenses based on a misrepresentation made to the purchaser of Lot 13T that the title to the property was clear. At trial, a number of the seized documents were admitted as evidence after being authenticated by the prosecution's witnesses. Andresen was found guilty, and the Maryland Court of Special Appeals affirmed the conviction. The United States Supreme Court granted certiorari.
Does the warrant lack sufficient particularity regarding the items to be seized? See *Andresen v. Maryland*, 427 U.S. 463 (1976).

Box 4.4 Summary of Requirements for a Search Warrant

Neutral and Detached Magistrate

Not required via the Fourth Amendment but added by the Court in *Johnson v. United States* (1948). An objective judicial officer, and not someone acting as a rubber stamp for the police, or someone with a personal connection or stake in the outcome, should be making determinations about the validity of a warrant application.

Oath or Affirmation

The affiant on the affidavit must affirm that the information located in the warrant application is accurate to the best of their knowledge. Frequently, the judicial officer will swear the affiant in under oath, but formal swearing-in is generally not required.

Probable Cause

Based upon the facts and information presented, the warrant application should establish that evidence of a crime is likely located in a specific location.

Particularity

The warrant application must describe, with specificity, the place to be searched and the objects to be seized. The objects must be described with enough specificity that a reasonable officer will be able to locate the objects in question.

Executing a Search Warrant

Knock and Announce

Assume the police have reason to believe that an individual has illegal drugs in the form of pills in their home, and that police secure a search warrant authorizing a search of the house. How should they go about executing the warrant? What might happen to the drugs if they knock on the door, identify themselves as police officers, and announce that they have a search warrant for the premises? On the other hand, what might happen if they simply burst through the door unannounced to surprise the resident? What if the police have reason to believe that the resident might be armed? Would that possibly make a "no-knock" entry more or less advisable? Does the manner in which the police gain entry to a dwelling under the authority of a search warrant affect the "reasonableness" of the search? The Court confronted this basic question in *Wilson v. Arkansas.*

Wilson v. Arkansas

514 U.S. 927 (1995)

JUSTICE THOMAS delivered the opinion of the Court.

At the time of the framing, the common law of search and seizure recognized a law enforcement officer's authority to break open the doors of a dwelling, but generally indicated that he first ought to announce his presence and authority. In this case, we hold that this common-law "**knock and announce**" principle forms a part of the reasonableness inquiry under the Fourth Amendment.

I

During November and December 1992, petitioner Sharlene Wilson made a series of narcotics sales to an informant acting at the direction of the Arkansas State Police. In late November, the informant purchased marijuana and methamphetamine at the home that petitioner shared with Bryson Jacobs. On December 30, the informant telephoned petitioner at her home and arranged to meet her at a local store to buy some marijuana. According to testimony presented below, petitioner produced a semiautomatic pistol at this meeting and waved it in the informant's face, threatening to kill her if she turned out to be working for the police. Petitioner then sold the informant a bag of marijuana.

The next day, police officers applied for and obtained warrants to search petitioner's home and to arrest both petitioner and Jacobs. Affidavits filed in support of the warrants set forth the details of the narcotics transactions and stated that Jacobs had previously been convicted of arson and firebombing. The search was conducted later that afternoon. Police officers found the main door to petitioner's home open. While opening an unlocked screen door and entering the residence, they identified themselves as police officers and stated that they had a warrant. Once inside the home, the officers seized marijuana, methamphetamine, valium, narcotics paraphernalia, a gun, and ammunition. They also found petitioner in the bathroom, flushing marijuana down the toilet. Petitioner and Jacobs were arrested and charged with the delivery of marijuana, delivery of methamphetamine, possession of drug paraphernalia, and possession of marijuana.

Before trial, petitioner filed a motion to suppress the evidence seized during the search. Petitioner asserted that the search was invalid on various grounds, including that the officers had failed to "knock and announce" before entering her home. The trial court summarily denied the suppression motion. After a jury trial, petitioner was convicted of all charges and sentenced to 32 years in prison.

The Arkansas Supreme Court affirmed petitioner's conviction on appeal. The court noted that "the officers entered the home *while they were identifying themselves*," but it rejected petitioner's argument that "the Fourth Amendment requires officers to knock and announce prior to entering the residence." (Emphasis added). Finding "no authority for [petitioner's] theory that the knock and announce principle is required by the Fourth Amendment," the court concluded that neither Arkansas law nor the Fourth Amendment required suppression of the evidence.

We granted certiorari to resolve the conflict among the lower courts as to whether the common law knock and announce principle forms a part of the Fourth Amendment reasonableness inquiry. We hold that it does, and accordingly reverse and remand.

II

The Fourth Amendment to the Constitution protects "[t]he right of the people to be secure in their persons, houses, papers, and effects, against unreasonable searches and seizures." In evaluating the scope of this right, we have looked to the traditional protections against unreasonable searches and seizures afforded by the common law at the time of the framing. Although the underlying command of the Fourth Amendment is always that searches and seizures be reasonable, our effort to give content to this term may be guided by the meaning ascribed to it by the Framers of the Amendment. An examination of the common law of search and seizure leaves no doubt that the reasonableness of a search of a dwelling may depend in part on whether law enforcement officers announced their presence and authority prior to entering.

Although the common law generally protected a man's house as his castle of defense and asylum, common-law courts long have held that when the King is party, the sheriff (if the doors be not open) may break the party's house, either to arrest him, or to do other execution of the K[ing]'s process, if otherwise he cannot enter." To this rule, however, common-law courts appended an important qualification:

> "But before he breaks it, he ought to signify the cause of his coming, and to make request to open doors . . . , for the law without a default in the owner abhors the destruction or breaking of any house (which is for the habitation and safety of man) by which great damage and inconvenience might ensue to the party, when no default is in him; for perhaps he did not know of the process, of which, if he had notice, it is to be presumed that he would obey it." 77 Eng Rep, at 195-196.

At common law was that "the officer may break open the door, if he be sure the offender is there, if after acquainting them of the business, and demanding the prisoner, he refuses to open the door." The common-law knock-and-announce principle was woven quickly into the fabric of early American law. Most of the States that ratified the Fourth Amendment had enacted constitutional provisions or statutes generally incorporating English common law, and a few States had enacted statutes specifically embracing the common-law view that the breaking of the door of a dwelling was permitted once admittance was refused. Early American courts similarly embraced the common-law knock-and-announce principle.

Our own cases have acknowledged that the common-law principle of announcement is embedded in Anglo-American law, but we have never squarely held that this principle is an element of the reasonableness inquiry under the Fourth Amendment. We now so hold. Given the longstanding common-law endorsement of the practice of announcement, we have little doubt that the Framers of the Fourth Amendment thought that the method of an officer's entry into a dwelling was among the factors to be considered in assessing the reasonableness of a search or seizure. Contrary to the decision below, we hold that in some circumstances an officer's unannounced entry into a home might be unreasonable under the Fourth Amendment.

This is not to say, of course, that every entry must be preceded by an announcement. The Fourth Amendment's flexible requirement of reasonableness should not be read to mandate a rigid rule of announcement that ignores countervailing law enforcement interests. As even petitioner concedes, the common-law principle of announcement was never stated as an inflexible rule requiring announcement under all circumstances.

Indeed, at the time of the framing, the common-law admonition that an officer "ought to signify the cause of his coming," had not been extended conclusively to the context of felony arrests. The common-law principle gradually was applied to cases involving felonies, but at the same time the courts continued to recognize that under certain circumstances the presumption in favor of announcement necessarily would give way to contrary considerations.

Thus, because the common-law rule was justified in part by the belief that announcement generally would avoid "the destruction or breaking of any house by which great damage and inconvenience might ensue," courts acknowledged that the presumption in favor of announcement would yield under circumstances presenting a threat of physical violence.

Similarly, courts held that an officer may dispense with announcement in cases where a prisoner escapes from him and retreats to his dwelling. Proof of "demand and refusal" was deemed unnecessary in such cases because it would be a "senseless ceremony" to require an officer in pursuit of a recently escaped arrestee to make an announcement prior to breaking the door to retake him. Finally, courts have indicated that unannounced entry may be justified where police officers have reason to believe that evidence would likely be destroyed if advance notice were given.

We need not attempt a comprehensive catalog of the relevant countervailing factors here. For now, we leave to the lower courts the task of determining the circumstances under which an unannounced entry is reasonable under the Fourth Amendment. We simply hold that although a search or seizure of a dwelling might be constitutionally defective if police officers enter without prior announcement, law enforcement interests may also establish the reasonableness of an unannounced entry.

III

Respondent contends that the judgment below should be affirmed because the unannounced entry in this case was justified for two reasons. First, respondent argues that police officers reasonably believed that a prior announcement would have placed them in peril, given their knowledge that petitioner had threatened a government informant with a semiautomatic weapon and that Mr. Jacobs had previously been convicted of arson and firebombing. Second, respondent suggests that prior announcement would have produced an unreasonable risk that petitioner would destroy easily disposable narcotics evidence.

These considerations may well provide the necessary justification for the unannounced entry in this case. Because the Arkansas Supreme Court did not address their sufficiency, however, we remand to allow the state courts to make any necessary findings of fact and to make the determination of reasonableness in the first instance.

FURTHER CASE LAW, REFLECTIONS, AND QUESTIONS

1. What do you think is the most likely resolution of this case on remand to the state courts? Based on the facts presented in the opinion, would you be inclined to conclude that the officers' unannounced entry was reasonable or unreasonable?

2. Even if a search warrant is supported by probable cause and particularly describes the place to be searched and things to be seized, the way the search is conducted can present challenges. For example, what if a properly issued warrant authorizes the seizure of a named item (*e.g.*, drugs), but while searching for that item, the police discover other unrelated but illegal material (*e.g.*, child pornography) that is not named in the warrant? Can the police legally seize the unnamed item, or must they ignore it because the search warrant does not authorize its seizure? We will confront this issue when discussing the "plain-view" exception to the warrant requirement.

3. Sometimes, search warrants become "**stale**." For example, a warrant signed in January authorizing the search of a dwelling for illegal drugs may be hopelessly outdated if the police delay until April to search. Even if probable cause existed to believe that illegal drugs were in the named residence when the warrant was issued, there might be no basis to assume that the drugs remain there several months later. Although the Fourth Amendment imposes no strict time limit defining when a delay between the issuance and execution of a search warrant is "unreasonable," statutes in many jurisdictions dictate that search warrants remain valid no longer than a fixed period after they are signed. *See, e.g.*, Federal Rule of Criminal Procedure 41(c)(1) (search warrant shall command the officer to search "within a specified period of time not to exceed 10 days").

4. Statutes in many jurisdictions also require that search warrants be executed during daytime hours (generally 6:00 a.m. through 10:00 p.m.) unless the issuing judge or magistrate specifically approves a nighttime search. In *Gooding v. United States*, 416 U.S. 430 (1974), the Supreme Court ruled that a federal statute governing searches for controlled substances requires no special showing for a nighttime search other than a showing that the contraband is likely to be on the property or person to be searched at that time.

5. Do cases involving felony drug investigations present such an inherently great risk that evidence will be destroyed or violence will ensue if the police knock and announce their identity and purpose before executing a search warrant, that "no-knock" entries always are reasonable? The Wisconsin Supreme Court thought so, but the United States Supreme Court unanimously disagreed in *Richards v. Wisconsin*, 520 U.S. 385 (1997). The Court rejected the "considerable overgeneralization" that all felony drug cases require "no-knock" entries.

   In *Richards*, the police suspected Steiney Richards of possessing narcotics but could not receive a judge's approval for a "no-knock" warrant to search his hotel room. Instead, they obtained a standard search warrant requiring them to knock on the door and identify themselves as officers before entering by force. Once at the hotel, a police officer knocked on Richards' door, identifying himself as a hotel custodian. Upon opening the door, Richards saw a uniformed officer and quickly slammed it shut. The officers broke through the door, grabbed Richards, who was trying to escape, and found cocaine and cash in his bathroom. At trial, Richards challenged the constitutionality of the officer's search, but this was denied. On appeal, Wisconsin's Supreme Court affirmed, holding that when serving warrants for felony narcotics offenses, police need not knock and announce their presence before entering.

   After granting certiorari, the United States Supreme Court unanimously rejected Wisconsin's blanket exception for searches involving drug crimes. Instead, it held that police must have reasonable suspicion that knocking and announcing their presence would be dangerous or futile or would inhibit the effective investigation of the crime by facilitating escape or destruction of evidence. Additionally, this analysis should be done on a case-by-case basis. Accordingly, although the Court rejected the Wisconsin court's blanket exception to the knock-and-announce requirement, it concluded that "the officers' no-knock entry into Richards' hotel room did not violate the Fourth Amendment because the circumstances, in this case, show that the officers had a reasonable suspicion that Richards might destroy evidence if given further opportunity to do so.

6. On March 13, 2020, Louisville, Kentucky police officers served a no-knock warrant on the apartment of Breonna Taylor, looking for drugs. When police entered the home, they were shot at by Breonna's boyfriend, Kenneth Walker, who assumed someone was breaking into their apartment due to officers not announcing or knocking. The unarmed Breonna Taylor was shot eight times and died from her injuries. Even before the unfortunate death of Breonna Taylor, the use of no-knock warrants was heavily criticized, and since her death, scrutiny of the practice has increased. (Bates, 2022).

7. No-knock warrants are dangerous for citizens as well as the police. Over a six-year period, between 2010 and 2016, 94 people — including 13 officers — were

killed while serving a no-knock warrant (Sack, 2017). The police and proponents of no-knock warrants argue they are needed because of the danger associated with serving warrants, especially on residents involved in drug crimes. Opponents of no-knock warrants argue that no-knock warrants do not increase safety and present more of a danger for citizens and the police. Additionally, the danger of executing a warrant on a home associated with drug activity is grossly overestimated. As most citizens do, people should be allowed to answer the door and comply with the police. Lastly, the use of no-knock warrants has increased significantly, and the ease of obtaining one has increased. Some judicial officers approve them when the police have not even requested one. Some states have taken steps to reduce and restrict the use of no-knock warrants, but opponents argue that regulations are not enough and that abolishing their use is the only solution (Dolan, 2019). Four states have banned no-knock warrants — Connecticut, Florida, Oregon, and Virginia (Bates, 2022).

The Length of Time Between Knocking and Entering

When police officers must knock on a door and announce their presence and have a search warrant, how long must they wait for a response before forcibly entering the premises? The Supreme Court considered this question in *United States v. Banks*, 540 U.S. 31 (2003).

Las Vegas Police and FBI agents arrived at the home of Lashawn Banks with a warrant to search his apartment for drugs. Police officers knocked loudly on the front door and announced their presence and purpose. They waited between 15 and 20 seconds, and when Banks did not come to the door, they broke it down with a battering ram. Banks was arrested, but before his trial, he filed a motion to suppress the evidence found in his apartment because he claimed that the forced entry had been unlawful, since officers did not wait long enough before breaking down the door, and there was no evidence that waiting longer would have had negative consequences. The District Court disagreed and found the evidence admissible. On appeal, the Ninth Circuit Court of Appeals reversed the District Court's ruling and ordered the evidence seized suppressed because the police did not wait a reasonable time before entering.

The United States Supreme Court granted certiorari and unanimously held that the police acted reasonably under the circumstances. The Court found that given the ease with which drugs can be destroyed, the 15-to-20 second wait before entry was reasonable. The Court explicitly said that the outcome may have been different had a different crime and evidence that could not be destroyed so quickly been involved. For example, what if the police had a search warrant to look for a grand piano? The Court once again called for a case-by-case analysis based on the totality of circumstances.

Box 4.5 You Be the Judge

Police received the following information regarding two men from a confidential informant.

- He had previously been in their apartment when he had received and sold drugs.
- The men would be receiving a large (15 kg, 33 lbs.) delivery of cocaine soon.
- He had previously seen a gun on top of a refrigerator in the apartment
- The men had barricaded the door with a wooden board.

Based on this information, the police obtained a search warrant for the apartment. In executing the warrant, the police did not knock or announce their presence out of fear that the defendants would dispose of the cocaine before the officers could enter the Apartment. They were also fearful for their safety because of the gun being in the apartment. After entering the apartment, police found a large amount of cocaine and a gun. The defendants were arrested. They filed a motion with the court to exclude the seized evidence from the trial because the police improperly entered the apartment.

How should the court rule? Would having any additional information affect your ruling?

See *United States v. Bates*, 84 F.3d 790 (6th Cir (1996)

Detaining and Searching Occupants of a Dwelling

Another issue arises when law enforcement officers have a warrant to search a dwelling. In these circumstances, may they detain (not arrest) the occupant while conducting the search and then arrest them based on the search results? The United States Supreme Court upheld this practice in *Michigan v. Summers*, 452 U.S. 692 (1981). "A warrant to search for contraband founded on probable cause implicitly carries with it the limited authority to detain the occupants of the premises while a proper search is conducted." 452 U.S., at 705. Similarly, in *Illinois v. McArthur*, 531 U.S. 326 (2001), the justices ruled (8–1) that the police acted reasonably when, having probable cause to believe that a suspect had illegal drugs in his home, they denied the suspect entry into his house for a period of approximately two hours while they obtained a warrant authorizing them to search the home for the drugs.

Once the police decide they will detain individuals present at the scene when a search warrant is issued, do they have the right to search each person? This question was addressed in *Ybarra v. Illinois*, 444 U.S. 85 (1979). Police officers obtained a search warrant to search a tavern and the tavern owner for evidence of the offense of possession of a controlled substance. With a warrant in hand, seven or eight officers proceeded to the tavern. Upon entering it, the officers announced their purpose and advised all those present that they were going to conduct a "cursory search for weapons." One of the officers proceeded to pat down each of the 9 to 13 customers present in the tavern, while the remaining officers engaged in an extensive search of the premises. When the officer frisked Ybarra, one of the patrons, he felt what he described as "a cigarette pack with objects in it." After the officer had frisked the other patrons, he returned to Ybarra and removed the cigarette pack from his pants pocket. Inside the pack, the officer found heroin. Ybarra was charged with possession of narcotics. He filed a motion with the court to suppress the heroin, arguing that it had been seized via an illegal search.

In considering the matter, the Supreme Court held that the search of Ybarra was unconstitutional. The Court noted that each individual maintained their rights under the Constitution. As such, the requisite level of suspicion or probable cause was needed to conduct extensive searches of their clothing or persons. The Court found that although the frisk for weapons of each of the patrons was reasonable for officer safety reasons, there was no probable cause to believe anybody but the tavern owner possessed contraband. The search of Ybarra's cigarette pack went beyond the permissible scope of the *Terry* frisk.

Remedy for Improper Execution of a Warrant

What should happen if, for example, the police fail to knock and announce their presence when executing a search warrant? More specifically, assume the police act unreasonably while making entry to search a home via a valid search warrant, thereby violating the Fourth Amendment rights of the person or persons inside. Additionally, assume the police discover contraband after entering the premises, as anticipated in their search warrant. Should the evidence they discover be admissible as evidence against the defendant? Or should suppression of the evidence be required by applying the exclusionary rule? The Court addressed these questions in *Hudson v. Michigan*, 547 U.S. 586 (2006).

Hudson concerned a warrant-based search at the home of Booker Hudson that resulted in the seizure of large quantities of drugs and a loaded gun. Police knocked on the door and announced their presence. After waiting only three or four seconds, the police used force to enter the residence. The prosecution conceded that the short period between the knock and the home's entry violated the Fourth Amendment. However, the question the Court had to answer was whether excluding the evidence seized was the appropriate remedy for the violation. It was not contested that the Fourth Amendment was violated by the police officers' failure to wait more than three or four seconds after announcing their presence before entering Hudson's home.

The Court split 5–4, with the majority opinion written by Justice Scalia. The Supreme Court held that suppression was not an appropriate remedy for a knock-and-announce violation, This was based on the view that the interests protected by the knock-and-announce rule are to protect police officers from surprised residents retaliating in presumed self-defense, to protect private property from damage, and to protect the privacy and dignity of residents. On the other hand, the Court held that the knock-and-announce rule does not exist to promote one's interest in preventing the government from seeing or taking evidence described in a warrant.

The Court also argued that applying the exclusionary rule to violations of the knock and announce rule would increase the "cost" of the exclusionary rule too much. In other words, too many cases would likely get thrown out due to mistakes made by the police when executing a warrant. Furthermore, the Court also said a proper remedy exists for this type of violation. According to the Court, a person whose rights are violated in this circumstance can file a Title 42 §1983 lawsuit against the police. A Section 1983 lawsuit is a federal lawsuit that can be filed against any state actor who has violated a citizen's Constitutional rights. There are also state-equivalent lawsuits that can be filed as well. Do you think a potential Section 1983 lawsuit is enough to deter the police from violating the knock-and-announce rule? Do you think it is an effective remedy? In a dissenting opinion, Justice Breyer argued that if the exclusionary rule does not apply to knock and announce violations, there is no means to deter police from ignoring the knock and announce rule.

Conclusion

The Warrant Clause of the Fourth Amendment provides an essential protection and check on government power for citizens of the United States. While not required in all instances, the use of a warrant to authorize searches, seizures, and arrests is the preferred method of operation. Although frequently not required for an arrest, particularly when made outside the home, search warrants are often a prerequisite to conducting a valid search. The requirements that must be met for a search warrant to be issued are straightforward and explicitly stated in the Fourth Amendment. Search warrants require an objective judicial determination of probable cause made by a neutral and detached magistrate, based upon the oath or affirmation of a government official that particularly describes the place to be searched or the person or thing to be seized. As shown in this chapter, there have been instances where the Supreme Court has had to interpret the warrants clause and clarify its requirements. These instances are relatively rare, particularly after the adoption of the totality of circumstances test for determining the presence of probable cause.

Much more frequent conflicts arise when dealing with the execution of warrants. While the Supreme Court has made clear that an arrest of a person inside a home requires an arrest warrant, how police are to enter the home to execute the warrant has been more troubling. The same can be said for executing a search warrant for a residence. Once again, the Court has been required to balance the competing objectives of public safety and officer safety against individuals' rights to privacy within their homes.

The Supreme Court adopted the "knock and announce" rule to achieve this balance. By requiring police to knock and announce their presence before forcibly entering a home, the Court sought to serve law enforcement's and individuals' interests. Such a rule is not unreasonable. That being said, by ruling that a violation of the knock and announce rule is not grounds for excluding evidence found in the corresponding search or dismissal of charges against an improper arrest, the Court has removed any incentive police have to adhere to the entry requirement.

KEY TERMS

affiant
affidavit
Aguilar-Spinelli test
anticipatory warrant
arrest warrant
basis of knowledge
knock and announce
particularity requirement
reliability
search warrant
stale
totality of circumstances
veracity

REVIEW QUESTIONS

Directions: Please refer to what you learned in this chapter to help you respond.

1. What are the four requirements for a warrant? What requirement was added by the Court that is not mentioned in the Constitution?
2. What are the two types of particularity required to be contained in a search warrant?
3. What is the *Aguilar-Spinelli* test, and what is its purpose? What are the two different prongs to the test?
4. How did the *Gates* test change the *Aguilar-Spinelli* test? What would a proponent of the Crime Control perspective think of the change from the *Aguilar-Spinelli* test to the *Gates* test?
5. What is the procedure used if a court or defendant suspects a search warrant affidavit contained false statements?
6. Under what conditions can the police possibly obtain a "no-knock" warrant?
7. When executing a warrant on a home, and the police don't have a no-knock warrant, how long must the police wait after knocking before entering the house?

8. If the police violate the knock and announce rule, what is the remedy or possible repercussions for violating the law? Do you think the exclusionary rule should be used in this circumstance?
9. What is an anticipatory warrant?
10. Provide examples of a magistrate who is not neutral.

APPLYING THE LAW

Below are five hypothetical fact scenarios. To practice your understanding of the law that you learned in this chapter and your ability to apply it, answer each question posed by applying that law to the hypothetical scenarios. Your answers should be supported by relevant case law and judicially created rules and tests.

1. Lee robbed a local jewelry store, making off with 10 rings. That night, Lee gave his girlfriend Mary a ring worth $10,000. Knowing that Lee is a criminal justice graduate student living on a paltry stipend who could not afford such a ring, she told her police cadet supervisor Butch that she thinks Lee stole the ring. Butch applied for a search warrant for Lee's apartment providing the above information as probable cause. A magistrate signed the warrant and Butch went to search Lee's home. On Lee's dining room table, Butch found nine rings. When Lee and his two roommates got home a few minutes later, Butch placed Lee under arrest.

   Did the search of Lee's home violate the Fourth Amendment?

   Should the ring(s) be excluded from Lee's trial?

   Was the arrest of Lee constitutional?

2. Detectives Hank and Bobby obtain information sufficient for a search warrant to search for cocaine in Peggy's house. They arrive at Peggy's house with a SWAT team. Bobby knocks loudly. After waiting 5 seconds, Hank uses a battering ram to knock down the door and enters the house with the SWAT team. Hearing the commotion, Peggy runs down the stairs in a bathrobe and her hair in curlers. Police find the cocaine in the kitchen and arrest Peggy.

   Peggy's lawyer files a motion to exclude the cocaine from the trial. Should Peggy win? Why or why not?

3. Ted owns a 10-unit apartment building. Police received information from a reliable source that Ted is dealing cocaine out of one of the apartments in his building. Police obtain a warrant with this information to search the building and the apartments therein. Armed with the search warrant, they enter the lobby of the building and search each apartment. Police find cocaine in the apartment that Bob lives in. Ted is arrested.

Were Bob's rights violated under the Fourth Amendment? Should the evidence discovered be excluded from his trial?

4. Detective Sue receives a call from her confidential informant, Pam. Pam has been an informant for 5 years and has been correct with her information about half of the time. Pam tells Sue that her brother Joe hijacked a truck the day before and made off with 30 televisions. She tells Sue the details of the robbery, when it occurred, who Joe's accomplices were, and what the post-robbery plan was. She also says that Joe is storing the televisions in the garage at his house. Based on this information, Sue applies for a warrant to search Joe's house.

   Should the warrant be granted? Discuss arguments for and against the issuance of the warrant.

5. An affidavit supporting a search warrant describes the informant as "having provided accurate information in at least 10 prior investigations." Internal police records reveal the informant only assisted twice, and both times the tips were inaccurate. The warrant was issued, and drugs were found in the area described.

   The defense attorney files a motion to have the drugs suppressed due to the falsehood contained in the affidavit. Should the drugs be excluded from trial?

ORAL ARGUMENTS

Draper v. United States: www.oyez.org/cases/1958/136
Franks v. Delaware: www.oyez.org/cases/1977/77-5176
Groh v. Ramirez: www.oyez.org/cases/2003/02-811
Illinois v. Gates: www.oyez.org/cases/1980-1989/1982/1982_81_430/argument
Shadwick v. City of Tampa: www.oyez.org/cases/1971/71-5445
Wilson v. Arkansas: www.oyez.org/cases/1990-1999/1994/1994_94_5707/argument

REFERENCES

Bates, J. (2022, March 11). Breonna Taylor's killing and what happened to no-knock warrants. *Time.* Retrieved from: https://time.com/6156590/breonna-taylor-no-knock-warrants/

Dolan, B. (2019). To knock or not to knock? No-knock warrants and confrontational policing. 93 *St. John's Law Review, 93,* 201.

Duizend, R. V., Sutton, L., & Carter, C. (1986). *The search warrant process: Preconception, perceptions, and practice.* National Institute of Justice. Retrieved from: https://www.ojp.gov/pdffiles1/Digitization/93585NCJRS.pdf

Sack, K. (2017). Door-busting drug raids leave a trail of blood. *New York Times.* Retrieved from: https://www.nytimes.com/interactive/2017/03/18/us/forced-entry-warrant-drug-raid.html

CHAPTER 5

Seizures of People

LEARNING OBJECTIVES

After reading this chapter, students should be able to:

- Explain when an arrest or search warrant is required before an arrest may be made.
- Explain when warrantless arrests are permissible.
- Understand when force may be used in making an arrest.
- Define and describe a stop and a frisk.
- Comprehend the concept and nuances associated with reasonable suspicion.
- Describe and know the differences between seizure, stop, arrest, and when someone has been seized for Fourth Amendment purposes.
- Critically analyze the Fourth Amendment and issues linked to it.
- Describe the different nuances concerning when a "stop" has occurred, how long a stop may last, and when hearsay evidence may be used to make a stop.
- Explain when an officer may frisk a detainee, the permissible scope of the frisk, and when the police can seize contraband during a frisk.

Introduction

The Fourth Amendment regulates "seizures" of "persons." In this chapter, we will learn about two categories of seizures of the person: arrests and what is commonly referred to as "stops." An **arrest** and **stop** are both seizures within the meaning of the Fourth Amendment and run on a continuum of severity, with a "stop" considered the least intrusive and an arrest the most invasive. Although they are both considered seizures within the meaning of the Fourth Amendment, arrests and stops differ in important respects, including (1) the standard or test used to determine whether an arrest or stop is justified; (2) the factual showing required to satisfy the respective legal standards; and (3) what the police lawfully can (and cannot) do after making an arrest or stop, including (a) how long they can detain a suspect and (b) whether and how thoroughly a suspect can be searched.

As you read the materials in this chapter, think about how the Supreme Court tried to balance the interests of individual liberty and public safety. We begin by considering these issues in the more traditional context of arrests.

Arrests

In the context of criminal justice, an arrest is the act of taking an individual into custody to charge the arrestee with a criminal offense. As a fundamental aspect of law enforcement, arrests represent a critical juncture where the state's powers intersect with individuals' rights and liberties.

Arrests protect public safety and ensure the proper functioning of the criminal justice system. By apprehending those believed to have committed crimes, police officers aim to prevent further harm, maintain social order, and facilitate the administration of justice. Moreover, arrests enable authorities to investigate and gather crucial evidence to support criminal charges.

The Fourth Amendment to the United States Constitution is pivotal in regulating arrests, mandating that individuals be protected from "unreasonable searches and seizures." As such, law enforcement officers must have probable cause to believe that an individual has committed a crime before making an arrest. This standard requires more than mere suspicion; rather, it demands a reasonable belief based on credible information or direct observation.

Warrantless Arrests

While arrests may be made with or without an arrest warrant, the overwhelming majority are warrantless. There are limits to when a warrantless arrest is permissible. In general, there are four circumstances when an individual may be placed under arrest.

Direct Observation

Police may arrest a person without a warrant if they observe the arrestee committing a crime. While this common law principle seems obvious, it has evolved to include observations involving senses other than sight. Firsthand observations by an officer through any of their five senses: sight, hearing, smell, touch, or taste can be used in establishing probable cause that a crime was committed. (It is worth noting that taste rarely establishes probable cause.) Consider the following examples.

- Smell. A patrol officer can smell alcohol on the breath of a driver who was stopped for driving erratically. This observation can establish probable cause that the driver was operating a motor vehicle while intoxicated.
- Touch. A patrol officer stops and frisks an individual based on reasonable suspicion that they recently committed a crime. During the frisk, he feels a hard object in the individual's waistband and immediately identifies it as a gun.
- Hearing. A patrol officer hears someone making incriminating statements about the crime they recently committed.

While observations other than sight alone are insufficient to justify a warrantless arrest, they can support an arrest based on direct visual observation.

Arrests Made in Public Places

At common law, "[a] peace officer was permitted to arrest without a warrant for a misdemeanor or felony committed in his presence as well as for a felony not committed in his presence if there was reasonable grounds for making the arrest." *Watson*, 423 U.S., at 418. This rule was carried forward from colonial times and was widely recognized in the states. Indeed, Congress had granted numerous federal law enforcement authorities, including postal inspectors, who were responsible for the arrest in Watson, to make warrantless arrests on probable cause. One justification for the historical rule, as well as the decision in *Watson*, was the reality that "a constitutional rule permitting felony arrests only with a warrant. . . could severely hamper effective law enforcement." 423 U.S., at 431 (Powell, J., concurring). This rule is based on the lack of an expectation of privacy in a public setting.

Arrest Warrant Required

An arrest warrant is required to arrest a person in limited circumstances. As explained in *Payton v. New York*, the warrant requirement is generally limited to arrests made in the home.

Payton v. New York

445 U.S. 573 (1980)

MR. JUSTICE STEVENS delivered the opinion of the Court.

On January 14, 1970, after two days of intensive investigation, New York detectives had assembled evidence sufficient to establish probable cause to believe that Theodore Payton had murdered the manager of a gas station two days earlier. At about 7:30 a.m. on January 15, six officers went to Payton's apartment in the Bronx, intending to arrest him. They had not obtained a warrant. Although light and music emanated from the apartment, there was no response to their knock on the metal door. They summoned emergency assistance and, about 30 minutes later, used crowbars to break open the door and enter the apartment. No one was there. In plain view, however, was a .30-caliber shell casing that was seized and later admitted into evidence at Payton's murder trial.

In due course, Payton surrendered to the police, was indicted for murder, and moved to suppress the evidence taken from his apartment. The trial judge held that the warrantless and forcible entry was authorized by the New York Code of Criminal Procedure, and that the evidence in plain view was properly seized. He found that exigent circumstances justified the officers' failure to announce their purpose before entering the apartment, as required by the statute. He had no occasion, however, to decide whether those circumstances also would have justified the failure to obtain a warrant, because he concluded that the warrantless entry was adequately supported by the statute without regard to the circumstances. The Appellate Division, First Department, summarily affirmed....

II

It is familiar history that indiscriminate searches and seizures conducted under the authority of "general warrants" were the immediate evils that motivated the framing and adoption of the Fourth Amendment. Indeed, as originally proposed in the House of Representatives, the draft contained only one clause, which directly imposed limitations on the issuance of warrants, but imposed no express restrictions on warrantless searches or seizures. As it was ultimately adopted, however, the Amendment contained two separate clauses, the first protecting the basic right to be free from unreasonable searches and seizures and the second requiring that warrants be particular and supported by probable cause. The Amendment provides:

> The right of the people to be secure in their persons, houses, papers, and effects, against unreasonable searches and seizures, shall not be violated, and no Warrants shall issue, but upon probable cause, supported by Oath or affirmation, and particularly describing the place to be searched, and the persons or things to be seized.

It is thus perfectly clear that the evil the Amendment was designed to prevent was broader than the abuse of a general warrant. Unreasonable searches or seizures conducted without any warrant at all are condemned by the plain language of the first clause of the Amendment. Almost a century ago, the Court stated in resounding terms that the principles reflected in the Amendment "reached farther than the concrete form" of the specific cases that gave it birth, and "apply to all invasions on the part of the government and its employes of the sanctity of a man's home and the privacies of life." *Boyd v. United States,* 116 U.S. 616, 630 (1886). Without pausing to consider whether that broad language may require some qualification, it is sufficient to note that the warrantless arrest of a person is a species of seizure required by the Amendment to be reasonable.

The simple language of the Amendment applies equally to seizures of persons and to seizures of property. Our analysis in this case may therefore properly commence with rules that have been well established in Fourth Amendment litigation involving tangible items. As the Court reiterated just a few years ago, the physical entry of the home is the chief evil against which the wording of the Fourth Amendment is directed. And we have long adhered to the view that the warrant procedure minimizes the danger of needless intrusions of that sort.

It is a "basic principle of Fourth Amendment law" that searches and seizures inside a home without a warrant are presumptively unreasonable. As the late Judge Leventhal recognized, this distinction has equal force when the seizure of a person is involved. Writing on the constitutional issue now before us for the United States Court of Appeals for the District of Columbia Circuit sitting en banc, *Dorman v. United States,* 435 F.2d 385 (1970), Judge Leventhal first noted the settled rule that warrantless arrests in public places are valid. He immediately recognized, however, that "[a] greater burden is placed... on officials who enter a home or dwelling without consent. Freedom from intrusion into the home or dwelling is the archetype of the privacy protection secured by the Fourth Amendment." 435 F.2d at 389.

His analysis of this question then focused on the long-settled premise that, absent exigent circumstances, a warrantless entry to search for weapons or contraband is unconstitutional even when a felony has been committed and there is probable cause to believe that incriminating evidence will be found within. He reasoned that the constitutional protection afforded to the individual's interest in the privacy of his own home is equally applicable to a warrantless entry for the purpose of arresting a resident of the house; for it is inherent in such an entry that a search for the suspect may be required before he can be apprehended. Judge Leventhal concluded that an entry to arrest and an entry to search for and to seize property implicate the same interest in preserving the privacy and the sanctity of the home, and justify the same level of constitutional protection.

This reasoning has been followed in other Circuits. Thus, the Second Circuit recently summarized its position in *United States v. Reed,* 572 F.2d 412, 423 (1978).

> To be arrested in the home involves not only the invasion attendant to all arrests, but also an invasion of the sanctity of the home. This is simply too substantial an invasion to allow without a warrant, at least in the absence of exigent circumstances, even when it is accomplished under statutory authority and when probable cause is clearly present.

We find this reasoning to be persuasive and in accord with this Court's Fourth Amendment decisions.

The majority of the New York Court of Appeals, however, suggested that there is a substantial difference in the relative intrusiveness of an entry to search for property and an entry to search for a person. It is true that the area that may legally be searched is broader when executing a search warrant than when executing an arrest warrant in the home. This difference may be more theoretical than real, however, because the police may need to check the entire premises for safety reasons, and sometimes they ignore the restrictions on searches incident to arrest.

But the critical point is that any differences in the intrusiveness of entries to search and entries to arrest are merely ones of degree, rather than kind. The two intrusions share this fundamental characteristic: the breach of the entrance to an individual's home. The Fourth Amendment protects the individual's privacy in a variety of settings. In none is the zone of privacy more clearly defined than when bounded by the unambiguous physical dimensions of an individual's home — a zone that finds its roots in clear and specific constitutional terms: "The right of the people to be secure in their. . . houses. . . shall not be violated." That language unequivocally establishes the proposition that, at the very core [of the Fourth Amendment] stands the right of a man to retreat into his own home and there be free from unreasonable governmental intrusion.

In terms that apply equally to seizures of property and to seizures of persons, the Fourth Amendment has drawn a firm line at the entrance to the house. Absent exigent circumstances, that threshold may not reasonably be crossed without a warrant.

III

Without contending that *United States v. Watson,* decided the question presented by these appeals, New York argues that the reasons that support the *Watson* holding require a similar result here. In *Watson,* the Court relied on (a) the well settled common law rule that. a warrantless arrest in a public place is valid if the arresting officer had probable cause to believe the suspect is a felon; b) the clear consensus among the States adhering to that well settled common law rule; and (c) the expression of the judgment of Congress that such an arrest is "reasonable." We consider each of these reasons as it applies to a warrantless entry into a home for the purpose of making a routine felony arrest. . . .

B

A majority of the States that have taken a position on the question permit warrantless entry into the home to arrest even in the absence of exigent circumstances. At this time, 24 States permit such warrantless entries; 15 States clearly prohibit them, though 3 States do so on federal constitutional grounds alone; and 11 States have apparently taken no position on the question.

But these current figures reflect a significant decline during the last decade in the number of States permitting warrantless entries for arrest. Recent dicta in this Court raising questions about the practice, and Federal Courts of Appeals' decisions on point, have led state courts to focus on the issue. Virtually all of the state courts that have had to confront the constitutional issue directly have held warrantless entries into the home to arrest to be invalid in the absence of exigent circumstances. Three state courts have relied on Fourth Amendment grounds alone, while seven have squarely placed their decisions on both federal and state constitutional grounds.

A longstanding, widespread practice is not immune from constitutional scrutiny. But neither is it to be lightly brushed aside. This is particularly so when the constitutional standard is as amorphous as the word "reasonable," and when custom and contemporary norms necessarily play such a large role in the constitutional analysis. In this case, although the weight of state law authority is clear, there is by no means the kind of virtual unanimity on this question that was present in *United States v. Watson* with regard to warrantless arrests in public places. *See* 423 U.S. at 422-423. Only 24 of the 50 States currently sanction warrantless entries into the home to arrest, and there is an obvious declining trend. Further, the strength of the trend is greater than the numbers alone indicate. Seven state courts have recently held that warrantless home arrests violate their respective State Constitutions. That is significant because, by invoking a state constitutional provision, a state court immunizes its decision from review by this Court. This heightened degree of immutability underscores the depth of the principle underlying the result.

IV

The parties have argued at some length about the practical consequences of a warrant requirement as a precondition to a felony arrest in the home. In the absence of any evidence that effective law enforcement has suffered in those States that already have such a requirement, we are inclined to view such arguments with skepticism. More fundamentally, however, such arguments of policy must give way to a constitutional command that we consider to be unequivocal.

Finally, we note the State's suggestion that only a search warrant based on probable cause to believe the suspect is at home at a given time can adequately protect the privacy interests at stake, and since such a warrant requirement is manifestly impractical, there need be no warrant of any kind. We find this ingenious argument unpersuasive. It is true that an arrest warrant requirement may afford less protection than a search warrant requirement, but it will suffice to interpose the magistrate's determination of probable cause between the zealous officer and the citizen. If there is sufficient evidence of a citizen's participation in a felony to persuade a judicial officer that his arrest is justified, it is constitutionally reasonable to require him to open his doors to the officers of the law. Thus, for Fourth Amendment purposes, an arrest warrant founded on probable cause implicitly carries with it the limited authority to enter a dwelling in which the suspect lives when there is reason to believe the suspect is within.

Because no arrest warrant was obtained in either of these cases, the judgments must be reversed and the cases remanded to the New York Court of Appeals for further proceedings not inconsistent with this opinion.

FURTHER CASE LAW, REFLECTIONS, AND QUESTIONS

1. Why did the Supreme Court rule against New York and the policies of 23 other states? Note that under *Payton*, an arrest warrant suffices to allow the police entry to a home to make an arrest. A search warrant is not required. Suppose there is sufficient evidence of a person's involvement in a felony to persuade a judicial officer that his arrest is justified. In that case, it is constitutionally reasonable to require him to open his doors to the police. As such, an arrest warrant founded on probable cause implicitly carries with it the limited authority to enter a dwelling where the suspect lives when there is reason to believe the suspect is within.
2. What about the arrest of a suspect inside a third party's home? For example, if officers have an arrest warrant for X, may they enter Y's home under the authority of that warrant when they have probable cause to believe that X is inside? In *Steagald v. United States*, 451 U.S. 204 (1981), the United States Supreme Court answered this question no, they may not. Justice Marshall's majority opinion reasoned that a third party's (Y) right to privacy in their home should not be compromised by a suspect's (X) presence inside. Accordingly, a search warrant for a third party's home for a suspect who does not live there is required for the police to gain entry, absent the third party's consent or the existence of exigent circumstances. A warrant for the suspect's arrest is not sufficient. Were the rule otherwise, the police, "armed solely with an arrest warrant for a single person, could search all the homes of that individual's friends and acquaintances." 451 U.S., at 215.
3. When law enforcement officers have a warrant to search a dwelling, may they detain (not arrest) the occupant while conducting the search and then arrest them based on the results of the search? The United States Supreme Court upheld this practice in *Michigan v. Summers*, 452 U.S. 692 (1981). "A warrant to search for contraband founded on probable cause implicitly carries with it the limited authority to detain the occupants of the premises while a proper search is conducted." 452 U.S., at 705. Similarly, in *Illinois v. McArthur*, 531 U.S. 326 (2001), the justices ruled (8–1) that the police acted reasonably when, having probable cause to believe that a suspect had illegal drugs in his home, they denied the suspect entry into his house for a period of approximately two hours while they obtained a warrant authorizing them to search the home for the drugs.

Once the police decide to detain individuals present at the scene after a search warrant is issued, do they have the right to search each person? This question was addressed in *Ybarra v. Illinois,* 444 U.S. 85 (1979). Police officers obtained a search warrant to search a tavern and the tavern owner for evidence of the offense of possession of a controlled substance. With a warrant in hand, seven or eight officers proceeded to the tavern. Upon entering it, the officers announced their purpose and advised all present that they would conduct a "cursory search for weapons." One of the officers proceeded to pat down each of the 9 to 13 customers present in the tavern, while the remaining officers engaged in an extensive search of the premises. When the officer frisked Ybarra, one of the patrons, he felt what he described as "a cigarette pack with objects in it." After the officer had frisked the other patrons, he returned to Ybarra and removed the cigarette pack from his pants pocket. Inside the pack, the officer found heroin. Ybarra was charged with possession of narcotics. He filed a motion with the court to suppress the heroin, arguing that it had been seized via an illegal search.

In considering the matter, the Supreme Court held that the search of Ybarra was unconstitutional. The Court noted that each individual maintained their rights under the Constitution. As such, the requisite level of suspicion or probable cause was needed to conduct extensive searches of their clothing or persons. The Court found that although the frisk for weapons of each of the patrons was reasonable for officer safety reasons, there was no probable cause to believe anybody but the tavern owner possessed contraband. The search of Ybarra's cigarette pack went beyond the permissible scope of the *Terry* frisk (See *Minnesota v Dickerson,* 508 U.S. 366 (1993) later in this chapter.)

Use of Force During an Arrest

From time to time, police must use force to detain or arrest a suspect. On occasions where such force is deemed unreasonable, its use violates the Fourth Amendment.

Typically, the use of force by law enforcement officers becomes necessary and is permitted in certain situations. Police may use reasonable force to defend themselves or others. Police may also use force to effect an arrest when a suspect resists arrest or attempts to flee, provided the force used is proportionate to the resistance encountered. Additionally, officers may use force to maintain control during volatile situations where it becomes necessary to gain or maintain control of the scene.

In *Graham v. Connor*, 490 U.S. 386 (1989), the Supreme Court held that police may use only objectively reasonable force, assessed based on the totality of the circumstances from the perspective of a reasonable officer on the scene. These circumstances include the severity of the crime at issue, the immediacy of the threat posed by the suspect, whether there is active resistance or an attempt to evade arrest, and the totality of circumstances surrounding the encounter.

Exactly when the circumstances considered by the police occurred has been a point of contention among the federal circuit courts of appeal. While eight circuits rejected a specific time limitation during which the circumstances involved in the use of force must have taken place, four circuits chose to evaluate whether a Fourth

Amendment violation had occurred using the "moment of the threat doctrine." In the recent case *Barnes v. Felix* (2025), the Supreme Court resolved this circuit split, clarifying the appropriate temporal scope courts should consider when evaluating the reasonableness of force under the Fourth Amendment.

Barnes v. Felix

605 U.S. ___ (May 15, 2025)

JUSTICE KAGAN delivered the opinion of the Court.

A police officer's use of deadly force violates the Fourth Amendment when it is not "objectively reasonable." Graham v. Connor, 490 U.S. 386, 397 (1989). And that inquiry into reasonableness, we have held, requires assessing the "totality of the circumstances." Id., at 396 (quoting Tennessee v. Garner, 471 U.S. 1, 9 (1985)).

The question here is whether that framework permits courts, in evaluating a police shooting (or other use of force), to apply the so-called moment-of-threat rule used in the courts below. Under that rule, a court looks only to the circumstances existing at the precise time an officer perceived the threat inducing him to shoot. Today, we reject that approach as improperly narrowing the requisite Fourth Amendment analysis. To assess whether an officer acted reasonably in using force, a court must consider all the relevant circumstances, including facts and events leading up to the climactic moment.

I

On the afternoon of April 28, 2016, Roberto Felix, Jr., a law enforcement officer patrolling a highway outside Houston, received a radio alert about an automobile on the road with outstanding toll violations. Felix soon spotted the car, a Toyota Corolla, and turned on his emergency lights to initiate a traffic stop. The driver, Ashtian Barnes, pulled over to the highway's shoulder.

Parking his own car just behind, Felix walked to the Corolla's driver-side door and asked Barnes for his license and proof of insurance. Barnes replied that he did not have his license with him, and that the car was a rental in his girlfriend's name. As he spoke, Barnes rummaged through some papers inside the car, causing Felix to tell him several times to stop "digging around." Felix also commented that he smelled marijuana, and asked if there was anything in the car he should know about. Barnes responded that he might have some identification in the trunk. So Felix told him to open the trunk from his seat. Barnes did so, while also turning off the ignition. All that happened (as a dash-cam recording of the incident shows) in less than two minutes.

Then things began moving even faster. With his right hand resting on his holster, Felix told Barnes to get out of the car. Barnes opened the door but did not exit; instead, he turned the ignition back on. Felix unholstered his gun and, as the car began to move forward, jumped onto its door sill. He twice shouted, "Don't fucking move."

And with no visibility into the car (because his head was above the roof), he fired two quick shots inside. Barnes was hit, but managed to stop the car. Felix then radioed for back-up. By the time it arrived, Barnes was dead. All told, about five seconds elapsed between when the car started moving and when it stopped. And within that period, two seconds passed between the moment Felix stepped on the doorsill and the moment he fired his first shot.

Barnes's mother, Janice Barnes, sued Felix on her son's behalf. The suit, brought under 42 U.S.C. §1983, alleged that Felix had violated Ashtian Barnes's Fourth Amendment rights by using excessive force against him.

The District Court granted summary judgment to Felix. The court explained that to prevail on her claim, Mrs. Barnes needed to show that Felix's use of force was "objectively unreasonable." In the usual excessive-force case, the court noted, the inquiry into reasonableness would involve considering a variety of circumstances. But when an officer has used deadly force, the court continued, "the Fifth Circuit has developed a much narrower approach." Then, a court could ask only about the situation existing "at the moment of the threat" that sparked the fatal shooting. The District Court identified that moment as "the two seconds before Felix fired his first shot," when he was standing on the doorsill of a moving vehicle. At that moment, the court found, an officer could reasonably think himself "at risk of serious harm." And under the Fifth Circuit's rule, that fact alone concluded the analysis. The court explained that it could not consider "what had transpired up until" those last two seconds, including Felix's decision to jump onto the sill. Although a "more robust examination" might have aided in assessing the reasonableness of the shooting, the court was "duty bound" by "Circuit precedent" to "limit[its] focus" to the "exact moment Felix was hanging onto Barnes's" moving car.

The Court of Appeals affirmed, explaining that it too was "[b]ound" by "this Circuit's moment of threat doctrine." 91 F. 4th 393, 394, 397 (2024). Under that rule, the panel agreed, the "inquiry is confined to whether the officer" was "in danger at the moment of the threat that resulted in [his] use of deadly force." Id., at 397. Any prior events "leading up to the shooting," including actions the officer took, were simply "not relevant." Ibid. (quoting Harris v. Serpas, 745 F. 3d 767, 772 (CA5 2014)). And here, as the District Court found, the "precise moment of the threat" was the "two seconds" when Felix was clinging to a moving car. 91 F. 4th, at 397–398. Because Felix could then have reasonably believed his life in danger, the panel concluded, his decision to shoot did not violate Barnes's constitutional rights.

In a concurring opinion, Judge Higginbotham (who also authored the panel opinion) expressed "concern" with the Fifth Circuit's moment-of-threat doctrine. He thought that rule inconsistent with this Court's directive to assess the reasonableness of an officer's use of force, including deadly force, by looking to the totality of circumstances. Under the totality approach, Judge Higginbotham wrote, a court could consider not just the "precise millisecond" when an officer deploys force, but everything that "ha[d] transpired up until" that time. And with that wider focus, Judge Higginbotham would have found that Felix's shooting of Barnes was unreasonable.

We granted certiorari to address whether, in resolving Fourth Amendment excessive-force claims, courts may apply the moment-of-threat rule just described. We hold they may not because that rule constricts the proper inquiry into the "totality of the circumstances."

II

A claim that a law enforcement officer used excessive force during a stop or arrest is analyzed under the Fourth Amendment. The touchstone of the Fourth Amendment is reasonableness, as measured in objective terms. So the question in a case like this one, as this Court has often held, is whether the force deployed was justified from "the perspective of a reasonable officer on the scene," taking due account of both the individual interests and the governmental interests at stake. Graham, 490 U.S., at 396.

That inquiry into the reasonableness of police force requires analyzing the "totality of the circumstances." There is no "easy-to-apply legal test" or "on/off switch" in this context. Scott v. Harris, 550 U.S. 372, 382–383 (2007). Rather, the Fourth Amendment requires, as we once put it, that a court "slosh [its] way through" a "factbound morass." Id., at 383. Or said more prosaically, deciding whether a use of force was objectively reasonable demands "careful attention to the facts and circumstances" relating to the incident, as then known to the officer. Graham, 490 U.S., at 396. For example, the "severity of the crime" prompting the stop can carry weight in the analysis. See ibid.; Garner, 471 U.S., at 11. So too can actions the officer took during the stop, such as giving warnings or otherwise trying to control the encounter. And the stopped person's conduct is always relevant because it indicates the nature and level of the threat he poses, either to the officer or to others. See ibid.; Graham, 490 U.S., at 396.

Most notable here, the "totality of the circumstances" inquiry into a use of force has no time limit. Of course, the situation at the precise time of the shooting will often be what matters most; it is, after all, the officer's choice in that moment that is under review. But earlier facts and circumstances may bear on how a reasonable officer would have understood and responded to later ones. Those later, "in-the-moment" facts cannot be hermetically sealed off from the context in which they arose. Taking account of that context may benefit either party in an excessive-force case. Prior events may show, for example, why a reasonable officer would have perceived otherwise ambiguous conduct of a suspect as threatening. Or instead they may show why such an officer would have perceived the same conduct as innocuous. The history of the interaction, as well as other past circumstances known to the officer, thus may inform the reasonableness of the use of force.

The Court's decision in Plumhoff v. Rickard, 572 U.S. 765 (2014), well illustrates the point. The excessive-force claim there concerned the fatal shooting of a driver at the end of a "dangerous car chase" lasting more than five minutes. The driver had sped away from a traffic stop on a well-used road and tried to outrun as many as six police cruisers at speeds sometimes exceeding 100 miles per hour. Eventually, the fleeing car ran into one of the cruisers and came to a near standstill. The driver, though, still tried to escape, pumping the gas in a way that sent his wheels spinning and then putting the car into reverse. Ibid. At that point, one of the officers fired several shots into the car. In a suit brought against the officer, the driver's daughter contended that those shots were taken when the chase was already over. But this Court rejected that claim based on everything that had happened during the incident — the driver's "outrageously reckless" behavior over the prior "five minutes," as well as his last-second efforts to again take flight. Given all of those events, the Court explained, a reasonable officer would have concluded that the driver was "intent on resuming" his getaway and, if allowed to do so, would "again pose a deadly threat for others." Id., at 777. In short, the shooting was justified "at the moment" it occurred partly because of what had transpired in the preceding period. Ibid.

The moment-of-threat rule applied in the courts below prevents that sort of attention to context, and thus conflicts with this Court's instruction to analyze the totality of the circumstances. Recall that the District Court and Fifth Circuit limited their view to the two seconds before the shooting, after Felix had stepped onto the doorsill of Barnes's car. Those courts believed that, under Fifth Circuit precedent, they could not take into account anything preceding that final moment. So, for example, they could not consider the reasons for the stop or the earlier conduct of, and interactions between, the suspect and officer. And because of that limit, they could not address whether the final two seconds of the encounter would look different if set within a longer timeframe. It is as though the Court in Plumhoff could consider only the instant when the chased car was at a "near standstill," and not the earlier time when it zigzagged down a busy roadway at speed. 572 U.S., at 776. To be sure, historical facts will not often matter as much as they did there to the reasonableness analysis. And some of those facts may not be relevant at all. But no rule that precludes consideration of prior events in assessing a police shooting is reconcilable with the fact-dependent and context-sensitive approach we have prescribed. A court deciding a use-of-force case cannot review the totality of the circumstances if it has put on chronological blinders.

The question presented to us was one of timing alone: whether to look only at the encounter's final two seconds, or also to consider earlier events serving to put those seconds in context. With that matter resolved, we return everything else to the courts below. It is for them now to consider the reasonableness of the shooting, using the lengthier timeframe we have prescribed.

Accordingly, we vacate the judgment of the Court of Appeals and remand the case for further proceedings consistent with this opinion.

FURTHER CASE LAW, REFLECTIONS, AND QUESTIONS

1. In *Barnes v. Felix*, the Supreme Court was unanimous in rejecting the moment of the threat doctrine. Does this surprise you?
2. The standard established in *Graham* and reaffirmed in *Barnes* recognizes that police officers often must make split-second decisions under tense, uncertain, and rapidly evolving circumstances. However, this acknowledgment does not excuse the use of unreasonable force, and courts continue to scrutinize each case based on whether the officer's actions were objectively reasonable given the specific facts and circumstances they faced at the time of the incident.
3. Several important limitations govern police use of force. The force must be necessary, meaning officers cannot use force when reasonable alternatives exist. It must also be proportional to the threat and resistance encountered by the officer. When possible, officers have a duty to de-escalate situations before resorting to force. Any use of excessive force violates the Fourth Amendment and can result in both criminal charges and civil liability for the officer and their department.

The Use of Deadly Force and the Fleeing Felon

A subcategory of the standard established in *Graham* involves the question of when police may use deadly force to seize a person who is fleeing from the commission of a crime. Under the common law, the use of deadly force was justified to apprehend a suspect fleeing from the commission of a **felony**. This is known as the **fleeing felon rule**.

As weapons became more advanced and society matured, concern grew about the fleeing felon rule. By the late twentieth century, a majority of states and local police agencies had abolished the fleeing felon rule and limited the instances in which deadly force was authorized. Unfortunately, this resulted in a hodgepodge of standards being employed across the country.

In *Tennessee v. Garner*, 471 U.S. 1 (1985), the Supreme Court established specific limits on the use of deadly force. The case involved a 15-year-old suspect, Edward Garner, whom the police had probable cause to arrest for burglarizing a home. On leaving the house, Garner fled from patrol officer Hymon. As Garner was climbing a fence, Hymon fatally shot him in the back. It turned out that Graner was unarmed and had only taken a purse containing ten dollars.

Garner's father brought a civil suit seeking damages for violating his son's constitutional rights. The district court ruled against Garner because Tennessee law authorized Hymon's actions. The Sixth Circuit Court of Appeals reversed, holding that killing a fleeing suspect is a "seizure" under the Fourth Amendment, and such a seizure would only be reasonable if the suspect posed a threat to the safety of police officers or the community at large. The Supreme Court granted certiorari and affirmed.

The Court held that deadly force may be used to prevent escape of a suspect when the officer has probable cause to believe that the suspect poses a threat of serious physical harm, either to the officer or to others in the community. Given that Garner never threatened the officer and was unarmed, the deadly seizure violated the Fourth Amendment.

Box 5.2 You Be the Judge

Deputy Sheriff George clocked Harry driving 73 miles per hour in a 55-mile-per-hour zone. George activated his lights and took off after Harry, but Harry refused to stop. George called it in over his dispatch, and several deputies, including Scott, joined in. After six minutes and 10 miles of a high-speed chase, Scott employed an authorized precision intervention technique known as a pit maneuver to stop Harry. This involved rear-ending Harry's car to make it spin out. Unfortunately, after Scott rear-ended the vehicle, it spun and flipped over. Harry was severely injured and is now a quadriplegic. Harry filed a civil suit alleging that Scott's actions were an unconstitutional use of force.

Were Harry's rights violated? What legal test will you use to make this decision? See *Scott v. Harris*, 550 U.S. 372 (2007).

Stop and Frisk

We now consider seizures of the person that fall short of a formal arrest. We also explore the related issue involving less intrusive searches than a full-scale search incident to an arrest. In everyday terms, these are the subjects of "stop" and "frisk."

Probable cause to believe that a crime has been committed is a relatively high burden for law enforcement to meet to make an arrest. The United States Supreme Court thought a lower standard still accorded with the Fourth Amendment's "reasonableness" requirement was needed to prevent crime. Consistent with our study of arrests, we want to identify this lower legal standard (analogous to probable cause) required to justify a "stop" and gain a feel for the factual showing necessary to satisfy that standard.

The following case discusses the difference between a stop and an arrest, the different levels of certainty required for each, and the difference in the nature of police detention involved between the two.

Terry v. Ohio

392 U.S. 1 (1968)

Mr. Chief Justice Warren delivered the opinion of the Court.

This case presents serious questions concerning the role of the Fourth Amendment in the confrontation on the street between the citizen and the policeman investigating suspicious circumstances.

Petitioner Terry was convicted of carrying a concealed weapon and sentenced to the statutorily prescribed term of one to three years in the penitentiary. Following the denial of a pretrial motion to suppress, the prosecution introduced in evidence two revolvers and a number of bullets seized from Terry and a codefendant, Richard Chilton, by Cleveland Police Detective Martin McFadden. At the hearing on the motion to suppress this evidence, Officer McFadden testified that while he was patrolling in plain clothes in downtown Cleveland at approximately 2:30 in the afternoon of October 31, 1963, his attention was attracted by two men, Chilton and Terry, standing on the corner of Huron Road and Euclid Avenue. He had never seen the two men before, and he was unable to say precisely what first drew his eye to them. However, he testified that he had been a policeman for 39 years and a detective for 35 and that he had been assigned to patrol this vicinity of downtown Cleveland for shoplifters and pickpockets for 30 years. He explained that he had developed routine habits of observation over the years and that he would "stand and watch people or walk and watch people at many intervals of the day." He added: "Now, in this case when I looked over they didn't look right to me at the time."

His interest aroused, Officer McFadden took up a post of observation in the entrance to a store 300 to 400 feet away from the two men. "I get more purpose to watch them when I seen their movements," he testified. He saw one of the men leave the other one and walk southwest on Huron Road, past some stores. The man paused for a moment and looked in a store window, then walked on a short distance, turned around and walked back toward the corner, pausing once again to look in the same store window. He rejoined his companion at the corner, and the two conferred briefly. Then the second man went through the same series of motions, strolling down Huron Road, looking in the same window, walking on a short distance, turning back, peering in the store window again, and returning to confer with the first man at the corner. The two men repeated this ritual alternately between five and six times apiece — in all roughly a dozen trips. At one point, while the two were standing together on the corner, a third man approached them and engaged them briefly in conversation. This man then left the two others and walked west on Euclid Avenue. Chilton and Terry resumed their measured pacing, peering, and conferring. After this had gone on for 10 to 12 minutes, the two men walked off together, heading west on Euclid Avenue, following the path taken earlier by the third man.

By this time Officer McFadden had become thoroughly suspicious. He testified that after observing their elaborately casual and oft-repeated reconnaissance of the store window on Huron Road, he suspected the two men of "casing a job, a stick-up," and that he considered it his duty as a police officer to investigate further. He added that he feared "they may have a gun." Thus, Officer McFadden followed Chilton and Terry and saw them stop in front of Zucker's store to talk to the same man who had conferred with them earlier on the street corner. Deciding that the situation was ripe for direct action, Officer McFadden approached the three men, identified himself as a police officer and asked for their names. At this point his knowledge was confined to what he had observed. He was not acquainted with any of the three men by name or by sight, and he had received no information concerning them from any other source. When the men "mumbled something" in response to his inquiries, Officer McFadden grabbed petitioner Terry, spun him around so that they were facing the other two, with Terry between McFadden and the others, and patted down the outside of his clothing. In the left breast pocket of Terry's overcoat Officer McFadden felt a pistol. He reached inside the overcoat pocket, but was unable to remove the gun. At this point, keeping Terry between himself and the others, the officer ordered all three men to enter Zucker's store. As they went in, he removed Terry's overcoat completely, removed a .38-caliber revolver from the pocket and ordered all three men to face the wall with their hands raised. Officer McFadden proceeded to pat-down the outer clothing of Chilton and the third man, Katz. He discovered another revolver in the outer pocket of Chilton's overcoat, but no weapons were found on Katz. The officer testified that he only patted the men down to see whether they had weapons, and that he did not put his hands beneath the outer garments of either Terry or Chilton until he felt their guns. So far as appears from the record, he never placed his hands beneath Katz' outer garments. Officer McFadden seized Chilton's gun, asked the proprietor of the store to call a police wagon, and took all three men to the station, where Chilton and Terry were formally charged with carrying concealed weapons.

II

Our first task is to establish at what point in this encounter the Fourth Amendment becomes relevant. That is, we must decide whether and when Officer McFadden "seized" Terry and whether and when he conducted a "search." There is some suggestion in the use of such terms as "stop" and "frisk" that such police conduct is outside the purview of the Fourth Amendment because neither action rises to the level of a "search" or "seizure" within the meaning of the Constitution. We emphatically reject this notion. It is quite plain that the Fourth Amendment governs "seizures" of the person which do not eventuate in a trip to the station house and prosecution for crime — "arrests" in traditional terminology. It must be recognized that whenever a police officer accosts an individual and restrains his freedom to walk away, he has "seized" that person. And it is nothing less than sheer torture of the English language to suggest that a careful exploration of the outer surfaces of a person's clothing all over his or her body in an attempt to find weapons is not a "search." Moreover, it is simply fantastic to urge that such a procedure performed in public by a policeman while the citizen stands helpless, perhaps facing a wall with his hands raised, is a "petty indignity." It is a serious intrusion upon the sanctity of the person, which may inflict great indignity and arouse strong resentment, and it is not to be undertaken lightly.

The distinctions of classical "stop-and-frisk" theory thus serve to divert attention from the central inquiry under the Fourth Amendment — the reasonableness in all the circumstances of the particular governmental invasion of a citizen's personal security. "Search" and "seizure" are not talismans. We therefore reject the notions that the Fourth Amendment does not come into play at all as a limitation upon police conduct if the officers stop short of something called a "technical arrest" or a "full-blown search."

In this case there can be no question, then, that Officer McFadden "seized" petitioner and subjected him to a "search" when he took hold of him and patted down the outer surfaces of his clothing. We must decide whether at that point it was reasonable for Officer McFadden to have interfered with petitioner's personal security as he did. And in determining whether the seizure and search were "unreasonable" our inquiry is a dual one — whether the officer's action was justified at its inception, and whether it was reasonably related in scope to the circumstances which justified the interference in the first place.

III

In order to assess the reasonableness of Officer McFadden's conduct as a general proposition, it is necessary "first to focus upon the governmental interest which allegedly justifies official intrusion upon the constitutionally protected interests of the private citizen," for there is "no ready test for determining reasonableness other than by balancing the need to search [or seize] against the invasion which the search [or seizure] entails." And in justifying the particular intrusion the police officer must be able to point to specific and articulable facts which, taken together with rational inferences from those facts, reasonably warrant that intrusion. The scheme of the Fourth Amendment becomes meaningful only when it is assured that at some point the conduct of those charged with enforcing the laws can be subjected to the more detached, neutral scrutiny of a judge who must evaluate the reasonableness of a particular search or seizure in light of the particular circumstances. And in making that assessment it is imperative that the facts be judged against an objective standard: would the facts available to the officer at the moment of the seizure or the search "warrant a man of reasonable caution in the belief" that the action taken was appropriate?

Anything less would invite intrusions upon constitutionally guaranteed rights based on nothing more substantial than inarticulate hunches, a result this Court has consistently refused to sanction. And simple "'good faith on the part of the arresting officer is not enough.' If subjective good faith alone were the test, the protections of the Fourth Amendment would evaporate, and the people would be 'secure in their persons, houses, papers, and effects,' only in the discretion of the police."

Applying these principles to this case, we consider first the nature and extent of the governmental interests involved. One general interest is of course that of effective crime prevention and detection; it is this interest which underlies the recognition that a police officer may in appropriate circumstances and in an appropriate manner approach a person for purposes of investigating possibly criminal behavior even though there is no probable cause to make an arrest. It was this legitimate investigation function Officer McFadden was discharging when he decided to approach petitioner and his companions. He had observed Terry, Chilton, and Katz go through a series of acts, each of them perhaps innocent in itself, but which taken together warranted further investigation. There is nothing unusual in two men standing together on a street corner, perhaps waiting for someone. Nor is there anything suspicious about people in such circumstances strolling up and down the street, singly or in pairs. Store windows, moreover, are made to be looked in. But the story is quite different where, as here, two men hover about a street corner for an extended period of time, at the end of which it becomes apparent that they are not waiting for anyone or anything; where these men pace alternately along an identical route, pausing to stare in the same store window roughly 24 times; where each completion of this route is followed immediately by a conference between the two men on the corner; where they are joined in one of these conferences by a third man who leaves swiftly; and where the two men finally follow the third and rejoin him a couple of blocks away. It would have been poor police work indeed for an officer of 30 years' experience in the detection of thievery from stores in this same neighborhood to have failed to investigate this behavior further.

The crux of this case, however, is not the propriety of Officer McFadden's taking steps to investigate petitioner's suspicious behavior, but rather, whether there was justification for McFadden's invasion of Terry's personal security by searching him for weapons in the course of that investigation. We are now concerned with more than the governmental interest in investigating crime; in addition, there is the more immediate interest of the police officer in taking steps to assure himself that the person with whom he is dealing is not armed with a weapon that could unexpectedly and fatally be used against him. Certainly it would be unreasonable to require that police officers take unnecessary risks in the performance of their duties. American criminals have a long tradition in armed violence, and every year in this country many law enforcement officers are killed in the line of duty, and thousands more are wounded. Virtually all of these deaths and a substantial portion of the injuries are inflicted with guns and knives.

In view of these facts, we cannot blind ourselves to the need for law enforcement officers to protect themselves and other prospective victims of violence in situations where they may lack probable cause for an arrest. When an officer is justified in believing that the individual whose suspicious behavior he is investigating at close range is armed and presently dangerous to the officers or to others, it would appear to be clearly unreasonable to deny the officer the power to take necessary measures to determine whether the person is in fact carrying a weapon and to neutralize the threat of physical harm.

We must still consider, however, the nature and quality of the intrusion on individual rights which must be accepted if police officers are to be conceded the right to search for weapons in situations where probable cause to arrest for crime is lacking. Even a limited search of the outer clothing for weapons constitutes a severe, though brief, intrusion upon cherished personal security, and it must surely be an annoying, frightening, and perhaps humiliating experience.

Petitioner does not argue that a police officer should refrain from making any investigation of suspicious circumstances until such time as he has probable cause to make an arrest; nor does he deny that police officers in properly discharging their investigative function may find themselves confronting persons who might well be armed and dangerous. Moreover, he does not say that an officer is always unjustified in searching a suspect to discover weapons. Rather, he says it is unreasonable for the policeman to take that step until such time as the situation evolves to a point where there is probable cause to make an arrest. When that point has been reached, petitioner would concede the officer's right to conduct a search of the suspect for weapons, fruits or instrumentalities of the crime, or "mere" evidence, incident to the arrest.

There are two weaknesses in this line of reasoning, however. First, it fails to take account of traditional limitations upon the scope of searches, and thus recognizes no distinction in purpose, character, and extent between a search incident to an arrest and a limited search for weapons. The former, although justified in part by the acknowledged necessity to protect the arresting officer from assault with a concealed weapon, is also justified on other grounds, and can therefore involve a relatively extensive exploration of the person. A search for weapons in the absence of probable cause to arrest, however, must, like any other search, be strictly circumscribed by the exigencies which justify its initiation. Thus it must be limited to that which is necessary for the discovery of weapons which might be used to harm the officer or others nearby, and may realistically be characterized as something less than a "full" search, even though it remains a serious intrusion.

A second, and related, objection to petitioner's argument is that it assumes that the law of arrest has already worked out the balance between the particular interests involved here — the neutralization of danger to the policeman in the investigative circumstance and the sanctity of the individual. But this is not so. An arrest is a wholly different kind of intrusion upon individual freedom from a limited search for weapons, and the interests each is designed to serve are likewise quite different. An arrest is the initial stage of a criminal prosecution. It is intended to vindicate society's interest in having its laws obeyed, and it is inevitably accompanied by future interference with the individual's freedom of movement, whether or not trial or conviction ultimately follows. The protective search for weapons, on the other hand, constitutes a brief, though far from inconsiderable, intrusion upon the sanctity of the person. It does not follow that because an officer may lawfully arrest a person only when he is apprised of facts sufficient to warrant a belief that the person has committed or is committing a crime, the officer is equally unjustified, absent that kind of evidence, in making any intrusions short of an arrest. Moreover, a perfectly reasonable apprehension of danger may arise long before the officer is possessed of adequate information to justify taking a person into custody for the purpose of prosecuting him for a crime. Petitioner's reliance on cases which have worked out standards of reasonableness with regard to "seizures" constituting arrests and searches incident therefore is thus misplaced. It assumes that the interests sought to be vindicated and the invasions of personal security may be equated in the two cases, and thereby ignores a vital aspect of the analysis of the reasonableness of particular types of conduct under the Fourth Amendment.

Our evaluation of the proper balance that has to be struck in this type of case leads us to conclude that there must be a narrowly drawn authority to permit a reasonable search for weapons for the protection of the police officer, where he has reason to believe that he is dealing with an armed and dangerous individual, regardless of whether he has probable cause to arrest the individual for a crime. The officer need not be absolutely certain that the individual is armed; the issue is whether a reasonably prudent man in the circumstances would be warranted in the belief that his safety or that of others was in danger. And in determining whether the officer acted reasonably in such circumstances, due weight must be given, not to his inchoate and unparticularized suspicion or "hunch," but to the specific reasonable inferences which he is entitled to draw from the facts in light of his experience.

IV

We must now examine the conduct of Officer McFadden in this case to determine whether his search and seizure of petitioner were reasonable, both at their inception and as conducted. We think on the facts and circumstances Officer McFadden detailed before the trial judge a reasonably prudent man would have been warranted in believing petitioner was armed and thus presented a threat to the officer's safety while he was investigating his suspicious behavior.

The manner in which the seizure and search were conducted is, of course, as vital a part of the inquiry as whether they were warranted at all. The Fourth Amendment proceeds as much by limitations upon the scope of governmental action as by imposing preconditions upon its initiation. Thus, evidence may not be introduced if it was discovered by means of a seizure and search which were not reasonably related in scope to the justification for their initiation.

The sole justification of the search in the present situation is the protection of the police officer and others nearby, and it must therefore be confined in scope to an intrusion reasonably designed to discover guns, knives, clubs, or other hidden instruments for the assault of the police officer.

The scope of the search in this case presents no serious problem in light of these standards. Officer McFadden patted down the outer clothing of petitioner and his two companions. He did not place his hands in their pockets or under the outer surface of their garments until he had felt weapons, and then he merely reached for and removed the guns. Officer McFadden confined his search strictly to what was minimally necessary to learn whether the men were armed and to disarm them once he discovered the weapons. He did not conduct a general exploratory search for whatever evidence of criminal activity he might find.

V

We conclude that the revolver seized from Terry was properly admitted in evidence against him. At the time he seized petitioner and searched him for weapons, Officer McFadden had reasonable grounds to believe that petitioner was armed and dangerous, and it was necessary for the protection of himself and others to take swift measures to discover the true facts and neutralize the threat of harm if it materialized. The policeman carefully restricted his search to what was appropriate to the discovery of the particular items which he sought. Each case of this sort will, of course, have to be decided on its own facts. We merely hold today that where a police officer observes unusual conduct which leads him reasonably to conclude in light of his experience that criminal activity may be afoot and that the persons with whom he is dealing may be armed and presently dangerous, where in the course of investigating this behavior he identifies himself as a policeman and makes reasonable inquiries, and where nothing in the initial stages of the encounter serves to dispel his reasonable fear for his own or others' safety, he is entitled for the protection of himself and others in the area to conduct a carefully limited search of the outer clothing of such persons in an attempt to discover weapons which might be used to assault him. Such a search is a reasonable search under the Fourth Amendment, and any weapons seized may properly be introduced in evidence against the person from whom they were taken.

Affirmed.

FURTHER CASE LAW, REFLECTIONS, AND QUESTIONS

1. *Terry* is a crucial case because, among other things, it unlinked the two principal clauses of the Fourth Amendment — the prohibition against unreasonable searches and seizures and the provision that no warrants shall issue but upon

probable cause. Before *Terry*, it generally was understood that because probable cause is necessary to justify a search or seizure under the Fourth Amendment's warrants clause, a warrantless search or seizure conducted without probable cause must certainly be "unreasonable" under the first clause of the Amendment. *Terry*, however, dispensed with the need for probable cause for some searches and seizures to aid law enforcement in preventing and fighting crime. The opinion instead approves of a balancing test that weighs law enforcement's interests against the degree of intrusion on the individual to determine whether a search or seizure is reasonable.

2. In *Terry*, the Court emphasized the need to balance individual rights with officer safety. How should that balance be maintained today, especially in communities with histories of over-policing?

Box 5.3 You Be the Judge

While patrolling on March 9, 1965, NYPD Officer Martin observed Nelson for several hours in the same location. During this period of time, he saw Nelson in conversation with six persons whom he knew from experience to be narcotics addicts. He did not overhear any of these conversations and saw nothing pass between Nelson and any of the others. Late in the evening, Nelson entered a restaurant where he spoke with three more known addicts. Once again, nothing was overheard, and nothing was seen to pass between Nelson and the addicts. Patrolman Martin approached him as Nelson ate and told him to come outside. Once outside, the officer said to Sibron, "You know what I am after." In response, Nelson "mumbled something and reached into his pocket." Simultaneously, Patrolman Martin thrust his hand into the same pocket, discovering several glassine envelopes, which, it turned out, contained heroin. Nelson was arrested and charged with possession of narcotics.

Did Officer Martin possess reasonable suspicion?

Assuming he did have reasonable suspicion, was the seizure of the heroin constitutional?

See *Sibron v. New York*, 392 U.S. 40 (1968), decided the same day as *Terry*.

Reasonable Suspicion

Terry established that police may **stop and frisk** a person based on **reasonable suspicion**. Similar to probable cause, reasonable suspicion is a fluid term. The Court said that reasonable suspicion is more than a hunch but below the standard of probable cause or the preponderance of the evidence. While establishing this standard, the Court did not provide details about what constitutes reasonable suspicion. Similar factors to establishing probable cause will be considered, but the factors do not need to be as definitive or reliable. Despite the somewhat elusive nature of reasonable suspicion, several facts can be stated:

1. It requires less evidence than probable cause;
2. It must be more than a mere hunch;
3. It must be based on articulable facts; and
4. The experience and training of a police officer may be taken into account.

Not surprisingly, *Terry* spawned a succession of follow-up cases confronting issues that had not been resolved in the Court's 1968 decision. These items include nuances of the reasonable suspicion standard, how long an individual may be detained before a *Terry* stop becomes an arrest, and what limits should be placed on the scope and nature of a frisk conducted as part of a stop.

We start our examination of these questions by asking what information may be considered in establishing reasonable suspicion.

Alabama v. White

496 U.S. 325 (1990)

Justice White delivered the opinion of the Court.

On April 22, 1987, at approximately 3 p.m., Corporal B. H. Davis of the Montgomery Police Department received a telephone call from an anonymous person, stating that Vanessa White would be leaving 235-C Lynwood Terrace Apartments at a particular time in a brown Plymouth station wagon with the right taillight lens broken, that she would be going to Dobey's Motel, and that she would be in possession of about an ounce of cocaine inside a brown attaché case. Corporal Davis and his partner, Corporal P. A. Reynolds, proceeded to the Lynwood Terrace Apartments. The officers saw a brown Plymouth station wagon with a broken right taillight in the parking lot in front of the 235 building. The officers observed respondent leave the 235 building, carrying nothing in her hands, and enter the station wagon. They followed the vehicle as it drove the most direct route to Dobey's Motel. When the vehicle reached the Mobile Highway, on which Dobey's Motel is located, Corporal Reynolds requested a patrol unit to stop the vehicle. The vehicle was stopped at approximately 4:18 p.m., just short of Dobey's Motel. Corporal Davis asked respondent to step to the rear of her car, where he informed her that she had been stopped because she was suspected of carrying cocaine in the vehicle. He asked if they could look for cocaine and respondent said they could look. The officers found a locked brown attaché case in the car and, upon request, respondent provided the combination to the lock. The officers found marijuana in the attaché case and placed respondent under arrest. During processing at the station, the officers found three milligrams of cocaine in respondent's purse.

Respondent was charged in Montgomery County court with possession of marijuana and possession of cocaine. The trial court denied respondent's motion to suppress and she pleaded guilty to the charges, reserving the right to appeal the denial of her suppression motion. The Court of Criminal Appeals of Alabama held that the officers did not have the reasonable suspicion necessary under *Terry v. Ohio*, 392 US 1 (1968), to justify the investigatory stop of respondent's car, and that the marijuana and cocaine were fruits of respondent's unconstitutional detention.

Adams v. Williams, 407 US 143 (1972), sustained a Terry stop and frisk undertaken on the basis of a tip given in person by a known informant who had provided information in the past. We concluded that, while the unverified tip may have been insufficient to support an arrest or search warrant, the information carried sufficient "indicia of reliability" to justify a forcible stop. We did not address the issue of anonymous tips in *Adams*, except to say that "[t]his is a stronger case than obtains in the case of an anonymous telephone tip."

Illinois v. Gates, 462 US 213 (1983), dealt with an **anonymous tip** in the probable cause context. The Court there abandoned the "two-pronged test" of *Aguilar v. Texas*, 378 US 108 (1964), and *Spinelli v. United States*, 393 US 410 (1969), in favor of a "totality of the circumstances" approach to determining whether an informant's tip establishes probable cause. *Gates* made clear, however, that those factors that had been considered critical under *Aguilar* and *Spinelli* — an informant's "veracity," "reliability," and "basis of knowledge" — remain "highly relevant in determining the value of his report." These factors are also relevant in the reasonable suspicion context, although allowance must be made in applying them for the lesser showing required to meet that standard.

The opinion in *Gates* recognized that an anonymous tip alone seldom demonstrates the informant's basis of knowledge or veracity. Simply put, a tip such as this one, standing alone, would not warrant a man of reasonable caution in the belief' that a stop was appropriate.

As there was in *Gates*, however, in this case there is more than the tip itself. The tip was not as detailed, and the corroboration was not as complete, as in *Gates*, but the required degree of suspicion was likewise not as high.

Reasonable suspicion is a less demanding standard than probable cause not only in the sense that reasonable suspicion can be established with information that is different in quantity or content than that required to establish probable cause, but also in the sense that reasonable suspicion can arise from information that is less reliable than that required to show probable cause. Reasonable suspicion, like probable cause, is dependent upon both the content of information possessed by police and its degree of reliability. Both factors — quantity and quality — are considered in the "totality of the circumstances — the whole picture," *United States v. Cortez*, 449 US 411 (1981), that must be taken into account when evaluating whether there is reasonable suspicion. Thus, if a tip has a relatively low degree of reliability, more information will be required to establish the requisite quantum of suspicion than would be required if the tip were more reliable.

Contrary to the court below, we conclude that when the officers stopped respondent, the anonymous tip had been sufficiently corroborated to furnish reasonable suspicion that respondent was engaged in criminal activity and that the investigative stop therefore did not violate the Fourth Amendment.

It is true that not every detail mentioned by the tipster was verified, such as the name of the woman leaving the building or the precise apartment from which she left; but the officers did corroborate that a woman left the 235 building and got into the particular vehicle that was described by the caller. With respect to the time of departure predicted by the informant, Corporal Davis testified that the caller gave a particular time when the woman would be leaving, but he did not state what that time was. He did testify that, after the call, he and his partner proceeded to the Lynwood Terrace Apartments to put the 235 building under surveillance. Given the fact that the officers proceeded to the indicated address immediately after the call and that respondent emerged not too long thereafter, it appears from the record before us that respondent's departure from the building was within the time frame predicted by the caller. As for the caller's prediction of respondent's destination it is true that the officers stopped her just short of Dobey's Motel and did not know whether she would have pulled in or continued on past it. But given that the four-mile route driven by respondent was the most direct route possible to Dobey's Motel, but nevertheless involved several turns, we think respondent's destination was significantly corroborated.

The Court's opinion in *Gates* gave credit to the proposition that because an informant is shown to be right about some things, he is probably right about other facts that he has alleged, including the claim that the object of the tip is engaged in criminal activity. Thus, it is not unreasonable to conclude in this case that the independent corroboration by the police of significant aspects of the informer's predictions imparted some degree of reliability to the other allegations made by the caller.

We think it also important that, as in *Gates*, the anonymous tip contained a range of details relating not just to easily obtained facts and conditions existing at the time of the tip, but to future actions of third parties ordinarily not easily predicted. The fact that the officers found a car precisely matching the caller's description in front of the 235 building is an example of the former. Anyone could have "predicted" that fact because it was a condition presumably existing at the time of the call. What was important was the caller's ability to predict respondent's future behavior because it demonstrated inside information — a special familiarity with respondent's affairs. The general public would have had no way of knowing that respondent would shortly leave the building, get in the described car, and drive the most direct route to Dobey's Motel. Because only a small number of people are generally privy to an individual's itinerary, it is reasonable for police to believe that a person with access to such information is likely to also have access to reliable information about that individual's illegal activities. When significant aspects of the caller's predictions were verified, there was reason to believe not only that the caller was honest but also that he was well informed, at least well enough to justify the stop.

Although it is a close case, we conclude that under the totality of the circumstances the anonymous tip, as corroborated, exhibited sufficient indicia of reliability to justify the investigatory stop of respondent's car.

FURTHER CASE LAW, REFLECTIONS, AND QUESTIONS

1. *Alabama v. White* established that reasonable suspicion does not have to be based on a police officer's firsthand observations. It may be based on an informant's tip, as long as sufficient reliability exists.

2. As we saw in *Illinois v. Gates*, the reliability of the information considered may be established in multiple ways. How was it established in *White*?

3. Does the anonymous tip in *Alabama v. White*, coupled with the police follow-up investigation, give you confidence that White was not just "the target of a prank" or was not simply being set up by someone with "a grudge against her?" Most people follow routines. Perhaps you routinely leave your residence at approximately the same time on particular days of the week to make it to one of your classes. You may even carry the same backpack or "attaché case" each time you go. Could an anonymous tip to the police that you were carrying contraband and would leave your residence with your backpack, headed toward class, at a specific time, in combination with the police's confirmation of the latter details, give the police "reasonable suspicion" to stop you?

4. **Drug courier profiles** were initially employed in the early 1970s by the Drug Enforcement Agency ("DEA") for use in investigating airline passengers suspected of carrying illegal narcotics. Since their development, they have been adopted by police at airports nationwide. These profiles involve a set of characteristics found to be typical of persons transporting illegal drugs. While the specifics of drug courier profiles vary across the nation, they are generally quite similar. Although these characteristics do not automatically establish reasonable suspicion that the drugs are being transported, they may be considered in assessing the situation.

   In *United States v. Sokolow*, 490 U.S. 1 (1989), the Supreme Court held that law enforcement officials, in determining if reasonable suspicion is present to stop a person at an airport, may use elements of a drug courier profile to evaluate the totality of circumstances involved in a stop. In Sokolow, the following items fell into a drug courier profile: (1) he paid $2,100 for two airplane tickets from a roll of $20 bills; (2) he traveled under a name that did not match the name under which his telephone number was listed; (3) his original destination was Miami, a source city for illicit drugs; (4) he stayed in Miami for only 48 hours, even though a round-trip flight from Honolulu to Miami takes 20 hours; (5) he appeared nervous during his trip; and (6) he checked none of his luggage. Even though Sokolow did not exhibit any criminal behavior, and each item may have an innocent explanation, the Supreme Court found that these items, taken in their totality, were sufficient to establish reasonable suspicion.

5. Factors that may be used in finding reasonable suspicion are presented in Box 5.4.

Box 5.4 Factors Considered for Reasonable Suspicion

Flight from the scene	Evasive or contradictory responses
Furtive gestures or movements	Clear attempt to hide or evade police
Statement of Eyewitness	Tip from a confidential informant
Elements of the profile	Anonymous tip
Possession of contraband or illegal material in plain view	Presence in a high-crime area
Out late at night	

Box 5.5 You Be the Judge

A police officer receives an anonymous tip about possible drug activity at a house. The officer decides to conduct surveillance of the home and observes many different signs that indicate drug activity: short-duration stops, and many vehicles coming and going. The officer observes the house for a week and sees these various signs of possible drug activity. While conducting surveillance, the officer observes a single adult male leave the residence. The officer did not see the male enter the home and didn't know how long he had been there. The officer approaches and detains the male in a nearby park and asks him, "What were you doing at that house?" The officer then asks for identification from the male.

Did the police officer possess the requisite reasonable suspicion to initiate a stop of the male leaving the residence? Articulate two reasons why you think he either did or did not possess reasonable suspicion to make a stop.

See *Utah v. Strieff*, 579 U.S. 232 (2016).

Pretextual Stops and Arrests

If the police have probable cause to believe an offense has been committed, is the suspect's arrest always lawful? For example, suppose that the police observe a suspect committing a minor offense — one that gives them the authority to make an arrest but that they ordinarily would decline to make. If they have a hunch that the suspect may be involved in more serious criminal activity and are "really" interested in investigating their hunch, would arresting the person for the minor offense be an illegitimate "pretext" for looking into the suspected serious activity, for which they lack probable cause? The Court considered this issue in the following case.

Whren v. United States

517 U.S. 806 (1996)

JUSTICE SCALIA delivered the opinion of the Court.

In this case we decide whether the temporary detention of a motorist who the police have probable cause to believe has committed a civil traffic violation is inconsistent with the Fourth Amendment's prohibition against unreasonable seizures unless a reasonable officer would have been motivated to stop the car by a desire to enforce the traffic laws.

I

On the evening of June 10, 1993, plainclothes vice-squad officers of the District of Columbia Metropolitan Police Department were patrolling a "high drug area" of the city in an unmarked car. Their suspicions were aroused when they passed a dark Pathfinder truck with temporary license plates and youthful occupants waiting at a stop sign, the driver looking down into the lap of the passenger at his right. The truck remained stopped at the intersection for what seemed an unusually long time — more than 20 seconds. When the police car executed a U-turn in order to head back toward the truck, the Pathfinder turned suddenly to its right, without signaling, and sped off at an "unreasonable" speed. The policemen followed, and in a short while overtook the Pathfinder when it stopped behind other traffic at a red light. They pulled up alongside, and Officer Ephraim Soto stepped out and approached the driver's door, identifying himself as a police officer and directing the driver, petitioner Brown, to put the vehicle in park. When Soto drew up to the driver's window, he immediately observed two large plastic bags of what appeared to be crack cocaine in petitioner Whren's hands. Petitioners were arrested, and quantities of several types of illegal drugs were retrieved from the vehicle.

Petitioners were charged in a four-count indictment with violating various federal drug laws. At a pretrial suppression hearing, they challenged the legality of the stop and the resulting seizure of the drugs. They argued that the stop had not been justified by probable cause to believe, or even reasonable suspicion, that petitioners were engaged in illegal drug-dealing activity; and that Officer Soto's asserted ground for approaching the vehicle — to give the driver a warning concerning traffic violations — was pretextual. The District Court denied the suppression motion. Petitioners were convicted of the counts at issue here. The Court of Appeals affirmed the convictions. We granted certiorari.

II

Petitioners accept that Officer Soto had probable cause to believe that various provisions of the District of Columbia traffic code had been violated. They argue, however, that "in the unique context of civil traffic regulations" probable cause is not enough. Since, they contend, the use of automobiles is so heavily and minutely regulated that total compliance with traffic and safety rules is nearly impossible, a police officer will almost invariably be able to catch any given motorist in a technical violation. This creates the temptation to use traffic stops as a means of investigating other law violations, as to which no probable cause or even **articulable suspicion** exists. Petitioners, who are both black, further contend that police officers might decide which motorists to stop based on decidedly impermissible factors, such as the race of the car's occupants. To avoid this danger, they say, the Fourth Amendment test for traffic stops should be, not the normal one of whether probable cause existed to justify the stop; but rather, whether a police officer, acting reasonably, would have made the stop for the reason given.

A

Petitioners contend that the standard they propose is consistent with our past cases' disapproval of police attempts to use valid bases of action against citizens as pretexts for pursuing other investigatory agendas. But only an undiscerning reader would regard these cases as endorsing the principle that ulterior motives can invalidate police conduct that is justifiable on the basis of probable cause to believe that a violation of law has occurred. In each case we were addressing the validity of a search conducted in the absence of probable cause. Our quoted statements simply explain that the exemption from the need for probable cause (and warrant), which is accorded to searches made for the purpose of inventory or administrative regulation, is not accorded to searches that are not made for those purposes.

Not only have we never held, outside the context of inventory search or administrative inspection that an officer's motive invalidates objectively justifiable behavior under the Fourth Amendment; but we have repeatedly held and asserted the contrary.

We think these cases foreclose any argument that the constitutional reasonableness of traffic stops depends on the actual motivations of the individual officers involved. We of course agree with petitioners that the Constitution prohibits selective enforcement of the law based on considerations such as race. But the constitutional basis for objecting to intentionally discriminatory application of laws is the Equal Protection

Clause, not the Fourth Amendment. Subjective intentions play no role in ordinary, probable cause Fourth Amendment analysis.

Recognizing that we have been unwilling to entertain Fourth Amendment challenges based on the actual motivations of individual officers, petitioners disavow any intention to make the individual officer's subjective good faith the touchstone of "reasonableness." They insist that the standard they have put forward — whether the officer's conduct deviated materially from usual police practices, so that a reasonable officer in the same circumstances would not have made the stop for the reasons given — is an "objective" one.

But although framed in empirical terms, this approach is plainly and indisputably driven by subjective considerations. Its whole purpose is to prevent the police from doing under the guise of enforcing the traffic code what they would like to do for different reasons. Petitioners' proposed standard may not use the word "pretext," but it is designed to combat nothing other than the perceived "danger" of the pretextual stop, albeit only indirectly and over the run of cases. Instead of asking whether the individual officer had the proper state of mind, the petitioners would have us ask, in effect, whether (based on general police practices) it is plausible to believe that the officer had the proper state of mind.

Why one would frame a test designed to combat pretext in such fashion that the court cannot take into account actual and admitted pretext is a curiosity that can only be explained by the fact that our cases have foreclosed the more sensible option. If those cases were based only upon the evidentiary difficulty of establishing subjective intent, petitioners' attempt to root out subjective vices through objective means might make sense. But they were not based only upon that, or indeed even principally upon that. Their principal basis — which applies equally to attempts to reach subjective intent through ostensibly objective means — is simply that the Fourth Amendment's concern with "reasonableness" allows certain actions to be taken in certain circumstances, whatever the subjective intent.

But even if our concern had been only an evidentiary one, petitioners' proposal would by no means assuage it. Indeed, it seems to us somewhat easier to figure out the intent of an individual officer than to plumb the collective consciousness of law enforcement in order to determine whether a "reasonable officer" would have been moved to act upon the traffic violation. While police manuals and standard procedures may sometimes provide objective assistance, ordinarily one would be reduced to speculating about the hypothetical reaction of a hypothetical constable — an exercise that might be called virtual subjectivity.

Moreover, police enforcement practices, even if they could be practicably assessed by a judge, vary from place to place and from time to time. We cannot accept that the search and seizure protections of the Fourth Amendment are so variable, and can be made to turn upon such trivialities. The difficulty is illustrated by petitioners' arguments in this case. Their claim that a reasonable officer would not have made this stop is based largely on District of Columbia police regulations which permit plainclothes officers in unmarked vehicles to enforce traffic laws "only in the case of a violation that is so grave as to pose an immediate threat to the safety of others." This basis of invalidation would not apply in jurisdictions that had a different practice. And it would not have applied even in the District of Columbia if Officer Soto had been wearing a uniform or patrolling in a marked police cruiser.

III

In what would appear to be an elaboration on the "reasonable officer" test, petitioners argue that the balancing inherent in any Fourth Amendment inquiry requires us to weigh the governmental and individual interests implicated in a traffic stop such as we have here. That balancing, petitioners claim, does not support investigation of minor traffic infractions by plainclothes police in unmarked vehicles; such investigation only minimally advances the government's interest in traffic safety, and may indeed retard it by producing motorist confusion and alarm — a view said to be supported by the Metropolitan Police Department's own regulations generally prohibiting this practice.

It is of course true that in principle every Fourth Amendment case, since it turns upon a "reasonableness" determination, involves a balancing of all relevant factors. With rare exceptions not applicable here, however, the result of that balancing is not in doubt where the search or seizure is based upon probable cause.

Where probable cause has existed, the only cases in which we have found it necessary actually to perform the "balancing" analysis involved searches or seizures conducted in an extraordinary manner, unusually harmful to an individual's privacy or even physical interests — such as, for example, seizure by means of deadly force, *see Tennessee v. Garner*, 471 US 1 (1985), unannounced entry into a home, *see Wilson v. Arkansas*, 514 US 927 (1995), entry into a home without a warrant, *see Welsh v. Wisconsin*, 466 US 740 (1984), or physical penetration of the body, *see Winston v. Lee*, 470 US 753 (1985). The making of a traffic stop out-of-uniform does not remotely qualify as such an extreme practice, and so is governed by the usual rule that probable cause to believe the law has been broken "outbalances" private interest in avoiding police contact.

Petitioners urge as an extraordinary factor in this case that the "multitude of applicable traffic and equipment regulations" is so large and so difficult to obey perfectly that virtually everyone is guilty of violation, permitting the police to single out almost whomever they wish for a stop. But we are aware of no principle that would allow us to decide at what point a code of law becomes so expansive and so commonly violated that infraction itself can no longer be the ordinary measure of the lawfulness of enforcement. And even if we could identify such exorbitant codes, we do not know by what standard (or what right) we would decide, as petitioners would have us do, which particular provisions are sufficiently important to merit enforcement.

For the run-of-the-mill case, which this surely is, we think there is no realistic alternative to the traditional common-law rule that probable cause justifies a search and seizure.

Here the District Court found that the officers had probable cause to believe that petitioners had violated the traffic code. That rendered the stop reasonable under the Fourth Amendment, the evidence thereby discovered admissible, and the upholding of the convictions by the Court of Appeals for the District of Columbia Circuit correct.

FURTHER CASE LAW, REFLECTIONS, AND QUESTIONS

1. Why should police officers' "subjective intentions play no role in ordinary, probable cause Fourth Amendment analysis"? The defendants in *Whren* were young African Americans who were driving in a "high-drug area" of Washington, D.C. Do you think the police (especially plainclothes officers in an unmarked car) would have stopped a middle-aged couple in a suburban area of the city for making a turn without signaling or for traveling at an "unreasonable" speed?
2. What dangers are associated with "pretextual" stops? Did the defendants in *Whren* offer workable ground rules for identifying when a stop is "pretextual"? Does the Court offer a workable solution to the risk that African Americans or other discrete groups may be singled out and arrested for traffic violations so that the police can investigate other possible wrongdoing?
3. Do you think the Supreme Court's ruling in *Whren v. United States* creates a legal framework that enables pretextual traffic stops? How should the law address situations where minor infractions are used to justify broader searches?

Seizure

The cases we have read in this chapter have undoubtedly involved "stops" that implicate the Fourth Amendment. In *Terry v. Ohio,* the Court stated that the Fourth Amendment becomes relevant only when "by means of physical force or show of authority, has in some way restrained the liberty" of a person. By implication, interactions that are less intrusive than a "stop" do not implicate the Fourth Amendment and, therefore, need not be based on reasonable suspicion or probable cause. Such interactions are classified as consensual or voluntary encounters with the police. The critical thing to remember about a voluntary encounter with the police is that a person can extinguish the encounter at any time. In contrast, the same cannot be said for a stop or an arrest where a person is not free to leave.

However, this gives rise to two critical questions regarding a stop. (1) When exactly has the suspect been "seized" (if at all), and (2) if so, does the seizure qualify as a limited "stop" or as a more intrusive "arrest"? We begin by considering the meaning of a "**seizure**" and when exactly a suspect has been seized for Fourth Amendment purposes.

California v. Hodari D.

499 U.S. 621 (1991)

JUSTICE SCALIA delivered the opinion of the Court.

Late one evening in April 1988, Officers Brian McColgin and Jerry Pertoso were on patrol in a high-crime area of Oakland, California. They were dressed in street clothes but wearing jackets with "Police" embossed on both front and back. Their unmarked car proceeded west on Foothill Boulevard, and turned south onto 63rd Avenue. As they rounded the corner, they saw four or five youths huddled around a small red car parked at the curb. When the youths saw the officers' car approaching they apparently panicked and took flight. The respondent here, Hodari D., and one companion ran west through an alley; the others fled south. The red car also headed south, at a high rate of speed.

The officers were suspicious and gave chase. McColgin remained in the car and continued south on 63rd Avenue; Pertoso left the car, ran back north along 63rd, then west on Foothill Boulevard, and turned south on 62nd Avenue. Hodari, meanwhile, emerged from the alley onto 62nd and ran north. Looking behind as he ran, he did not turn and see Pertoso until the officer was almost upon him, whereupon he tossed away what appeared to be a small rock. A moment later, Pertoso tackled Hodari, handcuffed him, and radioed for assistance. Hodari was found to be carrying $130 in cash and a pager; and the rock he had discarded was found to be crack cocaine.

In the juvenile proceeding brought against him, Hodari moved to suppress the evidence relating to the cocaine. The court denied the motion without opinion. The California Court of Appeal reversed, holding that Hodari had been "seized" when he saw Officer Pertoso running towards him, that this seizure was unreasonable under the Fourth Amendment, and that the evidence of cocaine had to be suppressed as the fruit of that illegal seizure.

As this case comes to us, the only issue presented is whether, at the time he dropped the drugs, Hodari had been "seized" within the meaning of the Fourth Amendment.[1] If so, respondent argues, the drugs were the fruit of that seizure and the evidence concerning them was properly excluded. If not, the drugs were abandoned by Hodari and lawfully recovered by the police, and the evidence should have been admitted.

We have long understood that the Fourth Amendment's protection against "unreasonable seizures" includes seizure of the person. From the time of the founding to the present, the word "seizure" has meant "taking possession." For most purposes at common law, the word connoted not merely grasping, or applying physical force to, the animate or inanimate object in question, but actually bringing it within physical control. To constitute an arrest, however — the quintessential "seizure of the person" under our Fourth Amendment jurisprudence — the mere grasping or application of physical force with lawful authority, whether or not it succeeded in subduing the arrestee, was sufficient.

To say that an arrest is effected by the slightest application of physical force, despite the arrestee's escape, is not to say that for Fourth Amendment purposes there is a *continuing* arrest during the period of fugitivity. If, for example, Pertoso had laid his hands upon Hodari to arrest him, but Hodari had broken away and had *then* cast away the cocaine, it would hardly be realistic to say that that disclosure had been made during the course of an arrest. The present case, however, is even one step further removed. It does not involve the application of any physical force; Hodari was untouched by Officer Pertoso at the time he discarded the cocaine. His defense relies instead upon the proposition that a seizure occurs "when the officer, by means of physical force *or show of authority*, has in some way restrained the liberty of a citizen." *Terry v. Ohio*, 392 US 1 (1968) (emphasis added). Hodari contends (and we accept as true for purposes of this decision) that Pertoso's pursuit qualified as a "show of authority" calling upon Hodari to halt. The narrow question before us is whether, with respect to a show of authority as with respect to application of physical force, a seizure occurs even though the subject does not yield. We hold that it does not.

The language of the Fourth Amendment, of course, cannot sustain respondent's contention. The word "seizure" readily bears the meaning of a laying on of hands or application of physical force to restrain movement, even when it is ultimately unsuccessful. It does not remotely apply, however, to the prospect of a policeman yelling "Stop, in the name of the law!" at a fleeing form that continues to flee. That is no seizure. An arrest requires either physical force (as described above) or, where that is absent, *submission* to the assertion of authority.

We do not think it desirable, even as a policy matter, to stretch the Fourth Amendment beyond its words and beyond the meaning of arrest, as respondent urges. Street pursuits always place the public at some risk, and compliance with police orders to stop should therefore be encouraged. Only a few of those orders, we must presume, will be without adequate basis, and since the addressee has no ready means of identifying the deficient ones it almost invariably is the responsible course to comply. Unlawful orders will not be deterred, moreover, by sanctioning through the exclusionary rule those of them that are not obeyed. Since policemen do not command "Stop!" expecting to be ignored, or give chase hoping to be outrun, it fully suffices to apply the deterrent to their genuine, successful seizures.

Respondent contends that his position is sustained by the so-called *Mendenhall* test, formulated by Justice Stewart's opinion in *United States v. Mendenhall*, 446 US 544 (1980), and adopted by the Court in later cases, "A person has been 'seized' within the meaning of the Fourth Amendment only if, in view of all the circumstances surrounding the incident, a reasonable person would have believed that he was not free to leave." In seeking to rely upon that test here, respondent fails to read it carefully. It says that a person has been seized "only if," not that he has been seized "whenever;" it states a *necessary*, but not a *sufficient* condition for seizure or, more precisely, for seizure effected through a "show of authority." *Mendenhall* established that the test for existence of a "show of authority" is an objective one: not whether the citizen perceived that he was being ordered to restrict his movement, but whether the officer's words and actions would have conveyed that to a reasonable person.

In sum, assuming that Pertoso's pursuit in the present case constituted a "show of authority" enjoining Hodari to halt, since Hodari did not comply with that injunction he was not seized until he was tackled. The cocaine abandoned while he was running was in this case not the fruit of the seizure, and his motion to exclude evidence of it was properly denied.

FURTHER CASE LAW, REFLECTIONS, AND QUESTIONS

1. The Court's conclusion in *Hodari D.* that Hodari had not been seized until he was tackled, which was after he had discarded the rock of crack cocaine, relieved them of having to decide whether the police had reasonable suspicion to support a *Terry* stop. Recall that California had conceded that Officer Pertoso lacked reasonable suspicion to stop Hodari. Justice Scalia appeared to question whether such a concession was well-founded. Should a suspect's "flight" on seeing an approaching police officer give the police a reasonable basis to stop the suspect on suspicion of criminal wrongdoing? Or is such an apparent effort to avoid coming into contact with the police sufficiently ambiguous that it should not, standing alone, satisfy *Terry's* standard of reasonable suspicion?

   The Court came close to but did not directly answer this unresolved question nearly a decade later. In *Illinois v. Wardlow*, 528 U.S. 119 (2000), four police cars and eight officers patrolled an area of Chicago known for heavy narcotics trafficking. One officer observed Sam Wardlow standing beside a building holding an opaque bag. Wardlow looked in the direction of the officers and fled. Two officers followed, eventually cornering and stopping him. The police immediately conducted a protective pat-down search for weapons because, in his experience, it was common for there to be weapons in the near vicinity of narcotics transactions. During the frisk, police discovered Wardlow was carrying a .38-caliber handgun with five live rounds of ammunition. The officers arrested Wardlow.

Wardlow filed a motion to suppress the gun before his trial for unlawful possession of the weapon. The trial court denied the motion, ruling that the gun was discovered during a lawful stop and frisk. Wardlow was convicted of the offense, but his conviction was reversed on appeal. The Illinois Supreme Court concluded that "flight may simply be an exercise of the right to 'go on one's way,' and, thus, could not constitute reasonable suspicion justifying a Terry stop," even if it occurred in a high-crime area. A 5–4 majority of the U.S. Supreme Court reversed, finding that the police had reasonable suspicion to stop and frisk Wardlow.

Chief Justice Rehnquist, writing for the majority, said that a person's presence in a high-crime area is insufficient to support a reasonable, particularized suspicion that the person is committing a crime. But, he continued, police officers may consider the relevant characteristics of a location in deciding whether the circumstances are sufficiently suspicious to warrant further investigation. The fact that a stop occurred in a "high crime area" is a relevant contextual consideration in a *Terry* analysis.

The Court noted that in addition to Wardlow's presence in an area of heavy narcotics trafficking, his unprovoked flight upon noticing the police increased their suspicion that he was up to no good.

According to the Court, nervous, evasive behavior is pertinent in determining reasonable suspicion. "Headlong flight — wherever it occurs — is the consummate act of evasion: It is not necessarily indicative of wrongdoing, but it is certainly suggestive of such." As such, the Court concluded that Officer Nolan was justified in suspecting that Wardlow was involved in criminal activity and, therefore, in investigating further.

Justice Stevens, concurring and dissenting in part, observed that the Court had "wisely" declined to endorse the proposition that a citizen's apparent flight from a police officer automatically provides reasonable suspicion to justify a *Terry* stop. He also rejected Wardlow's argument that flight alone is so inherently ambiguous that it could never amount to reasonable suspicion under *Terry*. Instead, he wrote that an unprovoked flight should be considered a factor in determining if a *Terry* stop was constitutional.

Parting company with the majority opinion, he disputed the conclusion that the police were justified in stopping Wardlow because of the additional fact that his flight occurred in a "high crime area."

> [E]ven in a high crime neighborhood unprovoked flight does not invariably lead to reasonable suspicion. On the contrary, because many factors

> providing innocent motivations for unprovoked flight are concentrated in high crime areas, the character of the neighborhood arguably makes an inference of guilt less appropriate, rather than more so. Like unprovoked flight itself, presence in a high crime neighborhood is a fact too generic and susceptible to innocent explanation to satisfy the reasonable suspicion inquiry. *Illinois v. Wardlow*, 528 U.S. at 139.

What "innocent motivations" might exist for a citizen to run from approaching police officers, as Wardlow did? What does Justice Stevens mean when he suggests that a citizen's flight from the police in "high crime areas arguably makes an inference of guilt less appropriate, rather than more so." What, precisely, is a "high crime area"? And what is "flight" from a police officer? If instead of running when the police approached, Wardlow had turned and begun to walk away, or if he had turned and stepped into his car on the curbside, would such activity amount to "flight"? Even if Wardlow began running as the police approached, how certain must we be that he ran in response to the police presence, as opposed to some other reason (such as being late for work or wanting to catch a bus)?

2. Assume that you are on a bus trip from Miami to Atlanta, with the bus making numerous stops at cities in between to pick up and drop off passengers. At one of those stops, two police officers board the bus and walk down its narrow aisle. The officers approach where you are seated, eye you, and then ask to inspect your ticket and see some identification. You comply, and your ticket and ID are returned to you. The officers then "explain their presence as narcotics agents on the lookout for illegal drugs" and ask permission to search your luggage. They further advise you that you are not required to give them permission. What would you do? At this point, have you been "seized" by the officers? Would you (as a reasonable person) feel "free to leave" the officers' presence? As you are miles away from both your starting point and your destination, where would you go? Could you even get past the officers in the bus aisle?

   These were the essential facts and issues in *Florida v. Bostick*, 501 U.S. 429 (1991). Bostick consented to the search of his luggage, and the police found cocaine inside it. He subsequently argued that the consent resulted from his unlawful "seizure" by the police on the bus. The Florida Supreme Court agreed, ruling that "bus sweeps" conducted by the police in all cases constitute seizures within the meaning of the Fourth Amendment. The U.S. Supreme Court reversed in an opinion written by Justice O'Connor.

   > Our cases make it clear that a seizure does not occur simply because a police officer approaches an individual and asks a few questions. So long as a reasonable person would feel free "to disregard the police and go about his business," *California v. Hodari D.*, 499 US 621 (1991), the en-

> counter is consensual and no reasonable suspicion is required. The encounter will not trigger Fourth Amendment scrutiny unless it loses its consensual nature.
>
> Here, the mere fact that Bostick did not feel free to leave the bus does not mean that the police seized him. Bostick was a passenger on a bus that was scheduled to depart. He would not have felt free to leave the bus even if the police had not been present. Bostick's movements were "confined" in a sense, but this was the natural result of his decision to take the bus; it says nothing about whether or not the police conduct at issue was coercive.
>
> Accordingly, the "free to leave" analysis on which Bostick relies is inapplicable. In such a situation, the appropriate inquiry is whether a reasonable person would feel free to decline the officers' requests or otherwise terminate the encounter — *Florida v. Bostick*, 501 U.S. at 436.

The majority opinion expressed doubt that Bostick had been "seized" under this definition but remanded the case so the Florida Supreme Court could consider the issue, applying the appropriate test. A decade later, in *United States v. Drayton*, 536 U.S. 194 (2002), the justices ruled (6–3) that bus passengers confronting a bus sweep similar to the one conducted in *Bostick* had not been "seized" when officers approached them and requested permission to search them and their luggage, even though the officers did not specifically advise them that they had the right to refuse to cooperate. On what basis did the Court make these holdings?

3. The law regarding stops and arrests is presented in Box 5.6.

Box 5.6 Arrests versus Stops

	Arrest	Stop
Legal Standard	Probable Cause	Reasonable Suspicion
Objective	Take the suspect into custody for the suspected commission of a crime	To investigate and determine if a crime has or is about to take place
Duration	Lengthy to process and book the suspect	Brief and no longer than reasonable to either confirm or dispel suspicion
Movement	Transported to a detention facility	Investigation generally takes place where the encounter began
Accompanying Search	Search incident to a lawful arrest	Frisk the suspect for weapons if the suspect presents a danger

Length of Detention

Assuming, now, that a citizen has been "seized" within the meaning of the Fourth Amendment, when is that seizure a "stop," and when is it an "arrest"? One factor considered when deciding on a stop versus an arrest is the length of the detention. Differentiating between a stop and an arrest can be critically important. First, whereas a stop can be justified on reasonable suspicion, an arrest must meet the more demanding probable cause standard. Second, as we shall consider directly, and as *Terry* makes clear, the permissible scope of a frisk falls far short of a search incident to an arrest. The issue of how and whether a brief investigative stop might be transformed into a *de facto* arrest arises in the following case.

United States v. Sharpe

470 U.S. 675 (1985)

CHIEF JUSTICE BURGER delivered the opinion of the Court.

[While patrolling the coast near the border of North Carolina and South Carolina, Agent Cooke of the Drug Enforcement Administration (DEA) spotted a blue pickup truck with an attached camper shell driving down the highway in tandem with a Pontiac. Sharpe was driving the Pontiac, and Savage was driving the pickup truck. Quilted material covered the windows of the truck, which appeared to be heavily loaded. After Agent Cooke followed the two vehicles for approximately 20 miles, he decided to make an "investigative stop" and radioed the South Carolina State Highway Patrol for assistance. Officer Thrasher, driving a marked patrol car, responded and joined the procession. Almost immediately, the Pontiac and the pickup turned off of the highway onto a campground road, maintaining a speed of 55 to 60 miles an hour, although the speed limit was 35 mph. When the vehicles eventually rejoined the highway, Officer Thrasher turned on his squad car's flashing light and motioned for Sharpe, the lead driver, to bring the Pontiac to a stop. "As Sharpe moved the Pontiac into the right lane, the pickup truck cut between the Pontiac and Thrasher's patrol car, nearly hitting the patrol car, and continued down the highway." Officer Thrasher pursued the pickup and succeeded in stopping it about one half mile from where the Pontiac had pulled over. Agent Cooke remained behind with the Pontiac. Cooke radioed for additional assistance, which arrived approximately 10 minutes later. Cooke thereupon joined Officer Thrasher, who had secured Savage's driver's license and the truck's vehicle registration. Savage earlier had requested permission to leave, but Officer Thrasher informed him that he was not free to do so.]

Agent Cooke arrived at the scene approximately 15 minutes after the truck had been stopped. Thrasher handed Cooke Savage's license and the bill of sale for the truck; Cooke noted that the bill of sale bore the same name as Sharpe's license. Cooke identified himself to Savage as a DEA agent and said that he thought the truck was loaded with marihuana. Cooke twice sought permission to search the camper, but Savage declined to give it, explaining that he was not the owner of the truck. Cooke then stepped on the rear of the truck and, observing that it did not sink any lower, confirmed his suspicion that it was probably overloaded. He put his nose against the rear window, which was covered from the inside, and reported that he could smell marihuana. Without seeking Savage's permission, Cooke removed the keys from the ignition, opened the rear of the camper, and observed a large number of burlap-wrapped bales resembling bales of marihuana that Cooke had seen in previous investigations. Agent Cooke then placed Savage under arrest and left him with Thrasher.

Cooke returned to the Pontiac and arrested Sharpe. That evening, DEA agents took the truck to the Federal Building in Charleston, South Carolina. Several days later, Cooke supervised the unloading of the truck, which contained 43 bales weighing a total of 2,629 pounds. Acting without a search warrant, Cooke had eight randomly selected bales opened and sampled. Chemical tests showed that the samples were marihuana.

Sharpe and Savage were charged with possession of a controlled substance with intent to distribute it. The United States District Court for the District of South Carolina denied respondents' motion to suppress the contraband, and respondents were convicted.

A divided panel of the Court of Appeals for the Fourth Circuit reversed the convictions.

The Fourth Amendment is not, of course, a guarantee against all searches and seizures, but only against unreasonable searches and seizures. In *Terry v. Ohio*, we adopted a dual inquiry for evaluating the reasonableness of an investigative stop. Under this approach, we examine whether the officer's action was justified at its inception, and whether it was reasonably related in scope to the circumstances which justified the interference in the first place.

As to the first part of this inquiry, the Court of Appeals assumed that the police had an articulable and reasonable suspicion that Sharpe and Savage were engaged in marihuana trafficking, given the setting and all the circumstances when the police attempted to stop the Pontiac and the pickup. That assumption is abundantly supported by the record. As to the second part of the inquiry, however, the court concluded that the 30- to 40-minute detention of Sharpe and the 20-minute detention of Savage failed to meet the Fourth Amendment's requirement of brevity.

The Court of Appeals did not question the reasonableness of Officer Thrasher's or Agent Cooke's conduct during their detention of Savage. Rather, the court concluded that the length of the detention alone transformed it from a Terry stop into a *de facto* arrest.

Obviously, if an investigative stop continues indefinitely, at some point it can no longer be justified as an investigative stop. But our cases impose no rigid time limitation on *Terry* stops. While it is clear that the brevity of the invasion of the individual's Fourth Amendment interests is an important factor in determining whether the seizure is so minimally intrusive as to be justifiable on reasonable suspicion, we have emphasized the need to consider the law enforcement purposes to be served by the stop as well as the time reasonably needed to effectuate those purposes. Much as a "bright line" rule would be desirable, in evaluating whether an investigative detention is unreasonable, common sense and ordinary human experience must govern over rigid criteria.

The Court of Appeals' decision would effectively establish a per se rule that a 20-minute detention is too long to be justified under the *Terry* doctrine. Such a result is clearly and fundamentally at odds with our approach in this area.

In assessing whether a detention is too long in duration to be justified as an investigative stop, we consider it appropriate to examine whether the police diligently pursued a means of investigation that was likely to confirm or dispel their suspicions quickly, during which time it was necessary to detain the defendant. A court making this assessment should take care to consider whether the police are acting in a swiftly developing situation, and in such cases the court should not indulge in unrealistic second-guessing. The question is not simply whether some other alternative was available, but whether the police acted unreasonably in failing to recognize or to pursue it.

We readily conclude that, given the circumstances facing him, Agent Cooke pursued his investigation in a diligent and reasonable manner. During most of Savage's 20-minute detention, Cooke was attempting to contact Thrasher and enlisting the help of the local police who remained with Sharpe while Cooke left to pursue Officer Thrasher and the pickup. Once Cooke reached Officer Thrasher and Savage, he proceeded expeditiously: within the space of a few minutes, he examined Savage's driver's license and the truck's bill of sale, requested (and was denied) permission to search the truck, stepped on the rear bumper and noted that the truck did not move, confirming his suspicion that it was probably overloaded. He then detected the odor of marihuana.

Clearly this case does not involve any delay unnecessary to the legitimate investigation of the law enforcement officers. Respondents presented no evidence that the officers were dilatory in their investigation. The delay in this case was attributable almost entirely to the evasive actions of Savage, who sought to elude the police as Sharpe moved his Pontiac to the side of the road. Except for Savage's maneuvers, only a short and certainly permissible pre-arrest detention would likely have taken place. The somewhat longer detention was simply the result of a "graduated response to the demands of the particular situation".

We reject the contention that a 20-minute stop is unreasonable when the police have acted diligently and a suspect's actions contribute to the added delay about which he complains. The judgment of the Court of Appeals is reversed, and the case is remanded for further proceedings consistent with this opinion.

FURTHER CASE LAW, REFLECTIONS, AND QUESTIONS

1. The Court rejected the notion that a twenty-minute stop was *per se* unreasonable. What should be the outer limits that police may detain a person stopped based on reasonable suspicion? Is it possible that a 16-hour detention could ever be considered reasonable without probable cause?

2. In a unique context involving an international traveler seeking entry to this country at the border, the Supreme Court ruled that a detention of this duration was justifiable on reasonable suspicion. In *United States v. Montoya de Hernandez*, 473 U.S. 531 (1985), U.S. Customs agents detained Montoya de Hernandez on her arrival at the Los Angeles Airport on a flight from Colombia. She possessed a large amount of cash and gave a dubious account of her presence in the country. The agents suspected that she was "a 'balloon swallower,' one who attempts to smuggle narcotics into this country hidden in her alimentary canal." Her distended abdomen lent credence to this supposition. Montoya de Hernandez was given the choice of submitting to an X-ray inspection or waiting in a room with a wastebasket and no toilet facilities until "nature took its course." The resulting 16-hour wait ended with a court-ordered physician's examination, during which a balloon containing a foreign substance was removed from Montoya de Hernandez's rectum. Over the next several days, she passed 88 balloons containing a total of 528 grams of 80% pure cocaine hydrochloride.

   In upholding the legality of the 16-hour detention based on reasonable suspicion, Justice Rehnquist's opinion for the Court recognized that neither the duration nor the degree of intrusiveness of Montoya de Hernandez's detention was "routine" but concluded that they were justified under the "reasonable suspicion" standard under the circumstances.

   > Here, respondent was detained incommunicado for almost 16 hours before inspectors sought a warrant; the warrant then took a number of hours to procure, through no apparent fault of the inspectors. This length of time undoubtedly exceeds any other detention we have approved under reasonable suspicion. But we have also consistently rejected hard-and-fast time limits. Instead, "common sense and ordinary human experience must govern over rigid criteria."
   >
   > The rudimentary knowledge of the human body which judges possess in common with the rest of humankind tells us that alimentary canal smug-

gling cannot be detected in the amount of time in which other illegal activity may be investigated through brief *Terry*-type stops. It presents few, if any external signs; a quick frisk will not do, nor will even a strip search. In the case of respondent the inspectors had available, as an alternative to simply awaiting her bowel movement, an x-ray. They offered her the alternative of submitting herself to that procedure. But when she refused that alternative, the customs inspectors were left with only two practical alternatives: detain her for such time as necessary to confirm their suspicions, a detention which would last much longer than the typical *Terry* stop or turn her loose into the interior carrying the reasonably suspected contraband drugs.

The inspectors in this case followed this former procedure. They no doubt expected that respondent, having recently disembarked from a 10-hour direct flight with a full and stiff abdomen, would produce a bowel movement without extended delay. But her visible efforts to resist the call of nature, which the court below labeled "heroic," disappointed this expectation and in turn caused her humiliation and discomfort. Our prior cases have refused to charge police with delays in investigatory detention attributable to the suspect's evasive actions, and that principle applies here as well. Respondent alone was responsible for much of the duration and discomfort of the seizure.

Under these circumstances, we conclude that the detention in this case was not unreasonably long.

United States v. Montoya de Hernandez, 473 U.S 542–44.

3. *Montoya de Hernandez* left open the question of how long a person can be detained as part of a *Terry* stop. Bearing in mind that *Terry* stops are not based on probable cause but merely a reasonable suspicion, does the fact that there is no specific time limit on the length of a detention trouble you?

4. Miami Airport police were suspicious that Place was transporting drugs. As Place's plane was due to take off for New York's LaGuardia Airport within minutes, they let him check his bags and fly to New York. The police notified the Drug Enforcement Administration agents at LaGuardia Airport about their suspicions. When Place landed in New York, DEA agents asked to search Place's luggage. Place refused. The agents then seized his luggage and transported it to JFK Airport, where trained dogs were available to conduct a "sniff test" on the bags. A full 90 minutes after the initial stop in New York, the dogs alerted to the presence of illegal narcotics in one of the suitcases. As these events occurred on a Friday, the agents kept the luggage in police custody until a federal judge could issue a search warrant the following Monday. After obtaining and executing the search warrant, agents found 1,125 grams of cocaine. Place was subsequently indicted for possession of cocaine with intent to distribute.

In the district court, Place moved to suppress the cocaine, arguing that the warrantless seizure of the luggage violated his Fourth Amendment rights. The district court disagreed, and Place was convicted of drug possession. On appeal, the Second Circuit reversed, holding that the prolonged seizure of Place's bags violated the principles of *Terry v. Ohio* (1968). The U.S. Supreme Court granted certiorari.

The Court's opinion in *United States v. Place*, 462 U.S. 696 (1983), contained two important holdings. First, the Court held that using drug-sniffing dogs to detect narcotics in a public place does not intrude upon a person's reasonable expectation of privacy and therefore does not constitute a search under the Fourth Amendment. As long as the process is part of a "brief and limited detention" based on reasonable suspicion, the limited investigative detention and sniffing are permissible.

That being said, the Court also held that the 90-minute seizure based on reasonable suspicion was far too long to be constitutional and violated the Fourth Amendment. Given that the agents knew what time Place's plane was scheduled to land and had ample time to arrange their investigation, moving the luggage between airports should not have been necessary. Accordingly, the 90-minute warrantless seizure was unconstitutional.

Do you agree that the use of drug-sniffing dogs does not constitute a search? See *Illinois v. Caballes*, 543 U.S. 405 (2005) and *Rodriguez v. United States*, 575 U.S. 348 (2015).

How long is a reasonable amount of time for a Terry stop? Unfortunately, the Court has never provided a specific time limit.

Box 5.7 You Be the Judge

Roy fit a drug courier profile. He was a 25–35-year-old man, purchased a one-way airline ticket to New York City at Miami International Airport under an assumed name, paid cash for the ticket, was nervous, and was carrying a specific type of luggage with only his name and destination on its tag. After purchasing the ticket and checking his two bags, Roy went to the concourse leading to the airline boarding area. He was stopped by two detectives, who had previously observed him and believed that his characteristics fit the so-called "drug courier profile." The detectives asked to see his identification and noted that the name on his driver's license did not match his airline ticket. They took Roy's identification and airline ticket and asked him to go with them into a small room next to the concourse. Once in the room, they obtained his consent to search his bags, where they found a large amount of marijuana.

Was the stop and seizure of Roy constitutional?

See *Florida v. Royer*, 460 U.S. 491 (1983)

The Frisk

So far, this chapter has examined the level of suspicion police must possess to conduct an arrest or an investigatory stop. We have also considered how long a person may be detained during a Terry stop. The final section will focus on what types of searches may be conducted as part of an investigatory stop.

A **frisk** is a light pat-down of the outer clothing to look for weapons. In *Terry v. Ohio* and *Sibron v. New York*, the Court explained that the object of a protective frisk must be to detect weapons and that the scope of a frisk initially is limited to a pat-down of the suspect's outer garments and person. A frisk is not an automatic consequence of a stop. In other words, once an officer has stopped someone based on reasonable suspicion, they must possess separate justification above and beyond the purpose for initiating the stop and have reason to believe the person is presently armed and dangerous in order to frisk them for weapons. However, there is one exception to this, as alluded to by Justice Harlan in his concurrence in *Terry*. If an officer possesses reasonable suspicion to stop a person for committing a dangerous or violent crime, the frisk can be automatic.

However, what should an officer do if, while conducting a frisk for weapons, they detect not a knife or a gun but an object that feels like drugs or some other form of contraband? Furthermore, what if a frisk of the suspect's person produces no evidence of a weapon but another area — say, the interior of a car, or a bag, or a purse — is immediately accessible to the suspect and might contain a weapon? Is the officer strictly limited to frisking the suspect's person, or may the "frisk" extend to adjoining areas and accessible containers? The first question is addressed in *Minnesota v. Dickerson.*

Minnesota v. Dickerson

508 U.S. 366 (1993)

Justice White delivered the opinion of the Court.

On the evening of November 9, 1989, two Minneapolis police officers were patrolling an area on the city's north side in a marked squad car. At about 8:15 p.m., one of the officers observed respondent leaving a notorious "crack house." According to testimony credited by the trial court, respondent began walking toward the police but, upon spotting the squad car and making eye contact with one of the officers, abruptly halted and began walking in the opposite direction. His suspicion aroused, this officer watched as respondent turned and entered an alley on the other side of the apartment building. Based upon respondent's seemingly evasive actions and the fact that he had just left a building known for cocaine traffic, the officers decided to stop respondent and investigate further.

The officers pulled their squad car into the alley and ordered respondent to stop and submit to a patdown search. The search revealed no weapons, but the officer conducting the search did take an interest in a small lump in respondent's nylon jacket. The officer later testified, "As I pat-searched the front of his body, I felt a lump, a small lump, in the front pocket. I examined it with my fingers and it slid and it felt to be a lump of crack cocaine in cellophane."

The officer then reached into respondent's pocket and retrieved a small plastic bag containing one fifth of one gram of crack cocaine. Respondent was arrested and charged in Hennepin County District Court with possession of a controlled substance.

Before trial, respondent moved to suppress the cocaine. The trial court first concluded that the officers were justified under *Terry v. Ohio*, 392 US 1 (1968), in stopping respondent to investigate whether he might be engaged in criminal activity. The court further found that the officers were justified in frisking respondent to ensure that he was not carrying a weapon. Finally, analogizing to the "plain-view" doctrine, under which officers may make a warrantless seizure of contraband found in plain view during a lawful search for other items, the trial court ruled that the officers' seizure of the cocaine did not violate the Fourth Amendment. His suppression motion having failed, respondent proceeded to trial and was found guilty.

On appeal, the Minnesota Court of Appeals reversed and the Minnesota Supreme Court affirmed. The court appeared to adopt a categorical rule barring the seizure of any contraband detected by an officer through the sense of touch during a patdown search for weapons. The court further noted that "[e]ven if we recognized a 'plain feel' exception, the search in this case would not qualify" because "[t]he pat search of the defendant went far beyond what is permissible under *Terry*." As the State Supreme Court read the record, the officer conducting the search ascertained that the lump in respondent's jacket was contraband only after probing and investigating what he certainly knew was not a weapon.

We granted certiorari, to resolve a conflict among the state and federal courts over whether contraband detected through the sense of touch during a patdown search may be admitted into evidence. We now affirm.

Terry held that when an officer is justified in believing that the individual whose suspicious behavior he is investigating at close range is armed and presently dangerous to the officer or to others, the officer may conduct a patdown search "to determine whether the person is in fact carrying a weapon. The purpose of this limited search is not to discover evidence of crime, but to allow the officer to pursue his investigation without fear of violence. Rather, a protective search — permitted without a warrant and on the basis of reasonable suspicion less than probable cause — must be strictly "limited to that which is necessary for the discovery of weapons which might be used to harm the officer or others nearby." If the protective search goes beyond what is necessary to determine if the suspect is armed, it is no longer valid under *Terry* and its fruits will be suppressed.

These principles were settled 25 years ago when, on the same day, the Court announced its decisions in *Terry* and *Sibron*. The question presented today is whether police officers may seize nonthreatening contraband detected during a protective patdown search of the sort permitted by *Terry*. We think the answer is clearly that they may, so long as the officer's search stays within the bounds marked by *Terry*.

Police officers, at least under certain circumstances, may seize contraband detected during the lawful execution of a *Terry* search. The Court has justified this latter holding by reference to our cases under the "plain-view" doctrine. Under that doctrine, if police are lawfully in a position from which they view an object, if its incriminating character is immediately apparent, and if the officers have a lawful right of access to the object, they may seize it without a warrant.

If, however, the police lack probable cause to believe that an object in plain view is contraband without conducting some further search of the object — *i.e.*, if its incriminating character is not immediately apparent, the plain-view doctrine cannot justify its seizure.

We think that this doctrine has an obvious application by analogy to cases in which an officer discovers contraband through the sense of touch during an otherwise lawful search. The rationale of the plain-view doctrine is that if contraband is left in open view and is observed by a police officer from a lawful vantage point, there has been no invasion of a legitimate expectation of privacy and thus no "search" within the meaning of the Fourth Amendment — or at least no search independent of the initial intrusion that gave the officers their vantage point. The warrantless seizure of contraband that presents itself in this manner is deemed justified by the realization that resort to a neutral magistrate under such circumstances would often be impracticable and would do little to promote the objectives of the Fourth Amendment. The same can be said of tactile discoveries of contraband. If a police officer lawfully pats down a suspect's outer clothing and feels an object whose contour or mass makes its identity immediately apparent, there has been no invasion of the suspect's privacy beyond that already authorized by the officer's search for weapons; if the object is contraband, its warrantless seizure would be justified by the same practical considerations that inhere in the plain-view context.

III

It remains to apply these principles to the facts of this case. Respondent has not challenged the finding made by the trial court and affirmed by both the Court of Appeals and the State Supreme Court that the police were justified under *Terry* in stopping him and frisking him for weapons. Thus, the dispositive question before this Court is whether the officer who conducted the search was acting within the lawful bounds marked by *Terry* at the time he gained probable cause to believe that the lump in respondent's jacket was contraband. The State District Court did not make precise findings on this point, instead finding simply that the officer, after feeling "a small, hard object wrapped in plastic" in respondent's pocket, "formed the opinion that the object was crack cocaine." The District Court also noted that the officer made "no claim that he suspected this object to be a weapon." The Minnesota Supreme Court, after "a close examination of the record," held that the officer's own testimony "belies any notion that he 'immediately'" recognized the lump as crack cocaine. Rather, the court concluded, the officer determined that the lump was contraband only after "squeezing, sliding and otherwise manipulating the contents of the defendant's pocket" a pocket which the officer already knew contained no weapon.

Under the State Supreme Court's interpretation of the record before it, it is clear that the court was correct in holding that the police officer in this case overstepped the bounds of the "strictly circumscribed" search for weapons allowed under *Terry*. Where, as here an officer who is executing a valid search for one item seizes a different item," this Court rightly "has been sensitive to the danger that officers will enlarge a specific authorization, furnished by a warrant or an exigency, into the equivalent of a general warrant to rummage and seize at will. Here, the officer's continued exploration of respondent's pocket after having concluded that it contained no weapon was unrelated to the sole justification of the search under *Terry*: the protection of the police officer and others nearby. It therefore amounted to the sort of evidentiary search that *Terry* expressly refused to authorize, and that we have condemned in subsequent cases.

Although the officer was lawfully in a position to feel the lump in respondent's pocket because *Terry* entitled him to place his hands upon respondent's jacket, the court below determined that the incriminating character of the object was not immediately apparent to him. Rather, the officer determined that the item was contraband only after conducting a further search, one not authorized by *Terry* or by any other exception to the warrant requirement. Because this further search of respondent's pocket was constitutionally invalid, the seizure of the cocaine that followed is likewise unconstitutional.

For these reasons, the judgment of the Minnesota Supreme Court is affirmed.

FURTHER CASE LAW, REFLECTIONS, AND QUESTIONS

1. The standard laid out in *Dickerson* is commonly referred to as "plain feel." As the Court noted, this is closely related to the "plain-view" doctrine discussed in Chapter 6.
2. Although the court established a plain feel doctrine in *Dickerson*, remember that the Court ultimately decided the seizure of the drugs was illegal in this case

because the officer went beyond the scope of the search when he continued to manipulate what he knew was not a weapon.

3. How should a court determine if an item felt by an officer was immediately recognized to be contraband or a weapon? Once an officer says, "I immediately knew it was contraband," can the assertion be disproven? How?

Breadth of Terry *Frisks*

We now consider a second question relating to the proper scope of a *Terry* frisk. Assuming that a police officer reasonably may frisk the person for weapons, must the frisk stop there, or can it ever extend to an area within the suspect's reach where a weapon could be stored, such as the passenger compartment of a vehicle?

Michigan v. Long

463 U.S. 1032 (1983)

JUSTICE O'CONNOR delivered the opinion of the Court.

Deputies Howell and Lewis were on patrol in a rural area one evening when, shortly after midnight, they observed a car traveling erratically, and at excessive speed. The officers observed the car turning down a side road, where it swerved off into a shallow ditch. The officers stopped to investigate. Long, the only occupant of the automobile, met the deputies at the rear of the car, which was protruding from the ditch onto the road. The door on the driver's side of the vehicle was left open.

Deputy Howell requested Long to produce his operator's license, but he did not respond. After the request was repeated, Long produced his license. Long again failed to respond when Howell requested him to produce the vehicle registration. After another repeated request, Long, whom Howell thought "appeared to be under the influence of something," turned from the officers and began walking toward the open door of the vehicle. The officers followed Long and both observed a large hunting knife on the floorboard of the driver's side of the car. The officers then stopped Long's progress and subjected him to a *Terry* protective pat-down, which revealed no weapons.

Long and Deputy Lewis then stood by the rear of the vehicle while Deputy Howell shined his flashlight into the interior of the vehicle, but did not actually enter it. The purpose of Howell's action was "to search for other weapons." The officer noticed that something was protruding from under the armrest on the front seat. He knelt in the vehicle and lifted the armrest. He saw an open pouch on the front seat, and upon flashing his light on the pouch, determined that it contained what appeared to be marijuana. After Deputy Howell showed the pouch and its contents to Deputy Lewis, Long was arrested for possession of marijuana. A further search of the interior of the vehicle, including the glovebox, revealed neither more contraband nor the vehicle registration. The officers decided to impound the vehicle. Deputy Howell opened the trunk, which did not have a lock, and discovered inside it approximately 75 pounds of marijuana.

The Barry County Circuit Court denied Long's motion to suppress the marijuana taken from both the interior of the car and its trunk. He was subsequently convicted of possession of marijuana. The Michigan Supreme Court reversed.

We granted certiorari in this case to consider the important question of the authority of a police officer to protect himself by conducting a *Terry*-type search of the passenger compartment of a motor vehicle during the lawful investigatory stop of the occupant of the vehicle.

The court below held, and respondent Long contends, that Deputy Howell's entry into the vehicle cannot be justified under the principles set forth in *Terry* because "*Terry* authorized only a limited pat-down search of a person suspected of criminal activity" rather than a search of an area. Although *Terry* did involve the protective frisk of a person, we believe that the police action in this case is justified by the principles that we have already established in *Terry* and other cases.

Our past cases indicate that protection of police and others can justify protective searches when police have a reasonable belief that the suspect poses a danger, that roadside encounters between police and suspects are especially hazardous, and that danger may arise from the possible presence of weapons in the area surrounding a suspect. These principles compel our conclusion that the search of the passenger compartment of an automobile, limited to those areas in which a weapon may be placed or hidden, is permissible if the police officer possesses a reasonable belief based on specific and articulable facts which, taken together with the rational inferences from those facts, reasonably warrant the officers in believing that the suspect is dangerous and the suspect may gain immediate control of weapons. The issue is whether a reasonably prudent man in the circumstances would be warranted in the belief that his safety or that of others was in danger. If a suspect is "dangerous," he is no less dangerous simply because he is not arrested. If, while conducting a legitimate *Terry* search of the interior of the automobile, the officer should, as here, discover contraband other than weapons, he clearly cannot be required to ignore the contraband, and the Fourth Amendment does not require its suppression in such circumstances.

The circumstances of this case clearly justified Deputies Howell and Lewis in their reasonable belief that Long posed a danger if he were permitted to reenter his vehicle. The hour was late and the area rural. Long was driving his automobile at excessive speed, and his car swerved into a ditch. The officers had to repeat their questions to Long, who appeared to be "under the influence" of some intoxicant. Long was not frisked until the officers observed that there was a large knife in the interior of the car into which Long was about to reenter. The subsequent search of the car was restricted to those areas to which Long would generally have immediate control, and that could contain a weapon. The trial court determined that the leather pouch containing marijuana could have contained a weapon. It is clear that the intrusion was strictly circumscribed by the exigencies which justified its initiation.

In evaluating the validity of an officer's investigative or protective conduct under *Terry*, the touchstone of our analysis is always 'the reasonableness of all circumstances of the particular governmental intrusion of a citizen's personal security. In this case, the officers did not act unreasonably in taking preventive measures to ensure that there were no other weapons within Long's immediate grasp before permitting him to reenter his automobile. Therefore, the balancing required by *Terry* clearly weighs in favor of allowing the police to conduct an area search of the passenger compartment to uncover weapons, as long as they possess an articulable and objectively reasonable belief that the suspect is potentially dangerous.

The Michigan Supreme Court appeared to believe that it was not reasonable for the officers to fear that Long could injure them, because he was effectively under their control during the investigative stop and could not get access to any weapons that might have been located in the automobile. This reasoning is mistaken in several respects. During any investigative detention, the suspect is in the control of the officers in the sense that he may be briefly detained against his will. Just as a *Terry* suspect on the street may, despite being under the brief control of a police officer, reach into his clothing and retrieve a weapon, so might a *Terry* suspect in Long's position break away from police control and retrieve a weapon from his automobile. In addition, if the suspect is not placed under arrest, he will be permitted to reenter his automobile, and he will then have access to any weapons inside. Or, as here, the suspect may be permitted to reenter the vehicle before the *Terry* investigation is over, and again, may have access to weapons. In any event, we stress that a *Terry* investigation such as the one that occurred here, involves a police investigation at close range when the officer remains particularly vulnerable in part because a full custodial arrest has not been effected, and the officer must make a quick decision as to how to protect himself and others from possible danger. In such circumstances, we have not required that officers adopt alternative means to ensure their safety in order to avoid the intrusion involved in a *Terry* encounter.

FURTHER CASE LAW, REFLECTIONS, AND QUESTIONS

1. What gave the officers in *Long* a reasonable basis for believing that he posed a danger? Would the hunting knife spotted in the car, by itself, justify the protective frisk? Is it important that "the hour was late and the area rural"? That "Long was driving his automobile at excessive speed, and his car swerved into a ditch"? That Long "appeared to be 'under the influence' of some intoxicant"?

2. Remember, this case concerns a frisk that extends to an automobile. Additionally, the holding in this case is relatively narrow. This case does not fall under the "automobile exception" to the search warrant requirement. We will look extensively at searches of automobiles in Chapter 6.

Conclusion

As with many areas of criminal procedure, the law surrounding arrests, probable cause, and stop and frisk requires a balance between individual rights and the government's ability to enforce the law. This balance frequently involves a sliding scale, with increased evidence and judicial oversight required as the level of intrusion on citizens' freedom of privacy increases.

Although probable cause is a "fluid concept," *District of Columbia v. Wesby*, 583 U.S. 48 (2018), that only requires a fair probability that a person has committed a crime for an arrest to take place, police often face situations where they suspect a person is up to no good but lack demonstrable probable cause that a crime is afoot. Police routinely need to stop citizens on the street or pull them over in their vehicles to question them briefly or enforce traffic laws. If probable cause were required to be present in these situations, such investigative stops would be impermissible in most cases. In the 1960s, the Supreme Court realized this conundrum and acted using the flexibility of the Fourth Amendment and the need to make room for stops and frisks.

In establishing what standard police should meet to justify brief investigative detentions, the Court balanced the governmental interest in conducting stops and frisks against the interference with individual liberty. As investigative detentions, or "stops and frisks," involve a significantly lower level of intrusion than an arrest, the Court determined that a lower standard of suspicion would be appropriate. The Court concluded that the officer must be able to articulate specific facts giving rise to "reasonable suspicion" that criminal activity may be occurring. Mere hunches and speculation are insufficient for an investigatory stop to be constitutional. Moreover, because the additional step of patting down constitutes an additional intrusion, it requires separate justification: reasonable suspicion that the suspect may be armed and dangerous.

KEY TERMS

anonymous tip
articulable suspicion
arrest
drug courier profile
exigent circumstances
felony
fleeing felon rule
frisk
hot pursuit
plain touch doctrine
pretextual arrest
probable cause
reasonable suspicion
seizure
stop
stop and frisk

REVIEW QUESTIONS

Directions: Please refer to what you learned in this chapter to help you respond.

1. Define and describe reasonable suspicion and probable cause. What are the significant differences between the two levels of justification?
2. What exactly is a seizure of a person, according to the Fourth Amendment? When has a suspect been seized?
3. What is the difference between a stop and an arrest?
4. What are the four situations when a warrantless arrest is permissible?
5. When is deadly force permissible to stop a fleeing felon?
6. What is the purpose of a frisk? What is the scope of a frisk? When, if ever, can the police seize drugs during a frisk?
7. What factors do the courts consider when determining if a stop turned into a de facto arrest?
8. How do profiles relate to stops and frisks?
9. How long can a stop last before it becomes an arrest?
10. What are pretext stops? Are they permissible under the Fourth Amendment?

APPLYING THE LAW

Below are five hypothetical fact scenarios. To practice your understanding of the law that you learned in this chapter and your ability to apply it, answer each question posed by applying that law to the hypothetical scenarios. Your answers should be supported by relevant case law and judicially created rules and tests.

1. Patrol officers Bob and Ray are on patrol in a bad area of town when they observe Jesse driving down the road. Bob and Ray know Jesse to be a drug dealer and suspect he probably has drugs and weapons in his car. Knowing this is insufficient to justify a stop, the officers follow Jesse from a distance. A few minutes later, they observe Jesse roll through a stop sign. The officers look at each other, fist bump, and stop Jesse's car. As they approach the car on foot, they smell marijuana in the air. As Jesse exits the car, they look inside and find bricks or marijuana in the backseat. Jesse is arrested.

   Jesse files a motion to suppress the marijuana on the grounds that the stop made by the officers was pretextual and violated the Fourth Amendment. Is Jesse correct? Explain why or why not.

2. Police received an anonymous call that a man was going to go into a bakery and shoot his ex-wife, who worked there. The caller explained that the man was standing beside a gray four-door sedan parked outside the bakery, wearing a navy-blue jacket, white shirt, and tan pants. The caller also told the police that she knew the man well and sincerely believed he was dangerous.

   An officer rushed to the bakery and saw a man matching the caller's description leaning against the gray four-door sedan. The man was talking on his phone and facing the bakery. The officer walked up to the man, frisked him, and found a gun in his jacket pocket. After the man was charged with illegal possession of a handgun, his attorney filed a motion to suppress the handgun.

   How will the court rule on the motion?

3. A police officer arrested an elderly woman for bank robbery without first obtaining an arrest warrant. While the officer did not witness the woman robbing the bank, he knew what she looked like because her photograph had been taken by the bank cameras and distributed to all local police officers.

   Did the arrest of the woman violate her constitutional rights?

4. Detective Duck received an anonymous telephone call asserting that Spike was dealing narcotics in a local park. Duck observed Spike talking with several people in the park, but could not confirm that he was engaged in illegal activity. Since he had a hunch that Spike was up to no good, Duck decided to check whether Spike

had a criminal record and learned that he had two prior convictions for narcotics offenses and one for weapons possession.

Based on this information, does Duck have a legal basis to do any of the following?

a. Stop Spike

b. Frisk Spike

c. Handcuff Spike

d. Arrest Spike

5. Officer Tom is on patrol in a high-crime area when he notices a man, John, walking down the street. Officer Tom observes that John is wearing a heavy jacket, despite the warm weather, and appears to be looking around nervously. Based on these observations and the fact that the area is known for drug activity, Officer Tom decides to conduct a stop and frisk.

   During the pat-down, Officer Tom feels a small, hard object in John's pocket. Suspecting that it might be a weapon, he reaches into the pocket and discovers a plastic bag containing illegal drugs. Officer Tom arrests John for drug possession.

   John's defense attorney files a motion to suppress the evidence of the drugs, arguing that Officer Tom's search violated John's Fourth Amendment rights because it exceeded the scope of a permissible stop and frisk. The prosecution contends that the search was lawful, as Officer Tom had reasonable suspicion to conduct the stop and frisk and that the search was limited to a pat-down for weapons.

   How should the court rule?

ORAL ARGUMENTS

Alabama v. White: www.oyez.org/cases/1980-1989/1989/1989_89_789/argument

California v. Hodari D.: www.oyez.org/cases/1990-1999/1990/1990_89_1632/argument

Michigan v. Long: www.oyez.org/cases/1980-1989/1982/1982_82_256/argument

Minnesota v. Dickerson: www.oyez.org/cases/1990-1999/1992/1992_91_2019/argument

Terry v. Ohio: www.oyez.org/cases/1960-1969/1967/1967_67/argument

United States v. Sharpe: www.oyez.org/cases/1980-1989/1984/1984_83_529/argument

Whren v. United States: www.oyez.org/cases/1990-1999/1995/1995_95_5841/argument

CHAPTER 6

Exceptions to the Warrant "Requirement"

LEARNING OBJECTIVES

After reading this chapter, students should be able to:

- Explain when an arrest or search warrant is required before an arrest may be made
- Explain the exceptions to the search warrant requirement and the logic behind the exceptions
- Explain what a search incident to arrest is, the justifications for the search, as well as the timing, and scope
- Understand who may give consent to search and the requirements for valid consent
- Discuss the importance of exigent circumstances in justifying warrantless searches and the parameters placed around them
- Apply the three factors required for a lawful plain view search
- Explain the justifications and reasoning for the automobile exception
- Describe the scope of a search in association with the automobile exception and how containers are treated

Introduction

We have repeatedly encountered the United States Supreme Court's pronouncement from *Katz* that warrantless searches are *per se* unreasonable under the Fourth Amendment — subject only to a few specifically established and well-delineated exceptions. We now consider the exceptions to the search warrant requirement and related issues and nuances about these searches. For example, questions we will continue to return to about most of these exceptions are the timing and scope of the search. At the end of this chapter, you may wish to evaluate whether you agree with the Court's assessment that these exceptions are few, specifically established, and well-delineated, or whether the number of exceptions has diluted the Fourth Amendment.

Search Incident to Lawful Arrest

The first exception to the search warrant requirement we discuss is Search Incident to Lawful Arrest. According to this exception, the police are authorized to search individuals they have lawfully arrested without securing a search warrant. This includes making an arrest for even minor offenses; however, to perform a search incident to a lawful arrest, the suspect must be taken into full custody. *Knowles v. Iowa*, 525. U.S. 113 (1998).

A warrantless search incident to an arrest is justified by the need for the police to secure potential weapons, evidence, and the need for a bright-line rule. The Court reasoned the police should not have to "second guess" when they can and cannot perform a search incident to a lawful arrest, so drawing a metaphorical line in the sand was necessary. The arrest has significantly diminished the suspect's privacy rights. However, we have yet to consider the permissible *scope* of the search that an officer is authorized to make incident to an arrest.

Is such a search strictly confined to the arrestee's person, and is a warrant required if the search extends to effects or the surrounding area or premises? Can a warrantless search be made of the arrestee's car if the arrest occurs following a motor vehicle violation? Can packages and other containers within the arrestee's possession be searched without a warrant? Issues like these are important aspects of the "search incident to a lawful arrest" exception to the warrant requirement.

Chimel v. California

395 U.S. 752 (1969)

MR. JUSTICE STEWART delivered the opinion of the Court.

Three police officers arrived at the Santa Ana, California, home of the petitioner with a warrant authorizing his arrest for the burglary of a coin shop. The officers knocked on the door, identified themselves to the petitioner's wife, and asked if they might come inside. She ushered them into the house, where they waited 10 or 15 minutes until the petitioner returned home from work. When the petitioner entered the house, one of the officers handed him the arrest warrant and asked for permission to "look around." The petitioner objected, but was advised that "on the basis of the lawful arrest," the officers would nonetheless conduct a search. No search warrant had been issued.

Accompanied by the petitioner's wife, the officers then looked through the entire three-bedroom house, including the attic, the garage, and a small workshop. In some rooms the search was relatively cursory. In the master bedroom and sewing room, however, the officers directed the petitioner's wife to open drawers and "to physically move contents of the drawers from side to side so that [they] might view any items that would have come from [the] burglary." After completing the search, they seized numerous items — primarily coins, but also several medals, tokens, and a few other objects. The entire search took between 45 minutes and an hour.

At the petitioner's subsequent state trial on two charges of burglary, the items taken from his house were admitted into evidence against him, over his objection that they had been unconstitutionally seized. He was convicted, and the judgments of conviction were affirmed by both the California Court of Appeal and the California Supreme Court.

Without deciding the question, we proceed on the hypothesis that the California courts were correct in holding that the arrest of the petitioner was valid under the Constitution. This brings us directly to the question whether the warrantless search of the petitioner's entire house can be constitutionally justified as incident to that arrest. The decisions of this Court bearing upon that question have been far from consistent, as even the most cursory review makes evident.

Only last Term in *Terry v Ohio*, 392 US 1 (1968) we emphasized that the police must, whenever practicable, obtain advance judicial approval of searches and seizures through the warrant procedure, and that "[t]he scope of [a] search must be 'strictly tied to and justified by' the circumstances which rendered its initiation permissible. The search undertaken by the officer in that "stop and frisk" case was sustained under that test, because it was no more than a protective search for weapons."

A similar analysis underlies the "search incident to arrest" principle and marks its proper extent. When an arrest is made, it is reasonable for the arresting officer to search the person arrested in order to remove any weapons that the latter might seek to use in order to resist arrest or effect his escape. Otherwise, the officer's safety might well be endangered, and the arrest itself frustrated. In addition, it is entirely reasonable for the arresting officer to search for and seize any evidence on the arrestee's person in order to prevent its concealment or destruction. And the area into which an arrestee might reach in order to grab a weapon or evidentiary items must, of course, be governed by a like rule. A gun on a table or in a drawer in front of one who is arrested can be as dangerous to the arresting officer as one concealed in the clothing of the person arrested. There is ample justification, therefore, for a search of the arrestee's person and the area "within his immediate control" construing that phrase to mean the area from within which he might gain possession of a weapon or destructible evidence.

There is no comparable justification, however, for routinely searching any room other than that in which an arrest occurs — or, for that matter, for searching through all the desk drawers or other closed or concealed areas in that room itself. Such searches, in the absence of well-recognized exceptions, may be made only under the authority of a search warrant. The "adherence to judicial processes" mandated by the Fourth Amendment requires no less.

It is argued in the present case that it is "reasonable" to search a man's house when he is arrested in it. But that argument is founded on little more than a subjective view regarding the acceptability of certain sorts of police conduct, and not on considerations relevant to Fourth Amendment interests. Under such an unconfined analysis, Fourth Amendment protection in this area would approach the evaporation point. It is not easy to explain why, for instance, it is less subjectively "reasonable" to search a man's house when he is arrested on his front lawn — or just down the street — than it is when he happens to be in the house at the time of arrest.

No consideration relevant to the Fourth Amendment suggests any point of rational limitation, once the search is allowed to go beyond the area from which the person arrested might obtain weapons or evidentiary items. The only reasoned distinction is one between a search of the person arrested and the area within his reach on the one hand, and more extensive searches on the other.

The general point so forcefully made by Judge Learned Hand in *United States v. Kirschenblatt*, 16 F2d 202, 203 (2nd Cir. 1926) remains:

> After arresting a man in his house, to rummage at will among his papers in search of whatever will convict him, appears to us to be indistinguishable from what might be done under a general warrant; indeed, the warrant would give more protection, for presumably it must be issued by a magistrate. True, by hypothesis the power would not exist, if the supposed offender were not found on the premises; but it is small consolation to know that one's papers are safe only so long as one is not at home.

Application of sound Fourth Amendment principles to the facts of this case produces a clear result. The search here went far beyond the petitioner's person and the area from within which he might have obtained either a weapon or something that could have been used against him. There was no constitutional justification, in the absence of a search warrant, for extending the search beyond that area. The scope of the search was, therefore, "unreasonable" under the Fourth and Fourteenth Amendments, and the petitioner's conviction cannot stand.

Reversed.

FURTHER CASE LAW, REFLECTIONS, AND QUESTIONS

1. The Supreme Court had struggled for years about the permissible scope of a search incident to a lawful arrest. Overruling prior precedent that permitted the search of an entire residence incident to arrest so long as it was reasonable, *Chimel's* limitation of a search incident to arrest to the arrestee's "**grabbing area**" has prevailed. However, the practical application of this rule is not always easy.
2. Before *Chimel*, the Court held that whether a search incident to arrest was reasonable should be considered on a case-by-case basis. If you were a police officer, would you prefer the clarity of the grabbing area rule established in *Chimel* or the flexible but uncertain standard used before 1969?
3. *Chimel* left open several questions. (1) Is a search of an arrestee's person limited to a pat down of their outer clothing as provided for in *Terry*? (2) Can packages and other containers within the arrestee's possession be searched without a warrant? The Supreme Court answered these questions four years after *Chimel* in *United States v. Robinson*, 414 U.S. 218 (1973).

    Police stopped Robinson for a motor vehicle violation. After the police confirmed that he was driving with a revoked driver's license, Robinson was arrested. A police officer frisked Robinson for weapons and found a crumpled container that contained capsules of heroin in his pocket. Robinson was convicted on narcotics charges. The United States Supreme Court found the search to be constitutional. The Court found that the officer was authorized to reach into Robinson's coat as part of his search since the officer had probable cause to arrest Robinson. Once probable cause to arrest was established, a full search incident to that arrest, including opening packages in the arrestee's possession, was authorized to protect the officer's safety and preserve evidence. In short, the Court held that a police officer with probable cause to arrest a suspect, even where the arrest was for a traffic violation, was not limited to a protective frisk of the suspect's clothes for weapons but rather was authorized to conduct a full search incident to the arrest.

4. *Robinson* established two clear precedents. First, police may search a person incident to a custodial arrest. Second, police may open and inspect containers found in an arrestee's possession at the time of the arrest. This includes containers located within *Chimel's* reach limitation. However, it will not come as a surprise that these precedents are not absolute.

5. While the police are permitted to search a person and the area near the person, they are not permitted to conduct strip searches or body cavity searches simply because the suspect was placed under arrest. Why do you suspect this is the case?

6. After an arrest, police are generally limited to searching the area in the immediate vicinity of an arrestee without first obtaining a search warrant. An exception to this rule involves arrests made inside a building where accomplices to the arrestee may be present and cause potential danger to the police. Such a search, whose scope is very limited, is known as a **protective sweep**.

   In *Maryland v. Buie*, 494 U.S. 325, 327 (1990), the Court defined a protective sweep as "a quick and limited search of a premises, incident to an arrest and conducted to protect the safety of police officers or others." According to the Court, the police, without reasonable suspicion or probable cause, may search those areas immediately adjoining the place of arrest where a possibly dangerous person could launch an attack. The Court also allowed a further protective sweep justified by reasonable suspicion that "the area swept harbored an individual posing a danger to the officers or others." In other words, police may search through the entire building based on reasonable suspicion that someone poses a danger in the home but may only search areas where a person could hide.

Box 6.1 You Be the Judge

Police officers, possessing warrants for Hal's arrest, were watching the house where he resided. They observed what they suspected was an exchange of narcotics between a known addict and Hal outside the house after Hal had gone into the house and brought something out to the addict. They arrested Hal on the front steps and told him that they would search the house. A search of the then-unoccupied house disclosed narcotics in a bedroom.

Were Hal's rights violated by the search of his house? Why?

What is Hal's best argument?

What arguments might the state raise?

See *Vale v Louisiana*, 399 U.S. 30 (1970).

Search of Containers and Electronics Incident to Lawful Arrest

For police to lawfully search a container in possession of an arrestee without a warrant, it must be done contemporaneously with the arrest. In *United States v. Chadwick*, 433 U.S. 1 (1977), federal agents arrested Chadwick for possession of marijuana. The agents possessed probable cause to believe that a locked footlocker being transported by a train passenger contained marijuana. The agents arrested Chadwick after he departed the train and transported the footlocker to the federal building. Over an hour later, they conducted a warrantless search of the footlocker, finding a "large quantity" of marijuana. The Supreme Court found the search unconstitutional because it was not conducted contemporaneously or "incident" to arrest, but after the arrest when the need for a warrantless search had dissipated. The Court held that once the police took possession of the footlocker and held it for a significant time post-arrest, the police should have obtained a search warrant before searching it.

To be contemporaneous, a search incident to an arrest must be conducted in close proximity to the time and location where the arrest took place. However, police may separate the arrestee from the container to be searched before performing the search, thereby alleviating officer safety concerns.

Similar standards apply to the search of electronic communication devices incident to an arrest. In the 21st century, the nature of items or containers possessed by people has changed dramatically. As technology advances, courts have been forced to consider what limits should be imposed on the authority of police to search items in an arrestee's possession without a warrant. In *Riley v. California*, 573 U.S. 373 (2014), the Supreme Court considered whether police may search a cell phone in possession of an arrestee incident to a custodial arrest.

David Riley was arrested for driving on a suspended license. At the time of his arrest, police found two guns in the car he was driving and a cell phone in his pocket. A gang unit detective analyzed videos and photographs located on his phone. The detective saw Riley making gang signs and other gang indicia stored on the phone. Based on this, the detective determined Riley was gang-affiliated. Riley was subsequently tied to a drive-by shooting via ballistics tests, and separate charges were brought, including shooting at an occupied vehicle, attempted murder, and assault with a semi-automatic firearm. Before trial, Riley moved to suppress the evidence regarding his gang affiliation acquired through his cell phone. His motion was denied. At trial, a gang expert testified to Riley's membership in the Lincoln Park gang, the rivalry between the gangs involved, and why the shooting could have been gang-related.

After granting certiorari, a unanimous Supreme Court held that the warrantless search of the cell phone was unconstitutional. The Court held that the warrantless search exception following an arrest exists to protect officer safety and preserve evidence, neither of which is at issue when searching digital data. For this type of evidence, including tablets, laptop computers, and other electronic devices, the police have the ability to preserve the evidence while waiting for a search warrant. The Court viewed cell phones as minicomputers filled with massive amounts of private information and are therefore different from the traditional items that can be seized from an arrestee's person, such as a wallet. The Court did conclude that some warrantless searches of cell phones might be permitted in an emergency, but only when the government's interests are so compelling that a warrantless search would be reasonable.

Search Incident to Lawful Arrest and Automobiles

Not infrequently, drivers or passengers in and around an automobile are arrested. Following *Chimel*, courts were forced to consider what constitutes a reaching distance for a person arrested in a vehicle. For example, what if an officer makes a custodial arrest of the driver of a car? Can all or parts of the vehicle be searched incident to the arrest? Should the permissible scope of the search be determined on a case-by-case basis, or should a general rule that can be applied in all cases govern? Keep in mind, in this section, we are discussing searches incident to arrest and a vehicle. This is not the vehicle exception to the search warrant requirement, which is discussed later in the chapter.

In *New York v. Belton*, 453 U.S. 454 (1981), a police officer stopped a car for speeding. When the officer approached the vehicle, he smelled burnt marijuana and saw other evidence of marijuana use. The officer ordered the four men who occupied the vehicle out of the car and separated them so they would not be in physical contact. Additionally, he patted them down and, while the men remained standing outside of the vehicle, placed them under arrest. He then searched the passenger compartment of the car. He found a black leather jacket belonging to Belton on the back seat. He unzipped one of the pockets of the jacket and discovered cocaine. The trial court subsequently denied Belton's motion to suppress the cocaine, and Belton pleaded guilty to a related offense, preserving his right to appeal. The New York Court of Appeals reversed, holding that "a warrantless search of the zippered pockets of an inaccessible jacket may not be upheld as a search incident to a lawful arrest where there is no longer any danger that the arrestee or a confederate might gain access to the article."

The Supreme Court granted certiorari and reversed. Justice Stewart's majority opinion emphasized the need for a "bright-line" rule that would give the police guidance in the recurring situation involving "the proper scope of a search of the interior of an automobile incident to a lawful custodial arrest of its occupants." Accordingly, the majority held that when a police officer has made a lawful custodial arrest of the occupant of an automobile, they may, as a contemporaneous incident of that arrest, search the passenger compartment of the automobile.

The majority further held that the police may examine the contents of any containers found within the passenger compartment. The justification for the search is not that the arrestee has no privacy interest in the container but that the lawful custodial arrest justifies the infringement of any privacy interest the arrestee may have. Such a container may be searched, whether it is open or closed. The Court concluded:

> It is not questioned that the respondent was the subject of a lawful custodial arrest on a charge of possessing marijuana. The search of the respondent's jacket followed immediately upon that arrest. The jacket was located inside the passenger compartment of the car in which the respondent had been a passenger just before he was arrested. The jacket was thus within the area which we have concluded was "within the arrestee's immediate control" within the meaning of the *Chimel* case. The search of the jacket, therefore, was a search incident to a lawful custodial arrest, and it did not violate the Fourth and Fourteenth Amendments. *Id.* at 1031

The so-called *Belton* rule was somewhat controversial and was not as straightforward as Justice Stewart assumed it would be. The Court confronted one of the lingering questions about *Belton's* applicability in *Thornton v. United States,* 541 U.S. 615 (2004). In this case, a police officer spotted Thornton while Thornton was driving a car with license plates registered to a different vehicle. However, when the officer caught up with Thornton, Thornton parked the car in a parking lot and was walking away from the vehicle. Thornton appeared nervous and apprehensive. He consented to the officer patting him down, admitted that he was carrying illegal drugs, and then produced both marijuana and crack cocaine concealed in one of his pockets. The officer thereupon arrested Thornton, handcuffed him, and placed him in the back seat of his squad car. He then searched Thornton's car and found a handgun under the driver's seat. Following Thornton's indictment on federal drug and firearms charges, a district court judge, in reliance on *Belton,* denied Thornton's motion to suppress the gun found in his car. The court of appeals affirmed. Chief Justice Rehnquist's majority opinion identified the issue before the Supreme Court as "whether *Belton's* rule is limited to situations where the officer makes contact with the occupant while the occupant is inside the vehicle, or whether it applies as well when the officer first makes contact with the arrestee after the latter has stepped out of his vehicle." The Court concluded that "*Belton* governs even when an officer does not make contact until the person arrested has left the vehicle."

> [W]e placed no reliance on the fact that the officer in *Belton* ordered the occupants out of the vehicle, or initiated contact with them while they remained within it. Nor do we find such a factor persuasive in distinguishing the current situation, as it bears no logical relationship to *Belton's* rationale. There is simply no basis to conclude that the span of the area generally within the arrestee's immediate possession is determined by

> whether the arrestee exited the vehicle at the officer's direction, or whether the officer-initiated contact with him while he remained in the car. So long as an arrestee is the sort of "recent occupant" of a vehicle such as petitioner was here, officers may search that vehicle incident to the arrest. *Thornton*, 541 U.S. at 620.

The rulings in *Belton* and *Thornton* were widely criticized, starting with the Justices themselves. While concurring in the judgment in *Thornton*, Justice Scalia, joined by Justice Ginsburg, disavowed allegiance to *Belton*, arguing that the Court should "limit *Belton* searches to cases where it is reasonable to believe evidence relevant to the crime of arrest might be found in the vehicle." Justice O'Connor, concurring in part, and Justices Stevens and Souter, dissenting, also expressed doubt about *Belton's* continuing viability. *Belton's* denouement came five years later, in *Arizona v. Gant.*

Arizona v. Gant

556 U.S. 332 (2009)

JUSTICE STEVENS delivered the opinion of the Court.

After Rodney Gant was arrested for driving with a suspended license, handcuffed, and locked in the back of a patrol car, police officers searched his car and discovered cocaine in the pocket of a jacket on the backseat. Because Gant could not have accessed his car to retrieve weapons or evidence at the time of the search, the Arizona Supreme Court held that the search-incident-to-arrest exception to the Fourth Amendment's warrant requirement, as defined in *Chimel v. California,* 395 U.S. 752 (1969), and applied to vehicle searches in *New York v. Belton,* 453 U.S. 454 (1981), did not justify the search in this case. We agree with that conclusion.

Under *Chimel,* police may search incident to arrest only the space within an arrestee's immediate control, meaning "the area from within which he might gain possession of a weapon or destructible evidence." The safety and evidentiary justifications underlying *Chimel's* reaching-distance rule determine *Belton* 's scope. Accordingly, we hold that *Belton* does not authorize a vehicle search incident to a recent occupant's arrest after the arrestee has been secured and cannot access the interior of the vehicle. Consistent with the holding in *Thornton v. United States,* 541 U.S. 615 (2004), and following the suggestion in Justice Scalia's opinion concurring in the judgment in that case, we also conclude that circumstances unique to the automobile context justify a search incident to arrest when it is reasonable to believe that evidence of the offense of arrest might be found in the vehicle.

I

Acting on an anonymous tip that the residence at 2524 North Walnut Avenue was being used to sell drugs, Tucson police officers Griffith and Reed knocked on the front door and asked to speak to the owner. Gant answered the door and, after identifying himself, stated that he expected the owner to return later. The officers left the residence and conducted a records check, which revealed that Gant's driver's license had been suspended and there was an outstanding warrant for his arrest for driving with a suspended license.

When the officers returned to the house that evening, they found a man near the back of the house and a woman in a car parked in front of it. After a third officer arrived, they arrested the man for providing a false name and the woman for possessing drug paraphernalia. Both arrestees were handcuffed and secured in separate patrol cars when Gant arrived. The officers recognized his car as it entered the driveway, and Officer Griffith confirmed that Gant was the driver by shining a flashlight into the car as it drove by him. Gant parked at the end of the driveway, got out of his car, and shut the door. Griffith, who was about 30 feet away, called to Gant, and they approached each other, meeting 10-to-12 feet from Gant's car. Griffith immediately arrested Gant and handcuffed him.

Because the other arrestees were secured in the only patrol cars at the scene, Griffith called for backup. When two more officers arrived, they locked Gant in the backseat of their vehicle. After Gant had been handcuffed and placed in the back of a patrol car, two officers searched his car: One of them found a gun, and the other discovered a bag of cocaine in the pocket of a jacket on the backseat.

Gant was charged with two offenses — possession of a narcotic drug for sale and possession of drug paraphernalia (*i.e.*, the plastic bag in which the cocaine was found). He moved to suppress the evidence seized from his car on the ground that the warrantless search violated the Fourth Amendment. Among other things, Gant argued that *Belton* did not authorize the search of his vehicle because he posed no threat to the officers after he was handcuffed in the patrol car and because he was arrested for a traffic offense for which no evidence could be found in his vehicle. When asked at the suppression hearing why the search was conducted, Officer Griffith responded: "Because the law says we can do it."

The trial court rejected the State's contention that the officers had probable cause to search Gant's car for contraband when the search began, but it denied the motion to suppress. Relying on the fact that the police saw Gant commit the crime of driving without a license and apprehended him only shortly after he exited his car, the court held that the search was permissible as a search incident to arrest. A jury found Gant guilty on both drug counts, and he was sentenced to a 3-year term of imprisonment.

After protracted state-court proceedings, the Arizona Supreme Court concluded that the search of Gant's car was unreasonable within the meaning of the Fourth Amendment.

II

The Arizona Supreme Court read our decision in *Belton* as merely delineating "the proper scope of a search of the interior of an automobile" incident to an arrest. That is, *when* the passenger compartment is within an arrestee's reaching distance, *Belton* supplies the generalization that the entire compartment and any containers therein may be reached. On that view of *Belton,* the state court concluded that the search of Gant's car was unreasonable because Gant clearly could not have accessed his car at the time of the search. It also found that no other exception to the warrant requirement applied in this case.

III

Despite the textual and evidentiary support for the Arizona Supreme Court's reading of *Belton,* our opinion has been widely understood to allow a vehicle search incident to the arrest of a recent occupant even if there is no possibility the arrestee could gain access to the vehicle at the time of the search.

Under this broad reading of *Belton,* a vehicle search would be authorized incident to every arrest of a recent occupant notwithstanding that in most cases the vehicle's passenger compartment will not be within the arrestee's reach at the time of the search. To read *Belton* as authorizing a vehicle search incident to every recent occupant's arrest would thus untether the rule from the justifications underlying the *Chimel* exception — a result clearly incompatible with our statement in *Belton* that it in no way alters the fundamental principles established in the *Chimel* case regarding the basic scope of searches incident to lawful custodial arrests. Accordingly, we reject this reading of *Belton* and hold that the *Chimel* rationale authorizes police to search a vehicle incident to a recent occupant's arrest only when the arrestee is unsecured and within reaching distance of the passenger compartment at the time of the search.

Although it does not follow from *Chimel,* we also conclude that circumstances unique to the vehicle context justify a search incident to a lawful arrest when it is reasonable to believe evidence relevant to the crime of arrest might be found in the vehicle. In many cases, as when a recent occupant is arrested for a traffic violation, there will be no reasonable basis to believe the vehicle contains relevant evidence. But in others, including *Belton* and *Thornton,* the offense of arrest will supply a basis for searching the passenger compartment of an arrestee's vehicle and any containers therein.

Neither the possibility of access nor the likelihood of discovering offense-related evidence authorized the search in this case. Unlike in *Belton,* which involved a single officer confronted with four unsecured arrestees, the five officers in this case outnumbered the three arrestees, all of whom had been handcuffed and secured in separate patrol cars before the officers searched Gant's car. Under those circumstances, Gant clearly was not within reaching distance of his car at the time of the search. An evidentiary basis for the search was also lacking in this case. Whereas Belton and Thornton were arrested for drug offenses, Gant was arrested for driving with a suspended license — an offense for which police could not expect to find evidence in the passenger compartment of Gant's car. Because police could not reasonably have believed either that Gant could have accessed his car at the time of the search or that evidence of the offense for which he was arrested might have been found therein, the search in this case was unreasonable.

IV

The State argues that *Belton* searches are reasonable regardless of the possibility of access in a given case because that expansive rule correctly balances law enforcement interests, including the interest in a bright-line rule, with an arrestee's limited privacy interest in his vehicle.

For several reasons, we reject the State's argument. First, the State seriously undervalues the privacy interests at stake. Although we have recognized that a motorist's privacy interest in his vehicle is less substantial than in his home, the former interest is nevertheless important and deserving of constitutional protection. It is particularly significant that *Belton* searches authorize police officers to search not just the passenger compartment but every purse, briefcase, or other container within that space. A rule that gives police the power to conduct such a search whenever an individual is caught committing a traffic offense, when there is no basis for believing evidence of the offense might be found in the vehicle, creates a serious and recurring threat to the privacy of countless individuals. Indeed, the character of that threat implicates the central concern underlying the Fourth Amendment — the concern about giving police officers unbridled discretion to rummage at will among a person's private effects.

At the same time as it undervalues these privacy concerns, the State exaggerates the clarity that its reading of *Belton* provides. Courts that have read *Belton* expansively are at odds regarding how close in time to the arrest and how proximate to the arrestee's vehicle an officer's first contact with the arrestee must be to bring the encounter within *Belton*'s purview and whether a search is reasonable when it commences or continues after the arrestee has been removed from the scene. The rule has thus generated a great deal of uncertainty, particularly for a rule touted as providing a "bright line."

Contrary to the State's suggestion, a broad reading of *Belton* is also unnecessary to protect law enforcement safety and evidentiary interests. Under our view, *Belton* and *Thornton* permit an officer to conduct a vehicle search when an arrestee is within reaching distance of the vehicle or it is reasonable to believe the vehicle contains evidence of the offense of arrest. Other established exceptions to the warrant requirement authorize a vehicle search under additional circumstances when safety or evidentiary concerns demand.

These exceptions together ensure that officers may search a vehicle when genuine safety or evidentiary concerns encountered during the arrest of a vehicle's recent occupant justify a search. Construing *Belton* broadly to allow vehicle searches incident to any arrest would serve no purpose except to provide a police entitlement, and it is anathema to the Fourth Amendment to permit a warrantless search on that basis. For these reasons, we are unpersuaded by the State's arguments that a broad reading of *Belton* would meaningfully further law enforcement interests and justify a substantial intrusion on individuals' privacy.

VI

Police may search a vehicle incident to a recent occupant's arrest only if the arrestee is within reaching distance of the passenger compartment at the time of the search or it is reasonable to believe the vehicle contains evidence of the offense of arrest. When these justifications are absent, a search of an arrestee's vehicle will be unreasonable unless police obtain a warrant or show that another exception to the warrant requirement applies. The Arizona Supreme Court correctly held that this case involved an unreasonable search. Accordingly, the judgment of the State Supreme Court is affirmed.

FURTHER CASE LAW, REFLECTIONS, AND QUESTIONS

1. The rule established by the Court in *Gant* is police may search a vehicle incident to a recent occupant's arrest only if the arrestee is (1) within reaching distance of the passenger compartment at the time of the search or (2) it is reasonable to believe the vehicle contains evidence of the offense of arrest.

2. Take note of the importance of the specific facts of *Gant* and how they differ from *Chimel*, *Belton*, and *Thornton*.

   Gant was not within reach of the car to justify a search incident to arrest, as Chimel requires.

   Gant was arrested by five police officers, handcuffed, and placed inside a police car prior to the search of his vehicle. Belton was arrested by a police officer and was standing on the side of the road when his car and jacket were searched.

   Gant was arrested for driving with a suspended license, while Thornton was arrested on narcotics charges.

   Given those facts, could the Court have arrived at the same outcome without overruling Belton's precedential value?

3. Be sure to keep in mind that *Belton* and *Gant* involve searches incident to an arrest exception to the search warrant requirement. The Court did not apply the "automobile exception," which we will consider later in this chapter.

Box 6.2 Summary of Search Incident to Lawful Arrest

Justification

Officer safety, the potential destruction of evidence, and the need for a bright-line rule.

Probable Cause and Custodial Arrest

The arrest must be lawful and based on probable cause.

The officer must also make a full custodial arrest and take the person into custody.

Scope

The search is limited to the person arrested and any containers or areas within their immediate control; or

A protective sweep of the home where officers may look for individuals located immediately adjoining the area of arrest; or

Based upon reasonable suspicion, search any area in the home where a dangerous person could be located.

If the arrest is made of an occupant or recent occupant of a vehicle, the suspect must be unsecured and within reaching distance of the passenger compartment, or it must be reasonable for the officer to believe that evidence of the crime of arrest will be located in the vehicle.

Timing

The timing of the search must be contemporaneous with the arrest.

The Court defined "contemporaneous" in *Rawlings v. Kentucky,* 448 U.S. 98 (1980) as "immediately before the arrest, at the same time as the arrest, or immediately after the arrest."

Consent Searches

The protections in the Bill of Rights are generally designed to safeguard individual liberties. Accordingly, an individual who does not feel the need for a particular safeguard may choose to relinquish it. In subsequent chapters, we will study how people can effectively waive their constitutional protections, including "*Miranda* rights," in the context of self-incrimination issues, the right to counsel, and others. In other words, **consent searches** are technically not exceptions to the search warrant requirement. There are two different legal reasons why some do not consider consent searches as exceptions to the warrant requirement: (1) if a person has voluntarily consented to a search and waived their right, the search warrant requirement does not apply; and (2) if an individual gives valid consent to the search of their person, effects, or premises, the ensuing search is not "unreasonable" according to the Fourth Amendment, even in the absence of a warrant, probable cause, or exigent circumstances. However, despite this semantic argument, consent searches are frequently discussed and treated as exceptions to the search warrant requirement because many of the same questions, rules, and issues apply.

We now take up the topic of consent searches. Two significant issues surround consent searches. The first involves the prerequisites for valid or effective consent. In other words, the voluntariness of the consent. For example, should we take at face value a person's affirmative response to a police officer's request to search her purse? Or their home? Does it matter if the person does not understand that they need not agree to the request? Does it matter if the person (reasonably) believes that withholding consent would be futile because the police will go ahead and search anyway?

The second issue concerns who is authorized to consent to a search or what is frequently referred to as "third-party consent." Assume, for example, that you share an apartment or dormitory room with a roommate. Can your roommate give legally valid consent for the police to search your common living area? What about your bedroom? Can parents consent to the search of their child's room or belongings? Conversely, can a child consent to the search of their parents' home or possessions? Does it matter whether the person permitting the search actually lacks the authority to consent? Is the search lawful if the police (reasonably) believe that the person granting permission is authorized to consent?

The Requirements for Effective Consent

For a person's consent to search to be legally valid, the consent must pass constitutional muster. In other words, it must, at a minimum, be given voluntarily. However, what does voluntary mean, and how is it defined? Could it be safe to say that whenever a private citizen provides consent to the police, there is always an element of coercion? In the following case, the United States Supreme Court considers what must be proven for consent to be considered voluntary.

Schneckloth v. Bustamonte

412 U.S. 218 (1973)

MR. JUSTICE STEWART delivered the opinion of the Court.

The respondent was brought to trial in a California court upon a charge of possessing a check with intent to defraud. He moved to suppress the introduction of certain material as evidence against him on the ground that the material had been acquired through an unconstitutional search and seizure. In response to the motion, the trial judge conducted an evidentiary hearing where it was established that the material in question had been acquired by the State under the following circumstances:

While on routine patrol in Sunnyvale, California, at approximately 2:40 in the morning, Police Officer James Rand stopped an automobile when he observed that one headlight and its license plate light were burned out. Six men were in the vehicle. Joe Alcala and the respondent, Robert Bustamonte, were in the front seat with Joe Gonzales, the driver. Three older men were seated in the rear. When, in response to the policeman's question, Gonzales could not produce a driver's license, Officer Rand asked if any of the other five had any evidence of identification. Only Alcala produced a license, and he explained that the car was his brother's. After the six occupants had stepped out of the car at the officer's request and after two additional policemen had arrived, Officer Rand asked Alcala if he could search the car. Alcala replied, "Sure, go ahead." Wadded up under the left rear seat, the police officers found three checks that had previously been stolen from a car wash.

The trial judge denied the motion to suppress, and the checks in question were admitted in evidence at Bustamonte's trial. On the basis of this and other evidence he was convicted, and the California Court of Appeal for the First Appellate District affirmed the conviction. [Bustamonte filed for federal habeas relief. The Ninth Circuit Court of Appeals granted him relief and remanded the case to the trial court on the grounds that the State must affirmatively prove that the subject of the search knew that he had a right to refuse consent. The United States Supreme Court granted certiorari.]

II

The respondent concedes that a search conducted pursuant to a valid consent is constitutionally permissible. And similarly the State concedes that "[w]hen a prosecutor seeks to rely upon consent to justify the lawfulness of a search, he has the burden of proving that the consent was, in fact, freely and voluntarily given."

The precise question in this case, then, is what must the prosecution prove to demonstrate that a consent was "voluntarily" given. And upon that question there is a square conflict of views between the state and federal courts that have reviewed the search involved in the case before us. The Court of Appeals for the Ninth Circuit concluded that it is an essential part of the State's initial burden to prove that a person knows he has a right to refuse consent. The California courts have followed the rule that voluntariness is a question of fact to be determined from the totality of all the circumstances, and that the state of a defendant's knowledge is only one factor to be taken into account in assessing the voluntariness of a consent.

The most extensive judicial exposition of the meaning of "voluntariness" has been developed in those cases in which the Court has had to determine the "voluntariness" of a defendant's confession for purposes of the Fourteenth Amendment. It is to that body of case law to which we turn for initial guidance on the meaning of "voluntariness" in the present context.

In determining whether a defendant's will was overborne in a particular case, the Court has assessed the totality of all the surrounding circumstances — both the characteristics of the accused and the details of the interrogation.

The significant fact about all of these decisions is that none of them turned on the presence or absence of a single controlling criterion; each reflected a careful scrutiny of all the surrounding circumstances.

Similar considerations lead us to agree with the courts of California that the question whether a consent to a search was in fact "voluntary" or was the product of duress or coercion, express or implied, is a question of fact to be determined from the totality of all the circumstances. While knowledge of the right to refuse consent is one factor to be taken into account, the government need not establish such knowledge as the *sine qua non* of an effective consent. As with police questioning, two competing concerns must be accommodated in determining the meaning of a "voluntary" consent — the legitimate need for such searches and the equally important requirement of assuring the absence of coercion.

In situations where the police have some evidence of illicit activity, but lack probable cause to arrest or search, a search authorized by a valid consent may be the only means of obtaining important and reliable evidence. In the present case for example, while the police had reason to stop the car for traffic violations, the State does not contend that there was probable cause to search the vehicle or that the search was incident to a valid arrest of any of the occupants. Yet, the search yielded tangible evidence that served as a basis for a prosecution, and provided some assurance that others, wholly innocent of the crime, were not mistakenly brought to trial. And in those cases where there is probable cause to arrest or search but where the police lack a warrant, a consent search may still be valuable. If the search is conducted and proves fruitless, that in itself may convince the police that an arrest with its possible stigma and embarrassment is unnecessary, or that a far more extensive search pursuant to a warrant is not justified. In short, a search pursuant to consent may result in considerably less inconvenience for the subject of the search, and properly conducted, is a constitutionally permissible and wholly legitimate aspect of effective police activity.

But the Fourth and Fourteenth Amendments require that a consent not be coerced, by explicit or implicit means, by implied threat or covert force. For, no matter how subtly the coercion was applied, the resulting "consent" would be no more than a **pretext** for the unjustified police intrusion against which the Fourth Amendment is directed.

The problem of reconciling the recognized legitimacy of consent searches with the requirement that they be free from any aspect of official coercion cannot be resolved by any infallible touchstone. Just as was true with confessions, the requirement of a "voluntary" consent reflects a fair accommodation of the constitutional requirements involved. In examining all the surrounding circumstances to determine if in fact the consent to search was coerced, account must be taken of subtly coercive police questions, as well as the possibly vulnerable subjective state of the person who consents. Those searches that are the product of police coercion can thus be filtered out without undermining the continuing validity of consent searches. In sum, there is no reason for us to depart in the area of consent searches, from the traditional definition of "voluntariness."

The approach of the Court of Appeals for the Ninth Circuit finds no support in any of our decisions that have attempted to define the meaning of "voluntariness." Its ruling, that the State must affirmatively prove that the subject of the search knew that he had a right to refuse consent, would, in practice, create serious doubt whether consent searches could continue to be conducted. There might be rare cases where it could be proved from the record that a person in fact affirmatively knew of his right to refuse. But more commonly where there was no evidence of any coercion, explicit or implicit, the prosecution would nevertheless be unable to demonstrate that the subject of the search in fact had known of his right to refuse consent.

One alternative that would go far toward proving that the subject of a search did know he had a right to refuse consent would be to advise him of that right before eliciting his consent. That, however, is a suggestion that has been almost universally repudiated by both federal and state courts, and, we think, rightly so. For it would be thoroughly impractical to impose on the normal consent search the detailed requirements of an effective warning. Consent searches are part of the standard investigatory techniques of law enforcement agencies. They normally occur on the highway, or in a person's home or office, and under informal and unstructured conditions. These situations are a far cry from the structured atmosphere of a trial where, assisted by counsel if he chooses, a defendant is informed of his trial rights. And, while surely a closer question, these situations are still immeasurably far removed from "custodial interrogation."

In short, neither this Court's prior cases, nor the traditional definition of "voluntariness" requires proof of knowledge of a right to refuse as the *sine qua non* of an effective consent to a search.

Our decision today is a narrow one. We hold only that when the subject of a search is not in custody and the State attempts to justify a search on the basis of his consent, the Fourth and Fourteenth Amendments require that it demonstrate that the consent was in fact voluntarily given, and not the result of duress or coercion, express or implied. Voluntariness is a question of fact to be determined from all the circumstances, and while the subject's knowledge of a right to refuse is a factor to be taken into account, the prosecution is not required to demonstrate such knowledge as a prerequisite to establishing a voluntary consent. Because the California court followed these principles in affirming the respondent's conviction, and because the Court of Appeals for the Ninth Circuit in remanding for an evidentiary hearing required more, its judgment must be reversed.

FURTHER CASE LAW, REFLECTIONS, AND QUESTIONS

1. Whether consent is given voluntarily must be considered under the totality of circumstances present in a given case. If questioned, it must be proven by the prosecution, based on the preponderance of the evidence, that consent was given voluntarily. *Schneckloth* listed several factors that may be taken into account to determine if consent was given voluntarily, including the youth of the accused, *Haley* v. *Ohio,* 332 U. S. 596 (1948); his low intelligence, *Fikes v. Alabama*, 352 U. S. 191 (1957); his lack of education, *Payne* v. *Arkansas,* 356 U. S. 560 (1958); the lack of any advice to the accused of his constitutional rights, *Davis v. North Carolina*, 384 U. S. 737 (1966); the repeated and prolonged nature of the questioning, *Ashcraft v. Tennessee*, 322 U. S. 143 (1944); and the use of physical punishment such as the deprivation of food or sleep, *Reck v. Pate*, 367 U. S. 433 (1961). What other factors do you believe should be taken into account by a court in determining whether consent was given voluntarily?
2. Even if a person voluntarily consents to a search, they may place limits on the scope of the search. These include limiting the length of time police will be permitted to conduct the search, specific portions of a house or car for which consent has been granted, and the intensity of the search. Additionally, a person may withdraw consent at any time after it has been granted.
3. In your opinion, should the police be required to inform individuals that they have the right to refuse consent? Would such a rule have a significant impact on law enforcement?
4. Can you imagine how you might respond if, following a police officer's stopping you for a traffic violation, the officer asked for your permission to search your car? Or if, while walking at night, a police officer asked, "if you would mind," allowing the officer to see what you had inside your backpack? Would you be concerned about what might happen if you said "no"?

Box 6.3 You Be the Judge

Bumper lived with his 66-year-old grandmother in rural North Carolina. Several days after an alleged rape, four white police officers went to the Bumper's house. When his grandmother answered the door, the police told her that they had a search warrant to search the house. No such warrant existed. Not knowing this, she stepped aside and let them conduct their search. Inside the house, police found a .22 caliber rifle allegedly used in the commission of the crime. Bumper was subsequently arrested.

During a suppression hearing, the officers testified that they relied not on the search warrant, but on the grandmother's consent to search. The grandmother testified that she believed the officers had a valid search warrant.

How should the trial court rule on the motion to suppress the evidence seized during the search? See *Bumper v. North Carolina*, 391 U.S. 543 (1968).

Who Has the Authority to Give Consent?

Let us now assume that a person "voluntarily" consents to a police search of premises or effects, but that the search affects someone else's interests. For example, can the proprietor of a hotel consent to the authorities' search of a room rented by a patron? In answering this question in the negative, the Supreme Court observed, "It is important to bear in mind that it was the [guest's] constitutional right which was at stake here, and not the night clerk's nor the hotel's. It was a right, therefore, which only the petitioner could waive by word or deed, either directly or through an agent. *Stoner v. California*, 376 U.S. 483, 489 (1964).

This principle received elaboration in *United States v. Matlock*, 415 U.S. 164 (1974). In *Matlock*, the woman with whom the defendant shared living arrangements consented to authorities' search of a bedroom that she and the defendant jointly occupied. In a diaper bag stored in a closet in this room, law enforcement officers found money that linked the defendant to the robbery of a bank. The Court concluded that the consent to search the room given by the woman was valid and binding against the defendant.

> The voluntary consent of any joint occupant of a residence to search the premises jointly occupied is valid against the co-occupant, permitting evidence discovered in the search to be admitted against him at a criminal trial. When the prosecution seeks to justify a warrantless search by proof of voluntary consent, it is not limited to proof that consent was given by the defendant, but may show that permission to search was obtained from a third party who possessed common authority over or other sufficient relation to the premises or effects sought to be inspected.
>
> "Common authority" is, of course, not to be implied from the mere property interest a third party has in the property. The authority which justifies the third-party consent does not rest upon the law of property with its attendant historical and legal refinements but rests rather on mutual use of the property by persons generally having joint access or control for most purposes, so that it is reasonable to recognize that any of the co-inhabitants has the right to permit the inspection in his own right and

that the others have assumed the risk that one of their number might permit the common area to be searched. *Id.* at 171.

In *Matlock*, the party consenting to the search had the *actual* authority to do so, based on her joint occupancy and use of the premises and its effects. However, what of the situation involving a person who has the ***apparent authority*** to consent but lacks the actual authority to do so? If the police (reasonably) rely on the apparent authority, conduct a search, and seize incriminating evidence, may that evidence be admitted against the person who actually retained the right to exclude the police and did not consent to their entry and search?

Box 6.4 Who Has Authority to Give Consent?

Husband-Wife	Either spouse may consent to the search of the entire premises, except for areas under exclusive control by one spouse (e.g., locked drawer, password-protected computer).
Roommates	Roommates can consent to searches of common areas. However, they can only consent to searches of their own containers and property.
Driver Passenger	The driver may consent to a search of the entire case except for containers identified as belonging to the passenger.
Employer-Employee	An employer may consent to the search of an employee's work area other than areas where the worker has a clear expectation of privacy.
Landlord-Tenant	A landlord may not consent to a search of a tenant's residence.
Hotel Clerk-Guest	Hotel clerks may not consent to a search of a guest's room The guest may consent to a search of the entire rented area.

Illinois v. Rodriguez

497 U.S. 177 (1990)

JUSTICE SCALIA delivered the opinion of the Court.

Respondent Edward Rodriguez was arrested at his apartment by law enforcement officers and charged with possession of illegal drugs. The police gained entry to the apartment with the consent and assistance of Gail Fischer, who had lived there with respondent for several months. The relevant facts leading to the arrest are as follows.

Police were summoned to the residence of Dorothy Jackson on South Wolcott in Chicago. They were met by Ms. Jackson's daughter, Gail Fischer, who showed signs of a severe beating. She told the officers that she had been assaulted by respondent Edward Rodriguez earlier that day in an apartment in South California. Fischer stated that Rodriguez was then asleep in the apartment, and she consented to travel there with the police in order to unlock the door with her key so that the officers could enter and arrest him. During this conversation, Fischer several times referred to the apartment in South California as "our" apartment, and said that she had clothes and furniture there. It is unclear whether she indicated that she currently lived at the apartment, or only that she used to live there.

The police officers drove to the apartment in South California, accompanied by Fischer. They did not obtain an arrest warrant for Rodriguez, nor did they seek a search warrant for the apartment. At the apartment, Fischer unlocked the door with her key and gave the officers permission to enter. They moved through the door into the living room, where they observed in plain view drug paraphernalia and containers filled with white powder that they believed (correctly, as later analysis showed) to be cocaine. They proceeded to the bedroom, where they found Rodriguez asleep and discovered additional containers of white powder in two open attaché cases. The officers arrested Rodriguez and seized the drugs and related paraphernalia.

Rodriguez was charged with possession of a controlled substance with intent to deliver. He moved to suppress all evidence seized at the time of his arrest, claiming that Fischer had vacated the apartment several weeks earlier and had no authority to consent to the entry. The Cook County Circuit Court granted the motion, holding that at the time she consented to the entry Fischer did not have common authority over the apartment. The Circuit Court also rejected the State's contention that, even if Fischer did not possess common authority over the premises, there was no Fourth Amendment violation if the police reasonably believed at the time of their entry that Fischer possessed the authority to consent.

The Appellate Court of Illinois affirmed the Circuit Court in all respects.

II

The Fourth Amendment generally prohibits the warrantless entry of a person's home, whether to make an arrest or to search for specific objects. The prohibition does not apply, however, to situations in which voluntary consent has been obtained, either from the individual whose property is searched, or from a third party who possesses common authority over the premises. The State of Illinois contends that that exception applies in the present case.

Common authority rests on mutual use of the property by persons generally having joint access or control for most purposes. The burden of establishing that common authority rests upon the State. On the basis of this record, it is clear that burden was not sustained. The evidence showed that although Fischer, with her two small children, had lived with Rodriguez beginning in December 1984, she had moved out on July 1, 1985, almost a month before the search at issue here, and had gone to live with her mother. She took her and her children's clothing with her, though leaving behind some furniture and household effects. During the period after July 1 she sometimes spent the night at Rodriguez's apartment, but never invited her friends there, and never went there herself when he was not home. Her name was not on the lease nor did she contribute to the rent. She had a key to the apartment, which she said at trial she had taken without Rodriguez's knowledge (though she testified at the preliminary hearing that Rodriguez had given her the key). On these facts the State has not established that, with respect to the South California apartment, Fischer had "joint access or control for most purposes." To the contrary, the Appellate Court's determination of no common authority over the apartment was obviously correct.

III

On the merits of the issue, respondent asserts that permitting a reasonable belief of common authority to validate an entry would cause a defendant's Fourth Amendment rights to be "vicariously waived." We disagree.

We have been unyielding in our insistence that a defendant's waiver of his trial rights cannot be given effect unless it is "knowing" and "intelligent."

What Rodriguez is assured by the trial right of the exclusionary rule, where it applies, is that no evidence seized in violation of the Fourth Amendment will be introduced at his trial unless he consents. What he is assured by the Fourth Amendment itself, however, is not that no government search of his house will occur unless he consents; but that no such search will occur that is "unreasonable." There are various elements, of course, that can make a search of a person's house "reasonable" — one of which is the consent of the person or his co-tenant. The essence of respondent's argument is that we should impose upon this element a requirement that we have not imposed upon other elements that regularly compel government officers to exercise judgment regarding the facts: namely, the requirement that their judgment be not only responsible but correct.

It is apparent that in order to satisfy the "reasonableness" requirement of the Fourth Amendment, what is generally demanded of the many factual determinations that must regularly be made by agents of the government — whether the magistrate issuing a warrant, the police officer executing a warrant, or the police officer conducting a search or seizure under one of the exceptions to the warrant requirement — is not that they always be correct, but that they always be reasonable. As we put it in *Brinegar v. United States*, 338 U.S. 160, 176, (1949):

> Because many situations which confront officers in the course of executing their duties are more or less ambiguous, room must be allowed for some mistakes on their part. But the mistakes must be those of reasonable men, acting on facts leading sensibly to their conclusions of probability.

We see no reason to depart from this general rule with respect to facts bearing upon the authority to consent to a search. Whether the basis for such authority exists is the sort of recurring factual question to which law enforcement officials must be expected to apply their judgment; and all the Fourth Amendment requires is that they answer it reasonably.

What we hold today does not suggest that law enforcement officers may always accept a person's invitation to enter premises. Even when the invitation is accompanied by an explicit assertion that the person lives there, the surrounding circumstances could conceivably be such that a reasonable person would doubt its truth and not act upon it without further inquiry. As with other factual determinations bearing upon search and seizure, determination of consent to enter must "be judged against an objective standard: would the facts available to the officer at the moment 'warrant a man of reasonable caution in the belief'" that the consenting party had authority over the premises? If not, then warrantless entry without further inquiry is unlawful unless authority actually exists. But if so, the search is valid.

In the present case, the Appellate Court found it unnecessary to determine whether the officers reasonably believed that Fischer had the authority to consent, because it ruled as a matter of law that a reasonable belief could not validate the entry. Since we find that ruling to be in error, we remand for consideration of that question.

FURTHER CASE LAW, REFLECTIONS, AND QUESTIONS

1. What should be required before the police's reliance on the apparent authority of a third person to consent to a search is considered "reasonable"? Was the officers' reliance on Gail Fischer's apparent authority in Rodriguez reasonable? Should the police be expected to collect information similar to that cited by Justice Scalia to demonstrate that Fischer lacked the actual authority to consent to the search — for example, to determine whether her name was on the lease to the apartment or whether she contributed to the rent?

2. The courts generally recognize consent given by parents to search a child's room in their dwelling, at least when the child is not an adult or when a part of the dwelling has not exclusively been reserved for the child. Children typically are not able to give effective consent to a search of their parents' home, although exceptions sometimes are made.

Disagreement among co-tenants regarding consent

The defendant in *Matlock* was not home (he was being secured in a police squad car, not far away) when his live-in companion consented to the search of their shared premises. In *Rodriguez,* the defendant was asleep when the police entered his apartment in reliance on Gail Fischer's apparent authority to consent to the entry. What would have happened in these cases if Matlock had been at home, or Rodriguez had been awake, and they had objected to the police's entry? Would the "assumption of risk" rationale result in the third-party consent being effective, notwithstanding the protests of the objecting occupant? Or, under such circumstances, should the police have to respect the wishes of the occupant who refuses to give consent to a search? In short, what if two parties possess actual authority over a home, both parties are present, one consents to a search, and one declines? The Court takes up this issue in the following case.

Georgia v. Randolph

547 U.S. 103 (2006)

JUSTICE SOUTER delivered the opinion of the Court.

Respondent Scott Randolph and his wife, Janet, separated in late May 2001, when she left the marital residence and went to stay with her parents, taking their son and some belongings. In July, she returned to their house with the child, though the record does not reveal whether her object was reconciliation or retrieval of remaining possessions.

On the morning of July 6, she complained to the police that after a domestic dispute her husband took their son away, and when officers reached the house she told them that her husband was a cocaine user whose habit had caused financial troubles. She mentioned the marital problems and said that she and their son had only recently returned after a stay of several weeks with her parents. Shortly after the police arrived, Scott Randolph returned and explained that he had removed the child to a neighbor's house out of concern that his wife might take the boy out of the country again; he denied cocaine use, and countered that it was in fact his wife who abused drugs and alcohol.

One of the officers, Sergeant Murray, went with Janet Randolph to reclaim the child, and when they returned she not only renewed her complaints about her husband's drug use, but also volunteered that there were "'items of drug evidence'" in the house. Sergeant Murray asked Scott Randolph for permission to search the house, which he unequivocally refused.

The sergeant turned to Janet Randolph for consent to search, which she readily gave. She led the officer upstairs to a bedroom that she identified as Scott's, where the sergeant noticed a section of a drinking straw with a powdery residue he suspected was cocaine. The police took the straw to the police station, along with the Randolph's. After getting a search warrant, they returned to the house and seized further evidence of drug use, on the basis of which Scott Randolph was indicted for possession of cocaine.

He moved to suppress the evidence, as products of a warrantless search of his house unauthorized by his wife's consent over his express refusal. The trial court denied the motion, ruling that Janet Randolph had common authority to consent to the search. The Court of Appeals of Georgia reversed principally on the ground that "the consent to conduct a warrantless search of a residence given by one occupant is not valid in the face of the refusal of another occupant who is physically present at the scene to permit a warrantless search."

We granted certiorari to resolve a split of authority on whether one occupant may give law enforcement effective consent to search shared premises, as against a co-tenant who is present and states a refusal to permit the search. We now affirm.

II

None of our co-occupant consent-to-search cases, however, has presented the further fact of a second occupant physically present and refusing permission to search, and later moving to suppress evidence so obtained. The significance of such a refusal turns on the underpinnings of the co-occupant consent rule, as recognized since *Matlock*.

A

The defendant in that case was arrested in the yard of a house where he lived with a Mrs. Graff and several of her relatives, and was detained in a squad car parked nearby. When the police went to the door, Mrs. Graff admitted them and consented to a search of the house. In resolving the defendant's objection to use of the evidence taken in the warrantless search, we said that "the consent of one who possesses common authority over premises or effects is valid as against the absent, nonconsenting person with whom that authority is shared

The constant element in assessing Fourth Amendment reasonableness in the consent cases is the great significance given to widely shared social expectations, which are naturally enough influenced by the law of property, but not controlled by its rules. *Matlock* accordingly not only holds that a solitary co-inhabitant may sometimes consent to a search of shared premises, but stands for the proposition that the reasonableness of such a search is in significant part a function of commonly held understanding about the authority that co-inhabitants may exercise in ways that affect each other's interests.

B

Matlock's example of common understanding is readily apparent. When someone comes to the door of a domestic dwelling with a baby at her hip, as Mrs. Graff did, she shows that she belongs there, and that fact standing alone is enough to tell a law enforcement officer or any other visitor that if she occupies the place along with others, she probably lives there subject to the assumption tenants usually make about their common authority when they share quarters. They understand that any one of them may admit visitors, with the consequence that a guest obnoxious to one may nevertheless be admitted in his absence by another. As *Matlock* put it, shared tenancy is understood to include an "assumption of risk," on which police officers are entitled to rely, and although some group living together might make an exceptional arrangement that no one could admit a guest without the agreement of all, the chance of such an eccentric scheme is too remote to expect visitors to investigate a particular household's rules before accepting an invitation to come in. So, *Matlock* relied on what was usual and placed no burden on the police to eliminate the possibility of atypical arrangements, in the absence of reason to doubt that the regular scheme was in place.

It is also easy to imagine different facts on which, if known, no common authority could sensibly be suspected. A person on the scene who identifies himself, say, as a landlord or a hotel manager calls up no customary understanding of authority to admit guests without the consent of the current occupant. A tenant in the ordinary course does not take rented premises subject to any formal or informal agreement that the landlord may let visitors into the dwelling, and a hotel guest customarily has no reason to expect the manager to allow anyone but his own employees into his room. In these circumstances, neither state-law property rights, nor common contractual arrangements, nor any other source points to a common understanding of authority to admit third parties generally without the consent of a person occupying the premises. And when it comes to searching through bureau drawers, there will be instances in which even a person clearly belonging on premises as an occupant may lack any perceived authority to consent; a child of eight might well be considered to have the power to consent to the police crossing the threshold into that part of the house where any caller, such as a pollster or salesman, might well be admitted, but no one would reasonably expect such a child to be in a position to authorize anyone to rummage through his parents' bedroom.

C

It is fair to say that a caller standing at the door of shared premises would have no confidence that one occupant's invitation was a sufficiently good reason to enter when a fellow tenant stood there saying, "stay out."

The visitor's reticence without some such good reason would show not timidity but a realization that when people living together disagree over the use of their common quarters, a resolution must come through voluntary accommodation, not by appeals to authority. Unless the people living together fall within some recognized hierarchy, like a household of parent and child or barracks housing military personnel of different grades, there is no societal understanding of superior and inferior, a fact reflected in a standard formulation of domestic property law, that each co-tenant has the right to use and enjoy the entire property as if he or she were the sole owner, limited only by the same right in the other co-tenants. The want of any recognized superior authority among disagreeing tenants is also reflected in the law's response when the disagreements cannot be resolved. The law does not ask who has the better side of the conflict; it simply provides a right to any co-tenant, even the most unreasonable, to obtain a decree partitioning the property. And while a decree of partition is not the answer to disagreement among rental tenants, this situation resembles co-ownership in lacking the benefit of any understanding that one or the other rental co-tenant has a superior claim to control the use of the quarters they occupy together. In sum, there is no common understanding that one co-tenant generally has a right or authority to prevail over the express wishes of another, whether the issue is the color of the curtains or invitations to outsiders.

E

Although the *Matlock* defendant was not present with the opportunity to object, he was in a squad car not far away; the *Rodriguez* defendant was actually asleep in the apartment, and the police might have roused him with a knock on the door before they entered with only the consent of an apparent co-tenant. If those cases are not to be undercut by today's holding, we have to admit that we are drawing a fine line; if a potential defendant with self-interest in objecting is in fact at the door and objects, the co-tenant's permission does not suffice for a reasonable search, whereas the potential objector, nearby but not invited to take part in the threshold colloquy, loses out.

This is the line we draw, and we think the formalism is justified. So long as there is no evidence that the police have removed the potentially objecting tenant from the entrance for the sake of avoiding a possible objection, there is practical value in the simple clarity of complementary rules, one recognizing the co-tenant's permission when there is no fellow occupant on hand, the other according dispositive weight to the fellow occupant's contrary indication when he expresses it. For the very reason that *Rodriguez* held it would be unjustifiably impractical to require the police to take affirmative steps to confirm the actual authority of a consenting individual whose authority was apparent, we think it would needlessly limit the capacity of the police to respond to ostensibly legitimate opportunities in the field if we were to hold that reasonableness required the police to take affirmative steps to find a potentially objecting co-tenant before acting on the permission they had already received. There is no ready reason to believe that efforts to invite a refusal would make a difference in many cases, whereas every co-tenant consent case would turn into a test about the adequacy of the police's efforts to consult with a potential objector. Better to accept the formalism of distinguishing *Matlock* from this case than to impose a requirement, time-consuming in the field and in the courtroom, with no apparent systemic justification.

III

This case invites a straightforward application of the rule that a physically present inhabitant's express refusal of consent to a police search is dispositive as to him, regardless of the consent of a fellow occupant.

The judgment of the Supreme Court of Georgia is therefore affirmed.

FURTHER CASE LAW, REFLECTIONS, AND QUESTIONS

1. *Fernandez v. California*, 571 U.S. 292 (2014) reiterated the Court's position in *Randolph* that it is limited to situations where a co-occupant refuses to consent to a search when the other occupant is present at the scene.

   In *Fernandez*, police officers observed a suspect in an armed robbery run into an apartment. A few minutes later, they heard screams coming from inside the apartments. They knocked on the apartment door, and Roxanne Rojas answered. She appeared to have been battered and bleeding. When the officers asked her for permission to search the apartment, Walter Fernandez came to the door and refused them entry. Suspecting that he had assaulted Rojas, the officers removed Fernandez from the apartment and placed him under arrest. He was then identified as the perpetrator of the earlier robbery and taken to the police station.

   Police returned to the apartment an hour later and searched the premises after obtaining Rojas' consent. Inside, they found several items linking Fernandez to the robbery as well as gang paraphernalia, bullets, and a sawed-off shotgun. At trial in California state court, Fernandez filed a motion to suppress that evidence, which the trial court denied. Fernandez was convicted of robbery. The California Court of Appeals affirmed the trial court's judgment, holding that because Fernandez was not present when Rojas consented to the search, the exception to permissible warrantless consent searches of jointly occupied premises was present. Thus, his motion to suppress was properly denied.

   The United States Supreme Court affirmed. The Court held that an occupant absent due to a lawful detention or arrest stood in the same shoes as an occupant absent for any other reason. When multiple occupants are involved, the rule extends to the search of the premises or effects of an absent, nonconsenting occupant, so long as the consent of one who possessed common authority over the premises or effects was obtained if they are the only occupant present. Refusing consent while not at the scene has no impact on the other occupant's ability to consent to a search, even if the absence was involuntary.

2. Does it seem fair that a co-tenant who is not present cannot refuse consent? What if one tenant wrote a note to the other tenant that stated, "Under no circumstances do I consent to a search of our home." Should such a written refusal from an absent tenant carry any weight?

Investigation-Related Exigencies: Destruction of Evidence

A second basis for permitting warrantless entries involves the need to prevent the destruction of evidence or what is sometimes called evanescent evidence. For a warrantless entry into a home to prevent the destruction of evidence, police need more than speculation. In *Kentucky v. King*, 563 U.S. 452, 461 (2011), the Supreme Court explained:

> In applying the imminent destruction of evidence exception to the search warrant requirement for the creation or manufacturing of an exigency by the police, courts require something more than mere proof that fear of detection by the police caused the destruction of evidence. An additional showing is obviously needed because in some sense the police always create the exigent circumstances. That is to say, in the vast majority of cases in which evidence is destroyed by persons who are engaged in illegal conduct, the reason for the destruction is fear that the evidence will fall into the hands of law enforcement.

Courts must not presume that someone in possession of illegal contraband will destroy it once it is discovered that police are closing in. Instead, police must show proof of affirmative conduct by individuals in possession of the contraband that shows evidence will be imminently destroyed.

Police-Created Exigencies

While *King* involved the potential destruction of evidence, it is best known for addressing police-created exigencies. For instance, if a person is preparing to distribute cocaine in their apartment and they hear the police banging on the door demanding entry, they may attempt to destroy the evidence before the police can enter. Since there were no exigent circumstances present prior to the police knocking on the door and demanding to be let in, it could be said the police created the exigent circumstances. In such situations, may police act on the exigency they created and enter the apartment without a warrant?

Kentucky v. King

563 U.S. 452 (2011)

JUSTICE ALITO delivered the opinion of the Court.

This case concerns the search of an apartment in Lexington, Kentucky. Police officers set up a controlled buy of crack cocaine outside an apartment complex. Undercover Officer Gibbons watched the deal take place from an unmarked car in a nearby parking lot. After the deal occurred, Gibbons radioed uniformed officers to move in on the suspect. He told the officers that the suspect was moving quickly toward the breezeway of an apartment building, and he urged them to "hurry up and get there" before the suspect entered an apartment.

In response to the radio alert, the uniformed officers drove into the nearby parking lot, left their vehicles, and ran to the breezeway. Just as they entered the breezeway, they heard a door shut and detected a very strong odor of burnt marijuana. At the end of the breezeway, the officers saw two apartments, one on the left and one on the right, and they did not know which apartment the suspect had entered. Gibbons had radioed that the suspect was running into the apartment on the right, but the officers did not hear this statement because they had already left their vehicles. Because they smelled marijuana smoke emanating from the apartment on the left, they approached the door of that apartment.

Officer Steven Cobb, one of the uniformed officers who approached the door, testified that the officers banged on the left apartment door "as loud as [they] could" and announced, "'This is the police'" or "'Police, police, police.'" Cobb said that "[a]s soon as [the officers] started banging on the door," they "could hear people inside moving," and "[i]t sounded as [though] things were being moved inside the apartment." These noises, Cobb testified, led the officers to believe that drug-related evidence was about to be destroyed.

At that point, the officers announced that they "were going to make entry inside the apartment." Cobb then kicked in the door, the officers entered the apartment, and they found three people in the front room: respondent Hollis King, respondent's girlfriend, and a guest who was smoking marijuana. The officers performed a protective sweep of the apartment during which they saw marijuana and powder cocaine in plain view. In a subsequent search, they also discovered crack cocaine, cash, and drug paraphernalia.

Police eventually entered the apartment on the right. Inside, they found the suspected drug dealer who was the initial target of their investigation.

B

In the Fayette County Circuit Court, a grand jury charged respondent with trafficking in marijuana, first-degree trafficking in a controlled substance, and second-degree persistent felony offender status. Respondent filed a motion to suppress the evidence from the warrantless search, but the Circuit Court denied the motion. Respondent then entered a conditional guilty plea, reserving his right to appeal the denial of his suppression motion. The court sentenced respondent to 11 years' imprisonment.

The Kentucky Court of Appeals affirmed. It held that exigent circumstances justified the warrantless entry because the police reasonably believed that evidence would be destroyed. The police did not impermissibly create the exigency, the court explained, because they did not deliberately evade the warrant requirement.

The Supreme Court of Kentucky reversed. 302 S.W.3d 649 (2010).

Although the court found no evidence of bad faith, it held that exigent circumstances could not justify the search because it was reasonably foreseeable that the occupants would destroy evidence when the police knocked on the door and announced their presence.

II

This Court has identified several exigencies that may justify a warrantless search of a home. Under the "emergency aid" exception, for example, "officers may enter a home without a warrant to render emergency assistance to an injured occupant or to protect an occupant from imminent injury." Police officers may enter premises without a warrant when they are in hot pursuit of a fleeing suspect. And — what is relevant here — the need "to prevent the imminent destruction of evidence" has long been recognized as a sufficient justification for a warrantless search.

Over the years, lower courts have developed an exception to the exigent circumstances rule, the so-called "police-created exigency" doctrine. Under this doctrine, police may not rely on the need to prevent destruction of evidence when that exigency was "created" or "manufactured" by the conduct of the police.

In applying this exception for the "creation" or "manufacturing" of an exigency by the police, courts require something more than mere proof that fear of detection by the police caused the destruction of evidence. An additional showing is obviously needed because "in some sense the police always create the exigent circumstances." *United States v. Duchi*, 906 F.2d 1278, 1284 (C.A.8 1990). That is to say, in the vast majority of cases in which evidence is destroyed by persons who are engaged in illegal conduct, the reason for the destruction is fear that the evidence will fall into the hands of law enforcement. Destruction of evidence issues probably occur most frequently in drug cases because drugs may be easily destroyed by flushing them down a toilet or rinsing them down a drain. Persons in possession of valuable drugs are unlikely to destroy them unless they fear discovery by the police. Consequently, a rule that precludes the police from making a warrantless entry to prevent the destruction of evidence whenever their conduct causes the exigency would unreasonably shrink the reach of this well-established exception to the warrant requirement.

Presumably for the purpose of avoiding such a result, the lower courts have held that the police-created exigency doctrine requires more than simple causation, but the lower courts have not agreed on the test to be applied.

III

Warrantless searches are allowed when the circumstances make it reasonable, within the meaning of the Fourth Amendment, to dispense with the warrant requirement. Therefore, the answer to the question before us is that the exigent circumstances rule justifies a warrantless search when the conduct of the police preceding the exigency is reasonable in the same sense. Where, as here, the police did not create the exigency by engaging or threatening to engage in conduct that violates the Fourth Amendment, warrantless entry to prevent the destruction of evidence is reasonable and thus allowed.

Respondent [also] contends that law enforcement officers impermissibly create an exigency when they "engage in conduct that would cause a reasonable person to believe that entry is imminent and inevitable." In respondent's view, relevant factors include the officers' tone of voice in announcing their presence and the forcefulness of their knocks. But the ability of law enforcement officers to respond to an exigency cannot turn on such subtleties.

Police officers may have a very good reason to announce their presence loudly and to knock on the door with some force. A forceful knock may be necessary to alert the occupants that someone is at the door. Furthermore, unless police officers identify themselves loudly enough, occupants may not know who is at their doorstep. Officers are permitted — indeed, encouraged — to identify themselves to citizens, and "in many circumstances this is cause for assurance, not discomfort." Citizens who are startled by an unexpected knock on the door or by the sight of unknown persons in plain clothes on their doorstep may be relieved to learn that these persons are police officers. Others may appreciate the opportunity to make an informed decision about whether to answer the door to the police.

If respondent's test were adopted, it would be extremely difficult for police officers to know how loudly they may announce their presence or how forcefully they may knock on a door without running afoul of the police-created exigency rule. And in most cases, it would be nearly impossible for a court to determine whether that threshold had been passed. The Fourth Amendment does not require the nebulous and impractical test that respondent proposes.

D

For these reasons, we conclude that the exigent circumstances rule applies when the police do not gain entry to premises by means of an actual or threatened violation of the Fourth Amendment. This holding provides ample protection for the privacy rights that the Amendment protects.

When law enforcement officers who are not armed with a warrant knock on a door, they do no more than any private citizen might do. And whether the person who knocks on the door and requests the opportunity to speak is a police officer or a private citizen, the occupant has no obligation to open the door or to speak. When the police knock on a door but the occupants choose not to respond or to speak, "the investigation will have reached a conspicuously low point," and the occupants "will have the kind of warning that even the most elaborate security system cannot provide." *United States v. Chambers*, 395 F.3d 563 577 (C.A. 6 2005) (Sutton, J., dissenting). And even if an occupant chooses to open the door and speak with the officers, the occupant need not allow the officers to enter the premises and may refuse to answer any questions at any time.

Occupants who choose not to stand on their constitutional rights but instead elect to attempt to destroy evidence have only themselves to blame for the warrantless exigent-circumstances search that may ensue.

IV

In this case, we see no evidence that the officers either violated the Fourth Amendment or threatened to do so prior to the point when they entered the apartment. Officer Cobb testified without contradiction that the officers "banged on the door as loud as [they] could" and announced either "'Police, police, police'" or "'This is the police.'" This conduct was entirely consistent with the Fourth Amendment, and we are aware of no other evidence that might show that the officers either violated the Fourth Amendment or threatened to do so (for example, by announcing that they would break down the door if the occupants did not open the door voluntarily).

Finally, respondent claims that the officers "explained to [the occupants that the officers] were going to make entry inside the apartment," but the record is clear that the officers did not make this statement until after the exigency arose. As Officer Cobb testified, the officers "knew that there was possibly something that was going to be destroyed inside the apartment," and "*[a]t that point*, . . . [they] explained . . . [that they] were going to make entry." (emphasis added). Given that this announcement was made *after* the exigency arose, it could not have created the exigency.

Like the court below, we assume for purposes of argument that an exigency existed. Because the officers in this case did not violate or threaten to violate the Fourth Amendment prior to the exigency, we hold that the exigency justified the warrantless search of the apartment.

The judgment of the Kentucky Supreme Court is reversed, and the case is remanded for further proceedings not inconsistent with this opinion.

JUSTICE GINSBURG, dissenting.

The Court today arms the police with a way routinely to dishonor the Fourth Amendment's warrant requirement in drug cases. In lieu of presenting their evidence to a neutral magistrate, police officers may now knock, listen, then break the door down, nevermind that they had ample time to obtain a warrant. I dissent from the Court's reduction of the Fourth Amendment's force.

This case involves a principal exception to the warrant requirement, the exception applicable in "exigent circumstances." "[C]arefully delineated," the exception should govern only in genuine emergency situations. Circumstances qualify as "exigent" when there is an imminent risk of death or serious injury, or danger that evidence will be immediately destroyed, or that a suspect will escape. The question presented: May police, who could pause to gain the approval of a neutral magistrate, dispense with the need to get a warrant by themselves creating exigent circumstances? I would answer no, as did the Kentucky Supreme Court. The urgency must exist, I would rule, when the police come on the scene, not subsequent to their arrival, prompted by their own conduct.

I

Two pillars of our Fourth Amendment jurisprudence should have controlled the Court's ruling: First, whenever practical, [the police must] obtain advance judicial approval of searches and seizures through the warrant procedure; second, unwarranted searches and seizures inside a home bear heightened scrutiny. The Court has declared warrantless searches, in the main, *per se* unreasonable. The police bear a heavy burden, the Court has cautioned, when attempting to demonstrate an urgent need that might justify warrantless searches.

That heavy burden has not been carried here. There was little risk that drug-related evidence would have been destroyed had the police delayed the search pending a magistrate's authorization. As the Court recognizes, "[p]ersons in possession of valuable drugs are unlikely to destroy them unless they fear discovery by the police." Nothing in the record shows that, prior to the knock at the apartment door, the occupants were apprehensive about police proximity.

How "secure" do our homes remain if police, armed with no warrant, can pound on doors at will and, on hearing sounds indicative of things moving, forcibly enter and search for evidence of unlawful activity?

II

Under an appropriately reined-in "emergency" or "exigent circumstances" exception, the result in this case should not be in doubt. The target of the investigation's entry into the building, and the smell of marijuana seeping under the apartment door into the hallway, the Kentucky Supreme Court rightly determined, gave the police "probable cause . . . sufficient . . . to obtain a warrant to search the . . . apartment." 302 S.W.3d 649, 653 (2010). As that court observed, nothing made it impracticable for the police to post officers on the premises while proceeding to obtain a warrant authorizing their entry.

I agree, and would not allow an expedient knock to override the warrant requirement. Instead, I would accord that core requirement of the Fourth Amendment full respect. When possible, "a warrant must generally be secured," the Court acknowledges. There is every reason to conclude that securing a warrant was entirely feasible in this case, and no reason to contract the Fourth Amendment's dominion.

FURTHER CASE LAW, REFLECTIONS, AND QUESTIONS

1. Imagine a loud knock on your door, followed by a shout: "This is the police," or "Police, police, police." What would your likely response be? Is it conceivable that you might make some sounds "as [though] things were being moved"? Would you concur that "[w]hen law enforcement officers who are not armed with a warrant knock on a door, they do no more than any private citizen might do"? Would you be confident doing nothing, understanding that "whether the person who knocks on the door and requests the opportunity to speak is a police officer or a private citizen, [you would have] no obligation to open the door or to speak"? If you chose "to open the door and speak with the officers," would you be aware that you "need not allow the officers to enter the premises and may refuse to answer any questions at any time"? Might you "be relieved to learn that these persons are police officers" and "appreciate the opportunity to make an informed decision about whether to answer the door to the police"? Are the assumptions made in Justice Alito's majority opinion in *Kentucky v. King* consistent with how you believe that you, or most citizens, would respond to the police knocking on your door and announcing their presence in the way that occurred in this case?
2. Is the position advocated by Justice Ginsburg in her dissent too restrictive ("The urgency must exist when the police come on the scene, not subsequent to their arrival, prompted by their own conduct") in that it would prohibit the police from even knocking on a citizen's door to ask a question? How satisfactory is the rule adopted by the Kentucky Supreme Court "that exigent circumstances could not justify the search because it was reasonably foreseeable that the occupants would destroy evidence when the police knocked on their door and announced their presence"?

Emergency Aid

The third category of exigent circumstances involves warrantless entries into a home to provide emergency aid. An example of the **emergency aid doctrine** is presented in the following scenario. If a police officer looks in a house window and sees a person bleeding profusely, we expect them to enter the house to provide aid. Should the officer do so, and while in the house, see contraband in plain view, should the contraband be excluded from use in a subsequent prosecution because of the warrantless entry? Consider the following case where the United States Supreme Court overturned a decision by the Utah Supreme Court.

Brigham City, Utah v. Stuart

547 U.S. 398 (2006)

Chief Justice Roberts delivered the opinion of the Court.

In this case we consider whether police may enter a home without a warrant when they have an objectively reasonable basis for believing that an occupant is seriously injured or imminently threatened with such injury. We conclude that they may.

I

This case arises out of a melee that occurred in a Brigham City, Utah, home in the early morning hours of July 23, 2000. At about 3 a.m., four police officers responded to a call regarding a loud party at a residence. Upon arriving at the house, they heard shouting from inside, and proceeded down the driveway to investigate. There, they observed two juveniles drinking beer in the backyard. They entered the backyard, and saw — through a screen door and windows — an altercation taking place in the kitchen of the home. According to the testimony of one of the officers, four adults were attempting, with some difficulty, to restrain a juvenile. The juvenile eventually "broke free, swung a fist and struck one of the adults in the face." The officer testified that he observed the victim of the blow spitting blood into a nearby sink. The other adults continued to try to restrain the juvenile, pressing him up against a refrigerator with such force that the refrigerator began moving across the floor. At this point, an officer opened the screen door and announced the officers' presence. Amid the tumult, nobody noticed. The officer entered the kitchen and again cried out, and as the occupants slowly became aware that the police were on the scene, the altercation ceased.

The officers subsequently arrested respondents and charged them with contributing to the delinquency of a minor, disorderly conduct, and intoxication. In the trial court, respondents filed a motion to suppress all evidence obtained after the officers entered the home, arguing that the warrantless entry violated the Fourth Amendment. The court granted the motion, and [both] the Utah Court of Appeals and Supreme Court of Utah affirmed.

We granted certiorari, in light of differences among state courts and the Courts of Appeals concerning the appropriate Fourth Amendment standard governing warrantless entry by law enforcement in an emergency situation.

II

It is a "'basic principle of Fourth Amendment law that searches and seizures inside a home without a warrant are presumptively unreasonable.'" *Groh v. Ramirez,* 540 U.S.

551, 559 (2004). Nevertheless, because the ultimate touchstone of the Fourth Amendment is "reasonableness," the warrant requirement is subject to certain exceptions. We have held, for example, that law enforcement officers may make a warrantless entry onto private property to fight a fire and investigate its cause, *Michigan v. Tyler*, 436 U.S. 499 (1978), to prevent the imminent destruction of evidence, *Ker v. California*, 374 U.S. 23 (1963), or to engage in "'hot pursuit'" of a fleeing suspect, *United States v. Santana*, 427 U.S. 38 (1976). "[W]arrants are generally required to search a person's home or his person unless 'the exigencies of the situation' make the needs of law enforcement so compelling that the warrantless search is objectively reasonable under the Fourth Amendment." *Mincey v. Arizona*, 437 U.S. 385 (1978).

One exigency obviating the requirement of a warrant is the need to assist persons who are seriously injured or threatened with such injury. Accordingly, law enforcement officers may enter a home without a warrant to render emergency assistance to an injured occupant or to protect an occupant from imminent injury.

Respondents do not take issue with these principles, but instead advance two reasons why the officers' entry here was unreasonable. First, they argue that the officers were more interested in making arrests than quelling violence. They urge us to consider, in assessing the reasonableness of the entry, whether the officers were "indeed motivated primarily by a desire to save lives and property."

Our cases have repeatedly rejected this approach. An action is "reasonable" under the Fourth Amendment, regardless of the individual officer's state of mind, "as long as the circumstances, viewed *objectively*, justify [the] action." *Scott v. United States*, 436 U.S. 128, 138 (1978). The officer's subjective motivation is irrelevant. It therefore does not matter here — even if their subjective motives could be so neatly unraveled — whether the officers entered the kitchen to arrest respondents and gather evidence against them or to assist the injured and prevent further violence.

Respondents further contend that their conduct was not serious enough to justify the officers' intrusion into the home. They rely on *Welsh v. Wisconsin*, 466 U.S. 740 (1984), in which we held that "an important factor to be considered when determining whether any exigency exists is the gravity of the underlying offense for which the arrest is being made." This contention, too, is misplaced. *Welsh* involved a warrantless entry by officers to arrest a suspect for driving while intoxicated. There, the "only potential emergency" confronting the officers was the need to preserve evidence (*i.e.*, the suspect's blood-alcohol level) — an exigency that we held insufficient under the circumstances to justify entry into the suspect's home. Here, the officers were confronted with *ongoing* violence occurring *within* the home. *Welsh* did not address such a situation.

We think the officers' entry here was plainly reasonable under the circumstances. The officers were responding, at 3 o'clock in the morning, to complaints about a loud party. As they approached the house, they could hear from within "an altercation occurring, some kind of a fight." "It was loud and it was tumultuous." The officers heard "thumping and crashing" and people yelling "stop, stop" and "get off me." As the trial court found, "it was obvious that . . . knocking on the front door" would have been futile. The noise seemed to be coming from the back of the house; after looking in the front window and seeing nothing, the officers proceeded around back to investigate further. They found two juveniles drinking beer in the backyard. From there, they could see that a fracas was taking place inside the kitchen. A juvenile, fists clenched, was being held back by several adults. As the officers watch, he breaks free and strikes one of the adults in the face, sending the adult to the sink spitting blood.

In these circumstances, the officers had an objectively reasonable basis for believing both that the injured adult might need help and that the violence in the kitchen was just beginning. Nothing in the Fourth Amendment required them to wait until another blow rendered someone "unconscious" or "semi-conscious" or worse before entering. The role of a peace officer includes preventing violence and restoring order, not simply rendering first aid to casualties; an officer is not like a boxing (or hockey) referee, poised to stop a bout only if it becomes too one-sided.

The manner of the officers' entry was also reasonable. After witnessing the punch, one of the officers opened the screen door and yelled in "police." When nobody heard him, he stepped into the kitchen and announced himself again. Only then did the tumult subside. The officer's announcement of his presence was at least equivalent to a knock on the screen door. Indeed, it was probably the only option that had even a chance of rising above the din. Under these circumstances, there was no violation of the Fourth Amendment's knock-and-announce rule. Furthermore, once the announcement was made, the officers were free to enter; it would serve no purpose to require them to stand dumbly at the door awaiting a response while those within brawled on, oblivious to their presence.

Accordingly, we reverse the judgment of the Supreme Court of Utah, and remand the case for further proceedings not inconsistent with this opinion.

FURTHER CASE LAW, REFLECTIONS, AND QUESTIONS

1. In *Brigham City*, the justices appeared interested in the exigent circumstances that justified the police's warrantless entry into the home and how the entry was made after those circumstances became apparent. *Brigham City* was decided a few weeks before *Hudson v. Michigan*, 547 U.S. 586 (2006), where the Court ruled that the exclusionary rule should not be applied when the police have a search warrant yet act unreasonably by entering a home too quickly after knocking and announcing their presence. What implications, if any, does the ruling in *Hudson* have for how the police should enter a home under circumstances like those in *Brigham City*?

Box 6.5 You Be the Judge

Police responded to a complaint of a disturbance. As they approached the residence, they observed broken windows, other property damage, and traces of blood. Looking through a window, the officers saw Jeremy Fisher inside the house. He was "screaming and throwing things." He refused to answer when the officers knocked on the door. Seeing that Fisher's hand was cut, the officers asked whether he needed medical assistance. Fisher did not respond and instead demanded, with accompanying profanity, that the officers go to get a search warrant. Officer Goolsby then opened the front door and ventured into the house. He encountered Fisher, who pointed a gun at him. Fisher was subsequently charged with assault with a dangerous weapon.

Was Goolsby's entry into the home a constitutional response to an exigent circumstance??

See *Michigan v. Fisher*, 558 U.S. 45 (2009).

Plain View

The **plain view doctrine** provides that if a police officer sees an item in plain view while in a place they have a legal right to be, they may seize the item without obtaining a warrant specific to the item. An item in "plain view" technically cannot be "searched" within the meaning of the Fourth Amendment because what is exposed for others to see cannot support a legitimate expectation of privacy. Like consent searches, the plain-view doctrine does not qualify as an exception to the search warrant requirement. Instead, it allows the police to make a warrantless seizure of items exposed to their view. Nevertheless, the plain-view doctrine is intimately related to the search warrant requirement. Because virtually everything seized by the police at some point is visible to them — that is, it is in their "plain view" — limitations must be placed on their authority to be in a position to come across contraband or other incriminating evidence in the first place. As we shall see, the application of the plain-view doctrine is largely designed to ensure that the police do not engage in general, exploratory searches prior to seizing an item they see.

The plain-view doctrine has several important applications, many of which we have encountered earlier in this chapter. For example, the Court approved a "protective sweep" of a house in *Maryland v. Buie* , on reasonable suspicion, to allow the police to look for other persons who might pose a danger to them. Yet the officer in *Buie* spotted not a dangerous confederate but a red running suit. Why could the running suit be seized? Similarly, in *Warden v. Hayden*, an officer found incriminating items of clothing while in hot pursuit of a fleeing felon and in search of the felon's gun. Why could the clothing be seized? Relying by analogy on the plain-view doctrine, the state in *Minnesota v. Dickerson* argued that crack cocaine lawfully could be seized even though the officer's pat-down search was justified solely to detect the presence of weapons. Conceptually, is that argument sound?

Several conditions must be present for the plain view doctrine to be applicable. First, as mentioned before, the police must be in a location where they are lawfully permitted to be — a lawful vantage point. During their jobs, police encounter many situations in which they may encounter contraband located in plain view. Beyond protective sweeps and consent searches, these include many different activities: inside automobiles during a routine traffic stop, inside a home or business during an unrelated investigation, at the entryway of a dwelling while canvassing a neighborhood following a crime, during an unrelated search or a parolee or probationer's home, or during an administrative inspection of a business. As long as police are in a place they are legally permitted to be, the plain view doctrine can be applied.

The second condition requires that the item be observed while the police are confining their activities to the permissible scope of that intrusion and have a right to gain lawful access to it. For example, a police officer might be able to see inside a home from the street and see some contraband. However, if the officer sees the item while in a public place, they may not gain access to it without entering a person's home. In other words, lawful access is lacking. Such an entry into a house may not be made in most circumstances without a court-issued warrant or an exception to the search warrant requirement, which is lacking here. Accordingly, the item may not be seized until a warrant has been issued. Similarly, if the officer in *Buie* saw the running suit in a closet while conducting a protective sweep, the running suit could be seized — there was lawful access. However, if the officer discovered the running suit inside a dresser drawer that the officer opened, they could not legally seize it — lawful access is lacking. While the officer had the right to be in the bedroom as part of a brief search for accomplices, looking inside a dresser drawer goes beyond a protective sweep, thereby prohibiting the seizure of the running suit.

The third condition required for a seizure under the plain view doctrine is that it must be immediately apparent that the item to be seized is contraband or evidence of a criminal act. Recall that in *Dickerson,* the drugs found as part of a frisk could not be seized because it was not immediately apparent that the substance found was contraband. However, what does it mean for something to be immediately apparent? How is this defined?

There is no dispute regarding the nature of the first two conditions for a lawful plain view seizure. However, the United States Supreme Court has found it necessary to clarify what standard to use in applying the requirement that it is immediately apparent that an item is contraband or evidence of a crime. Consider the following case and what is required before the Court will find the police have met the immediately apparent requirement for a lawful plain view seizure.

Arizona v. Hicks

480 U.S. 321 (1987)

JUSTICE SCALIA delivered the opinion of the Court.

On April 18, 1984, a bullet was fired through the door of respondent's apartment, striking and injuring a man in the apartment below. Police officers arrived and entered respondent's apartment to search for the shooter, for other victims, and for weapons. They found and seized three weapons, including a sawed-off rifle, and in the course of their search also discovered a stocking-cap mask.

One of the policemen, Officer Nelson, noticed two sets of expensive stereo components, which seemed out of place in the squalid and otherwise ill-appointed four-room apartment. Suspecting that they were stolen, he read and recorded their serial numbers — moving some of the components, including a Bang and Olufsen turntable, in order to do so — which he then reported by phone to his headquarters. On being advised that the turntable had been taken in an armed robbery, he seized it immediately. It was later determined that some of the other serial numbers matched those on other stereo equipment taken in the same armed robbery, and a warrant was obtained and executed to seize that equipment as well. Respondent was subsequently indicted for the robbery.

The state trial court granted respondent's motion to suppress the evidence that had been seized. The Court of Appeals of Arizona affirmed. Both courts — the trial court explicitly and the Court of Appeals by necessary implication — rejected the State's contention that Officer Nelson's actions were justified under the "plain view" doctrine of *Coolidge v New Hampshire*.

II

As an initial matter, the State argues that Officer Nelson's actions constituted neither a "search" nor a "seizure" within the meaning of the Fourth Amendment. We agree that the mere recording of the serial numbers did not constitute a seizure. To be sure, that was the first step in a process by which respondent was eventually deprived of the stereo equipment. In and of itself, however, it did not "meaningfully interfere" with respondent's possessory interest in either the serial numbers or the equipment, and therefore did not amount to a seizure.

Officer Nelson's moving of the equipment, however, did constitute a "search" separate and apart from the search for the shooter, victims, and weapons that was the lawful objective of his entry into the apartment. Merely inspecting those parts of the turntable that came into view during the latter search would not have constituted an independent search, because it would have produced no additional invasion of respondent's privacy interest. But taking action, unrelated to the objectives of the authorized intrusion, which exposed to view concealed portions of the apartment or its contents, did produce a new invasion of respondent's privacy unjustified by the exigent circumstance that validated the entry. This is why, contrary to Justice Powell's suggestion, the "distinction between 'looking' at the suspicious object in plain view and 'moving' it even a few inches" is much more than trivial for purposes of the Fourth Amendment. It matters not that the search uncovered nothing of any great personal value to the respondent — serial numbers rather than (what might conceivably have been hidden behind or under the equipment) letters or photographs. A search is a search, even if it happens to disclose nothing but the bottom of a turntable.

III

The remaining question is whether the search was "reasonable" under the Fourth Amendment.

On this aspect of the case we reject, at the outset, the apparent position of the Arizona Court of Appeals that because the officers' action directed to the stereo equipment was unrelated to the justification for their entry into respondent's apartment, it was *ipso facto* unreasonable. That lack of relationship always exists with regard to action validated under the "plain view" doctrine; where action is taken for the purpose justifying the entry, invocation of the doctrine is superfluous.

We turn, then, to application of the doctrine to the facts of this case. "It is well established that under certain circumstances the police may *seize* evidence in plain view without a warrant," *Coolidge v New Hampshire*, 403 US, at 465 (plurality) (emphasis added). Those circumstances include situations "[w]here the initial intrusion that brings the police within plain view of such [evidence] is supported by one of the recognized exceptions to the warrant requirement," *ibid.*, such as the exigent-circumstances intrusion here. It would be absurd to say that an object could lawfully be seized and taken from the premises, but could not be moved for closer examination. It is clear, therefore, that the search here was valid if the "plain view" doctrine would have sustained a seizure of the equipment.

There is no doubt it would have done so if Officer Nelson had probable cause to believe that the equipment was stolen. The State has conceded, however, that he had only a "reasonable suspicion," by which it means something less than probable cause. We have not ruled on the question whether probable cause is required in order to invoke the "plain view" doctrine.

We now hold that probable cause is required. To say otherwise would be to cut the "plain view" doctrine loose from its theoretical and practical moorings. The theory of that doctrine consists of extending to nonpublic places such as the home, where searches and seizures without a warrant are presumptively unreasonable, the police's longstanding authority to make warrantless seizures in public places of such objects as weapons and contraband. And the practical justification for that extension is the desirability of sparing police, whose viewing of the object in the course of a lawful search is as legitimate as it would have been in a public place, the inconvenience and the risk — to themselves or to preservation of the evidence — of going to obtain a warrant. Dispensing with the need for a warrant is worlds apart from permitting a lesser standard of *cause* for the seizure than a warrant would require, *i.e.*, the standard of probable cause. No reason is apparent why an object should routinely be seizable on lesser grounds, during an unrelated search and seizure, than would have been needed to obtain a warrant for the same object if it had been known to be on the premises.

The same considerations preclude us from holding that, even though probable cause would have been necessary for a seizure, the search of objects in plain view that occurred here could be sustained on lesser grounds. A dwelling-place search, no less than a dwelling-place seizure, requires probable cause, and there is no reason in theory or practicality why application of the plain-view doctrine would supplant that requirement. Although the interest protected by the Fourth Amendment injunction against unreasonable searches is quite different from that protected by its injunction against unreasonable seizures, neither the one nor the other is of inferior worth or necessarily requires only lesser protection. We have not elsewhere drawn a categorical distinction between the two insofar as concerns the degree of justification needed to establish the reasonableness of police action, and we see no reason for a distinction in the particular circumstances before us here. Indeed, to treat searches more liberally would especially erode the plurality's warning in *Coolidge* that "the 'plain view' doctrine may not be used to extend a general exploratory search from one object to another until something incriminating at last emerges." In short, whether legal authority to move the equipment could be found only as an inevitable concomitant of the authority to seize it, or also as a consequence of some independent power to search certain objects in plain view, probable cause to believe the equipment was stolen was required.

FURTHER CASE LAW, REFLECTIONS, AND QUESTIONS

1. Why does moving a piece of stereo equipment constitute a "search?" Did the information obtained from the search — the unit's serial number — in any way implicate Hicks' privacy interests? Is Justice O'Connor's point well taken, that the intrusion on individual privacy is so slight that a lower standard of justification — reasonable suspicion — should allow the police to take such action?

2. If it must be "immediately apparent" that an object in plain view is contraband, evidence of a crime, or otherwise properly subject to seizure, what if Officer Nelson had probable cause to believe the stereo was stolen: Would he then have been justified in moving parts of the stereo to see the serial numbers?

3. Police must have the right to access the object itself observed in plain view for the exception to apply. Consider a situation where Lisa, a police officer, sees and

smells a large amount of marijuana inside a neighbor's home while walking her dog. Lisa is in a place that she is allowed to be, and based on her observations, it is immediately apparent that she saw marijuana in the house. Lisa may not enter the house without a search warrant because she has no lawful right to access the object.

4. While the three conditions discussed above — lawful vantage point, lawful access, and immediately apparent — must be present for an object found in plain view to be seized, there is no requirement that the police stumble upon the item inadvertently. However, this was not always the case. Before 1990, it was assumed, although not explicitly required, that the police did not know or suspect in advance that an inculpatory piece of evidence would be found while at a specific location. However, this requirement was abandoned in *Horton v. California*, 496 U.S. 128 (1990). So long as the other conditions required under the plain view doctrine are met, the Court held that the subjective intent of the police is of limited value when compared to the benefits of following objective standards.

The Automobile Exception

The **automobile exception** is one of the most recognized exceptions to the warrant requirement. According to this exception, police may search a vehicle without a warrant if there is probable cause to believe it contains contraband or evidence of criminal activity. The automobile exception was established in 1926 in the case of *Carroll v. United States*, 267 U.S. 132 (1926). The *Carroll* court held that it would be impractical to require police to obtain a search warrant before searching "a ship, motor boat, wagon, or automobile" based on probable cause due to their inherent mobility.

The "*Carroll* Doctrine" was premised on a vehicle's inherent mobility; questions arose regarding whether a warrant would be required to search an immobilized car. The Court addressed this question in Chambers v. Maroney, 399 US 42 (1970).

The facts in *Chambers* are straightforward. Two men robbed a Pennsylvania gas station at gunpoint, taking the currency from the cash register and ordering the attendant to place the coins from the register in one of their gloves and then turn the glove over to them. Witnesses reported seeing a blue station wagon circling the block and later speeding away from a parking lot close to the gas station. Four men reportedly were in the car. The gas station attendant said that one of the robbers wore a green sweater and the other a trench coat. Within an hour of the robbery, police stopped a blue station wagon approximately two miles from the gas station. Four men were in the car. One wore a green sweater, and a trench coat was in the car. The occupants of the vehicle were arrested. The car was not immediately searched; instead, it was driven by a police officer to the police station. At the station house, the vehicle was thoroughly searched. Concealed within it were two revolvers, a glove with change in it, and cards bearing the attendant's name at a gas station that had been robbed a week earlier. The defendant, Chambers, was convicted of both gas station robberies. Evidence seized from the car was introduced at his trial.

On appeal, Chambers argued that since the police had immobilized the car by seizing it, there was no longer an exigency justifying the warrantless search. The Supreme Court disagreed, holding that the police had probable cause to believe the car contained evidence of the robbery. "For constitutional purposes, we see no difference between, on the one hand, seizing and holding a car before presenting the probable cause issue to a magistrate and, on the other hand, carrying out an immediate search without a warrant. Given probable cause to search, either course is reasonable under the Fourth Amendment."

Chambers has been interpreted to mean that a car's mobility is not a controlling factor in justifying the automobile exception and has also been heavily criticized. The following case extrapolates on the second justification for allowing warrantless searches of vehicles: the lowered expectation of privacy over a licensed automobile.

California v. Carney

471 U.S. 386 (1985)

CHIEF JUSTICE BURGER delivered the opinion of the Court.

Drug Enforcement Agency Agent Robert Williams watched respondent, Charles Carney, approach a youth in downtown San Diego. The youth accompanied Carney to a Dodge Mini Motor Home parked in a nearby lot. Agent Williams had previously received uncorroborated information that the same motor home was used by another person who was exchanging marihuana for sex. Williams, with assistance from other agents, kept the motorhome under surveillance for the entire one and one-quarter hours that Carney and the youth remained inside. When the youth left the motor home, the agents followed and stopped him. The youth told the agents that he had received marihuana in return for allowing Carney sexual contacts.

At the agents' request, the youth returned to the motor home and knocked on its door; Carney stepped out. The agents identified themselves as law enforcement officers. Without a warrant or consent, one agent entered the motor home and observed marihuana, plastic bags, and a scale of the kind used in weighing drugs on a table. Agent Williams took Carney into custody and took possession of the motorhome. A subsequent search of the motorhome at the police station revealed additional marihuana in the cupboards and refrigerator.

Respondent was charged with possession of marihuana for sale. Respondent then pleaded *nolo contendere* to the charges against him and was placed on probation for three years. Respondent appealed from the order placing him on probation. The California Court of Appeal affirmed, reasoning that the vehicle exception applied to respondent's motor home.

The California Supreme Court reversed the conviction. The Supreme Court did not disagree with the conclusion of the trial court that the agents had probable cause to arrest respondent and to believe that the vehicle contained evidence of a crime; however, the court held that the search was unreasonable because no warrant was obtained, rejecting the State's argument that the vehicle exception to the warrant requirement should apply. That court reached its decision by concluding that the mobility of a vehicle "is no longer the prime justification for the automobile exception; rather, the answer lies in the diminished expectation of privacy which surrounds the automobile." The California Supreme Court held that the expectations of privacy in a motor home are more like those in a dwelling than in an automobile because the primary function of motor homes is not to provide transportation but to "provide the occupant with living quarters." We granted certiorari, 465 U.S. 1098 (1984). We reverse.

II

The Fourth Amendment protects the "right of the people to be secure in their persons, houses, papers, and effects, against unreasonable searches and seizures." This fundamental right is preserved by a requirement that searches be conducted pursuant to a warrant issued by an independent judicial officer. There are, of course, exceptions to the general rule that a warrant must be secured before a search is undertaken; one is the so-called "automobile exception" at issue in this case. This exception to the warrant requirement was first set forth by the Court 60 years ago in *Carroll v. United States,* 267 U.S. 132 (1925). There, the Court recognized that the privacy interests in an automobile are constitutionally protected; however, it held that the ready mobility of the automobile justifies a lesser degree of protection of those interests. The Court rested this exception on a long-recognized distinction between stationary structures and vehicles.

The capacity to be "quickly moved" was clearly the basis of the holding in *Carroll,* and our cases have consistently recognized ready mobility as one of the principal bases of the automobile exception. In *Chambers,* for example, commenting on the rationale for the vehicle exception, we noted that "the opportunity to search is fleeting since a car is readily movable." More recently, in *United States v. Ross,* 456 U. S. 798 (1982), we once again emphasized that "an immediate intrusion is necessary" because of "the nature of an automobile in transit." The mobility of automobiles, we have observed, "creates circumstances of such exigency that, as a practical necessity, rigorous enforcement of the warrant requirement is impossible."

However, although ready mobility alone was perhaps the original justification for the vehicle exception, our later cases have made clear that ready mobility is not the only basis for the exception. The reasons for the vehicle exception, we have said, are twofold.

Besides the element of mobility, less rigorous warrant requirements govern because the expectation of privacy with respect to one's automobile is significantly less than that relating to one's home or office. Even in cases where an automobile was not immediately mobile, the lesser expectation of privacy resulting from its use as a readily mobile vehicle justified application of the vehicular exception. These reduced expectations of privacy derive not from the fact that the area to be searched is in plain view, but from the pervasive regulation of vehicles capable of traveling on the public highways.

Automobiles, unlike homes, are subjected to pervasive and continuing governmental regulation and controls, including periodic inspection and licensing requirements. As an everyday occurrence, police stop and examine vehicles when license plates or inspection stickers have expired, or if other violations, such as exhaust fumes or excessive noise, are noted, or if headlights or other safety equipment are not in proper working order.

The public is fully aware that it is accorded less privacy in its automobiles because of this compelling governmental need for regulation. Historically, individuals have always been on notice that movable vessels may be stopped and searched on facts giving rise to probable cause that the vehicle contains contraband, without the protection afforded by a magistrate's prior evaluation of those facts. In short, the pervasive schemes of regulation, which necessarily lead to reduced expectations of privacy, and the exigencies attendant to ready mobility justify searches without prior recourse to the authority of a magistrate so long as the overriding standard of probable cause is met.

When a vehicle is being used on the highways, or if it is readily capable of such use and is found stationary in a place not regularly used for residential purposes — temporary or otherwise — the two justifications for the vehicle exception come into play. First, the vehicle is obviously readily mobile by the turn of an ignition key, if not actually moving. Second, there is a reduced expectation of privacy stemming from its use as a licensed motor vehicle subject to a range of police regulation inapplicable to a fixed dwelling. At least in these circumstances, the overriding societal interests in effective law enforcement justify an immediate search before the vehicle and its occupants become unavailable.

While it is true that respondent's vehicle possessed some, if not many of the attributes of a home, it is equally clear that the vehicle falls clearly within the scope of the exception laid down in *Carroll* and applied in succeeding cases. Like the automobile in *Carroll,* respondent's motorhome was readily mobile. Absent the prompt search and seizure, it could readily have been moved beyond the reach of the police. Furthermore, the vehicle was licensed to "operate on public streets; was serviced in public places, and was subject to extensive regulation and inspection. And the vehicle was so situated that an objective observer would conclude that it was being used not as a residence, but as a vehicle.

Respondent urges us to distinguish his vehicle from other vehicles within the exception because it was *capable of functioning as a home.* In our increasingly mobile society, many vehicles used for transportation can be and are being used not only for transportation but for shelter, *i.e.,* as a "home" or "residence." To distinguish between respondent's motor home and an ordinary sedan for purposes of the vehicle exception would require that we apply the exception depending upon the size of the vehicle and the quality of its appointments. Moreover, to fail to apply the exception to vehicles such as a motorhome ignores the fact that a motor home lends itself easily to use as an instrument of illicit drug traffic and other illegal activity. In *United States v. Ross,* 456 U.S. at 822 we declined to distinguish between "worthy" and "unworthy" containers, noting that "the central purpose of the Fourth Amendment forecloses such a distinction." We decline today to distinguish between "worthy" and "unworthy" vehicles which are either on the public roads and highways or situated such that it is reasonable to conclude that the vehicle is not being used as a residence.

Our application of the vehicle exception has never turned on the other uses to which a vehicle might be put. The exception has historically turned on the ready mobility of the vehicle, and on the presence of the vehicle in a setting that objectively indicates that the vehicle is being used for transportation. These two requirements for application of the exception ensure that law enforcement officials are not unnecessarily hamstrung in their efforts to detect and prosecute criminal activity, and that the legitimate privacy interests of the public are protected. Applying the vehicle exception in these circumstances allows the essential purposes served by the exception to be fulfilled, while assuring that the exception will acknowledge legitimate privacy interests.

III

The question remains whether, apart from the lack of a warrant, this search was unreasonable. Under the vehicle exception to the warrant requirement, only the prior approval of the magistrate is waived; the search otherwise [must be such] as the magistrate could authorize.

This search was not unreasonable; it was plainly one that the magistrate could authorize if presented with these facts. The DEA agents had fresh, direct, uncontradicted evidence that the respondent was distributing a controlled substance from the vehicle, apart from evidence of other possible offenses. The agents thus had abundant probable cause to enter and search the vehicle for evidence of a crime notwithstanding its possible use as a dwelling place.

The judgment of the California Supreme Court is reversed, and the case is remanded for further proceedings not inconsistent with this opinion.

FURTHER CASE LAW, REFLECTIONS, AND QUESTIONS

1. In *Collins v. Virginia*, 584 U.S. 586 (2018), the Supreme Court considered whether police may conduct a warrantless search of a vehicle located within the curtilage of a residence. During the investigation of two traffic incidents involving a unique-looking orange and black motorcycle with an extended frame, Officer Rhodes learned that the motorcycle was stolen and in the possession of Ryan Collins. Officer Rhodes discovered photographs on Collins' Facebook profile of an orange and black motorcycle parked in the driveway of a house. Officer Rhodes drove to the house and parked on the street, where he could see what appeared to be the motorcycle under a white tarp parked in the exact location of the motorcycle in the photograph. Without obtaining a search warrant, Officer Rhodes walked to the top of the driveway and removed the tarp. He confirmed the bike was stolen by running the license plate and vehicle identification numbers. He returned to his car to wait for Collins. When Collins returned, Officer Rhodes arrested him.

   At trial, Collins moved to suppress the motorcycle as evidence because the police officer conducted an illegal warrantless search (by lifting the tarp covering the motorcycle parked in the driveway) that led to its discovery. The trial court held that the search was based on probable cause and was justified under the exigent circumstances automobile exceptions to the Fourth Amendment's warrant requirement. The appeals court affirmed on the grounds of exigent circumstances, and the Virginia Supreme Court also affirmed, but under the automobile exception only. The Virginia Supreme Court reasoned that the automobile exception applies to vehicles parked on private property.

   In an 8–1 decision, the United States Supreme Court reversed. The Court held that the Fourth Amendment's automobile exception does not permit a police officer without a warrant to enter private property to search a vehicle parked a few feet from the house. The fact that the motorcycle was located in the home's curtilage prevents police from entering and searching without a warrant, even if the object searched is an automobile. The Court found that since the area searched was the curtilage of the Collins' home, the Fourth Amendment's highest degree of protection applies. The Court concluded that although a warrantless search of an automobile is permitted in limited circumstances, the warrantless search of a car parked within the curtilage of one's home is not permissible.

2. Apply the facts of *Carney* to the holding of *Collins*. Suppose Carney's motorhome was housed in a residential mobile home park that he rented on a month-to-month basis. Was the warrantless search unconstitutional under the precedent set by *Collins*? Would this be so for all motor homes housed in a semi-permanent residential location?

Looking Inside Closed Containers

A question that frequently arises in cases involving the automobile exception is whether a warrantless search of a car, based on probable cause, extends not only to items readily visible in the vehicle but also to closed packages and containers inside the car.

As we consider this question, be sure to distinguish this issue from *Arizona v. Gant* and related cases, which we considered earlier in this chapter. An important skill to develop in learning criminal procedure is to recognize and know what legal doctrine applies. Recall that *Gant* ruled that under appropriate circumstances, containers found within the passenger area of a car may be searched incident to the arrest of the car's occupant. *Gant* and related cases have to do with search incident to lawful arrest and vehicles, which (1) presume a lawful arrest, (2) apply only to containers found in the auto's passenger area and not the trunk, and (3) do not require probable cause to search the car. Under such circumstances, the search can automatically follow incident to the suspect's lawful arrest.

The question we now raise is different. What if, for example, the police have probable cause to believe that drugs are located somewhere within a suspect's car during a lawful stop? On searching the car's trunk, they find a closed box, bag, suitcase, or other containers that might contain the drugs. Can they open the container without a warrant? Does an individual's "expectation of privacy" in a sealed container carried inside a car survive the "automobile exception" to the search warrant requirement? What does *United States v. Chadwick*, presented earlier in this chapter, suggest the rule would be if the police came across the container outside of the car? Could they search it on probable cause alone, without a warrant? Must they seize the container and then apply for a warrant? If a container located outside of a car normally cannot be searched without a warrant (absent exigent circumstances), does the act of placing it inside of the vehicle somehow cause the package to lose its individual identity so that it essentially merges with "the car" and thus can be searched without a warrant? Should it matter if the police have probable cause to search a specific container instead of the whole car?

The Court struggled for several years over the limits and requirements associated with container searches and the automobile exception to the search warrant requirement. The following case discusses these contradictions and concludes by stating a simplified, singular rule for when police may search closed containers based on probable cause but without a search warrant.

California v. Acevedo

500 U.S. 565 (1991)

JUSTICE BLACKMUN delivered the opinion of the Court.

[J.R. Daza picked up a package from a federal express office that the police knew contained marijuana and took it to his apartment. Several hours later Acevedo went to Daza's apartment. After staying a few minutes Acevedo left carrying a brown paper bag the size of one of the wrapped marijuana packages. He placed the paper bag in the trunk of his car and drove off. Shortly thereafter the police stopped him, opened the trunk and the paper bag, and found marijuana. Acevedo was arrested and charged with possession of marijuana for sale.

Acevedo pled guilty but appealed the legality of the search of the paper bag and seizure of the marijuana. The California Court of Appeal, Fourth District, agreed, concluding that the marijuana found in the paper bag in the car's trunk should have been suppressed. The California Supreme Court denied review and the U.S. Supreme Court granted certiorari to reexamine the law applicable to a closed container in an automobile.]

In *United States* v. *Ross,* 456 U.S. 798, decided in 1982, we held that a warrantless search of an automobile under the *Carroll* doctrine could include a search of a container or package found inside the car when such a search was supported by probable cause. The warrantless search of Ross' car occurred after an informant told the police that he had seen Ross complete a drug transaction using drugs stored in the trunk of his car. The police stopped the car, searched it, and discovered in the trunk a brown paper bag containing drugs. We decided that the search of Ross' car was not unreasonable under the Fourth Amendment: "The scope of a warrantless search based on probable cause is no narrower — and no broader — than the scope of a search authorized by a warrant supported by probable cause." Thus, "[i]f probable cause justifies the search of a lawfully stopped vehicle, it justifies the search of every part of the vehicle and its contents that may conceal the object of the search." In *Ross,* therefore, we clarified the scope of the *Carroll* doctrine as properly including a "probing search" of compartments and containers within the automobile so long as the search is supported by probable cause.

In addition to this clarification, *Ross* distinguished the *Carroll* doctrine from the separate rule that governed the search of closed containers. The Court had announced this separate rule, unique to luggage and other closed packages, bags, and containers, in *United States* v. *Chadwick,* 433 U.S. 1 (1977). In *Chadwick,* federal narcotics agents had probable cause to believe that a 200-pound double-locked footlocker contained marijuana. The agents tracked the locker as the defendants removed it from a train and carried it through the station to a waiting car. As soon as the defendants lifted the locker into the trunk of the car, the agents arrested them, seized the locker, and searched it. In this Court, the United States did not contend that the locker's brief contact with the automobile's trunk sufficed to make the *Carroll* doctrine applicable. Rather, the United States urged that the search of movable luggage could be considered analogous to the search of an automobile.

The Court rejected this argument because, it reasoned, a person expects more privacy in his luggage and personal effects than he does in his automobile. Moreover, it concluded that as "may often not be the case when automobiles are seized," secure storage facilities are usually available when the police seize luggage.

In *Arkansas* v. *Sanders,* 442 U.S. 753 (1979), the Court extended *Chadwick's* rule to apply to a suitcase actually being transported in the trunk of a car. In *Sanders,* the police had probable cause to believe a suitcase contained marijuana. They watched as the defendant placed the suitcase in the trunk of a taxi and was driven away. The police pursued the taxi for several blocks, stopped it, found the suitcase in the trunk, and searched it. Although the Court had applied the *Carroll* doctrine to searches of integral parts of the automobile itself, it did not extend the doctrine to the warrantless search of personal luggage "merely because it was located in an automobile lawfully stopped by the police." Again, the *Sanders* majority stressed the heightened privacy expectation in personal luggage and concluded that the presence of luggage in an automobile did not diminish the owner's expectation of privacy in his personal items.

In *Ross,* the Court endeavored to distinguish between *Carroll,* which governed the *Ross* automobile search, and *Chadwick,* which governed the *Sanders* automobile search. It held that the *Carroll* doctrine covered searches of automobiles when the police had probable cause to search an entire vehicle but that the *Chadwick* doctrine governed searches of luggage when the officers had probable cause to search only a container within the vehicle. Thus, in a *Ross* situation, the police could conduct a reasonable search under the Fourth Amendment without obtaining a warrant, whereas in a *Sanders* situation, the police had to obtain a warrant before they searched.

Ross held that closed containers encountered by the police during a warrantless search of a car pursuant to the automobile exception could also be searched. Thus, this Court in *Ross* took the critical step of saying that closed containers in cars could be searched without a warrant because of their presence within the automobile. Despite the protection that *Sanders* purported to extend to closed containers, the privacy interest in those closed containers yielded to the broad scope of an automobile search.

III

This Court in *Ross* rejected *Chadwick's* distinction between containers and cars. It concluded that the expectation of privacy in one's vehicle is equal to one's expectation of privacy in the container, and noted that "the privacy interests in a car's trunk or glove compartment may be no less than those in a movable container." It also recognized that it was arguable that the same exigent circumstances that permit a warrantless search of an automobile would justify the warrantless search of a movable container. In deference to the rule of *Chadwick* and *Sanders*, however, the Court put that question to one side. It concluded that the time and expense of the warrant process would be misdirected if the police could search every cubic inch of an automobile until they discovered a paper sack, at which point the Fourth Amendment required them to take the sack to a magistrate for permission to look inside. We now must decide the question deferred in *Ross*: whether the Fourth Amendment requires the police to obtain a warrant to open the sack in a movable vehicle simply because they lack probable cause to search the entire car. We conclude that it does not.

IV

Dissenters in *Ross* asked why the suitcase in *Sanders* was "more private, less difficult for police to seize and store, or in any other relevant respect more properly subject to the warrant requirement, than a container that police discover in a probable-cause search of an entire automobile?" We now agree that a container found after a general search of the automobile and a container found in a car after a limited search for the container are equally easy for the police to store and for the suspect to hide or destroy. In fact, we see no principled distinction in terms of either the privacy expectation or the exigent circumstances between the paper bag found by the police in *Ross* and the paper bag found by the police here. Furthermore, by attempting to distinguish between a container for which the police are specifically searching and a container which they come across in a car, we have provided only minimal protection for privacy and have impeded effective law enforcement.

The line between probable cause to search a vehicle and probable cause to search a package in that vehicle is not always clear, and separate rules that govern the two objects to be searched may enable the police to broaden their power to make warrantless searches and disserve privacy interests. We noted this in *Ross* in the context of a search of an entire vehicle. Recognizing that under *Carroll*, the "entire vehicle itself could be searched without a warrant," we concluded that "prohibiting police from opening immediately a container in which the object of the search is most likely to be found and instead forcing them first to comb the entire vehicle would actually exacerbate the intrusion on privacy interests.

Finally, the search of a paper bag intrudes far less on individual privacy than does the incursion sanctioned long ago in *Carroll*. In that case, prohibition agents slashed the upholstery of the automobile. This Court nonetheless found their search to be reasonable under the Fourth Amendment. If destroying the interior of an automobile is not unreasonable, we cannot conclude that looking inside a closed container is. In light of the minimal protection to privacy afforded by the *Chadwick-Sanders* rule, and our serious doubt whether that rule substantially serves privacy interests, we now hold that the Fourth Amendment does not compel separate treatment for an automobile search that extends only to a container within the vehicle.

V

The *Chadwick-Sanders* rule not only has failed to protect privacy but it has also confused courts and police officers and impeded effective law enforcement. The conflict between the *Carroll* doctrine cases and the *Chadwick-Sanders* line has been criticized in academic commentary.

The discrepancy between the two rules has led to confusion for law enforcement officers. For example, when an officer, who has developed probable cause to believe that a vehicle contains drugs, begins to search the vehicle, and immediately discovers a closed container, which rule applies? The defendant will argue that the fact that the officer first chose to search the container indicates that his probable cause extended only to the container and that *Chadwick* and *Sanders* therefore require a warrant. On the other hand, the fact that the officer first chose to search in the most obvious location should not restrict the propriety of the search. The *Chadwick* rule, as applied in *Sanders,* has devolved into an anomaly such that the more likely the police are to discover drugs in a container, the less authority they have to search it. We have noted the virtue of providing "clear and unequivocal" guidelines to the law enforcement profession. The *Chadwick-Sanders* rule is the antithesis of a "clear and unequivocal guideline."

VI

The interpretation of the *Carroll* doctrine set forth in *Ross* now applies to all searches of containers found in an automobile. In other words, the police may search without a warrant if their search is supported by probable cause. The Court in *Ross* put it this way: "The scope of a warrantless search of an automobile is not defined by the nature of the container in which the contraband is secreted. Rather, it is defined by the object of the search and the places in which there is probable cause to believe that it may be found."

It went on to note: "Probable cause to believe that a container placed in the trunk of a taxi contains contraband or evidence does not justify a search of the entire cab." We reaffirm that principle. In the case before us, the police had probable cause to believe that the paper bag in the automobile's trunk contained marijuana. That probable cause now allows a warrantless search of the paper bag. The facts in the record reveal that the police did not have probable cause to believe that contraband was hidden in any other part of the automobile and a search of the entire vehicle would have been without probable cause and unreasonable under the Fourth Amendment.

Our holding today neither extends the *Carroll* doctrine nor broadens the scope of the permissible automobile search delineated in *Carroll, Chambers,* and *Ross.* It remains a "cardinal principle that 'searches conducted outside the judicial process, without prior approval by judge or magistrate, are *per se* unreasonable under the

Fourth Amendment — subject only to a few specifically established and well-delineated exceptions.

Until today, this Court has drawn a curious line between the search of an automobile that coincidentally turns up a container and the search of a container that coincidentally turns up in an automobile. The protections of the Fourth Amendment must not turn on such coincidences. We therefore interpret *Carroll* as providing one rule to govern all automobile searches. The police may search an automobile and the containers within it where they have probable cause to believe contraband or evidence is contained.

FURTHER CASE LAW, REFLECTIONS, AND QUESTIONS

1. Would the police in *Acevedo* have been justified in searching the entire car?
2. If the police in *Ross* had probable cause to believe that Ross was transporting stolen television sets instead of illegal drugs, could they have searched the paper bag and the leather pouch? The answer is no. Why not?
3. Assume the police have probable cause to believe drugs are in a car. Further, assume that they stop the vehicle and encounter the driver who admits to drug-related activity and a passenger who makes no such admission. May they search the passenger's purse, assuming, of course, that the precise whereabouts of the drugs are unknown and that the purse is large enough that it could contain drugs? This is the situation the Court considered in *Wyoming v. Houghton*, 526 U.S. 295 (1999).

   In *Houghton*, a Wyoming Highway Patrol officer stopped an automobile for speeding and driving with a faulty brake light. Three passengers were in the car's front seat: David Young (the driver), his girlfriend, and the respondent. While questioning Young, the officer noticed a hypodermic needle in Young's shirt pocket. Young admitted he used the needle to take drugs.

   In light of Young's admission, the officer searched the car's passenger compartment for contraband. On the back seat, he found a purse Houghton claimed was hers. The officer searched inside the purse and found a syringe containing methamphetamine and other drug paraphernalia. He placed Houghton under arrest.

   The trial court denied her motion to suppress, ruling that "the officer had probable cause to search the car for contraband, and, by extension, any containers therein that could hold such contraband," including Houghton's purse. The Wyoming Supreme Court reversed, holding that "the officer 'knew or should have known that the purse did not belong to the driver, but to one of the passengers,' and 'there was no probable cause to search the passengers' personal effects and no reason to believe that contraband had been placed within the purse.'" The U.S. Supreme Court granted certiorari and reversed. Writing for a six-member majority, Justice Scalia held:

> When there is probable cause to search for contraband in a car, it is reasonable for police officers to examine packages and containers without a showing of individualized probable cause for each one. A passenger's personal belongings, just like the driver's belongings or containers attached to the car like a glove compartment, are "in" the car, and the officer has probable cause to search for contraband in the car. *Id.* at 302. . .
>
> Effective law enforcement would be appreciably impaired without the ability to search a passenger's personal belongings when there is reason to believe contraband or evidence of criminal wrongdoing is hidden in the car. A criminal might be able to hide contraband in a passenger's belongings as readily as in other containers in the car — perhaps even surreptitiously, without the passenger's knowledge or permission. *Id.* at 304–5.
>
> We hold that police officers with probable cause to search a car may inspect passengers' belongings found in the car that are capable of concealing the object of the search. *Id.* at 307.

Box 6.6 Car Searches

Vehicle Exception: Probable cause to believe that a readily mobile vehicle has evidence or contraband in it, a search of that vehicle may be conducted without first obtaining a warrant.

Area of the Car — If probable cause justifies the search of a lawfully stopped vehicle, it justifies the search of every part of the vehicle and its contents.

Containers — Police may search locked or unlocked containers that may conceal the object of the search.

Search Incident to Arrest: Police may contemporaneously search the vehicle with a custodial search.

Area of the Car — During a search incident to arrest the occupant of a vehicle, the vehicle's passenger compartment may be searched.

Containers — Containers found in the passenger compartment may be searched.

Traffic Stop: Police may look in the vehicle and seize contraband observed in plain view.

Area of Car — Passenger compartment only

Containers — Containers may not be opened without consent, probable cause, or arrest.

Conclusion

The Fourth Amendment provides that searches must not be unreasonable; it says nothing about the constitutionality of searches made without a warrant. Over time, the Supreme Court has viewed this silence as permitting warrantless searches so long as they are reasonable. As we have seen in this chapter, the underlying basis for finding specific types of searches reasonable includes exigency, practicality, and logic. The ability to search a vehicle or stop a fleeing suspect requires action before a warrant can realistically be obtained. Limited warrantless searches made incident to arrest are practical and necessary for officer safety. Allowing a search to be conducted based on a property owner's consent is logical. While each of these search categories are reasonable, they also illustrate a troubling trend.

Over 50 years ago, the Supreme Court stated that "searches conducted outside the judicial process, without prior approval by judge or magistrate, are per se unreasonable under the Fourth Amendment — subject only to a few specifically established and well-delineated exceptions." *Katz v. United States*, 389 U.S. 347, 357 (1967). Over the past half-century, the Court has backed away from the foundational statement and approved the types of searches that may be conducted without a warrant. This movement led Justice Stevens to argue that the Court majority is paying only "lip service" to the fundamental principle that warrantless searches are per se unreasonable under the Fourth Amendment. See *California v. Acevedo*, 500 U.S. 565, 585 (1991) (Stevens, J., dissenting). In fact, so long as a warrantless search falls into one of the categories discussed in this chapter, it is considered reasonable per se.

This may not be a bad thing. The Court has practically applied the law by using the reasonableness standard for determining the constitutionality of warrantless searches. The effect of case-by-case analyses of the reasonableness of warrantless searches is unclear. The ability to employ the Court's analyses in the coming years will be crucial for those working in the criminal justice system.

KEY TERMS

apparent authority
automobile exception
consent search
emergency aid
grabbing area
plain view doctrine
protective sweep
search incident to arrest

REVIEW QUESTIONS

Directions: Please refer to what you learned in this chapter to help you respond.

1. What are the purposes or justifications for allowing the police to perform a search incident to a lawful arrest of a person? Also, what is the scope and the timing of the search?
2. What are the two conditions when the police can conduct a search incident to a lawful arrest on an arrested person's vehicle?
3. How do the courts determine if consent to search was given voluntarily? What would consent that was not given voluntarily look like? What is the scope of a consent search?
4. What are the differences between real, common, and apparent authority?
5. What three exceptions to the search warrant requirement fall under exigent circumstances? What do these have in common?
6. According to the Court, why do people have a reduced expectation of privacy in a vehicle? What is the scope of the search under the vehicle exception?
7. Can containers located in the vehicle be searched when conducting a search under the vehicle exception? What about containers or a bag owned by a passenger in the car?
8. What is a protective sweep? What is it limited to?
9. When can police search electronic devices incident to an arrest?
10. What are the requirements for an item to be seized under the plain view doctrine?

APPLYING THE LAW

Below are five hypothetical fact scenarios. To practice your understanding of the law that you learned in this chapter and your ability to apply it, answer each question posed by applying that law to the hypothetical scenarios. Your answers should be supported by relevant case law and judicially created rules and tests.

1. Sheriff's Deputy Sal stops Paul for driving with expired tags. Sal runs Paul's license and discovers he has a bench warrant for failing to pay a speeding ticket. Sal would not usually take someone in on such a trivial matter, but he has had a bad day and feels like giving somebody else a bad day. Sal has Paul step out of the car and explains that he is under arrest. Sal places Paul in handcuffs and searches him, but finds nothing. Sal then secures Paul in the back of his patrol car and then

searches Paul's vehicle. Inside the car, Sal finds drugs, drug paraphernalia, and an assault rifle.

Was the arrest of Paul and the search of his car constitutional?

2. Jacob, an undercover police officer, made a controlled purchase of cocaine from Hannah at Hannah's house. As he drove away from the house, Jacob called his partner, Esau, and told him that the sale had been completed. Esau drove to Hannah's house and saw her standing on the sidewalk, speaking to a neighbor. Esau stopped the car, identified himself as a police officer, and told Hannah she was under arrest. Hannah turned and ran into her house. Esau caught her in the entryway just inside the front door. In a subsequent search incident to arrest, the partner found cash and packets of cocaine in Hannah's pocket. A minute after the arrest, Jacob arrived and searched the entire house. In one of the upstairs bedrooms, he discovered evidence of drug dealing.

    Were the searches and arrest of Hannah constitutional?

3. Police obtained a search warrant to search a home for evidence related to a bank robbery, specifically, a black ski mask, canvas bags belonging to the bank, and weapons. During the search, an officer was looking through a dresser in an upstairs bedroom when he saw a small square jewelry box sitting in the corner of the drawer next to a pile of underwear. The officer opened the box and found a small plastic bag containing white powder. Suspecting that the bag contained cocaine, the officer seized the bag and continued looking for evidence related to the bank robbery. Later testing revealed that the powder was in fact cocaine.

    Was the cocaine legally seized?

4. Police developed probable cause to believe that a man was using drugs to lure teenagers into his parked motor home and was trading the drugs for sex. After waiting to ensure the man was alone in the motor home, two officers approached it and knocked on the door. The man answered, and the officers, without asking for consent, stepped inside and searched it. The officers found drugs and drug paraphernalia. After the man was charged with various crimes, his attorney filed a motion to suppress. Arguing that since the motorhome was capable of being a home, the police were required to get a warrant for the search.

    What is the most likely ruling on the suppression motion?

5. Officer Otto pulled over Ethan for speeding. While speaking with him, Otto developed probable cause to believe that drug evidence would be found in the car. Otto searched the car and found 3 kilos of heroin and two loaded semi-automatic weapons in the trunk. He then placed Ethan under arrest. Ethan's attorney filed a motion to suppress the heroin and guns.

    How should the court rule?

ORAL ARGUMENTS

Arizona v. Gant: www.oyez.org/cases/2000-2009/2008/2008_07_542/argument
Arizona v. Hicks: www.oyez.org/cases/1980-1989/1986/1986_85_1027/argument
Brigham City, Utah v. Stuart: www.oyez.org/cases/2005/05-502
Bumper v. North Carolina: www.oyez.org/cases/1967/1016
California v. Acevedo: www.oyez.org/cases/1990-1999/1990/1990_89_1690/argument
Chimel v. California: www.oyez.org/cases/1960-1969/1968/1968_770/argument
Collins v Virginia: www.oyez.org/cases/2017/16-1027
Fernandez v. California: www.oyez.org/cases/2013/12-7822
Georgia v Randolph: www.oyez.org/cases/2005/04-1067
Horton v. California: www.oyez.org/cases/1980-1989/1989/1989_88_7164/argument
Hudson v. Michigan: www.oyez.org/cases/2000-2009/2005/2005_04_1360/argument
Illinois v. Rodriguez: www.oyez.org/cases/1980-1989/1989/1989_88_2018/argument
Kentucky v. King: www.oyez.org/cases/2010-2019/2010/2010_09_1272/argument
Lange v. California: www.oyez.org/cases/2020/20-18
Maryland v. Buie: www.oyez.org/cases/1989/88-1369
United States v. Chadwick: www.oyez.org/cases/1976/75-1721
United States v. Leon: www.oyez.org/cases/1980-1989/1983/1983_82_1771/argument
United States v. Robinson: www.oyez.org/cases/1973/72-936
United States v. Ross: www.oyez.org/cases/1980-1989/1981/1981_80_2209/argument
Vale v. Louisiana: www.oyez.org/cases/1969/727

CHAPTER 7

Administrative and Regulatory Searches

LEARNING OBJECTIVES

After reading this chapter, students should be able to:

- Understand what an administrative search is and why administrative searches do not typically trigger Fourth Amendment protections
- Comprehend what special needs searches are and how they are different from administrative searches
- Explain the legality of and the rules that regulate border searches and motor vehicle checkpoints
- Discuss the legality and rules that regulate school searches and suspicionless drug testing
- Describe what an inventory search is, why inventory searches are permitted, and the rules that regulate inventory searches

Introduction

Prior to the United States Supreme Court's decision in *Terry v. Ohio*, probable cause was required before a search undertaken by a government actor could be legally conducted. In ruling that a *Terry* stop or frisk was permitted based on the lower reasonable suspicion standard, the Supreme Court opened the door to specific types of searches occurring, not based on probable cause but still falling well within the bounds of the Fourth Amendment.

The Supreme Court has primarily focused on the reasonableness of a search as required by the Fourth Amendment. It has adopted a balancing test to determine if a search is reasonable. This balancing test involves weighing the type and amount of intrusion against the benefit provided by the search. For example, as we learned previously, searches involving criminal investigations require probable cause — because the level of intrusion, arrest or full search is so high, and we hold freedom sacrosanct in the United States. Furthermore, to stop or frisk, the police only need to possess reasonable suspicion because the level of intrusion is not as extensive. Clearly, the seriousness of the intrusion must be commensurate with the level of justification for the intrusion. However, what about an intrusion that lacks any justification?

In the half-century since *Terry*, the United States Supreme Court has considered the constitutionality of searches where government officials lack probable cause or any suspicion and conduct a search. While rare, there are a finite number of areas where warrantless, suspicionless searches are permissible. These searches fall into two general categories: administrative searches and "special needs" or regulatory searches. This chapter will examine such searches, the basis for the Court permitting them to occur, and the limits imposed on their usage. While reading the chapter, consider if you think the searches still fall within the reasonableness clause of the Fourth Amendment or if you believe this is another way the United States Supreme Court has continued to weaken and chip away at the Fourth Amendment.

Administrative Searches

Searches conducted by government officials designed to determine whether there are violations of governmental codes or regulations are known as **administrative searches**. Administrative searches are predominantly conducted pursuant to local codes and ordinances and consist of inspections to ensure compliance with regulations. Since administrative searches are not done as part of a criminal investigation, they may be conducted without probable cause. However, despite the need for probable cause, limitations are still placed on administrative searches. For example, they cannot be undertaken arbitrarily and without authorization.

Administrative searches do not generally involve criminal law enforcement, so police officers do not usually conduct them. Instead, they are performed by investigators for specific government agencies. Rather than looking for evidence of criminal activity, investigators generally inspect for code violations associated with the safety and well-being of individuals and the public. There are three broad categories of administrative searches: Inspections of private housing for code violations, inspections of businesses for code violations, and searches of closely regulated businesses.

Safety Inspection of Homes

The first type of administrative search we will examine involves inspections of private residences for local code and ordinance violations. The United States Supreme Court established what a governmental agency must do to legally conduct a home inspection in *Camara v. Municipal Court*, 387 U.S. 523 (1967). In *Camara*, an inspector of the San Francisco Department of Public Health entered an apartment building to make a routine annual inspection for possible violations of the city's Housing Code. Camara refused to let the inspector enter the building without a warrant. The inspector returned several more times without a warrant and was refused entry on each occasion. About a month after the first visit, a complaint was filed against Camara for violating the San Francisco Housing Code (SFHC) by refusing to allow the inspection. The superior court denied Camara's motion to dismiss, and the court of appeals affirmed.

After granting certiorari, the United States Supreme Court reversed the California courts. The Court wrote, "[A]dministrative searches of the kind at issue here are significant intrusions upon the interests protected by the Fourth Amendment, that such searches, when authorized and conducted without a warrant procedure, lack the traditional safeguards which the Fourth Amendment guarantees to the individual." *Id.* at 534.

While the Court held that allowing such warrantless inspections violated the Fourth Amendment, the Court agreed that the community's public safety needs might outweigh the blanket prohibition on such searches. If a valid public interest justifies the intrusion contemplated, then there is probable cause to issue a suitably restricted search warrant. Such an approach neither endangers time-honored doctrines applicable to criminal investigations nor makes a nullity of the probable cause requirement in this area. It merely gives full recognition to the competing public and private interests here at stake and, in so doing, best fulfills the historic purposes behind the constitutional right to be free from unreasonable government invasions of privacy.

The Court concluded that a warrant is required for such a search if consent is refused. While required, such a warrant may be issued not based on probable cause specific to the residence in question but on the need for inspections to ensure public safety.

Business Inspections

The same day it decided *Camara*, the United States Supreme Court issued its opinion in *See v. City of Seattle*, 387 U.S. 541 (1967). In *See*, an inspector for the City of Seattle Fire Department was denied permission to inspect a locked warehouse without a warrant or probable cause to believe a violation of the relevant city ordinance had occurred. Rather than being based on traditional probable cause, the inspection was part of a routine, periodic citywide canvas to ensure compliance with the city's fire code. The defendant, See, was convicted for refusing to allow the warrantless inspection, which violated the city fire code.

As with *Camara*, the United States Supreme Court held that inspections of commercial premises that are not open to the public must follow a suitable warrant procedure. The Court held that individual probable cause is not necessary to obtain a warrant; rather, evidence that the building to be inspected fell into a class of structure that is reasonably regulated. "[T]he agency's particular demand for access will of course be measured, in terms of probable cause to issue a warrant, against a flexible standard of reasonableness that takes into account the public need for effective enforcement of the particular regulation involved." *See v. City of Seattle*, 387 U.S. at 545. Should an entry be denied by the owner, entry may be made after a search warrant is obtained based on this reasonableness standard.

Searches of Closely Regulated Businesses

The third category of administrative searches involves inspections of closely regulated businesses. While inspections of homes and most businesses require probable cause and a warrant, government inspections of **closely regulated businesses** require neither. Instead, due to the nature of the industry — for example, racetracks, railroads, and liquor stores — the government has a substantial interest in regulating businesses that operate within it. The leading case on closely regulated businesses is *New York v. Burger*, 482 U.S. 691 (1987).

New York v. Burger

482 U.S. 691 (1987)

JUSTICE BLACKMUN delivered the opinion of the Court.

Respondent Joseph Burger is the owner of a junkyard in Brooklyn, N.Y. His business consists, in part, of the dismantling of automobiles and the selling of their parts. His junkyard is an open lot with no buildings. A high metal fence surrounds it, wherein are located, among other things, vehicles and parts of vehicles. At approximately noon on November 17, 1982, Officer Joseph Vega and four other plainclothes officers, all members of the Auto Crimes Division of the New York City Police Department, entered respondent's junkyard to conduct an inspection pursuant to N. Y. Veh. & Traf. Law §415-a5. On any given day, the Division conducts from 5 to 10 inspections of vehicle dismantlers, automobile junkyards, and related businesses.

Upon entering the junkyard, the officers asked to see Burger's license and his "police book" — the record of the automobiles and vehicle parts in his possession. Burger replied that he had neither a license nor a police book. The officers then announced their intention to conduct a §415-a5 inspection. Burger did not object. In accordance with their practice, the officers copied down the Vehicle Identification Numbers (VINs) of several vehicles and parts of vehicles that were in the junkyard. After checking these numbers against a police computer, the officers determined that respondent was in possession of stolen vehicles and parts. Accordingly, Burger was arrested and charged with five counts of possession of stolen property and one count of unregistered operation as a vehicle dismantler, in violation of §415-a1.

In the Kings County Supreme Court, Burger moved to suppress the evidence obtained as a result of the inspection, primarily on the ground that §415-a5 was unconstitutional. After a hearing, the court denied the motion. It reasoned that the junkyard business was a "pervasively regulated" industry in which warrantless administrative inspections were appropriate, that the statute was properly limited in "time, place and scope," and that, once the officers had reasonable cause to believe that certain vehicles and parts were stolen, they could arrest Burger and seize the property without a warrant.

The New York Court of Appeals reversed. Because of the important state interest in administrative schemes designed to regulate the vehicle-dismantling or automobile-junkyard industry, we granted certiorari.

II

The Court long has recognized that the Fourth Amendment's prohibition on unreasonable searches and seizures is applicable to commercial premises, as well as to private homes. An owner or operator of a business thus has an expectation of privacy in commercial property, which society is prepared to consider to be reasonable. This expectation exists not only with respect to traditional police searches conducted for the gathering of criminal evidence but also with respect to administrative inspections designed to enforce regulatory statutes. An expectation of privacy in commercial premises, however, is different from, and indeed less than, a similar expectation in an individual's home. This expectation is particularly attenuated in commercial property employed in "closely regulated" industries. The Court [has] observed Certain industries have such a history of government oversight that no reasonable expectation of privacy could exist for a proprietor over the stock of such an enterprise.

B

Because the owner or operator of commercial premises in a "closely regulated" industry has a reduced expectation of privacy, the warrant and probable-cause requirements, which fulfill the traditional Fourth Amendment standard of reasonableness for a government search, have lessened application in this context. Rather, we conclude that, as in other situations of "special need" where the privacy interests of the owner are weakened and the government interests in regulating particular businesses are concomitantly heightened, a warrantless inspection of commercial premises may well be reasonable within the meaning of the Fourth Amendment.

This warrantless inspection, however, even in the context of a pervasively regulated business, will be deemed to be reasonable only so long as three criteria are met.

First, there must be a "substantial" government interest that informs the regulatory scheme pursuant to which the inspection is made.

Second, the warrantless inspections must be necessary to further the regulatory scheme.

Finally, the statute's inspection program, in terms of the certainty and regularity of its application, must provide a constitutionally adequate substitute for a warrant. In other words, the regulatory statute must perform the two basic functions of a warrant: it must advise the owner of the commercial premises that the search is being made pursuant to the law and has a properly defined scope, and it must limit the discretion of the inspecting officers. To perform this first function, the statute must be sufficiently comprehensive and defined that the owner of commercial property cannot help but be aware that his property will be subject to periodic inspections undertaken for specific purposes. In addition, in defining how a statute limits the discretion of the inspectors, we have observed that it must be carefully limited in time, place, and scope.

III

The New York regulatory scheme satisfies the three criteria necessary to make reasonable warrantless inspections pursuant to §415-a5. First, the State has a substantial interest in regulating the vehicle-dismantling and automobile-junkyard industry because motor vehicle theft has increased in the State and because the problem of theft is associated with this industry. In this day, automobile theft has become a significant social problem, placing enormous economic and personal burdens upon the citizens of different States. For example, when approving the 1979 amendment to §415-a5, which added the provision for inspections of records and inventory of junkyards, the Governor of the State explained:

"Motor vehicle theft in New York State has become a multimillion dollar industry. In 1976, over 130,000 automobiles were reported stolen in New York, resulting in losses in excess of $225 million. Stolen automobiles are often used in the commission of other crimes and there is a high incidence of accidents resulting in property damage and bodily injury involving stolen automobiles."

Second, regulation of the vehicle-dismantling industry reasonably serves the State's substantial interest in eradicating automobile theft. It is well established that the theft problem can be addressed effectively by controlling the receiver of, or market in, stolen property. Thus, the State rationally may believe that it will reduce car theft by regulations that prevent automobile junkyards from becoming markets for stolen vehicles and that help trace the origin and destination of vehicle parts.

Moreover, the warrantless administrative inspections pursuant to §415-a5 are necessary to further the regulatory scheme. In this respect, we see no difference between these inspections and those approved by the Court in *United States* v. *Biswell* and *Donovan* v. *Dewey*. We explained in *Biswell*, "If inspection is to be effective and serve as a credible deterrent, unannounced, even frequent, inspections are essential. In this context, the prerequisite of a warrant could easily frustrate inspection; and if the necessary flexibility as to time, scope, and frequency is to be preserved, the protections afforded by a warrant would be negligible." 406 U.S., at 316.

Similarly, in the present case, a warrant requirement would interfere with the statute's purpose of deterring automobile theft accomplished by identifying vehicles and parts as stolen and shutting down the market in such items. Because stolen cars and parts often pass quickly through an automobile junkyard, "frequent" and "unannounced" inspections are necessary in order to detect them. In sum, surprise is crucial if the regulatory scheme aimed at remedying this major social problem is to function at all.

Third, §415-a5 provides a constitutionally adequate substitute for a warrant. The statute informs the operator of a vehicle dismantling business that inspections will be made on a regular basis. Thus, the vehicle dismantler knows that the inspections to which he is subject do not constitute discretionary acts by a government official but are conducted pursuant to statute. Section 415-a5 also sets forth the scope of the inspection and, accordingly, places the operator on notice as to how to comply with the statute. In addition, it notifies the operator as to who is authorized to conduct an inspection.

Finally, the "time, place, and scope" of the inspection is limited to place appropriate restraints upon the discretion of the inspecting officers. The officers are allowed to conduct an inspection only during the regular and usual business hours. The inspections can be made only of vehicle-dismantling and related industries. And the permissible scope of these searches is narrowly defined: the inspectors may examine the records, as well as any vehicles or parts of vehicles which are subject to the record requirements of this section, and which are on the premises.

V

The judgment of the New York Court of Appeals is reversed, and the case is remanded to that court for further proceedings not inconsistent with this opinion.

FURTHER CASE LAW, REFLECTIONS, AND QUESTIONS

1. Administrative searches differ from police-based searches in that the former aim to enhance public safety, not investigate criminal activity. Remember, however, that if an administrative search uncovers criminal activity or evidence associated with a crime, it may be used to obtain appropriate search warrants and as part of a prosecution.

2. Examples of closely regulated industries include gun shops, pawn shops, liquor stores, mining, railroads, commercial trucking, and airlines. This list continuously expands as new industries take root in society. Can you think of new industries that have been developed in your lifetime that are likely to be closely regulated?

Special Needs Searches

Administrative searches are generally not conducted by the police and are performed to enhance and ensure public safety. However, there are similar searches undertaken by the police, which are also not based on probable cause or reasonable suspicion. The United States Supreme Court has found that occasionally governmental interests in safety outweigh the intrusion on individual privacy. This is the personification of the delicate balancing act between individual liberties and public safety and security that we discussed in Chapter 1. These searches conducted by the police and other law enforcement officials are referred to as "**special needs searches**." We begin our examination of special needs searches with searches conducted at the Nation's border.

Border Searches

Border security is a critical function of any sovereign nation. This truism has been accepted throughout American history. Since the 1st Congress in 1789, the Federal Government has been given extensive power to conduct warrantless and suspicionless searches of individuals, vehicles, and other items at the Nation's borders. As explained by Chief Justice Rehnquist in *United States v. Ramsey*, 431 U.S. 606, 618 (1977),

> **Border searches**... from before the adoption of the Fourth Amendment, have been considered to be "reasonable" by the single fact that the person or item in question had entered into our country from outside. There has never been any additional requirement that the reasonableness of a border search depended on the existence of probable cause. This longstanding recognition that searches at our borders without probable cause and without a warrant are nonetheless "reasonable" has a history as old as the Fourth Amendment itself. We reaffirm it now.

As you might suspect, the border search exception is not limited to the area immediately adjacent to the border. The border search exception extends to those searches conducted at the "functional equivalent" of the border. The "functional equivalent" of a border is generally the first practical detention point after a border crossing or the final port of entry, typically an airport that has flights arriving from other countries. It is justified because it is comparable to a search conducted at the border but only occurs because it is impossible to require the subject to be searched at the physical border.

It must be noted, however, that the ability of the government to conduct suspicionless searches at the border is not absolute. While significant leeway is given to how and when such searches are performed, such searches must still be "reasonable" to be considered constitutional. This reasonableness analysis has required courts to consider where the search is conducted, what exactly is being searched, and how intrusive the search is based on the length of time associated with a specific search. In examining the constitutionality of border searches, courts have distinguished between routine and non-routine searches. The distinction between these two categories revolves around the level of intrusion each involves. The following case discusses the breadth of **routine border searches.**

United States v. Flores-Montano

541 U.S. 149 (2004)

CHIEF JUSTICE REHNQUIST delivered the opinion of the Court.

Customs officials seized 37 kilograms — a little more than 81 pounds — of marijuana from respondent Manuel Flores-Montano's gas tank at the international border. The Court of Appeals for the Ninth Circuit, relying on an earlier decision by a divided panel of that court, *United States* v. *Molina-Tarazon*, 279 F.3d 709 (2002), held that the Fourth Amendment forbade the fuel tank search absent reasonable suspicion. We hold that the search in question did not require reasonable suspicion.

Respondent, driving a 1987 Ford Taurus station wagon, attempted to enter the United States at the Otay Mesa Port of Entry in southern California. A customs inspector conducted an inspection of the station wagon, and requested respondent to leave the vehicle. The vehicle was then taken to a secondary inspection station.

At the secondary station, a second customs inspector inspected the gas tank by tapping it, and noted that the tank sounded solid. Subsequently, the inspector requested a mechanic under contract with Customs to come to the border station to remove the tank. Within 20 to 30 minutes, the mechanic arrived. He raised the car on a hydraulic lift, loosened the straps and unscrewed the bolts holding the gas tank to the undercarriage of the vehicle, and then disconnected some hoses and electrical connections. After the gas tank was removed, the inspector hammered off bondo (a putty-like hardening substance that is used to seal openings) from the top of the gas tank. The inspector opened an access plate underneath the bondo and found 37 kilograms of marijuana bricks. The process took 15 to 25 minutes.

A grand jury for the Southern District of California indicted respondent on one count of unlawfully importing marijuana and one count of possession of marijuana with intent to distribute. Relying on *Molina-Tarazon*, respondent filed a motion to suppress the marijuana recovered from the gas tank. In *Molina-Tarazon*, a divided panel of the Court of Appeals held that removal of a gas tank requires reasonable suspicion in order to be consistent with the Fourth Amendment.

The Government advised the District Court that it was not relying on reasonable suspicion as a basis for denying respondent's suppression motion, but that it believed *Molina-Tarazon* was wrongly decided. The District Court, relying on *Molina-Tarazon*, held that reasonable suspicion was required to justify the search and, accordingly, granted respondent's motion to suppress. The Court of Appeals, citing *Molina-Tarazon*, summarily affirmed the District Court's judgment. We granted certiorari and now reverse.

In *Molina-Tarazon*, the Court of Appeals decided a case presenting similar facts to the one at bar. It asked "whether [the removal and dismantling of the defendant's fuel tank] is a 'routine' border search for which no suspicion whatsoever is required." 279 F.3d, at 711. The Court of Appeals stated that "[i]n order to conduct a search that goes beyond the routine, an inspector must have reasonable suspicion," and the "critical factor" in determining whether a search is "routine" is the "degree of intrusiveness."

The Court of Appeals seized on language from our opinion in *United States* v. Montoya de Hernandez, 473 U.S. 531 (1985), in which we used the word "routine" as a descriptive term in discussing border searches. ("Routine searches of the persons and effects of entrants are not subject to any requirement of reasonable suspicion, probable cause, or warrant"). The Court of Appeals took the term "routine," fashioned a new balancing test, and extended it to searches of vehicles. But the reasons that might support a requirement of some level of suspicion in the case of highly intrusive searches of the person–dignity and privacy interests of the person being searched–simply do not carry over to vehicles. Complex balancing tests to determine what is a "routine" search of a vehicle, as opposed to a more "intrusive" search of a person, have no place in border searches of vehicles.

The Government's interest in preventing the entry of unwanted persons and effects is at its zenith at the international border. Time and again, we have stated that searches made at the border, pursuant to the longstanding right of the sovereign to protect itself by stopping and examining persons and property crossing into this country, are reasonable simply by virtue of the fact that they occur at the border." Congress, since the beginning of our Government, has granted the Executive plenary authority to conduct routine searches and seizures at the border, without probable cause or a warrant, in order to regulate the collection of duties and to prevent the introduction of contraband into this country. It is axiomatic that the United States, as sovereign, has the inherent authority to protect, and a paramount interest in protecting, its territorial integrity.

That interest in protecting the borders is illustrated in this case by the evidence that smugglers frequently attempt to penetrate our borders with contraband secreted in their automobiles' fuel tank. Over the past 5 1/2 fiscal years, there have been 18,788 vehicle drug seizures at the southern California ports of entry. Of those 18,788, gas tank drug seizures have accounted for 4,619 of the vehicle drug seizures, or approximately 25%. In addition, instances of persons smuggled in and around gas tank compartments are discovered at the ports of entry of San Ysidro and Otay Mesa at a rate averaging 1 approximately every 10 days.

Respondent asserts two main arguments with respect to his Fourth Amendment interests. First, he urges that he has a privacy interest in his fuel tank, and that the suspicionless disassembly of his tank is an invasion of his privacy. But on many occasions, we have noted that the expectation of privacy is less at the border than it is in the interior. *Montoya de Hernandez, supra,* at 538. We have long recognized that automobiles seeking entry into this country may be searched. See *Carroll* v. *United States,* 267 U.S. 132, 154 (1925) ("Travelers may be so stopped in crossing an international boundary because of national self-protection reasonably requiring one entering the country to identify himself as entitled to come in, and his belongings as effects which may be lawfully brought in"). It is difficult to imagine how the search of a gas tank, which should be solely a repository for fuel, could be more of an invasion of privacy than the search of the automobile's passenger compartment.

Second, respondent argues that the Fourth Amendment protects property as well as privacy and that the disassembly and reassembly of his gas tank is a significant deprivation of his property interest because it may damage the vehicle. He does not, and on the record cannot, truly contend that the procedure of removal, disassembly, and reassembly of the fuel tank in this case or any other has resulted in serious damage to, or destruction of, the property. According to the Government, for example, in fiscal year 2003, 348 gas tank searches conducted along the southern border were negative (*i.e.*, no contraband was found), the gas tanks were reassembled, and the vehicles continued their entry into the United States without incident.

Respondent cites not a single accident involving the vehicle or motorist in the many thousands of gas tank disassemblies that have occurred at the border. A gas tank search involves a brief procedure that can be reversed without damaging the safety or operation of the vehicle. If damage to a vehicle were to occur, the motorist might be entitled to recovery. The interference with a motorist's possessory interest is not insignificant when the Government removes, disassembles, and reassembles his gas tank, it nevertheless is justified by the Government's paramount interest in protecting the border.

For the reasons stated, we conclude that the Government's authority to conduct suspicionless inspections at the border includes the authority to remove, disassemble, and reassemble a vehicle's fuel tank. While it may be true that some searches of property are so destructive as to require a different result, this was not one of them. The judgment of the United States Court of Appeals for the Ninth Circuit is therefore reversed, and the case is remanded for further proceedings consistent with this opinion.

FURTHER CASE LAW, REFLECTIONS, AND QUESTIONS

1. Manual searches of electronic equipment, such as cell phones and laptop computers, are considered routine border searches. On the other hand, forensic inspections of these items are classified as non-routine searches. That being said, if conducted on an item that was seized at the border, law enforcement only needs reasonable suspicion that illegal materials are housed within the object. Moreover, if seized at the border, law enforcement officials may send the seized item to a forensics lab for examination based solely on reasonable suspicion.
2. In your opinion, are government officials given too much leeway in conducting suspicionless searches at the border?

Non-Routine Border Searches

Non-routine border searches go beyond the scope and intensity of a routine search. They are significantly more invasive of an individual's privacy. Beyond being highly intrusive and invasive, non-routine searches may involve actions that impact an individual's dignity and privacy interests or are conducted in a particularly offensive manner. Accordingly, the Supreme Court has held that government agents need at least some level of suspicion to justify such searches. Box 7.1 compares routine and non-routine border searches.

Non-routine border searches are constitutional so long as government officials possess reasonable suspicion of criminal activity to justify the intrusion. However, it is not always clear what makes a search non-routine. Courts have regularly found searches involving bodily intrusions, involuntary X-rays, and strip searches to be non-routine. Additionally, a longer-than-normal detention of a person at the border can transform a search from routine to non-routine. It is important to remember that just because a search is considered non-routine, even in seemingly extreme cases, courts are likely to give deference to government searches at the border as long as reasonable suspicion is present.

This fact is exemplified in *United States v. Montoya de Hernandez*, 473 U.S. 531 (1985). Customs inspectors stopped Rosa Montoya de Hernandez at the Los Angeles International Airport, where she arrived on a flight from Bogota, Colombia. Montoya de Hernandez's passport revealed she had made eight recent trips to Los Angeles or Miami from Bogota. Noticing that she had a bulge in her abdomen, she was wearing two sets of elastic underpants in a manner frequently worn by drug mules. In conjunction with her frequent travels from Colombia, inspectors detained Montoya de Hernandez under suspicion that she was smuggling drugs in her alimentary canal or "body packing." After 16 hours of detention, during which Montoya de Hernandez managed not to use the bathroom, officials obtained a court order for an X-ray and other tests. A doctor removed a balloon filled with cocaine from her rectum at the hospital. Over the next several days, she passed 88 balloons filled with cocaine.

On appeal from her conviction for drug smuggling, the United States Supreme Court held that the lengthy detention was not unreasonably prolonged. Such lengthy incommunicado detention is undoubtedly non-routine. However, the fact that the event occurred at an international border, the government had reasonable, articulable suspicion that she was carrying drugs in her alimentary canal, the Court determined that detaining her for many hours was necessary to dispel or confirm the inspectors' suspicions, and this was not unreasonable.

Box 7.1 Comparing Routine and Non-Routine Border Searches

Routine Border Search No Suspicion Required	Non-Routine Border Search Articulable Suspicion Required
Inspection of travel documents	Forensic search of electronic devices
Inspection of luggage and bags	Body cavity search
X-ray scan of personal items	Strip search
Vehicle inspection	Detention for extended questioning
Basic pat-down of an individual	Inspection of digital cloud storage
Collect fingerprints and photos	Vehicle disassembly
Swabbing luggage for explosives or narcotics	Search of personal journals or documents

Box 7.2 You Be the Judge

David was the target of a criminal investigation into a series of stock manipulation schemes. Following a business trip to Panama, David flew into Miami International Airport. At the airport, United States Customs and Border Protection (CBP) officers detained David and escorted him to a holding area without interrogating him. The officers had received information about the investigation of David from a Drug Enforcement Administration (DEA) task force, which was primarily responsible for looking into David's role in the manipulation schemes. Outside his presence, the officers inspected David's luggage, focusing on a spiral-bound notebook containing eighteen pages of handwritten notes on various subjects, including travel information, business contacts, bank and trading account data, and limited details of his personal affairs. One of the CBP officers examined and photocopied the notebook. After about two hours, the CBP officers returned the original notebook and other items to David, who was still in the holding area and allowed him to leave the airport.

David was subsequently indicted on charges of securities fraud, wire fraud, and conspiracy to commit money laundering. Prior to trial, David filed a motion to suppress the photocopies of the notebook made at the airport.

Were David's rights violated by the search and photocopying of his notebook? See *United States v. Levy*, 803 F.3d 120 (2nd Cir. 2015).

Motor Vehicle Checkpoints

As we have seen in previous chapters, before police may legally stop a vehicle, they need reasonable suspicion that the driver or an occupant is involved in criminal activity. A limited exception to this rule consists of law enforcement officials' use of **motor vehicle checkpoints** under certain conditions. So long as such stops meet specific requirements and limitations prescribed by the United States Supreme Court, using checkpoints and roadblocks is constitutional.

To limit illegal immigration from Mexico, the United States Border Patrol set up a series of checkpoints between sixty and one hundred miles north of Mexico on major highways frequently used in transporting illegal aliens to major American cities. All vehicles that passed through the checkpoint were stopped, and their occupants were briefly questioned. The vast majority of cars were allowed to pass through, but a small number were forwarded to a secondary inspection area for further questioning.

United States v. Martinez-Fuerte, 428 U.S. 543 (1976) involved the prosecution of three people arrested at a checkpoint for illegally transporting aliens. They each appealed to the United States Supreme Court following their convictions, arguing that the suspicionless stop at the fixed checkpoints violated the Fourth Amendment. In a 6–3 decision, the Court disagreed and found using fixed checkpoints near the border constitutional. In its decision, the Court balanced the need for such checkpoints to curb illegal immigration against the limited intrusion on drivers' privacy. Moreover, the Court noted that officers had minimal discretion in operating the checkpoints, and any inconvenience and invasion of privacy were limited. The Court concluded that the importance of the checkpoints outweighed any privacy interests held by motorists.

Three years later, the Supreme Court took a step back while reaffirming the prohibition against suspicionless stops of vehicles. In *Delaware v. Prouse,* 440 U.S. 648 (1979), the Supreme Court held that police could not perform random, suspicionless vehicle stops and detain the driver to check their driver's license and car registration. The Court emphasized that while the state has a legitimate goal of ensuring only licensed drivers and registered cars drive on the Nation's roads, the individual driver's right to privacy outweighs the state's use of suspicionless traffic stops performed at the whim of individual officers.

While ruling that the ad hoc stops at issue in *Prouse* were unconstitutional, in the last paragraph of its opinion, the Court stated, "This holding does not preclude the State of Delaware or other States from developing methods for spot checks that involve less intrusion or that do not involve the unconstrained exercise of discretion. Questioning of all oncoming traffic at roadblock-type stops is one possible alternative." *Id.* at 663. In other words, fixed checkpoints to check drivers' licenses and registration may be permitted under certain circumstances. The Court in *Prouse* discussed officers stopping all oncoming traffic to reduce officer discretion concerning who gets stopped. However, in a concurring opinion, Justice Blackburn said that stopping all oncoming traffic is likely unnecessary, but the police should be systematic and use neutral criteria when deciding who gets stopped to reduce officer discretion (e.g., every 5th car).

Local and state police departments around the country took the invitation to use roadblocks in *Prouse* to heart. Across the country, roadblock policies were developed and put into practice. The policies varied in terms of specific goals and techniques employed. In 1990, the Supreme Court helped clarify what was necessary for roadblocks to pass constitutional muster.

Michigan Department of State Police v. Sitz., 496 U.S. 444 (1990) involved a multi-jurisdictional program to implement sobriety checkpoints across Michigan. Under the program, checkpoints would be set up at multiple sites along state highways. All vehicles passing through a checkpoint would be stopped, and their drivers briefly examined for signs of intoxication. When an officer observed signs of intoxication, the motorist would be directed to the side, and an officer would check the motorist's driver's license and car registration and, if warranted, conduct further standardized field sobriety tests. Should the field tests and the police observations suggest that the driver was intoxicated, an arrest would be made. All others would be permitted to resume their journey immediately. The Supreme Court was asked to determine whether using highway sobriety checkpoints violates the Fourth and Fourteenth Amendments to the United States Constitution.

In upholding the legality of sobriety checkpoints, the Court adopted the balancing test it had used in *Prouse*. In considering the constitutionality of checkpoints, the courts should balance (a) the seriousness of the problem being addressed; (b) the degree to which the state action advances the state's interest; and (c) the severity of the action and the interference with individual liberty. DUI checkpoints involve a balance of the state's interest in preventing accidents caused by drunk drivers, the effectiveness of sobriety checkpoints in achieving that goal, and the level of intrusion on an individual's privacy caused by the checkpoints.

In applying this standard to the Michigan checkpoints, the Court found that drunk driving was a serious problem facing the Nation. On the other hand, the brief stop at checkpoints minimally intrudes on individual liberty. Finally, the Court found that the program effectively prevented drunk driving. For these reasons, the Court held that DUI checkpoints akin to the Michigan program do not violate the Fourth Amendment.

Several years later, the Court considered the constitutionality of checkpoints designed to detect whether vehicles were transporting illegal drugs. As explained in the following case, the Supreme Court found that checkpoints designed to address general criminal activity, such as drug trafficking, went too far.

Indianapolis v. Edmond

531 U.S. 32 (2000)

JUSTICE O'CONNOR delivered the opinion of the Court.

In *Michigan Dept. of State Police* v. *Sitz*, 496 U.S. 444 (1990), and *United States v. Martinez-Fuerte*, 428 U.S. 543 (1976), we held that brief, suspicionless seizures at highway checkpoints for the purposes of combating drunk driving and intercepting illegal immigrants were constitutional. We now consider the constitutionality of a highway checkpoint program whose primary purpose is the discovery and interdiction of illegal narcotics.

I

In August 1998, the city of Indianapolis began to operate vehicle checkpoints on Indianapolis roads in an effort to interdict unlawful drugs. The city conducted six such roadblocks between August and November that year, stopping 1,161 vehicles and arresting 104 motorists. Fifty-five arrests were for drug-related crimes, while 49 were for offenses unrelated to drugs. The overall "hit rate" of the program was thus approximately nine percent.

At each checkpoint location, the police stop a predetermined number of vehicles. Approximately 30 officers are stationed at the checkpoint. Pursuant to written directives issued by the chief of police, at least one officer approaches the vehicle, advises the driver that he or she is being stopped briefly at a drug checkpoint, and asks the driver to produce a license and registration. The officer also looks for signs of impairment and conducts an open-view examination of the vehicle from the outside. A narcotics-detection dog walks around the outside of each stopped vehicle.

The directives instruct the officers that they may conduct a search only by consent or based on the appropriate quantum of particularized suspicion. The officers must conduct each stop in the same manner until particularized suspicion develops, and the officers have no discretion to stop any vehicle out of sequence.

The affidavit of Indianapolis Police Sergeant Marshall DePew provides further insight concerning the operation of the checkpoints. According to Sergeant DePew, checkpoint locations are selected weeks in advance based on such considerations as area crime statistics and traffic flow. The checkpoints are generally operated during daylight hours and are identified with lighted signs reading, "NARCOTICS CHECKPOINT ___ MILE AHEAD, NARCOTICS K-9 IN USE, BE PREPARED TO STOP." Once a group of cars has been stopped, other traffic proceeds without interruption until all the stopped cars have been processed or diverted for further processing. Sergeant DePew also stated that the average stop for a vehicle not subject to further processing lasts two to three minutes or less.

Respondents were each stopped at a narcotics checkpoint in late September 1998. Respondents then filed a lawsuit on behalf of themselves and the class of all motorists who had been stopped or were subject to being stopped in the future at the Indianapolis drug checkpoints. Respondents claimed that the roadblocks violated the Fourth Amendment of the United States Constitution and the search and seizure provision of the Indiana Constitution. Respondents requested declaratory and injunctive relief for the class, as well as damages and attorney's fees for themselves.

Respondents then moved for a preliminary injunction. The United States District Court for the Southern District of Indiana denied the motion for a preliminary injunction, holding that the checkpoint program did not violate the Fourth Amendment. A divided panel of the United States Court of Appeals for the Seventh Circuit reversed, holding that the checkpoints contravened the Fourth Amendment. We granted certiorari and now affirm.

II

The Fourth Amendment requires that searches and seizures be reasonable. A search or seizure is ordinarily unreasonable in the absence of individualized suspicion of wrongdoing. While such suspicion is not an "irreducible" component of reasonableness, *Martinez-Fuerte,* 428 U.S., at 561, we have recognized only limited circumstances in which the usual rule does not apply. For example, we have upheld certain regimes of suspicionless searches where the program was designed to serve "special needs, beyond the normal need for law enforcement." We have also allowed searches for certain administrative purposes without particularized suspicion of misconduct, provided that those searches are appropriately limited.

We have also upheld brief, suspicionless seizures of motorists at a fixed Border Patrol checkpoint designed to intercept illegal aliens, and at a sobriety checkpoint aimed at removing drunk drivers from the road, *Michigan Dept. of State Police* v. *Sitz,* 496 U.S. 444 (1990). In addition, in *Delaware* v. *Prouse,* 440 U.S. 648, 663 (1979), we suggested that a similar type of roadblock with the purpose of verifying drivers' licenses and vehicle registrations would be permissible. In none of these cases, however, did we indicate approval of a checkpoint program whose primary purpose was to detect evidence of ordinary criminal wrongdoing.

III

What principally distinguishes these checkpoints from those we have previously approved is their primary purpose.

As petitioners concede, the Indianapolis checkpoint program unquestionably has the primary purpose of interdicting illegal narcotics. In their stipulation of facts, the parties repeatedly refer to the checkpoints as "drug checkpoints" and describe them as "being operated by the City of Indianapolis in an effort to interdict unlawful drugs in Indianapolis."

We have never approved a checkpoint program whose primary purpose was to detect evidence of ordinary criminal wrongdoing. Rather, our checkpoint cases have recognized only limited exceptions to the general rule that a seizure must be accompanied by some measure of individualized suspicion. Each of the checkpoint programs that we have approved was designed primarily to serve purposes closely related to the problems of policing the border or the necessity of ensuring roadway safety. Because the primary purpose of the Indianapolis narcotics checkpoint program is to uncover evidence of ordinary criminal wrongdoing, the program contravenes the Fourth Amendment.

Petitioners propose several ways in which the narcotics-detection purpose of the instant checkpoint program may instead resemble the primary purposes of the checkpoints in *Sitz* and *Martinez-Fuerte*. Petitioners state that the checkpoints in those cases had the same ultimate purpose of arresting those suspected of committing crimes. Securing the border and apprehending drunk drivers are, of course, law enforcement activities, and law enforcement officers employ arrests and criminal prosecutions in pursuit of these goals. If we were to rest the case at this high level of generality, there would be little check on the ability of the authorities to construct roadblocks for almost any conceivable law enforcement purpose. Without drawing the line at roadblocks designed primarily to serve the general interest in crime control, Fourth Amendment would do little to prevent such intrusions from becoming a routine part of American life.

Petitioners also emphasize the severe and intractable nature of the drug problem as justification for the checkpoint program. There is no doubt that traffic in illegal narcotics creates social harms of the first magnitude. But the gravity of the threat alone cannot be dispositive of questions concerning what means law enforcement officers may employ to pursue a given purpose. Rather, in determining whether individualized suspicion is required, we must consider the nature of the interests threatened and their connection to the particular law enforcement practices at issue. We are particularly reluctant to recognize exceptions to the general rule of individualized suspicion where governmental authorities primarily pursue their general crime control ends.

Nor can the narcotics-interdiction purpose of the checkpoints be rationalized in terms of a highway safety concern similar to that present in *Sitz*. The detection and punishment of almost any criminal offense serves broadly the safety of the community, and our streets would no doubt be safer but for the scourge of illegal drugs. Only with respect to a smaller class of offenses, however, is society confronted with the type of immediate, vehicle-bound threat to life and limb that the sobriety checkpoint in *Sitz* was designed to eliminate.

Petitioners also liken the anti-contraband agenda of the Indianapolis checkpoints to the anti-smuggling purpose of the checkpoints in *Martinez-Fuerte*. Petitioners cite this Court's conclusion in *Martinez-Fuerte* that the flow of traffic was too heavy to permit "particularized study of a given car that would enable it to be identified as a possible carrier of illegal aliens," and claim that this logic has even more force here. The problem with this argument is that the same logic prevails any time a vehicle is employed to conceal contraband or other evidence of a crime. This type of connection to the roadway is very different from the close connection to roadway safety that was present in *Sitz* and *Prouse*. Further, the Indianapolis checkpoints are far removed from the border context that was crucial in *Martinez-Fuerte*.

The primary purpose of the Indianapolis narcotics checkpoints is in the end to advance the general interest in crime control. We decline to suspend the usual requirement of individualized suspicion where the police seek to employ a checkpoint primarily for the ordinary enterprise of investigating crimes. We cannot sanction stops justified only by the generalized and ever-present possibility that interrogation and inspection may reveal that any given motorist has committed some crime.

Of course, there are circumstances that may justify a law enforcement checkpoint where the primary purpose would otherwise, but for some emergency, relate to ordinary crime control. For example the Fourth Amendment would almost certainly permit an appropriately tailored roadblock set up to thwart an imminent terrorist attack or to catch a dangerous criminal who is likely to flee by way of a particular route. The exigencies created by these scenarios are far removed from the circumstances under which authorities might simply stop cars as a matter of course to see if there just happens to be a felon leaving the jurisdiction. While we do not limit the purposes that may justify a checkpoint program to any rigid set of categories, we decline to approve a program whose primary purpose is ultimately indistinguishable from the general interest in crime control.

Petitioners argue that the Indianapolis checkpoint program is justified by its lawful secondary purposes of keeping impaired motorists off the road and verifying licenses and registrations. If this were the case, however, law enforcement authorities would be able to establish checkpoints for virtually any purpose so long as they also included a license or sobriety check. For this reason, we examine the available evidence to determine the primary purpose of the checkpoint program. While we recognize the challenges inherent in a purpose inquiry, courts routinely engage in this enterprise in many areas of constitutional jurisprudence as a means of sifting abusive governmental conduct from that which is lawful. As a result, a program driven by an impermissible purpose may be proscribed while a program impelled by licit purposes is permitted, even though the challenged conduct may be outwardly similar. While reasonableness under the Fourth Amendment is predominantly an objective inquiry, our special needs and administrative search cases demonstrate that purpose is often relevant when suspicionless intrusions pursuant to a general scheme are at issue.

It goes without saying that our holding today does nothing to alter the constitutional status of the sobriety and border checkpoints that we approved in *Sitz* and *Martinez-Fuerte*, or of the type of traffic checkpoint that we suggested would be lawful in *Prouse*. The constitutionality of such checkpoint programs still depends on a balancing of the competing interests at stake and the effectiveness of the program.

Because the primary purpose of the Indianapolis checkpoint program is ultimately indistinguishable from the general interest in crime control, the checkpoints violate the Fourth Amendment The judgment of the Court of Appeals is accordingly affirmed.

FURTHER CASE LAW, REFLECTIONS, AND QUESTIONS

1. Do you think the Court's holding in *Edmond* is consistent with the precedents established in *Prouse, Martinez-Fuerte*, and *Sitz*?
2. Why is the Court so concerned with limiting police discretion?
3. In *Illinois v Lidster*, 540 U.S. 419 (2004), police in Illinois set up a checkpoint to obtain information from people about a fatal hit-and-run accident that took place in the same general area a week before. In finding the checkpoint constitutional, the Court noted the difference between it and the checkpoints used in *Edmond*. The roadblock in *Lidster* was not designed to determine if motorists were committing a crime but rather to obtain information from members of the public about a crime committed by others. Additionally, checkpoints for gathering information are likely to cause less stress and consume less time than checkpoints designed to "elicit self-incriminating information." The Court applied the balancing test used previously and found these types of checkpoints minimally intrusive and served the purpose of advancing a specific matter of grave public concern. The checkpoints were therefore found to be reasonable.

School Searches

Special needs searches allow government officials to search with less than probable cause if the primary purpose of the search is to advance a special need beyond mere law enforcement. In *New Jersey v. T.L.O.*, 469 U.S. 325 (1985), the Supreme Court considered whether the need of school officials to maintain discipline is such a special need and, if so, what level of suspicion, if any, would justify the search of a student.

In *T.L.O.*, a high school student was accused of violating school rules by smoking in the restroom. After she denied smoking, an assistant principal searched her purse for cigarettes, admittedly without probable cause or a warrant. In addition to finding cigarettes, the vice principal discovered marijuana and other items that implicated the student in dealing marijuana, which was illegal. The police were called, and T.L.O. was charged with possession of marijuana. The Supreme Court was asked whether the search of T.L.O.'s purse without probable cause violated the Fourth Amendment.

The Court first noted that students do not lose their constitutional rights while at school. However, the Court held that the special needs of teachers and school administrators to maintain order in a school require searches to be permitted on less than probable cause. However, for a search to take place, the search must be reasonable. Reasonableness is determined by balancing the legitimate expectation of privacy of the student and the school's interest in maintaining order and discipline. This requires a reasonable belief that the search will turn up evidence that the student has violated the law or a school rule. It also requires that the scope and intensity of the search be conducted in a reasonable manner.

In the following case, the Supreme Court used the *T.L.O.* framework in considering a school's ability to conduct a much more intrusive search of a young girl.

Safford Unified School District v. Redding

557 U.S. 364 (2009)

JUSTICE SOUTER delivered the opinion of the Court.

The events immediately prior to the search in question began in 13-year-old Savana Redding's math class at Safford Middle School one October day in 2003. The assistant principal of the school, Kerry Wilson, came into the room and asked Savana to go to his office. There, he showed her a day planner, unzipped and open flat on his desk, in which there were several knives, lighters, a permanent marker, and a cigarette. Wilson asked Savana whether the planner was hers; she said it was, but that a few days before she had lent it to her friend, Marissa Glines. Savana stated that none of the items in the planner belonged to her.

Wilson then showed Savana four white prescription-strength ibuprofen 400-mg pills, and one over-the-counter blue naproxen 200-mg pill, all used for pain and inflammation but banned under school rules without advance permission. He asked Savana if she knew anything about the pills. Savana answered that she did not. Wilson then told Savana that he had received a report that she was giving these pills to fellow students; Savana denied it and agreed to let Wilson search her belongings. Helen Romero, an administrative assistant, came into the office, and together with Wilson they searched Savana's backpack, finding nothing.

At that point, Wilson instructed Romero to take Savana to the school nurse's office to search her clothes for pills. Romero and the nurse, Peggy Schwallier, asked Savana to remove her jacket, socks, and shoes, leaving her in stretch pants and a T-shirt (both without pockets), which she was then asked to remove. Finally, Savana was told to pull her bra out and to the side and shake it, and to pull out the elastic on her underpants, thus exposing her breasts and pelvic area to some degree. No pills were found.

Savana's mother filed suit against Safford Unified School District #1, Wilson, Romero, and Schwallier for conducting a strip search in violation of Savana's Fourth Amendment rights. The individuals (hereinafter petitioners) moved for summary judgment, raising a defense of qualified immunity. The District Court for the District of Arizona granted the motion on the ground that there was no Fourth Amendment violation. A closely divided Circuit sitting en banc, however, reversed. The Ninth Circuit held that the strip search was unjustified under the Fourth Amendment test for searches of children by school officials set out in *New Jersey* v. *T.L.O.*, 469 U. S. 325 (1985). We granted certiorari.

II

In *T.L.O.*, we recognized that the school setting requires some modification of the level of suspicion of illicit activity needed to justify a search, and held that for searches by school officials a careful balancing of governmental and private interests suggests that the public interest is best served by a Fourth Amendment standard of reasonableness that stops short of probable cause. We have thus applied a standard of reasonable suspicion to determine the legality of a school administrator's search of a student and have held that a school search will be permissible in its scope when the measures adopted are reasonably related to the objectives of the search and not excessively intrusive in light of the age and sex of the student and the nature of the infraction.

III

In this case, the school's policies strictly prohibit the nonmedical use, possession, or sale of any drug on school grounds, including '[a]ny prescription or over-the-counter drug, except those for which permission to use in school has been granted pursuant to Board policy.' A week before Savana was searched, another student, Jordan Romero (no relation of the school's administrative assistant), told the principal and Assistant Principal Wilson that "certain students were bringing drugs and weapons on campus," and that he had been sick after taking some pills that "he got from a classmate." On the morning of October 8, the same boy handed Wilson a white pill that he said Marissa Glines had given him. He told Wilson that students were planning to take the pills at lunch.

Wilson learned from Peggy Schwallier, the school nurse, that the pill was Ibuprofen 400 mg, available only by prescription. Wilson then called Marissa out of class. Outside the classroom, Marissa's teacher handed Wilson the day planner, found within Marissa's reach, containing various contraband items. Wilson escorted Marissa back to his office.

In the presence of Helen Romero, Wilson requested Marissa to turn out her pockets and open her wallet. Marissa produced a blue pill, several white ones, and a razor blade. Wilson asked where the blue pill came from, and Marissa answered, "I guess it slipped in when *she* gave me the IBU 400s." When Wilson asked whom she meant, Marissa replied, "Savana Redding." Wilson then enquired about the day planner and its contents; Marissa denied knowing anything about them.

Schwallier did not immediately recognize the blue pill, but information provided through a poison control hotline indicated that the pill was a 200-mg dose of an anti-inflammatory drug, generically called naproxen, available over the counter. At Wilson's direction, Marissa was then subjected to a search of her bra and underpants by Romero and Schwallier, as Savana was later on. The search revealed no additional pills.

It was at this juncture that Wilson called Savana into his office and showed her the day planner. Their conversation established that Savana and Marissa were on friendly terms: while she denied knowledge of the contraband, Savana admitted that the day planner was hers and that she had lent it to Marissa. Wilson had other reports of their friendship from staff members, who had identified Savana and Marissa as part of an unusually rowdy group at the school's opening dance in August, during which alcohol and cigarettes were found in the girls' bathroom. Wilson had reason to connect the girls with this contraband, for Wilson knew that Jordan Romero had told the principal that before the dance, he had been at a party at Savana's house where alcohol was served. Marissa's statement that the pills came from Savana was thus sufficiently plausible to warrant suspicion that Savana was involved in pill distribution.

This suspicion of Wilson's was enough to justify a search of Savana's backpack and outer clothing. If a student is reasonably suspected of giving out contraband pills, she is reasonably suspected of carrying them on her person and in the carryall that has become an item of student uniform in most places today. If Wilson's reasonable suspicion of pill distribution were not understood to support searches of outer clothes and backpack, it would not justify any search worth making. And the look into Savana's bag, in her presence and in the relative privacy of Wilson's office, was not excessively intrusive, any more than Romero's subsequent search of her outer clothing.

B

Here it is that the parties part company, with Savana's claim that extending the search at Wilson's behest to the point of making her pull out her underwear was constitutionally unreasonable. The exact label for this final step in the intrusion is not important, though strip search is a fair way to speak of it. Romero and Schwallier directed Savana to remove her clothes down to her underwear, and then "pull out" her bra and the elastic band on her underpants. The very fact of Savana's pulling her underwear away from her body in the presence of the two officials who were able to see her necessarily exposed her breasts and pelvic area to some degree, and both subjective and reasonable societal expectations of personal privacy support the treatment of such a search as categorically distinct, requiring distinct elements of justification on the part of school authorities for going beyond a search of outer clothing and belongings.

Savana's subjective expectation of privacy against such a search is inherent in her account of it as embarrassing, frightening, and humiliating. The reasonableness of her expectation (required by the Fourth Amendment standard) is indicated by the consistent experiences of other young people similarly searched, whose adolescent vulnerability intensifies the patent intrusiveness of the exposure.

The indignity of the search does not, of course, outlaw it, but it does implicate the rule of reasonableness as stated in *T.L.O.*, that "the search as actually conducted be reasonably related in scope to the circumstances which justified the interference in the first place." The scope will be permissible, that is, when it is "not excessively intrusive in light of the age and sex of the student and the nature of the infraction."

Here, the content of the suspicion failed to match the degree of intrusion. Wilson knew beforehand that the pills were prescription-strength ibuprofen and over-the-counter naproxen, common pain relievers equivalent to two Advil, or one Aleve. He must have been aware of the nature and limited threat of the specific drugs he was searching for, and while just about anything can be taken in quantities that will do real harm, Wilson had no reason to suspect that large amounts of the drugs were being passed around, or that individual students were receiving great numbers of pills.

Nor could Wilson have suspected that Savana was hiding common painkillers in her underwear. Petitioners suggest, as a truth universally acknowledged, that "students ... hid[e] contraband in or under their clothing," But when the categorically extreme intrusiveness of a search down to the body of an adolescent requires some justification in suspected facts, general background possibilities fall short; a reasonable search that extensive calls for suspicion that it will pay off. But nondangerous school contraband does not raise the specter of stashes in intimate places, and there is no evidence in the record of any general practice among Safford Middle School students of hiding that sort of thing in underwear.

In sum, what was missing from the suspected facts that pointed to Savana was any indication of danger to the students from the power of the drugs or their quantity, and any reason to suppose that Savana was carrying pills in her underwear. We think that the combination of these deficiencies was fatal to finding the search reasonable.

To make it clear that the *T.L.O.* concern to limit a school search to reasonable scope requires the support of reasonable suspicion of danger or of resort to underwear for hiding evidence of wrongdoing before a search can reasonably make the quantum leap from outer clothes and backpacks to exposure of intimate parts. The meaning of such a search, and the degradation its subject may reasonably feel, place a search that intrusive in a category of its own demanding its own specific suspicions.

FURTHER CASE LAW, REFLECTIONS, AND QUESTIONS

1. Under the circumstances, what should the assistant principal have done?
2. Would it ever be permissible for a school official to conduct a strip search of a student? Under what circumstances, if any?
3. Do you agree with the Court that students should have reduced Fourth Amendment protections while in school compared to the rest of society?

Suspicionless Drug Testing

In the latter part of the twentieth century, the United States embarked on a war against drugs. Well-known components of this war include increased punishments for drug crimes, increased spending on law enforcement, and increased efforts to secure the border to prevent drugs from entering the country. A lesser-known strategy used in the war on drugs has involved the suspicionless drug testing of individuals active in specific industries or activities.

This strategy was first accepted as constitutional by the Supreme Court in two 1989 cases. In *Skinner v. Railway Labor Executives Association,* 489 U.S. 602 (1989,), the Federal Railway Administration imposed several policies to address railroad employees' perceived widespread drug use. Concerned that drug and alcohol policies that restricted drug and alcohol use for decades were ineffective — citing dozens of injuries and fatalities during the previous decade that occurred in railway accidents where drugs or alcohol were a contributing factor — the FRA implemented a policy whereby employees involved in a major railway accident or accidents resulting in serious injury or death would be required to submit to a blood or urine test to determine if they had recently used drugs or consumed alcohol. The railroad workers' union went to court to halt the regulation on the grounds that suspicionless drug and alcohol testing violated the Fourth Amendment.

The Supreme Court found the regulation to be constitutional. The Court held that the government's interest in assuring safety on the country's railroads is compelling and was a "special need" which justified a departure from warrant and probable-cause requirements. Employees subject to the tests perform tasks fraught with risks of injury to others that even a momentary lapse of attention can have disastrous consequences. The Court concluded that the benefit achieved by the testing protocol greatly exceeds any intrusion on the workers' expectation of privacy.

In *National Treasury Employees Union v. Von Raab*, 489 U.S. 656 (1989), decided on the same day as *Skinner*, the Court considered the legality of U.S. Customs Service's suspicionless drug testing of employees applying for promotion to positions directly involving the interdiction of drugs or that require the carrying of a firearm. It observed that the policy was not designed to serve the general needs of law enforcement but rather to deter drug use among employees or potential employees in sensitive positions within the Customs Service.

The Court found that the "substantial interests" of the government in limiting illegal drugs entering the country justified departure from the ordinary warrant and probable cause requirements associated with searches. The Court also noted that the program only applied to those seeking promotions and was carefully designed to protect privacy. Moreover, given the Nation's drug abuse epidemic, the danger inherent in drug users misusing their firearms, and the danger that employees using illegal drugs could be bribed or blackmailed, the Court held that the government had demonstrated a compelling interest in safeguarding the borders and public safety sufficiently to outweigh the privacy expectations of those employees who sought promotions.

The Supreme Court has considered the issue of suspicionless drug testing in several different areas. One such area is the wide-scale implementation of drug tests of students by school districts. We have already seen that while students have a decreased expectation of privacy while at school, they retain some protection under the Fourth Amendment. The level of these protections and specifically the use of drug tests was explored further in the following case.

Board of Education v. Earls

536 U.S. 822 (2002)

JUSTICE THOMAS delivered the opinion of the Court.

In the fall of 1998, the School District adopted the Student Activities Drug Testing Policy (Policy), which requires all middle and high school students to consent to drug testing in order to participate in any extracurricular activity. In practice, the Policy has been applied only to competitive extracurricular activities sanctioned by the Oklahoma

Secondary Schools Activities Association. Under the Policy, students are required to take a drug test before participating in an extracurricular activity, must submit to random drug testing while participating in that activity, and must agree to be tested at any time upon reasonable suspicion. The urinalysis tests are designed to detect only the use of illegal drugs, including amphetamines, marijuana, cocaine, opiates, and barbiturates, not medical conditions or the presence of authorized prescription medications.

At the time of their suit, both respondents attended Tecumseh High School. Respondent Lindsay Earls was a member of the show choir, the marching band, the Academic Team, and the National Honor Society. Respondent Daniel James sought to participate in the Academic Team. Together with their parents, Earls and James brought an action against the School District, challenging the Policy. They alleged that the Policy violates the Fourth Amendment as incorporated by the Fourteenth Amendment and requested injunctive and declarative relief.

II

Given that the School District's Policy is not in any way related to the conduct of criminal investigations, respondents do not contend that the School District requires probable cause before testing students for drug use. Respondents instead argue that drug testing must be based at least on some level of individualized suspicion. It is true that we generally determine the reasonableness of a search by balancing the nature of the intrusion on the individual's privacy against the promotion of legitimate governmental interests. In certain limited circumstances, the Government's need to discover such latent or hidden conditions, or to prevent their development, is sufficiently compelling to justify the intrusion on privacy entailed by conducting such searches without any measure of individualized suspicion. Therefore, in the context of safety and administrative regulations, a search unsupported by probable cause may be reasonable when special needs, beyond the normal need for law enforcement, make the warrant and probable-cause requirement impracticable.

Significantly, this Court has previously held that "special needs" inhere in the public school context. While schoolchildren do not shed their constitutional rights when they enter the schoolhouse, Fourth Amendment rights are different in public schools than elsewhere; the `reasonableness' inquiry cannot disregard the schools' custodial and tutelary responsibility for children. In particular, a finding of individualized suspicion may not be necessary when a school conducts drug testing.

In *Vernonia School District 47 v. Acton*, 515 U.S. 646 (1985), this Court held that the suspicionless drug testing of athletes was constitutional. The Court, however, did not simply authorize all school drug testing, but rather conducted a fact-specific balancing of the intrusion on the children's Fourth Amendment rights against the promotion of legitimate governmental interests. Applying the principles of *Vernonia* to the somewhat different facts of this case, we conclude that Tecumseh's Policy is also constitutional.

A

We first consider the nature of the privacy interest allegedly compromised by the drug testing. As in *Vernonia,* the context of the public school environment serves as the backdrop for the analysis of the privacy interest at stake and the reasonableness of the drug testing policy in general.

A student's privacy interest is limited in a public school environment where the State is responsible for maintaining discipline, health, and safety. Schoolchildren are routinely required to submit to physical examinations and vaccinations against disease. Securing order in the school environment sometimes requires that students be subjected to greater controls than those appropriate for adults.

Respondents argue that because children participating in nonathletic extracurricular activities are not subject to regular physicals and communal undress, they have a stronger expectation of privacy than the athletes tested in *Vernonia.* This distinction, however, was not essential to our decision in *Vernonia,* which depended primarily upon the school's custodial responsibility and authority.

In any event, students who participate in competitive extracurricular activities voluntarily subject themselves to many of the same intrusions on their privacy as do athletes. Some of these clubs and activities require occasional off campus travel and communal undress. All of them have their own rules and requirements for participating students that do not apply to the student body as a whole. For example, each of the competitive extracurricular activities governed by the Policy must abide by the rules of the Oklahoma Secondary Schools Activities Association, and a faculty sponsor monitors the students for compliance with the various rules dictated by the clubs and activities. This regulation of extracurricular activities further diminishes the expectation of privacy among schoolchildren. Somewhat like adults who choose to participate in a closely regulated industry, students who voluntarily participate in school athletics have reason to expect intrusions upon normal rights and privileges, including privacy. We therefore conclude that the students affected by this Policy have a limited expectation of privacy.

Next, we consider the character of the intrusion imposed by the Policy. Urination is an excretory function traditionally shielded by great privacy. But the "degree of intrusion" on one's privacy caused by collecting a urine sample depends upon the manner in which production of the urine sample is monitored.

Under the Policy, a faculty monitor waits outside the closed restroom stall for the student to produce a sample and must "listen for the normal sounds of urination in order to guard against tampered specimens and to insure an accurate chain of custody." This procedure is virtually identical to that reviewed in *Vernonia,* except that it additionally protects privacy by allowing male students to produce their samples behind a closed stall. Given that we considered the method of collection in *Vernonia* a "negligible" intrusion, the method here is even less problematic.

In addition, the Policy clearly requires that the test results be kept in confidential files separate from a student's other educational records and released to school personnel only on a "need to know" basis.

The test results are not turned over to any law enforcement authority. Nor do the test results here lead to the imposition of discipline or have any academic consequences. Rather, the only consequence of a failed drug test is to limit the student's privilege of participating in extracurricular activities. Indeed, a student may test positive for drugs twice and still be allowed to participate in extracurricular activities. After the first positive test, the school contacts the student's parent or guardian for a meeting. The student may continue to participate in the activity if within five days of the meeting the student shows proof of receiving drug counseling and submits to a second drug test in two weeks. For the second positive test, the student is suspended from participation in all extracurricular activities for 14 days, must complete four hours of substance abuse counseling, and must submit to monthly drug tests. Only after a third positive test will the student be suspended from participating in any extracurricular activity for the remainder of the school year, or 88 school days, whichever is longer. Given the minimally intrusive nature of the sample collection and the limited uses to which the test results are put, we conclude that the invasion of students' privacy is not significant.

Finally, this Court must consider the nature and immediacy of the government's concerns and the efficacy of the Policy in meeting them. This Court has already articulated in detail the importance of the governmental concern in preventing drug use by schoolchildren. The drug abuse problem among our Nation's youth has hardly abated since *Vernonia* was decided in 1995. In fact, evidence suggests that it has only grown worse. As in *Vernonia,* the necessity for the State to act is magnified by the fact that this evil is being visited not just upon individuals at large, but upon children for whom it has undertaken a special responsibility of care and direction. The health and safety risks identified in *Vernonia* apply with equal force to Tecumseh's children. Indeed, the nationwide drug epidemic makes the war against drugs a pressing concern in every school.

III

Within the limits of the Fourth Amendment, local school boards must assess the desirability of drug testing schoolchildren. In upholding the constitutionality of the Policy, we express no opinion as to its wisdom. Rather, we hold only that Tecumseh's Policy is a reasonable means of furthering the School District's important interest in preventing and deterring drug use among its schoolchildren.

FURTHER CASE LAW, REFLECTIONS, AND QUESTIONS

1. Do you agree that drug use among high school students is an evil that supersedes students' rights?
2. How does *Earls* compare to *Safford*? Why does one require reasonable suspicion to allow a search while the other does not?
3. Not all suspicionless drug testing policies have been validated by the Supreme Court. In *Chandler v. Miller*, 550 U.S. 305 (1997), the Supreme Court held that Georgia's policy that candidates for state office must pass a drug test within 30 days of an election was unconstitutional. The Court found that the policy did not address a pressing problem and that, if implemented, the policy would not be effective in preventing state officeholders from using drugs once in office.
4. In the fall of 1988, staff members at the Charleston public hospital operated by the Medical University of South Carolina became concerned about an apparent increase in the use of cocaine by patients who were receiving prenatal treatment. The incidence of cocaine use among maternity patients remained unchanged despite referrals for counseling and treatment of patients who tested positive. In response, hospital staff offered to cooperate with the city in prosecuting mothers whose children tested positive for drugs at birth. Accordingly, a task force made up of hospital representatives, police, and local officials developed a policy that set forth procedures for identifying and testing pregnant patients suspected of drug use; contained police procedures and criteria for arresting patients who tested positive; and prescribed prosecutions for drug offenses and/or child neglect, depending on the stage of the defendant's pregnancy. Obstetrical patients arrested after testing positive for cocaine filed suit challenging the policy's validity based on the theory that warrantless and nonconsensual drug tests conducted for criminal investigatory purposes were unconstitutional searches.

   In *Ferguson v. City of Charleston*, 532 U.S. 67 (2001), the Supreme Court found the testing program unconstitutional. The Court found that the program's primary purpose was to use the threat of arrest and prosecution to force women into treatment. Additionally, given the extensive involvement of law enforcement officials at every stage of the policy, the case did not fit within the category of "special needs."

Box 7.3 You Be the Judge

A Georgia law requires all candidates running for public office to submit to drug testing. Waller, a candidate for governor, sues on the grounds that such a requirement violates her Fourth Amendment rights.

Is the Georgia statute constitutional?

See *Chandler v Miller*, 520 U.S. 305 (1997).

Inventory "Searches"

Even though the automobile exception allows the police to search a car without a warrant, they still need probable cause to believe the car or a container in the car contains contraband or another seizable item. Of course, under *Gant* and related cases, the police, under appropriate circumstances, may search the passenger compartment of a car, including containers, without probable cause incident to the arrest of the car's occupant. *See also Michigan v. Long* (which we also considered earlier, permitting a protective search of a vehicle when *Terry v. Ohio's* reasonable suspicion test is met). Are there additional circumstances under which a car can be searched without probable cause? Consider *South Dakota v. Opperman*, below, and the "**inventory search.**"

South Dakota v. Opperman

428 U.S. 364 (1976)

MR. CHIEF JUSTICE BURGER delivered the opinion of the Court.

We review the judgment of the Supreme Court of South Dakota, holding that local police violated the Fourth Amendment to the Federal Constitution, as applicable to the States under the Fourteenth Amendment, when they conducted a routine inventory search of an automobile lawfully impounded by police for violations of municipal parking ordinances.

(1)

Local ordinances prohibit parking in certain areas of downtown Vermillion, S.D., between the hours of 2 a.m. and 6 a.m. During the early morning hours of December 10, 1973, a Vermillion police officer observed respondent's unoccupied vehicle illegally parked in the restricted zone. At approximately 3 a.m., the officer issued an overtime parking ticket and placed it on the car's windshield. The citation warned:

"Vehicles in violation of any parking ordinance may be towed from the area."

At approximately 10 o'clock on the same morning, another officer issued a second ticket for an overtime parking violation. These circumstances were routinely reported to police headquarters, and after the vehicle was inspected, the car was towed to the city impound lot.

From outside the car at the impound lot, a police officer observed a watch on the dashboard and other items of personal property located on the back seat and back floorboard. At the officer's direction, the car door was then unlocked and, using a standard inventory form pursuant to standard police procedures, the officer inventoried the contents of the car, including the contents of the glove compartment, which was unlocked. There he found marihuana contained in a plastic bag. All items, including the contraband, were removed to the police department for safekeeping. During the late afternoon of December 10, respondent appeared at the police department to claim his property. The marihuana was retained by police. Respondent was subsequently arrested on charges of possession of marihuana. His motion to suppress the evidence yielded by the inventory search was denied; he was convicted after a jury trial and sentenced to a fine of $100 and 14 days of incarceration in the county jail.

(2)

This Court has traditionally drawn a distinction between automobiles and homes or offices in relation to the Fourth Amendment. Although automobiles are "effects" and thus within the reach of the Fourth Amendment, warrantless examinations of automobiles have been upheld in circumstances in which a search of a home or office would not.

The reason for this well-settled distinction is twofold. First, the inherent mobility of automobiles creates circumstances of such exigency that, as a practical necessity, rigorous enforcement of the warrant requirement is impossible. But the Court has also upheld warrantless searches where no immediate danger was presented that the car would be removed from the jurisdiction. Besides the element of mobility, less rigorous warrant requirements govern because the expectation of privacy with respect to one's automobile is significantly less than that relating to one's home or office. In discharging their varied responsibilities for ensuring the public safety, law enforcement officials are necessarily brought into frequent contact with automobiles. Most of this contact is distinctly noncriminal in nature. Automobiles, unlike homes, are subjected to pervasive and continuing governmental regulation and controls, including periodic inspection and licensing requirements. As an everyday occurrence, police stop and examine vehicles when license plates or inspection stickers have expired, or if other violations, such as exhaust fumes or excessive noise, are noted, or if headlights or other safety equipment are not in proper working order.

The expectation of privacy as to automobiles is further diminished by the obviously public nature of automobile travel .

In the interests of public safety and as part of what the Court has called "community caretaking functions," automobiles are frequently taken into police custody. Vehicle accidents present one such occasion. To permit the uninterrupted flow of traffic and in some circumstances to preserve evidence, disabled or damaged vehicles will often be removed from the highways or streets at the behest of police engaged solely in caretaking and traffic-control activities. Police will also frequently remove and impound automobiles which violate parking ordinances and which thereby jeopardize both the public safety and the efficient movement of vehicular traffic. The authority of police to seize and remove from the streets vehicles impeding traffic or threatening public safety and convenience is beyond challenge.

When vehicles are impounded, local police departments generally follow a routine practice of securing and inventorying the automobiles' contents. These procedures developed in response to three distinct needs: the protection of the owner's property while it remains in police custody, the protection of the police against claims or disputes over lost or stolen property, and the protection of the police from potential danger. The practice has been viewed as essential to respond to incidents of theft or vandalism. In addition, police frequently attempt to determine whether a vehicle has been stolen and thereafter abandoned.

These caretaking procedures have almost uniformly been upheld by the state courts, which by virtue of the localized nature of traffic regulation have had considerable occasion to deal with the issue. Applying the Fourth Amendment standard of "reasonableness," the state courts have overwhelmingly concluded that, even if an inventory is characterized as a "search," the intrusion is constitutionally permissible.

The majority of the Federal Courts of Appeals have likewise sustained inventory procedures as reasonable police intrusions.

(3)

The decisions of this Court point unmistakably to the conclusion reached by both federal and state courts that inventories pursuant to standard police procedures are reasonable.

In *Cady v. Dombrowski*, 413 US 433 (1973), the Court upheld a warrantless search of an automobile towed to a private garage even though no probable cause existed to believe that the vehicle contained fruits of a crime. The sole justification for the warrantless incursion was that it was incident to the caretaking function of the local police to protect the community's safety. Indeed, the protective search was instituted solely because local police "were under the impression" that the incapacitated driver, a Chicago police officer, was required to carry his service revolver at all times; the police had reasonable grounds to believe a weapon might be in the car, and thus available to vandals. The Court carefully noted that the protective search was carried out in accordance with standard procedures in the local police department, a factor tending to ensure that the intrusion would be limited in scope to the extent necessary to carry out the caretaking function.

The Vermillion police were indisputably engaged in a caretaking search of a lawfully impounded automobile. The inventory was conducted only after the car had been impounded for multiple parking violations. The owner, having left his car illegally parked for an extended period, and thus subject to impoundment, was not present to make other arrangements for the safekeeping of his belongings. The inventory itself was prompted by the presence in plain view of a number of valuables inside the car. As in *Cady*, there is no suggestion whatever that this standard procedure, essentially like that followed throughout the country, was a pretext concealing an investigatory police motive.

On this record we conclude that in following standard police procedures, prevailing throughout the country and approved by the overwhelming majority of courts, the conduct of the police was not "unreasonable" under the Fourth Amendment.

FURTHER CASE LAW, REFLECTIONS, AND QUESTIONS

1. On remand, the South Dakota Supreme Court held that the inventory search of Opperman's car violated the defendant's search and seizure protections under the South Dakota Constitution. *State v. Opperman*, 247 N.W.2d 673 (S.D. 1976).

2. The key to a police department being allowed to conduct an inventory search is whether the agency has a clear policy regarding conducting an inventory search. In *Colorado v. Bertine*, 479 U.S. 367 (1987), the Court permitted the scope of an inventory search to extend to closed containers within a vehicle under police department policy.

3. Inventory searches do not invariably involve motor vehicles. For example, in *Illinois v. Lafayette*, 462 U.S. 640 (1983), the defendant was arrested for disturbing the peace and taken to a police station. As he was being booked, a police officer opened the shoulder bag the arrestee had in his possession and found 10 amphetamine pills inside the plastic wrap of a cigarette package. The Supreme Court upheld the search of the shoulder bag as a valid inventory procedure.

Searches of Probationers, Parolees, and Inmates

Searches of individuals under state supervision or confinement fall into a category of special need searches. Regarding people on probation (community supervision instead of incarceration), the Supreme Court has held that a probation officer may search a probationer's home without a warrant if based on reasonable grounds, *Griffin v. Wisconsin*, 493 U.S. 868 (1987). While the Court did not specifically define what "reasonable grounds" meant, it was clear that it was significantly less than probable cause.

A number of years later, the Court clarified the matter somewhat. In *United States v. Knights*, 534 U.S. 112 (2001), the Court held that a warrantless search of a probationer's home qualifies as a special needs search and is constitutional if based on reasonable suspicion. As stated by the Court, "When an officer has reasonable suspicion that a probationer subject to a search condition is engaged in criminal activity, there is enough likelihood that criminal conduct is occurring that an intrusion on the probationer's significantly diminished privacy interests is reasonable." *Id.* at 121.

In searches of individuals on parole (early release from prison after serving part of the total sentence), the Supreme Court has held that a warrantless, suspicionless search of a parolee's home is valid under the Fourth Amendment, *Samson v. California*, 547 U.S. 843 (2006). The Court based its decision on the view that parolees are technically in the custody of the Department of Corrections. The Court explained that under the continuum of state-imposed punishments, parolees have fewer expectations of privacy than probationers because parole is more like imprisonment than probation.

It should not come as a surprise that prison inmates have a lower expectation of privacy in their cells than parolees have in their homes. In fact, in Hudson v. Palmer, 468 U.S. 517 (1984), they have no Fourth Amendment protections concerning their cells. Accordingly, an inmate's prison cell may be searched anytime without justification.

Conclusion

In examining administrative and special needs searches that may be conducted without probable cause, it is important that you consider several things. As a threshold requirement, the search program must have public welfare as its primary objective, not criminal law enforcement. Assuming the search meets this requirement, you must balance the nature of the privacy interest implicated, the character of the privacy intrusion, the nature and immediacy of the government concerns, and the effectiveness of the search protocol that addresses the governmental concerns. The greater the privacy intrusion involved in the search, the greater the likelihood that the government's concerns need to be effectively addressed. This sliding scale analysis is once again an example of the Court trying to implement a flexible reasonableness standard for the Fourth Amendment.

KEY TERMS

administrative search	non-routine border search
border search	routine border search
closely regulated business	special needs search
motor vehicle checkpoint	inventory search

REVIEW QUESTIONS

Directions: Please refer to what you learned in this chapter to help you respond.

1. What is the primary difference between an administrative and special needs search?
2. What justifications does the Court rely on to allow administrative searches? What are the three administrative searches discussed in the chapter?
3. What is the balancing test used by the Court to analyze the Constitutionality of special needs searches?

4. What did the Court rule concerning the Constitutionality of static suspicionless stops near the border?
5. What did the Court decide concerning the Constitutionality of roving suspicionless stops to check a driver's license and registration? Would a static roadblock designed to check the license and registration of every third car be legal?
6. What did the Court decide about the legality of sobriety checkpoints? What justification or reasoning did the Court rely on to make its ruling? Do you agree or disagree with the decision of the Court?
7. Do children attending public school have a reasonable expectation of privacy? Can school officials ever search a child? If so, what level of justification is needed?
8. What justifications does the Court rely on to permit the police to perform an inventory search of a vehicle? What parameters or regulations has the Court put on this type of search?
9. What are the rules for inspecting a closely regulated business?
10. What limits are there on the government requiring drug tests for employees of specific industries? How about government employees?

APPLYING THE LAW

Below are five hypothetical fact scenarios. To practice your understanding of the law that you learned in this chapter and your ability to apply it, answer each question posed by applying that law to the hypothetical scenarios. Your answers should be supported by relevant case law and judicially created rules and tests.

1. A federal statute permitted warrantless drug and alcohol testing of all airport employees. The Airport Workers' Union sued to prevent such testing from occurring, arguing that it violates the Fourth Amendment. Will this suit be successful?

2. Lucy was detained at Miami International Airport because she was suspected of smuggling drugs in her alimentary canal. She had swelling in her abdomen, was wearing three pairs of adult diapers, had $10,000 of cash, spoke no English, had a return ticket to Columbia for the next day, and had made 10 roundtrips between Miami and Columbia during the past year. Upon request, she refused to allow authorities to x-ray her abdomen or perform any other medical procedure. Finally, after being detained for 20 hours, nature called, and she passed 80 bags of heroin during a bowel movement. Did the 20-hour detention of Lucy violate the Constitution?

3. Ed was a housing inspector. One day, he inspected an apartment building for code and occupancy ordinances. While inspecting the basement, the building's owner, Al, approached him and told him to leave unless he had a search warrant. Ed refused and told Al he could search wherever and whenever he wanted. Who, if anybody, is correct?

4. Sixteen-year-old Betty was caught smoking in a school bathroom. Betty was taken to Vice Principal Wetherbee's office, where she denied that she had been smoking. Enraged, Wetherbee grabbed her backpack and looked inside. He immediately saw a pack of cigarettes, a lighter, and a marijuana pipe. Suspecting she was also using marijuana, he looked through her entire backpack for weed.

   Is the search of Betty's backpack unconstitutional?

5. Police established a surprise DUI checkpoint on Highway 1. As part of the checkpoint, police stopped every car and had the driver blow into a portable alcohol tester. Bud was stopped at such a checkpoint and arrested for DUI. Was the Highway 1 checkpoint constitutional?

ORAL ARGUMENTS

Board of Education v. Earls: www.oyez.org/cases/2001/01-332
Camara v. Municipal Court: www.oyez.org/cases/1966/92
Chandler v Miller: www.oyez.org/cases/1996/96-126
Ferguson v. City of Charleston: www.oyez.org/cases/2000/99-936
Indianapolis v. Edmond: www.oyez.org/cases/2000/99-1030
National Treasury Employees Union v. Von Raab https://www.oyez.org/cases/1988/86-1879
New Jersey v. T.L.O: www.oyez.org/cases/1983/83-712
New York v. Burger: www.oyez.org/cases/1986/86-80
Safford Unified School District v. Redding: www.oyez.org/cases/2008/08-479
Skinner v. Railway Labor Executives' Association www.oyez.org/cases/1988/87-1555
South Dakota v. Opperman: www.oyez.org/cases/1970-1979/1975/1975_75_76/argument
Samson v. California: www.oyez.org/cases/2005/04-9728
United States v. Flores-Montano: www.oyez.org/cases/2003/02-1794
United States v. Montoya de Hernandez: www.oyez.org/cases/1984/84-755

CHAPTER 8

Interrogation, Confessions, and Self-Incrimination

LEARNING OBJECTIVES

After reading this chapter, students should be able to:

- Recognize the role the Fourteenth Amendment and voluntariness play in the admission of confessions at trial
- Understand the history, requirements, protections, exceptions, and logic behind *Miranda* rights
- Discuss when a person is in custody for the purposes of *Miranda*
- Explain what interrogation is and when a suspect is interrogated for the purposes of *Miranda*
- Understand how the Court treats silence in association with *Miranda*
- Understand the requirements for a suspect to invoke or waive *Miranda*
- Comprehend how the right to counsel relates to interrogation and *Miranda*

Introduction

In this chapter, we examine police interrogation practices, confessions, and the use of incriminating statements in criminal trials. These issues implicate different constitutional safeguards, including the Fourteenth Amendment's due process clause, the Fifth Amendment's right against compelled self-incrimination, and the Sixth Amendment's right to counsel.

The right against compelled self-incrimination has roots that date at least as far back as thirteenth-century England. The Catholic Church, which exerted tremendous influence over the Crown and in matters of government, adopted the *inquisitio* proceeding to discover and sanction misconduct among the clergy. From this practice sprang the more widespread Inquisition, the mission of which was to identify heretics who were untrue to the Church's religious teachings. The inquisitional method of proof had several characteristic features. It relied heavily on an oath that suspected heretics were required to swear, known as the oath *de veritate,* or the oath *ex officio,* obligating them to respond truthfully to all questions asked.

> **Confession** of guilt was central to the whole inquisitional process, and the oath, which was administered at the very outset of the proceedings, was reckoned as indispensable to the confession. The accused, knowing neither the charges against him, nor his accusers, nor the evidence, was immediately placed between hammer and anvil: he must take the oath or be condemned as guilty, yet if he took the oath he exposed himself to the nearly certain risk of punishment for perjury — and his lies were evidence of his guilt — or condemned himself by admissions which his judge regarded as damaging, perhaps as a confession to the unnamed crime. L. Levy, *Origins of the Fifth Amendment,* 23–24 (1968).

Suspects unwilling to confess their infidelity were frequently tortured. Inquisitional procedures were not used in the common-law courts that dispensed the king's justice throughout England, but they were adopted by the King's Council, composed of prominent nobility, bishops, and jurists, which sometimes acted as a court. The judicial branch of the council came to be known as the infamous Court of **Star Chamber**, where torture, the oath, and other cruel techniques were commonly used to coerce confessions. The methods of the Inquisition eventually were recognized as a gross abuse of official authority. The memory of those abuses was largely responsible for the right against compelled **self-incrimination** that is embedded in the Fifth Amendment.

The Supreme Court has utilized three provisions in the Bill of Rights to protect people's privilege against self-incrimination.

The due process clause of the Fourteenth Amendment

The self-incrimination clause of the Fifth Amendment

The right to counsel of the Sixth Amendment

We begin with the Court's reliance on due process to condemn **involuntary confessions**. This rationale, which used the Due Process Clauses of the Fourteenth Amendment, was applied most commonly to state cases that arose between the 1930s and the early 1960s. As we shall see, however, involuntariness remains a viable means for challenging incriminating statements even today. We devote most of our attention to the Fifth Amendment's right against compelled self-incrimination, to the Court's 1966 decision of Miranda v. Arizona, 384 U.S. 436 (1966), and to the *post-Miranda* cases that have dominated the law of police interrogation and confessions for the past several decades. Lastly, we examine the Court's use of the Sixth Amendment right to counsel to oversee the questioning of criminal suspects.

Involuntary Confessions

The Supreme Court reviewed convictions in which confessions were challenged in important federal cases decided toward the end of the nineteenth century. In *Hopt v. Utah,* 110 U.S. 574 (1884), which arose when Utah was still a federal territory, the justices relied on common-law evidentiary principles to express disapproval of confessions obtained by 'inducements, threats, or promises," citing the dubious trustworthiness of such statements.

In *Bram v. United States,* 168 U.S. 532 (1897), the Court invoked the Fifth Amendment's protection against compelled self-incrimination to bar the admission of an involuntary confession in a federal criminal trial. However, shortly thereafter, the justices refused to apply the Fifth Amendment's self-incrimination clause to state trials. Even in its federal case decisions, the Court failed to develop or build on the Fifth Amendment groundwork laid in Bram for many years to come.

The Court first invalidated a state court's use of a confession in *Brown* v. *Mississippi,* 297 U.S. 278 (1936). We considered *Brown* in Chapter 1. You will recall that in this case, a Mississippi deputy sheriff unabashedly admitted whipping the (African American) suspects in a murder, hanging them from a tree, and otherwise using physical coercion to produce confessions that led to convictions and death sentences. The Supreme Court ruled that the use of coerced confessions as evidence was unconstitutional. However, Chief Justice Hughes's decision did not rest on the Fifth Amendment's guarantee against compelled self-incrimination, but rather the due process clause of the Fourteenth Amendment.

> The state is free to regulate the procedure of its courts in accordance with its own conceptions of policy, unless in so doing it offends some principle of justice so rooted in the traditions and conscience of our people as to be ranked as fundamental.
>
> The state may abolish trial by jury. It may dispense with indictment by a grand jury and substitute complaint or information. But the freedom of the state in establishing its policy is the freedom of constitutional government and is limited by the requirement of due process of law. Because a state may dispense with a jury trial, it does not follow that it may substitute trial by ordeal. The rack and torture chamber may not be substituted for the witness stand.
>
> The due process clause requires that state action, whether through one agency or another, shall be consistent with the fundamental principles of

> liberty and justice which lie at the base of all our civil and political institutions. It would be difficult to conceive of methods more revolting to the sense of justice than those taken to procure the confessions of these petitioners, and the use of the confessions thus obtained as the basis for conviction and sentence was a clear denial of due process. *Brown* v. *Mississippi,* 297 U.S. at 285–287.

What is the precise basis for Brown's conclusion that the use of the confessions violated the defendant's due process rights? Is it the implicit assumption that incriminating statements produced by such methods may be unreliable? Could interrogation methods short of physical coercion offend due process? Would the statements be admissible if corroborated and proven to be trustworthy?

Brown stood for the principle that due process prohibits using "involuntary" confessions to prove guilt. The Court struggled over the next three decades to give meaning to the concept of involuntariness. Rules providing general guidance proved elusive because only careful consideration of each case's "totality of the circumstances" could resolve whether a confession was involuntary. Relevant factors included police interrogation tactics and the characteristics of the individual being questioned. (See Box 8.1).

Box 8.1: Items Considered in Determining Voluntariness of a Confession

Police Conduct	Suspect Characteristics
Length of pre-trial detention	Age
Duration of the interrogation	Pain
Location of interrogation	Education
Intensity of interrogation	Pain
Promises made	Intoxication/impairment
Use of deception	Fatigue
Psychological or physical threats	Mental disabilities
Isolation from others	Experience in the justice system
Number of officers	

In addition to the outright brutality that was evident in *Brown,* other interrogation methods used by the police inspired the Court's disapproval. For example, the interrogation tactics used in *Ashcraft* v. *Tennessee,* 322 U.S. 143 (1944), were considered to be so inherently coercive as to render a confession involuntary and hence inadmissible under due process of law: "For thirty-six hours after the defendant's seizure during which period he was held incommunicado, without sleep or rest, relays of officers, experienced investigators, and highly trained lawyers questioned him without respite." *Id.* at 153. Other physical deprivations, such as prolonged denial of food, *Payne v. Arkansas,* 356 U.S. 560 (1958), clothing, *Malinski* v. *New York,* 324 U.S. 401 (1945), and seclusion from counsel, family, and friends, *Haynes* v. Washington, 373 U.S. 503 (1963); *Ward* v. *Texas*, 316 U.S. 547 (1942), could help support the conclusion that a confession was involuntary. Yet the Court also made clear that psychological pressures, no less than physical ones, could undermine the voluntariness of a statement.

> If the confession is the product of sustained pressure by the police it does not issue from a free choice. When a suspect speaks because he is overborne, it is immaterial whether he has been subjected to a physical or mental ordeal. Eventual yielding to questioning under such circumstances is plainly the product of the suction process of interrogation and therefore the reverse of voluntary *Watts* v. *Indiana*, 338 U.S. 49, 53 (1949).

The characteristics of the suspect being interrogated also helped determine whether a confession was considered to be involuntary. Statements were less likely to be found involuntary if the suspect was relatively well educated, *Crooker v. California*, 357 U.S. 433 (1958) (suspect had completed one year of law school), or was an experienced criminal, *Stein* v. New *York*, 346 U.S. 156 (1953). On the other hand, the voluntariness of a confession was more closely scrutinized if a suspect was youthful, *Gallegos* v. *Colorado*, 370 U.S.49 (1962) (14 years old); *Haley v. Ohio*, 332 U.S. 596 (1948) (15 years old); had little education or was of low intelligence, *Culombe v. Connecticut*, 367 U.S. 568 (1961); was ill, Jackson v. *Denno*, 378 U.S. 368 (1964).

The Court thus considered an ill-defined mix of police interrogation tactics and the characteristics of the suspect in the totality of the circumstances that determined the voluntariness of a statement. The justices eventually clarified whether their central concern involved the reliability of confessions, or the methods used to obtain them. In *Spano v. New York*, 360 U.S. 315, 320–321 (1959), Chief Justice Warren explained that:

> The abhorrence of society to the use of involuntary' confessions does not turn alone on their inherent untrustworthiness. It also turns on the deep-rooted feeling that the police must obey the law while enforcing the law; that in the end life and liberty can be as much endangered from illegal methods used to convict those thought to be criminals as from the actual criminals themselves.

The voluntariness test had many drawbacks. The biggest problem was its unclarity and its consequent inability to give meaningful guidance to law enforcement officials and the lower courts about the ground rules governing police questioning of suspected criminals. This lack of clarity was virtually unavoidable since the test depended on such abstract concepts as whether a suspect's will had been overborne or whether a statement was the product of free choice.

Even if those concepts could be defined adequately, application of the voluntariness standard depended on the idiosyncratic facts — the totality of the circumstances — of each case in which a confession was challenged. What actually happened over the course of an interrogation was often vigorously disputed and impossible to reconstruct. "Swearing contests" between the police and suspects almost always were resolved in favor of the police. The fact-bound nature of the voluntariness inquiry made it especially difficult for appellate courts, including the Supreme Court, to regulate the behavior of the police. Trial courts, which first ruled on the admissibility of confessions, suffered from doctrinal unclarity and could not always be trusted to promote the due process norms underlying the High Court's decisions.

Acutely aware of these problems, the Supreme Court began to explore alternative rules to bring order to the self-incrimination area.

The Fifth Amendment Privilege Against Self-Incrimination

The *Miranda* Rule, which is based on the Fifth Amendment Privilege Against Self-Incrimination was established by the United States Supreme Court in 1966. The Court's decision in *Miranda v. Arizona involved* four different cases involving custodial interrogations:

- *State v. Miranda, 98* Ariz. 18, 401 P.2d 721 (1965)
- *People v. Vignera,* 21 A.D.2d 752, 252 N.Y.S.2d 19 (1964)
- *Westover v. United States,* 342 F. 2d 684 (9th Cir 1965)
- *People v. Stewart,* 43 Cal. 201, 400 P.2d 97 (1965)

In each case, the defendant was questioned by law enforcement officials in a room that was isolated from the outside world. None of the defendants was given a full and effective warning of their rights before the interrogation. In each case, the defendant confessed orally and in writing. Each was found guilty of a serious felony and sentenced to a number of years in prison. The convictions were affirmed in three of the four cases (the California Supreme Court reversed the conviction in *California v. Stewart.*

The Supreme Court granted certiorari for each case to consider the admissibility of statements obtained from an individual who is subjected to custodial police interrogation and the necessity for procedures that assure that the individual is accorded his privilege under the Fifth Amendment to the Constitution not to be compelled to incriminate himself.

Due to the similarity in the issues presented, when these cases wound their way up to the U.S. Supreme Court, they were consolidated for decision in the case now universally known as *Miranda* v. *Arizona,* 384 U.S. 436 (1966). *Miranda* sprawls over 109 pages in the United States Reports. It was decided by a 5–4 vote. As you read in *Miranda,* be sure to keep in mind the pre-1966 law governing confessions. Approach *Miranda* not simply as "the answer" to the general challenges raised by police interrogation practices and confessions in criminal cases, but with a critical eye attuned to the several intertwined issues of law and fact that figure in this revolutionary decision.

Miranda v. Arizona
384 U.S. 436 (1966)

MR. CHIEF JUSTICE WARREN delivered the opinion of the Court.

The cases before us raise questions which go to the roots of our concepts of American criminal jurisprudence: the restraints society must observe consistent with the Federal Constitution in prosecuting individuals for crime. More specifically, we deal with the admissibility of statements obtained from an individual who is subjected to custodial police interrogation and the necessity for procedures which assure that the individual is accorded his privilege under the Fifth Amendment to the Constitution not to be compelled to incriminate himself.

Our holding will be spelled out with some specificity in the pages which follow but briefly stated it is this: the prosecution may not use statements, whether exculpatory or inculpatory, stemming from **custodial interrogation** of the defendant unless it demonstrates the use of procedural safeguards effective to secure the privilege against self-incrimination. By custodial interrogation, we mean questioning initiated by law enforcement officers after a person has been taken into custody or otherwise deprived of his freedom of action in any significant way. As for the procedural safeguards to be employed, unless other fully effective means are devised to inform accused persons of their right of silence and to assure a continuous opportunity to exercise it, the following measures are required. Prior to any questioning, the person must be warned that he has a right to remain silent, that any statement he does make may be used as evidence against him, and that he has a right to the presence of an attorney, either retained or appointed. The defendant may waive effectuation of these rights, provided the waiver is made voluntarily, knowingly, and intelligently. If, however, he indicates in any manner and at any stage of the process that he wishes to consult with an attorney before speaking there can be no questioning. Likewise, if the individual is alone and indicates in any manner that he does not wish to be interrogated, the police may not question him. The mere fact that he may have answered some questions or volunteered some statements on his own does not deprive him of the right to refrain from answering any further inquiries until he has consulted with an attorney and thereafter consents to be questioned.

I

The constitutional issue we decide in each of these cases is the admissibility of statements obtained from a defendant questioned while in custody or otherwise deprived of his freedom of action in any significant way. In each, the defendant was questioned by police officers, detectives, or a prosecuting attorney in a room in which he was cut off from the outside world. In none of these cases was the defendant given a full and effective warning of his rights at the outset of the interrogation process. In all the cases, the questioning elicited oral admissions, and in three of them, signed statements as well which were admitted at their trials. They all thus share salient features — incommunicado interrogation of individuals in a police-dominated atmosphere, resulting in self-incriminating statements without full warnings of constitutional rights.

An understanding of the nature and setting of this in-custody interrogation is essential to our decisions today. The difficulty in depicting what transpires at such interrogations stems from the fact that in this country they have largely taken place incommunicado. From extensive factual studies undertaken in the early 1930's, including the famous Wickersham Report to Congress by a Presidential Commission, it is clear that police violence and the "third degree" flourished at that time.

The officers are told by the manuals that the principal psychological factor contributing to a successful interrogation is privacy — being alone with the person under interrogation. To highlight the isolation and unfamiliar surroundings, the manuals instruct the police to display an air of confidence in the suspect's guilt and from outward appearance to maintain only an interest in confirming certain details. The guilt of the subject is to be posited as a fact. The interrogator should direct his comments toward the reasons why the subject committed the act, rather than court failure by asking the subject whether he did it. Like other men, perhaps the subject has had a bad family life, had an unhappy childhood, had too much to drink, had an unrequited desire for women. The officers are instructed to minimize the moral seriousness of the offense, to cast blame on the victim or on society. These tactics are designed to put the subject in a psychological state where his story is but an elaboration of what the police purport to know already — that he is guilty. Explanations to the contrary are dismissed and discouraged.

The manuals suggest that the suspect be offered legal excuses for his actions in order to obtain an initial admission of guilt.

When the techniques described above prove unavailing, the texts recommend they be alternated with a show of some hostility.

The interrogators sometimes are instructed to induce a confession out of trickery. The technique here is quite effective in crimes which require identification or which run in series. In the identification situation, the interrogator may take a break in his questioning to place the subject among a group of men in a line-up. The witness or complainant (previously coached, if necessary) studies the line-up and confidently points out the subject as the guilty party. Then the questioning resumes as though there were now no doubt about the guilt of the subject. A variation on this technique is called the "reverse line-up": the accused is placed in a line-up, but this time he is identified by several fictitious witnesses or victims who associated him with different offenses. It is expected that the subject will become desperate and confess to the offense under investigation in order to escape from the false accusations.

Even without employing brutality, the "third degree" or the specific stratagems described above, the very fact of custodial interrogation exacts a heavy toll on individual liberty and trades on the weakness of individuals.

In the cases before us today, given this background, we concern ourselves primarily with this interrogation atmosphere and the evils it can bring.

In these cases, we might not find the defendants' statements to have been involuntary in traditional terms. Our concern for adequate safeguards to protect precious Fifth Amendment rights is, of course, not lessened in the slightest. In each of the cases, the defendant was thrust into an unfamiliar atmosphere and run through menacing police interrogation procedures. The potentiality for compulsion is forcefully apparent. To be sure, the records do not evince overt physical coercion or patent psychological ploys. The fact remains that in none of these cases did the officers undertake to afford appropriate safeguards at the outset of the interrogation to insure that the statements were truly the product of free choice.

It is obvious that such an interrogation environment is created for no purpose other than to subjugate the individual to the will of his examiner. This atmosphere carries its own badge of intimidation. To be sure, this is not physical intimidation, but it is equally destructive of human dignity. The current practice of incommunicado interrogation is at odds with one of our Nation's most cherished principles — that the individual may not be compelled to incriminate himself. Unless adequate protective devices are employed to dispel the compulsion inherent in custodial surroundings, no statement obtained from the defendant can truly be the product of his free choice.

From the foregoing, we can readily perceive an intimate connection between the privilege against self-incrimination and police custodial questioning. It is fitting to turn to history and precedent underlying the Self-Incrimination Clause to determine its applicability in this situation.

The question in these cases is whether the privilege is fully applicable during a period of custodial interrogation. In this Court, the privilege has consistently been accorded a liberal construction. We are satisfied that all the principles embodied in the privilege apply to informal compulsion exerted by law-enforcement officers during in-custody questioning. An individual swept from familiar surroundings into police custody, surrounded by antagonistic forces, and subjected to the techniques of persuasion described above cannot be otherwise than under compulsion to speak.

In addition to the expansive historical development of the privilege and the sound policies which have nurtured its evolution, judicial precedent thus clearly establishes its application to incommunicado interrogation. The presence of counsel, in all the cases before us today, would be the adequate protective device necessary to make the process of police interrogation conform to the dictates of the privilege. His presence would insure that statements made in the government-established atmosphere are not the product of compulsion. That counsel is present when statements are taken from an individual during interrogation obviously enhances the integrity of the fact-finding processes in court. The presence of an attorney, and the warnings delivered to the individual, enable the defendant under otherwise compelling circumstances to tell his story without fear, effectively, and in a way that eliminates the evils in the interrogation process.

III

Today, then, there can be no doubt that the Fifth Amendment privilege is available outside of criminal court; proceedings and serves to protect persons in all settings in which their freedom of action is curtailed in any significant way from being compelled to incriminate themselves. We have concluded that without proper safeguards the process of in-custody interrogation of persons suspected or accused of crime contains inherently compelling pressures which work to undermine the individual's will to resist and to compel him to speak where he would not otherwise do so freely. In order to combat these pressures and to permit a full opportunity to exercise the privilege against self-incrimination, the accused must be adequately and effectively apprised of his rights and the exercise of those rights must be fully honored.

It is impossible for us to foresee the potential alternatives for protecting the privilege which might be devised by Congress or the States in the exercise of their creative rulemaking capacities. Therefore, we cannot say that the Constitution necessarily requires adherence to any particular solution for the inherent compulsions of the interrogation process as it is presently conducted. Our decision in no way creates a constitutional straitjacket which will handicap sound efforts at reform, nor is it intended to have this effect. We encourage Congress and the States to continue their laudable search for increasingly effective ways of protecting the rights of the individual while promoting efficient enforcement of our criminal laws. However, unless we are shown other procedures which are at least as effective in apprising accused persons of their right of silence and in assuring a continuous opportunity to exercise it, the following safeguards must be observed.

At the outset, if a person in custody is to be subjected to interrogation, he must first be informed in clear and unequivocal terms that he has the right to remain silent. For those unaware of the privilege, the warning is needed simply to make them aware of it — the threshold requirement for an intelligent decision as to its exercise. More importantly, such a warning is an absolute prerequisite in overcoming the inherent pressures of the interrogation atmosphere. It is not just the subnormal or woefully ignorant who succumb to an interrogator's imprecations, whether implied or expressly stated, that the interrogation will continue until a confession is obtained or that silence in the face of accusation is itself damning and will bode ill when presented to a jury. Further, the warning will show the individual that his interrogators are prepared to recognize his privilege should he choose to exercise it.

The Fifth Amendment privilege is so fundamental to our system of constitutional rule and the expedient of giving an adequate warning as to the availability of the privilege so simple, we will not pause to inquire in individual cases whether the defendant was aware of his rights without a warning being given. Assessments of the knowledge the defendant possessed, based on information as to his age, education, intelligence, or prior contact with authorities, can never be more than speculation; a warning is a clearcut fact. More important, whatever the background of the person interrogated, a warning at the time of the interrogation is indispensable to overcome its pressures and to insure that the individual knows he is free to exercise the privilege at that point in time.

The warning of the right to remain silent must be accompanied by the explanation that anything said can and will be used against the individual in court. This warning is needed in order to make him aware not only of the privilege, but also of the consequences of forgoing it. It is only through an awareness of these consequences that there can be any assurance of real understanding and intelligent exercise of the privilege. Moreover, this warning may serve to make the individual more acutely aware that he is faced with a phase of the adversary system — that he is not in the presence of persons acting solely in his interest. The circumstances surrounding in-custody interrogation can operate very quickly to overbear the will of one merely made aware of his privilege by his interrogators. Therefore, the right to have counsel present at the interrogation is indispensable to the protection of the Fifth Amendment privilege under the system we delineate today. Our aim is to assure that the individual's right to choose between silence and speech remains unfettered throughout the interrogation process. A once-stated warning, delivered by those who will conduct the interrogation, cannot itself suffice to that end among those who most require knowledge of their rights. A mere warning given by the interrogators is not alone sufficient to accomplish that end. Thus, the need for counsel to protect the Fifth Amendment privilege comprehends not merely a right to consult with counsel prior to questioning, but also to have counsel present during any questioning if the defendant so desires.

The presence of counsel at the interrogation may serve several significant subsidiary functions as well. If the accused decides to talk to his interrogators, the assistance of counsel can mitigate the dangers of untrustworthiness. With a lawyer present the likelihood that the police will practice coercion is reduced, and if coercion is nevertheless exercised the lawyer can testify to it in court. The presence of a lawyer can also help to guarantee that the accused gives a fully accurate statement to the police and that the statement is rightly reported by the prosecution at trial.

An individual need not make a pre-interrogation request for a lawyer. While such request affirmatively secures his right to have one, his failure to ask for a lawyer does not constitute a waiver. No effective waiver of the right to counsel during interrogation can be recognized unless specifically made after the warnings we here delineate have been given. The accused who does not know his rights and therefore does not make a request may be the person who most needs counsel.

Accordingly, we hold that an individual held for interrogation must be clearly informed that he has the right to consult with a lawyer and to have the lawyer with him during interrogation under the system for protecting the privilege we delineate today. As with the warnings of the right to remain silent and that anything stated can be used in evidence against him, this warning is an absolute prerequisite to interrogation. No amount of circumstantial evidence that the person may have been aware of this right will suffice to stand in its stead. Only through such a warning is there ascertainable assurance that the accused was aware of this right.

If an individual indicates that he wishes the assistance of counsel before any interrogation occurs, the authorities cannot rationally ignore or deny his request on the basis that the individual does not have or cannot afford a retained attorney. The financial ability of the individual has no relationship to the scope of the rights involved here. The privilege against self-incrimination secured by the Constitution applies to all individuals. The need for counsel in order to protect the privilege exists for the indigent as well as the affluent. In fact, were we to limit these constitutional rights to those who can retain an attorney, our decisions today would be of little significance. The cases before us as well as the vast majority of confession cases with which we have dealt in the past involve those unable to retain counsel. While authorities are not required to relieve the accused of his poverty, they have the obligation not to take advantage of indigence in the administration of justice.

In order fully to apprise a person interrogated of the extent of his rights under this system then, it is necessary to warn him not only that he has the right to consult with an attorney, but also that if he is indigent a lawyer will be appointed to represent him. Without this additional warning, the admonition of the right to consult with counsel would often be understood as meaning only that he can consult with a lawyer if he has one or has the funds to obtain one. As with the warnings of the right to remain silent and of the general right to counsel, only by effective and express explanation to the indigent of this right can there be assurance that he was truly in a position to exercise it.

Once warnings have been given, the subsequent procedure is clear. If the individual indicates in any manner, at any time prior to or during questioning, that he wishes to remain silent, the interrogation must cease. At this point he has shown that he intends to exercise his Fifth Amendment privilege; any statement taken after the person invokes his privilege cannot be other than the product of compulsion, subtle or otherwise. Without the right to cut off questioning, the setting of in-custody interrogation operates on the individual to overcome free choice in producing a statement after the privilege has been once invoked. If the individual states that he wants an attorney, the interrogation must cease until an attorney is present. At that time, the individual must have an opportunity to confer with the attorney and to have him present during any subsequent questioning. If the individual cannot obtain an attorney and he indicates that he wants one before speaking to police, they must respect his decision to remain silent.

If the interrogation continues without the presence of an attorney and a statement is taken, a heavy burden rests on the government to demonstrate that the defendant knowingly and intelligently waived his privilege against self-incrimination and his right to retained or appointed counsel. This Court has always set high standards of proof for the waiver of constitutional rights and we reassert these standards as applied to in-custody interrogation. Since the State is responsible for establishing the isolated circumstances under which the interrogation takes place and has the only means of making available corroborated evidence of warnings given during incommunicado interrogation, the burden is rightly on its shoulders. An express statement that the individual is willing to make a statement and does not want an attorney followed closely by a statement could constitute a waiver. But a valid waiver will not be presumed simply from the silence of the accused after warnings are given or simply from the fact that a confession was in fact eventually obtained.

Whatever the testimony of the authorities as to waiver of rights by an accused, the fact of lengthy interrogation or incommunicado incarceration before a statement is made is strong evidence that the accused did not validly waive his rights. In these circumstances the fact that the individual eventually made a statement is consistent with the conclusion that the compelling influence of the interrogation finally forced him to do so. It is inconsistent with any notion of a voluntary relinquishment of the privilege. Moreover, any evidence that the accused was threatened, tricked, or cajoled into a waiver will, of course, show that the defendant did not voluntarily waive his privilege. The requirement of warnings and waiver of rights is fundamental with respect to the Fifth Amendment privilege and not simply a preliminary ritual to existing methods of interrogation.

The warnings required and the waiver necessary in accordance with our opinion today are, in the absence of a fully effective equivalent, prerequisites to the admissibility of any statement made by a defendant. No distinction can be drawn between statements which are direct confessions and statements which amount to "admissions" of part or all of an offense. The privilege against self-incrimination protects the individual from being compelled to incriminate himself in any manner; it does not distinguish degrees of incrimination. Similarly, for precisely the same reason, no distinction may be drawn between inculpatory statements and statements alleged to be merely "exculpatory."

The principles announced today deal with the protection which must be given to the privilege against self-incrimination when the individual is first subjected to police interrogation while in custody at the station or otherwise deprived of his freedom of action in any significant way. It is at this point that our adversary system of criminal proceedings commences, distinguishing itself at the outset from the inquisitorial system recognized in some countries. Under the system of warnings we delineate today or under any other system which may be devised and found effective, the safeguards to be erected about the privilege must come into play at this point.

Our decision is not intended to hamper the traditional function of police officers in investigating crime. When an individual is in custody on probable cause, the police may, of course, seek out evidence in the field to be used at trial against him.

In dealing with statements obtained through interrogation, we do not purport to find all confessions inadmissible. Confessions remain a proper element in law enforcement. Any statement given freely and voluntarily without any compelling influences is, of course, admissible in evidence.

To summarize, we hold that when an individual is taken into custody, or otherwise deprived of his freedom by the authorities in any significant way and is subjected to questioning, the privilege against self-incrimination is jeopardized. Procedural safeguards must be employed to protect the privilege, and unless other fully effective means are adopted to notify the person of his right of silence and to assure that the exercise of the right will be scrupulously honored, the following measures are required. He must be warned prior to any questioning that he has the right to remain silent, that anything he says can be used against him in a court of law, that he has the right to the presence of an attorney, and that if he cannot afford an attorney one will be appointed for him prior to any questioning if he so desires. The opportunity to exercise these rights must be afforded to him throughout the interrogation. After such warnings have been given, and such opportunity afforded him, the individual may knowingly and intelligently waive these rights and agree to answer questions or make a statement. But unless and until such warnings and waiver are demonstrated by the prosecution at trial, no evidence obtained as a result of interrogation can be used against him.

FURTHER CASE LAW, REFLECTIONS, AND QUESTIONS

1. *The problem.* On what sources or authorities does Chief Justice Warren's majority opinion in *Miranda* rely to make the case that police interrogation tactics threaten the Fifth Amendment prohibition against compelled self-incrimination? Does the opinion rely on testimony about those practices? Does it depend on the facts of the four cases before the Court? What difficulties does the Chief Justice note

in obtaining reliable evidence about the methods that police officers use to question suspects? What does the Court resort to to fill the gap in our knowledge as to what goes on in interrogation rooms? What assurance is given that these sources describe representative interrogation procedures?

How should "the problem" to which the Court attempts to respond in *Miranda* be described? Does the problem involve confessions generally or some smaller subset of confessions? Does it affect all confessions produced by police questioning, or is it limited to the products of a specific type of questioning? Does it extend to all types of statements or only to statements that are directly incriminating?

How does the Court's definition of "the problem" relate to the constitutional right against compelled self-incrimination? Does the concern seem to be with physical compulsion or a different kind of compulsion? What conditions identified by the Court combine to produce that compulsion?

2. *The solution.* After defining how the police interrogation practices at issue threaten the right against compelled self-incrimination, the majority opinion in *Miranda* details its solution to the problem. You undoubtedly were familiar with the *Miranda* "warnings" long before reading this decision. The Court's desire to give concrete constitutional guidelines for law enforcement agencies and courts to follow motivated the use of the specific warnings as a partial response to a problem that had existed for many years and had defied resolution through the other approaches we have considered.

   The enforcement of *Miranda* rights is an essential part of, but not the entire remedy that the Court fashions. Another facet of the solution involves the *waiver* of those rights. To be effective, how must a suspect's waiver, or willingness to relinquish the specified rights, be made? What are the prerequisites of an effective decision to forgo those rights? Who has the burden of establishing whether a valid waiver of the *Miranda* rights occurred, and how can such proof be made?

3. There is considerable dispute over how effective *Miranda* has been either in bringing clarity to the rules governing police interrogation of suspected criminals or in providing meaningful protections for individuals' rights against compelled self-incrimination. Another aspect *of Miranda* also concerned the Court, as well as the general public, when the decision was announced. The dissenting opinions of Justices Harlan and White darkly warned about the adverse impact that *Miranda* would have on law enforcement. Nevertheless, research studies published shortly after the decision suggested that *Miranda* had had a negligible effect in reducing the number of confessions, guilty pleas, or trial convictions.

One of the primary reasons the Supreme Court adopted the Miranda rule was to standardize the admissibility of confessions made during an interrogation at trial. By moving away from the subjective nature of the voluntariness inquiry, the court hoped to implement the rules regarding the admissibility of confessions.

This has not been the case. In focusing on custodial interrogation, the court gave rise to a number of sub-issues that must be dealt with in implementing Miranda. These issues include:

1. How is custody defined when considering custodial interrogations?
2. What constitutes an interrogation?
3. What specifically must be included in warnings given to a suspect?
4. What is required for a valid waiver of the privilege?
5. What is required for an effective invocation of the privilege?
6. Under what circumstances may a waiver or invocation of the privilege be withdrawn?

Addressing these issues has not been as straightforward and simple as one might have hoped. The next several sections in this chapter will address these complexities and the rules the Court has established. We start this analysis by considering what constitutes custody for purposes of considering Miranda.

Custody

The *Miranda* requirements apply only to "custodial" interrogation. "By custodial interrogation, we mean questioning initiated by law enforcement officers *after a person has been taken* into custody or *otherwise deprived of his freedom of action in any significant way.*" 384 U.S., at 444 (emphasis added). The Court elaborated:

> Our decision is not intended to hamper the traditional function of police officers in investigating crime. General on-the-scene questioning as to facts surrounding a crime or other general questioning of citizens in the fact-finding process is not affected by our holding. It is an act of responsible citizenship for individuals to give whatever information they may have to aid in law enforcement. In such situations the compelling atmosphere inherent in the process of in-custody interrogation is not necessarily present. 384 U.S., at 477–478.

When a police officer approaches an individual on the street and asks, "What's going on here?" (obviously a form of interrogation), *Miranda* warnings do not necessarily have to be administered for the answer to be admissible in a criminal trial. This is true even if the response is highly incriminating. If you have ever been in a situation like this, with a police officer posing questions to you at arm's length, you might feel considerable pressure to respond. Even if, as the *Miranda* Court suggested, such an atmosphere is not as "compelling" as a custodial interrogation, might it still produce such pressure that most people would have great difficulty in not responding? Whatever the answer is to this question, which we leave to your introspection, a crucial legal distinction remains between custodial and noncustodial interrogation. *Miranda* warnings are required only in the former context.

Miranda rights are triggered once a person is placed in custody. Whether a person is in fact in custody is decided by an objective assessment from the totality of circumstances at the time of the interrogation. Courts will consider whether a reasonable person under the totality of circumstances would believe they are free to leave. Note that what the police officer or individual involved in the interrogation actually believes does not matter. Rather, courts will evaluate what a reasonable person would believe.

Courts will consider all of the circumstances present in determining if a custodial interrogation requires cases to be considered on a case-by-case basis. In conducting this objective analysis, courts have considered the following items:

- Where the interrogation takes place;
- How long the interrogation lasted;
- The intensity of the questioning;
- The number of police officers involved;
- Whether physical force was used in detaining the person; and
- Whether the questioning took place in public.

Courts will consider the totality of circumstances involving these and other relevant facts. The following case excerpts illustrate how an objective analysis of the circumstances surrounding an interrogation can lead to surprising results.

Orozco v. Texas

394 U.S. 324 (1969)

MR. JUSTICE BLACK delivered the opinion of the Court.

The petitioner, Reyes Arias Orozco, was convicted in the Criminal District Court of Dallas County, Texas, of murder without malice and was sentenced to serve in the state prison not less than two nor more than 10 years. The Court of Criminal Appeals of Texas affirmed the conviction, rejecting petitioner's contention that a material part of the evidence against him was obtained in violation of the provision of the Fifth Amendment to the United States Constitution, made applicable to the States by the Fourteenth Amendment, that: "No person... shall be compelled in any criminal case to be a witness against himself."

The evidence introduced at trial showed that petitioner and the deceased had quarreled outside the El Farleto Cafe in Dallas shortly before midnight on the date of the shooting. The deceased had apparently spoken to petitioner's female companion inside the restaurant. In the heat of the quarrel outside, the deceased is said to have beaten petitioner about the face and called him "Mexican Grease." A shot was fired killing the deceased. Petitioner left the scene and returned to his boardinghouse to sleep. At about 4 a.m. four police officers arrived at petitioner's boardinghouse, were admitted by an unidentified woman, and were told that petitioner was asleep in the bedroom. All four officers entered the bedroom and began to question petitioner. From the moment he gave his name, according to the testimony of one of the officers, petitioner was not free to go where he pleased but was "under arrest." The officers asked him if he had been to the El Farleto restaurant that night and when he answered "yes" he was asked if he owned a pistol. Petitioner admitted owning one. After being asked a second time where the pistol was located, he admitted that it was in the washing machine in a back room of the boarding house. Ballistics tests indicated that the gun found in the washing machine was the gun that fired the fatal shot. At petitioner's trial, held after the effective date of this Court's decision in *Miranda v. Arizona,* 384 U. S. 436 (1966), the trial court allowed one of the officers, over the objection of petitioner's lawyer, relate the statements made by petitioner concerning the gun and petitioner's presence at the scene of the shooting.

The trial testimony clearly shows that the officers questioned petitioner about incriminating facts without first informing him of his right to remain silent, his right to have the advice of a lawyer before making any statement, and his right to have a lawyer appointed to assist him if he could not afford to hire one. We hold that the use of these admissions obtained in the absence of the required warnings was a flat violation of the Self-Incrimination Clause of the Fifth Amendment as construed in *Miranda.*

The State has argued here that, since petitioner was interrogated on his own bed, in familiar surroundings, our *Miranda* holding should not apply. It is true that the Court did say in *Miranda* that "compulsion to speak in the isolated setting of the police station may well be greater than in courts or other official investigations, where there are often impartial observers to guard against intimidation or trickery." 384 U.S. at 461. But the opinion iterated and reiterated the absolute necessity for officers interrogating people "in custody" to give the described warnings.

According to the officer's testimony, petitioner was under arrest, and not free to leave, when he was questioned in his bedroom in the early hours of the morning. The *Miranda* opinion declared that the warnings were required when the person being interrogated was "in custody at the station *or otherwise deprived of his freedom of action in any significant way.*" 384 U.S. at 384 U. S. 477. (Emphasis supplied.) The decision of this Court in *Miranda* was reached after careful consideration, and lengthy opinions were announced by both the majority and dissenting Justices. There is no need to canvass those arguments again. We do not, as the dissent implies, expand or extend to the slightest extent our *Miranda* decision. We do adhere to our well considered holding in that case, and therefore reverse the conviction below.

FURTHER CASE LAW, REFLECTIONS, AND QUESTIONS

1. In *Beckwith v. United States*, 425 U.S. 341 (1976), two Internal Revenue Service (IRS) special agents investigating potential criminal tax violations interviewed Beckwith in a private residence. During the interview, Beckwith was informed of his Fifth Amendment rights, though not with complete Miranda warnings. The agents advised him of their investigation into his tax liability and ensured he understood his rights.

   The interview was described as friendly and relaxed, with no evidence of coercion. Beckwith later sought to suppress the statements made during the interview, arguing that they were obtained without the necessary Miranda warnings. The District Court denied the motion, ruling that Miranda warnings were not required as the situation was non-custodial. The U.S. Court of Appeals affirmed this decision, and the case was brought to the U.S. Supreme Court to resolve whether such warnings were necessary.

   The Supreme Court agreed with the lower courts, ruling that the statements made by Beckwith were admissible as evidence, as the interview was non-custodial and Miranda warnings were not required.

   What makes *Beckwith* different from *Orozco* warranting different outcomes?

Just as *Orozco* confirms that questioning need not be conducted within the confines of a police station to be considered "custodial," the next case confirms the converse: merely because questioning does occur at a police station, it is not necessarily "custodial" within the meaning of *Miranda.*

Oregon v. Mathiason

429 U.S. 492 (1977)

Per Curiam.

An officer of the State Police investigated a theft at a residence near Pendleton. He asked the lady of the house which had been burglarized if she suspected anyone. She replied that the defendant was the only one she could think of. The defendant was a parolee and a 'close associate' of her son. The officer tried to contact defendant on three or four occasions with no success. Finally, about 25 days after the burglary, the officer left his card at defendant's apartment with a note asking him to call because 'I'd like to discuss something with you.' The next afternoon the defendant did call. The officer asked where it would be convenient to meet. The defendant had no preference; so the officer asked if the defendant could meet him at the state patrol office in about an hour and a half, about 5:00 p.m. The patrol office was about two blocks from defendant's apartment. The building housed several state agencies.

The officer met defendant in the hallway, shook hands and took him into an office. The defendant was told he was not under arrest. The door was closed. The two sat across a desk. The police radio in another room could be heard. The officer told defendant he wanted to talk to him about a burglary and that his truthfulness would possibly be considered by the district attorney or judge. The officer further advised that the police believed defendant was involved in the burglary and falsely stated that defendant's fingerprints were found at the scene. The defendant sat for a few minutes and then said he had taken the property. This occurred within five minutes after defendant had come to the office. The officer then advised defendant of his *Miranda* rights and took a taped confession.

At the end of the taped conversation the officer told defendant he was not arresting him at this time; he was released to go about his job and return to his family. The officer said he was referring the case to the district attorney for him to determine whether criminal charges would be brought. It was 5:30 p.m. when the defendant left the office.

The Supreme Court of Oregon reasoned from these facts that:

> We hold the interrogation took place in a 'coercive environment.' The parties were in the offices of the State Police; they were alone behind closed doors; the officer informed the defendant he was a suspect in a theft and the authorities had evidence incriminating him in the crime; and the defendant was a parolee under supervision. We are of the opinion that this evidence is not overcome by the evidence that the defendant came to the office in response to a request and was told he was not under arrest.

Our decision in *Miranda* set forth rules of police procedure applicable to "custodial interrogation." "By custodial interrogation, we mean questioning initiated by law enforcement officers after a person has been taken into custody or otherwise deprived of his freedom of action in any significant way." 384 U.S., at 444

In the present case, however, there is no indication that the questioning took place in a context where respondent's freedom to depart was restricted in any way. He came voluntarily to the police station, where he was immediately informed that he was not under arrest. At the close of a 1/2 hour interview respondent did in fact leave the police station without hindrance. It is clear from these facts that Mathiason was not in custody or otherwise deprived of his freedom of action in any significant way.

Any interview of one suspected of a crime by a police officer will have coercive aspects to it, simply by virtue of the fact that the police officer is part of a law enforcement system which may ultimately cause the suspect to be charged with a crime. But police officers are not required to administer *Miranda* warnings to everyone whom they question. Nor is the requirement of warnings to be imposed simply because the questioning takes place in the station house, or because the questioned person is one whom the police suspect. *Miranda* warnings are required only where there has been such a restriction on a person's freedom as to render him "in custody." It was that sort of coercive environment to which *Miranda* by its terms was made applicable, and to which it is limited.

The officer's false statement about having discovered Mathiason's fingerprints at the scene was found by the Supreme Court of Oregon to be another circumstance contributing to the coercive environment which makes *the Miranda* rationale applicable. Whatever relevance this fact may have to other issues in the case, it has nothing to do with whether respondent was in custody for purposes of the *Miranda* rule.

FURTHER CASE LAW, REFLECTIONS, AND QUESTIONS

1. As a parolee, Mathiason faced an almost inevitable return to prison on a showing that he had committed another crime. The police officer questioning him led Mathiason to believe that his fingerprints had been found at the scene of the crime and suggested that his truthfulness might receive favorable consideration by the prosecutor or judge. Is it reasonable to assume that Mathiason would have experienced significant psychological pressure when the officer asked about his involvement in the burglary?
2. Does Mathiason's likely state of mind make a difference to the Court? Should it? Is the "in-custody" aspect of *Miranda* best characterized as a physical condition? As a psychological condition? As some combination of objective physical circumstances and subjective psychological experiences?

Box 8.2 You Be the Judge

Robert was taken to the police station for questioning as a potential witness in the investigation of the killing of a 10-year-old girl. Robert was not a suspect in the death and was not given the Miranda warnings. While being questioned by a detective, Robert said that he had used his housemate's turquoise American-made car on the night of the murder. This statement aroused the detective's suspicion that Robert may have been involved in the homicide because a car matching such a description had been implicated in the homicide. Later during the interview, when Robert admitted to having prior convictions for rape, kidnapping, and child molestation, the detective terminated the questioning and read Robert his Miranda rights. Robert invoked his right to remain silent and requested an attorney. The detective immediately arrested Robert.

Prior to trial, Robert moved to suppress his statements because he was not advised of his Miranda rights. The prosecution argued that while being questioned as a witness and not considered a suspect by the police, Robert was not in custody for Miranda purposes and therefore not entitled to be read his rights under *Miranda*.

Who do you agree with? Explain the strength of each argument and the basis for your decision.

See *Stansbury v. California*, 511 U.S. 318 (1994).

In our study of the Fourth Amendment in the preceding chapters, we devoted considerable attention to the concept of a seizure of a person. Is it fair to assume that an individual who has been "seized" under the terms of the Fourth Amendment also is "in custody" for purposes of *Miranda*"? This issue is considered in the following case, which further defines *Miranda's* "in-custody" component.

Berkemer v. McCarty

468 U.S. 420 (1984)

JUSTICE MARSHALL delivered the opinion of the Court.

On the evening of March 31, 1980, Trooper Williams of the Ohio State Highway Patrol observed respondent's car weaving in and out of a lane on Interstate Highway 270. After following the car for two miles, Williams forced respondent to stop and asked him to get out of the vehicle. When respondent complied, Williams noticed that he was having difficulty standing. At that point, Williams concluded that respondent would be charged with a traffic offense and, therefore, his freedom to leave the scene was terminated. However, respondent was not told that he would be taken into custody. Williams then asked respondent to perform a field sobriety test, commonly known as a "balancing test." Respondent could not do so without falling.

While still at the scene of the traffic stop, Williams asked respondent whether he had been using intoxicants. Respondent replied that he had consumed two beers and had smoked several joints of marijuana a short time before. Respondent's speech was slurred, and Williams had difficulty understanding him. Williams thereupon formally placed respondent under arrest and transported him in the patrol car to the Franklin County Jail.

At the jail, respondent was given an intoxilyzer test to determine the concentration of alcohol in his blood. The test did not detect any alcohol whatsoever in respondent's system. Williams then resumed questioning respondent in order to obtain information for inclusion in the State Highway Patrol Alcohol Influence Report. Respondent answered a question about whether he had been drinking affirmatively. When asked if he was under the influence of alcohol, he said, "I guess, barely." Williams next asked respondent to indicate on the form whether the marijuana he had smoked had been treated with any chemicals. In the section of the report headed "Remarks," respondent wrote, "No angel dust or PCP in the pot. Rick McCarty."

At no point in this sequence of events did Williams or anyone else tell respondent that he had a right to remain silent, to consult with an attorney, and to have an attorney appointed for him if he could not afford one.

Respondent was charged with operating a motor vehicle while under the influence of alcohol and/or drugs. Under Ohio law, that offense is a first- degree misdemeanor and is punishable by fine or imprisonment for up to 6 months.

Respondent moved to exclude the various incriminating statements he had made to Patrolman Williams on the ground that introduction into evidence of those statements would violate the Fifth Amendment insofar as he had not been informed of his constitutional rights prior to his interrogation.

[The trial court denied the motion, and McCarty was convicted, sentenced to 90 days in jail, 80 of which were suspended, and fined. The Ohio Supreme Court affirmed his conviction, and a federal district court denied his petition for a writ of habeas corpus. The Sixth Circuit Court of Appeals reversed, ruling that McCarty's post-arrest statements were obtained in violation of *Miranda*. The court was less clear regarding the admissibility of the statements McCarty made before he was formally placed under arrest.]

To assess the admissibility of the self-incriminating statements made by respondent prior to his formal arrest, we are obliged to address a second issue concerning the scope of our decision in *Miranda:* whether the roadside questioning of a motorist detained pursuant to a routine traffic stop should be considered "custodial interrogation." Respondent urges that it should, on the ground that *Miranda* by its terms applies whenever a person has been taken into custody or otherwise deprived of his freedom of action in any significant way.

It must be acknowledged at the outset that a traffic stop significantly curtails the "freedom of action" of the driver and the passengers, if any, of the detained vehicle. Under the law of most States, it is a crime either to ignore a policeman's signal to stop one's car or, once having stopped, to drive away without permission. Certainly few motorists would feel free either to disobey a directive to pull over or to leave the scene of a traffic stop without being told they might do so. Partly for these reasons, we have long acknowledged that stopping an automobile and detaining its occupants constitute a 'seizure' within the meaning of the Fourth Amendment, even though the purpose of the stop is limited and the resulting detention quite brief.

However, we decline to accord talismanic power to the phrase in the *Miranda* opinion emphasized by respondent. Fidelity to the doctrine announced in *Miranda* requires that it be enforced strictly, but only in those types of situations in which the concerns that powered the decision are implicated. Thus, we must decide whether a traffic stop exerts upon a detained person pressures that sufficiently impair his free exercise of his privilege against self-incrimination to require that he be warned of his constitutional rights.

Two features of an ordinary traffic stop mitigate the danger that a person questioned will be induced to speak where he would not otherwise do so freely. First, detention of a motorist pursuant to a traffic stop is presumptively temporary and brief. The vast majority of roadside detentions last only a few minutes. A motorist's expectations, when he sees a policeman's light flashing behind him, are that he will be obliged to spend a short period of time answering questions and waiting while the officer checks his license and registration, that he may then be given a citation, but that in the end he most likely will be allowed to continue on his way. In this respect, questioning incident to an ordinary traffic stop is quite different from stationhouse interrogation, which frequently is prolonged, and in which the detainee often is aware that questioning will continue until he provides his interrogators the answers they seek.

Second, circumstances associated with the typical traffic stop are not such that the motorist feels completely at the mercy of the police. To be sure, the aura of authority surrounding an armed, uniformed officer and the knowledge that the officer has some discretion in deciding whether to issue a citation, in combination, exert some pressure on the detainee to respond to questions. But other aspects of the situation substantially offset these forces. Perhaps most importantly, the typical traffic stop is public, at least to some degree. Passersby, on foot or in other cars, witness the interaction of officer and motorist. This exposure to public view both reduces the ability of an unscrupulous policeman to use illegitimate means to elicit self-incriminating statements and diminishes the motorist's fear that, if he does not cooperate, he will be subjected to abuse. The fact that the detained motorist typically is confronted by only one or at most two policemen further mutes his sense of vulnerability. In short, the atmosphere surrounding an ordinary traffic stop is substantially less "police dominated" than that surrounding the kinds of interrogation at issue in *Miranda* itself, and in the subsequent cases in which we have applied *Miranda.*

In both of these respects, the usual traffic stop is more analogous to a so-called "*Terry* stop" than to a formal arrest. Under the Fourth Amendment, we have held, a policeman who lacks probable cause but whose observations lead him reasonably to suspect that a particular person has committed, is committing, or is about to commit a crime, may detain that person briefly in order to investigate the circumstances that provoke suspicion. Typically, this means that the officer may ask the detainee a moderate number of questions to determine his identity and to try to obtain information confirming or dispelling the officer's suspicions. But the detainee is not obliged to respond. And, unless the detainee's answers provide the officer with probable cause to arrest him, he must then be released. The comparatively nonthreatening character of detentions of this sort explains the absence of any suggestion in our opinions that *Terry* stops are subject to the dictates *of Miranda.* The similarly non- coercive aspect of ordinary traffic stops prompts us to hold that persons temporarily detained pursuant to such stops are not "in custody" for the purposes of *Miranda.*

Turning to the case before us, we find nothing in the record that indicates that respondent should have been given *Miranda* warnings at any point prior to the time Trooper Williams placed him under arrest. For the reasons indicated above, we reject the contention that the initial stop of respondent's car, by itself, rendered him "in custody." And respondent has failed to demonstrate that, at any time between the initial stop and the arrest, he was subjected to restraints comparable to those associated with a formal arrest. Only a short period of time elapsed between the stop and the arrest. At no point during that interval was respondent informed that his detention would not be temporary. Although Trooper Williams apparently decided as soon as respondent stepped out of his car that respondent would be taken into custody and charged with a traffic offense, Williams never communicated his intention to respondent. A policeman's unarticulated plan has no bearing on the question whether a suspect was "in custody" at a particular time; the only relevant inquiry is how a reasonable man in the suspect's position would have understood his situation. Nor do other aspects of the interaction of Williams and respondent support the contention that respondent was exposed to "custodial interrogation" at the scene of the stop. From aught that appears in the stipulation of facts, a single police officer asked respondent a modest number of questions and requested him to perform a simple balancing test at a location visible to passing motorists. Treatment of this sort cannot fairly be characterized as the functional equivalent of formal arrest.

We conclude, in short, that respondent was not taken into custody for the purposes *of Miranda* until Williams arrested him. Consequently, the statements respondent made prior to that point were admissible against him.

FURTHER CASE LAW, REFLECTIONS, AND QUESTIONS

1. How persuasive do you find Justice Marshall's argument that traffic stops such as occurred in *McCarty* are not sufficiently "police dominated" to merit *Miranda's* protections? In particular, what relevance is the fact that the typical traffic stop is public? Is the interaction between officer and citizen during a traffic stop truly "public" in nature when motorists presumably view it while driving by at a speed of 55 mph? What about the fact that "only one or at most two" police officers are involved in typical traffic stops? Why should the number of officers matter?

2. If the Court is not adopting a *per se* rule that a traffic stop can never represent "custody" for purposes of *Miranda,* under what circumstances would such a stop require the warnings and a waiver before a suspect can be questioned?

3. Trooper Williams concluded that he would charge McCarty and thus not allow him to leave the scene of the stop well before McCarty was formally arrested and before the pre-arrest statements were obtained in response to questioning. Once the officer had decided that McCarty would not be allowed to leave, why wasn't McCarty "in custody"?

It is important to remember that *Miranda* is required prior to a custodial interrogation because questioning in a custodial environment is "inherently coercive." Limited circumstances exist under which an interrogation of a person held in custody is not actually coercive. One such situation is discussed in the following case.

Illinois v. Perkins

496 U.S. 292 (1990)

JUSTICE KENNEDY delivered the opinion of the Court.

In November 1984, Richard Stephenson was murdered in a suburb of East St. Louis, Illinois. The murder remained unsolved until March 1986, when one Donald Charlton told police that he had learned about a homicide from a fellow inmate at the Graham Correctional Facility, where Charlton had been serving a sentence for burglary. The fellow inmate was Lloyd Perkins, who is the respondent here.

By the time the police heard Charlton's account, respondent had been released from Graham, but police traced him to a jail in Montgomery County, Illinois, where he was being held pending trial on a charge of aggravated battery, unrelated to the Stephenson murder. The police wanted to investigate further respondent's connection to the Stephenson murder, but feared that the use of an eavesdropping device would prove impracticable and unsafe. They decided instead to place an undercover agent in the cellblock with respondent and Charlton. The plan was for Charlton and undercover agent John Parisi to pose as escapees from a work release program who had been arrested in the course of a burglary. Parisi and Charlton were instructed to engage respondent in casual conversation and report anything he said about the Stephenson murder.

Parisi, using the alias "Vito Bianco," and Charlton, both clothed in jail garb, were placed in the cellblock with respondent at the Montgomery County Jail. Respondent greeted Charlton who, after a brief conversation with respondent, introduced Parisi by his alias. Parisi told respondent that he wasn't going to do any more time, and suggested that the three of them escape. Respondent replied that the Montgomery County jail was "rinky-dink" and that they could "break out." The trio met in respondent's cell later that evening, after the other inmates were asleep, to refine their plan. Respondent said that his girlfriend could smuggle in a pistol. Charlton said "Hey, I'm not a murderer. I'm a burglar. That's your guys' profession." After telling Charlton that he would be responsible for any murder that occurred, Parisi asked respondent if he had ever "done" anybody. Respondent said that he had, and proceeded to describe at length the events of the Stephenson murder. Parisi and respondent then engaged in some casual conversation before respondent went to sleep. Parisi did not give respondent *Miranda* warnings before the conversations.

Respondent was charged with the Stephenson murder. Before trial, he moved to suppress the statements made to Parisi in the jail. The trial court granted the motion to suppress, and the State appealed. The Appellate Court of Illinois affirmed, holding *that Miranda v. Arizona,* 384 US 436 (1966), prohibits all undercover contacts with incarcerated suspects which are reasonably likely to elicit an incriminating response.

We granted certiorari, to decide whether an undercover law enforcement officer must give *Miranda* warnings to an incarcerated suspect before asking him questions that may elicit an incriminating response. We now reverse.

The warning mandated by *Miranda* was meant to preserve the privilege during incommunicado interrogation of individuals in a police-dominated atmosphere. That atmosphere is said to generate "inherently compelling pressures which work to undermine the individual's will to resist and to compel him to speak where he would not otherwise do so freely." "Fidelity to the doctrine announced in *Miranda* requires that it be enforced strictly, but only in those types of situations in which the concerns that powered the decision are implicated." *Berkemer v. McCarty,* 468 US 420, 437 (1984).

Conversations between suspects and undercover agents do not implicate the concerns underlying *Miranda.* The essential ingredients of a "police dominated atmosphere" and compulsion are not present when an incarcerated person speaks freely to someone that he believes to be a fellow inmate. Coercion is determined from the perspective of the suspect. When a suspect considers himself in the company of cellmates and not officers, the coercive atmosphere is lacking. There is no empirical basis for the assumption that a suspect speaking to those whom he assumes are not officers will feel compelled to speak by the fear of reprisal for remaining silent or in the hope of more lenient treatment should he confess.

It is the premise of *Miranda* that the danger of coercion results from the interaction of custody and official interrogation. We reject the argument that *Miranda* warnings are required whenever a suspect is in custody in a technical sense and converses with someone who happens to be a government agent. Questioning by captors, who appear to control the suspect's fate, may create mutually reinforcing pressures that the Court has assumed will weaken the suspect's will, but where a suspect does not know that he is conversing with a government agent, these pressures do not exist. *Miranda* forbids coercion, not mere strategic deception by taking advantage of a suspect's misplaced trust in one he supposes to be a fellow prisoner. As we recognized in *Miranda,* confessions remain a proper element in law enforcement. Any statement given freely and voluntarily without any compelling influences is, of course, admissible in evidence. Ploys to mislead a suspect or lull him into a false sense of security that do not rise to the level of compulsion or coercion to speak are not within *Miranda's* concerns.

The tactic employed here to elicit a voluntary confession from a suspect does not violate the Self- Incrimination Clause. We held in *Hoffa* v. *United States,* 385 US 293 (1966), that placing an undercover agent near a suspect in order to gather incriminating information was permissible under the Fifth Amendment. The only difference between this case and *Hoffa* is that the suspect here was incarcerated, but detention, whether or not for the crime in question, does not warrant a presumption that the use of an undercover agent to speak with an incarcerated suspect makes any confession thus obtained involuntary. Where the suspect does not know that he is speaking to a government agent there is no reason to assume the possibility that the suspect might feel coerced. (The bare fact of custody may not in every instance require a warning even when the suspect is aware that he is speaking to an official, but we do not have occasion to explore that issue here.)

We hold that an undercover law enforcement officer posing as a fellow inmate need not give *Miranda* warnings to an incarcerated suspect before asking questions that may elicit an incriminating response. The statements at issue in this case were voluntary, and there is no federal obstacle to their admissibility at trial. We now reverse and remand for proceedings not inconsistent with our opinion.

FURTHER CASE LAW, REFLECTIONS, AND QUESTIONS

1. How clear-cut is the line between "coercion" and "strategic deception"? Is it fair to allow the police to use deception to deny a suspect knowledge of a fact that almost certainly would cause the suspect to refrain from making incriminating statements?
2. It is important to remember that when considering whether a person is in custody for custodial interrogation purposes, courts will use an objective standard, taking into account the totality of circumstances, in considering whether a reasonable person would believe they are free to leave.

Interrogation

Recall *Miranda's* caveat concerning "volunteered" statements — those offered spontaneously rather than in response to questioning.

> In dealing with statements obtained through interrogation, we do not purport to find all confessions inadmissible. Confessions remain a proper element in law enforcement. Any statement given freely and voluntarily without any compelling influences is, of course, admissible in evidence. The fundamental import of the privilege, while an individual is in custody,

> is not whether he is allowed to talk to the police without the benefit of warnings and counsel, but whether he can be interrogated. There is no requirement that police stop a person who enters a police station and states that he wishes to confess to a crime or a person who calls the police to offer a confession or any other statement he desires to make. Volunteered statements of any kind are not barred by the Fifth Amendment and their admissibility is not affected by our holding today 383 U.S., at 478.

It is the *interplay* or combination of "custody" and "interrogation" that creates the police-dominated, psychologically coercive environment that was of concern to the *Miranda* court. Cases such as *Oregon* v. *Mathiason, Berkemer v. McCarty,* and *Illinois v. Perkins* clearly establish that the police may interrogate a criminal suspect without first giving *Miranda* warnings as long as the suspect is not "in custody." The converse is also true. The incriminating statements made by a person in police custody are admissible without the prior administration of *Miranda* warnings as long as those statements are not the product of "interrogation."

We still must distinguish between a "volunteered" statement and a statement made in response to "interrogation." *Rhode Island v. Innis,* presented below, defines "**interrogation.**"

Rhode Island v. Innis

446 U.S. 291(1980)

MR. JUSTICE STEWART delivered the opinion of the Court.

[A Rhode Island taxicab driver disappeared after being dispatched to pick up a customer. Four days later, his body was discovered in a shallow grave. He had been killed by a shotgun blast to the back of his head. The following day, another taxicab driver reported to the police that he had been robbed by a man brandishing a sawed-off shotgun. He identified a photograph of the respondent, Thomas Innis, as the robber. Just hours after Innis's photo had been identified, a police officer on patrol spotted Innis standing on the side of a street. The officer placed Innis under arrest and advised him of his *Miranda* rights.]

Captain Leyden also advised the respondent of *his Miranda* rights. The respondent stated that he understood those rights and wanted to speak with a lawyer. Captain Leyden then directed that the respondent be placed in a "caged wagon," a four-door police car with a wire screen mesh between the front and rear seats, and be driven to the central police station. Three officers, Patrolmen Gleckman, Williams, and McKenna, were assigned to accompany the respondent to the central station. They placed the respondent in the vehicle and shut the doors. Captain Leyden then instructed the officers not to question the respondent or intimidate or coerce him in any way. The three officers then entered the vehicle, and it departed.

While en route to the central station. Patrolman Gleckman initiated a conversation with Patrolman McKenna concerning the missing shotgun. As Patrolman Gleckman later testified:

> "A. At this point, I was talking back and forth with Patrolman McKenna stating that I frequent this area while on patrol and [that because a school for handicapped children is located nearby,] there's a lot of handicapped children running around in this area, and God forbid one of them might find a weapon with shells and they might hurt themselves."

> Patrolman McKenna apparently shared his fellow officer's concern:

> "A. I more or less concurred with him [Gleckman] that it was a safety factor and that we should, you know, continue to search for the weapon and try to find it."

While Patrolman Williams said nothing, he overheard the conversation between the two officers:

> "A. He [Gleckman] said it would be too bad if the little — I believe he said a girl — would pick up the gun, maybe kill herself."

The respondent then interrupted the conversation, stating that the officers should turn the car around so he could show them where the gun was located. At this point. Patrolman McKenna radioed back to Captain Leyden that they were returning to the scene of the arrest, and that the respondent would inform them of the location of the gun. At the time the respondent indicated that the officers should turn back, they had traveled no more than a mile, a trip encompassing only a few minutes.

The police vehicle then returned to the scene of the arrest where a search for the shotgun was in progress. There, Captain Leyden again advised the respondent of his *Miranda* rights. The respondent replied that he understood those rights but that he "wanted to get the gun out of the way because of the kids in the area in the school." The respondent then led the police to a nearby field, where he pointed out the shotgun under some rocks by the side of the road.

[Innis subsequently was convicted of the robbery, kidnapping, and murder of the first taxi driver. The trial court admitted the shotgun and testimony about Innis's statements into evidence. By vote of 3-2, the Rhode Island Supreme Court reversed, concluding that Innis had invoked his *Miranda* rights and that the police had violated those rights by "interrogating" him in the absence of counsel. The U.S. Supreme Court granted certiorari "to address for the first time the meaning of 'interrogation' under *Miranda v. Arizona*."]

In the present case, the parties are in agreement that the respondent was fully informed of his *Miranda* rights and that he invoked his *Miranda* right to counsel when he told Captain Leyden that he wished to consult with a lawyer. It is also uncontested that the respondent was "in custody" while being transported to the police station. The issue, therefore, is whether the respondent was "interrogated" by the police officers in violation of the respondent's undisputed right under *Miranda* to remain silent until he had consulted with a lawyer. In resolving this issue, we first define the term "interrogation" under *Miranda* before turning to a consideration of the facts of this case.

The starting point for defining "interrogation" in this context is, of course, the Court's *Miranda* opinion. There the Court observed that by custodial interrogation, we mean *questioning* initiated by law enforcement officers after a person has been taken into custody or otherwise deprived of his freedom of action in any significant way. This passage and other references throughout the opinion to "questioning" might suggest that the *Miranda* rules were to apply only to those police interrogation practices that involve express questioning of a defendant while in custody.

We do not, however, construe the *Miranda* opinion so narrowly. The concern of the Court in *Miranda* was that the "interrogation environment" created by the interplay of interrogation and custody would "subjugate the individual to the will of his examiner" and thereby undermine the privilege against compulsory self-incrimination.

The police practices that evoked this concern included several that did not involve express questioning. For example, one of the practices discussed in *Miranda* was the use of line-ups in which a coached witness would pick the defendant as the perpetrator. This was designed to establish that the defendant was in fact guilty as a predicate for further interrogation. A variation on this theme discussed in *Miranda* was the so-called "reverse line-up" in which a defendant would be identified by coached witnesses as the perpetrator of a fictitious crime, with the object of inducing him to confess to the actual crime of which he was suspected in order to escape the false prosecution. The Court in *Miranda* also included in its survey of interrogation practices the use of psychological ploys, such as to posit the guilt of the subject to minimize the moral seriousness of the offense, and to cast blame on the victim or on society. It is clear that these techniques of persuasion, no less than express questioning, were thought, in a custodial setting, to amount to interrogation.

This is not to say, however, that all statements obtained by the police after a person has been taken into custody are to be considered the product of interrogation. As the Court in *Miranda* noted:

> Confessions remain a proper element in law enforcement. Any statement given freely and voluntarily without any compelling influences is, of course, admissible in evidence.
>
> *The fundamental import of the privilege while an individual is in custody is not whether he is allowed to talk to the police without the benefit of warnings and counsel, but whether he can be interrogated. Volunteered statements of any kind are not barred by the Fifth Amendment and their admissibility is not affected by our holding today. Id.*, at 478 (emphasis added).

It is clear therefore that the special procedural safeguards outlined in *Miranda* are required not where a suspect is simply taken into custody, but rather where a suspect in custody is subjected to interrogation. "Interrogation," as conceptualized in the *Miranda* opinion, must reflect a measure of compulsion above and beyond that inherent in custody itself.

We conclude that the *Miranda* safeguards come into play whenever a person in custody is subjected to either express questioning or its functional equivalent. That is to say, the term "interrogation" under *Miranda* refers not only to express questioning, but also to any words or actions on the part of the police (other than those normally attendant to arrest and custody) that the police should know are reasonably likely to elicit an incriminating response from the suspect. The latter portion of this definition focuses primarily upon the perceptions of the suspect, rather than the intent of the police. This focus reflects the fact that the *Miranda* safeguards were designed to vest a suspect in custody with an added measure of protection against coercive police practices, without regard to objective proof of the underlying intent of the police. A practice that the police should know is reasonably likely to evoke an incriminating response from a suspect thus amounts to interrogation.[7] But, since the police surely cannot be held accountable for the unforeseeable results of their words or actions, the definition of interrogation can extend only to words or actions on the part of police officers that they should have known were reasonably likely to elicit an incriminating response.[8]

B

Turning to the facts of the present case, we conclude that the respondent was not "interrogated" within the meaning of *Miranda*. It is undisputed that the first prong of the definition of "interrogation" was not satisfied, for the conversation between Patrolmen Gleckman and McKenna included no express questioning of the respondent. Rather, that conversation was, at least in form, nothing more than a dialogue between the two officers to which no response from the respondent was invited.

Moreover, it cannot be fairly concluded that the respondent was subjected to the **functional equivalent of questioning**. It cannot be said, in short, that Patrolmen Gleckman and McKenna should have known that their conversation was reasonably likely to elicit an incriminating response from the respondent. There is nothing in the record to suggest that the officers were aware that the respondent was peculiarly sus-

---

7. This is not to say that the intent of the police is irrelevant, for it may well have a bearing on whether the police should have known that their words or actions were reasonably likely to evoke an incriminating response. In particular, where a police practice is designed to elicit an incriminating response from the accused, it is unlikely that the practice will not also be one which the police should have known was reasonably likely to have that effect.

8. Any knowledge the police may have had concerning the unusual susceptibility of a defendant to a particular form of persuasion might be an important factor in determining whether the police should have known that their words or actions were reasonably likely to elicit an incriminating response from the suspect.

ceptible to an appeal to his conscience concerning the safety of handicapped children. Nor is there anything in the record to suggest that the police knew that the respondent was unusually disoriented or upset at the time of his arrest.

The case thus boils down to whether, in the context of a brief conversation, the officers should have known that the respondent would suddenly be moved to make a self-incriminating response. Given the fact that the entire conversation appears to have consisted of no more than a few offhand remarks, we cannot say that the officers should have known that it was reasonably likely that Innis would so respond. This is not a case where the police carried on a lengthy harangue in the presence of the suspect. Nor does the record support the respondent's contention that, under the circumstances, the officers' comments were particularly evocative. It is our view, therefore, that the respondent was not subjected by the police to words or actions that the police should have known were reasonably likely to elicit an incriminating response from him.

The Rhode Island Supreme Court erred, in short, in equating subtle compulsion with interrogation. That the officers' comments struck a responsive chord is readily apparent. Thus, it may be said, as the Rhode Island Supreme Court did say, that the respondent was subjected to subtle compulsion. But that is not the end of the inquiry. It must also be established that a suspect's incriminating response was the product of words or actions on the part of the police that they should have known were reasonably likely to elicit an incriminating response. This was not established in the present case.

For the reasons stated, the judgment of the Supreme Court of Rhode Island is vacated, and the case is remanded to that court for further proceedings not inconsistent with this opinion.

MR. JUSTICE MARSHALL, with whom MR. JUSTICE BRENNAN joins, dissenting.

I am substantially in agreement with the Court's definition of "interrogation" within the meaning *of Miranda v. Arizona.* The Court requires an objective inquiry into the likely effect of police conduct on a typical individual, taking into account any special susceptibility of the suspect to certain kinds of pressure of which the police know or have reason to know.

I am utterly at a loss, however, to understand how this objective standard as applied to the facts before us can rationally lead to the conclusion that there was no interrogation.

One can scarcely imagine a stronger appeal to the conscience of a suspect — any suspect — than the assertion that if the weapon is not found an innocent person will be hurt or killed. And not just any innocent person, but an innocent child — a little girl-a helpless, handicapped little girl on her way to school. The notion that such an appeal could not be expected to have any effect unless the suspect were known to have some special interest in handicapped children verges on the ludicrous. As a matter of fact, the appeal to a suspect to confess for the sake of others, to display some evidence of decency and honor, is a classic interrogation technique.

Gleckman's remarks would obviously have constituted interrogation if they had been explicitly directed to respondent, and the result should not be different because they were nominally addressed to McKenna. This is not a case where police officers speaking among themselves are accidentally overheard by a suspect. These officers were talking back and forth in close quarters with the handcuffed suspect, traveling past the very place where they believed the weapon was located. They knew respondent would hear and attend to their conversation, and they are chargeable with knowledge of and responsibility for the pressures to speak which they created.

FURTHER CASE LAW, REFLECTIONS, AND QUESTIONS

1. Is *Innis's* definition of "interrogation" an objective test, a subjective test (relying on the intent of the involved officers and/or the impact of the police's words or actions on a particular suspect), or some combination thereof? In this regard, consider footnotes 7 and 8 in Justice Stewart's majority opinion.
2. Extracting the test for "interrogation" from *Innis* is much less difficult than applying that test to the facts of the case. Who has the more convincing argument concerning whether Innis was "interrogated": Justice Stewart, in his majority opinion, or Justice Marshall, in his dissent?
3. What if no school for handicapped children actually existed in the area, and Officers Gleckman and McKenna had just made up this story? Would (should) that change the majority's decision about whether their exchange was the functional equivalent of express questioning?

Box 8.3 You Be the Judge

Will was arrested for killing his son. He was taken to the police station where he was advised of his *Miranda* rights. Will asked to speak with a lawyer before making any statements. Will's wife, who had been talking with a detective in another room, insisted she be allowed to speak with her husband. The police were reluctant to permit the meeting but did so after telling Will and Mrs. Mauro that a police officer would have to be present in the room to observe and hear what was going on. An officer stationed himself in the room with a clearly visible tape recorder while the two conversed. A recording of the conversation was later played at Will's murder trial.

Were Will's rights under the Fifth Amendment violated? Why or why not?

What are the key facts that led you to your decision?

See *Arizona v. Mauro*, 481 U.S. 520 (1987).

The *Miranda* Warnings

The ***Miranda* warnings** involve important constitutional rights. As such, they must be given in a clear and unambiguous manner. While you may be familiar with the protections they afford from your education or television viewing, not everyone knows they have a privilege against self-incrimination, a right to remain silent, and the right to have an attorney appointed to them. Given their importance, exactly how the warnings are communicated to suspects is a concern for the Supreme Court. The following case discusses the precision with which the warnings must be conveyed.

Duckworth v. Eagan

492 U.S. 195 (1989)

CHIEF JUSTICE REHNQUIST delivered the opinion of the Court.

[The respondent Eagan was convicted of attempted murder in an Indiana state court. Among the evidence supporting his conviction was his confession to stabbing the victim, along with the knife and several items of clothing associated with the stabbing. He was sentenced to 35 years in prison. The state courts and the U.S. District Court upheld Eagan's conviction, but the U.S. Court of Appeals for the Seventh Circuit reversed, concluding that the warnings given Eagan prior to his confession were inadequate under *Miranda* v. *Arizona.* The warnings appeared on a waiver form used by the Hammond, Indiana, police. The form provided:]

> Before we ask you any questions, you must understand your rights. You have the right to remain silent. Anything you say can be used against you in court. *You have the right to talk to a lawyer for advice before we ask you any questions, and to have him with you during questioning.* You have this right to the advice and presence of a lawyer even if you cannot afford to hire one. *have no way of giving you a lawyer, but one will be appointed for you, if you wish, if and when you go to court.* If you wish to answer questions now without a lawyer present, you have the right to stop answering questions at any time. You also have the right to stop answering at any time until you've talked to a lawyer. (Emphasis added by court.)

In *Miranda v. Arizona* the Court established certain procedural safeguards that require police to advise criminal suspects of their rights under the Fifth and Fourteenth Amendments before commencing custodial interrogation. In now-familiar words, the Court said that the suspect must be told that "he has the right to remain silent, that anything he says can be used against him in a court of law, that he has the right to the presence of an attorney, and that if he cannot afford an attorney one will be appointed for him prior to any questioning if he so desires." *Id.*, at 479.

We have never insisted that *Miranda* warnings be given in the exact form described in that decision. In *Miranda* itself, the Court said that "[t]he warnings required and the waiver necessary in accordance with our opinion today are, *in the absence of a fully ef-*

fective equivalent, prerequisites to the admissibility of any statement made by a defendant. In *California v. Prysock,* 453 U.S. 355 (1981), we stated that "the 'rigidity" of *Miranda* [does not] exten[d]to the precise formulation of the warnings given a criminal defendant," and that no talismanic incantation [is] required to satisfy its strictures.

The prophylactic *Miranda* warnings are not themselves rights protected by the Constitution but are instead measures to insure that the right against compulsory self-incrimination is protected. Reviewing courts therefore need not examine *Miranda* warnings as if construing a will or defining the terms of an easement. The inquiry is simply whether the warnings reasonably convey to a suspect his rights as required by Miranda

We think the initial warnings given to respondent touched all of the bases required by *Miranda.* The police told respondent that he had the right to remain silent, that anything he said could be used against him in court, that he had the right to speak to an attorney before and during questioning, that he had "this right to the advice and presence of a lawyer even if he could not afford to hire one," and that he had the "right to stop answering at any time until he talked to a lawyer." As noted, the police also added that they could not provide respondent with a lawyer, but that one would be appointed "if and when you go to court." The Court of Appeals thought this "if and when you go to court" language suggested that "only those accused who can afford an attorney have the right to have one present before answering any questions," and "implied that if the accused does not 'go to court,' *i.e.,* the government does not file charges, the accused is not entitled to counsel at all."

In our view, the Court of Appeals misapprehended the effect of the inclusion of "if and when you go to court" language in *Miranda* warnings. First, this instruction accurately described the procedure for the appointment of counsel in Indiana. Under Indiana law, counsel is appointed at the defendant's initial appearance in court, and formal charges must be filed at or before that hearing. We think it must be relatively commonplace for a suspect, after receiving *Miranda* warnings, to ask when he will obtain counsel. The "if and when you go to court" advice simply anticipates that question. Second, *Miranda* does not require that attorneys be producible on call, but only that the suspect be informed, as here, that he has the right to an attorney before and during questioning, and that an attorney would be appointed for him if he could not afford one. The Court in *Miranda* emphasized that it was not suggesting that each police station must have a 'station house lawyer' present at all times to advise prisoners. If the police cannot provide appointed counsel, *Miranda* requires only that the police not question a suspect unless he waives his right to counsel. Here, respondent did just that.

We hold that the initial warnings given to respondent, in their totality, satisfied *Miranda,* and therefore that his statement as well as the knife and the clothing were all properly admitted into evidence.

FURTHER CASE LAW, REFLECTIONS, AND QUESTIONS

1. Police officers often carry a small card containing the Miranda warnings. By reading directly from the card each time they give the warnings, the officers can ensure that they state the warnings correctly and enhance their credibility in court if a defendant complains that the full, accurate warnings were not given.

2. Is the ruling in *Duckworth* v. *Eagan* more likely to promote or detract from *Miranda's* goal of providing clear, consistent, and easily followed rules to regulate police interrogation procedures?

Box 8.4 You Be the Judge

Powell was arrested by police in Tampa, Florida for illegally possessing a handgun. Before questioning, the police advised him of his rights as follows:

> You have the right to remain silent. If you give up the right to remain silent, anything you say can be used against you in court. You have the right to talk to a lawyer before answering any of our questions. If you cannot afford to hire a lawyer, one will be appointed for you without cost and before any questioning. You have the right to use any of these rights at any time you want during this interview.

Powell agreed to speak with the police and confessed to possessing a handgun in violation of state law. His confession was admitted into evidence at his trial, and he was convicted. Powell appealed his conviction on the grounds that the advice given to him was misleading and inadequate.

Do the warnings given to Powell meet the requirements of Duckworth and Miranda? If not, what items render them unconstitutional?

See Florida v. Powell, 559 U.S. 50 (2010).

Invocation of Miranda *Protections*

The Supreme Court has been willing to give police significant leeway in how the *Miranda* warnings are administered. The Court has been more restrictive on the language needed for a person invoking those rights. The Court has applied a strict invocation requirement in two distinct areas: who a suspect wishes to speak with before or have present during an interrogation, and the clarity and definitiveness of a statement invoking the *Miranda* rights must be.

In *Fare v. Michael C.*, 442 U.S. 707 (1979), sixteen-year-old Michael C. was arrested by police on suspicion of murder. Before being questioned, he was fully advised of his rights under *Miranda* v. *Arizona*. Prior to being questioned, Michael, who was on probation to the Juvenile Court, asked to talk to his probation officer. After the police denied this request, he stated he would answer their questions without consulting an attorney. He proceeded to make statements implicating himself in the murder.

After being charged in Juvenile Court with the murder, he moved to suppress the incriminating statements on the ground that they had been obtained in violation of *Miranda, arguing* that his request to see his probation officer constituted an invocation of his Fifth Amendment right to remain silent, just as if he had requested an attorney. The trial court denied the motion, holding that the facts showed that respondent had waived his right to remain silent, notwithstanding his request to see his probation officer. The California Supreme Court reversed, holding that his request for his probation officer was a *per se* invocation of his Fifth Amendment rights in the same way the request for an attorney was found to be in *Miranda.* This was based on the court's view that a probation officer occupies a position as a trusted guardian figure in a juvenile's life that would make it normal for the juvenile to turn to the officer when apprehended by the police and was also based on the state-law requirement that the officer represent the juvenile's interests.

The United States Supreme Court granted review and reversed. What follows is an excerpt from the Court's decision.

Fare v. Michael C

442 U.S. 707 (1979)

MR. JUSTICE BLACKMUN delivered the opinion of the Court.

The rule in *Miranda* was based on this Court's perception that the lawyer occupies a critical position in our legal system because of his unique ability to protect the Fifth Amendment rights of a client undergoing custodial interrogation. Because of this special ability of the lawyer to help the client preserve his Fifth Amendment rights once the client becomes enmeshed in the adversary process, the Court found that the right to have counsel present at the interrogation is indispensable to the protection of the Fifth Amendment privilege under the system established by the Court. Moreover, the lawyer's presence helps guard against overreaching by the police and ensures that any statements actually obtained are accurately transcribed for presentation into evidence.

The per se aspect of *Miranda* was thus based on the unique role the lawyer plays in the adversary system of criminal justice in this country. Whether it is a minor or an adult who stands accused, the lawyer is the one person to whom society as a whole looks as the protector of the legal rights of that person in his dealings with the police and the courts. For this reason, the Court fashioned in *Miranda* the rigid rule that an accused's request for an attorney is per se an invocation of his Fifth Amendment rights, requiring that all interrogation cease.

A probation officer is not in the same posture with regard to either the accused or the system of justice as a whole. Often he is not trained in the law, and so is not in a position to advise the accused as to his legal rights. Neither is he a trained advocate, skilled in the representation of the interests of his client before both police and courts. He does not assume the power to act on behalf of his client by virtue of his status as adviser, nor are the communications of the accused to the probation officer shielded by the lawyer-client privilege.

Moreover, the probation officer is the employee of the State which seeks to prosecute the alleged offender. He is a peace officer, and as such is allied, to a greater or lesser extent, with his fellow peace officers. He owes an obligation to the State, notwithstanding the obligation he may also owe the juvenile under his supervision. In most cases, the probation officer is duty bound to report wrongdoing by the juvenile when it comes to his attention, even if by communication from the juvenile himself. Indeed, when this case arose, the probation officer had the responsibility for filing the petition alleging wrongdoing by the juvenile and seeking to have him taken into the custody of the Juvenile Court. It was respondent's probation officer who filed the petition against him, and it is the acting chief of probation for the State of California, a probation officer, who is petitioner in this Court today.

We thus believe it clear that the probation officer is not in a position to offer the type of legal assistance necessary to protect the Fifth Amendment rights of an accused undergoing custodial interrogation that a lawyer can offer. The Court in *Miranda* recognized that "the attorney plays a vital role in the administration of criminal justice under our Constitution." 384 US, at 481. It is this pivotal role of legal counsel that justifies the per se rule established *in Miranda,* and that distinguishes the request for counsel from the request for a probation officer, a clergyman, or a close friend. A probation officer simply is not necessary, in the way an attorney is, for the protection of the legal rights of the accused, juvenile or adult. He is significantly handicapped by the position he occupies in the juvenile system from serving as an effective protector of the rights of a juvenile suspected of a crime.

We hold, in short, that the California Supreme Court erred in finding that a juvenile's request for his probation officer was a *per se* invocation of that juvenile's Fifth Amendment rights under *Miranda.* We conclude, rather, that whether the statements obtained during subsequent interrogation of a juvenile who has asked to see his probation officer, but who has not asked to consult an attorney or expressly asserted his right to remain silent, are admissible on the basis of waiver remains a question to be resolved on the totality of the circumstances surrounding the interrogation. On the basis of the record in this case, we hold that the Juvenile Court's findings that respondent voluntarily and knowingly waived his rights and consented to continued interrogation, and that the statements obtained from him were voluntary, were proper, and that the admission of those statements in the proceeding against respondent in Juvenile Court was correct.

The judgment of the Supreme Court of California is reversed, and the case is remanded for further proceedings not inconsistent with this opinion.

FURTHER CASE LAW, REFLECTIONS, AND QUESTIONS

1. Would you expect a different result in *Fare v. Michael C.* if Michael C. had asked to see his father or mother? In what respects is a parent unlike a probation officer? Unlike an attorney?
2. Many states, through legislation, provide that a juvenile cannot waive his or her self-incrimination rights without first consulting with a parent or guardian. Is this appropriate, or does it unreasonably hinder law enforcement?

Under the holding in *Fare,* for a suspect to effectively invoke their right to an attorney during a custodial interrogation, the suspect must specifically ask for an attorney. The Supreme Court rarely presents such a bright-line rule. No such clarity has been provided by the Court in its rulings regarding what verbiage must be used by a suspect in invoking their *Miranda* rights.

As we have discussed, the *Miranda* protections do not go into effect until a suspect has invoked either their right to remain silent or their right to an attorney. While not mandating the use of specific language, the Court has held that for an invocation to be accepted, it must be clear, unambiguous, and unequivocal. What exactly constitutes a valid invocation of a person's *Miranda* rights has proven to be far from clear, as evidenced by decisions made by state and federal courts

In *Davis v. United States,* 512 U.S. 452 (1994), Davis was brought in for questioning about a murder. After being read the Miranda warnings, he waived his rights in writing and orally. After being questioned for over an hour, during which he made an incriminating statement, Davis said, "Maybe I should talk to a lawyer." When the interrogator asked for clarification on whether Davis was asking for an attorney, Davis said that he was not, and the interview continued. An hour later, Davis asked to speak to an attorney.

The Supreme Court found that Davis' statement "Maybe I should talk to a lawyer" was equivocal, and insufficient to serve as an invocation of his Miranda rights.

> The suspect must unambiguously request counsel. He must articulate his desire to have counsel present sufficiently clearly that a reasonable police officer in the circumstances would understand the statement to be a request for an attorney. If the statement fails to meet the requisite level of clarity, *we will* not require that the officers stop questioning the suspect. *Davis v. United States,* 512 U.S. at 459.

Based on this standard, police need not stop questioning a suspect until a clear and unambiguous invocation has been made. As noted above, exactly what constitutes a clear and unequivocal invocation has proven to be difficult to ascertain. There has been a lack of consistency among both state and federal courts at all levels in applying facts to the standard established by the Supreme Court. In fact, as illustrated in Box 8.5 leaving decisions in specific cases without additional guidance has led to seemingly absurd outcomes. Can you explain the basis for the differing results from the statements presented?

Box 8.5 Effective and Ineffective Invocation of Rights

Invocation Found to be Effective

- "I have to get me a good lawyer, man. Can I make a phone call?" *Shedelbower v. Estelle*, 885 F.2d 570, 571 (9th Cir. 1989).
- "You know, I'm scared now. I think I should call an attorney," *Smith v. Endell* 860 F.2d 1528, 1529 (9th Cir. 1988).
- "I have to get me a good lawyer, man. Can I make a phone call?" *Robinson v. Borg*, 918 F.2d 1387 (9th Cir. 1988).
- I should call my lawyer," *United States v. de la Jara*, 973 F.2d 746, 750 (9th Cir. 1992)

Invocation Found to be Ineffective

- "I think I'll probably stop talking now." *State v. Hernandez*, 911 N.W.2d 524, 536 (Neb. 2018).
- "It would be nice to have an attorney." *Ledbetter v. Edwards*, 35 F.3d 1062, 1070 (6th Cir. 1994).
- "I think I would like to talk to a lawyer," "should I be telling you, or should I talk to an attorney?" *Clark v. Murphy*, 331 F.3d 1062, 1071–72 (9th Cir. 2003).
- "I think I need a lawyer," *Diaz v. Senkowski*, 76 F.3d 61, 63–65 (2d Cir. 1996).

Box 8.6 You Be the Judge

Warren was questioned at the police station regarding two sexual assaults. Warren was read his Miranda rights, waived them, and answered the questions posed. Shortly thereafter and before making any admissions, according to a transcript of the interrogation, Warren said, "If y'all, this is how I feel, if y'all think I did it, I know that I didn't do it so why don't you just give me a lawyer dog cause this is not what's up." The police ignored this statement and continued the questioning. Warren made several admissions that the prosecution wishes to use at trial.

Did Warren invoke his right to an attorney?

Should his admissions be admissible in his prosecution?

See *State of Louisiana v. Demesme*, 2017-KK-954 (La., decided Oct. 31, 2017).

Tabler, N. (2018). The Unspeakable Comma, *The Federal Lawyer, May 2018, 18.*

Silence as an Invocation

If a person stands silent and refuses to answer any questions by remaining silent, have they effectively invoked their right to remain silent? In short, no. In *Berghuis v. Thompkins*, 560 U.S. 370 (2010), the Supreme Court expanded the requirement of a clear and unambiguous statement to invoke *Miranda*.

Thompkins was a suspect in a fatal shooting in Southfield, Michigan. After advising Thompkins of his *Miranda* rights, police officers interrogated him. Thompkins had been almost completely silent during the three-hour interrogation and the few sporadic comments he made had no bearing on the case. Near the end of the interview when asked "Did he pray to God to forgive him for shooting the victim., "Thompkins replied, "yes."

Thompkins moved to suppress his statements, claiming that he had invoked his Fifth Amendment right to remain silent, that he had not waived that right, and that his inculpatory statements were involuntary. The trial court denied his motion and Thompkins was found guilty by a jury and sentenced to life imprisonment without the possibility of parole. The Supreme Court agreed to consider whether Thompkins' silence served as an invocation of his *Miranda* right to remain silent. The Court said it did not. A five-member majority found that staying silent for most of an interrogation does not mean that a suspect invoked his right to remain silent for purposes of *Miranda*. Relying on *Davis v. United States*, the Court held that silence in and of itself is not an "unambiguous" invocation of the right. As Thompkins's conduct was ambiguous, the police were permitted to continue questioning him.

Does this seem appropriate? Is it odd that a person who remains silent has not invoked the right to remain silent? Or to put it another way, should a person have to break their silence to invoke their right to that silence?

Resumption of Questioning Following the Invocation of Right to Remain Silent

As *Davis* v. *United States* suggests, a suspect initially may decide to waive his or her *Miranda* rights, respond to questioning, and then later invoke his or her right to counsel or silence. This is because the original waiver is not irrevocable. "The mere fact that the suspect may have answered some questions or volunteered some statements on his own does not deprive him of the right to refrain from answering any further inquiries until he has consulted with an attorney and thereafter consents to be questioned." *Miranda v. Arizona,* 384 U.S., at 445.

In this section, we consider the reverse situation. What of the suspect who initially requests an attorney or invokes his or her right to silence? Do the police forever lose the opportunity to question the suspect? May the police resume questioning if they administer a fresh set of warnings and the suspect then agrees to waive his or her rights? Should it matter whether it is the police or the suspect who takes the initiative in the resumption of questioning? Should it matter how much time passes between the suspect's request and law enforcement officers' attempt to resume questioning? We first consider the case of suspects who are questioned after they invoke the right to remain silent.

The respondent in *Michigan* v. *Mosley*, 423 U.S. 96 (1975), was arrested for two robberies. He was given *Miranda* warnings and stated that he did not want to talk about the robberies. The police terminated their attempt to question him, and he was locked in a jail cell. About two hours later, a homicide detective, who had not been involved in the prior events, had Mosley brought from his cell to an office in the homicide bureau. The detective's purpose was to question Mosley about an unrelated holdup murder. The detective readministered the *Miranda* warnings, and Mosley signed a *Miranda* rights waiver form. He subsequently made statements implicating himself in the murder. Those statements helped support his conviction for first-degree murder.

The Michigan Court of Appeals reversed, holding that the homicide detective's interrogation was improper because Mosley had invoked his right to silence in response to prior attempts to question him about the robbery charges. The Supreme Court reversed (7–2) in an opinion authored by Justice Stewart.

The re-initiation of interrogation after a suspect has invoked his right to silence is not a per se violation of the Fifth Amendment. Given that *Miranda* did not clearly establish the circumstances under which questioning may be resumed, the Court held that *Miranda* only required that the suspect's right to refuse to answer questions be scrupulously honored once the refusal is communicated.

Concerning the specific facts in *Mosley*, the Court found that Mosley's Fifth Amendment rights were not violated. Once he invoked his right to remain silent during the first interrogation, questioning ceased. The second interrogation occurred after a significant time lapse, was directed at a different crime unrelated to the subject of the initial interrogation, was conducted by a different officer, and was done at a different location. Moreover, Mosley voluntarily waived his right to remain silent before the second interrogation. Under this set of facts, his initial request to remain silent had been scrupulously honored.

The fact-specific nature of Mosley has left open a number of questions. How important was it in *Mosley* that the second interrogation pertained "to a crime that had not been a subject of the earlier interrogation" attempt? That more than two hours passed between Mosley's invocation of his right to silence and the second round of questioning? That "another police officer" conducted the new questioning, "at another location"? Which of these factors seems essential to the Court's conclusion that Mosley's "right to cut off questioning" had been "scrupulously honored"? What other factors could be important? That the police officer who initially attempted to question Mosley about the robbery promptly respected Mosley's expression that he did not want to talk? That Mosley waived his rights after a new set of *Miranda* warnings was given?

It is important to keep in mind that Mosley invoked his right to silence instead of requesting the assistance of an attorney. The Court has treated the two types of requests differently. We will consider the latter later in this chapter.

The Waiver of *Miranda* Rights

The suspect may elect to waive their Miranda rights at any time. The government has a heavy burden in proving that a suspect waived their rights. Not only must the government show that a waiver was actually made, but it must also prove that it was made voluntarily, knowingly, and intelligently. We consider the law surrounding whether a waiver was voluntary, knowing, and intelligent in the next section of this chapter. In this section, we examine what must be proven before a court will find that a waiver was made.

Express and Implied Waiver

A waiver may be either express or implied. The following case addresses this distinction and what is required for a waiver to be considered executed.

Berghuis v. Thompkins

560 U.S. 370 (2010)

Justice Kennedy delivered the opinion of the Court.

On January 10, 2000, a shooting occurred outside a mall in Southfield, Michigan. Among the victims was Samuel Morris, who died from multiple gunshot wounds. The other victim, Frederick France, recovered from his injuries and later testified. Thompkins, who was a suspect, fled. About one year later he was found in Ohio and arrested there.

Two Southfield police officers traveled to Ohio to interrogate Thompkins, then awaiting transfer to Michigan. The interrogation began around 1:30 p.m. and lasted about three hours. The interrogation was conducted in a room that was 8 by 10 feet, and Thompkins sat in a chair that resembled a school desk (it had an arm on it that swings around to provide a surface to write on). At the beginning of the interrogation, one of the officers. Detective Helgert, presented Thompkins with a form derived from the *Miranda* rule. Thompkins declined to sign the form.

Officers began an interrogation. Thompkins was largely silent during the interrogation, which lasted about three hours. He did give a few limited verbal responses, however, such as "yeah," "no," or "I don't know."

About 2 hours and 45 minutes into the interrogation, Helgert asked Thompkins, "Do you believe in God?" Thompkins made eye contact with Helgert and said "Yes," as his eyes "welled up with tears." Helgert asked, "Do you pray to God?" Thompkins said "Yes." Helgert asked, "Do you pray to God to forgive you for shooting that boy down?" Thompkins answered "Yes" and looked away. Thompkins refused to make a written confession, and the interrogation ended about 15 minutes later.

Thompkins was charged with first-degree murder, assault with intent to commit murder, and certain firearms-related offenses. He moved to suppress the statements made during the interrogation. He argued that he had not waived his right to remain silent. The jury found Thompkins guilty on all counts. He was sentenced to life in prison without parole.

Thompkins appealed the trial court's refusal to suppress his pretrial statements under *Miranda*. The Michigan Court of Appeals rejected the *Miranda* claim, ruling that Thompkins had not invoked his right to remain silent and had waived it.

Thompkins filed a petition for a writ of habeas corpus in the United States District Court for the Eastern District of Michigan. The District Court rejected Thompkins's *Miranda* claims.

The United States Court of Appeals for the Sixth Circuit reversed. The Court of Appeals ruled that the state court, in rejecting Thompkins's *Miranda* claim, unreasonably applied clearly established federal law and based its decision on an unreasonable determination of the facts. We granted certiorari.

III

The *Miranda* Court formulated a warning that must be given to suspects before they can be subjected to custodial interrogation.

All concede that the warning given in this case was in full compliance with these requirements. The dispute centers on the response — or nonresponse — from the suspect.

We now consider whether Thompkins waived his right to remain silent. Even absent the accused's invocation of the right to remain silent, the accused's statement during a custodial interrogation is inadmissible at trial unless the prosecution can establish that the accused in fact knowingly and voluntarily waived *Miranda* rights when making the statement. The waiver inquiry has two distinct dimensions; waiver must be voluntary in the sense that it was the product of a free and deliberate choice rather than intimidation, coercion, or deception, and made with a full awareness of both the nature of the right being abandoned and the consequences of the decision to abandon it.

Some language in *Miranda* could be read to indicate that waivers are difficult to establish absent an explicit written waiver or a formal, express oral statement. *Miranda* said a valid waiver will not be presumed simply from the silence of the accused after warnings are given or simply from the fact that a confession was in fact eventually obtained. ("No effective waiver can be recognized unless specifically made after the *Miranda* warnings have been given"). In addition, the *Miranda* Court stated that a heavy burden rests on the government to demonstrate that the defendant knowingly and intelligently waived his privilege against self-incrimination and his right to retained or appointed counsel.

The course of decisions since *Miranda,* informed by the application *of Miranda* warnings in the whole course of law enforcement, demonstrates that waivers can be established even absent formal or express statements of waiver that would be expected in, say, a judicial hearing to determine if a guilty plea has been properly entered. The main purpose of *Miranda* is to ensure that an accused is advised of and understands the right to remain silent and the right to counsel. Thus, if anything, our subsequent cases have reduced the impact of the *Miranda* rule on legitimate law enforcement while reaffirming the decision's core ruling that unwarned statements may not be used as evidence in the prosecution's case in chief.

One of the first cases to decide the meaning and import of *Miranda* with respect to the question of waiver was *North Carolina* v. *Butler.* The *Butler* Court, after discussing some of the problems created by the language in *Miranda,* established certain important propositions. *Butler* interpreted the *Miranda* language concerning the heavy burden to show waiver, in accord with usual principles of determining waiver, which can include waiver implied from all the circumstances. And in a later case, the Court stated that this "heavy burden" is not more than the burden to establish waiver by a preponderance of the evidence.

The prosecution therefore does not need to show that a waiver of *Miranda* rights was expressed. An implicit waiver of the right to remain silent is sufficient to admit a suspect's statement into evidence. *Butler* made clear that a waiver of *Miranda* rights may be implied through the defendant's silence, coupled with an understanding of his rights and a course of conduct indicating waiver. The Court in *Butler* therefore retreated from the language and tenor of the *Miranda* opinion, which suggested that the Court would require that a waiver be specifically made.

If the State establishes that a *Miranda* warning was given and the accused made an uncoerced statement, this showing, standing alone, is insufficient to demonstrate a valid waiver of *Miranda* rights. The prosecution must make the additional showing that the accused understood these rights. Where the prosecution shows that a *Miranda* warning was given and that it was understood by the accused, an accused's uncoerced statement establishes an implied waiver of the right to remain silent.

Although *Miranda* imposes on the police a rule that is both formalistic and practical when it prevents them from interrogating suspects without first providing them with a *Miranda* warning, it does not impose a formalistic waiver procedure that a suspect must follow to relinquish those rights. As a general proposition, the law can presume that an individual who, with a full understanding of his or her rights, acts in a manner inconsistent with their exercise has made a deliberate choice to relinquish the protection those rights afford. As *Butler* recognized, *Miranda* rights can therefore be waived through means less formal than a typical waiver on the record in a courtroom, given the practical constraints and necessities of interrogation and the fact that Miranda's main protection lies in advising defendants of their rights.

The record in this case shows that Thompkins waived his right to remain silent. There is no basis in this case to conclude that he did not understand his rights; and on these facts it follows that he chose not to invoke or rely on those rights when he did speak. First, there is no contention that Thompkins did not understand his rights; and from this it follows that he knew what he gave up when he spoke. There was more than enough evidence in the record to conclude that Thompkins understood his *Miranda* rights. Thompkins received a written copy of the *Miranda* warnings; Detective Helgert determined that Thompkins could read and understand English, and Thompkins was given time to read the warnings. Thompkins, furthermore, read aloud the fifth warning, which stated that "you have the right to decide at any time before or during questioning to use your right to remain silent and your right to talk with a lawyer while you are being questioned." He was thus aware that his right to remain silent would not dissipate after a certain amount of time and that police would have to honor his right to be silent and his right to counsel during the whole course of interrogation. Those rights, the warning made clear, could be asserted at any time. Helgert, moreover, read the warnings aloud.

Second, Thompkins's answer to Detective Helgert's question about whether Thompkins prayed to God for forgiveness for shooting the victim is a course of conduct indicating waiver of the right to remain silent. If Thompkins wanted to remain silent, he could have said nothing in response to Helgert's questions, or he could have unambiguously invoked his *Miranda* rights and ended the interrogation. The fact that Thompkins made a statement about three hours after receiving a *Miranda* warning does not overcome the fact that he engaged in a course of conduct indicating waiver. Police are not required to rewarn suspects from time to time. Thompkins's answer to Helgert's question about praying to God for forgiveness for shooting the victim was sufficient to show a course of conduct indicating waiver. This is confirmed by the fact that before then Thompkins had given sporadic answers to questions throughout the interrogation.

Third, there is no evidence that Thompkins's statement was coerced. Thompkins knowingly and voluntarily made a statement to police, so he waived his right to remain silent.

Thompkins next argues that, even if his answer to Detective Helgert could constitute a waiver of his right to remain silent, the police were not allowed to question him until they obtained a waiver first. *Butler* forecloses this argument. The *Butler* Court held that courts can infer a waiver *of Miranda* rights from the actions and words of the person interrogated. This principle would be inconsistent with a rule that requires a waiver at the outset. The *Butler* Court thus rejected the rule proposed by the *Butler* dissent, which would have required the police to obtain an **express waiver** of *Miranda* rights before proceeding with interrogation. This holding also makes sense given that the primary protection afforded suspects subjected to custodial interrogation is the *Miranda* warnings themselves. The *Miranda* rule and its requirements are met if a suspect receives adequate *Miranda* warnings, understands them, and has an opportunity to invoke the rights before giving any answers or admissions. Any waiver, express or implied, may be contradicted by an invocation at any time. If the right to counsel or the right to remain silent is invoked at any point during questioning, further interrogation must cease.

Interrogation provides the suspect with additional information that can put his or her decision to waive, or not to invoke, into perspective. As questioning commences and then continues, the suspect has the opportunity to consider the choices he or she faces and to make a more informed decision, either to insist on silence or to cooperate. When the suspect knows that *Miranda* rights can be invoked at any time, he or she has the opportunity to reassess his or her immediate and long-term interests. Cooperation with the police may result in more favorable treatment for the suspect; the apprehension of accomplices; the prevention of continuing injury and fear; beginning steps towards relief or solace for the victims; and the beginning of the suspect's own return to the law and the social order it seeks to protect.

In order for an accused's statement to be admissible at trial, police must have given the accused a *Miranda* warning. If that condition is established, the court can proceed to consider whether there has been an express or implied waiver of *Miranda* rights. In making its ruling on the admissibility of a statement made during custodial questioning, the trial court, of course, considers whether there is evidence to support the conclusion that, from the whole course of questioning, an express or implied waiver has been established. Thus, after giving a Miranda warning, police may interrogate a suspect who has neither invoked nor waived his or her *Miranda* rights. On these premises, it follows the police were not required to obtain a waiver of Thompkins's *Miranda* rights before commencing the interrogation.

In sum, a suspect who has received and understood the *Miranda* warnings, and has not invoked his *Miranda* rights, waives the right to remain silent by making an uncoerced statement to the police. Thompkins did not invoke his right to remain silent and stop the questioning. Understanding his rights in full, he waived his right to remain silent by making a voluntary statement to the police. The police, moreover, were not required to obtain a waiver of Thompkins's right to remain silent before interrogating him.

The judgment of the Court of Appeals is reversed.

Justice Sotomayor dissenting.

The Court concludes today that a criminal suspect waives his right to remain silent if, after sitting tacit and uncommunicative through nearly three hours of police interrogation, he utters a few one-word responses. The Court also concludes that a suspect who wishes to guard his right to remain silent against such a finding of waiver must, counterintuitively, speak — and must do so with sufficient precision to satisfy a clear-statement rule that construes ambiguity in favor of the police. Both propositions mark a substantial retreat from the protection against compelled self-incrimination that *Miranda* v. *Arizona*, 384 U.S. 436 (1966), has long provided during custodial interrogation.

II

I begin with the question whether Thompkins waived his right to remain silent. Even if Thompkins did not invoke that right, he is entitled to relief because Michigan did not satisfy its burden of establishing waiver.

Rarely do this Court's precedents provide clearly established law so closely on point with the facts of a particular case. Together, *Miranda* and *Butler* establish that a court must presume that a defendant did not waive his rights; the prosecution bears a heavy burden in attempting to demonstrate waiver; the fact of a lengthy interrogation prior to obtaining statements is strong evidence against a finding of valid waiver; mere silence in response to questioning is not enough; and waiver may not be presumed simply from the fact that a confession was in fact eventually obtained.

It is undisputed here that Thompkins never expressly waived his right to remain silent. His refusal to sign even an acknowledgment that he understood his *Miranda* rights evinces, if anything, an intent not to waive those rights. That Thompkins did not make the inculpatory statements at issue until after approximately 2 hours and 45 minutes of interrogation serves as strong evidence against waiver. *Miranda* and *Butler* expressly preclude the possibility that the inculpatory statements themselves are sufficient to establish waiver.

In these circumstances, Thompkins' actions and words preceding the inculpatory statements simply do not evidence a course of conduct indicating waiver sufficient to carry the prosecution's burden. I believe it is objectively unreasonable under our clearly established precedents to conclude the prosecution met its "heavy burden" of proof on a record consisting of three one-word answers, following 2 hours and 45 minutes of silence punctuated by a few largely nonverbal responses to unidentified questions.

The Court concludes that when *Miranda* warnings have been given and understood, an accused's uncoerced statement establishes an **implied waiver** of the right to remain silent. More broadly still, the Court states that, as a general proposition, the law can presume that an individual who, with a full understanding of his or her rights, acts in a manner inconsistent with their exercise has made a deliberate choice to relinquish the protection those rights afford.

These principles flatly contradict our longstanding views that "a valid waiver will not be presumed simply from the fact that a confession was in fact eventually obtained," *Miranda,* 384 U.S., at 475, and that "the courts must presume that a defendant did not waive his rights," *Butler,* 441 U.S., at 373.

At best, the Court today creates an unworkable and conflicting set of presumptions that will undermine *Miranda's* goal of providing "concrete constitutional guidelines for law enforcement agencies and courts to follow," 384 U.S., at 442. At worst, it overrules *sub silentio,* an essential aspect of the protections *Miranda* has long provided for the constitutional guarantee against self-incrimination.

When waiver is to be inferred during a custodial interrogation, there are sound reasons to require evidence beyond inculpatory statements themselves. *Miranda* and our subsequent cases are premised on the idea that custodial interrogation is inherently coercive. Requiring proof of a course of conduct beyond the inculpatory statements themselves is critical to ensuring that those statements are voluntary admissions and not the dubious product of an overborne will.

III

Today's decision turns *Miranda* upside down. Criminal suspects must now unambiguously invoke their right to remain silent — which, counterintuitively, requires them to speak. At the same time, suspects will be legally presumed to have waived their rights even if they have given no clear expression of their intent to do so. Those results, in my view, find no basis in *Miranda* or our subsequent cases and are inconsistent with the fair-trial principles on which those precedents are grounded. Today's broad new rules are all the more unfortunate because they are unnecessary to the disposition of the case before us. I respectfully dissent.

FURTHER CASE LAW, REFLECTIONS, AND QUESTIONS

1. Does the Court's decision in *Thompkins* seem faithful to *Miranda's* premises and language or does it, in the words of Justice Sotomayor's dissenting opinion, "*sub silentio* an essential aspect of the protections *Miranda* has long provided for the constitutional guarantee against self-incrimination"?

2. What led the majority opinion to conclude that Thompkins knowingly, intelligently, and voluntarily waived his *Miranda* rights? Is it permissible to infer an effective waiver from the fact of a confession, or must something in addition be demonstrated? If there is an additional requirement, what, precisely, is it, and what sort

of evidence can establish it? What is the meaning of the following aspect of the Court's holding? If the State establishes that a *Miranda* warning was given and the accused made an uncoerced statement, this showing, standing alone, is insufficient to demonstrate a valid waiver of *Miranda* rights. The prosecution must make the additional showing that the accused understood these rights.

3. Thompkins made his incriminating statement two hours and forty-five minutes into the interrogation session. When, specifically, did he waive his *Miranda* protections?
4. If Thompkins invoked his right to silence before Detective Helgert's question, "Do you pray to God to forgive you for shooting that boy down?", the question should not have been posed, and Thompkins's incriminating response should be inadmissible. Justice Kennedy's majority opinion rejects the claim that Thompkins invoked his right to silence, explaining that "Thompkins did not say that he wanted to remain silent or that he did not want to talk with the police. Had he made either of these simple, unambiguous statements, he would have invoked his 'right to cut off questioning.'" Justice Sotomayor's dissent charges that this rule creates something of a constitutional Catch 22: "Criminal suspects must now unambiguously invoke their right to remain silent — which, counterintuitively, requires them to speak." Is the majority's application of the "clear statement" rule, derived from *Davis* v. *United States* and its ruling regarding how a suspect must invoke the right to counsel, appropriate in this context? Does it overlook the aspect of *Davis,* as noted in Justice Sotomayor's dissent, that "the suspect's equivocal reference to a lawyer in *Davis* occurred only *after* he had given express oral and written waivers of his rights"?

Knowing and Intelligent Waivers

A waiver of one's Miranda rights must be made knowingly, intelligently, and voluntarily. For a waiver to be knowing and intelligent, it must be made with full awareness of the nature of the right being abandoned and the consequences of the decision. In *Fare v. Michael C.*, the Supreme Court held that a determination of a waiver's knowing and intelligent nature must be made after considering the totality of circumstances. This includes items such as a suspect's age, level of education, intoxication, or other factors that may impact a person's ability to understand the warnings. Moreover, it does not involve a suspect having perfect knowledge of the events surrounding the interrogation.

In *Moran v. Burbine*, 475 U.S. 412 (1986), Brian Burbine was arrested for burglary as well as suspicion of murder. Burbine was read his Miranda rights. He waived his right to an attorney in writing, and after questioning, he also signed three written statements admitting to the murder. Unbeknownst to Burbine, that same night, his sister called the local public defender to get him a lawyer. The public defender contacted the police and informed them of his representation. The police responded that they were not questioning him at that time and that they would not be questioning him until the next day. This was untrue. Police never told Burbine that an attorney attempted to contact him and obtained a written confession.

The trial court denied a motion to suppress the statements made at the police station, holding that Burbine knowingly, intelligently, and voluntarily waived his right to counsel and privilege against self-incrimination. The U.S. District Court for the District of Rhode Island denied Burbine's petition for a writ of habeas corpus. The U.S. Court of Appeals for the First Circuit reversed, holding that the police officer's deliberate or reckless failure to inform Burbine that his counsel attempted to contact him invalidated his waiver of rights.

The Supreme Court reversed, holding that the failure to inform Burbine about the attorney's phone call did not affect the validity of his waiver of rights. The Court found that the waiver was not coerced, and Burbine was aware of his rights at all times. It held that the only requirement for police to protect a suspect's Fifth Amendment constitutional rights is to notify them of their rights under *Miranda* (including the right to counsel) and ensure they voluntarily and knowingly waived those rights. For a waiver to be knowing and intelligent, it must be made with a full awareness of the nature of the right being abandoned and the consequences of the decision. This does not mean that the suspect must be informed about what the interrogation will involve. Moreover, it does not include a suspect knowing of events occurring outside his presence and without his knowledge.

Another issue concerning the prerequisites of a knowing and intelligent waiver of *Miranda* rights arose in *Colorado v. Spring,* 479 U.S. 564 (1987). John Spring was arrested by federal agents from the Bureau of Alcohol, Tobacco, and Firearms (ATF) while making an illegal sale of firearms to an undercover agent. He was advised of his *Miranda* rights and waived them in writing. ATF agents first questioned him about the firearms sale that resulted in his arrest. Then, because they had received a tip that Spring had shot and killed a man in Colorado, they asked him if he had ever shot anyone. Spring admitted that he had shot another guy once, although he denied shooting Donald Walker, the man who had been killed in Colorado. During subsequent questioning, which was preceded by fresh *Miranda* warnings and a new waiver, Spring confessed to killing Donald Walker. His confession was admitted into evidence at his state court trial, and he was convicted of first-degree murder.

Spring moved to suppress both statements on the ground that his waiver of Miranda rights was not made knowingly. The trial court held that the ATF agents' failure to inform Spring before the first interview that they would question him about the Colorado murder did not affect the waiver and that, therefore, the statements should not be suppressed. The Colorado Court of Appeals reversed, holding that Spring's waiver of his Miranda rights before his first statement was invalid because he was not informed that he would be questioned about the Colorado murder and that the State had failed to prove the second statement was not the product of the prior illegal statement. The Colorado Supreme Court affirmed.

The Supreme Court reversed, holding that there was no evidence that Spring was coerced into signing the waiver of his Fifth Amendment rights or that he was prevented from understanding his rights and the consequences of waiving them. The Court stated that the Constitution does not require that a suspect understand every nuance of the consequences of waiving their rights, but rather that they understand that whatever they say may be used against them. The Court held that the Fifth Amendment did not require ATF agents to warn Spring of a possible murder charge before he waived his Miranda rights. The Court found that Spring knowingly waived his Miranda rights since he knew what his rights were, including the right to discontinue talking at any time.

Waivers Following Questioning in Violation of Miranda

Assume that the police obtain an initial confession (C1) from a suspect in violation of *Miranda*. After securing the confession, they administer the *Miranda* warnings, secure a waiver, and obtain a second confession (C2). Further, assume that the suspect has no idea that C1 would be inadmissible in evidence because of the *Miranda* violation, and, in fact, gave C2 to the police because the cat was already out of the bag. Has the suspect made a knowing waiver of their *Miranda* rights prior to the second confession so that C2 should be admissible in evidence? The Supreme Court addressed this question in *Oregon v. Elstad,* 470 U.S. 298 (1985), and *Missouri v. Seibert*, 542 U.S. 600 (2004).

Michael Elstad was suspected of committing a burglary. After obtaining a witness's tip, two officers went to Elstad's home with a warrant for his arrest. The Respondent's mother answered the door and led the officers to her son's bedroom. The officers asked Elstad to get dressed and accompany them to the living room. After one of the officers took Elstad's mother into another room, the other officer, without giving Elstad his Miranda warnings, got him to admit he was present during the robbery.

Subsequently, Elstad was transported to the police station where one of the officers finally advised him of his Miranda rights. Elstad said he understood his rights and agreed to speak to the officers. Thereafter, he recounted to the officers how he participated in the burglary. The statement was then put in writing. Before trial, Elstad moved to suppress his oral statement and signed confession.

He argued that "the statement he made in response to questioning at his house, 'let the cat out of the bag,' and tainted the subsequent confession as 'fruit of the poisonous tree.' The trial court ruled against him, and a jury found him guilty.

The Oregon Court of Appeals reversed the conviction. The United States Supreme Court granted certiorari and reversed the court of appeals. At the outset, the Court held that Elstad's statements made in his house were obtained in violation of *Miranda*. The Court held that his statement at the police station did not violate the Constitution. It stated that a suspect who had once responded to unwarned yet noncoercive questioning was not thereby disabled from waiving his rights and confessing after he had been given the *Miranda* warnings.

Importantly, the Court stated,

> Absent deliberately coercive tactics in obtaining the initial statement, the mere fact that a suspect has made an unwarned admission does not warrant a presumption of compulsion. A subsequent administration of *Miranda* warnings to a suspect who has given a voluntary but unwarned statement ordinarily should suffice to remove conditions that precluded admission of the earlier statement.

Twenty years later, the Supreme Court considered the impact of police deliberately interrogating a suspect without giving Miranda warnings with the goal of obtaining an admission during a subsequent interrogation.

Missouri v. Seibert

542 U.S. 600 (2004)

JUSTICE SOUTER announced the judgment of the Court and delivered an opinion, in which JUSTICE STEVENS, JUSTICE GINSBURG, and JUSTICE BREYER join.

This case tests a police protocol for custodial interrogation that calls for giving no warnings of the rights to silence and counsel until interrogation has produced a confession. Although such a statement is generally inadmissible, since taken in violation of Miranda v. Arizona, 384 U.S. 436 (1966), the interrogating officer follows it with Miranda warnings and then leads the suspect to cover the same ground a second time. The question here is the admissibility of the repeated statement. Because this midstream recitation of warnings after interrogation and unwarned confession could not effectively comply with Miranda's constitutional requirement, we hold that a statement repeated after a warning in such circumstances is inadmissible.

I

Respondent Patrice Seibert's 12-year-old son Jonathan had cerebral palsy, and when he died in his sleep she feared charges of neglect because of bedsores on his body. In her presence, two of her teenage sons and two of their friends devised a plan to conceal the facts surrounding Jonathan's death by incinerating his body in the course of burning the family's mobile home, in which they planned to leave Donald Rector, a mentally ill teenager living with the family, to avoid any appearance that Jonathan had been unattended. Seibert's son Darian and a friend set the fire, and Donald died.

Five days later, the police awakened Seibert at 3 a.m. at a hospital where Darian was being treated for burns. In arresting her, Officer Kevin Clinton followed instructions from Rolla, Missouri, officer Richard Hanrahan that he refrain from giving Miranda warnings. After Seibert had been taken to the police station and left alone in an interview room for 15 to 20 minutes, Hanrahan questioned her without Miranda warnings for 30 to 40 minutes, squeezing her arm and repeating "Donald was also to die in his sleep." After Seibert finally admitted she knew Donald was meant to die in the fire, she was given a 20-minute coffee and cigarette break. Officer Hanrahan then turned on a tape recorder, gave Seibert the Miranda warnings, and obtained a signed waiver of rights from her. He resumed the questioning with "Ok, 'trice, we've been talking for a little while about what happened on Wednesday the twelfth, haven't we?," and confronted her with her prewarning statements:

Hanrahan: In discussion you told us, you told us that there was an understanding about Donald.

Seibert: Yes.

Hanrahan: Did that take place earlier that morning?

Seibert: Yes.

Hanrahan: And what was the understanding about Donald?

Seibert: If they could get him out of the trailer, to take him out of the trailer.

Hanrahan: And if they couldn't?

Seibert: I, I never even thought about it. I just figured they would.

Hanrahan: 'Trice, didn't you tell me that he was supposed to die in his sleep?

Seibert: If that would happen, 'cause he was on that new medicine.

Hanrahan: The Prozac? And it makes him sleepy. So he was supposed to die in his sleep?

Seibert: Yes.

After being charged with first-degree murder for her role in Donald's death, Seibert sought to exclude both her prewarning and postwarning statements. At the suppression hearing, Officer Hanrahan testified that he made a "conscious decision" to withhold Miranda warnings, thus resorting to an interrogation technique he had been taught: question first, then give the warnings, and then repeat the question "until I get the answer that she's already provided once." He acknowledged that Seibert's ultimate statement was "largely a repeat of information . . . obtained" prior to the warning.

The trial court suppressed the prewarning statement but admitted the responses given after the Miranda recitation. A jury convicted Seibert of second-degree murder. On appeal, the Missouri Court of Appeals affirmed, treating this case as indistinguishable from Oregon v. Elstad, 470 U.S. 298 (1985).

The Supreme Court of Missouri reversed, holding that "[i]n the circumstances here, where the interrogation was nearly continuous, . . . the second statement, clearly the product of the invalid first statement, should have been suppressed." We granted certiorari and now affirm.

III

The technique of interrogating in successive, unwarned and warned phases raises a new challenge to Miranda. Although we have no statistics on the frequency of this practice, it is not confined to Rolla, Missouri. The Police Law Institute, for example, instructs that "officers may conduct a two-stage interrogation. At any point during the pre-Miranda interrogation, usually after arrestees have confessed, officers may then read the Miranda warnings and ask for a waiver. If the arrestees waive their Miranda rights, officers will be able to repeat any subsequent incriminating statements later in court." Police Law Institute, Illinois Police Law Manual 83 (Jan. 2001–Dec. 2003). The upshot of all this advice is a question-first practice of some popularity.

IV

When a confession so obtained is offered and challenged, attention must be paid to the conflicting objects of Miranda and question-first. Miranda addressed interrogation practices likely to disable an individual from making a free and rational choice about speaking, and held that a suspect must be adequately and effectively advised of the choice the Constitution guarantees. The object of question-first is to render Miranda warnings ineffective by waiting for a particularly opportune time to give them, after the suspect has already confessed.

The threshold issue when interrogators question first and warn later is thus whether it would be reasonable to find that in these circumstances the warnings could function effectively as Miranda requires. Could the warnings effectively advise the suspect that he had a real choice about giving an admissible statement at that juncture? Could they reasonably convey that he could choose to stop talking even if he had talked earlier? For unless the warnings could place a suspect who has just been interrogated in a position to make such an informed choice, there is no practical justification for accepting the formal warnings as compliance with Miranda, or for treating the second stage of interrogation as distinct from the first, unwarned and inadmissible segment.

There is no doubt about the answer that proponents of question-first give to this question about the effectiveness of warnings given only after successful interrogation, and we think their answer is correct. By any objective measure, applied to circumstances exemplified here, it is likely that if the interrogators employ the technique of withholding warnings until after interrogation succeeds in eliciting a confession, the warnings will be ineffective in preparing the suspect for successive interrogation, close in time and similar in content. After all, the reason that question-first is catching on is as obvious as its manifest purpose, which is to get a confession the suspect would not make if he understood his rights at the outset; the sensible underlying assumption is that with one confession in hand before the warnings, the interrogator can count on getting its duplicate, with trifling additional trouble. Upon hearing warnings only in the aftermath of interrogation and just after making a confession, a suspect would hardly think he had a genuine right to remain silent, let alone persist in so believing once the police began to lead him over the same ground again. A more likely reaction on a suspect's part would be perplexity about the reason for discussing rights at that point, bewilderment being an unpromising frame of mind for a knowledgeable decision. What is worse, telling a suspect that "anything you say can and will be used against you," without expressly excepting the statement just given, could lead to an entirely reasonable inference that what he has just said will be used, with subsequent silence being of no avail. Thus, when Miranda warnings are inserted in the midst of coordinated and continuing interrogation, they are likely to mislead and deprive a defendant of knowledge essential to his ability to understand the nature of his rights and the consequences of abandoning them. By the same token, it would ordinarily be unrealistic to treat two spates of integrated and proximately conducted questioning as independent interrogations subject to independent evaluation simply because Miranda warnings formally punctuate them in the middle.

V

Missouri argues that a confession repeated at the end of an interrogation sequence envisioned in a question-first strategy is admissible on the authority of Oregon v. Elstad, 470 U. S. 298 (1985), but the argument disfigures that case. In Elstad, the police went to the young suspect's house to take him into custody on a charge of burglary. Before the arrest, one officer spoke with the suspect's mother, while the other one joined the suspect in a brief stop in the living room, where the officer said he felt the young man was involved in a burglary. The suspect acknowledged he had been at the scene. This Court noted that the pause in the living room was not to interrogate the suspect but to notify his mother of the reason for his arrest, and described the incident as having none of the earmarks of coercion. The Court, indeed, took care to mention that the officer's initial failure to warn was an oversight that may have been the result of confusion as to whether the brief exchange qualified as 'custodial interrogation' or may simply have reflected reluctance to initiate an alarming police procedure before an officer had spoken with respondent's mother. At the outset of a later and systematic station house interrogation going well beyond the scope of the laconic prior admission, the suspect was given Miranda warnings and made a full confession. In holding the second statement admissible and voluntary, Elstad rejected the cat out of the bag theory that any short, earlier admission, obtained in arguably innocent neglect of Miranda, determined the character of the later, warned confession; on the facts of that case, the Court thought any causal connection between the first and second responses to the police was speculative and attenuated. Although the Elstad Court expressed no explicit conclusion about either officer's state of mind, it is fair to read Elstad as treating the living room conversation as a good-faith Miranda mistake, not only open to correction by careful warnings before systematic questioning in that particular case, but posing no threat to warn-first practice generally.

The contrast between Elstad and this case reveals a series of relevant facts that bear on whether Miranda warnings delivered midstream could be effective enough to accomplish their object: the completeness and detail of the questions and answers in the first round of interrogation, the overlapping content of the two statements, the timing and setting of the first and the second, the continuity of police personnel, and the degree to which the interrogator's questions treated the second round as continuous with the first. In Elstad, it was not unreasonable to see the occasion for questioning at the station house as presenting a markedly different experience from the short conversation at home; since a reasonable person in the suspect's shoes could have seen the station house questioning as a new and distinct experience, the Miranda warnings could have made sense as presenting a genuine choice whether to follow up on the earlier admission.

At the opposite extreme are the facts here, which by any objective measure reveal a police strategy adapted to undermine the Miranda warnings. The unwarned interrogation was conducted in the station house, and the questioning was systematic, exhaustive, and managed with psychological skill. When the police were finished there was little, if anything, of incriminating potential left unsaid. The warned phase of questioning proceeded after a pause of only 15 to 20 minutes, in the same place as the unwarned segment. When the same officer who had conducted the first phase recited the Miranda warnings, he said nothing to counter the probable misimpression that the advice that anything Seibert said could be used against her also applied to the details of the inculpatory statement previously elicited. In particular, the police did not advise that her prior statement could not be used. Nothing was said or done to dispel the oddity of warning about legal rights to silence and counsel right after the police had led her through a systematic interrogation, and any uncertainty on her part about a right to stop talking about matters previously discussed would only have been aggravated by the way Officer Hanrahan set the scene by saying "we've been talking for a little while about what happened on Wednesday the twelfth, haven't we?" The impression that the further questioning was a mere continuation of the earlier questions and responses was fostered by references back to the confession already given. It would have been reasonable to regard the two sessions as parts of a continuum, in which it would have been unnatural to refuse to repeat at the second stage what had been said before. These circumstances must be seen as challenging the comprehensibility and efficacy of the Miranda warnings to the point that a reasonable person in the suspect's shoes would not have understood them to convey a message that she retained a choice about continuing to talk.

VI

Strategists dedicated to draining the substance out of Miranda cannot accomplish by training instructions what Dickerson held Congress could not do by statute. Because the question-first tactic effectively threatens to thwart Miranda's purpose of reducing the risk that a coerced confession would be admitted, and because the facts here do not reasonably support a conclusion that the warnings given could have served their purpose, Seibert's postwarning statements are inadmissible. The judgment of the Supreme Court of Missouri is affirmed.

JUSTICE KENNEDY, concurring in the judgment.

The interrogation technique used in this case is designed to circumvent Miranda v. Arizona, 384 U. S. 436 (1966). It undermines the Miranda warning and obscures its meaning. The plurality opinion is correct to conclude that statements obtained through the use of this technique are inadmissible. Although I agree with much in the careful and convincing opinion for the plurality, my approach does differ in some respects, requiring this separate statement.

The Miranda rule has become an important and accepted element of the criminal justice system. At the same time, not every violation of the rule requires suppression of the evidence obtained. Evidence is admissible when the central concerns of Miranda are not likely to be implicated and when other objectives of the criminal justice system are best served by its introduction.

Oregon v. Elstad reflects this approach. In Elstad, a suspect made an initial incriminating statement at his home. The suspect had not received a Miranda warning before making the statement, apparently because it was not clear whether the suspect was in custody at the time. The suspect was taken to the station house, where he received a proper warning, waived his Miranda rights, and made a second statement. He later argued that the postwarning statement should be suppressed because it was related to the unwarned first statement, and likely induced or caused by it. The Court held that, although a Miranda violation made the first statement inadmissible, the postwarning statements could be introduced against the accused because neither the general goal of deterring improper police conduct nor the Fifth Amendment goal of assuring trustworthy evidence would be served by suppression given the facts of that case.

In my view, Elstad was correct in its reasoning and its result. Elstad reflects a balanced and pragmatic approach to enforcement of the Miranda warning.

This case presents different considerations. The police used a two-step questioning technique based on a deliberate violation of Miranda. The Miranda warning was withheld to obscure both the practical and legal significance of the admonition when finally given. As Justice Souter points out, the two-step technique permits the accused to conclude that the right not to respond did not exist when the earlier incriminating statements were made. The strategy is based on the assumption that Miranda warnings will tend to mean less when recited mid-interrogation, after inculpatory statements have already been obtained. This tactic relies on an intentional misrepresentation of the protection that Miranda offers and does not serve any legitimate objectives that might otherwise justify its use.

Further, the interrogating officer here relied on the defendant's prewarning statement to obtain the postwarning statement used against her at trial. This shows the temptations for abuse inherent in the two-step technique. Reference to the prewarning statement was an implicit suggestion that the mere repetition of the earlier statement was not independently incriminating. The implicit suggestion was false.

The technique used in this case distorts the meaning of Miranda and furthers no legitimate countervailing interest. The Miranda rule would be frustrated were we to allow police to undermine its meaning and effect. When an interrogator uses this deliberate, two-step strategy, predicated upon violating Miranda during an extended interview, postwarning statements that are related to the substance of prewarning statements must be excluded absent specific, curative steps.

The plurality concludes that whenever a two-stage interview occurs, admissibility of the postwarning statement should depend on whether the Miranda warnings delivered midstream could have been effective enough to accomplish their objective given the specific facts of the case. This test envisions an objective inquiry from the perspective of the suspect, and applies in the case of both intentional and unintentional two-stage interrogations. In my view, this test cuts too broadly. Miranda's clarity is one of its strengths, and a multifactor test that applies to every two-stage interrogation may serve to undermine that clarity. I would apply a narrower test applicable only in the infrequent case, such as we have here, in which the two-step interrogation technique was used in a calculated way to undermine the Miranda warning.

The admissibility of postwarning statements should continue to be governed by the principles of Elstad unless the deliberate two-step strategy was employed. If the deliberate two-step strategy has been used, postwarning statements that are related to the substance of prewarning statements must be excluded unless curative measures are taken before the postwarning statement is made. Curative measures should be designed to ensure that a reasonable person in the suspect's situation would understand the import and effect of the Miranda warning and of the Miranda waiver. For example, a substantial break in time and circumstances between the prewarning statement and the Miranda warning may suffice in most circumstances, as it allows the accused to distinguish the two contexts and appreciate that the interrogation has taken a new turn. Alternatively, an additional warning that explains the likely inadmissibility of the prewarning custodial statement may be sufficient. No curative steps were taken in this case, however, so the postwarning statements are inadmissible and the conviction cannot stand.

For these reasons, I concur in the judgment of the Court.

JUSTICE O'CONNOR, with whom THE CHIEF JUSTICE, JUSTICE SCALIA, and JUSTICE THOMAS join, dissenting.

The plurality devours Oregon v. Elstad, even as it accuses petitioner's argument of disfiguring that decision. I believe that we are bound by Elstad to reach a different result, and I would vacate the judgment of the Supreme Court of Missouri.

On two preliminary questions I am in full agreement with the plurality. First, the plurality appropriately follows Elstad in concluding that Seibert's statement cannot be held inadmissible under a "fruit of the poisonous tree" theory. Second, the plurality correctly declines to focus its analysis on the subjective intent of the interrogating officer.

Although the analysis the plurality ultimately espouses examines the same facts and circumstances that a "fruits" analysis would consider (such as the lapse of time between the two interrogations and change of questioner or location), it does so for entirely different reasons. The fruits analysis would examine those factors because they are relevant to the balance of deterrence value versus the drastic and socially costly course of excluding reliable evidence. The plurality, by contrast, looks to those factors to inform the psychological judgment regarding whether the suspect has been informed effectively of her right to remain silent. The analytical underpinnings of the two approaches are thus entirely distinct, and they should not be conflated just because they function similarly in practice.

The plurality's rejection of an intent-based test is also, in my view, correct. Freedom from compulsion lies at the heart of the Fifth Amendment and requires us to assess whether a suspect's decision to speak truly was voluntary. Because voluntariness is a matter of the suspect's state of mind, we focus our analysis on the way in which suspects experience interrogation.

Thoughts kept inside a police officer's head cannot affect that experience. A suspect who experienced the exact same interrogation as Seibert, save for a difference in the undivulged, subjective intent of the interrogating officer when he failed to give Miranda warnings, would not experience the interrogation any differently.

Because the isolated fact of Officer Hanrahan's intent could not have had any bearing on Seibert's capacity to comprehend and knowingly relinquish her right to remain silent, it could not by itself affect the voluntariness of her confession. Moreover, recognizing an exception to Elstad for intentional violations would require focusing constitutional analysis on a police officer's subjective intent, an unattractive proposition that we all but uniformly avoid.

Because I believe that the plurality gives insufficient deference to Elstad and that Justice Kennedy places improper weight on subjective intent, I respectfully dissent.

FURTHER CASE LAW, REFLECTIONS, AND QUESTIONS

1. It appears that Justice Kennedy, who cast the decisive fifth vote to uphold the suppression of Seibert's post-warning confession, believes that it is critical that the police deliberately withheld the *Miranda* warnings as a tactic to secure an initial admission based on his assumption that the post warning confession would be admissible under *Elstad.*
2. Should it matter that police use loopholes in constitutional rules and ignore the spirit of the rule to obtain a confession? Why is this problematic?

Voluntary Waivers

Beyond being knowingly and intelligently made, a waiver of one's Fifth Amendment rights must be voluntary. A confession will be considered involuntary only if it is obtained through coercion by a state actor. The following case examines several nuances of voluntary waivers.

Colorado v. Connelly

479 U.S. 157 (1986)

CHIEF JUSTICE REHNQUIST delivered the opinion of the Court.

On August 18, 1983, Officer Patrick Anderson of the Denver Police Department was in uniform, working in an off-duty capacity in downtown Denver. Respondent Francis Connelly approached Officer Anderson and, without any prompting, stated that he had murdered someone and wanted to talk about it. Anderson immediately advised respondent that he had the right to remain silent, that anything he said could be used against him in court, and that he had the right to an attorney prior to any police questioning. Respondent stated that he understood these rights but he still wanted to talk about the murder. Understandably bewildered by this confession, Officer Anderson asked respondent several questions. Connelly denied that he had been drinking, denied that he had been taking any drugs, and stated that, in the past, he had been a patient in several mental hospitals. Officer Anderson again told Connelly that he was under no obligation to say anything. Connelly replied that it was all right, and that he would talk to Officer Anderson because his conscience had been bothering him. To Officer Anderson, respondent appeared to understand fully the nature of his acts.

Shortly thereafter. Homicide Detective Stephen Antuna arrived. Respondent was again advised of his rights, and Detective Antuna asked him "what he had on his mind." Respondent answered that he had come all the way from Boston to confess to the murder of MaryAnn Junta, a young girl whom he had killed in Denver sometime during November 1982. Respondent was taken to police headquarters, and a search of police records revealed that the body of an unidentified female had been found in April 1983. Respondent openly detailed his story to Detective Antuna and Sergeant Thomas Haney, and readily agreed to take the officers to the scene of the killing. Under Connelly's sole direction, the two officers and respondent proceeded in a police vehicle to the location of the crime. Respondent pointed out the exact location of the murder. Throughout this episode. Detective Antuna perceived no indication whatsoever that respondent was suffering from any kind of mental illness.

Respondent was held overnight. During an interview with the public defender's office the following morning, he became visibly disoriented. He began giving confused answers to questions, and for the first time, stated that "voices" had told him to come to Denver and that he had followed the directions of these voices in confessing. Respondent was sent to a state hospital for evaluation. He was initially found incompetent to assist in his own defense. By March 1984, however, the doctors evaluating respondent determined that he was competent to proceed to trial.

At a preliminary hearing, respondent moved to suppress all of his statements. Doctor Jeffrey Metzner, a psychiatrist employed by the state hospital, testified that respondent was suffering from chronic schizophrenia and was in a psychotic state at least as of August 17, 1983, the day before he confessed. Metzner's interviews with respondent revealed that respondent was following the "voice of God." This voice instructed respondent to withdraw money from the bank, to buy an airplane ticket, and to fly from Boston to Denver. When respondent arrived from Boston, God's voice became stronger and told respondent either to confess to the killing or to commit suicide. Reluctantly following the command of the voices, respondent approached Officer Anderson and confessed.

Dr. Metzner testified that, in his expert opinion, respondent was experiencing "command hallucinations." This condition interfered with respondent's "volitional abilities; that is, his ability to make free and rational choices." Dr. Metzner further testified that Connelly's illness did not significantly impair his cognitive abilities. Thus, respondent understood the rights he had when Officer Anderson and Detective Antuna advised him that he need not speak.

On the basis of this evidence the Colorado trial court decided that respondent's statements must be suppressed because they were involuntary. The court ruled that a confession is admissible only if it is a product of the defendant's rational intellect and free will. Although the court found that the police had done nothing wrong or coercive in securing respondent's confession, Connelly's illness destroyed his volition and compelled him to confess. The trial court also found that Connelly's mental state vitiated his attempted waiver of the right to counsel and the privilege against compulsory self-incrimination. Accordingly, respondent's initial statements and his custodial confession were suppressed. The Colorado Supreme Court affirmed.

The Due Process Clause of the Fourteenth Amendment provides that no State shall "deprive any person of life, liberty, or property, without due process of law." Just last Term, in *Miller* v. *Fenton,* 474 US 104 (1985), we held that by virtue of the Due Process clause "certain interrogation techniques, either in isolation or as applied to the unique characteristics of a particular suspect, are so offensive to a civilized system of justice that they must be condemned." *Id.* at 109

Indeed, coercive government misconduct was the catalyst for this Court's seminal confession case. *Brown* v. *Mississippi,* 297 US 278 (1936). In that case, police officers extracted confessions from the accused through brutal torture. The Court had little difficulty concluding that even though the Fifth Amendment did not at that time apply to the States, the actions of the police were "revolting to the sense of justice." *Id., at* 286.

Thus the cases considered by this Court over the 50 years since *Brown* v. *Mississippi* have focused upon the crucial element of police overreaching.' While each confession case has turned on its own set of factors justifying the conclusion that police conduct was oppressive, all have contained a substantial element of coercive police conduct. Absent police conduct causally related to the confession, there is simply no basis for concluding that any state actor has deprived a criminal defendant of due process of law.

Our involuntary confession jurisprudence is entirely consistent with the settled law requiring some sort of state action to support a claim of violation of the Due Process Clause of the Fourteenth Amendment. The Colorado trial court, of course, found that the police committed no wrongful acts, and that finding has been neither challenged by the respondent nor disturbed by the Supreme Court of Colorado. The latter court, however, concluded that sufficient state action was present by virtue of the admission of the confession into evidence in a court of the State.

The difficulty with the approach of the Supreme Court of Colorado is that it fails to recognize the essential link between coercive activity of the State, on the one hand, and a resulting confession by a defendant, on the other. The flaw in respondent's constitutional argument is that it would expand our previous line of voluntariness cases into a far-ranging requirement that courts must divine a defendant's motivation for speaking or acting as he did even though there be no claim that governmental conduct coerced his decision.

Moreover, suppressing respondent's statements would serve absolutely no purpose in enforcing constitutional guarantees. The purpose of excluding evidence seized in violation of the Constitution is to substantially deter future violations of the Constitution. Only if we were to establish a brand new constitutional right — the right of a criminal defendant to confess to his crime only when totally rational and properly motivated — could respondent's present claim be sustained.

A statement rendered by one in the condition of respondent might be proved to be quite unreliable, but this is a matter to be governed by the evidentiary laws of the forum, and not by the Due Process Clause of the Fourteenth Amendment.

We hold that coercive police activity is a necessary predicate to the finding that a confession is not voluntary within the meaning of the Due Process Clause of the Fourteenth Amendment. We also conclude that the taking of respondent's statements, and their admission into evidence, constitute no violation of that Clause.

The judgment of the Supreme Court of Colorado is accordingly reversed, and the cause remanded for further proceedings not inconsistent with this opinion.

JUSTICE BRENNAN, dissenting.

The respondent's seriously impaired mental condition is clear on the record of this case. At the time of his confession, Mr. Connelly suffered from a longstanding severe mental disorder, diagnosed as chronic paranoid schizophrenia. He had been hospitalized for psychiatric reasons five times prior to his confession; his longest hospitalization lasted for seven months. Mr. Connelly heard imaginary voices and saw nonexistent objects. He believed that his father was God, and that he was a reincarnation of Jesus.

Today's decision restricts the application of the term involuntary to those confessions obtained by police coercion. Confessions by mentally ill individuals or by persons coerced by parties other than police officers are now considered voluntary. The Court's failure to recognize all forms of involuntariness or coercion as antithetical to due process reflects a refusal to acknowledge free will as a value of constitutional consequence. But due process derives much of its meaning from a conception of **fundamental fairness** that emphasizes the right to make vital choices voluntarily: "The Fourteenth Amendment secures against state invasion of the right of a person to remain silent unless he chooses to speak in the unfettered exercise of his own will." *Malloy v. Hogan*, 378 US 1, 8 (1964). This right requires vigilant protection if we are to safeguard the values of private conscience and human dignity.

Since the Court redefines voluntary confessions to include confessions by mentally ill individuals, the reliability of these confessions becomes a central concern. A concern for reliability is inherent in our criminal justice system, which relies upon accusatorial rather than inquisitorial practices. While an inquisitorial system prefers obtaining confessions from criminal defendants, an accusatorial system must place its faith in determinations of "guilt by evidence independently and freely secured."

Because the admission of a confession so strongly tips the balance against the defendant in the adversarial process, we must be especially careful about a confession's reliability.

FURTHER CASE LAW, REFLECTIONS, AND QUESTIONS

1. Chief Justice Rehnquist's majority opinion and Justice Brennan's dissent identify different policy objectives promoted by suppressing involuntary statements. Do those differences help explain the divergent conclusions reached in their opinions?

2. If a police officer had threatened to kill Connelly if he did not confess, it would be clear that the confession would not be the product of Connelly's free will and that it should be suppressed as involuntary. What would result if the murder victim's father put a gun to Connelly's head and produced a confession by threatening to kill him? Would the confession be a product of Connelly's free will? Should it be considered involuntary in the psychological meaning of that term? Should it be deemed involuntary to the legal sense of that term? If the Constitution did not require suppression of the confession, might Connelly invoke other legal rules or principles to keep the statement out of evidence?

Box 8.7 You Be the Judge

One day, while walking home from work, Omar, a typical 18-year-old from the inner city of Baltimore, is stopped by the police and questioned about a mugging that just happened a few blocks away. The police question Omar, and he denies any involvement. While this occurs, the police drive the victim by Omar in an unmarked police vehicle. The victim states that they cannot say with 100% certainty, but they think that Omar is the one who mugged them.

Based on the identification and Omar's proximity to the crime scene, the police placed him under arrest and transported him to the police station for interrogation. Before the interrogation, the police read Omar the *Miranda* warnings, and he voluntarily waived his rights and agreed to speak with the police. The police engage in a lengthy and contentious interrogation of Omar, where they continue to tell Omar that the victim has identified him as the mugger. Omar continues to profess his innocence throughout the interrogation but frequently breaks down crying and has intermittent panic attacks. Due to the length of the interrogation, three officers continue to switch off interrogators to give themselves a break. After 10 hours of interrogation, Omar finally confesses to the crime. The police get Omar to sign a confession, but only after he takes a needed break due to a panic attack.

After being given a new lawyer Omar recants his confession and professes his innocence.

Should Omar's confession be suppressed?

See *Spano v. New York*, 360 U.S. 315 (1959) and *Payne v. Arkansas*, 356 U.S. 560 (1958).

Nontestimonial Evidence

The Fifth Amendment right against compelled self-incrimination, which *Miranda* is designed to safeguard, clearly applies to verbal expressions, such as oral and written confessions. We now consider whether the Fifth Amendment extends to other types of evidence that might be used to incriminate suspects, such as their fingerprints, a handwriting sample, a recording of their voice, a dental impression, a DNA sample, or their blood. These forms of evidence are classified as "nontestimonial." Should the Fifth Amendment protect an individual from being "compelled" to supply such potentially incriminating evidence from his or her person? This important question has relevance beyond the *Miranda* context but also figures significantly in cases raising *Miranda* issues.

The principal case addressing this issue, *Schmerber* v. *California,* was decided just one week after *Miranda.* Schmerber was convicted of driving while intoxicated, a conviction based in part on an alcohol content analysis performed on blood drawn from Schmerber by a hospital physician at the direction of the police. Schmerber contended that this evidence was obtained in violation of due process of law under the Fourteenth Amendment, as well as his privilege against self-incrimination under the Fifth Amendment; his right to counsel under the Sixth Amendment; and his right not to be subjected to unreasonable searches and seizures in violation of the Fourth Amendment. We focus on the Fifth Amendment claim.

Schmerber v. California

384 U.S. 757 (1966)

MR. JUSTICE BRENNAN delivered the opinion of the Court.

Petitioner was convicted in Los Angeles Municipal Court of the criminal offense of driving an automobile while under the influence of intoxicating liquor. He had been arrested at a hospital while receiving treatment for injuries suffered in an accident involving the automobile that he had apparently been driving. At the direction of a police officer, a blood sample was then withdrawn from petitioner's body by a physician at the hospital. The chemical analysis of this sample revealed a percent by weight of alcohol in his blood at the time of the offense which indicated intoxication, and the report of this analysis was admitted in evidence at the trial. Petitioner objected to receipt of this evidence of the analysis on the ground that the blood had been withdrawn despite his refusal, on the advice of his counsel, to consent to the test.

In *Malloy v. Hogan,* 378 US 1(1964), we held that the Fourteenth Amendment secures against state invasion the same privilege that the Fifth Amendment guarantees against federal infringement — the right of a person to remain silent unless he chooses to speak in the unfettered exercise of his own will, and to suffer no penalty for such silence. We therefore must now decide whether the withdrawal of the blood and admission in evidence of the analysis involved in this case violated petitioner's privilege.

We hold that the privilege protects an accused only from being compelled to testify against himself, or otherwise provide the State with evidence of a testimonial or communicative nature, and that the withdrawal of blood and use of the analysis in question in this case did not involve compulsion to these ends.

It could not be denied that in requiring petitioner to submit to the withdrawal and chemical analysis of his blood the State compelled him to submit to an attempt to discover evidence that might be used to prosecute him for a criminal offense. He submitted only after the police officer rejected his objection and directed the physician to proceed. The officer's direction to the physician to administer the test over petitioner's objection constituted compulsion for the purposes of the privilege. The critical question, then, is whether petitioner was thus compelled to be a witness against himself.

If the scope of the privilege coincided with the complex of values it helps to protect, we might be obliged to conclude that the privilege was violated. *In Miranda v. Arizona.* 384 US 436 (1966) the Court said of the interests protected by the privilege; "All these policies point to one overriding thought: the constitutional foundation underlying the privilege is the respect a government — state or federal — must accord to the dignity and integrity of its citizens. To maintain a 'fair state-individual balance,' to require the government 'to shoulder the entire load' to respect the inviolability of the human personality, our accusatory system of criminal justice demands that the government seeking to punish an individual produce the evidence against him by its own independent labors, rather than by the cruel, simple expedient of compelling it from his own mouth." *Id.* at 460. The withdrawal of blood necessarily involves puncturing the skin for extraction, and the percent by weight of alcohol in the blood, as established by chemical analysis, is evidence of criminal guilt. Compelled submission fails on one view to respect the "inviolability of the human personality." Moreover, since it enables the State to rely on evidence forced from the accused, the compulsion violates at least one meaning of the requirement that the State procure the evidence against an accused by its own independent labors.

As the passage in *Miranda* implicitly recognizes, however, the privilege has never been given the full scope which the values it helps to protect suggest. History and a long line of authorities in lower courts have consistently limited its protection to situations in which the State seeks to submerge those values by obtaining the evidence against an accused through the cruel, simple expedient of compelling it from his own mouth. In sum, the privilege is fulfilled only when the person is guaranteed the right to remain silent unless he chooses to speak in the unfettered exercise of his own will. The leading case in this Court is *Holt* v. *United States,* 218 US 245 (1910). There the question was whether evidence was admissible that the accused, prior to trial and over his protest, put on a blouse that fitted him. It was contended that compelling the accused to submit to the demand that he model the blouse violated the privilege. Mr. Justice Holmes, speaking for the Court, rejected the argument as based upon an extravagant extension of the Fifth Amendment, and went on to say: "The prohibition of compelling a man in a criminal court to be witness against himself is a prohibition of the use of physical or moral compulsion to extort communications from him, not an exclusion of his body as evidence when it may be material. The objection in principle would forbid a jury to look at a prisoner and compare his features with a photograph in proof." 218 US, at 252-253.

It is clear that the protection of the privilege reaches an accused's communications, whatever form they might take, and the compulsion of responses which are also communications, for example, compliance with a subpoena to produce one's papers. On the other hand, both federal and state courts have usually held that it offers no protection against compulsion to submit to fingerprinting, photographing, or measurements, to write or speak for identification, to appear in court, to stand, to assume a stance, to walk, or to make a particular gesture. The distinction which has emerged, often expressed indifferent ways, is that the privilege is a bar against compelling communications or testimony, but that compulsion which makes a suspect or accused the source of real or physical evidence does not violate it.

Although we agree that this distinction is a helpful framework for analysis, we are not to be understood to agree with past applications in all instances. There will be many cases in which such a distinction is not readily drawn. Some tests seemingly directed to obtain physical evidence, for example, lie detector tests measuring changes in body function during interrogation, may actually be directed to eliciting responses which are essentially testimonial. To compel a person to submit to testing in which an effort will be made to determine his guilt or innocence on the basis of physiological responses, whether willed or not, is to evoke the spirit and history of the Fifth Amendment. Such situations call to mind the principle that the protection of the privilege is as broad as the mischief against which it seeks to guard. In the present case, however, no such problem of application is presented. Not even a shadow of testimonial compulsion upon or enforced communication by the accused was involved either in the extraction or in the chemical analysis. Petitioner's testimonial capacities were in no way implicated; indeed, his participation, except as a donor, was irrelevant to the results of the test, which depend on chemical analysis and on that alone. Since the blood test evidence, although an incriminating product of compulsion, was neither petitioner's testimony nor evidence relating to some communicative act or writing by the petitioner, it was not inadmissible on privilege grounds.

MR. JUSTICE BLACK, dissenting.

In the first place it seems to me that the compulsory extraction of petitioner's blood for analysis so that the person who analyzed it could give evidence to convict him had both a testimonial and a communicative nature. The sole purpose of this project which proved to be successful was to obtain testimony from some persons to prove that petitioner had alcohol in his blood at the time he was arrested. And the purpose of the project was certainly communicative in that the analysis of the blood was to supply information to enable a witness to communicate to the court and jury that petitioner was more or less drunk.

I think it unfortunate that the Court rests so heavily for its very restrictive reading of the Fifth Amendment's privilege against self-incrimination on the words testimonial and communicative. These words are not models of clarity and precision as the Court's rather labored explication shows. Nor can the Court, so far as I know, find precedent in the former opinions of this Court for using these particular words to limit the scope of the Fifth Amendment's protection.

It concedes, as it must so long as *Boyd v. United States,* 116 US 616 (1886) stands, that the Fifth Amendment bars a State from compelling a person to produce papers he has that might tend to incriminate him. It is a strange hierarchy of values that allows the State to extract a human being's blood to convict him of a crime because of the blood's content but proscribes compelled the production of his lifeless papers. Certainly, there could be few papers that would have any more testimonial value to convict a man of drunken driving than would an analysis of the alcoholic content of a human being's blood introduced in evidence at a trial for driving while under the influence of alcohol. In such a situation blood, of course, is not oral testimony given by an accused but it can certainly communicate to a court and jury the fact of guilt.

FURTHER CASE LAW, REFLECTIONS, AND QUESTIONS

1. As the Court noted in *Schmerber,* several situations in which an accused has been compelled to produce self-incriminating evidence have been held to concern nontestimonial, or physical, or real evidence, thus not violating rights protected by the Fifth Amendment. The Supreme Court has considered the following types of evidence to be nontestimonial: the physical display of suspects in lineups. *United States* v. *Wade,* 388 U.S. 218 (1967); the production of handwriting exemplars, *Gilbert v. California,* 388 U.S. 263 (1967); *United States v. Mara,* 410 U.S. 19 (1973); and the production of voice exemplars. *United States v. Dionisio,* 410 U.S. 1 (1973).

2. In *Pennsylvania v. Muniz,* 496 U.S. 582 (1990), a police officer arrested Muniz for intoxicated driving. The officer transported Muniz to a booking center, where Muniz was asked to provide his name, address, height, weight, eye color, date of

birth, and current age. Each of these questions is routinely asked as part of the booking process. Muniz was then asked, "Do you know the date of your sixth birthday?" After Muniz offered an inaudible reply, the officer repeated, "When you turned six years old, do you remember what the date was?" Muniz responded, "No, I don't." Muniz was then asked to perform three sobriety tests, each of which he failed. After Muniz refused to take a breathalyzer test he was read his Miranda rights. This process was both videotaped and audio-taped.

At trial, the video and audio recordings of Muniz's behavior at the booking center were admitted into evidence, along with the officer's reports of Muniz's failure of the field sobriety tests and his incriminating statements. Muniz was convicted of driving under the influence of alcohol. The Superior Court of Pennsylvania reversed and held that the testimony regarding Muniz's behavior and the results of the field sobriety tests was physical in nature, not testimonial, but that the audio portion of the recording should have been suppressed. The Pennsylvania Supreme Court denied the application for review.

After granting certiorari, the Supreme Court held that when the officer asked the defendant for his name, height, etc. before reading him his *Miranda* rights, it did not violate the 5th Amendment because these questions are part of the police booking routine. The court also found that the defendant's drunken style of speech was part of the physical evidence and not protected under *Miranda*. On the other hand, the Court ruled that the question about Muniz's sixth birthday should be suppressed because it can be considered **testimonial evidence** that should have been obtained after Muniz was read his Miranda rights. The Court reasoned that since the jury could infer from the fact that Muniz did not know the date of his sixth birthday that his mental state was impaired, his response to the sixth birthday question was testimonial. "Whenever a suspect is asked for a response requiring him to communicate an express or implied assertion of fact or belief, the suspect confronts the 'trilemma' of truth, falsity, or silence, and hence the response (whether based on truth or falsity) contains a testimonial component." *Muniz* 496 U.S at 596. Accordingly, as the sixth birthday question required a testimonial response, the Court held that the response should have been suppressed.

Permitted Use of Statements Obtained in Violation of Miranda

Just as there are a number of exceptions to the exclusionary rule regarding Fourth Amendment violations, there are also exceptions to the exclusion of evidence obtained in violation of the Fifth Amendment. The first such exception involves using a suspect's confession obtained in violation of Miranda to address an immediate threat to public safety.

The Public Safety Exception

We have seen that statements secured in violation of *Miranda* can be used to impeach the credibility of a defendant whose trial testimony is inconsistent with those earlier statements. However, we were careful to distinguish between using the unlawful confession for impeachment purposes and using it as part of the prosecution's "case-in-chief," or evidence used to prove guilt, which generally is forbidden. Are there any circumstances under which an accused's incriminating statements should be admissible to prove guilt, even though the police violated his or her *Miranda* rights during custodial interrogation?

On April 15, 2013, a bomb went off near the finish line of the Boston Marathon. Three days later, images of two suspects were released. During the manhunt for the two terrorist suspects — brothers Dzhokhar Tsarnaev and Tamerlan Tsarnaev — Tamerlan was killed. His brother, Dzhokhar, was eventually caught but was severely injured and taken to the hospital. From his bedside, he was questioned and responded to police questioning without being read *Miranda rights,* which was purposefully done by the police. How was this so? Clearly, Dzhokhar was in custody, and there was direct questioning about the crime. The answer is based on the next case, *New York v. Quarles*, where the police concede a *Miranda* violation. The Court nevertheless considers — and recognizes — a "**public safety exception**" to the normal rule that a confession produced in violation of *Miranda* cannot be used in a criminal trial as evidence of guilt.

New York v. Quarles

467 U.S. 649 (1984)

JUSTICE REHNQUIST delivered the opinion of the Court.

On September 11, 1980, at approximately 12:30 am. Officer Frank Kraft and Officer Sal Scarring were on road patrol in Queens, New York, when a young woman approached their car. She told them that she had just been raped by a black male, approximately six feet tall, who was wearing a black jacket with the name "Big Ben" printed in yellow letters on the back. She told the officers that the man had just entered an A & P supermarket located nearby and that the man was carrying a gun.

The officers drove the woman to the supermarket, and Officer Kraft entered the store while Officer Scarring radioed for assistance. Officer Kraft quickly spotted respondent, who matched the description given by the woman, approaching a checkout counter. Apparently upon seeing the officer, respondent turned and ran toward the rear of the store, and Officer Kraft pursued him with a drawn gun. When respondent turned the corner at the end of an aisle. Officer Kraft lost sight of him for several seconds, and upon regaining sight of respondent, ordered him to stop and put his hands over his head.

Although more than three other officers had arrived on the scene by that time. Officer Kraft was the first to reach respondent. He frisked him and discovered that he was wearing a shoulder holster which was then empty. After handcuffing him. Officer Kraft asked him where the gun was. Respondent nodded in the direction of some empty cartons and responded, "the gun is over there." Officer Kraft thereafter retrieved a loaded .38 caliber revolver from one of the cartons, formally placed respondent under arrest, and read him his *Miranda* rights from a printed card. Respondent indicated that he would be willing to answer questions without an attorney present. Officer Kraft then asked respondent if he owned the gun and where he had purchased it. Respondent answered that he did own it and that he had purchased it in Miami, Florida.

In the subsequent prosecution of respondent for criminal possession of a weapon, the judge excluded the statement, "the gun is over there," and the gun because the officer had not given respondent the warnings required by our decision in *Miranda* v. *Arizona* before asking him where the gun was located. The judge excluded the other statements about respondent's ownership of the gun and the place of purchase, as evidence tainted by the prior *Miranda* violation. The Appellate Division of the Supreme Court of New York affirmed without opinion. The Court of Appeals granted leave to appeal and affirmed.

The New York Court of Appeals was undoubtedly correct in deciding that the facts of this case come within the ambit of the *Miranda* decision as we have subsequently interpreted it. We agree that respondent was in police custody. Here Quarles was surrounded by at least four police officers and was handcuffed when the questioning at issue took place. As the New York Court of Appeals observed, there was nothing to suggest that any of the officers were any longer concerned for their own physical safety. The New York Court of Appeals' majority declined to express an opinion as to whether there might be an exception to the *Miranda* rule if the police had been acting to protect the public, because the lower courts in New York had made no factual determination that the police had acted with that motive.

We hold that on these facts there is a "public safety" exception to the requirement that *Miranda* warnings be given before a suspect's answers may be admitted into evidence, and that the availability of that exception does not depend upon the motivation of the individual officers involved. In a kaleidoscopic situation such as the one confronting these officers. where spontaneity rather than adherence to a police manual is necessarily the order of the day, the application of the exception which we recognize today should not be made to depend on post hoc findings at a suppression hearing concerning the subjective motivation of the arresting officer. Undoubtedly most police officers, if placed in Officer Kraft's position, would act out of a host of different, instinctive, and largely unverifiable motives — their own safety, the safety of others, and perhaps as well the desire to obtain incriminating evidence from the suspect.

Whatever the motivation of individual officers in such a situation, we do not believe that the doctrinal underpinnings *of Miranda* require that it be applied in all its rigor to a situation in which police officers ask questions reasonably prompted by a concern for the public safety. The *Miranda* decision was based in large part on this Court's view that the warnings which it required police to give to suspects in custody would reduce the likelihood that the suspects would fall victim to constitutionally impermissible practices of police interrogation in the presumptively coercive environment of the station house. The dissenters warned that the requirement of *Miranda* warnings would have the effect of decreasing the number of suspects who respond to police questioning. The *Miranda* majority, however, apparently felt that whatever the cost to society in terms of fewer convictions of guilty suspects, that cost would simply have to be borne in the interest of enlarged protection for the Fifth Amendment privilege.

The police in this case, in the very act of apprehending a suspect, were confronted with the immediate necessity of ascertaining the whereabouts of a gun which they had every reason to believe the suspect had just removed from his empty holster and discarded in the supermarket. So long as the gun was concealed somewhere in the supermarket, with its actual whereabouts unknown, it obviously posed more than one danger to the public safety: an accomplice might make use of it, a customer or employee might later come upon it.

In such a situation, if the police are required to recite the familiar *Miranda* warnings before asking the whereabouts of the gun, suspects in Quarles' position might well be deterred from responding. Procedural safeguards which deter a suspect from responding were deemed acceptable in *Miranda* in order to protect the Fifth Amendment privilege; when the primary social cost of those added protections is the possibility of fewer convictions, the *Miranda* majority was willing to bear that cost. Here, had *Miranda* warnings deterred Quarles from responding to Officer Kraft's question about the whereabouts of the gun, the cost would have been something more than merely the failure to obtain evidence useful in convicting Quarles. Officer Kraft needed an answer to his question not simply to make his case against Quarles but to insure that further danger to the public did not result from the concealment of the gun in a public area.

We conclude that the need for answers to questions in a situation posing a threat to public safety outweighs the need for the prophylactic rule protecting the Fifth Amendment's privilege against self-incrimination. We decline to place officers such as Officer Kraft in the untenable position of having to consider, often in a matter of seconds, whether it best serves society for them to ask the necessary questions without the *Miranda* warnings and render whatever probative evidence they uncover inadmissible, or for them to give the warnings in order to preserve the admissibility of evidence they might uncover but possibly damage or destroy their ability to obtain that evidence and neutralize the volatile situation confronting them.

In recognizing a narrow exception to *the Miranda* rule in this case, we acknowledge that to some degree we lessen the desirable clarity of that rule. As we have in other contexts, we recognize here the importance of a workable rule to guide police officers, who have only limited time and expertise to reflect on and balance the social and individual interests involved in the specific circumstances they confront. But as we have pointed out, we believe that the exception which we recognize today lessens the necessity of that on-the-scene balancing process. The exception will not be difficult for police officers to apply because in each case it will be circumscribed by the exigency which justifies it. We think police officers can and will distinguish almost instinctively between questions necessary to secure their own safety or the safety of the public and questions designed solely to elicit testimonial evidence from a suspect.

The facts of this case clearly demonstrate that distinction and an officer's ability to recognize it. Officer Kraft asked only the question necessary to locate the missing gun before advising respondent of his rights. It was only after securing the loaded revolver and giving the warnings that he continued with investigatory questions about the ownership and place of purchase of the gun. The exception which we recognize today, far from complicating the thought processes and the on-the-scene judgments of police officers, will simply free them to follow their legitimate instincts when confronting situations presenting a danger to the public safety.

We hold that the Court of Appeals in this case erred in excluding the statement, the gun is over there, and the gun because of the officer's failure to read respondent his Miranda rights before attempting to locate the weapon. Accordingly, we hold that it also erred in excluding the subsequent statements as illegal fruits of a Miranda violation.

FURTHER CASE LAW, REFLECTIONS, AND QUESTIONS

1. What if Officer Kraft had asked Quarles where he purchased the gun before administering his *Miranda* rights? Would Quarles's response, that he had bought the gun in Miami, be admissible under the public safety exception? What if the officer, after retrieving the gun, had shown it to Quarles and asked him, "Is this your gun?" Would Quarles's affirmative reply be admissible if this exchange occurred prior to his receiving *Miranda* warnings? How confident are you that "police officers can and will distinguish almost instinctively between questions necessary to secure their own safety or the safety of the public and questions designed solely to elicit testimonial evidence from a suspect"? Into which category of questioning would the inquiry "Is this your gun?" fall?
2. Under the benefit-cost analysis used by the *Quarles* majority, why not allow the police to ask questions motivated by a concern for their own or the public safety

without administering *Miranda* warnings — to reduce the risk that a suspect will withhold information — but then prohibit the use of the evidence in court after the safety-related crisis has disappeared? Would this practice, which Justice Marshall suggests in dissent, allow the police to realize the benefits of dispensing *with Miranda* without imposing a cost on suspects' rights? What drawbacks, if any, would there be to such an approach?

3. When is a question "reasonably prompted by a concern for the public safety"? What if Quarles had been suspected of having discarded a knife instead of a gun? What if his alleged weapon had been a metal pipe or a set of brass knuckles? What if he had not been accused of rape but instead had been suspected of being a heroin user and police had reason to believe that he once had in his possession a syringe and needle? Would police questioning to discover the whereabouts of those different items without complying with *Miranda* have been permissible under the public safety exception? Should it matter if Quarles was cornered in a deserted store at midnight as opposed to one teeming with business at noon? Do the facts in *Quarles* present a convincing case for applying the public safety exception to *Miranda?*

4. Recall the actions of Dirty Harry examined in Chapter 1. Would Harry's interrogation of Scorpio to rescue the kidnapped girl fall under the public safety exception?

5. Why would the Court treat involuntary confessions differently from statements obtained in violation of *Miranda?* Is one type of violation worse than the other?

Impeachment

Any witness who testifies at a trial must abide by an oath to tell the truth. This rule applies to defendants who choose to testify, no less than to other witnesses. Defendants in criminal cases cannot be required to testify, but once they decide to relinquish their right to silence, they are subject to cross-examination and, in most other respects, are treated like other witnesses.

In all trials, it is common for the lawyer cross-examining a witness to try to impeach the witness's credibility or to raise doubts about the truthful nature of the witness or her or his testimony. Efforts to impeach testimony take many different forms. Thus, witnesses may be asked to reveal prior criminal convictions, on the theory that the jury or judge may doubt the truthfulness of one who has been convicted of a crime. Attempts often are made to expose witnesses' potential interest in the outcome of a trial or their biases against a party or to show that they are testifying with the expectation of getting some benefit or reward in return.

One of the most common methods of attempting to impeach witnesses' credibility is by demonstrating that their testimony is inconsistent with prior statements that they have made. Witnesses whose courtroom testimony is diametrically in conflict with statements they have made on prior occasions may not be believable. Attorneys who succeed in getting a witness to admit that she or he has made prior statements that are contrary to her or his trial testimony frequently go for the jugular by demanding to know (with great flourish and an appropriate tone of indignation), "So, were you lying then, or are you lying now?"

We have learned that if a defendant's statements have been obtained in violation of *Miranda*, they usually must be suppressed from evidence; that is, the prosecution may not use those statements to prove the defendant's guilt. But does it follow that statements produced in violation of *Miranda* cannot be used for any purpose at all? Even if they are inadmissible to prove guilt, might they be used to impeach the defendant's credibility?

Assume, for example, that a defendant confesses to possessing a large quantity of heroin but that the confession is found to be inadmissible because of a *Miranda* violation. The defendant, knowing that the confession has been suppressed, testifies at her trial that she has "never seen heroin in my life." Can the prosecutor cross-examine her about her prior admission about possessing a large quantity of heroin to impeach the credibility of her trial testimony, or is the prior statement entirely "off limits" because it was obtained in violation of *Miranda?*

Note the dilemma if the statement is admissible to impeach her credibility but cannot be considered to prove guilt. The jury must be instructed that it is allowed to consider the defendant's earlier admission that she possessed heroin only to evaluate her credibility. The jurors must further be instructed that they cannot consider her admission to prove guilt — that is, to establish that she in fact possessed the heroin. Another question is whether jurors can perform such mental gymnastics and follow instructions of this nature, try as they might to comply.

We consider the use of statements obtained in violation of *Miranda* to impeach a defendant's credibility in the following case.

Harris v. New York

401 U.S. 222 (1971)

MR. CHIEF JUSTICE BURGER delivered the opinion of the Court.

The State of New York charged petitioner in a two-count indictment with twice selling heroin to an undercover police officer. At a subsequent jury trial the officer was the State's chief witness, and he testified as to details of the two sales. A second officer verified collateral details of the sales, and a third offered testimony about the chemical analysis of the heroin.

Petitioner took the stand in his own defense. He admitted knowing the undercover police officer but denied a sale on January 4, 1966. He admitted making a sale of contents of a glassine bag to the officer on January 6 but claimed it was baking powder and part of a scheme to defraud the purchaser.

On cross-examination petitioner was asked seriatim whether he had made specific statements to the police immediately following his arrest on January 7 — statements that partially contradicted petitioner's direct testimony at trial. In response to the cross-examination, petitioner testified that he could not remember virtually any of the questions or answers recited by the prosecutor. At the request of petitioner's counsel the written statement from which the prosecutor had read questions and answers in his impeaching process was placed in the record for possible use on appeal; the statement was not shown to the jury.

The trial judge instructed the jury that the statements attributed to petitioner by the prosecution could be considered only in passing on petitioner's credibility and not as evidence of guilt. In closing summations both counsel argued the substance of the impeaching statements. The jury then found petitioner guilty on the second count of the indictment. The New York Court of Appeals affirmed.

At trial the prosecution made no effort in its case in chief to use the statements allegedly made by petitioner, conceding that they were inadmissible under Miranda v. *Arizona.* The transcript of the interrogation used in the impeachment, but not given to the jury, shows that no warning of a right to appointed counsel was given before questions were put to petitioner when he was taken into custody. Petitioner makes no claim that the statements made to the police were coerced or involuntary.

Some comments in the *Miranda* opinion can indeed be read as indicating a bar to use of an uncounseled statement for any purpose, but discussion of that issue was not at all necessary to the Court's holding and cannot be regarded as controlling. *Miranda* banned the prosecution from making its case with statements of an accused made while in custody prior to having or effectively waiving counsel. It does not follow from *Miranda* that evidence inadmissible against an accused in the prosecution's case in chief is barred for all purposes, provided of course that the trustworthiness of the evidence satisfies legal standards.

In *Walder v. United States,* 347 US 62 (1954), the Court permitted physical evidence, inadmissible in the case in chief, to be used for impeachment purposes.

> It is one thing to say that the Government cannot make an affirmative use of evidence unlawfully obtained. It is quite another to say that the defendant can turn the illegal method by which evidence in the Government's possession was obtained to his own advantage, and provide himself with a shield against contradiction of his untruths. Such an extension of the *Weeks* doctrine would be a perversion of the Fourth Amendment.
>
> There is hardly justification for letting the defendant affirmatively resort to perjurious testimony in reliance on the Government's disability to challenge his credibility. 347 US, at 65.

It is true that Walder was impeached as to collateral matters included in his direct examination, whereas petitioner here was impeached as to testimony bearing more directly on the crimes charged. We are not persuaded that there is a difference in principle that warrants a result different from that reached by the Court in *Walder.* Petitioner's testimony on his own behalf concerning the events of January 7 contrasted sharply with what he told the police shortly after his arrest. The impeachment process here undoubtedly provided valuable aid to the jury in assessing petitioner's credibility, and the benefits of this process should not be lost, in our view, because of the speculative possibility that impermissible police conduct will be encouraged thereby. Assuming that the exclusionary rule has a deterrent effect on proscribed police conduct, sufficient deterrence flows when the evidence in question is made unavailable to the prosecution in its case in chief.

Every criminal defendant is privileged to testify in his own defense, or to refuse to do so. But that privilege cannot be construed to include the right to commit perjury. Having voluntarily taken the stand, petitioner was under an obligation to speak truthfully and accurately, and the prosecution here did no more than utilize the traditional truth-testing devices of the adversary process.

The shield provided by *Miranda* cannot be perverted into a license to use perjury by way of a defense, free from the risk of confrontation with prior inconsistent utterances. We hold, therefore, that petitioner's credibility was appropriately impeached by use of his earlier conflicting statements. Affirmed.

Mr. Justice Brennan dissenting.

Walder v. *United States* was not a case where tainted evidence was used to impeach an accused's direct testimony on matters directly related to the case against him. In *Walder* the evidence was used to impeach the accused's testimony on matters collateral to the crime charged. The Court was careful to distinguish the situation of an accused whose testimony, as in the instant case, was a denial of complicity in the crimes of which he was charged, that is, where illegally obtained evidence was used to impeach the accused's direct testimony on matters directly related to the case against him. As to that situation, the Court said:

> Of course, the Constitution guarantees a defendant the fullest opportunity to meet the accusation against him. He must be free to deny all the elements of the case against him without thereby giving leave to the Government to introduce by way of rebuttal evidence illegally secured by it, and therefore not available for its case in chief. 347 US, at 65.

While *Walder* did not identify the constitutional specifics that guarantee "a defendant the fullest opportunity to meet the accusation against him and permit him to be free to deny all the elements of the case against him," in my view *Miranda* v. *Arizona* identified the Fifth Amendment's privilege against self-incrimination as one of those specifics. It is fulfilled only when an accused is guaranteed the right to remain silent unless he chooses to speak in the unfettered exercise of his own will. The choice of whether to testify in one's own defense must therefore be unfettered, since that choice is an exercise of constitutional privilege.

The prosecution's use of the tainted statement "]cuts down on the privilege by making its assertion costly. Thus, the accused is denied an "unfettered" choice when the decision whether to take the stand is burdened by the risk that an illegally obtained prior statement may be introduced to impeach his direct testimony denying complicity in the crime charged against him. We settled this proposition in *Miranda* where we said:

> The privilege against self-incrimination protects the individual from being compelled to incriminate himself in any manner. Statements merely intended to be exculpatory by the defendant are often *used to impeach his testimony at trial. These statements are incriminating in any meaningful sense of the word and may not be used without the full warnings and effective waiver required for any other statement.* 384 US, at 476-477 (emphasis added).

This language completely disposes of any distinction between statements used in direct as opposed to cross-examination.

The objective of deterring improper police conduct is only part of the larger objective of safeguarding the integrity of our adversary system. The essential mainstay of that system, *Miranda v. Arizona,* 384 US, at 460, is the privilege against self-incrimination, which for that reason has occupied a central place in our jurisprudence since before the Nation's birth. Moreover, we may view the historical development of the privilege as one which groped for the proper scope of governmental power over the citizen. All these policies point to one overriding thought: the constitutional foundation underlying the privilege is the respect a government must accord to the dignity and integrity of its citizens.. These values are plainly jeopardized if an exception against admission of tainted statements is made for those used for impeachment purposes. Moreover, it is monstrous that courts should aid or abet the lawbreaking police officer. It is an abiding truth that "nothing can destroy a government more quickly than its failure to observe its own laws, or worse, its disregard of the charter of its own existence." *Mapp v. Ohio,* 367 US 648, 659 (1961). Thus, even to the extent that *Miranda* was aimed at deterring police practices in disregard of the Constitution, I fear that today's holding will seriously undermine the achievement of that objective. The Court today tells the police that they may freely interrogate an accused incommunicado and without counsel and know that although any statement they obtain in violation of *Miranda* cannot be used on the State's direct case, it may be introduced if the defendant has the temerity to testify in his own defense. This goes far toward undoing much of the progress made in conforming police methods to the Constitution. I dissent.

FURTHER CASE LAW, REFLECTIONS, AND QUESTIONS

1. Compare *Harris v. New York* with other landmark cases involving Miranda rights and the exclusionary rule, such as *Miranda v. Arizona* (1966) and *Oregon v. Elstad* (1985). What common themes or tensions emerge in these cases, and what do they reveal about the evolution of Fifth Amendment jurisprudence?

Oregon v. Hass

420 U.S. 714 (1975)

MR. JUSTICE BLACKMUN delivered the opinion of the Court.

This case presents a variation of the fact situation encountered by the Court in *Harris* v. *New York*, 401 US 222 (1971): When a suspect, who is in the custody of a state police officer, has been given full *Miranda* warnings and accepts them, and then later states that he would like to telephone a lawyer but is told that this cannot be done until the officer and the suspect reach the station, and the suspect then provides inculpatory information, is that information admissible in evidence solely for impeachment purposes after the suspect has taken the stand and testified contrarily to the inculpatory information, or is it inadmissible under the Fifth and Fourteenth Amendments?

We see no valid distinction to be made in the application of the principles of *Harris* to that case and to Hass' case. Hass' statements were made after the defendant knew the police officer's opposing testimony had been ruled inadmissible for the prosecution's case in chief.

As in *Harris*, it does not follow from *Miranda* that evidence inadmissible against Hass in the prosecution's case in chief is barred for all purposes, always provided that "the trustworthiness of the evidence satisfies legal standards." 401 US, at 224. Again, the impeaching material would provide valuable aid to the jury in assessing the defendant's credibility; again, "the benefits of this process should not be lost" *id.*, at 225, and, again, making the deterrent-effect assumption, there is sufficient deterrence when the evidence in question is made unavailable to the prosecution in its case in chief. If all this sufficed for the result in *Harris*, it supports and demands a like result in Hass' case. Here, too, the shield provided *by Miranda* is not to be perverted to a license to testify inconsistently, or even perjuriously, free from the risk of confrontation with prior inconsistent utterances.

We are, after all, always engaged in a search for truth in a criminal case so long as the search is surrounded with the safeguards provided by our Constitution.

MR. JUSTICE BRENNAN dissenting.

The Court's decision today goes beyond *Harris* in undermining *Miranda*. Even after *Harris*, police had some incentive for following *Miranda* by warning an accused of his right to remain silent and his right to counsel. If the warnings were given, the accused might still make a statement which could be used in the prosecution's case in chief. Under today's holding, however, once the warnings are given, police have almost no incentive for following *Miranda's* requirement that if the individual states that he wants an attorney, the interrogation must cease until an attorney is present. If the requirement is followed there will almost surely be no statement since the attorney will advise the accused to remain silent. If, however, the requirement is disobeyed, the police may obtain a statement which can be used for impeachment if the accused has the temerity to testify in his own defense. Thus, after today's decision, if an individual states that he wants an attorney, police interrogation will doubtless be vigorously pressed to obtain statements before the attorney arrives. I am unwilling to join this fundamental erosion of Fifth and Sixth Amendment rights and therefore dissent.

FURTHER CASE LAW, REFLECTIONS, AND QUESTIONS

1. In light of the seemingly unequivocal language from *Miranda* quoted in Justice Brennan's dissent in *Harris v. New York*, how does the majority justify the conclusion that allowing the use of the improperly obtained statement for impeachment purposes is consistent with Miranda?
2. The *Miranda* violation in *Harris* involved the failure to administer adequate warnings. In Oregon v. Hass, the violation involved the police's failure to respect the suspect's invocation of his right to counsel. What significance, if any, is the different nature of these violations?
3. In his dissenting opinion in *Hass*, Justice Brennan argues that "after today's decision, if an individual states that he wants an attorney, police interrogation will doubtless be vigorously pressed to obtain statements before the attorney arrives." Is this outcome a risk? Do *Harris* and *Hass* have the potential to encourage the police to "circumvent" *Miranda?*

Impeachment with Coerced Confessions

Is there a difference between a confession obtained in violation of a suspect's rights under *Miranda* and a confession made involuntarily as a result of police coercion? Should they be treated similarly by courts? A classic example of an involuntary confession arose in *Mincey v. Arizona*, in which the Court considered whether a coerced statement — as opposed to one resulting simply from a *Miranda* violation — can be used for impeachment purposes.

Mincey v. Arizona

437 U.S. 385 (1978)

MR. JUSTICE STEWART delivered the opinion of the Court.

Mincey was brought to the hospital after the shooting and taken immediately to the emergency room where he was examined and treated. He had sustained a wound in his hip, resulting in damage to the sciatic nerve and partial paralysis of his right leg. Tubes were inserted into his throat to help him breathe, and through his nose into his stomach to keep him from vomiting; a catheter was inserted into his bladder. He received various drugs, and a device was attached to his arm so that he could be fed intravenously. He was then taken to the intensive care unit.

At about eight o'clock that evening. Detective Hust of the Tucson Police Department came to the intensive care unit to interrogate him. Mincey was unable to talk because of the tube in his mouth, and so he responded to Detective Hust's questions by writing answers on pieces of paper provided by the Hospital.

Hust told Mincey he was under arrest for the murder of a police officer, gave him the warnings required by *Miranda* v. *Arizona*, and began to ask questions about the events that had taken place in Mincey's apartment a few hours earlier. Although Mincey asked repeatedly that the interrogation stop until he could get a lawyer, Hust continued to question him until almost midnight.

After a pretrial hearing, the trial court found that Mincey had responded to this interrogation voluntarily. When Mincey took the witness stand at his trial his statements in response to Detective Hust's questions were used in an effort to impeach his testimony in several respects.

Statements made by a defendant in circumstances violating the strictures *of Miranda v. Arizona* are admissible for impeachment if their "trustworthiness satisfies legal standards." *Harris* v. *New York*, 401 U.S. 222, 224. But any criminal trial use against a defendant of his involuntary statement is a denial of due process of law even though there is ample evidence aside from the confession to support the conviction. If, therefore, Mincey's statements to Detective Hust were not the product of a rational intellect and a free will, his conviction cannot stand.

It is hard to imagine a situation less conducive to the exercise of a rational intellect and a free will than Mincey's. He had been seriously wounded just a few hours earlier, and had arrived at the hospital depressed almost to the point of coma, according to his attending physician. Although he had received some treatment, his condition at the time of Hust's interrogation was still sufficiently serious that he was in the intensive care unit. He complained to Hust that the pain in his leg was unbearable. He was evidently confused and unable to think clearly about either the events of that afternoon or the circumstances of his interrogation, since some of his written answers were on their face not entirely coherent. Finally, while Mincey was being questioned he was lying on his back on a hospital bed, encumbered by tubes, needles, and breathing apparatus. He was, in short, at the complete mercy of Detective Hust, unable to escape or resist the thrust of Hust's interrogation.

Despite Mincey's entreaties to be let alone, Hust ceased the interrogation only during intervals when Mincey lost consciousness or received medical treatment, and after each such interruption returned relentlessly to his task. The statements at issue were thus the result of virtually continuous questioning of a seriously and painfully wounded man on the edge of consciousness.

There were not present in this case some of the gross abuses that have led the Court in other cases to find confessions involuntary, such as beatings, or truth serums. But the blood of the accused is not the only hallmark of an unconstitutional inquisition. Determination of whether a statement is involuntary requires more than a mere color-matching of cases. It requires careful evaluation of all the circumstances of the interrogation.

It is apparent from the record in this case that Mincey's statements were not the product of his free and rational choice. To the contrary, the undisputed evidence makes clear that Mincey wanted *not* to answer Detective Hust. But Mincey was weakened by pain and shock, isolated from family, friends, and legal counsel, and barely conscious, and his will was simply overborne. Due process of law requires that statements obtained as these were cannot be used in any way against a defendant at his trial.

FURTHER CASE LAW, REFLECTIONS, AND QUESTIONS

1. The Court said in *Mincey* that "any criminal trial use against a defendant of his involuntary statement is a denial of due process" (emphasis in original). If an involuntary confession is erroneously admitted into evidence at trial, must the defendant's conviction automatically be reversed, or can the conviction stand if a reviewing court determines that the error was "harmless" — that is, if it is clear "beyond a reasonable doubt that the error complained of did not contribute to the verdict obtained"? *Chapman* v. *California,* 386 U.S. 18, 24 (1967). In *Arizona* v. *Fulminante,* 499 U.S. 279 (1991), the Court rejected a rule of automatic reversal in favor of the "harmless error" analysis. However, concluding that admission of the defendant's involuntary confession was not harmless beyond a reasonable doubt, the Court refused to reinstate the defendant's conviction.

Box 8.8 You Be the Judge

Kevin was lawfully arrested for burglary. Kevin is a well-known drug user and broke into homes primarily looking for drugs, money, and guns, but would take other small valuables to support his heroin addiction. After spending the night in jail, Kevin woke up with severe sweating, nausea, diarrhea, and vomiting. At 10:00 am, correctional officers took him to the emergency room, where he was diagnosed with heroin withdrawal. He was given morphine and fluids and primarily recovered. He was discharged and in good condition, with the doctor later testifying that he was "alert and with the program" upon release.

Kevin was released into the custody of correctional officers and transported back to jail around 1:45 pm. While being transported back to jail, Kevin vomited twice in the vehicle. At the jail, officers read Kevin *Miranda* warnings, which he waived, and began interrogating him. During the interrogation, he vomited three times. Officers gave him a plastic bag to vomit in. It was clear he was ill and going through withdrawal. Kevin confessed orally and in writing to a series of burglaries.

Kevin's attorney files a motion to suppress his confession because it was not given voluntarily due to Kevin's physical pain and distress from the heroin withdrawal. The officer who conducted the interrogation testifies that Kevin seemed to be in a clear state of mind and coherent in his thinking. The officer also states that Kevin never complained about feeling sick or that he needed medical attention.

Should Kevin's confession be suppressed from the prosecutor's case in chief? Can it be used for impeachment? Why or why not?

See *United States v. Walker*, 272 F.3d 407, (7th Cir. 2001)

Conclusion

Issues surrounding confessions and self-incrimination involve a complex mix of values. The law strives to further those values by achieving the appropriate balance between law enforcement interests, fairness, and individual freedoms. Justice Goldberg summarized "the policies of the privilege" against compelled self-incrimination in an oft-quoted passage from *Murphy v. Waterfront Commission,* 378 U.S. 52, 55, (1964).

> The privilege against self-incrimination registers an important advance in the development of our liberty — one of the great landmarks in man's struggle to make himself civilized. It reflects many of our fundamental values and most noble aspirations: our unwillingness to subject those suspected of crime to the cruel trilemma of self-accusation, perjury or contempt; our preference for an accusatorial, rather than an inquisitorial, sys-

> tem of criminal justice; our fear that self-incriminating statements will be elicited by inhumane treatment and abuses; our sense of fair play which dictates a fair state-individual balance by requiring the government to leave the individual alone until good cause is shown for disturbing him and by requiring the government in its contest with the individual to shoulder the entire load, our respect for the inviolability of the human personality and of the right of each individual to a private enclave where he may lead a private life, our distrust of self-deprecatory statements; and our realization that the privilege, while sometimes a shelter to the guilty, is often a protection to the innocent.

Justice Goldberg's statement is conspicuously silent about the legitimate law enforcement objectives associated with securing confessions. Suspects' statements obviously assist the police in their investigation of crimes. Confessions are powerful evidence of guilt and facilitate the arrest, prosecution, conviction, and punishment of wrongdoers. The confessions of guilty parties also help ensure that innocent people will not be wrongly accused or convicted of crimes. Some scholars (and judges) believe that "the law governing police interrogation in the United States is overly restrictive and formalistic." J. Grano, *Confessions, Truth, and the Law* 3 (1993). They believe that "the goal of discovering the truth should play a dominant role in designing the rules that govern criminal procedure." *Id.* at 6. Similarly, while dissenting from the Supreme Court's famous decision regulating police interrogation of criminal suspects, *Miranda v. Arizona,* 384 U.S. 436, 537, 539 (1966), Justice White argued that:

> The Court's duty to assess the consequences of its action is not satisfied by the utterance of the truth that a value of our system of criminal justice is "to respect the inviolability of the human personality" and to require the government to produce the evidence against the accused by its own independent labors. More than the human dignity of the accused is involved; the human personality of others in the society must also be preserved. Thus, the values reflected by the privilege are not the sole desideratum; society's interest in the general security is of equal weight.
>
> The most basic function of any government is to provide for the security of the individual and of his property. These ends of society are served by the criminal laws which for the most part are aimed at the prevention of crime. Without the reasonably effective performance of the task of preventing private violence and retaliation, it is idle to talk about human dignity and civilized values.

It should not be difficult to categorize Justice Goldberg's and Justice White's respective views about the law governing self-incrimination on the continuum of "due process" and "crime control" values. Which principles and policy objectives should the law prioritize in this context? If someone is suspected of committing a crime, what more straightforward way could there be of resolving the matter than simply asking the person to confirm or deny his or her involvement? Should it not be presumed that the innocent will make a convincing denial and that the guilty will falter and thus justly face punishment? What harm can there be in asking — and expecting an answer from — an individual about suspected criminal activity? Addressing these questions in a fair, consistent manner is a critical component of criminal procedure law.

KEY TERMS

- break in custody
- confession
- custodial interrogation
- express waiver
- functional equivalent of questioning
- fundamental fairness
- implied waiver
- interrogation
- involuntary confessions
- Miranda warnings
- non-testimonial evidence
- public safety exception
- self-incrimination
- Star Chamber
- testimonial evidence

REVIEW QUESTIONS

1. When do *Miranda* warnings have to be given?
2. What is the purpose of administering *Miranda* warnings?
3. How is interrogation defined for the purposes of *Miranda*?
4. What is an example of a statement that would not be an effective request for an attorney for *Miranda* purposes?
5. How is "in custody" defined for the purposes of *Miranda*? What factors are considered in determining if someone was in custody?
6. What is the difference between waiving and invoking *Miranda*?
7. If a suspect initially waives their *Miranda* rights, can they decide to invoke them later? How does this process occur, and how should the police respond to a delayed invocation of rights?
8. What is required to effectively invoke *Miranda?*
9. What is required to waive *Miranda?*
10. What does "deliberately elicit" mean?

APPLYING THE LAW

Below are five hypothetical fact scenarios. To practice your understanding of the law you learned in this chapter and your ability to apply it, answer each question posed by applying it to hypothetical scenarios. Your answers should be supported by relevant case law and judicially created rules and tests.

1. In the movie *Filthy Larry*, the bad guy, Aries, is a serial bomber. He has planted a bomb somewhere in Pullman. Desperate to find the bomb, Larry breaks into Aries' home and searches for evidence of where the bomb might be. He sees a note that says BOOM TIME 10 a.m., only one hour away. Fortuitously, he looks out the window and sees Scorpio running away. Larry proceeds to shoot Aries in the leg. Larry approaches a screaming Aries and asks where the bomb is. When Aries refuses to reveal the location and demands a lawyer, Larry stands on the wounded leg yelling, "Tell me so we can save lives." After 10 minutes, Aries relents and reveals the whereabouts. Larry jumps in his car, locates the bomb, and defuses it before it can detonate. Aries is prosecuted, and Larry is hailed as a hero. Does Aries's confession fall under the public safety exception in *New York v. Quarles?*

2. Officer Ted went to Kim's house with an arrest warrant for robbery. Based on what he was taught at the police academy, Ted decided he would question Kim before arresting her. Ted knocked on the door and asked if he could come in and ask Kim a few questions. Kim said yes and invited him in. Once in the living room, Kim said, "I think I may need a lawyer." Ted replied, "Are you sure? Only guilty people need lawyers." After a minute, Kim said she was not guilty and agreed to answer Ted's questions. Her answers provided incriminatory information and made the state's prosecution much easier. After 20 minutes of questioning, Ted pulled out the arrest warrant and placed her under arrest. At trial, the prosecution sought to use her statements against her. Should the judge allow the statements to be used by the prosecution?

3. Dr. Phil, a college professor, suspected a student submitted a term paper that had been plagiarized. Under college rules, the punishment for plagiarism can include a failing grade, suspension, or expulsion. As required by college procedures, Dr. Phil referred the matter to the Dean of Students. The Dean met with the student to discuss the paper. At the meeting, the Dean confronted the student with her paper and the evidence of plagiarism and demanded an explanation. The student, realizing she had been caught, replied that she would not answer the Dean's questions and was invoking her Fifth Amendment privilege against self-incrimination.

   Does the student have a Fifth Amendment right to remain silent in this situation?

4. Jen was a 20-year-old college student. After having one beer, she was pulled over while driving her motorcycle. The officer, Rich, asked her if she had been

drinking, and Jen responded, "Only one beer." He told her to get off her motorcycle and lie on the sidewalk spread-eagled while he checked out her information. She complained, at which point Rich yelled, "Do it, or I'll cuff you." She proceeded to do as told. After her license and registration had come back clean, being satisfied she was not intoxicated, Rich went back to her, told her to get up, and said, "It's not smart to ride this thing while you are drinking." She stood up and replied, "It must make you feel like a big man being able to lecture and boss around college kids." Rich proceeded to cite her for being a minor in possession of alcohol for the beer she admitted to drinking. Jen fought the ticket and filed a motion with the Court to have the case dismissed because the only evidence she had been drinking was obtained in violation of her Miranda rights.

How should the judge rule on her motion?

5. Shortly after an Uber driver who had been robbed by a man wielding a Colt 45 automatic handgun identified a picture of Butch as that of his assailant, a Pullman patrolman spotted Butch, who was unarmed, on the street, arrested him and advised him of his rights under Miranda. While driving Butch to the station, two of the officers engaged in a conversation between themselves concerning the missing gun. One of the officers said to the other that there were "a lot of special needs children running around in this area" because a school for such children was located nearby; in addition, he said, "God forbid one of them might find a weapon with bullets and they might hurt themselves." Butch interrupted the conversation, telling the officers to turn the car around so that he could show them where the gun was located.

   Was Butch "interrogated" within the meaning of Miranda?

ORAL ARGUMENTS

Arizona v. Mauro: www.oyez.org/cases/1986/85-2121
Berghuis v. Thompkins: www.oyez.org/cases/2009/08-1470
Berkemer v. McCarty: www.oyez.org/cases/1983/83-710
Brewer v. Williams: www.oyez.org/cases/1976/74-1263
Colorado v. Connelly: www.oyez.org/cases/1986/85-660
Duckworth v. Eagan: www.oyez.org/cases/1988/88-317
Edwards v. Arizona: www.oyez.org/cases/1980/79-5269
Fare v. Michael C.: www.oyez.org/cases/1978/78-334
Florida v. Powell: www.oyez.org/cases/2009/08-1175
Harris v. New York: www.oyez.org/cases/1970/206
Illinois v. Perkins: www.oyez.org/cases/1989/88-1972
Kuhlmann v. Wilson: www.oyez.org/cases/1985/84-1479
Mincey v. Arizona: www.oyez.org/cases/1977/77-5353

Miranda v. Arizona: www.oyez.org/cases/1965/759
Missouri v. Seibert: www.oyez.org/cases/2003/02-1371
Moran v. Burbine: www.oyez.org/cases/1985/84-1485
New York v. Quarles: www.oyez.org/cases/1983/82-1213
Oregon v. Bradshaw: www.oyez.org/cases/1982/81-1857
Oregon v. Elstad: www.oyez.org/cases/1984/83-773
Rhode Island v. Innis: www.oyez.org/cases/1979/78-1076
Stansbury v. California: www.oyez.org/cases/1993/93-5770
United States v. Henry: www.oyez.org/cases/1959/17

REFERENCES

Grano, J. D. (1996). *Confessions, truth, and the law*. University of Michigan Press.
Levy, L. (1968). *Origins of the Fifth Amendment*. Oxford University Press.
Police Law Institute .(Jan. 2001–Dec. 2003). *Illinois Police Law Manual*.
Tabler, N. (2018). The Unspeakable Comma, *The Federal Lawyer*, May 2018, 18.

CHAPTER 9

Eyewitness Identification

LEARNING OBJECTIVES

After reading this chapter, students should be able to:

- Understand the inherent fallibility of eyewitness identifications
- Explain how the Sixth Amendment right to counsel applies to eyewitness identifications
- Comprehend the due process protections given to defendants when eyewitness testimony is used in court
- Recognize the limitations on the use of eyewitness identification in court
- Determine when and why expert testimony is allowed at trial

Introduction

When a crime is committed, several essential components factor into whether an arrest is made and a conviction secured. Only around 40% of crimes committed in the United States are reported to the police (Sheldon et al., 2016). Additionally, despite spending over $123 billion on policing annually in the United States (Urban Institute, 2022), only approximately 20% of reported index crimes are cleared yearly (Sheldon et al., 2016).

The existence of an **eyewitness** to a crime is often a vital component of a criminal investigation and prosecution (President's Commission on Law Enforcement and Administration of Justice, 1967). Not only does such a witness provide law enforcement and prosecutorial agencies with information upon which to base an arrest and indictment, but the **testimony** of the witnesses at trial also can be critical. Studies have repeatedly shown that juries give great weight to the testimony of an eyewitness (Wells et al., 1980).

As can be seen from the statistics presented in Box 9.1 regarding the presence of mistaken identifications and wrongful convictions, the importance of ensuring eyewitness identification is critical. Unfortunately, "[T]he vagaries of **eyewitness identification** are well known; the annals of criminal law are rife with instances of mistaken identification." *United States v. Wade*, 388 U.S. 218, 228 (1967). Faced with this reality, the Supreme Court has taken the opportunity to indirectly regulate aspects of several procedures (primarily **lineups**) used by police and prosecutors when witnesses identify suspects. While not requiring the police to use specific identification procedures, the Court has taken steps to help ensure the reliability of eyewitness identification testimony presented at criminal trials.

The Court has focused on two constitutional approaches in this effort: the Sixth Amendment's right to counsel and the due process guarantees of the Fifth and Fourteenth Amendments. This chapter examines these constitutional protections as they apply to identification procedures and eyewitness testimony at criminal trials. We also consider how state courts have interpreted their own constitutions in these areas. The first section of the chapter examines a suspect's right to counsel during different eyewitness identification procedures. The second section covers due-process protections given to defendants when eyewitness testimony is offered in a court. The last section considers the use of expert testimony in the field of eyewitness identification.

Box 9.1 Statistics Regarding Mistaken Identification and Exonerations 1995–2021

Original Sentence	Death	31 cases
	Life	216 cases
	Minimum 40 years	124 cases
Race	White	20.4%
	Black	63.6%
	Latinx	14.2%
	Other	1.8%
Sex Assigned at Birth	Male	98.6%
Average Time Imprisoned Before Exonerated		13.85 years

Data obtained from National Registry of Exonerations, https://exonerationregistry.org/

The Right to Counsel at Pretrial Identification Procedures

A defendant's Sixth Amendment right to counsel applies during **critical stages** of a criminal prosecution. Does a crime suspect, therefore, have the right to counsel at a lineup? What purpose would counsel serve at a lineup? Does the right to counsel at a lineup attach once a suspected criminal is taken to the police station for questioning? After they are arrested? Following an indictment? The Supreme Court addressed these issues in 1967 in three cases known as the "Wade trilogy."

United States v. Wade

388 U.S. 218 (1967)

MR. JUSTICE BRENNAN delivered the opinion of the Court.

The question here is whether courtroom identifications of an accused at trial are to be excluded from evidence because the accused was exhibited to the witnesses before trial at a post-indictment lineup conducted for identification purposes without notice to and in the absence of the accused's appointed counsel.

The federally insured bank in Eustace, Texas, was robbed on September 21, 1964. A man with a small strip of tape on each side of his face entered the bank, pointed a pistol at the female cashier and the vice president, the only persons in the bank at the time, and forced them to fill a pillowcase with the bank's money. The man then drove away with an accomplice who had been waiting in a stolen car outside the bank. On March 23, 1965, an indictment was returned against respondent, Wade, and two others for conspiring to rob the bank, and against Wade and the accomplice for the robbery itself. Wade was arrested on April 2, and counsel was appointed to represent him on April 26. Fifteen days later an FBI agent, without notice to Wade's lawyer, arranged to have the two bank employees observe a lineup made up of Wade and five or six other prisoners and conducted in a courtroom of the local county courthouse. Each person in the line wore strips of tape such as allegedly worn by the robber and, upon direction, each said something like "put the money in the bag," the words allegedly uttered by the robber. Both bank employees identified Wade in the lineup as the bank robber.

At trial, the two employees, when asked on direct examination if the robber was in the courtroom, pointed to Wade. The prior lineup identification was then elicited from both employees on cross-examination. At the close of testimony, Wade's counsel moved for a judgment of acquittal or, alternatively, to strike the bank officials' courtroom identifications on the ground that conduct of the lineup, without notice to and in the absence of his appointed counsel, violated his Fifth Amendment privilege against self-incrimination and his Sixth Amendment right to the assistance of counsel. The motion was denied, and Wade was convicted.

I

Neither the lineup itself nor anything shown by this record that Wade was required to do in the lineup violated his privilege against self-incrimination. We have only recently reaffirmed that the privilege protects an accused only from being compelled to testify against himself, or otherwise provide the State with evidence of a testimonial or communicative nature.

We have no doubt that compelling the accused merely to exhibit his person for observation by a prosecution witness prior to trial involves no compulsion of the accused to give evidence having testimonial significance. It is compulsion of the accused to exhibit his physical characteristics, not compulsion to disclose any knowledge he might have.

II

The fact that the lineup involved no violation of Wade's privilege against self-incrimination does not, however, dispose of his contention that the courtroom identifications should have been excluded because the lineup was conducted without notice to and in the absence of his counsel. In this case it is urged that the assistance of counsel at the lineup was indispensable to protect Wade's most basic right as a criminal defendant — his right to a fair trial at which the witnesses against him might be meaningfully cross-examined.

The principle of *Powell v. Alabama* and succeeding cases requires that we scrutinize any pretrial confrontation of the accused to determine whether the presence of his counsel is necessary to preserve the defendant's basic right to a fair trial as affected by his right meaningfully to cross-examine the witnesses against him and to have effective assistance of counsel at the trial itself. It calls upon us to analyze whether potential substantial prejudice to defendant's rights inheres in the particular confrontation and the ability of counsel to help avoid that prejudice.

III

The Government characterizes the lineup as a mere preparatory step in the gathering of the prosecution's evidence, not different — for Sixth Amendment purposes — from various other preparatory steps, such as systematized or scientific analyzing of the accused's fingerprints, blood sample, clothing, hair, and the like. We think there are differences which preclude such stages being characterized as critical stages at which the accused has the right to the presence of his counsel. Knowledge of the techniques of science and technology is sufficiently available, and the variables in techniques few enough, that the accused has the opportunity for a meaningful confrontation of the Government's case at trial through the ordinary processes of cross examination of the Government's expert witnesses and the presentation of the evidence of his own experts. The denial of a right to have his counsel present at such analyses does not therefore violate the Sixth Amendment; they are not critical stages since there is minimal risk that his counsel's absence at such stages might derogate from his right to a fair trial.

But the confrontation compelled by the State between the accused and the victim or witnesses to a crime to elicit identification evidence is peculiarly riddled with innumerable dangers and variable factors which might seriously, even crucially, derogate from a fair trial. The vagaries of eyewitness identification are well-known; the annals of criminal law are rife with instances of mistaken identification. Mr. Justice Frankfurter once said: "What is the worth of identification testimony even when uncontradicted? The identification of strangers is proverbially untrustworthy. The hazards of such testimony are established by a formidable number of instances in the records of English and American trials. These instances are recent — not due to the brutalities of ancient criminal procedure." A major factor contributing to the high incidence of miscarriage of justice from mistaken identification has been the degree of suggestion inherent in the manner in which the prosecution presents the suspect to witnesses for pretrial identification. A commentator has observed that "[t]he influence of improper suggestion upon identifying witnesses probably accounts for more miscarriages of justice than any other single factor — perhaps it is responsible for more such errors than all other factors combined." Wall, Eye-Witness Identification in Criminal Cases 26. Suggestion can be created intentionally or unintentionally in many subtle ways. And the dangers for the suspect are particularly grave when the witness' opportunity for observation was insubstantial, and thus his susceptibility to suggestion the greatest.

Moreover, it is a matter of common experience that, once a witness has picked out the accused at the line-up, he is not likely to go back on his word later on, so that in practice the issue of identity may (in the absence of other relevant evidence) for all practical purposes be determined there and then, before the trial.

The pretrial confrontation for purpose of identification may take the form of a lineup, also known as an "identification parade" or "**showup**," as in the present case, or presentation of the suspect alone to the witness, as in *Stovall v. Denno*, 388 US 293. It is obvious that risks of suggestion attend either form of confrontation and increase the dangers inhering in eyewitness identification. But as is the case with secret interrogations, there is serious difficulty in depicting what transpires at lineups and other forms of identification confrontations: "Privacy results in secrecy and this in turn results in a gap in our knowledge as to what in fact goes on." For the same reasons, the defense can seldom reconstruct the manner and mode of lineup identification for a judge or jury at trial. Those participating in a lineup with the accused may often be police officers; in any event, the participants' names are rarely recorded or divulged at trial. The impediments to an objective observation are increased when the victim is the witness. Lineups are prevalent in rape and robbery prosecutions and present a particular hazard that a victim's understandable outrage may excite vengeful or spiteful motives. In any event, neither witnesses nor lineup participants are apt to be alert for conditions prejudicial to the suspect. And if they were, it would likely be of scant benefit to the suspect since neither witnesses nor lineup participants are likely to be schooled in the detection of suggestive influences. Improper influences may go undetected by a suspect, guilty or not, who experiences the emotional tension which we might expect in one being confronted with potential accusers. Even when he does observe abuse, if he has a criminal record he may be reluctant to take the stand and open up the admission of prior convictions. Moreover, any protestations by the suspect of the fairness of the lineup made at trial are likely to be in vain; the jury's choice is between the accused's unsupported version and that of the police officers present. In short, the accused's inability effectively to reconstruct at trial any unfairness that occurred at the lineup may deprive him of his only opportunity meaningfully to attack the credibility of the witness' courtroom identification.

The potential for improper influence is illustrated by the circumstances, insofar as they appear, surrounding the prior identifications in the three cases we decide today. In the present case, the testimony of the identifying witnesses elicited on cross-examination revealed that those witnesses were taken to the courthouse and seated in the courtroom to await assembly of the lineup. The courtroom faced on a hallway observable to the witnesses through an open door. The cashier testified that she saw Wade "standing in the hall" within sight of an FBI agent. Five or six other prisoners later appeared in the hall. The vice president testified that he saw a person in the hall in the custody of the agent who "resembled the person that we identified as the one that had entered the bank."

The few cases that have surfaced therefore reveal the existence of a process attended with hazards of serious unfairness to the criminal accused and strongly suggest the plight of the more numerous defendants who are unable to ferret out suggestive influences in the secrecy of the confrontation. We do not assume that these risks are the result of police procedures intentionally designed to prejudice an accused. Rather we assume they derive from the dangers inherent in eyewitness identification and the suggestibility inherent in the context of the pretrial identification. Williams & Hammelmann, in one of the most comprehensive studies of such forms of identification, said, "[T]he fact that the police themselves have, in a given case, little or no doubt that the man put up for identification has committed the offense, and that their chief preoccupation is with the problem of getting sufficient proof, because he has not 'come clean,' involves a danger that this persuasion may communicate itself even in a doubtful case to the witness in some way." Identification Parades, Part I, [1963] Crim L Rev 479, 483.

Insofar as the accused's conviction may rest on a courtroom identification in fact the fruit of a suspect pretrial identification which the accused is helpless to subject to effective scrutiny at trial, the accused is deprived of that right of cross-examination which is an essential safeguard to his right to confront the witnesses against him. *Pointer v Texas*, 380 US 400. And even though cross-examination is a precious safeguard to a fair trial, it cannot be viewed as an absolute assurance of accuracy and reliability. Thus in the present context, where so many variables and pitfalls exist, the first line of defense must be the prevention of unfairness and the lessening of the hazards of eyewitness identification at the lineup itself. The trial which might determine the accused's fate may well not be that in the courtroom but that at the pretrial confrontation, with the State aligned against the accused, the witness the sole jury, and the accused unprotected against the over-reaching, intentional or unintentional, and with little or no effective appeal from the judgment there rendered by the witness — "that's the man."

Since it appears that there is grave potential for prejudice, intentional or not, in the pretrial lineup, which may not be capable of reconstruction at trial, and since presence of counsel itself can often avert prejudice and assure a meaningful confrontation at trial, there can be little doubt that for Wade the post-indictment lineup was a critical stage of the prosecution at which he was "as much entitled to such aid [of counsel] as at the trial itself." Thus both Wade and his counsel should have been notified of the impending lineup, and counsel's presence should have been a requisite to conduct of the lineup, absent an "intelligent waiver." No substantial countervailing policy considerations have been advanced against the requirement of the presence of counsel.

In our view counsel can hardly impede legitimate law enforcement; on the contrary, for the reasons expressed, law enforcement may be assisted by preventing the infiltration of taint in the prosecution's identification evidence. That result cannot help the guilty avoid conviction but can only help assure that the right man has been brought to justice.

Legislative or other regulations, such as those of local police departments, which eliminate the risks of abuse and unintentional suggestion at lineup proceedings and the impediments to meaningful confrontation at trial may also remove the basis for regarding the stage as "critical." But neither Congress nor the federal authorities have seen fit to provide a solution. What we hold today "in no way creates a constitutional straitjacket which will handicap sound efforts at reform, nor is it intended to have this effect."

V

We come now to the question whether the denial of Wade's motion to strike the courtroom identification by the bank witnesses at trial because of the absence of his counsel at the lineup required, as the Court of Appeals held, the grant of a new trial at which such evidence is to be excluded. We do not think this disposition can be justified without first giving the Government the opportunity to establish by clear and convincing evidence that the in-court identifications were based upon observations of the suspect other than the lineup identification. Where, as here, the admissibility of evidence of the lineup identification itself is not involved, a per se rule of exclusion of courtroom identification would be unjustified. A rule limited solely to the exclusion of testimony concerning identification at the lineup itself, without regard to admissibility of the courtroom identification, would render the right to counsel an empty one. The lineup is most often used, as in the present case, to crystallize the witnesses' identification of the defendant for future reference. We have already noted that the lineup identification will have that effect. The State may then rest upon the witnesses' unequivocal courtroom identification, and not mention the pretrial identification as part of the State's case at trial. Counsel is then in the predicament in which Wade's counsel found himself — realizing that possible unfairness at the lineup may be the sole means of attack upon the unequivocal courtroom identification, and having to probe in the dark in an attempt to discover and reveal unfairness, while bolstering the government witness' courtroom identification by bringing out and dwelling upon his prior identification. Since counsel's presence at the lineup would equip him to attack not only the lineup identification but the courtroom identification as well, limiting the impact of violation of the right to counsel to exclusion of evidence only of identification at the lineup itself disregards a critical element of that right.

We think it follows that the proper test to be applied in these situations is that quoted in *Wong Sun v. United States*, 371 US 471, 488, " '[W]hether, granting establishment of the primary illegality, the evidence to which instant objection is made has been come at by exploitation of that illegality or instead by means sufficiently distinguishable to be purged of the primary taint.'" Application of this test in the present context requires consideration of various factors; for example, the prior opportunity to observe the alleged criminal act, the existence of any discrepancy between any pre-lineup description and the defendant's actual description, any identification prior to lineup of another person, the identification by picture of the defendant prior to the lineup, failure to identify the defendant on a prior occasion, and the lapse of time between the alleged act and the lineup identification. It is also relevant to consider those facts which, despite the absence of counsel, are disclosed concerning the conduct of the lineup.

On the record now before us we cannot make the determination whether the in-court identifications had an independent origin. This was not an issue at trial, although there is some evidence relevant to a determination. That inquiry is most properly made in the District Court. We therefore think the appropriate procedure to be followed is to vacate the conviction pending a hearing to determine whether the in-court identifications had an independent source, or whether, in any event, the introduction of the evidence was harmless error, and for the District Court to reinstate the conviction or order a new trial, as may be proper.

FURTHER CASE LAW, REFLECTIONS, AND QUESTIONS

1. Notice how limited the holding in *Wade* is and how many questions are left unanswered in the majority opinion. What are these unanswered questions, and how do you suppose the Court would (should) decide them?

2. In the companion case of *Gilbert v. California*, 388 U.S. 263 (1967), several witnesses who identified Gilbert in the courtroom testified that they had identified him previously at an uncounseled, post-indictment lineup. The court established a per se exclusionary rule for testimony regarding out-of-court identifications made in violation of a defendant's right to counsel. The Court reasoned that "only a per se exclusionary rule as to such testimony can be an effective sanction to assure that law enforcement authorities will respect the accused's constitutional right to the presence of counsel at the critical lineup." Id at 273.

3. The holdings in *Wade* and *Gilbert* established what is commonly referred to as the *Wade-Gilbert* rule. The ***Wade-Gilbert* rule** has three parts. First, a suspect has the right to have an attorney present at a post-indictment lineup. Second, if an attorney is not present at the lineup, testimony regarding the lineup is not admissible at trial. Third, an in-court identification of a suspect following an illegal lineup is permitted if the prosecution can prove by clear and convincing evidence that the in-court identification was made independent of the lineup.

4. What should the role of counsel be in the lineup procedure? Is counsel merely a passive observer to ensure fairness, or does he have a right, or even a duty, to take a proactive role in the process? Should this role involve making suggestions about the procedures, including making verbal objections at the time counsel feels an impropriety has occurred? Most courts have held that counsel is present for the sole purpose of observing the procedure and to ensure that the lineup is conducted fairly.

5. Should a suspect have a right to a lineup if they believe it will help exonerate them? Most appellate courts have held that granting such a request is within the trial court's discretion. Although allowing a defendant to have a lineup conducted upon request may seem fair, trial courts are hesitant to order them. The refusal to make such an order is rarely found to be reversible error.

6. In the third case in the *Wade* trilogy, *Stovall v. Denno*, 388 U.S. 293 (1967), the Supreme Court held that *Wade* would not be applied retroactively. In other words, defendants whose cases had been resolved prior to the decision in *Wade* would not benefit from the rule announced in the case.

In *Wade*, the Court found that the line-up was a critical stage of a criminal prosecution, and as such, a suspect had a Sixth Amendment right to have counsel present.

Importantly, the line-up in *Wade* was conducted after formal charges were filed. The Court's holding was unclear as to whether a preindictment lineup would also be considered a critical stage of a prosecution, thereby requiring the presence of an attorney. Specifically, at what stage of the criminal justice process does the right exist to have counsel present at a lineup was still an open question. Five years after *the Wade decision*, the Supreme Court answered this question. As you read *Kirby v. Illinois*, ponder which of the Justices' opinions most closely follows the spirit of *Wade*. Note that *Wade* was decided during the Warren Court era, whereas Kirby was decided during the reign of the Burger Court.

Kirby v. Illinois

406 U.S. 682 (1972)

MR. JUSTICE STEWART announced the judgment of the Court

In *United States v. Wade*, 388 US 218 and *Gilbert v. California*, 388 US 263, this Court held "that a post-indictment pretrial lineup at which the accused is exhibited to identifying witnesses is a critical stage of the criminal prosecution; that police conduct of such a lineup without notice to and in the absence of his counsel denies the accused his Sixth [and Fourteenth] Amendment right to counsel and calls in question the admissibility at trial of the in-court identifications of the accused by witnesses who attended the lineup." Those cases further held that no "in-court identifications" are admissible in evidence if their "source" is a lineup conducted in violation of this constitutional standard. "Only a per se exclusionary rule as to such testimony can be an effective sanction," the Court said, "to assure that law enforcement authorities will respect the accused's constitutional right to the presence of his counsel at the critical lineup." *Id.*, at 273. In the present case we are asked to extend the Wade-Gilbert per se exclusionary rule to identification testimony based upon a police station showup that took place before the defendant had been indicted or otherwise formally charged with any criminal offense.

On February 21, 1968, a man named Willie Shard reported to the Chicago police that the previous day two men had robbed him on a Chicago street of a wallet containing, among other things, traveler's checks, and a Social Security card. On February 22, two police officers stopped the petitioner and a companion, Ralph Bean, on West Madison Street in Chicago. When asked for identification, the petitioner produced a wallet that contained three traveler's checks and a Social Security card, all bearing the name of Willie Shard.

Only after arriving at the police station, and checking the records there, did the arresting officers learn of the Shard robbery. A police car was then dispatched to Shard's place of employment, where it picked up Shard and brought him to the police station. Immediately upon entering the room in the police station where the petitioner and Bean were seated at a table, Shard positively identified them as the men who had robbed him two days earlier. No lawyer was present in the room, and petitioner had not asked for legal assistance, or been advised of any right to the presence of counsel.

More than six weeks later, the petitioner and Bean were indicted for the robbery of Willie Shard. Upon arraignment, counsel was appointed to represent them, and they pleaded not guilty. A pretrial motion to suppress Shard's identification testimony was denied, and at the trial Shard testified as a witness for the prosecution. In his testimony he described his identification of the two men at the police station on February 22, and identified them again in the courtroom as the men who had robbed him on February 20. He was cross-examined at length regarding the circumstances of his identification of the two defendants. The jury found both defendants guilty, and the petitioner's conviction was affirmed on appeal.

In a line of constitutional cases in this Court stemming back to the Court's landmark opinion in *Powell v. Alabama*, 287 US 45, it has been firmly established that a person's Sixth and Fourteenth Amendment right to counsel attaches only at or after the time that adversary judicial proceedings have been initiated against him.

This is not to say that a defendant in a criminal case has a constitutional right to counsel only at the trial itself. The Powell case makes clear that the right attaches at the time of arraignment, and the Court has recently held that it exists also at the time of a preliminary hearing. But the point is that, while members of the Court have differed as to existence of the right to counsel in the contexts of some of the above cases, all of those cases have involved points of time at or after the initiation of adversary judicial criminal proceedings — whether by way of formal charge, preliminary hearing, indictment, information, or arraignment.

The initiation of judicial criminal proceedings is far from a mere formalism. It is the starting point of our whole system of adversary criminal justice. For it is only then that the government has committed itself to prosecute, and only then that the adverse positions of government and defendant have solidified. It is then that a defendant finds himself faced with the prosecutorial forces of organized society, and immersed in the intricacies of substantive and procedural criminal law. It is this point, therefore, that marks the commencement of the "criminal prosecutions" to which alone the explicit guarantees of the Sixth Amendment are applicable.

In this case we are asked to import into a routine police investigation an absolute constitutional guarantee historically and rationally applicable only after the onset of formal prosecutorial proceedings. We decline to do so. Less than a year after Wade and Gilbert were decided, the Court explained the rule of those decisions as follows: "The rationale of those cases was that an accused is entitled to counsel at any 'critical stage of the prosecution,' and that a post-indictment lineup is such a 'critical stage.'" (Emphasis supplied.) *Simmons v. United States*, 390 US 377, 382–383. We decline to depart from that rationale today by imposing a per se exclusionary rule upon testimony concerning an identification that took place long before the commencement of any prosecution whatever.

II

What has been said is not to suggest that there may not be occasions during the course of a criminal investigation when the police do abuse identification procedures. Such abuses are not beyond the reach of the Constitution.

The Due Process Clause of the Fifth and Fourteenth Amendments forbids a lineup that is unnecessarily suggestive and conducive to irreparable mistaken identification. *Stovall v. Denno*, 388 US 293; *Foster v. California*, 394 US 440. When a person has not been formally charged with a criminal offense, Stovall strikes the appropriate constitutional balance between the right of a suspect to be protected from prejudicial procedures and the interest of society in the prompt and purposeful investigation of an unsolved crime.

The judgment is affirmed.

MR. JUSTICE BRENNAN dissenting.

While it should go without saying, it appears necessary, in view of the plurality opinion today, to re-emphasize that Wade did not require the presence of counsel at pretrial confrontations for identification purposes simply on the basis of an abstract consideration of the words "criminal prosecutions" in the Sixth Amendment. Counsel is required at those confrontations because "the dangers inherent in eyewitness identification and the suggestibility inherent in the context of the pretrial identification," mean that protection must be afforded to the "most basic right [of] a criminal defendant — his right to a fair trial at which the witnesses against him might be meaningfully cross-examined," *Id.*, at 224. Hence, "the initiation of adversary judicial criminal proceedings" is completely irrelevant to whether counsel is necessary at a pretrial confrontation for identification in order to safeguard the accused's constitutional rights to confrontation and the effective assistance of counsel at his trial.

In view of *Wade*, it is plain, and the plurality today does not attempt to dispute it, that there inhere in a confrontation for identification conducted after arrest the identical hazards to a fair trial that inhere in such a confrontation conducted "after the onset of formal prosecutorial proceedings." *Id.*, at 690. The plurality apparently considers an arrest, which for present purposes we must assume to be based upon probable cause, to be nothing more than part of "a routine police investigation," and thus not "the starting point of our whole system of adversary criminal justice," *id.*, at 689. An arrest, according to the plurality, does not face the accused "with the prosecutorial forces of organized society," nor immerse him "in the intricacies of substantive and procedural criminal law." Those consequences ensue, says the plurality, only with "[t]he initiation of judicial criminal proceedings," "[f]or it is only then that the government has committed itself to prosecute, and only then that the adverse positions of government and defendant have solidified." If these propositions do not amount to "mere formalism," it is difficult to know how to characterize them. An arrest evidences the belief of the police that the perpetrator of a crime has been caught. A post-arrest confrontation for identification is not "a mere preparatory step in the gathering of the prosecution's evidence." *Wade*, supra, at 227. A primary, and frequently sole, purpose of the confrontation for identification at the stage is to accumulate proof to buttress the conclusion of the police that they have the offender in hand. The plurality offers no reason, and I can think of none, for concluding that a post-arrest confrontation for identification, unlike a post-charge confrontation, is not among those "critical confrontations of the accused by the prosecution at pretrial proceedings where the results might well settle the accused's fate and reduce the trial itself to a mere formality."

The highly suggestive form of confrontation employed in this case underscores the point. This showup was particularly fraught with the peril of mistaken identification. In the setting of a police station squad room where all present except petitioner and Bean were police officers, the danger was quite real that Shard's understandable resentment might lead him too readily to agree with the police that the pair under arrest, and the only persons exhibited to him, were indeed the robbers. "It is hard to imagine a situation more clearly conveying the suggestion to the witness that the one presented is believed guilty by the police." The State had no case without Shard's identification testimony, and safeguards against that consequence were therefore of critical importance. Shard's testimony itself demonstrates the necessity for such safeguards. On direct examination, Shard identified petitioner and Bean not as the alleged robbers on trial in the courtroom, but as the pair he saw at the police station. His testimony thus lends strong support to the observation, quoted by the Court in *Wade*, that "[i]t is a matter of common experience that, once a witness has picked out the accused at the line-up, he is not likely to go back on his word later on, so that in practice the issue of identity may (in the absence of other relevant evidence) for all practical purposes be determined there and then, before the trial." Williams & Hammelman, Identification Parades, Part I, [1963] Crim L Rev 479, 482.

Wade and *Gilbert*, of course, happened to involve post-indictment confrontations. Yet even a cursory perusal of the opinions in those cases reveals that nothing at all turned upon that particular circumstance. In short, it is fair to conclude that rather than "declin[ing] to depart from [the] rationale" of *Wade* and *Gilbert*, the plurality today, albeit purporting to be engaged in "principled constitutional adjudication," refuses even to recognize that "rationale." For my part, I do not agree that we "extend" *Wade* and *Gilbert*, by holding that the principles of those cases apply to confrontations for identification conducted after arrest. Because Shard testified at trial about his identification of petitioner at the police station show up, the exclusionary rule of *Gilbert* requires reversal.

FURTHER CASE LAW, REFLECTIONS, AND QUESTIONS

1. On which constitutional grounds was *Kirby* decided? Can the opinion be harmonized with the Court's opinion in *Miranda*?
2. What are the main problems with showups? Do these problems outweigh the efficiency they provide to law enforcement?
3. A vast majority of lineups are conducted prior to the institution of formal proceedings against a defendant. Does this surprise you? Do you think this is done intentionally by law enforcement?

Photographic Lineups

After *Wade* and *Kirby*, it is clear that a defendant has a right to counsel at a post-indictment lineup. Is this right limited to a live lineup (often referred to as a **corporeal lineup**), or does it also apply to **photographic lineups**? The Supreme Court answered this question in *United States v. Ash*.

United States v. Ash

413 U.S. 300 (1973)

MR. JUSTICE BLACKMUN delivered the opinion of the Court.

In this case the Court is called upon to decide whether the Sixth Amendment grants an accused the right to have counsel present whenever the Government conducts a post-indictment photographic display, containing a picture of the accused, for the purpose of allowing a witness to attempt an identification of the offender. The United States Court of Appeals for the District of Columbia Circuit, sitting en banc, held, by a 5-to-4 vote, that the accused possesses this right to counsel.

[Two men wearing ski masks robbed a bar in Washington, D.C., at gunpoint. Law enforcement officials received a tip from an informant that Ash was one of the robbers. On the basis of this information, police showed four people who witnessed the robbery black-and-white mug shots of five individuals, one of whom was Ash. All four witnesses identified Ash and his codefendant John Bailey as being the robbers. Both were subsequently indicted.]

In preparing for trial, the prosecutor decided to use a photographic display to determine whether the witnesses he planned to call would be able to make in-court identifications. Shortly before the trial, an FBI agent and the prosecutor showed five color photographs to the four witnesses who previously had tentatively identified the black-and-white photograph of Ash. Three of the witnesses selected the picture of Ash, but one was unable to make any selection. None of the witnesses selected the picture of Bailey which was in the group. This post-indictment[3] identification provides the basis for respondent Ash's claim that he was denied the right to counsel at a "critical stage" of the prosecution.

At trial, the three witnesses who had been inside the bank identified Ash as the gunman, but they were unwilling to state that they were certain of their identifications. None of these made an in-court identification of Bailey. The fourth witness, who had been in a car outside the bank and who had seen the fleeing robbers after they had removed their masks made positive in-court identifications of both Ash and Bailey. The jury convicted Ash on all counts.

The five-member majority of the Court of Appeals held that Ash's right to counsel, guaranteed by the Sixth Amendment, was violated when his attorney was not given the opportunity to be present at the photographic displays conducted in May 1968 before the trial. The majority relied on this Court's lineup cases, *United States v. Wade*, 388 U.S. 218 (1967), and *Gilbert v. California*, 388 U.S. 263 (1967), and on *Stovall v. Denno*, 388 U.S. 293 (1967).

II

The Court of Appeals relied exclusively on that portion of the Sixth Amendment providing, "In all criminal prosecutions, the accused shall enjoy the right to have the Assistance of Counsel for his defence." The right to counsel in Anglo-American law has a rich historical heritage, and this Court has regularly drawn on that history in construing the counsel guarantee of the Sixth Amendment.

The Court frequently has interpreted the Sixth Amendment to assure that the "guiding hand of counsel" is available to those in need of its assistance. The core purpose of the counsel guarantee was to assure "Assistance" at trial when the accused was confronted with both the intricacies of the law and the advocacy of the public prosecutor. Later developments have led this Court to recognize that "Assistance" would be less than meaningful if it were limited to the formal trial itself.

This extension of the right to counsel to events before trial has resulted from changing patterns of criminal procedure and investigation that have tended to generate pretrial events that might appropriately be considered to be parts of the trial itself. At these newly emerging and significant events, the accused was confronted, just as at trial, by the procedural system, or by his expert adversary, or by both. In *Wade*, the Court explained the process of expanding the counsel guarantee to these confrontations:

> "When the Bill of Rights was adopted, there were no organized police forces as we know them today. The accused confronted the prosecutor and the witnesses against him, and the evidence was marshalled largely at the trial

> itself. In contrast, today's law enforcement machinery involves critical confrontations of the accused by the prosecution at pretrial proceedings where the results might well settle the accused's fate and reduce the trial itself to a mere formality. In recognition of these realities of modern criminal prosecution, our cases have construed the Sixth Amendment guarantee to apply to 'critical' stages of the proceedings."

The Court consistently has applied a historical interpretation of the guarantee, and has expanded the constitutional right to counsel only when new contexts appear presenting the same dangers that gave birth initially to the right itself.

The function of counsel in rendering "Assistance" at the lineup [was] under consideration in Wade and its companion cases. Although the accused was not confronted there with legal questions, the lineup offered opportunities for prosecuting authorities to take advantage of the accused. Counsel was seen by the Court as being more sensitive to, and aware of, suggestive influences than the accused himself, and as better able to reconstruct the events at trial. Counsel present at lineup would be able to remove disabilities of the accused in precisely the same fashion that counsel compensated for the disabilities of the layman at trial. Thus, the Court mentioned that the accused's memory might be dimmed by "emotional tension," that the accused's credibility at trial would be diminished by his status as defendant, and that the accused might be unable to present his version effectively without giving up his privilege against compulsory self-incrimination. It was in order to compensate for these deficiencies that the Court found the need for the assistance of counsel.

III

Although the Court of Appeals' majority recognized the argument that "a major purpose behind the right to counsel is to protect the defendant from errors that he himself might make if he appeared in court alone," the court concluded that "other forms of prejudice," mentioned and recognized in Wade, could also give rise to a right to counsel. These forms of prejudice were felt by the court to flow from the possibilities for mistaken identification inherent in the photographic display.

We conclude that the dangers of mistaken identification, mentioned in Wade, were removed from context by the Court of Appeals and were incorrectly utilized as a sufficient basis for requiring counsel. Although Wade did discuss possibilities for suggestion and the difficulty for reconstructing suggestivity, this discussion occurred only after the Court had concluded that the lineup constituted a trial-like confrontation, requiring the "Assistance of Counsel" to preserve the adversary process by compensating for advantages of the prosecuting authorities.

After the Court in *Wade* held that a lineup constituted a trial-like confrontation requiring counsel, a more difficult issue remained in the case for consideration. The same changes in law enforcement that led to lineups and pretrial hearings also generated other events at which the accused was confronted by the prosecution. The Government had argued in Wade that if counsel was required at a lineup, the same forceful considerations would mandate counsel at other preparatory steps in the "gathering of the prosecution's evidence," such as, for particular example, the taking of fingerprints or blood samples.

The structure of *Wade*, viewed in light of the careful limitation of the Court's language to "confrontations," makes it clear that lack of scientific precision and inability to reconstruct an event are not the tests for requiring counsel in the first instance. These are, instead, the tests to determine whether confrontation with counsel at trial can serve as a substitute for counsel at the pretrial confrontation. If accurate reconstruction is possible, the risks inherent in any confrontation still remain, but the opportunity to cure defects at trial causes the confrontation to cease to be "critical." The opinion of the Court even indicated that changes in procedure might cause a lineup to cease to be a "critical" confrontation.

Legislative or other regulations, such as those of local police departments, which eliminate the risks of abuse and unintentional suggestion at lineup proceedings and the impediments to meaningful confrontation at trial may also remove the basis for regarding the stage as critical.

We now undertake the threshold analysis that must be addressed.

A substantial departure from the historical test would be necessary if the Sixth Amendment were interpreted to give Ash a right to counsel at the photographic identification in this case. Since the accused himself is not present at the time of the photographic display, and asserts no right to be present, no possibility arises that the accused might be misled by his lack of familiarity with the law or overpowered by his professional adversary. Similarly, the counsel guarantee would not be used to produce equality in a trial like adversary confrontation.

Even if we were willing to view the counsel guarantee in broad terms as a generalized protection of the adversary process, we would be unwilling to go so far as to extend the right to a portion of the prosecutor's trial-preparation interviews with witnesses. Although photography is relatively new, the interviewing of witnesses before trial is a procedure that predates the Sixth Amendment.

That adversary mechanism remains as effective for a photographic display as for other parts of pretrial interviews. No greater limitations are placed on defense counsel in constructing displays, seeking witnesses, and conducting photographic identifications than those applicable to the prosecution. Selection of the picture of a person other than the accused, or the inability of a witness to make any selection, will be useful to the defense in precisely the same manner that the selection of a picture of the defendant would be useful to the prosecution.

The argument has been advanced that requiring counsel might compel the police to observe more scientific procedures or might encourage them to utilize corporeal rather than photographic displays. This Court has recognized that improved procedures can minimize the dangers of suggestion. *Simmons v. United States*, 390 U.S. 377, 386 n. 6 (1968). Commentators have also proposed more accurate techniques.

Pretrial photographic identifications, however, are hardly unique in offering possibilities for the actions of the prosecutor unfairly to prejudice the accused. Evidence favorable to the accused may be withheld: testimony of witnesses may be manipulated; the results of laboratory tests may be contrived. In many ways the prosecutor, by accident or by design, may improperly subvert the trial. The primary safeguard against abuses of this kind is the ethical responsibility of the prosecutor, who, as so often has been said, may "strike hard blows" but not "foul ones." If that safeguard fails, review remains available under due process standards. These same safeguards apply to misuse of photographs. *See Simmons v. United States*, 390 U.S., at 384.

We are not persuaded that the risks inherent in the use of photographic displays are so pernicious that an extraordinary system of safeguards is required.

We hold, then, that the Sixth Amendment does not grant the right to counsel at photographic displays conducted by the Government for the purpose of allowing a witness to attempt an identification of the offender. This holding requires reversal of the judgment of the Court of Appeals. Although respondent Ash has urged us to examine this photographic display under the due process standard enunciated in *Simmons v. United States*, 390 U.S., at 384, the Court of Appeals, expressing the view that additional findings would be necessary, refused to decide the issue. We decline to consider this question on this record in the first instance. It remains open, of course, on the Court of Appeals' remand to the District Court.

Reversed and remanded.

MR. JUSTICE STEWART, concurring in the judgment.

A photographic identification is quite different from a lineup, for there are substantially fewer possibilities of impermissible suggestion when photographs are used, and those unfair influences can be readily reconstructed at trial. It is true that the defendant's photograph may be markedly different from the others displayed, but this unfairness can be demonstrated at trial from an actual comparison of the photographs used or from the witness' description of the display. Similarly, it is possible that the photographs could be arranged in a suggestive manner, or that by comment or gesture the prosecuting authorities might single out the defendant's picture. But these are the kinds of overt influence that a witness can easily recount and that would serve to impeach the identification testimony. In short, there are few possibilities for unfair suggestiveness — and those rather blatant and easily reconstructed. Accordingly, an accused would not be foreclosed from an effective cross-examination of an identification witness simply because his counsel was not present at the photographic display. For this reason, a photographic display cannot fairly be considered a "critical stage" of the prosecution.

Mr. Justice Brennan dissenting.

The Court holds today that a pretrial display of photographs to the witnesses of a crime for the purpose of identifying the accused, unlike a lineup, does not constitute a "critical stage" of the prosecution at which the accused is constitutionally entitled to the presence of counsel. In my view, today's decision is wholly unsupportable in terms of such considerations as logic, consistency, and, indeed, fairness. As a result, I must reluctantly conclude that today's decision marks simply another step towards the complete evisceration of the fundamental constitutional principles established by this Court, only six years ago, in *United States v. Wade*, 388 U.S. 218 (1967); *Gilbert v. California*, 388 U.S. 263 (1967); and *Stovall v. Denno*, 388 U.S. 293 (1967). I dissent.

III

As the Court of Appeals recognized, "the dangers of mistaken identification set forth in Wade are applicable in large measure to photographic as well as corporeal identifications." To the extent that misidentification may be attributable to a witness' faulty memory or perception, or inadequate opportunity for detailed observation during the crime, the risks are obviously as great at a photographic display as at a lineup. But "[b]ecause of the inherent limitations of photography, which presents its subject in two dimensions rather than the three dimensions of reality, a photographic identification, even when properly obtained, is clearly inferior to a properly obtained corporeal identification." P. Wall, Eye-Witness Identification in Criminal Cases 70 (1965). Indeed, noting "the hazards of initial identification by photograph," we have expressly recognized that "a corporeal identification is normally more accurate" than a photographic identification. *Simmons v. United States*, 390 U.S. 377, 384, 386 n. 6, (1968). Thus, in this sense at least, the dangers of misidentification are even greater at a photographic display than at a lineup.

Moreover, as in the lineup situation, the possibilities for impermissible suggestion in the context of a photographic display are manifold. Such suggestion, intentional or unintentional, may derive from three possible sources. First, the photographs themselves might tend to suggest which of the pictures is that of the suspect. For example, differences in age, pose, or other physical characteristics of the persons represented, and variations in the mounting, background, lighting, or markings of the photographs all might have the effect of singling out the accused.

Second, impermissible suggestion may inhere in the manner in which the photographs are displayed to the witness. The danger of misidentification is, of course, increased if the police display to the witness the pictures of several persons among which the photograph of a single such individual recurs or is in some way emphasized. And, if the photographs are arranged in an asymmetrical pattern, or if they are displayed in a time sequence that tends to emphasize a particular photograph, any identification of the photograph which stands out from the rest is no more reliable than an identification of a single photograph, exhibited alone.

Third, gestures or comments of the prosecutor at the time of the display may lead an otherwise uncertain witness to select the "correct" photograph. For example, the prosecutor might "indicate to the witness that [he has] other evidence that one of the persons pictured committed the crime," and might even point to a particular photograph and ask whether the person pictured "looks familiar." More subtly, the prosecutor's inflection, facial expressions, physical motions, and myriad other almost imperceptible means of communication might tend, intentionally or unintentionally, to compromise the witness' objectivity. Thus, as is the case with lineups, improper photographic identification procedures, by exerting a suggestive influence upon the witnesses, can often lead to an erroneous identification. And regardless of how the initial misidentification comes about, the witness thereafter is apt to retain in his memory the image of the photograph rather than of the person actually seen. As a result, the issue of identity may (in the absence of other relevant evidence) for all practical purposes be determined there and then before the trial.

Moreover, as with lineups, the defense can "seldom reconstruct" at trial the mode and manner of photographic identification. It is true, of course, that the photographs used at the pretrial display might be preserved for examination at trial. But "it may also be said that a photograph can preserve the record of a lineup; yet this does not justify a lineup without counsel." Indeed, in reality, preservation of the photographs affords little protection to the unrepresented accused. For, although retention of the photographs may mitigate the dangers of misidentification due to the suggestiveness of the photographs themselves, it cannot in any sense reveal to defense counsel the more subtle, and therefore more dangerous, suggestiveness that might derive from the manner in which the photographs were displayed or any accompanying comments or gestures.

Finally, and unlike the lineup situation, the accused himself is not even present at the photographic identification, thereby reducing the likelihood that irregularities in the procedures will ever come to light. Indeed, in *Wade*, the Government itself observed:

> When the defendant is present — as he is during a lineup — he may personally observe the circumstances, report them to his attorney, and (if he chooses to take the stand) testify about them at trial. In the absence of an accused, on the other hand, there is no one present to verify the fairness of the interview or to report any irregularities. If the prosecution were tempted to engage in 'sloppy or biased or fraudulent' conduct , it would be far more likely to do so when the accused is absent than when he is himself being 'used.' Brief for United States 24-25 in *United States v. Wade*, No. 334, O.T. 1966.

Thus, the difficulties of reconstructing at trial an uncounseled photographic display are at least equal to, and possibly greater than, those involved in reconstructing an uncounseled lineup.

IV

The fundamental premise underlying all of this Court's decisions holding the right to counsel applicable at "critical" pretrial proceedings, is that a "stage" of the prosecution must be deemed "critical" for the purposes of the Sixth Amendment if it is one at which the presence of counsel is necessary to protect the fairness of the trial itself.

This established conception of the Sixth Amendment guarantee is, of course, in no sense dependent upon the physical "presence of the accused," at a "trial-like confrontation" with the Government, at which the accused requires the "guiding hand of counsel." On the contrary, in *Powell v. Alabama*, 287 U.S. 45 (1932), the seminal decision in this area, we explicitly held the right to counsel applicable at a stage of the pretrial proceedings involving none of the three criteria set forth by the Court today. In Powell, the defendants in a state felony prosecution were not appointed counsel until the very eve of trial. This Court held, in no uncertain terms, that such an appointment could not satisfy the demands of the Sixth Amendment, for " '[i]t is vain to guarantee [the accused] counsel without giving the latter any opportunity to acquaint himself with the facts or law of the case.' " *Id.*, at 59. In other words, Powell made clear that, in order to preserve the accused's right to a fair trial and to "effective and substantial" assistance of counsel at that trial, the Sixth Amendment guarantee necessarily encompasses a reasonable period of time before trial during which counsel might prepare the defense. Yet it can hardly be said that this preparatory period of research and investigation involves the physical "presence of the accused," at a "trial-like confrontation" with the Government, at which the accused requires the "guiding hand of counsel."

There is something ironic about the Court's conclusion today that a pretrial lineup identification is a "critical stage" of the prosecution because counsel's presence can help to compensate for the accused's deficiencies as an observer, but that a pretrial photographic identification is not a "critical stage" of the prosecution because the accused is not able to observe at all. In my view, there simply is no meaningful difference, in terms of the need for attendance of counsel, between corporeal and photographic identifications. And applying established and well-reasoned Sixth Amendment principles, I can only conclude that a pretrial photographic display, like a pretrial lineup, is a "critical stage" of the prosecution at which the accused is constitutionally entitled to the presence of counsel.

FURTHER CASE LAW, REFLECTIONS, AND QUESTIONS

1. Which identification procedure is more reliable, a corporeal lineup or a photographic array? Why?
2. Why did the Court find that there should be counsel present at a post-indictment corporeal lineup (*Wade*), but that counsel was unnecessary at a photographic lineup (*Ash*)?
3. A summary of the legal protections provided to a suspect during eyewitness identification procedures is provided in Box 9.2
4. If counsel must be present at a post-indictment lineup but does not need to be present at a photographic array presented to witnesses, is there a built-in incentive for police to use the latter practice rather than the former? This possibility, coupled with doubts about the reliability of photographic identifications, has led several states to grant more protections to suspects under their state constitutions than are afforded under *Ash*. In *People v. Anderson*, 205 N.W.2d 461, 476 (Mich. 1973), the Michigan Supreme Court held that the Michigan state constitution requires the following limitations on the use of photographic lineups:
    a. Subject to certain exceptions, identification by photograph should not be used where the accused is in custody. Some of the situations which may, in a particular case, possibly justify the use of photographs are:
        i. It is not possible to arrange a proper lineup.
        ii. There are insufficient number of persons available with defendant's physical characteristics.
        iii. The nature of the case requires immediate identification.
        iv. The witnesses are at a place far distant from the location of the in-custody accused.
        v. The subject refuses to participate in a lineup and by his actions would seek to destroy the value of the identification.
    b. Where there is a legitimate reason to use photographs for identification of an in-custody accused, he has the right to counsel as much as he would for corporeal identification procedures.

Does this approach seem unduly restrictive of the law enforcement process? If counsel were required at a photographic lineup conducted prior to the suspect's arrest, would the investigatory process be unnecessarily hindered?

Box 9.2 Summary of Legal Protections for Eyewitness Identification Procedures

Sixth Amendment Assistance of Counsel

A defendant has a Sixth Amendment right to the presence of counsel at any post-indictment lineup

Counsel is not mandatory at a post-arrest lineup, and the defendant can waive the assistance of counsel, but they must do so knowingly, intelligently, and voluntarily

If the defendant is denied counsel at a post-indictment lineup, the prosecution is barred from an open court identification of the defendant by the victim or an eyewitness unless the prosecution can prove by clear and convincing evidence that the identification is based on independent information from the illegal lineup.

There is no right to counsel for a photographic lineup

Fifth and Fourteenth Amendments and Due Process

Protects the defendant from biased or prejudicial procedures and ensures the identification process is reliable

Applies at any time during the adjudication process when eye-witness identification is used and regardless of the presence of counsel

To make a showing that the identification violated due process the defendant must demonstrate:

- The identification was unnecessarily suggestive; and
- The police procedures created a substantial likelihood of misidentification

The Due-Process Approach

Regardless of whether counsel is required or even present at an identification procedure, a defendant has a right to challenge the admissibility at trial of an identification that followed an **unduly suggestive procedure**. Although this notion seems logical, in the decade following the *Wade* trilogy, the lower courts struggled to determine when such an identification should be excluded from evidence. Should the fact that the police unnecessarily used suggestive identification procedures require that testimony about the out-of-court identification be excluded? Or should the reliability of the out-of-court identification remain the crucial issue because a witness still might be able to make a dependable identification of a suspect that they had a good opportunity to observe or even had previously known if the identification procedures were unnecessarily suggestive? In 1977, the Supreme Court resolved this controversy in *Manson v. Brathwaite.*

Manson v. Brathwaite

432 U.S. 98 (1977)

MR. JUSTICE BLACKMUN delivered the opinion of the Court.

This case presents the issue as to whether the Due Process Clause of the Fourteenth Amendment compels the exclusion, in a state criminal trial, apart from any consideration of reliability, of pretrial identification evidence obtained by a police procedure that was both suggestive and unnecessary.

I

Jimmy D. Glover, a full-time trooper of the Connecticut State Police, in 1970 was assigned to the Narcotics Division in an undercover capacity. On May 5 of that year, about 7:45 p.m., and while there was still daylight, Glover and Henry Alton Brown, an informant, went to an apartment building at 201 Westland, in Hartford, for the purpose of purchasing narcotics from "Dickie Boy" Cicero, a known narcotics dealer. Cicero, it was thought, lived on the third floor of that apartment building. Glover and Brown entered the building, observed by backup Officers D'Onofrio and Gaffey, and proceeded by stairs to the third floor. Glover knocked at the door of one of the two apartments served by the stairway. The area was illuminated by natural light from a window in the third-floor hallway. The door was opened 12 to 18 inches in response to the knock. Glover observed a man standing at the door and, behind him, a woman. Brown identified himself. Glover then asked for "two things" of narcotics. The man at the door held out his hand, and Glover gave him two $10 bills. The door closed. Soon the man returned and handed Glover two glassine bags. While the door was open, Glover stood within two feet of the person from whom he made the purchase and observed his face. Five to seven minutes elapsed from the time the door first opened until it closed the second time.

Glover and Brown then left the building. This was about eight minutes after their arrival. Glover drove to headquarters where he described the seller to D'Onofrio and Gaffey. Glover at that time did not know the identity of the seller. He described him as being "a colored man, approximately five feet eleven inches tall, dark complexion, black hair, short Afro style, and having high cheekbones, and of heavy build. He was wearing at the time blue pants and a plaid shirt." D'Onofrio, suspecting from this description that respondent might be the seller, obtained a photograph of respondent from the Records Division of the Hartford Police Department. He left it at Glover's office. D'Onofrio was not acquainted with respondent personally, but did know him by sight and had seen him "[s]everal times" prior to May 5. Glover, when alone, viewed the photograph for the first time upon his return to headquarters on May 7; he identified the person shown as the one from whom he had purchased the narcotics.

The toxicological report on the contents of the glassine bags revealed the presence of heroin. The report was dated July 16, 1970. Respondent was arrested on July 27 while visiting at the apartment of a Mrs. Ramsey on the third floor of 201 Westland. This was the apartment at which the narcotics sale had taken place on May 5.

Respondent was charged, in a two-count information, with possession and sale of heroin. At his trial in January 1971, the photograph from which Glover had identified respondent was received in evidence without objection on the part of the defense. Glover also testified that, although he had not seen respondent in the eight months that had elapsed since the sale, "there [was] no doubt whatsoever" in his mind that the person shown on the photograph was respondent. Glover also made a positive in-court identification without objection.

No explanation was offered by the prosecution for the failure to utilize a photographic array or to conduct a lineup.

Respondent, who took the stand in his own defense, testified that on May 5, the day in question, he had been ill at his Albany Avenue apartment, and that at no time on that particular day had he been at 201 Westland. His wife testified that she recalled, after her husband had refreshed her memory, that he was home all day on May 5.

The jury found respondent guilty on both counts of the information. He received a sentence of not less than six nor more than nine years. His conviction was affirmed by the Supreme Court of Connecticut.

Fourteen months later, respondent filed a petition for habeas corpus in the United States District Court for the District of Connecticut. He alleged that the admission of the identification testimony at his state trial deprived him of due process of law to which he was entitled under the Fourteenth Amendment. The District Court, by an unreported written opinion based on the court's review of the state trial transcript, dismissed respondent's petition. On appeal, the United States Court of Appeals for the Second Circuit reversed.

In brief summary, the court felt that evidence as to the photograph should have been excluded, regardless of reliability, because the examination of the single photograph was unnecessary and suggestive. And, in the court's view, the evidence was unreliable in any event. We granted certiorari.

II

Stovall v. Denno, supra, decided in 1967, concerned a petitioner who had been convicted in a New York court of murder. He was arrested the day following the crime and was taken by the police to a hospital where the victim's wife, also wounded in the assault, was a patient. After observing Stovall and hearing him speak, she identified him as the murderer. She later made an in-court identification.

On the identification issue, the Court reviewed the practice of showing a suspect singly for purposes of identification, and the claim that this was so unnecessarily suggestive and conducive to irreparable mistaken identification that it constituted a denial of due process of law. The Court noted that the practice "has been widely condemned," but it concluded that "a claimed violation of due process of law in the conduct of a confrontation depends on the totality of the circumstances surrounding it." In that case, showing Stovall to the victim's spouse "was imperative." The Court then quoted the observations of the Court of Appeals to the effect that the spouse was the only person who could possibly exonerate the accused; that the hospital was not far from the courthouse and jail; that no one knew how long she might live; that she was not able to visit the jail; and that taking Stovall to the hospital room was the only feasible procedure, and, under the circumstances, "'the usual police station line-up was out of the question.'"

Neil v. Biggers, decided in 1972, concerned a respondent who had been convicted in a Tennessee court of rape, on evidence consisting in part of the victim's visual and voice identification of Biggers at a station-house show up seven months after the crime. The victim had been in her assailant's presence for some time and had directly observed him indoors and under a full moon outdoors. She testified that she had "no doubt" that Biggers was her assailant. She previously had given the police a description of the assailant. She had made no identification of others presented at previous show ups, lineups, or through photographs. On federal habeas, the District Court held that the confrontation was so suggestive as to violate due process. The Court of Appeals affirmed. This Court reversed on that issue, and held that the evidence properly had been allowed to go to the jury. The Court reviewed Stovall and certain later cases where it had considered the scope of due process protection against the admission of evidence derived from suggestive identification procedures.

The Court concluded that general guidelines emerged from these cases as to the relationship between suggestiveness and misidentification. The admission of evidence of a showup without more does not violate due process. The Court expressed concern about the lapse of seven months between the crime and the confrontation and observed that this would be a seriously negative factor in most cases. The central question, however, was "whether under the 'totality of the circumstances' the identification was reliable even though the confrontation procedure was suggestive." *Id.*, at 199. Applying that test, the Court found no substantial likelihood of misidentification. The evidence was properly allowed to go to the jury.

III

In the present case the District Court observed that the sole evidence tying Brathwaite to the possession and sale of the heroin consisted in his identifications by the police undercover agent, Jimmy Glover. On the constitutional issue, the court stated that the first inquiry was whether the police used an impermissibly suggestive procedure in obtaining the out-of-court identification. If so, the second inquiry is whether, under all the circumstances, that suggestive procedure gave rise to a substantial likelihood of irreparable misidentification.

The court concluded that there was no substantial likelihood of irreparable misidentification. It referred to the facts: Glover was within two feet of the seller. The duration of the confrontation was at least a couple of minutes. There was natural light from a window or skylight and there was adequate light to see clearly in the hall. Glover certainly was paying attention to identify the seller. He was a trained police officer who realized that later he would have to find and arrest the person with whom he was dealing. He gave a detailed description to D'Onofrio. The reliability of this description was supported by the fact that it enabled D'Onofrio to pick out a single photograph that was thereafter positively identified by Glover. Only two days elapsed between the crime and the photographic identification. Despite the fact that another eight months passed before the in-court identification, Glover had "no doubt" that Brathwaite was the person who had sold him heroin.

The Court of Appeals confirmed that the exhibition of the single photograph to Glover was impermissibly suggestive, and felt that, in addition, it was unnecessarily so. There was no emergency and little urgency.

Evidence of an identification unnecessarily obtained by impermissibly suggestive means must be excluded under Stovall. No rules less stringent than these can force police administrators and prosecutors to adopt procedures that will give fair assurance against the awful risks of misidentification. Finally, the court said, even if this conclusion were wrong, the writ, nevertheless, should issue. It took judicial notice that on May 5, 1970, sunset at Hartford was at 7:53 p.m. It characterized Glover's duty as an undercover agent as one to cause arrests to be made, and his description of the suspect as one that could have applied to hundreds of Hartford black males. The in-court identification had little meaning, for Brathwaite was at the counsel table. The fact that respondent was arrested in the very apartment where the sale was made was subject to a not implausible explanation from the respondent, although evidently not credited by the jury. And the court was troubled by the long and unexplained delay in the arrest. It was too great a danger that the respondent was convicted because he was a man D'Onofrio had previously observed near the scene, was thought to be a likely offender, and was arrested when he was known to be in Mrs. Ramsey's apartment, rather than because Glover really remembered him as the seller.

IV

Petitioner at the outset acknowledges that "the procedure in the instant case was suggestive [because only one photograph was used] and unnecessary" [because there was no emergency or exigent circumstance]. Brief for Petitioner 10; Tr of Oral Arg 7. The respondent, in agreement with the Court of Appeals, proposes a per se rule of exclusion that he claims is dictated by the demands of the Fourteenth Amendment's guarantee of due process. He rightly observes that this is the first case in which this Court has had occasion to rule upon strictly post-Stovall out-of-court identification evidence of the challenged kind.

Since the decision in Biggers, the Courts of Appeals appear to have developed at least two approaches to such evidence. The first, or per se approach, employed by the Second Circuit in the present case, focuses on the procedures employed and requires exclusion of the out-of-court identification evidence, without regard to reliability, whenever it has been obtained through unnecessarily suggestive confrontation procedures. The justifications advanced are the elimination of evidence of uncertain reliability, deterrence of the police and prosecutors, and the stated fair assurance against the awful risks of misidentification.

The second, or more lenient, approach is one that continues to rely on the totality of the circumstances. It permits the admission of the confrontation evidence if, despite the suggestive aspect, the out-of-court identification possesses certain features of reliability. Its adherents feel that the per se approach is not mandated by the Due Process Clause of the Fourteenth Amendment. This second approach, in contrast to the other, is ad hoc and serves to limit the societal costs imposed by a sanction that excludes relevant evidence from consideration and evaluation by the trier of fact.

The respondent here stresses the need for deterrence of improper identification practice, a factor he regards as preeminent. Photographic identification, it is said, continues to be needlessly employed. He notes that the legislative regulation the Court had *Wade* would engender, has not been forthcoming. He argues that a totality rule cannot be expected to have a significant deterrent impact; only a strict rule of exclusion will have direct and immediate impact on law enforcement agents. Identification evidence is so convincing to the jury that sweeping exclusionary rules are required. Fairness of the trial is threatened by suggestive confrontation evidence, and thus, it is said, an exclusionary rule has an established constitutional predicate.

There are, of course, several interests to be considered and taken into account. Usually the witness must testify about an encounter with a total stranger under circumstances of emergency or emotional stress. The witness' recollection of the stranger can be distorted easily by the circumstances or by later actions of the police. Thus, Wade and its companion cases reflect the concern that the jury not hear eyewitness testimony unless that evidence has aspects of reliability. It must be observed that both approaches before us are responsive to this concern. The per se rule, however, goes too far since its application automatically and peremptorily, and without consideration of alleviating factors, keeps evidence from the jury that is reliable and relevant.

The second factor is deterrence. Although the per se approach has the more significant deterrent effect, the totality approach also has an influence on police behavior. The police will guard against unnecessarily suggestive procedures under the totality rule, as well as the per se one, for fear that their actions will lead to the exclusion of identifications as unreliable.

The third factor is the effect on the administration of justice. Here the per se approach suffers serious drawbacks. Since it denies the trier reliable evidence, it may result, on occasion, in the guilty going free.

Certainly, inflexible rules of exclusion, that may frustrate rather than promote justice, have not been viewed recently by this Court with unlimited enthusiasm.

The standard, after all, is that of fairness as required by the Due Process Clause of the Fourteenth Amendment. Stovall, with its reference to the totality of the circumstances, and Biggers, with its continuing stress on the same totality, did not, singly or together, establish a strict exclusionary rule or new standard of due process.

We therefore conclude that reliability is the linchpin in determining the admissibility of identification testimony for both pre- and post-Stovall confrontations. The factors to be considered are set out in Biggers. These include the opportunity of the witness to view the criminal at the time of the crime, the witness' degree of attention, the accuracy of his prior description of the criminal, the level of certainty demonstrated at the confrontation, and the time between the crime and the confrontation. Against these factors is to be weighed the corrupting effect of the suggestive identification itself.

V

We turn, then, to the facts of this case and apply the analysis:

1. The opportunity to view. Glover testified that for two to three minutes he stood at the apartment door, within two feet of the respondent. The door opened twice, and each time the man stood at the door. The moments passed, the conversation took place, and payment was made. Glover looked directly at his vendor. It was near sunset, to be sure, but the sun had not yet set, so it was not dark or even dusk or twilight. Natural light from outside entered the hallway through a window. There was natural light, as well, from inside the apartment.

2. The degree of attention. Glover was not a casual or passing observer, as is so often the case with eyewitness identification. Trooper Glover was a trained police officer on duty — and specialized and dangerous duty — when he called at the third floor of 201 Westland in Hartford on May 5, 1970. It is true that Glover's duty was that of ferreting out narcotics offenders and that he would be expected in his work to produce results. But it is also true that, as a specially trained, assigned, and experienced officer, he could be expected to pay scrupulous attention to detail, for he knew that subsequently he would have to find and arrest his vendor. In addition, he knew that his claimed observations would be subject later to close scrutiny and examination at any trial.

3. The accuracy of the description. Glover's description was given to D'Onofrio within minutes after the transaction. It included the vendor's race, his height, his build, the color and style of his hair, and the high cheekbone facial feature. It also included clothing the vendor wore. No claim has been made that respondent did not possess the physical characteristics so described. D'Onofrio reacted positively at once. Two days later, when Glover was alone, he viewed the photograph D'Onofrio produced and identified its subject as the narcotics seller.

4. The witness' level of certainty. There is no dispute that the photograph in question was that of respondent. Glover, in response to a question whether the photograph was that of the person from whom he made the purchase, testified: there is no question whatsoever. This positive assurance was repeated.

5. The time between the crime and the confrontation. Glover's description of his vendor was given to D'Onofrio within minutes of the crime. The photographic identification took place only two days later. We do not have here the passage of weeks or months between the crime and the viewing of the photograph.

These indicators of Glover's ability to make an accurate identification are hardly outweighed by the corrupting effect of the challenged identification itself. Although identifications arising from single-photograph displays may be viewed in general with suspicion, we find in the instant case little pressure on the witness to acquiesce in the suggestion that such a display entails. D'Onofrio had left the photograph at Glover's office and was not present when Glover first viewed it two days after the event. There thus was little urgency and Glover could view the photograph at his leisure. And since Glover examined the photograph alone, there was no coercive pressure to make an identification arising from the presence of another. The identification was made in circumstances allowing care and reflection.

Surely, we cannot say that under all the circumstances of this case there is a very substantial likelihood of irreparable misidentification. Short of that point, such evidence is for the jury to weigh. We are content to rely upon the good sense and judgment of American juries, for evidence with some element of untrustworthiness is customary grist for the jury mill. Juries are not so susceptible that they cannot intelligently measure the weight of identification testimony that has some questionable feature.

Of course, it would have been better had D'Onofrio presented Glover with a photographic array including "so far as practicable a reasonable number of persons similar to any person then suspected whose likeness is included in the array." Model Code, §160.2(2). The use of that procedure would have enhanced the force of the identification at trial and would have avoided the risk that the evidence would be excluded as unreliable. But we are not disposed to view D'Onofrio's failure as one of constitutional dimension to be enforced by a rigorous and unbending exclusionary rule. The defect, if there be one, goes to weight and not to substance.

Mr. Justice Marshall dissenting.

Today's decision can come as no surprise to those who have been watching the Court dismantle the protections against mistaken eyewitness testimony erected a decade ago in *United States v. Wade*, 388 US 218 (1967); *Gilbert v. California*, 388 US 263 (1967); and *Stovall v. Denno*, 388 US 293 (1967). But it is still distressing to see the Court virtually ignore the teaching of experience embodied in those decisions and blindly uphold the conviction of a defendant who may well be innocent.

In determining the admissibility of the post-Stovall identification in this case, the Court considers two alternatives, a per se exclusionary rule and a totality-of-the-circumstances approach. The Court weighs three factors in deciding that the totality approach, which is essentially the test used in Biggers, should be applied. In my view, the Court wrongly evaluates the impact of these factors.

First, the Court acknowledges that one of the factors, deterrence of police use of unnecessarily suggestive identification procedures, favors the per se rule. Indeed, it does so heavily, for such a rule would make it unquestionably clear to the police they must never use a suggestive procedure when a fairer alternative is available. I have no doubt that conduct would quickly conform to the rule.

Second, the Court gives passing consideration to the dangers of eyewitness identification recognized in the Wade trilogy. It concludes, however, that the grave risk of error does not justify adoption of the per se approach because that would too often result in exclusion of relevant evidence. In my view, this conclusion totally ignores the lessons of Wade. The dangers of mistaken identification are, as Stovall held, simply too great to permit unnecessarily suggestive identifications. Neither Biggers nor the Court's opinion today points to any contrary empirical evidence. Studies since Wade have only reinforced the validity of its assessment of the dangers of identification testimony. While the Court is content to rely on the good sense and judgment of American juries, the impetus for Stovall and Wade was repeated miscarriages of justice resulting from juries' willingness to credit inaccurate eyewitness testimony.

Finally, the Court errs in its assessment of the relative impact of the two approaches on the administration of justice. The Court relies most heavily on this factor, finding that reversal is a Draconian sanction in cases where the identification is reliable despite an unnecessarily suggestive procedure used to obtain it. Relying on little more than a strong distaste for inflexible rules of exclusion, the Court rejects the per se test.

In my view, the Court's totality test will allow seriously unreliable and misleading evidence to be put before juries. Equally important, it will allow dangerous criminals to remain on the streets while citizens assume that police action has given them protection. According to my calculus, all three of the factors upon which the Court relies point to acceptance of the per se approach.

Even more disturbing than the Court's reliance on the totality test, however, is the analysis it uses, which suggests a reinterpretation of the concept of due process of law in criminal cases. The decision suggests that due process violations in identification procedures may not be measured by whether the government employed procedures violating standards of fundamental fairness. By relying on the probable accuracy of a challenged identification, instead of the necessity for its use, the Court seems to be ascertaining whether the defendant was probably guilty.

The Court holds, as *Neil v. Biggers* failed to, that a due process identification inquiry must take account of the suggestiveness of a confrontation and the likelihood that it led to misidentification, as recognized in Stovall and Wade. Thus, even if a witness did have an otherwise adequate opportunity to view a criminal, the later use of a highly suggestive identification procedure can render his testimony inadmissible. Indeed, it is my view that, assuming applicability of the totality test enunciated by the Court, the facts of the present case require that result.

I consider first the opportunity that Officer Glover had to view the suspect. Careful review of the record shows that he could see the heroin seller only for the time it took to speak three sentences of four or five short words, to hand over some money, and later after the door reopened, to receive the drugs in return. The entire face-to-face transaction could have taken as little as 15 or 20 seconds. But during this time, Glover's attention was not focused exclusively on the seller's face. He observed that the door was opened 12 to 18 inches, that there was a window in the room behind the door, and, most importantly, that there was a woman standing behind the man. Glover was, of course, also concentrating on the details of the transaction — he must have looked away from the seller's face to hand him the money and receive the drugs. The observation during the conversation thus may have been as brief as 5 or 10 seconds.

As the Court notes, Glover was a police officer trained in and attentive to the need for making accurate identifications. Nevertheless, both common sense and scholarly study indicate that while a trained observer such as a police officer is somewhat less likely to make an erroneous identification than the average untrained observer, the mere fact that he has been so trained is no guarantee that he is correct in a specific case. His identification testimony should be scrutinized just as carefully as that of the normal witness. Moreover, identifications made by policemen in highly competitive activities, such as undercover narcotic agents, should be scrutinized with special care. Yet it is just such a searching inquiry that the Court fails to make here.

Another factor on which the Court relies — the witness' degree of certainty in making the identification — is worthless as an indicator that he is correct. Even if Glover had been unsure initially about his identification of respondent's picture, by the time he was called at trial to present a key piece of evidence for the State that paid his salary, it is impossible to imagine his responding negatively to such questions as is there any doubt in your mind whatsoever that the identification was correct. As the

Court noted in Wade: it is a matter of common experience that, once a witness has picked out the accused at the pretrial confrontation, he is not likely to go back on his word later on.

Next, the Court finds that because the identification procedure took place two days after the crime, its reliability is enhanced. While such temporal proximity makes the identification more reliable than one occurring months later, the fact is that the greatest memory loss occurs within hours after an event. After that, the drop-off continues much more slowly. Thus, the reliability of an identification is increased only if it was made within several hours of the crime. If the time gap is any greater, reliability necessarily decreases.

Finally, the Court makes much of the fact that Glover gave a description of the seller to D'Onofrio shortly after the incident. Despite the Court's assertion that because "Glover himself was a Negro and unlikely to perceive only general features of 'hundreds of Hartford black males,'" as the Court of Appeals stated, the description given by Glover was actually no more than a general summary of the seller's appearance. We may discount entirely the seller's clothing, for that was of no significance later in the proceeding. Indeed, to the extent that Glover noticed clothes, his attention was diverted from the seller's face. Otherwise, Glover merely described vaguely the seller's height, skin color, hairstyle, and build. He did say that the seller had "high cheekbones," but there is no other mention of facial features, nor even an estimate of age. Conspicuously absent is any indication that the seller was a native of the West Indies, certainly something which a member of the black community could immediately recognize from both appearance and accent.

From all of this, I must conclude that the evidence of Glover's ability to make an accurate identification is far weaker than the Court finds it. In contrast, the procedure used to identify respondent was both extraordinarily suggestive and strongly conducive to error. In dismissing the corrupting effect of the suggestive identification procedure here, the Court virtually grants the police license to convict the innocent. By displaying a single photograph of respondent to the witness Glover under the circumstances in this record almost everything that could have been done wrong was done wrong.

In the first place, there was no need to use a photograph at all. Because photos are static, two-dimensional, and often outdated, they are clearly inferior in reliability to corporeal procedures. While the use of photographs is justifiable and often essential where the police have no knowledge of an offender's identity, the poor reliability of photos makes their use inexcusable where any other means of identification is available.

Here, since Detective D'Onofrio believed that he knew the seller's identity, further investigation without resort to a photographic show-up was easily possible. With little inconvenience, a corporeal lineup including Brathwaite might have been arranged.

Properly conducted, such a procedure would have gone far to remove any doubt about the fairness and accuracy of the identification.

Worse still than the failure to use an easily available corporeal identification was the display to Glover of only a single picture, rather than a photo array. With good reason, such single-suspect procedures have been widely condemned. They give no assurance that the witness can identify the criminal from among a number of persons of similar appearance, surely the strongest evidence that there was no misidentification. In *Simmons v. United States*, our first decision involving photographic identification, we recognized the danger that a witness seeing a suggestively displayed picture will retain in his memory the image of the photograph rather than of the person actually seen. Subsequent identification of the accused then shows nothing except that the picture was a good likeness. As *Simmons* warned, the danger of error is at its greatest when the police display to the witness only the picture of a single individual and is also heightened if the police indicate to the witness that they have other evidence that the person pictured committed the crime.

The use of a single picture (or the display of a single live suspect, for that matter) is a grave error, of course, because it dramatically suggests to the witness that the person shown must be the culprit. Why else would the police choose the person? And it is deeply ingrained in human nature to agree with the expressed opinions of others — particularly others who should be more knowledgeable — when making a difficult decision. In this case, moreover, the pressure was not limited to that inherent in the display of a single photograph. Glover, the identifying witness, was a state police officer on special assignment. He knew that D'Onofrio, an experienced Hartford narcotics detective, presumably familiar with local drug operations, believed respondent to be the seller. There was at work, then, both loyalty to another police officer and deference to a better-informed colleague. Finally, of course, there was Glover's knowledge that without an identification and arrest, government funds used to buy heroin had been wasted.

The Court discounts this overwhelming evidence of suggestiveness, however. It reasons that because D'Onofrio was not present when Glover viewed the photograph, there was little pressure on the witness to acquiesce in the suggestion. That conclusion blinks psychological reality. There is no doubt in my mind that even in D'Onofrio's absence, a clear and powerful message was telegraphed to Glover as he looked at respondent's photograph. He was emphatically told that, this is the man, and he responded by identifying respondent then and at trial whether or not he was in fact 'the man.'

I must conclude that this record presents compelling evidence that there was a very substantial likelihood of misidentification of respondent Brathwaite. The suggestive display of respondent's photograph to the witness Glover likely erased any independent memory that Glover had retained of the seller from his barely adequate opportunity to observe the criminal.

FURTHER CASE LAW, REFLECTIONS, AND QUESTIONS

1. Does *Brathwaite* give the police incentive to scrupulously honor a defendant's rights at an identification procedure by avoiding even the possibility of suggestiveness? If the police act improperly, what is the likely result? Is this result good for the criminal justice system?

2. How is *Brathwaite* similar to and/or different from *Stovall v. Denno* and *Neil v. Biggers*?

3. What three factors were considered by the Court in reaching its opinion in *Brathwaite*? Do these factors support the Court's conclusions?

4. Is an identification that is highly suggestive admissible in court if the police had no part in arranging it? This question was considered in *Perry v. New Hampshire*, 565 U.S. 228 (2012). In the early hours of the morning, the Nashua, New Hampshire, Police Department received a report that an African-American male was trying to break into cars parked in an apartment building's parking lot. When the responding officer asked the caller's wife to describe the man, she pointed out of her kitchen window to the parking lot and said that the man was currently there.

   Barion Perry was subsequently arrested. Before trial, Perry moved to suppress the identification because admitting it at trial would violate due process. The trial court denied the motion, and the jury found him guilty of theft. On appeal, Perry argued that the trial court erred in requiring an initial showing that police arranged a suggestive identification procedure. Suggestive circumstances alone, Perry argued, were sufficient to require the court to conduct a preliminary evaluation of the reliability of an eyewitness identification before allowing it to be presented to the jury. The New Hampshire Supreme Court rejected that argument and affirmed his conviction. Perry petitioned for certiorari review.

   The United States Supreme Court affirmed. The Court held that the Due Process Clause did not require trial judges to conduct preliminary assessments of the reliability of eyewitness identifications that were made under suggestive circumstances when the circumstances were not created by law enforcement personnel.

   > Our decisions turn on the presence of state action and aim to deter police from rigging identification procedures. When no improper law enforcement activity is involved, we hold, it suffices to test reliability through the rights and opportunities generally designed for that purpose, notably, the presence of counsel at post indictment lineups, vigorous cross-examination, protective rules of evidence, and jury instructions on both the falli-

> bility of eyewitness identification and the requirement that guilt be proved beyond a reasonable doubt. 565 U.S. at 233.

Justice Sotomayor dissented. She stated that it is not merely the act of suggestion that creates a due process problem but rather the effect of an act of suggestion on the reliability of a resulting identification. She argued that the court's ruling draws an immaterial distinction between intentionally suggestive conduct and inadvertently suggestive conduct, either of which could lead to an unfair result.

Does Justice Sotomayor have a valid point? Does the fact that she was the only dissenter suggest that, in the eyes of the Court, deterring police misconduct is a more important goal than preventing the jury from reviewing unreliable identifications?

5. Since *Brathwaite* was decided in 1977, "scholars and scientists studying eyewitness identification have uniformly criticized the *Manson* test as doctrinally flawed and inconsistent with what psychological research has taught us about the nature of human memory" (Kahn-Fogel, 2012, at 176). Kahn-Fogel (2012) conducted an empirical study of 1,471 federal cases between 1977 and 2010 involving allegedly suggestive eyewitness identification procedures. A summary of his findings calls the Court's analysis into question.

> In the final analysis, the record is discouraging, and it reveals flaws both in Manson itself and in the ways federal courts have applied Manson. First, despite the Manson Court's insistence that the decision would provide deterrence against police using suggestive identification procedures, this seems unlikely. Amongst the federal cases, courts evaluating evidence of clearly unnecessarily suggestive procedures allowed eyewitnesses exposed to those procedures to identify defendants in court more than nine times out of ten. Additionally, most courts assessing clear evidence of unnecessarily suggestive procedures either held the procedures to be acceptable or failed to make a definitive determination as to whether the procedures were improper. By failing to specifically require courts to decide whether challenged procedures are unnecessarily suggestive and by failing to give lower courts any guidance on the kinds of procedures that are unacceptable, the Supreme Court in Manson and since has ensured that Manson would, in fact, provide little deterrence against law enforcement use of inadequate identification techniques.
>
> Furthermore, a lack of clarity in the Court's prescription for assessing eyewitness certainty has led many courts to examine certainty after the eyewitness is likely to have experienced an inflated sense of confidence because of suggestion. In about one of every seven of the federal cases in

which courts examined definitively suggestive procedures, those courts clearly relied on eyewitnesses' expressions of their certainty after the eyewitnesses had already viewed the suspect procedures. This unresponsiveness of federal courts to scientific evidence showing the lack of a correlation between certainty and accuracy under such circumstances is due at least in part to the failure of the Supreme Court to correct or clarify its muddled prescription for evaluating reliability in Manson. Without doubt, federal courts have also often made similar errors in their measurements of eyewitnesses' subjective accounts of opportunity to view and degree of attention.

The data from the 1,471 federal cases thus show that Manson has been an inadequate mechanism for protecting against the admission of unreliable eyewitness evidence. Not only have federal courts very rarely suppressed in-court identifications, but they have regularly evaluated eyewitness evidence in ways that contradict undeniable scientific proof of the best means of assessing the evidence before them, and they have made no discernible improvements in their jurisprudence despite the ever-increasing body of scientific data available to them. By verifying data from scientific experiments and anecdotal accounts from decades of previous legal scholarship, this study provides powerful new evidence of what psychologists, lawyers, and legal academicians have now been arguing for decades: Manson, at least as it is currently applied, is an inadequate tool for protecting against the admission of tainted procedures and unreliable evidence. *Id.* at 224-25.

Box 9.3 You Be the Judge

The defendant, John, was arrested on a bench warrant for failure to pay several fines. Additionally, the police suspect he might be involved in a series of robberies. Shortly after the arrest, the police decided to conduct a line-up. The police selected four individuals with characteristics similar to John's. They then instructed the victim that she would see five people, and if she believed one of them was the perpetrator from last night, she should indicate him by his assigned number.

John refused to stand up at the lineup even after multiple requests because his attorney was not present. After multiple refusals, two officers picked John up, put him on his feet, and stood behind him during the line-up. The victim identified John as the perpetrator of the robbery the night before. John's attorney filed a pretrial motion to suppress the identification.

How should the trial judge decide on the admissibility of the evidence? On what basis?

See *State v. Lanos*, 14 S.W.3d 90 (Mo. App. 1999).

Expert Testimony Regarding Eyewitness Identification

The courts in each case presented in this chapter have acknowledged the vagaries of eyewitness identification in reaching their decisions. Despite these vagaries, eyewitness testimony can be very persuasive to a jury. As a result of the combination of persuasiveness and potential for inaccuracy, experts increasingly have been used at trials to explain the fallibility and complexities of eyewitness identification. As you read the following case in this area, pay careful attention to the items that affect the reliability of an identification and their relationship to those factors listed by the Supreme Court in *Brathwaite*.

State v. Guilbert

49 A.3d 705 (Conn 2012)

PALMER, J.

At approximately 11:30 p.m. on October 8, 2004, Cedric Williams and Terry Ross arrived at a bar in New London known as Ernie's Cafe (bar). Before arriving at the bar, Ross had parked his Volvo station wagon in a nearby municipal parking lot. At approximately 11:45 p.m., William Robinson arrived at the bar. About one hour later, as Robinson walked to the restroom, he was shot in the face and suffered a life-threatening wound. Police and emergency medical personnel transported Robinson first to The William W. Backus Hospital in Norwich and then to Rhode Island Hospital in Providence, Rhode Island.

At approximately 12:40 a.m. on October 9, 2004, Officer Jose Olivero of the New London police department received a radio transmission about a disturbance at the bar. As he responded to the call, he saw the defendant running away from the bar, clutching something in both hands. At trial, Olivero testified that the defendant had been wearing light blue sweatpants, a white tee shirt, and a black or dark blue bomber jacket.

At approximately 12:51 a.m., the New London police department received a 911 call about a shooting at the intersection of Hope and Hempstead Streets in New London. Police officers responding to the call found Ross' Volvo station wagon crashed into a tree. Ross and Williams were inside the vehicle, and both had been shot in the head. An examiner with the state forensic science laboratory ultimately determined that Ross and Williams had been shot with the gun that had been used to shoot Robinson.

On the evening of October 9, 2004, Detective Keith Crandall and Officer George Potts of the New London police department visited Robinson at Rhode Island Hospital. Potts and Crandall then showed Robinson several photographic arrays, and Robinson identified the defendant as the person who had shot him. Robinson gave a statement to Crandall indicating that he had known the defendant "for a while" and had "had words" with him "a couple of months" earlier. Robinson said that, when he saw the defendant in the bar, he had "a bad feeling and knew something was going to happen." Crandall prepared a written statement, and Robinson signed it. At trial, Robinson denied knowing who had shot him, denied having signed the statement, and denied that the reason why he had picked the defendant's photograph from the array was that the defendant had shot him.

Nine days after the shooting, Lashon Baldwin saw the defendant's photograph in a newspaper and gave a statement to the New London police about the incident at the intersection of Hope and Hempstead Streets. At trial, Baldwin testified to the following. At the time of the shooting, Baldwin and her cousin, Jackie Gomez, were seated in a car parked on Hempstead Street. Baldwin saw a car traveling down Hempstead Street and, as the car reached Hope Street, she heard three "loud pops." The car then came to a stop after hitting another parked car, and the defendant exited through the back door on the driver's side. The defendant was wearing "a black flight [jacket]" and "a black skully hat." Baldwin recognized the defendant and knew him as "Fats" because she had seen him as a "regular customer" in a donut shop where she had worked for more than one and one-half years. Baldwin and Gomez left the area immediately. Shortly thereafter, Baldwin received telephone calls from family members indicating that Williams, who was Baldwin's cousin, had been in the car on Hempstead Street. Baldwin returned to the area and saw Williams' body in the car. Police were present, but Baldwin did not talk to them because she was "upset" and "scared."

Gomez gave a statement to the police nine days after the shooting. At trial, he testified to the following. At approximately 1 a.m. on October 9, 2004, Gomez was with Baldwin in the car on Hempstead Street when he heard three gunshots. He looked to see what was happening and saw a car drive up Hope Street and hit another car. A person wearing a "black hoodie" and "blue jeans" exited from the car and wiped the door handle with his sleeve. The person came toward the car that Gomez and Baldwin were in, and Gomez recognized him as the defendant. Gomez knew the defendant because they previously had lived together for "quite some time." Gomez then left the area but returned upon learning that his cousin, Williams, had been shot. Although police were present, Gomez did not speak to them because he was "in shock."

Ten days after the shootings, Scott Lang, who had been at the bar when Robinson was shot, saw the defendant's photograph in a newspaper and recognized him as the person who had shot Robinson. Lang then went to the police and gave a statement. At trial, he testified to the following. On the night of the shooting, Lang was waiting in line to use the restroom at the bar when he was shoved against a door and a shot was fired. Lang was "shoulder to shoulder" with the shooter and observed that he was wearing "a black quilted jacket, possibly North Face." At trial, Lang identified the defendant as the shooter.

On October 14, 2004, police apprehended the defendant in New York. Thereafter, the defendant was tried before a jury and convicted of two counts of murder in connection with the shooting deaths of Williams and Ross, capital felony arising out of that double killing, and assault in the first degree for the shooting of Robinson.

I

We first address the defendant's claim that the trial court improperly granted the state's motion to preclude **expert testimony** on the reliability of eyewitness identifications in reliance on our decisions in *Kemp* and *McClendon*. We agree that *Kemp* and *McClendon* should be overruled and that expert testimony on eyewitness identification is admissible upon a determination by the trial court that the expert is qualified and the proffered testimony is relevant and will aid the jury.

Before trial, defense counsel indicated that he intended to call Charles A. Morgan III as an expert on eyewitness identifications. The state filed a motion to preclude Morgan's testimony on the ground that the reliability of eyewitness identifications is within the knowledge of the average juror. The trial court then conducted an evidentiary hearing on the state's motion at which Morgan proffered testimony that he is a medical doctor with "specialty training" in psychiatry and that, for the last seventeen years, he has spent 50 percent of his time researching how stress affects thought processes and memory.

Morgan testified that stress hormones are detrimental to certain aspects of memory. According to his testimony, high levels of stress impair thinking and memory formation. Morgan explained that there are three phases of memory formation — encoding, storage and retrieval — and that stress can disrupt both encoding and storage. When a subject is exposed to information about the remembered event during the storage phase — for example, when, following the event, the subject discusses the observation with someone else or sees a photograph of the person in the newspaper — the subject may incorporate the information into his or her memory and come to believe that the information actually was obtained at an earlier time. This process is known as retrofitting. Furthermore, Morgan testified that the majority of eyewitness identification researchers agree that there is little or no correlation between confidence and accuracy; in other words, an eyewitness' confidence in the accuracy of an identification is not a reliable indicator of the identification's true accuracy. Although Morgan observed that, if an eyewitness is familiar with a person, the eyewitness' identification of that person is likely to be more accurate, he explained that an identification's accuracy may be adversely affected by such factors as the length of time during which the eyewitness was able to observe the person, lighting, distance, and whether the eyewitness was paying attention.

At the conclusion of the hearing, the trial court granted the state's motion to preclude Morgan's testimony.

On appeal, the defendant contends that the trial court improperly granted the state's motion to preclude Morgan's expert testimony. The defendant argues that we should overrule *State v. Kemp,* 507 A.2d (1387), and *State v. McClendon,* 730 A.2d 1107, in which we held that expert testimony on the reliability of eyewitness identifications is unnecessary because the average juror knows about the factors affecting the reliability of eyewitness identifications and that expert testimony on the issue is disfavored because it invades the province of the jury to determine what weight to give such evidence.

We first set forth the legal principles that govern our review. The trial court has wide discretion in ruling on the admissibility of expert testimony and, unless that discretion has been abused or the ruling involves a clear misconception of the law, the trial court's decision will not be disturbed. In determining whether there has been an abuse of discretion, the ultimate issue is whether the court could reasonably conclude as it did.

This court recently articulated the test for the admission of expert testimony, which is deeply rooted in common law. Expert testimony should be admitted when: (1) the witness has a special skill or knowledge directly applicable to a matter in issue, (2) that skill or knowledge is not common to the average person, and (3) the testimony would be helpful to the court or jury in considering the issues. In other words, [i]n order to render an expert opinion the witness must be qualified to do so and there must be a factual basis for the opinion.

It is well settled that [t]he true test of the admissibility of [expert] testimony is not whether the subject matter is common or uncommon, or whether many persons or few have some knowledge of the matter; but it is whether the witnesses offered as experts have any peculiar knowledge or experience, not common to the world, which renders their opinions founded on such knowledge or experience any aid to the court or the jury in determining the questions at issue. Implicit in this standard is the requirement that the expert's knowledge or experience be directly applicable to the matter specifically in issue.

Beyond these general requirements regarding the admissibility of expert testimony, [t]here is a further hurdle to the admissibility of expert testimony when that testimony is based on scientific [evidence]. In those situations, the scientific evidence that forms the basis for the expert's opinion must undergo a validity assessment to ensure reliability. Scientific evidence should be subjected to a flexible test, with differing factors that are applied on a case-by-case basis, to determine the reliability of the scientific evidence. Scientific evidence, and expert testimony based thereon, usually is to be evaluated under a threshold admissibility standard [relating to] the reliability of the methodology underlying the evidence.

This court first addressed the admissibility of expert testimony on eyewitness identification in *State v. Kemp*, in which we concluded that the trial court properly had precluded the testimony of the defendant's expert witness. We reasoned that the reliability of eyewitness identification is within the knowledge of jurors and expert testimony generally would not assist them in determining the question. We also explained that such testimony is disfavored because it invades the province of the jury to determine what weight or effect it wishes to give to eyewitness testimony. Although we acknowledged that, in many cases the determination of guilt or innocence depends in large part on the credibility assigned to eyewitness identifications, and that in many instances identifications may be unreliable, we recognized that criminal defendants have many protections against the risk of misidentification. We specifically observed that the weaknesses of identifications can be explored on cross-examination and during counsel's final arguments to the jury. Finally, we noted that the trial court may instruct the jury, as the court had done in *Kemp*, on the critical nature of eyewitness identifications and the various factors that might affect their reliability; including delay, performance under stress and inaccuracy of prior descriptions.

This court revisited the issue in *State v. McClendon*, a case in which the defendant had sought to introduce an expert witness' testimony that the confidence of an eyewitness does not correlate to the accuracy of observation, that variables such as lighting, stress and time to observe have an impact on accuracy, that leading questions and the repetition of testimony can increase an eyewitness' confidence but not accuracy, that people remember faces best when they analyze many features and characteristics of the face rather than just one, that misleading police questions can alter memories, and that the most accurate descriptions are given immediately after a crime. We concluded that the trial court properly had excluded the proffered testimony because it was nothing outside the common experience of mankind. As we had done in *Kemp*, we observed in *McClendon* that defense counsel had been able to explore weaknesses in the eyewitness identifications on cross-examination, and that the trial court had instructed the jury on several factors that could affect the reliability of the identifications.

We now conclude that *Kemp* and *McClendon* are out of step with the widespread judicial recognition that eyewitness identifications are potentially unreliable in a variety of ways unknown to the average juror. This broad based judicial recognition tracks a near perfect scientific consensus. The extensive and comprehensive scientific research, as reflected in hundreds of peer reviewed studies and meta-analyses, convincingly demonstrates the fallibility of eyewitness identification testimony and pinpoints an array of variables that are most likely to lead to a mistaken identification. "[T]he scientific evidence is both reliable and useful." *State v. Henderson*, 208 N.J. 208, 283, 27 A.3d 872 (2011).

> Experimental methods and findings have been tested and retested, subjected to scientific scrutiny through peer-reviewed journals, evaluated through the lens of meta-analyses, and replicated at times in real-world

> settings. [C]onsensus exists among the experts within the research community. [T]he science abundantly demonstrates the many vagaries of memory encoding, storage and retrieval; the malleability of memory; the contaminating effects of extrinsic information; the influence of police interview techniques and identification procedures; and the many other factors that bear on the reliability of eyewitness identifications. *Id.*

Courts across the country now accept that (1) there is at best a weak correlation between a witness' confidence in his or her identification and its accuracy, (2) the reliability of an identification can be diminished by a witness' focus on a weapon, (3) high stress at the time of observation may render a witness less able to retain an accurate perception and memory of the observed events, (4) cross-racial identifications are considerably less accurate than same race identifications, (5) a person's memory diminishes rapidly over a period of hours rather than days or weeks, (6) identifications are likely to be less reliable in the absence of a double-blind, sequential identification procedure, (7) witnesses are prone to develop unwarranted confidence in their identifications if they are privy to postevent or postidentification information about the event or the identification, and (8) the accuracy of an eyewitness identification may be undermined by unconscious transference, which occurs when a person seen in one context is confused with a person seen in another. This list is not exhaustive; courts have permitted expert testimony on other factors deemed to affect the accuracy of eyewitness identification testimony.

Although these findings are widely accepted by scientists, they are largely unfamiliar to the average person, and, in fact, many of the findings are counterintuitive. For example, people often believe that the more confident an eyewitness is in an identification, the more likely the identification is to be accurate. Similarly, the average person is likely to believe that eyewitnesses held at gunpoint or otherwise placed in fear are likely to have been acutely observant and therefore more accurate in their identifications. Most people also tend to think that cross-racial identifications are no less likely to be accurate than same race identifications. Yet none of these beliefs is true. Indeed, laypersons commonly are unaware of the effect of the other aforementioned factors, including the rate at which memory fades, the influence of postevent or postidentification information, the phenomenon of unconscious transference, and the risks inherent in the use by police of identification procedures that are not double-blind and sequential. Moreover, although there is little if any correlation between confidence and accuracy, an eyewitness' confidence "is the most powerful single determinant of whether observers will believe that the eyewitness made an accurate identification." (Citations omitted.) G. Wells et al., "Eyewitness Identification Procedures: Recommendations for Lineups and Photospreads," 22 Law & Hum. Behav. 603, 620 (1998).

As a result of this strong scientific consensus, federal and state courts around the country have recognized that the methods traditionally employed for alerting juries to the fallibility of eyewitness identifications — cross-examination, closing argument and generalized jury instructions on the subject — frequently are not adequate to inform them of the factors affecting the reliability of such identifications.

Cross-examination, the most common method, often is not as effective as expert testimony at identifying the weaknesses of eyewitness identification testimony because cross-examination is far better at exposing lies than at countering sincere but mistaken beliefs. An eyewitness who expresses confidence in the accuracy of his or her identification may of course believe sincerely that the identification is accurate. Furthermore, although cross-examination may expose the *existence* of factors that undermine the accuracy of eyewitness identifications, it cannot effectively educate the jury about the *import* of these factors. Thus, while skillful cross-examination may succeed in exposing obvious inconsistencies in an eyewitness' account, because nothing is obvious about the psychology of eyewitness identification and most people's intuitions on the subject of identification are wrong some circumstances undoubtedly call for more than mere cross-examination of the eyewitness.

Defense counsel's closing argument to the jury that an eyewitness identification is unreliable also is an inadequate substitute for expert testimony. In the absence of evidentiary support, such an argument is likely to be viewed as little more than partisan rhetoric. This is especially true if the argument relates to a factor that is counterintuitive.

Finally, research has revealed that jury instructions that direct jurors in broad terms to exercise caution in evaluating eyewitness identifications are less effective than expert testimony in apprising the jury of the potential unreliability of eyewitness identification testimony. Generalized instructions given at the end of what might be a long and fatiguing trial, and buried in an overall charge by the court, are unlikely to have much effect on the minds of the jurors.

We now recognize that, contrary to our reasoning in *Kemp* and *McClendon*, expert testimony on the reliability of eyewitness identifications does not invade the province of the jury to determine what weight or effect it wishes to give to eyewitness testimony. An expert should not be permitted to give an opinion about the credibility or accuracy of the eyewitness testimony itself; that determination is solely within the province of the jury. Rather, the expert should be permitted to testify only about factors that generally have an adverse effect on the reliability of eyewitness identifications and are relevant to the specific eyewitness identification at issue.

We depart from *Kemp* and *McClendon* mindful of recent studies confirming what courts have long suspected, namely, mistaken eyewitness identification testimony is by far the leading cause of wrongful convictions. A highly effective safeguard against this serious and well documented risk is the admission of expert testimony on the reliability of eyewitness identification.

In summary, we conclude that the reliability of eyewitness identifications frequently is not a matter within the knowledge of an average juror and that the admission of expert testimony on the issue does not invade the province of the jury to determine what weight to give the evidence. Many of the factors affecting the reliability of eyewitness identifications are either unknown to the average juror or contrary to common assumptions, and expert testimony is an effective way to educate jurors about the risks of misidentification. To the extent that *Kemp* and *McClendon* held to the contrary, they are hereby overruled.

In light of the numerous scientifically valid studies cited previously in this opinion, we also conclude that, as a general matter, competent expert testimony predicated on those studies' findings satisfies the threshold admissibility requirement that such testimony must be based on scientific knowledge rooted in the methods and procedures of science, at least with respect to the following propositions: (1) there is at best a weak correlation between a witness' confidence in his or her identification and the identification's accuracy; (2) the reliability of an identification can be diminished by a witness' focus on a weapon; (3) high stress at the time of observation may render a witness less able to retain an accurate perception and memory of the observed events; (4) cross-racial identifications are considerably less accurate than identifications involving the same race; (5) memory diminishes most rapidly in the hours immediately following an event and less dramatically in the days and weeks thereafter; (6) an identification may be less reliable in the absence of a double-blind, sequential identification procedure; (7) witnesses may develop unwarranted confidence in their identifications if they are privy to postevent or postidentification information about the event or the identification; and (8) the accuracy of an eyewitness identification may be undermined by unconscious transference, which occurs when a person seen in one context is confused with a person seen in another.

In *State v. Henderson* the New Jersey Supreme Court appointed a special master who conducted an extensive hearing for the sole purpose of evaluating scientific and other evidence about eyewitness identifications. The hearing, which spanned ten days and produced more than 2000 pages of transcripts, included testimony from seven expert witnesses concerning more than 200 published scientific studies, articles and books. On the basis of the evidence adduced at the hearing, the special master issued a comprehensive report, virtually all of which was adopted by a unanimous New Jersey Supreme Court. The report concluded that the science regarding eyewitness identifications — including the science regarding the variables previously discussed in this opinion — is reliable, definitive and unquestionably fit for use in the courtroom.

Of course, a trial court retains broad discretion in ruling on the qualifications of expert witnesses and determining whether their opinions are relevant. Consequently, whether to permit expert testimony concerning the reliability of eyewitness identification evidence in any individual case ultimately is a matter within the sound discretion of the trial court. A trial court may bar expert testimony on the fallibility of eyewitness identifications if it reasonably concludes that the witness does not qualify as an expert or that the witness, although otherwise qualified, lacks an adequate scientific foundation for one or more of his opinions concerning the eyewitness identification at issue. Similarly, the trial court may preclude such testimony if the court reasonably determines, upon due consideration of the facts and circumstances of the case, that the particular issue presented is not beyond the ken of the average juror or that the proffered testimony would not aid the jury in resolving the issues presented.

Having concluded that our prior case law is outmoded we turn to the defendant's claim that the trial court improperly granted the state's motion and precluded him from introducing Morgan's testimony on the reliability of eyewitness identifications. To resolve this issue, we must determine whether (1) Morgan had a special skill or knowledge directly applicable to a matter in issue, (2) that skill or knowledge is not common to the average person, and (3) Morgan's testimony would have been] helpful to the jury in considering the issues. In light of the foregoing discussion, it is evident that the trial court correctly concluded that Morgan had special skill or knowledge on the issue of the reliability of eyewitness identifications, and the state does not seriously claim to the contrary. It is equally evident, in light of the data that we have reviewed and in light of Morgan's unchallenged testimony, that the trial court abused its discretion in concluding that Morgan's proposed testimony about the reliability of eyewitness identifications concerned matters of common knowledge. Therefore, the only issues that we must address at any length are whether Morgan's testimony was directly applicable to a matter in issue and whether it would have been helpful to the jury in considering the issues.

The state contends that Morgan's testimony was not applicable to the specific facts of this case and would not have been helpful to the jury because most of the eyewitnesses knew the defendant and were therefore much less likely to render a mistaken identification. We agree with the state that, although there are exceptions, identification of a person who is well-known to the eyewitness generally does not give rise to the same risk of misidentification as does the identification of a person who is not well-known to the eyewitness. We also agree that four of the five eyewitnesses in the present case — Robinson, Olivero, Baldwin, and Gomez — were familiar enough with the defendant that the risk of misidentification was small. Accordingly, we conclude that the trial court did not abuse its discretion in precluding Morgan from testifying on the reliability of the identification testimony of these four witnesses. Because the state's case concerning the murders of Ross and Williams was predicated on the testimony of three of those eyewitnesses, Olivero, Baldwin and Gomez, the defendant's claim must fail with respect to the two murder charges and the related capital felony charge.

Unlike the other eyewitnesses, however, Lang, who testified that he had observed the defendant shoot Robinson, was not so familiar with the defendant that the risk of misidentification was insignificant. In fact, Lang did not know the defendant at all.

Moreover, according to Lang, he had been standing next to the shooter at the time of the shooting and saw the defendant's photograph in the newspaper before identifying him as the shooter. We conclude that, with respect to Lang, Morgan's proposed testimony on the effect of stress on memory, the risk of retrofitting based on postevent information, and the relationship, or lack thereof, between confidence and accuracy, was relevant and would have been helpful to the jury. The trial court therefore abused its discretion in precluding Morgan's expert testimony insofar as it pertained to Lang's identification of the defendant as Robinson's assailant.

Broadly speaking, when the identity of the perpetrator is disputed and the state seeks to use eyewitness testimony to identify the defendant as the perpetrator, the defendant should be permitted to adduce relevant expert testimony on the fallibility of the eyewitness' identification, at least in the absence of an adequate substitute for the testimony, such as comprehensive and focused jury instructions. A contrary rule would unfairly restrict the defendant's opportunity to mount a defense.

FURTHER CASE LAW, REFLECTIONS, AND QUESTIONS

1. What possible downsides do you see in allowing a defendant to present testimony from an expert on eyewitness identification?
2. It is important to remember that the jury ultimately decides what weight to give to an eyewitness identification. An expert cannot testify that the witness was correct or incorrect.
3. Instead, an expert can inform the jury about factors that may impact the accuracy and reliability of an identification. Additionally, as seen in *Guilbert*, only factors that are present in the case at trial may be considered.

Conclusion

Eyewitness identification testimony is often a critical aspect of a criminal trial. Jurors tend to give more credence to the testimony of a person who has personally seen an event than to any other type of evidence presented. Thus, it is imperative that the criminal justice system does all it can to ensure the accuracy and reliability of eyewitness identifications.

As presented in this chapter, the U.S. Supreme Court and state supreme courts have mandated several procedural safeguards. A defendant has the right to have an attorney present at a lineup conducted after the commencement of formal proceedings. The right to counsel at lineups, however, is far from limitless. There is no right to counsel at a lineup conducted prior to the commencement of formal criminal proceedings. Neither is there a right to counsel at photographic lineups.

The Supreme Court has also held that all identification procedures are subject to review to ensure they were not unnecessarily suggestive or untrustworthy. A totality-of-the-circumstances approach is used to determine if the identification was unduly suggestive and likely to lead to mistaken identification. Keep in mind that even if a procedure is unduly suggestive, so long as it is reliable, it may be used at trial. In making this determination, courts consider such items as the opportunity that the witness had to observe the perpetrator, the accuracy of prior descriptions given by the witness, the witness's level of certainty, and the elapsed time between the crime and the identification procedure.

The Supreme Court has stated that reliability of eyewitness identification testimony is paramount. Thus, procedures that might be unduly suggestive but do not adversely affect the reliability of the identification should not stand in the way of the witness testifying. If the identification is not found to be unduly suggestive and unreliable, it does not violate due process and may be used at trial, subject to cross-examination by the defendant, as discussed later in the text.

KEY TERMS

corporeal lineup
critical stage
expert testimony
eyewitness
eyewitness identification
lineups
photographic lineup
show up
unduly suggestive procedure
Wade-Gilbert rule

REVIEW QUESTIONS

1. What Amendments and Constitutional protections regulate identification procedures?
2. Under what conditions does a suspect have a Constitutional right to counsel when subjected to a police lineup?
3. What is the role or purpose of having counsel at a lineup? What protections does this give the defendant?
4. What remedy is used if the police violate a suspect's right to counsel during a lineup? Can the evidence ever be used against this suspect? If so, when?

5. Does a suspect ever possess the right to have counsel present during a photographic lineup? If so, under what conditions?
6. How does due process protect a suspect during a police lineup?
7. What would an unduly suggestive police lineup look like in practice?
8. Why do you think jurors place so much emphasis on eyewitness identification?

APPLYING THE LAW

Below are three hypothetical fact scenarios. To practice your understanding of the law that you learned in this chapter and your ability to apply it, answer each question posed by applying that law to the hypothetical scenarios. Your answers should be supported by relevant caselaw and judicially created rules and tests.

1. Neil was arrested for allegedly attempting to rape a jogger in a public park. According to the victim, she was jogging in the early morning and entered a public restroom in the park. Once she entered the bathroom, a man she had never seen before entered and attempted to rape her. Fortunately, she got away, called the police, and gave them a description of the suspect. The police responded in a few minutes and saw a man fitting most of the description given by the victim walking near the scene; however, his clothes did not match her description. Neil was arrested and charged with attempted rape. Following Neil's indictment, the victim picked him out of a lineup. The police did not offer Neil an attorney prior to the lineup. At trial, and during direct examination, the prosecution asked the victim to identify Neil in open court. The defense objected.

   How should the judge rule on the defense's objection to the victim identifying Neil in open court?

2. John was arrested on a bench warrant for failure to pay several fines. The police also suspected him of being involved in a series of robberies. The police decided to conduct a line-up. John was informed he was going to participate in a lineup. However, he refused to stand up during the lineup despite multiple requests. Two officers picked John up, put him on his feet, and stood behind him during the lineup so the victim could see him. The victim identified John as the perpetrator of the robbery the night before. John's attorney filed a pretrial motion to suppress the identification. How do you think the trial judge should decide on the admissibility of the evidence?

3. Bob, a confidential informant, purchased cocaine from a group of five men in an apartment. Bob reported this to the police, who obtained a search warrant for the apartment. In the apartment and the surrounding hallway, police found nine individuals. Police handcuffed all nine and paraded them in front of Bob, who

was sitting in a patrol car. Bob identified five of the suspects as being involved in the drug deal. Several days later, the police presented Bob with a series of photo arrays. Bob identified Ira as the person who sold him drugs. Ira was subsequently indicted and appointed a lawyer. At trial, Bob identified Ira in court.

Did any of the identifications violate Ira's rights?

ORAL ARGUMENTS

Kirby v. Illinois: www.oyez.org/cases/1970-1979/1971/1971_70_5061/argument
Manson v. Brathwaite: www.oyez.org/cases/1970-1979/1976/1976_75_871/argument
United States v. Ash: www.oyez.org/cases/1970-1979/1972/1972_71_1255/argument
United States v. Wade: www.oyez.org/cases/1966/334

REFERENCES

Kahn-Fogel, N. A. (2012). Manson and its progeny. An empirical analysis of American eyewitness law. *Alabama Civil Rights & Civil Liberties Review, 3*(1), 175–226.

President's Commission on Law Enforcement and Administration of Justice. (1967). *Task force report: The police.* U.S. Government Printing Office.

Sheldon, R. G., Brown, W. B., Miller, K. S., & Fritzler, R. B. (2016). *Crime and criminal justice in American society* (2nd ed.). Waveland Press.

Urban Institute. (2022, March 20). *Criminal justice expenditures: Police, corrections, and courts.* Retrieved from: www.urban.org/policy-centers/cross-center-initiatives/state-and-local-finance-initiative/state-and-local-backgrounders/criminal-justice-police-corrections-courts-expenditures

Wells, G. L., Small, M., Penrod, S., Malpass, R. S., Fulero, S. M., & Brimacombe, C. E. (1998). Eyewitness identification procedures: Recommendations for lineups and photospreads. *Law and Human Behavior, 22*(6), 603.

Williams, G., & Hammelmann, H. A. (1963). Identification parades. *Criminal Law Review*, 479, 545–555.

CHAPTER 10

The Accused's Right to Counsel

LEARNING OBJECTIVES

After reading this chapter, students should be able to:

- Understand the inherent fallibility of eyewitness identifications
- Explain the history of the Sixth Amendment right to counsel
- Understand when a defendant has a right to counsel and when it is triggered during criminal proceedings
- Comprehend the right of self-representation and the associated requirements
- Understand the standard for finding counsel constitutionally ineffective
- Determine when and why expert testimony is allowed at trial

Introduction

Today, it is almost unthinkable that a person who is too poor to be able to hire an attorney could be forced to go to trial on a serious criminal charge without the assistance of a lawyer. A skilled legal advocate seems indispensable to advise the accused, file motions, offer evidence, cross-examine witnesses, raise objections, present arguments to a judge and jury, and provide other essentials of representation. A trial pitting a trained prosecutor against an unassisted layperson would strike most people as being unfair and unjust. Yet it was only a little over a generation ago that the Supreme Court ruled, in *Gideon v. Wainwright*, 372 U.S. 335 (1963), that poor people are constitutionally entitled to court-appointed counsel to represent them at felony trials.

The English common-law rule governing the right to counsel that was effective at the time of the American Revolution was even less forgiving than the law in this country prior to *Gideon*. At common law, criminal defendants were flatly prohibited from being represented by a lawyer at felony trials, even if they could afford to hire one. This prohibition did not apply to misdemeanor trials or cases involving treason. It was justified on the theory that the trial judge would protect the accused's interests in felony trials. Additionally, because public prosecutors rarely appeared on behalf of the government or the alleged victim in criminal cases, the accused normally was not matched against a trained legal adversary.

The Sixth Amendment to the United States Constitution, which was modeled after similar state constitutional provisions, rejected the English rule. In relevant part, the Sixth Amendment provides: "In all criminal prosecutions, the accused shall enjoy the right to have the Assistance of Counsel for his defense."

This chapter focuses on the constitutional rights of people accused or convicted of crimes to be represented by counsel — during trials, appeals, and subsequent stages of the criminal justice process. We consider several issues. Does the right to the assistance of defense counsel necessarily include the right to court-appointed counsel for indigents, *i.e.*, people who lack the financial means to hire a lawyer? If poor people do have a constitutional right to court-appointed counsel, does that right apply to the trial of all crimes, or just serious ones such as felonies? Does it apply regardless of the threatened or actual punishment, or is it a provisional right that depends on the sentence that may be or actually is imposed? Does the right to court-appointed counsel extend beyond the trial, so that convicted offenders are guaranteed legal representation on appeal or to pursue judicial review of their cases after the first appeal?

We explore a number of related questions. If a defendant has the right to an attorney, is there an implicit corollary right to forgo the services of a lawyer so that an accused is entitled to represent himself or herself at a criminal trial? When defense lawyers appear on behalf of individuals charged with a crime, are there legal and ethical limits governing how vigorously or aggressively they can represent their clients? Can (and should) defense attorneys represent clients they know to be guilty? Must a lawyer meet minimum standards of performance to provide the assistance of counsel guaranteed under the Constitution? If so, how should minimal performance norms be defined and enforced?

We begin by examining the existence and scope of the accused's right to court-appointed counsel in trials, appeals, and subsequent stages of the criminal justice process.

The Right to Counsel: Trial and Beyond

The Road to *Gideon*

Like other provisions of the federal Constitution's Bill of Rights, the Sixth Amendment originally did not apply to the states. As we have seen, not until the 1960s did the Supreme Court begin to "incorporate" specific Bill of Rights protections through the Fourteenth Amendment to make those rights applicable to state criminal proceedings. The early, seminal case involving the right to court-appointed counsel in state criminal trials, *Powell v. Alabama*, 287 U.S. 45 (1932), did not rest on the Sixth Amendment's right-to-counsel provisions; it instead relied squarely on due process principles.

In *Powell*, nine young African Americans, who would become known as the "Scottsboro boys," were charged with raping two young white women on a freight train following an altercation with several white youths. Word of the alleged assaults spread as the train headed west through northern Alabama, en route to Memphis. A large posse met the train at its scheduled Paint Rock, Alabama stop. The nine African Americans who, like many Americans during the Great Depression, were "hoboing," or "riding the rails," were removed from the train and arrested. The young men were transported to jail in the nearby town of Scottsboro. An angry mob of whites soon gathered, causing the governor to call out the state militia to help maintain order.

The alleged rapes were committed on March 25, 1931. The nine young men were arrested that same day. Under Alabama law, rape could be punished with between 10 years imprisonment and death. The defendants were indicted and arraigned in less than a week. At their arraignment, they were not asked whether they had, or were able to employ, counsel, or wished to have counsel appointed; or whether they had friends or relatives who might assist in that regard if communicated with. The trial judge took the unusual move of appointing all the members of the bar for the purpose of arraigning the defendants, and indicated that he anticipated that the members of the bar would continue to help the defendants if no counsel appeared.

The defendants' trials commenced within the week. Four sets of trials would be conducted, involving different combinations of the defendants. On the morning the trials began, Stephen Roddy, a lawyer from out of state, appeared in court at the behest of "people who are interested in these boys from Chattanooga." 287 U.S. 45, at 55. Roddy emphasized that he had not been hired to represent the defendants, that he was not prepared to represent them, and that he was unfamiliar with Alabama law. The judge reiterated that he had appointed all willing members of the local bar to represent the defendants. One local attorney, Milo Moody, volunteered "to go ahead and help" the out-of-state lawyer.

All four trials were completed within three days, and Roddy and Moody represented all of the defendants. Eight of the young men were convicted and sentenced to death. The state courts affirmed the convictions and death sentences for seven of the eight remaining defendants. The seven defendants still under sentence of death sought review by the United States Supreme Court. The Supreme Court granted certiorari in *Powell v. Alabama* to consider "whether the defendants were in substance denied the right of counsel, and if so, whether such denial infringes the due process clause of the Fourteenth Amendment." 287 U.S. 45, at 52.

The Court's opinion recounted the circumstances surrounding the trial as follows.

> The defendants, young, ignorant, illiterate, surrounded by hostile sentiment, haled back and forth under guard of soldiers, charged with an atrocious crime regarded with especial horror in the community where they were to be tried, were thus put in peril of their lives within a few moments after counsel for the first time charged with any degree of responsibility began to represent them. 287 U.S. 45, at 57–58.

The Court then had to determine whether the essential denial of legal representation to the defendants violated their due process rights. This inquiry required an assessment of whether the right involved is of such a character that it cannot be denied without violating those fundamental principles of liberty and justice which lie at the base of all our civil and political institutions. Justice Sutherland's opinion made clear that the right to the aid of counsel is of this fundamental character.

> It never has been doubted by this court, or any other, so far as we know, that notice and hearing are preliminary steps essential to the passing of an enforceable judgment, and that they, together with a legally competent tribunal having jurisdiction of the case, constitute basic elements of the constitutional requirement of due process of law....
>
> What, then, does a hearing include? Historically and in practice, in our own country, at least, it has always included the right to the aid of counsel when desired and provided by the party asserting the right. The right to be heard would be, in many cases, of little avail if it did not comprehend the right to be heard by counsel. Even the intelligent and educated layman has small and sometimes no skill in the science of law. If charged with crime, he is incapable, generally, of determining for himself whether the indictment is good or bad. He is unfamiliar with the rules of evidence. Left without the aid of counsel, he may be put on trial without a proper charge, and convicted upon incompetent evidence, or evidence irrelevant to the issue or otherwise inadmissible. He lacks both the skill and knowledge adequately to prepare his defense, even though he have a perfect one. He requires the guiding hand of counsel at every step in the proceedings against him. Without it, though he be not guilty, he faces the danger of conviction because he does not know how to establish his innocence. If that be true

> of men of intelligence, how much more true is it of the ignorant and illiterate, or those of feeble intellect. . . .
>
> In the light of the facts outlined in the forepart of this opinion — the ignorance and illiteracy of the defendants, their youth, the circumstances of public hostility, the imprisonment and the close surveillance of the defendants by the military forces, the fact that their friends and families were all in other states and communication with them necessarily difficult, and, above all, that they stood in deadly peril of their lives — we think the failure of the trial court to give them reasonable time and opportunity to secure counsel was a clear denial of due process. . . .
>
> [W]e are of opinion that, under the circumstances just stated, the necessity of counsel was so vital and imperative that the failure of the trial court to make an effective appointment of counsel was likewise a denial of due process within the meaning of the Fourteenth Amendment. Whether this would be so in other criminal prosecutions, or under other circumstances, we need not determine. All that it is necessary now to decide, as we do decide, is that, in a capital case, where the defendant is unable to employ counsel and is incapable adequately of making his own defense because of ignorance, feeble mindedness, illiteracy, or the like, it is the duty of the court, whether requested or not, to assign counsel for him as a necessary requisite of due process of law, and that duty is not discharged by an assignment at such a time or under such circumstances as to preclude the giving of effective aid in the preparation and trial of the case. To hold otherwise would be to ignore the fundamental postulate, already adverted to, that there are certain immutable principles of justice which inhere in the very idea of free government which no member of the Union may disregard. 287 U.S. 45, at 68–72.

Powell v. Alabama was a momentous decision. It was one of the first cases in which the Supreme Court ruled that state criminal procedures had violated a fundamental tenet of the federal Constitution. The Court clearly perceived the need to proceed cautiously in regulating state trials. The justices pointedly refrained from establishing a general due process right to court-appointed counsel in all state trials, or even in all state capital trials. However, the Court was less hesitant about invoking the Sixth Amendment to require the appointment of counsel for indigent defendants charged with federal crimes. The justices ruled in *Johnson v. Zerbst*, 304 U.S. 458 (1938), that "the Sixth Amendment withholds from federal courts, in all criminal proceedings, the power and authority to deprive an accused of his life or liberty unless he has or waives the assistance of counsel."

The Court's comparative reluctance to "interfere" with state trials in the right-to-counsel context was apparent in *Betts v. Brady*, 316 U.S. 455 (1942), a case decided a decade after *Powell* and four years after *Johnson v. Zerbst*. Smith Betts was charged in a Maryland state court with robbery. Too poor to be able to hire a lawyer, he asked the trial judge to appoint him one. The judge declined Betts's request, explaining the court's practice of appointing counsel for indigent defendants only in murder and rape cases. Betts thus proceeded to trial representing himself. He cross-examined prosecution witnesses, trying to discredit testimony identifying him as the robber, and summoned and examined his own witnesses to establish an alibi. Betts was described as "not helpless, but a man forty-three years old, of ordinary intelligence and ability to take care of his own interests on that narrow issue. He had once before been in a criminal court, pleaded guilty to larceny and served a sentence, and was not wholly unfamiliar with criminal procedure." 316 U.S. 455, at 472. He was convicted of the robbery charge and sentenced to eight years in prison. The Supreme Court heard his case on certiorari.

Justice Roberts framed the issue before the Court as being whether Betts' "conviction and sentence [constituted] a deprivation of his liberty without due process of law, in violation of the Fourteenth Amendment, because of the court's refusal to appoint counsel at his request." 316 U.S. 455, at 461. He emphasized that due process:

> formulates a concept less rigid and more fluid than those envisaged in other specific and particular provisions of the Bill of Rights. Its application is less a matter of rule. Asserted denial is to be tested by an appraisal of the totality of facts in a given case. That which may, in one setting, constitute a denial of fundamental fairness, shocking to the universal sense of justice, may, in other circumstances, and in the light of other considerations, fall short of such denial. 316 U.S. 455, at 462.

The Court concluded that history demonstrated that "appointment of counsel is not a fundamental right, essential to a fair trial. We are unable to say that the concept of due process obligates the states, whatever may be their own views, to furnish counsel in every case." 316 U.S. 455, at 471. The Court thus declined to adopt a general rule requiring the appointment of counsel for indigents in all state criminal trials. Stressing the relatively straightforward nature of Betts' case, and in light of Betts' personal characteristics and experience, the majority opinion concluded that Betts' trial and conviction without the assistance of counsel did not violate fundamental fairness:

> [T]he Fourteenth Amendment prohibits the conviction and incarceration of one whose trial is offensive to the common and fundamental ideas of fairness and right, and while want of counsel in a particular case may result in a conviction lacking in such fundamental fairness, we cannot say that the amendment embodies an inexorable command that no trial for any offense, or in any court, can be fairly conducted and justice accorded a defendant who is not represented by counsel. 316 U.S. 455, at 473.

Justice Black dissented. Joined by Justices Douglas and Murphy, he argued that the Sixth Amendment right to counsel fully applied to the states by operation of the

Fourteenth Amendment's due process clause. He further concluded that even under the majority opinion's due process rationale, Betts' conviction without a lawyer was inconsistent with fundamental fairness.

The holding in *Betts v. Brady* developed into a "special circumstances" rule. Although due process did not automatically require the appointment of counsel for indigents facing state criminal trials, circumstances peculiar to the case — "such as the age and education of the defendant, the conduct of the court or the prosecuting officials, and the complicated nature of the offense charged and the possible defenses thereto — [could] render criminal proceedings without counsel so apt to result in injustice as to be fundamentally unfair." *Uveges v. Pennsylvania*, 335 U.S. 437, 441 (1948).

The "special circumstances" rule derived from *Betts* prevailed, at least nominally, for 20 years. However, it proved difficult to anticipate the precise circumstances that required the appointment of counsel. By allowing a case-by-case analysis of when a defendant was entitled to counsel, the Court facilitated wide variance between courts, both within a state as well as across states, regarding under what circumstances the appointment of an attorney is required.

Two decades after *Betts* was decided, in a decision authored by Justice Black, the Supreme Court reconsidered when the Sixth Amendment mandates that defendants charged with a felony must be provided with counsel

Gideon v. Wainwright

372 U.S. 335 (1963)

MR. JUSTICE BLACK delivered the opinion of the Court.

Petitioner was charged in a Florida state court with having broken and entered a poolroom with intent to commit a misdemeanor. This offense is a felony under Florida law. Appearing in court without funds and without a lawyer, petitioner asked the court to appoint counsel for him, whereupon the following colloquy took place:

"The Court: Mr. Gideon, I am sorry, but I cannot appoint Counsel to represent you in this case. Under the laws of the State of Florida, the only time the Court can appoint Counsel to represent a Defendant is when that person is charged with a capital offense.

"The Defendant: The United States Supreme Court says I am entitled to be represented by Counsel."

Put to trial before a jury, Gideon conducted his defense about as well as could be expected from a layman. He made an opening statement to the jury, cross-examined the State's witnesses, presented witnesses in his own defense, declined to testify himself, and made a short argument "emphasizing his innocence to the charge contained in the Information filed in this case." The jury returned a verdict of guilty, and petitioner was sentenced to serve five years in the state prison.

[Gideon's state court challenge to his conviction and sentence on the ground that the trial court had violated his federal constitutional rights by refusing to appoint counsel for him was denied.]

Since 1942, when *Betts v. Brady* was decided by a divided Court, the problem of a defendant's federal constitutional right to counsel in a state court has been a continuing source of controversy and litigation in both state and federal courts. To give this problem another review here, we granted certiorari. Since Gideon was proceeding in forma pauperis, we appointed counsel to represent him and requested both sides to discuss in their briefs and oral arguments the following: "Should this Court's holding in *Betts v. Brady*, 316 US 455 (1942), be reconsidered?"

We accept *Betts v. Brady's* assumption, based as it was on our prior cases, that a provision of the Bill of Rights which is "fundamental and essential to a fair trial" is made obligatory upon the States by the Fourteenth Amendment. We think the Court in *Betts* was wrong, however, in concluding that the Sixth Amendment's guarantee of counsel is not one of these fundamental rights. Ten years before *Betts v. Brady*, this Court, after full consideration of all the historical data examined in *Betts*, had unequivocally declared that "the right to the aid of counsel is of this fundamental character." *Powell v. Alabama*. While the Court at the close of its Powell opinion did by its language, as this Court frequently does, limit its holding to the particular facts and circumstances of that case, its conclusions about the fundamental nature of the right to counsel are unmistakable.

The fact is that in deciding as it did — that "appointment of counsel is not a fundamental right, essential to a fair trial" — the Court in *Betts v. Brady* made an abrupt break with its own well-considered precedents. In returning to these old precedents, sounder we believe than the new, we but restore constitutional principles established to achieve a fair system of justice. Not only these precedents but also reason and reflection require us to recognize that in our adversary system of criminal justice, any person haled into court, who is too poor to hire a lawyer, cannot be assured a fair trial unless counsel is provided for him. This seems to us to be an obvious truth. Governments, both state and federal, quite properly spend vast sums of money to establish machinery to try defendants accused of crime. Lawyers to prosecute are everywhere deemed essential to protect the public's interest in an orderly society. Similarly, there are few defendants charged with crime, few indeed, who fail to hire the best lawyers they can get to prepare and present their defenses. That the government hires lawyers to prosecute and defendants who have the money hire lawyers to defend are the strongest indications of the widespread belief that lawyers in criminal courts are necessities, not luxuries. The right of one charged with crime to counsel may not be deemed fundamental and essential to fair trials in some countries, but it is in ours. From the very beginning, our state and national constitutions and laws have laid great emphasis on procedural and substantive safeguards designed to assure fair trials before impartial tribunals in which every defendant stands equal before the law. This noble idea cannot be realized if the poor man charged with crime has to face his accusers without a lawyer to assist him.

The Court in *Betts v. Brady* departed from the sound wisdom upon which the Court's holding in *Powell v. Alabama* rested. Florida, supported by two other States, has asked that *Betts v. Brady* be left intact. Twenty-two States, as friends of the Court, argue that *Betts* was "an anachronism when handed down" and that it should now be overruled. We agree.

FURTHER CASE LAW, REFLECTIONS, AND QUESTIONS

1. Clarence Gideon wrote the petition for writ of certiorari filed in his case in his own hand, using a pencil, and mailed it to the Supreme Court from the Florida prison in which he was incarcerated. Abe Fortas, a prominent Washington, D.C., attorney who would later be named as a Supreme Court Justice, was appointed to represent Gideon before the Supreme Court. A different court-appointed lawyer represented Gideon when his case was retried in Florida following his victory before the Supreme Court. After deliberating for a little over an hour, the jury announced its verdict: not guilty. See A. Lewis, *Gideon's Trumpet* (1964).
2. The Supreme Court made *Gideon* fully retroactive. Thus, indigent defendants who had been tried without counsel and convicted of serious crimes before *Gideon* was decided were entitled to challenge their uncounseled convictions and have them vacated, absent an effective waiver of counsel. Most states had already provided for the appointment of counsel for indigents in felony cases prior to *Gideon*. This fact, in combination with the preexisting rule of *Betts v. Brady*, made *Gideon's* retroactive impact less dramatic than it otherwise would have been.

The Right to Court-Appointed Trial Counsel for Misdemeanors

Gideon involved a felony conviction and a five-year prison sentence. It remained to be seen how comprehensive the right to court-appointed counsel would be. Specifically, did this right extend to misdemeanor trials, or to trials not resulting in a sentence of imprisonment? The following cases addressed the questions and clarified the scope of *Gideon*.

Argersinger v. Hamlin

407 U.S. 25 (1972)

MR. JUSTICE DOUGLAS delivered the opinion of the Court.

Petitioner, an indigent, was charged in Florida with carrying a concealed weapon, an offense punishable by imprisonment up to six months, a $1,000 fine, or both. The trial was to a judge, and petitioner was unrepresented by counsel. He was sentenced to serve 90 days in jail, and brought this habeas corpus action in the Florida Supreme Court, alleging that, being deprived of his right to counsel, he was unable as an indigent layman properly to raise and present to the trial court good and sufficient defenses to the charges for which he stands convicted. The Florida Supreme Court by a four-to-three decision, in ruling on the right to counsel, followed the line we marked out in *Duncan v. Louisiana*, 391 US 145 (1968), as respects the right to trial by jury and held that the right to court-appointed counsel extends only to trials "for non-petty offenses punishable by more than six months imprisonment."

The case is here on a petition for certiorari. We reverse.

The right to trial by jury guaranteed by the Sixth Amendment by reason of the Fourteenth, was limited by *Duncan v. Louisiana* to trials where the potential punishment was imprisonment of six months or more. But, as the various opinions in *Baldwin v. New York*, 399 US 66 (1970), make plain, the right to trial by jury has a different genealogy and is brigaded with a system of trial to a judge alone. While there is historical support for limiting the "deep commitment" to trial by jury to "serious criminal cases," there is no such support for a similar limitation on the right to assistance of counsel.

The Sixth Amendment extended the right to counsel beyond its common-law dimensions. But there is nothing in the language of the Amendment, its history, or in the decisions of this Court, to indicate that it was intended to embody a retraction of the right in petty offenses wherein the common law previously did require that counsel be provided. We reject, therefore, the premise that since prosecutions for crimes punishable by imprisonment for less than six months may be tried without a jury, they may also be tried without a lawyer.

Both *Powell* and *Gideon* involved felonies. But their rationale has relevance to any criminal trial, where an accused is deprived of his liberty.

The requirement of counsel may well be necessary for a fair trial even in a petty-offense prosecution. We are by no means convinced that legal and constitutional questions involved in a case that actually leads to imprisonment even for a brief period are any less complex than when a person can be sent off for six months or more.

Beyond the problem of trials and appeals is that of the guilty plea, a problem which looms large in misdemeanor as well as in felony cases. Counsel is needed so that the accused may know precisely what he is doing, so that he is fully aware of the prospect of going to jail or prison, and so that he is treated fairly by the prosecution.

In addition, the volume of misdemeanor cases, far greater in number than felony prosecutions, may create an obsession for speedy dispositions, regardless of the fairness of the result. An inevitable consequence of volume that large is the almost total preoccupation in such a court with the movement of cases. The calendar is long, speed often is substituted for care, and casually arranged out-of-court compromise too often is substituted for adjudication. Inadequate attention tends to be given to the individual defendant, whether in protecting his rights, sifting the facts at trial, deciding the social risk he presents, or determining how to deal with him after conviction.

There is evidence of the prejudice which results to misdemeanor defendants from this "assembly-line justice." One study concluded that "misdemeanants represented by attorneys are five times as likely to emerge from police court with all charges dismissed as are defendants who face similar charges without counsel." American Civil Liberties Union, *Legal Counsel for Misdemeanants, Preliminary Report* 1 (1970).

We must conclude, therefore, that the problems associated with misdemeanor and petty offenses often require the presence of counsel to insure the accused a fair trial. Mr. Justice Powell suggests that these problems are raised even in situations where there is no prospect of imprisonment. We need not consider the requirements of the Sixth Amendment as regards the right to counsel where loss of liberty is not involved, however, for here petitioner was in fact sentenced to jail. And, as we said in *Baldwin v. New York*, 399 US, at 73, "the prospect of imprisonment for however short a time will seldom be viewed by the accused as a trivial or 'petty' matter and may well result in quite serious repercussions affecting his career and his reputation."

We hold, therefore, that absent a knowing and intelligent waiver, no person may be imprisoned for any offense, whether classified as petty, misdemeanor, or felony, unless he was represented by counsel at his trial.

We do not sit as an ombudsman to direct state courts how to manage their affairs but only to make clear the federal constitutional requirement. How crimes should be classified is largely a state matter. The fact that traffic charges technically fall within the category of "criminal prosecutions" does not necessarily mean that many of them will be brought into the class where imprisonment actually occurs.

Under the rule we announce today, every judge will know when the trial of a misdemeanor starts that no imprisonment may be imposed, even though local law permits it, unless the accused is represented by counsel. He will have a measure of the seriousness and gravity of the offense and therefore know when to name a lawyer to represent the accused before the trial starts.

Reversed.

MR. JUSTICE POWELL, with whom MR. JUSTICE REHNQUIST joins, concurring in the result.

I am unable to agree with the Supreme Court of Florida that an indigent defendant, charged with a petty offense, may in every case be afforded a fair trial without the assistance of counsel. Nor can I agree with the new rule of due process, today enunciated by the Court, that "absent a knowing and intelligent waiver, no person may be imprisoned unless he was represented by counsel at his trial." It seems to me that the line should not be drawn with such rigidity.

There is a middle course, between the extremes of Florida's six-month rule and the Court's rule, which comports with the requirements of the Fourteenth Amendment. I would adhere to the principle of due process that requires fundamental fairness in criminal trials, a principle which I believe encompasses the right to counsel in petty cases whenever the assistance of counsel is necessary to assure a fair trial.

While counsel is often essential to a fair trial, this is by no means a universal fact. Some petty offense cases are complex; others are exceedingly simple. As a justification for furnishing counsel to indigents accused of felonies, this Court noted, "That government hires lawyers to prosecute and defendants who have the money hire lawyers to defend are the strongest indications of the widespread belief that lawyers in criminal courts are necessities, not luxuries." Yet government often does not hire lawyers to prosecute petty offenses; instead the arresting police officer presents the case. Nor does every defendant who can afford to do so hire lawyers to defend petty charges. Where the possibility of a jail sentence is remote and the probable fine seems small, or where the evidence of guilt is overwhelming, the costs of assistance of counsel may exceed the benefits. It is anomalous that the Court's opinion today will extend the right of appointed counsel to indigent defendants in cases where the right to counsel would rarely be exercised by nonindigent defendants.

Although the new rule is extended today only to the imprisonment category of cases, the Court's opinion foreshadows the adoption of a broad prophylactic rule applicable to all petty offenses. No one can foresee the consequences of such a drastic enlargement of the constitutional right to free counsel. But even today's decision could have a seriously adverse impact upon the day-to-day functioning of the criminal justice system. The opinion is disquietingly barren of details as to how this rule will be implemented.

There are thousands of statutes and ordinances which authorize imprisonment for six months or less, usually as an alternative to a fine. These offenses include some of the most trivial of misdemeanors, ranging from spitting on the sidewalk to certain traffic offenses. They also include a variety of more serious misdemeanors. This broad spectrum of petty offense cases daily floods the lower criminal courts. The rule laid down today will confront the judges of each of these courts with an awkward dilemma. If counsel is not appointed or knowingly waived, no sentence of imprisonment for any duration may be imposed. The judge will therefore be forced to decide in advance of trial — and without hearing the evidence — whether he will forgo entirely his judicial discretion to impose some sentence of imprisonment and abandon his responsibility to consider the full range of punishments established by the legislature. His alternatives, assuming the availability of counsel, will be to appoint counsel and retain the discretion vested in him by law, or to abandon this discretion in advance and proceed without counsel.

If the latter course is followed, the first victim of the new rule is likely to be the concept that justice requires a personalized decision both as to guilt and the sentence. The notion that sentencing should be tailored to fit the crime and the individual would have to be abandoned in many categories of offenses. In resolving the dilemma as to how to administer the new rule, judges will be tempted arbitrarily to divide petty offenses into two categories — those for which sentences of imprisonment may be imposed and those in which no such sentence will be given regardless of the statutory authorization. In creating categories of offenses which by law are imprisonable but for which he would not impose jail sentences, a judge will be overruling de facto the legislative determination as to the appropriate range of punishment for the particular offense.

The new rule announced today also could result in equal protection problems. There may well be an unfair and unequal treatment of individual defendants, depending on whether the individual judge has determined in advance to leave open the option of imprisonment. Thus, an accused indigent would be entitled in some courts to counsel while in other courts in the same jurisdiction an indigent accused of the same offense would have no counsel. Since the services of counsel may be essential to a fair trial even in cases in which no jail sentence is imposed, the results of this type of pretrial judgment could be arbitrary and discriminatory.

To avoid these equal protection problems and to preserve a range of sentencing options as prescribed by law, most judges are likely to appoint counsel for indigents in all but the most minor offenses where jail sentences are extremely rare. It is doubtful that the States possess the necessary resources to meet this sudden expansion of the right to counsel.

Perhaps the most serious potential impact of today's holding will be on our already overburdened local courts. The primary cause of "assembly line" justice is a volume of cases far in excess of the capacity of the system to handle efficiently and fairly. The Court's rule may well exacerbate delay and congestion in these courts. We are familiar with the common tactic of counsel of exhausting every possible legal avenue, often without due regard to its probable payoff. In some cases this may be the lawyer's duty; in other cases it will be done for purposes of delay. The absence of direct economic impact on the client, plus the omnipresent ineffective assistance-of-counsel claim, frequently produces a decision to litigate every issue.

There is an additional problem. The ability of various States and localities to furnish counsel varies widely. Even if there were adequate resources on a national basis, the uneven distribution of these resources — of lawyers, of facilities, and available funding — presents the most acute problem.

To require that counsel be furnished virtually every indigent charged with an imprisonable offense would be a practical impossibility for many small town courts. The community could simply not enforce its own laws.

Perhaps it will be said that I give undue weight both to the likelihood of short-term "chaos" and to the possibility of long-term adverse effects on the system. The answer may be given that if the Constitution requires the rule announced by the majority, the consequences are immaterial. If I were satisfied that the guarantee of due process required the assistance of counsel in every case in which a jail sentence is imposed or that the only workable method of insuring justice is to adopt the majority's rule, I would not hesitate to join the Court's opinion despite my misgivings as to its effect upon the administration of justice.

I would hold that the right to counsel in petty offense cases is not absolute but is one to be determined by the trial courts exercising a judicial discretion on a case-by-case basis.

It is impossible, as well as unwise, to create a precise and detailed set of guidelines for judges to follow in determining whether the appointment of counsel is necessary to assure a fair trial. Certainly three general factors should be weighed. First, the court should consider the complexity of the offense charged. For example, charges of traffic law infractions would rarely present complex legal or factual questions, but charges that contain difficult intent elements or which raise collateral legal questions, such as search-and-seizure problems, would usually be too complex for an unassisted layman. If the offense were one where the State is represented by counsel and where most defendants who can afford to do so obtain counsel, there would be a strong indication that the indigent also needs the assistance of counsel.

Second, the court should consider the probable sentence that will follow if a conviction is obtained. The more serious the likely consequences, the greater is the probability that a lawyer should be appointed.

Third, the court should consider the individual factors peculiar to each case. These, of course, would be the most difficult to anticipate. One relevant factor would be the competency of the individual defendant to present his own case. The attitude of the community toward a particular defendant or particular incident would be another consideration. But there might be other reasons why a defendant would have a peculiar need for a lawyer which would compel the appointment of counsel in a case where the court would normally think this unnecessary. Obviously, the sensitivity and diligence of individual judges would be crucial to the operation of a rule of fundamental fairness requiring the consideration of the varying factors in each case.

FURTHER CASE LAW, REFLECTIONS, AND QUESTIONS

1. Justice Douglas hints that requiring counsel to be appointed for indigent defendants who face incarceration on conviction may induce the states to reconsider the range of conduct presently defined as "criminal" and entailing jail sentences. Would such a reexamination be healthy? Is it the Supreme Court's job to instigate such changes in state criminal justice systems?
2. Among the points made by Justice Powell in his concurring opinion is that limiting the right of court-appointed counsel only to cases resulting in actual incarceration — if, indeed, that is a correct reading of *Argersinger* (*see Scott v. Illinois*, below) — would present difficult problems of administration. He pointed out that "the judge will be forced to decide in advance of trial — and without hearing the evidence — whether he will forgo entirely his judicial discretion to impose some sentence of imprisonment." Is there any apparent solution to this problem?
3. Justice Powell also observed that many state and local criminal justice systems have limited resources and could find compliance with *Argersinger* to be difficult if not impossible. Should resource constraints be a legitimate consideration for establishing a constitutional rule defining the scope of the right to counsel?
4. We consider the Sixth Amendment right to a jury trial in criminal cases in Chapter 12. Note the Court's attempt in *Argersinger* to distinguish *Duncan v. Louisiana*, where the Court refrained from ruling that the right to trial by jury necessarily applies in all state criminal cases resulting in the defendant's incarceration.

The defendant in *Argersinger* faced a maximum jail sentence of six months and was actually sentenced to 90 days in jail. What if he had been charged with the same offense but the judge decided not to send him to jail? Would the Fourteenth Amendment still require the appointment of trial counsel if he were too poor to hire one? The Court addressed this issue in *Scott v. Illinois*.

Scott v. Illinois

440 U.S. 367 (1979)

MR. JUSTICE REHNQUIST delivered the opinion of the Court.

Petitioner Scott was convicted of theft and fined $50 after a bench trial in the Circuit Court of Cook County, Ill. His conviction was affirmed by the state intermediate appellate court and then by the Supreme Court of Illinois, over Scott's contention that the Sixth and Fourteenth Amendments to the United States Constitution required that Illinois provide trial counsel to him at its expense.

Petitioner Scott was convicted of shoplifting merchandise valued at less than $150. The applicable Illinois statute set the maximum penalty for such an offense at a $500 fine or one year in jail, or both. The petitioner argues that a line of this Court's cases culminating in *Argersinger v. Hamlin* requires State provision of counsel whenever imprisonment is an authorized penalty.

We agree with the Supreme Court of Illinois that the Federal Constitution does not require a state trial court to appoint counsel for a criminal defendant such as petitioner, and we therefore affirm its judgment.

The Court held in *Duncan v. Louisiana*, 391 US 145 (1968), that the right to jury trial in federal court guaranteed by the Sixth Amendment was applicable to the States by virtue of the Fourteenth Amendment. The Court held, however: "It is doubtless true that there is a category of petty crimes or offenses which is not subject to the Sixth Amendment jury trial provision and should not be subject to the Fourteenth Amendment jury trial requirement here applied to the States. Crimes carrying possible penalties up to six months do not require a jury trial if they otherwise qualify as petty offenses." *Id.*, at 159 *Baldwin v. New York*, 399 US 66 (1970), the controlling opinion of Mr. Justice White concluded that "no offense can be deemed 'petty' for purposes of the right to trial by jury where imprisonment for more than six months is authorized."

In *Argersinger* the Court rejected arguments that social cost or a lack of available lawyers militated against its holding, in some part because it thought these arguments were factually incorrect. But they were rejected in much larger part because of the Court's conclusion that incarceration was so severe a sanction that it should not be imposed as a result of a criminal trial unless an indigent defendant had been offered appointed counsel to assist in his defense, regardless of the cost to the States implicit in such a rule. The Court in its opinion repeatedly referred to trials "where an accused is deprived of his liberty," and to "a case that actually leads to imprisonment even for a brief period."

Although the intentions of the *Argersinger* Court are not unmistakably clear from its opinion, we conclude today that *Argersinger* did indeed delimit the constitutional right to appointed counsel in state criminal proceedings. Even were the matter *res nova*, we believe that the central premise of *Argersinger* — that actual imprisonment is a penalty different in kind from fines or the mere threat of imprisonment — is eminently sound and warrants adoption of actual imprisonment as the line defining the constitutional right to appointment of counsel. *Argersinger* has proved reasonably workable, whereas any extension would create confusion and impose unpredictable, but necessarily substantial, costs on 50 quite diverse States. We therefore hold that the Sixth and Fourteenth Amendments to the United States Constitution require only that no indigent criminal defendant be sentenced to a term of imprisonment unless the State has afforded him the right to assistance of appointed counsel in his defense.

Mr. Justice Brennan dissenting.

Gideon v. Wainwright held that, because representation by counsel in a criminal proceeding is "fundamental and essential to a fair trial," the Sixth Amendment right to counsel was applicable to the States through the Fourteenth Amendment.

Earlier precedents had recognized that the assistance of appointed counsel was critical, not only to equalize the sides in an adversary criminal process, but also to give substance to other constitutional and procedural protections afforded criminal defendants. *Gideon* established the right to appointed counsel for indigent accused as a categorical requirement, making the Court's former case-by-case due process analysis unnecessary in cases covered by its holding. *Gideon* involved a felony prosecution, but that fact was not crucial to the decision; its reasoning extended, in the words of the Sixth Amendment, to "all criminal prosecutions."

In my view, petitioner could prevail in this case without extending the right to counsel beyond what was assumed to exist in *Argersinger*. Neither party in that case questioned the existence of the right to counsel in trials involving "nonpetty" offenses punishable by more than six months in jail. The question the Court addressed was whether the right applied to some "petty" offenses to which the right to jury trial did not extend.

Argersinger thus established a "two dimensional" test for the right to counsel: the right attaches to any "nonpetty" offense punishable by more than six months in jail and in addition to any offense where actual incarceration is likely regardless of the maximum authorized penalty.

The offense of "theft" with which Scott was charged is certainly not a "petty" one. It is punishable by a sentence of up to one year in jail. Scott's right to the assistance of appointed counsel is thus plainly mandated by the logic of the Court's prior cases, including *Argersinger* itself.

But rather than decide consonant with the assumption in regard to nonpetty offenses that was both implicit and explicit in *Argersinger*, the Court today retreats to the indefensible position that the *Argersinger* "actual imprisonment" standard is the *only* test for determining the boundary of the Sixth Amendment right to appointed counsel in state misdemeanor cases, thus necessarily deciding that in many cases (such as this one) a defendant will have no right to appointed counsel even when he has a constitutional right to a jury trial. This is simply an intolerable result. Not only is the "actual imprisonment" standard unprecedented as the exclusive test, but the problems inherent in its application demonstrate the superiority of an "authorized imprisonment" standard that would require the appointment of counsel for indigents accused of any offense for which imprisonment for any time is authorized.

First, the "authorized imprisonment" standard more faithfully implements the principles of the Sixth Amendment identified in *Gideon*. The procedural rules established by state statutes are geared to the nature of the potential penalty for an offense, not to the actual penalty imposed in particular cases. The authorized penalty is also a better predictor of the stigma and other collateral consequences that attach to conviction of an offense. By contrast, the "actual imprisonment" standard, as the Court's opinion in this case demonstrates, denies the right to counsel in criminal prosecutions to accuseds who suffer the severe consequences of prosecution other than imprisonment.

Second, the "authorized imprisonment" test presents no problems of administration. It avoids the necessity for time-consuming consideration of the likely sentence in each individual case before trial and the attendant problems of inaccurate predictions, unequal treatment, and apparent and actual bias.

Finally, the "authorized imprisonment" test ensures that courts will not abrogate legislative judgments concerning the appropriate range of penalties to be considered for each offense.

The apparent reason for the Court's adoption of the "actual imprisonment" standard for all misdemeanors is concern for the economic burden that an "authorized imprisonment" standard might place on the States. But, with all respect, that concern is both irrelevant and speculative. This Court's role in enforcing constitutional guarantees for criminal defendants cannot be made dependent on the budgetary decisions of state governments.

In any event, the extent of the alleged burden on the States is speculative. Although more persons are charged with misdemeanors punishable by incarceration than are charged with felonies, a smaller percentage of persons charged with misdemeanors qualify as indigent, and misdemeanor cases as a rule require far less attorney time.

Perhaps the strongest refutation of respondent's alarmist prophecies that an "authorized imprisonment" standard would wreak havoc on the States is that the standard has not produced that result in the substantial number of States that already provide counsel in all cases where imprisonment is authorized — States that include a large majority of the country's population and a great diversity of urban and rural environments. Moreover, of those States that do not yet provide counsel in all cases where any imprisonment is authorized, many provide counsel when periods of imprisonment longer than 30 days, 3 months, or 6 months are authorized. In fact, Scott would be entitled to appointed counsel under the current laws of at least 33 States.

It may well be that adoption by this Court of an "authorized imprisonment" standard would lead state and local governments to re-examine their criminal statutes. A state legislature or local government might determine that it no longer desired to authorize incarceration for certain minor offenses in light of the expense of meeting the requirements of the Constitution. In my view this re-examination is long overdue.

FURTHER CASE LAW, REFLECTIONS, AND QUESTIONS

1. Is there a principled basis for denying indigents court-appointed trial counsel when a conviction does not result in incarceration?

2. What if Scott's case involved an unusually complicated search-and-seizure issue? What if he entered a plea of not guilty by reason of insanity? What if he were mentally retarded? Can you imagine any "special circumstances," akin to those considered in the aftermath of *Betts v. Brady*, where due process would require the appointment of trial counsel for an indigent who does not face incarceration, even if the Sixth Amendment does not impose such a requirement?

3. Scott's conviction resulted only in a $50 fine. We know that *Argersinger* requires the appointment of trial counsel for indigents charged with misdemeanors whenever a jail sentence will actually be imposed on conviction. What about cases that fall somewhere between *Scott* and *Argersinger*, where, following conviction, the defendant is sentenced to jail but the sentence is suspended, conditioned upon the defendant's compliance with the terms of probation? Is such a sentence valid when imposed on an indigent who has not been represented by trial counsel? The Supreme Court confronted this issue in *Alabama v. Shelton*, 535 U.S. 654 (2002).

   LeReed Shelton was convicted of assault in a state court trial. As the trial court did not offer him the assistance of counsel at state expense, he represented himself. Shelton was sentenced to a jail term of 30 days, which the trial court immediately suspended, placing Shelton on probation for two years. After the lower appeals court affirmed the conviction and sentence, the Alabama Supreme Court reversed the defendant's suspended sentence and vacated the probation. The Supreme Court granted certiorari.

   In a 5–4 decision, the Supreme Court held that a suspended sentence that may end up in the actual deprivation of a person's liberty may not be imposed unless the defendant was accorded "the right to counsel in the prosecution for the crime charged. The Court found that "a suspended sentence is a prison term imposed for the offense of conviction. Once the prison term is triggered, the defendant is incarcerated not for the probation violation, but for the underlying offense. This is precisely what the Sixth Amendment, as interpreted in *Argersinger* and *Scott*, does not allow."

4. The right to counsel includes the right to non-attorney components of being represented by counsel. If they are found to be needed, these include investigators, office staff and expenses, and importantly, the assistance of expert witnesses. The standards established by the Supreme Court for the assistance of expert testimony are discussed in Box 10.1.

Box 10.1 Must Indigent Defendants Have Access to Expert Witnesses?

In *Ake v. Oklahoma*, 470 U.S. 68 (1985), the Supreme Court considered whether a criminal defendant had a right to the assistance of an expert witness in preparing his defense. The Court held that "when a defendant demonstrates to the trial judge that his sanity at the time of the offense is to be a significant factor at trial, the State must, at a minimum, assure the defendant access to a competent psychiatrist who will conduct an appropriate examination and assist in evaluation, preparation, and presentation of the defense" *Id.* at 83.

Later that year James McWilliams was convicted of rape and murder. Prior to sentencing, McWilliams's court-appointed counsel asked that his client be given neurological and neuropsychological testing. The court granted the request, and McWilliams was examined by Dr. John Goff, a neuropsychologist employed by the State's Department of Mental Health. Dr. Goff concluded that McWilliams was probably exaggerating his symptoms, but did suffer from genuine neuro-psychological problems. Just before the hearing, counsel also received updated and previously requested mental health records. Defense counsel requested the hearing be continued to allow him to review the new material; counsel also asked for the assistance of someone with expertise in psychological matters to review the findings. The trial court denied both requests, and McWilliams was sentenced to death. McWilliams appealed, arguing that the trial court denied him the right to meaningful expert assistance guaranteed by *Ake*. His appeal was rejected by the Alabama appellate courts as was his petition for habeas review by the District Court and Eleventh Circuit Court of Appeals.

The U.S. Supreme Court granted certiorari, and in a 5–4 decision reversed, *McWilliams v. Dunn*, 137 S.Ct. 1790 (2017). The majority held that once it is established that a defendant is indigent and that his mental condition is relevant and in question, *Ake* requires the state to provide a defendant with access to a mental health expert who is sufficiently available to the defense and independent from the prosecution to effectively "conduct an appropriate examination and assist in evaluation, preparation, and presentation of the defense." The Court went on to state that the limited exam and assistance given to McWilliams by a doctor employed by the state were insufficient to satisfy the requirements mandated by *Ake*. *Ake* requires more than just an examination. It requires that the state provide the defense with "access to a competent psychiatrist who will conduct an appropriate (1) examination and assist in (2) evaluation, (3) preparation, and (4) presentation of the defense. Therefore, even assuming that Alabama met the examination requirement, it did not meet any of the other three requirements. No expert helped the defense evaluate the Goff report or McWilliams's extensive medical records and translate these data into a legal strategy. No expert helped the defense prepare and present arguments that might, for example, have explained that McWilliams's purported malingering was not necessarily inconsistent with mental illness. No expert helped the defense prepare direct or cross-examination of any witnesses or testify at the judicial sentencing hearing.

Because Alabama's provision of mental health assistance fell so short of *Ake*'s requirements that an independent expert be provided to the defendant if needed, the Alabama courts' decision affirming McWilliams's sentence was erroneous.

1. What are your thoughts on the Court's opinion?
2. Should an expert appointed by the court to assist the defense work solely for the defense? Can such an expert be neutral and work for both parties?
3. Who should pay for an appointed expert? Should a court consider the expense, or should an expert be appointed to assist the defense regardless of cost?

The Sixth Amendment Right to Counsel and Its Application to Confessions

The *Miranda* rights are designed to protect the Fifth Amendment's privilege against compelled self-incrimination. Although they include the right to counsel and a court-appointed lawyer if the suspect cannot afford to hire an attorney, *Miranda's* protections differ from the Sixth Amendment's counsel provision. The Sixth Amendment guarantees that "in all criminal prosecutions, the accused shall enjoy the right to have the Assistance of Counsel for his defense."

The role of the Sixth Amendment in this area can be traced to *Massiah v. United States*, 377 U.S. 201 (1964). In *Massiah,* the defendant and a man named Colson had been indicted on federal narcotics charges. Massiah retained an attorney, pleaded not guilty, posted bail, and was released pending trial. Colson also was released but, unbeknownst to Massiah, decided to cooperate with the government in its investigation of the alleged narcotics trafficking. Federal agents installed a radio transmitter under the seat of Colson's car, and an agent monitored the receiving end. By prearrangement, a law enforcement officer was thus able to listen in on a lengthy conversation between Massiah and Colson in Colson's car. Massiah made several incriminating statements during this conversation. The agent monitoring the conversation testified about it at Massiah's trial, and *Massiah* was convicted of various narcotics offenses.

Massiah challenged the admissibility of the incriminating statements based on the Fourth, Fifth, and Sixth Amendments. The Court seized on the latter ground in ruling that the statements had been obtained and admitted into evidence unlawfully. Justice Stewart's opinion emphasized that Massiah had been indicted and had retained the services of counsel and that the agents had acted deliberately in attempting to secure incriminating statements from him.

The Massiah Doctrine has two primary components. First, it applies after the commencement of formal criminal proceedings. The first component, the commencement of formal criminal proceedings, while not always clear, has not been highly controversial. In *Rothgery v. Gillespie County,* 554 U.S. 1 (2008), the Supreme Court established that formal criminal proceedings begin when the suspect initially appears before a judge following an arrest. It is at this point that the Sixth Amendment right to counsel attaches.

The second component is that the police may not interrogate a suspect without the presence of an attorney. In the following section, we address this component of the *Massiah* Doctrine.

The Meaning of "Deliberately Elicit"

A suspect in police custody who volunteers an incriminating statement without being "interrogated" does not benefit from *Miranda. (see Rhode Island v. Innis,* which we considered earlier). In the Sixth Amendment context, an individual who makes an incriminating statement does not violate his or her right to counsel unless law enforcement officials "deliberately elicit" the statement. The meaning of deliberately elicit is discussed in the next several cases.

Brewer v. Williams

430 U.S. 387 (1977)

MR. JUSTICE STEWART delivered the opinion of the Court.

On the afternoon of December 24, 1968, a 10-year-old girl named Pamela Powers went with her family to the YMCA in Des Moines, Iowa, to watch a wrestling tournament in which her brother was participating. When she failed to return from a trip to the washroom, a search for her began. The search was unsuccessful.

Robert Williams, who had recently escaped from a mental hospital, was a resident of the YMCA. Soon after the girl's disappearance Williams was seen in the YMCA lobby carrying some clothing and a large bundle wrapped in a blanket. He obtained help from a 14-year-old boy in opening the street door of the YMCA and the door to his automobile parked outside. When Williams placed the bundle in the front seat of his car the boy "saw two legs in it and they were skinny and white." Before anyone could see what was in the bundle Williams drove away. His abandoned car was found the following day in Davenport, Iowa, roughly 160 miles east of Des Moines. A warrant was then issued in Des Moines for his arrest on a charge of abduction.

On the morning of December 26, a Des Moines lawyer named Henry McKnight went to the Des Moines police station and informed the officers present that he had just received a long distance call from Williams, and that he had advised Williams to turn himself in to the Davenport police. Williams did surrender that morning to the police in Davenport, and they booked him on the charge specified in the arrest warrant and gave him the warnings required by *Miranda v. Arizona*, 384 US 436 (1966).

The Davenport police then telephoned their counterparts in Des Moines to inform them that Williams had surrendered. McKnight, the lawyer, was still in the Des Moines police headquarters, and Williams conversed with McKnight on the telephone. In the presence of the Des Moines chief of police and a police detective named Leaming, McKnight advised Williams that Des Moines police officers would be driving to Davenport to pick him up, that the officers would not interrogate him or mistreat him, and that Williams was not to talk to the officers about Pamela Powers until after consulting with McKnight upon his return to Des Moines. As a result of these conversations, it was agreed between McKnight and the Des Moines police officials that Detective Leaming and a fellow officer would drive to Davenport to pick up Williams, that they would bring him directly back to Des Moines, and that they would not question him during the trip.

In the meantime, Williams was arraigned before a judge in Davenport on the outstanding arrest warrant. The judge advised him of his Miranda rights and committed him to jail. Before leaving the courtroom, Williams conferred with a lawyer named Kelly, who advised him not to make any statements until consulting with McKnight back in Des Moines.

Detective Leaming and his fellow officer arrived in Davenport about noon to pick up Williams and return him to Des Moines. Soon after their arrival they met with Williams and Kelly, who, they understood, was acting as Williams' lawyer. Detective Leaming repeated the Miranda warnings, and told Williams:

"[W]e both know that you're being represented here by Mr. Kelly and you're being represented by Mr. McKnight in Des Moines, and I want you to remember this because we'll be visiting between here and Des Moines."

Williams then conferred again with Kelly alone, and after this conference Kelly reiterated to Detective Leaming that Williams was not to be questioned about the disappearance of Pamela Powers until after he had consulted with McKnight back in Des Moines. When Leaming expressed some reservations, Kelly firmly stated that the agreement with McKnight was to be carried out — that there was to be no interrogation of Williams during the automobile journey to Des Moines. Kelly was denied permission to ride in the police car back to Des Moines with Williams and the two officers.

The two detectives, with Williams in their charge, then set out on the 160-mile drive. At no time during the trip did Williams express a willingness to be interrogated in the absence of an attorney. Instead, he stated several times that "when I get to Des Moines and see Mr. McKnight, I am going to tell you the whole story." Detective

Leaming knew that Williams was a former mental patient and knew also that he was deeply religious.

The detective and his prisoner soon embarked on a wide-ranging conversation covering a variety of topics, including the subject of religion. Then, not long after leaving Davenport and reaching the interstate highway, Detective Leaming delivered what has been referred to in the briefs and oral arguments as the "Christian burial speech." Addressing Williams as "Reverend," the detective said:

"I want to give you something to think about while we're traveling down the road. Number one, I want you to observe the weather conditions, it's raining, it's sleeting, it's freezing, driving is very treacherous, visibility is poor, it's going to be dark early this evening. They are predicting several inches of snow for tonight, and I feel that you yourself are the only person that knows where this little girl's body is, that you yourself have only been there once, and if you get a snow on top of it you yourself may be unable to find it. And, since we will be going right past the area on the way into Des Moines, I feel that we could stop and locate the body, that the parents of this little girl should be entitled to a Christian burial for the little girl who was snatched away from them on Christmas Eve and murdered. And I feel we should stop and locate it on the way in rather than waiting until morning and trying to come back out after a snowstorm and possibly not being able to find it at all."

Williams asked Detective Leaming why he thought their route to Des Moines would be taking them past the girl's body, and Leaming responded that he knew the body was in the area of Mitchellville — a town they would be passing on the way to Des Moines. Leaming then stated: "I do not want you to answer me. I don't want to discuss it any further. Just think about it as we're riding down the road."

The car continued towards Des Moines, and as it approached Mitchellville, Williams said that he would show the officers where the body was. He then directed the police to the body of Pamela Powers.

Williams was indicted for first-degree murder. Before trial, his counsel moved to suppress all evidence relating to or resulting from any statements Williams had made during the automobile ride from Davenport to Des Moines. After an evidentiary hearing, the trial judge denied the motion. He found that "an agreement was made between defense counsel and the police officials to the effect that the Defendant was not to be questioned on the return trip to Des Moines," and that the evidence in question had been elicited from Williams during "a critical stage in the proceedings requiring the presence of counsel on his request." The judge ruled, however, that Williams had "waived his right to have an attorney present during the giving of such information." The evidence in question was introduced over counsel's continuing objection at the subsequent trial. The jury found Williams guilty of murder, and the judgment of conviction was affirmed by the Iowa Supreme Court.

Williams then petitioned for a writ of habeas corpus in the United States District Court for the Southern District of Iowa. The District Court made findings of fact as summarized above, and concluded as a matter of law that the evidence in question had been wrongly admitted at Williams' trial.

The Court of Appeals for the Eighth Circuit, with one judge dissenting, affirmed this judgment. We granted certiorari to consider the constitutional issues presented.

II

There is no need to review in this case the doctrine of *Miranda v. Arizona*, a doctrine designed to secure the constitutional privilege against compulsory self-incrimination. It is equally unnecessary to evaluate the ruling of the District Court that Williams' self-incriminating statements were, indeed, involuntarily made. For it is clear that the judgment before us must in any event be affirmed upon the ground that Williams was deprived of a different constitutional right — the right to the assistance of counsel.

There can be no doubt in the present case that judicial proceedings had been initiated against Williams before the start of the automobile ride from Davenport to Des Moines. A warrant had been issued for his arrest, he had been arraigned on that warrant before a judge in a Davenport courtroom, and he had been committed by the court to confinement in jail. The State does not contend otherwise.

There can be no serious doubt, either, that Detective Leaming deliberately and designedly set out to elicit information from Williams just as surely as — and perhaps more effectively than — if he had formally interrogated him. Detective Leaming was fully aware before departing for Des Moines that Williams was being represented in Davenport by Kelly and in Des Moines by McKnight. Yet he purposely sought during Williams' isolation from his lawyers to obtain as much incriminating information as possible. Indeed, Detective Leaming conceded as much when he testified at Williams' trial:

> "Q. In fact, Captain, whether he was a mental patient or not, you were trying to get all the information you could before he got to his lawyer, weren't you?
>
> "A. I was sure hoping to find out where that little girl was, yes, sir.
>
> "Q. Well, I'll put it this way: You was [sic] hoping to get all the information you could before Williams got back to McKnight, weren't you?
>
> "A. Yes, sir."

The circumstances of this case are thus constitutionally indistinguishable from those presented in *Massiah v. United States*, 377 US 201, (1964). The petitioner in that case was indicted for violating the federal narcotics law. He retained a lawyer, pleaded not guilty, and was released on bail. While he was free on bail a federal agent succeeded by surreptitious means in listening to incriminating statements made by him. Evidence of these statements was introduced against the petitioner at his trial, and he was convicted. This Court reversed the conviction, holding that the petitioner was denied the basic protections of that guarantee the right to counsel when there was used against him at his trial evidence of his own incriminating words, which federal agents had deliberately elicited from him after he had been indicted and in the absence of his counsel.

That the incriminating statements were elicited surreptitiously in the Massiah case, and otherwise here, is constitutionally irrelevant. Rather, the clear rule of Massiah is that once adversary proceedings have commenced against an individual, he has a right to legal representation when the government interrogates him. It thus requires no wooden or technical application of the Massiah doctrine to conclude that Williams was entitled to the assistance of counsel guaranteed to him by the Sixth and Fourteenth Amendments.

III

The Iowa courts recognized that Williams had been denied the constitutional right to the assistance of counsel. They held, however, that he had waived that right during the course of the automobile trip from Davenport to Des Moines.

The District Court and the Court of Appeals were also correct in their understanding of the proper standard to be applied in determining the question of waiver as a matter of federal constitutional law — that it was incumbent upon the State to prove an intentional relinquishment or abandonment of a known right or privilege. That standard has been reiterated in many cases. We have said that the right to counsel does not depend upon a request by the defendant, and that courts indulge in every reasonable presumption against waiver. This strict standard applies equally to an alleged waiver of the right to counsel whether at trial or at a critical stage of pretrial proceedings.

We conclude, finally, that the Court of Appeals was correct in holding that, judged by these standards, the record in this case falls far short of sustaining petitioner's burden. It is true that Williams had been informed of and appeared to understand his right to counsel. But waiver requires not merely comprehension but relinquishment, and Williams' consistent reliance upon the advice of counsel in dealing with the authorities refutes any suggestion that he waived that right.

Despite Williams' express and implicit assertions of his right to counsel, Detective Leaming proceeded to elicit incriminating statements from Williams. Leaming did not preface this effort by telling Williams that he had a right to the presence of a lawyer, and made no effort at all to ascertain whether Williams wished to relinquish that right. The circumstances of record in this case thus provide no reasonable basis for finding that Williams waived his right to the assistance of counsel.

The Court of Appeals did not hold, nor do we, that under the circumstances of this case Williams could not, without notice to counsel, have waived his rights under the Sixth and Fourteenth Amendments. It only held, as do we, that he did not.

IV

The crime of which Williams was convicted was senseless and brutal, calling for swift and energetic action by the police to apprehend the perpetrator and gather evidence with which he could be convicted. No mission of law enforcement officials is more important. Yet "disinterested zeal for the public good does not assure either wisdom or right in the methods it pursues." *Haley v. Ohio*, 332 US 596, 605 (1948) (Frankfurter, J., concurring in judgment). Although we do not lightly affirm the issuance of a writ of habeas corpus in this case, so clear a violation of the Sixth and Fourteenth Amendments as here occurred cannot be condoned. The pressures on state executive and judicial officers charged with the administration of the criminal law are great, especially when the crime is murder and the victim is a small child. But it is precisely the predictability of those pressures that makes imperative a resolute loyalty to the guarantees that the Constitution extends to us all.

FURTHER CASE LAW, REFLECTIONS, AND QUESTIONS

1. The Supreme Court has consistently held that police may not deliberately elicit an incriminating statement from a suspect after they have been indicted and in the absence of counsel. How does this differ from the standard used to determine whether an interrogation violated the Fifth Amendment as discussed in *Rhode Island v Innis*?
2. What factors influenced the Supreme Court's determination that the defendant's waiver of his right to counsel was invalid? How might this influence police procedures when obtaining waivers from suspects?
3. Was Williams actually questioned by Lemming?

Several Sixth Amendment issues are raised when defendants who have been indicted and have counsel are incarcerated with police informants while awaiting trial. Particularly, does information obtained by informants for the purpose of providing it to prosecutors violate the Sixth Amendment? The Supreme Court considered the meaning of "deliberately elicit" in addressing this question in two cases decided in the 1980s.

United States v. Henry

447 U.S. 264 (1980)

MR. CHIEF JUSTICE BURGER delivered the opinion of the Court.

[The Janaf Branch of a federally insured bank was robbed in Norfolk, Virginia in August 1972. Henry was arrested in November 1972 and was indicted for the bank robbery two weeks later. He was held pending trial in the Norfolk city jail. A lawyer was appointed to represent him on November 27.]

On November 21, 1972, shortly after Henry was incarcerated. Government agents working on the Janaf robbery contacted one Nichols, an inmate at the Norfolk city jail, who for some time prior to this meeting had been engaged to provide confidential information to the Federal Bureau of Investigation as a paid informant. Nichols was then serving a sentence on local forgery charges.

Nichols informed the agent that he was housed in the same cellblock with several federal prisoners awaiting trial, including Henry. The agent told him to be alert to any statements made by the federal prisoners, but not to initiate any conversation with or question Henry regarding the bank robbery. In early December, after Nichols had been released from jail, the agent again contacted Nichols, who reported that he and Henry had engaged in conversation and that Henry had told him about the robbery of the Janaf bank. Nichols was paid for furnishing the information.

Nichols testified at trial that he had "an opportunity to have some conversations with Mr. Henry while he was in the jail," and that Henry told him that on several occasions he had gone to the Janaf Branch to see which employees opened the vault. Nichols also testified that Henry described to him the details of the robbery and stated that the only evidence connecting him to the robbery was the rental receipt. The jury was not informed that Nichols was a paid Government informant.

On the basis of this testimony, Henry was convicted of bank robbery and sentenced to a term of imprisonment of 25 years.

On August 28, 1975, Henry moved to vacate his sentence pursuant to 28 USC §2255. At this stage, he stated that he had just learned that Nichols was a paid Government informant and alleged that he had been intentionally placed in the same cell with Nichols so that Nichols could secure information about the robbery. Thus, Henry contended that the introduction of Nichols' testimony violated his Sixth Amendment right to the assistance of counsel.

The District Court again denied Henry's §2255 motion, concluding that Nichols' testimony at trial did not violate Henry's Sixth Amendment right to counsel. The Court of Appeals reversed and remanded, holding that the actions of the Government impaired the Sixth Amendment rights of the defendant under *Massiah v. United States*, 377 U. S. 201 (1964). The court noted that Nichols had engaged in conversation with Henry and concluded that, if by association, by general conversation, or both,

Nichols had developed a relationship of trust and confidence with Henry such that Henry revealed incriminating information, this constituted interference with the right to the assistance of counsel under the Sixth Amendment.

II

This Court has scrutinized post-indictment confrontations between Government agents and the accused to determine whether they are "critical stages" of the prosecution at which the Sixth Amendment right to the assistance of counsel attaches. The present case involves incriminating statements made by the accused to an undisclosed and undercover Government informant while in custody and after indictment. The Government characterizes Henry's incriminating statements as voluntary and not the result of any affirmative conduct on the part of Government agents to elicit evidence. From this, the Government argues that Henry's rights were not violated, even assuming the Sixth Amendment applies to such surreptitious confrontations; in short, it is contended that the Government has not interfered with Henry's right to counsel.

This Court first applied the Sixth Amendment to post-indictment communications between the accused and agents of the Government in *Massiah* v. *United States*. There, after the accused had been charged, he made incriminating statements to his codefendant, who was acting as an agent of the Government. In reversing the conviction, the Court held that the accused was denied "the basic protections of the Sixth Amendment when there was used against him at his trial evidence of his own incriminating words, which federal agents had deliberately elicited from him." The *Massiah* holding rests squarely on interference with his right to counsel.

The question here is whether under the facts of this case, a Government agent "deliberately elicited" incriminating statements from Henry within the meaning of *Massiah*. Three factors are important. First, Nichols was acting under instructions as a paid informant for the Government; second, Nichols was ostensibly no more than a fellow inmate of Henry; and third, Henry was in custody and under indictment at the time he was engaged in conversation by Nichols.

The Court of Appeals viewed the record as showing that Nichols deliberately used his position to secure incriminating information from Henry when counsel was not present and held that conduct attributable to the Government. Nichols had been a paid Government informant for more than a year; moreover, the FBI agent was aware that Nichols had access to Henry and would be able to engage him in conversations without arousing Henry's suspicion. The arrangement between Nichols and the agent was on a contingent-fee basis; Nichols was to be paid only if he produced useful information.

This combination of circumstances is sufficient to support the Court of Appeals' determination. Even if the agent's statement that he did not intend that Nichols would take affirmative steps to secure incriminating information is accepted, he must have known that such propinquity likely would lead to that result.

The Government argues that the federal agents instructed Nichols not to question Henry about the robbery. Yet according to his own testimony, Nichols was not a passive listener; rather, he had "some conversations with Mr. Henry" while he was in jail and Henry's incriminatory statements were "the product of this conversation." While affirmative interrogation, absent waiver, would certainly satisfy *Massiah*, we are not persuaded, as the Government contends, that *Brewer* v. *Williams*, 430 US 387 (1977), modified *Massiah's* "deliberately elicited" test. In *Massiah*, no inquiry was made as to whether Massiah or his codefendant first raised the subject of the crime under investigation.

It is undisputed that Henry was unaware of Nichols' role as a Government informant. The Government argues that this Court should apply a less rigorous standard under the Sixth Amendment where the accused is prompted by an undisclosed undercover informant than where the accused is speaking in the hearing of persons he knows to be Government officers. That line of argument, however, seeks to infuse Fifth Amendment concerns against compelled self-incrimination into the Sixth Amendment protection of the right to the assistance of counsel. An accused speaking to a known Government agent is typically aware that his statements may be used against him. The adversary positions at that stage are well established; the parties are then "arm's-length" adversaries.

When the accused is in the company of a fellow inmate who is acting by prearrangement as a Government agent, the same cannot be said. Conversation stimulated in such circumstances may elicit information that an accused would not intentionally reveal to persons known to be Government agents.

Moreover, the concept of a knowing and voluntary waiver of Sixth Amendment rights does not apply in the context of communications with an undisclosed undercover informant acting for the Government. In that setting, Henry, being unaware that Nichols was a Government agent expressly commissioned to secure evidence, cannot be held to have waived his right to the assistance of counsel.

Finally, Henry's incarceration at the time he was engaged in conversation by Nichols is also a relevant factor. As a ground for imposing the prophylactic requirements in *Miranda v. Arizona*, 384 US 436, 467 (1966), this Court noted the powerful psychological inducements to reach for aid when a person is in confinement. While the concern in *Miranda* was limited to custodial police interrogation, the mere fact of custody imposes pressures on the accused; confinement may bring into play subtle influences that will make him particularly susceptible to the ploys of undercover Government agents. The Court of Appeals determined that on this record the incriminating conversations between Henry and Nichols were facilitated by Nichols' conduct and apparent status as a person sharing a common plight.

By intentionally creating a situation likely to induce Henry to make incriminating statements without the assistance of counsel, the Government violated Henry's Sixth Amendment right to counsel.

The judgment of the Court of Appeals for the Fourth Circuit is Affirmed.

FURTHER CASE LAW, REFLECTIONS, AND QUESTIONS

1. Analyze how *United States v. Henry* clarifies the boundaries of the Sixth Amendment right to counsel. In what ways did the Court define the limits of permissible government conduct in eliciting information from an indicted defendant?
2. Consider the distinction made in *Henry* between "deliberate elicitation" of information by government agents and passive listening. Why is this distinction critical in Sixth Amendment jurisprudence?

Several years later, the Court reexamined the constitutionality of using information obtained from an informant intentionally housed in a cell with a suspect.

Kuhlmann v. Wilson

477 U.S. 436 (1986)

Justice Powell delivered the opinion of the Court

In the early morning of July 4, 1970, respondent and two confederates robbed the Star Taxicab Garage in the Bronx, New York, and fatally shot the night dispatcher. Shortly before, employees of the garage had observed respondent, a former employee there, on the premises conversing with two other men. They also witnessed respondent fleeing after the robbery, carrying loose money in his arms. After eluding the police for four days, respondent turned himself in. Respondent admitted that he had been present when the crimes took place, claimed that he had witnessed the robbery, gave the police a description of the robbers, but denied knowing them. Respondent also denied any involvement in the robbery or murder, claiming that he had fled because he was afraid of being blamed for the crimes.

After his arraignment, respondent was confined in the Bronx House of Detention, where he was placed in a cell with a prisoner named Benny Lee. Unknown to respondent, Lee had agreed to act as a police informant. Respondent made incriminating statements that Lee reported to the police. Prior to trial, respondent moved to suppress the statements on the ground that they were obtained in violation of his right to counsel. The trial court held an evidentiary hearing on the suppression motion, which revealed that the statements were made under the following circumstances.

Before respondent arrived in the jail, Lee had entered into an arrangement with Detective Cullen, according to which Lee agreed to listen to respondent's conversations and report his remarks to Cullen. Since the police had positive evidence of respondent's participation, the purpose of placing Lee in the cell was to determine the identities of respondent's confederates. Cullen instructed Lee not to ask respondent any questions, but simply to "keep his ears open" for the names of the other perpetrators. Respondent first spoke to Lee about the crimes after he looked out the cellblock window at the Star Taxicab Garage, where the crimes had occurred. Respondent said "someone's messing with me," and began talking to Lee about the robbery, narrating the same story that he had given the police at the time of his arrest. Lee advised respondent that this explanation "didn't sound too good," but respondent did not alter his story. Over the next few days, however, respondent changed details of his original account. Respondent then received a visit from his brother, who mentioned that members of his family were upset because they believed that respondent had murdered the dispatcher. After the visit, respondent again described the crimes to Lee. Respondent now admitted that he and two other men, whom he never identified, had planned and carried out the robbery, and had murdered the dispatcher. Lee informed Cullen of respondent's statements and furnished Cullen with notes that he had written surreptitiously while sharing the cell with respondent.

After hearing the testimony of Cullen and Lee, the trial court found that Cullen had instructed Lee "to ask no questions of respondent about the crime but merely to listen as to what respondent might say in his presence." The court determined that Lee obeyed these instructions, that he "at no time asked any questions with respect to the crime," and that he "only listened to respondent and made notes regarding what respondent had to say." The trial court also found that respondent's statements to Lee were "spontaneous" and "unsolicited." Under state precedent, a defendant's volunteered statements to a police agent were admissible in evidence because the police were not required to prevent talkative defendants from making incriminating statements. The jury convicted respondent of common-law murder and felonious possession of a weapon.

[After the state courts affirmed Wilson's conviction and the U.S. District Court denied his habeas corpus petition, the Second Circuit Court of Appeals reversed.]

We conclude that the Court of Appeals erred in holding that respondent was entitled to relief under *United States v. Henry,* 447 US 264 (1980). As the District Court observed, Henry left open the question whether the Sixth Amendment forbids admission in evidence of an accused's statements to a jailhouse informant who was "placed in close proximity but made no effort to stimulate conversations about the crime charged."

The primary concern of the *Massiah* line of decisions is secret interrogation by investigatory techniques that are the equivalent of direct police interrogation. Since the Sixth Amendment is not violated whenever — by luck or happenstance — the State obtains incriminating statements from the accused after the right to counsel has attached a defendant does not make out a violation of that right simply by showing that an informant, either through prior arrangement or voluntarily, reported his incriminating statements to the police. Rather, the defendant must demonstrate that the police and their informant took some action, beyond merely listening, that was designed deliberately to elicit incriminating remarks.

It is thus apparent that the Court of Appeals erred in concluding that respondent's right to counsel was violated under the circumstances of this case.

The state court found that Officer Cullen had instructed Lee only to listen to respondent for the purpose of determining the identities of the other participants in the robbery and murder. The police already had solid evidence of respondent's participation. The court further found that Lee followed those instructions, that he "at no time asked any questions" of respondent concerning the pending charges, and that he "only listened" to respondent's "spontaneous" and "unsolicited" statements. The only remark made by Lee that has any support in this record was his comment that respondent's initial version of his participation in the crimes "didn't sound too good." The Court of Appeals focused on that one remark and gave a description of Lee's interaction with respondent that is completely at odds with the facts found by the trial court. In the Court of Appeals' view, "subtly and slowly, but surely, Lee's ongoing verbal intercourse with respondent served to exacerbate respondent's already troubled state of mind." After thus revising some of the trial court's findings, and ignoring other more relevant findings, the Court of Appeals concluded that the police "deliberately elicited" respondent's incriminating statements. This conclusion conflicts with the decision of every other state and federal judge who reviewed this record.

The judgment of the Court of Appeals is reversed, and the case is remanded for further proceedings consistent with this opinion.

FURTHER CASE LAW, REFLECTIONS, AND QUESTIONS

1. Chief Justice Burger, who authored the majority opinion in *United States v. Henry* and concluded that Henry's Sixth Amendment rights had been violated, found Henry to be "clearly distinguishable" from *Kuhlmann v. Wilson*. How different are *Henry* and *Wilson?*

2. The Court concludes in *Henry* that "by intentionally creating a situation likely to induce Henry to make incriminating statements without the assistance of counsel, the Government violated Henry's Sixth Amendment right to counsel." Does this "test" seem to survive *Kuhlmann* v. *Wilson* If it does, what result would be produced by a faithful application of the test to the facts in *Wilson?*

3. Why wasn't *Miranda* an issue in either *Henry* or *Wilson? (See Illinois v. Perkins,* presented in Chapter 8.)

Resumption of Questioning Following the Invocation of Right to Counsel

Earlier, we considered when police may resume questioning after a defendant has invoked their right to remain silent. *Edwards v. Arizona*, 451 U.S. 477 (1981) was the first in a line of cases that dealt with varying situations involving the resumption of questioning after counsel is requested.

Edwards was arrested for a series of offenses and given his *Miranda* warnings. He said that he understood his rights and agreed to respond to questioning. After being told that another suspect had implicated him in the crimes, Edwards attempted to "make a deal" with the authorities. He stated, however, that "I want an attorney before making a deal." Questioning then ceased, and Edwards was removed to the county jail. The next morning, a jail guard called upon Edwards at his cell and told him that detectives wanted to speak with him. Edwards replied that he did not want to talk with anyone, but the guard responded that he "had to" and took Edwards to where the detectives were waiting. Edwards had not had the chance to confer with an attorney. The detectives readvised Edwards of his *Miranda* rights and agreed to speak with them, eventually confessing to the crimes. The state courts upheld the admissibility of the confession at Edwards's trial. The Supreme Court reversed.

> Although we have held that after initially being advised of his *Miranda* rights, the accused may himself validly waive his rights and respond to interrogation, *see North Carolina* v. *Butler*, 441 U.S. 369 (1979) the Court has strongly indicated that additional safeguards are necessary when the accused asks for counsel; and we now hold that when an accused has invoked his right to have counsel present during custodial interrogation, a valid waiver of that right cannot be established by showing only that he responded to further police-initiated custodial interrogation even if he has been advised of his rights. We further hold that an accused, such as Edwards, having expressed his desire to deal with the police only through counsel, is not subject to further interrogation by the authorities until counsel has been made available to him, unless the accused himself initiates further communication, exchanges, or conversations with the police. *Edwards v. Arizona*, 451 U.S. at 484.

In the following case, we learn more about the policies underlying the Edwards rule and what it means for a suspect to "initiate further communication, exchanges, or conversations with the police. "

Oregon v. Bradshaw

462 U.S. 1039 (1983)

Justice Rehnquist announced the judgment of the Court.

In September 1980, Oregon police were investigating the death of one Lowell Reynolds in Tillamook County. Reynolds' body had been found in his wrecked pickup truck, in which he appeared to have been a passenger at the time the vehicle left the roadway, struck a tree and an embankment, and finally came to rest on its side in a shallow creek. During the investigation of Reynolds' death, respondent was asked to accompany a police officer to the Rockaway Police Station for questioning.

Once at the station, respondent was advised of his rights as required by *Miranda* v. *Arizona,* 384 US 436 (1966). Respondent then repeated to the police his earlier account of the events of the evening of Reynolds' death, admitting that he had provided Reynolds and others with liquor for a party at Reynolds' house, but denying involvement in the traffic accident that apparently killed Reynolds.

At this point, respondent was placed under arrest for furnishing liquor to Reynolds, a minor, and again advised of his *Miranda* rights. A police officer then told respondent the officer's theory of how the traffic accident that killed Reynolds occurred; a theory which placed respondent behind the wheel of the vehicle. Respondent again denied his involvement and said "I do want an attorney before it goes very much further." The officer immediately terminated the conversation.

Sometime later respondent was transferred from the Rockaway Police Station to the Tillamook County Jail, a distance of some 10 to 15 miles. Either just before, or during, his trip from Rockaway to Tillamook, respondent inquired of a police officer, "Well, what is going to happen to me now?" The officer answered by saying: "You do not have to talk to me. You have requested an attorney and I don't want you talking to me unless you so desire because anything you say — because — since you have requested an attorney, you know, it has to be at your own free will." Respondent said he understood. There followed a discussion between respondent and the officer concerning where respondent was being taken and the offense with which he would be charged. The officer suggested that respondent might help himself by taking a polygraph examination. Respondent agreed to take such an examination, saying that he was willing to do whatever he could to clear up the matter.

The next day, following another reading to respondent of his *Miranda* rights, and respondent's signing a written waiver of those rights, the polygraph was administered. At its conclusion, the examiner told respondent that he did not believe respondent was telling the truth. Respondent then recanted his earlier story, admitting that he had been at the wheel of the vehicle in which Reynolds was killed, that he had consumed a considerable amount of alcohol, and that he had passed out at the wheel before the vehicle left the roadway and came to rest in the creek.

Respondent was charged with first-degree manslaughter, driving while under the influence of intoxicants, and driving while his license was revoked. His motion to suppress the statements described above was denied, and he was found guilty after a bench trial. The Oregon Court of Appeals, relying on our decision in *Edwards* v. *Arizona,* reversed, concluding that the statements had been obtained in violation of respondent's Fifth Amendment rights. We now conclude that the Oregon Court of Appeals misapplied our decision in *Edwards.* Respondent's question in the present case, "Well, what is going to happen to me now?", admittedly was asked prior to respondent's being "subjected to further interrogation by the authorities."

We think the Oregon Court of Appeals misapprehended the test laid down in *Edwards.* We did not there hold that the "initiation" of a conversation by a defendant such as respondent would amount to a waiver of a previously invoked right to counsel; we held that after the right to counsel had been asserted by an accused, further interrogation of the accused should not take place "unless the accused himself initiates further communication, exchanges, or conversations with the police." This was in effect a prophylactic rule, designed to protect an accused in police custody from being badgered by police officers in the manner in which the defendant in *Edwards* was.

But even if a conversation taking place after the accused has "expressed his desire to deal with the police only through counsel," is initiated by the accused, where reinterrogation follows, the burden remains upon the prosecution to show that subsequent events indicated a waiver of the Fifth Amendment right to have counsel present during the interrogation.

There can be no doubt in this case that in asking, "Well, what is going to happen to me now?", respondent "initiated" further conversation in the ordinary dictionary sense of that word. While we doubt that it would be desirable to build a superstructure of legal refinements around the word "initiate" in this context, there are undoubtedly situations where a bare inquiry by either a defendant or by a police officer should not be held to "initiate" any conversation or dialogue. There are some inquiries, such as a request for a drink of water or a request to use a telephone, that are so routine that they cannot be fairly said to represent a desire on the part of an accused to open up a more generalized discussion relating directly or indirectly to the investigation. Such inquiries or statements, by either an accused or a police officer, relating to routine incidents of the custodial relationship, will not generally "initiate" a conversation in the sense in which that word was used in *Edwards.* Although ambiguous, the respondent's question in this case as to what was going to happen to him evinced a willingness and a desire for a generalized discussion about the investigation; it was not merely a necessary inquiry arising out of the incidents of the custodial relationship. It could reasonably have been interpreted by the officer as relating generally to the investigation. On these facts we believe that there was not a violation of the *Edwards* rule.

The judgment of the Oregon Court of Appeals is therefore reversed, and the cause is remanded for further proceedings.

Justice Marshall dissenting.

The significance of the invocation of the right to counsel is premised in part on a lawyer's "unique ability to protect the Fifth Amendment rights of a client undergoing custodial interrogation." The Oregon Court of Appeals properly applied *Edwards.* When this Court in *Edwards* spoke of "initiating further communication" with the police and "reopening the dialogue with the authorities," it obviously had in mind communication or dialogue about the subject matter of the criminal investigation. The rule announced in *Edwards* was designed to ensure that any interrogation subsequent to an invocation of the right to counsel be at the instance of the accused, not the authorities. Thus, a question or statement which does not invite further interrogation before an attorney is present cannot qualify as "initiation" under *Edwards.* To hold otherwise would drastically undermine the safeguards that *Miranda and Edwards* carefully erected around the right to counsel in the custodial setting.

I agree with the plurality that, in order to constitute "initiation" under *Edwards,* an accused's inquiry must demonstrate a desire to discuss the subject matter of the criminal investigation. I am baffled, however, at the plurality's application of that standard to the facts of this case. The plurality asserts that respondent's question, "what is going to happen to me now?" evinced both "a willingness and a desire for a generalized discussion about the investigation."

If respondent's question had been posed by Jean-Paul Sartre before a class of philosophy students, it might well have evinced a desire for a "generalized" discussion. But under the circumstances of this case, it is plain that respondent's only "desire" was to find out where the police were going to take him. As the Oregon Court of Appeals stated, respondent's query came only minutes after his invocation of the right to counsel and was simply "a normal reaction to being taken from the police station and placed in a police car, obviously for transport to some destination." On these facts, I fail to see how respondent's question can be considered "initiation of a conversation about the subject matter of the criminal investigation."

FURTHER CASE LAW, REFLECTIONS, AND QUESTIONS

1. The Court's 4-1-4 division in *Bradshaw* shows that reasonable people can disagree about whether the inquiry "Well, what is going to happen to me now?" demonstrates (in the words of Justice Rehnquist) "a willingness and a desire for a generalized discussion about the investigation" or whether (in Justice Marshall's words) "It is plain that Bradshaw's only 'desire' was to find out where the police were going to take him." The interpretation of facts requires the exercise of judgment. Do the different conclusions reached in *Bradshaw* arguably reflect the

crime control and due process orientations of the respective justices, or do logical grounds seem to support the divergent interpretations of Bradshaw's question?

2. Note that while the Court was sharply divided on Bradshaw's outcome, it did agree that to constitute "initiation" under *Edwards,* an accused's inquiry must demonstrate a desire to discuss the subject matter of the criminal investigation.

As noted above, in *Michigan* v. *Mosley* the Court held that an invocation of the right to remain silent must be scrupulously honored. From the holdings in *Edwards* and *Bradshaw* it is clear that the Court has found that this standard does not apply in instances where the suspect requests an attorney. The following cases examine this distinction.

In *Arizona v. Roberson*, 486 U.S. 675 (1988), Roberson was arrested for burglary. After being given his *Miranda* warnings, he said he wanted to speak with an attorney before answering any questions. Several days later, while still in custody, he was Mirandized and questioned by a different officer about a different burglary. The second officer was unaware that Roberson had previously invoked his right to counsel. During this second interrogation, an incriminating statement was obtained. The state argued that *Mosely* controlled and that the *Edwards* rule cutting off interrogation should not apply regarding a different crime.

The Supreme Court disagreed. The Court applied a bright line application of Edwards. The Court ruled that whether the re-interrogation concerned the same or a different offense, or whether the same or different law enforcement authorities were involved in the second investigation, once a suspect has requested counsel, police cannot question them unless they initiate contact.

A suspect who has indicated his inability to cope with the pressures of custodial interrogation by requesting counsel, any further interrogation without counsel having been provided will surely exacerbate whatever compulsion to speak the suspect may be feeling. Thus, we also disagree with petitioner's contention that fresh sets of *Miranda* warnings will "reassure" a suspect who has been denied the counsel he has clearly requested that his rights have remained untrammeled. *Arizona v. Roberson*, 486 U.S. at 686.

What precisely is the suspect who invokes his or her right to counsel entitled to in the *Edwards* context? What if the police terminate their interrogation attempts when the suspect asks for a lawyer, and the suspect thereafter is allowed to confer with counsel? After the lawyer leaves, may the police approach the suspect, readminister *Miranda* warnings, and attempt to secure a waiver and elicit incriminating statements? Or must the suspect still "initiate" subsequent conversations with the police, even after the suspect has consulted his or her lawyer?

In *Minnick* v. *Mississippi,* 498 U.S. 146 (1990), the Supreme Court held that once counsel is requested, no interrogation can occur without counsel being present unless the accused waives that right. The Court found that an attorney's presence ensures that statements made during a custodial interrogation are not the product of compulsion. Edwards's essence is to preserve the integrity of an accused's choice to communicate with police only through counsel. Accordingly, when an attorney is requested, questioning must cease, and police may not reinitiate interrogation without counsel being present, whether or not the accused has consulted with his attorney.

Does this cessation of questioning last forever once an attorney is requested, or is the invocation of *Miranda* rights limited in its duration? In *Maryland v. Shatzer*, 559 U.S. 98 (2010), the Court agreed to consider how long an invocation of the right to counsel is effective. In 2003, a detective sought to question Shatzer, who was incarcerated at a Maryland prison pursuant to a prior conviction, about allegations that he had sexually abused his son. Shatzer invoked his *Miranda* right to have counsel present during interrogation, so the detective terminated the interview. In 2006, another detective reopened the case, obtained new evidence, and attempted to interrogate Shatzer, who was still incarcerated. This time, Shatzer waived his *Miranda* rights and made inculpatory statements. The trial court refused to suppress those statements, reasoning that *Edwards* did not apply because Shatzer had experienced a break in custody before the 2006 interrogation. Shatzer was convicted of sexual child abuse. On appeal, the Court of Appeals of Maryland reversed, holding that the *Edwards* protections apply to an inmate who has been continually incarcerated and had previously invoked his Fifth Amendment rights, until either counsel is made available or the inmate initiates further conversation with police. Therefore, Shatzer's confession was inadmissible.

The United States Supreme Court granted certiorari and unanimously reversed. According to the Court, when a person has been released from custody and returned to everyday life before the police later attempt interrogation, there is no reason to believe that any agreement to be questioned was coerced. A **break in custody** that is of sufficient length dissipates any coercive effects. The Court then stated that a 14-day break in custody was of sufficient length for a person to be re-acclimated to normal life. In the case of Shatzer even though he was only released back into the general prison population, he returned to his everyday life and was free of the pressures of investigative custody. Accordingly, the *Edwards* mandate was no longer warranted.

Right to Court-Appointed Counsel Beyond Trial

To this point, we have considered cases involving the right to court-appointed counsel in criminal trials. Suppose an indigent (poor) defendant facing incarceration cannot be forced to stand trial without the assistance of counsel. Does it follow that the same defendant has a constitutional right to the assistance of counsel on appeal, to challenge the legality of a conviction and sentence? Does the right to counsel extend to additional proceedings, such as petitioning the Supreme Court for a writ of certiorari, or to "postconviction" proceedings in which the state courts are asked to review issues that could not be raised on appeal, such as prosecutorial misconduct, ineffective assistance of counsel, or newly discovered evidence?

The Supreme Court addressed one issue involving appellate review of an indigent's conviction in *Griffin v. Illinois*, 351 U.S. 12 (1956), a case that preceded *Gideon* by seven years. Under Illinois law, criminal defendants were not entitled to a full review of their convictions on appeal unless they paid for a transcript and record of the trial proceedings and filed those documents with the appellate court. Griffin and a codefendant were convicted of armed robbery and sentenced to prison. They maintained that they were too poor to pay for the transcript and record needed for the appeal. Justice Black's plurality opinion, a portion of which is presented below, ruled that Illinois' practice denied indigent defendants due process and equal protection of the law.

> Surely no one would contend that either a State or the Federal Government could constitutionally provide that defendants unable to pay court costs in advance should be denied the right to plead not guilty or to defend themselves in court. Such a law would make the constitutional promise of a fair trial a worthless thing. Notice, the right to be heard, and the right to counsel would under such circumstances be meaningless promises to the poor. In criminal trials, a State can no more discriminate on account of poverty than on account of religion, race, or color. Plainly the ability to pay costs in advance bears no rational relationship to a defendant's guilt or innocence and could not be used as an excuse to deprive a defendant of a fair trial.
>
> There is no meaningful distinction between a rule which would deny the poor the right to defend themselves in a trial court and one which effectively denies the poor an adequate appellate review accorded to all who have money enough to pay the costs in advance. It is true that a State is not required by the Federal Constitution to provide appellate courts or a right to appellate review at all. But that is not to say that a State that does grant appellate review can do so in a way that discriminates against some convicted defendants on account of their poverty. Appellate review has now become an integral part of the Illinois trial system of finally adjudicating the guilt or innocence of a defendant. Consequently, at all stages of the proceedings the Due Process and Equal Protection Clauses protect persons like petitioners from invidious discriminations.
>
> All of the States now provide some method of appeal from criminal convictions, recognizing the importance of appellate review to a correct adjudication of guilt or innocence. Statistics show that a substantial proportion of criminal convictions are reversed by state appellate courts. Thus to deny adequate review to the poor means that many of them may lose their

> life, liberty, or property because of unjust convictions which appellate courts would set aside. Many States have recognized this and provided aid for convicted defendants who have a right to appeal and need a transcript but are unable to pay for it. A few have not. Such a denial is a misfit in a country dedicated to affording equal justice to all and special privileges to none in the administration of its criminal law. There can be no equal justice where the kind of trial a man gets depends on the amount of money he has. Destitute defendants must be afforded as adequate appellate review as defendants who have money enough to buy transcripts. 351 U.S. 12, at 17–19.

Griffin set the stage for the Supreme Court to consider whether the Constitution guarantees indigent criminal defendants the right to court-appointed counsel to assist with the appeal of their convictions. This issue was confronted in *Douglas v. California*, which was decided the same day as *Gideon.*

Douglas v. California

372 U.S. 353 (1963)

Mr. Justice Douglas delivered the opinion of the Court.

The record shows that petitioners requested, and were denied, the assistance of counsel on appeal, even though it plainly appeared they were indigents. In denying petitioners' requests, the California District Court of Appeal stated that it had "gone through" the record and had come to the conclusion that "no good whatever could be served by appointment of counsel." The District Court of Appeal was acting in accordance with a California rule of criminal procedure which provides that state appellate courts, upon the request of an indigent for counsel, may make an independent investigation of the record and determine whether it would be of advantage to the defendant or helpful to the appellate court to have counsel appointed. After such investigation, appellate courts should appoint counsel if in their opinion it would be helpful to the defendant or the court, and should deny the appointment of counsel only if in their judgment such appointment would be of no value to either the defendant or the court.

In *Griffin v. Illinois,* we held that a State may not grant appellate review in such a way as to discriminate against some convicted defendants on account of their poverty. There the right to a free transcript on appeal was in issue. Here the issue is whether or not an indigent shall be denied the assistance of counsel on appeal. In either case the evil is the same: discrimination against the indigent. For there can be no equal justice where the kind of an appeal a man enjoys "depends on the amount of money he has." *Griffin v. Illinois* 351 U.S. at 19.

In spite of California's forward treatment of indigents, under its present practice the type of an appeal a person is afforded in the District Court of Appeal hinges upon whether or not he can pay for the assistance of counsel. If he can, the appellate court passes on the merits of his case only after having the full benefit of written briefs and oral argument by counsel. If he cannot, the appellate court is forced to prejudge the merits before it can even determine whether counsel should be provided. At this stage in the proceedings only the barren record speaks for the indigent, and, unless the printed pages show that an injustice has been committed, he is forced to go without a champion on appeal. Any real chance he may have had of showing that his appeal has hidden merit is deprived him when the court decides on an *ex parte* examination of the record that the assistance of counsel is not required.

We are not here concerned with problems that might arise from the denial of counsel for the preparation of a petition for discretionary or mandatory review beyond the stage in the appellate process at which the claims have once been presented by a lawyer and passed upon by an appellate court. We are dealing only with the first appeal, granted as a matter of right to rich and poor alike from a criminal conviction. We need not now decide whether California would have to provide counsel for an indigent seeking a discretionary hearing from the California Supreme Court after the District Court of Appeal had sustained his conviction or whether counsel must be appointed for an indigent seeking review of an appellate affirmance of his conviction in this Court by appeal as of right or by petition for a writ of certiorari which lies within the Court's discretion. But it is appropriate to observe that a State can, consistently with the Fourteenth Amendment, provide for differences so long as the result does not amount to a denial of due process or an "invidious discrimination." Absolute equality is not required; lines can be and are drawn and we often sustain them. But where the merits of the one and only appeal an indigent has as of right are decided without benefit of counsel, we think an unconstitutional line has been drawn between rich and poor.

When an indigent is forced to run this gauntlet of a preliminary showing of merit, the right to appeal does not comport with fair procedure. There is lacking that equality demanded by the Fourteenth Amendment where the rich man, who appeals as of right, enjoys the benefit of counsel's examination into the record, research of the law, and marshalling of arguments on his behalf, while the indigent, already burdened by a preliminary determination that his case is without merit, is forced to shift for himself. The indigent, where the record is unclear or the errors are hidden, has only the right to a meaningless ritual, while the rich man has a meaningful appeal.

FURTHER CASE LAW, REFLECTIONS, AND QUESTIONS

1. *Gideon* relied on the Sixth Amendment to hold that indigents are entitled to representation by court-appointed trial counsel in felony cases. *Douglas*, conversely, relied on Fourteenth Amendment due process and equal-protection principles. Why did the *Douglas* Court not base its decision on the Sixth Amendment? And why, do you suppose, did *Gideon* not invoke due process and

equal-protection grounds? If the Court had chosen the latter constitutional foundation for *Gideon*, would you expect a different resolution of *Scott v. Illinois*?

2. How far does the principle extend that "there can be no equal justice where the kind of appeal a man enjoys 'depends on the amount of money he has'"? Should poor people be entitled to the lawyer of their choice, or simply to a lawyer? Should the right to court-appointed counsel extend beyond the first appeal and also apply when indigents petition for certiorari or seek other post-appeal review of their cases?

3. Defendants have a right to counsel at **critical stages** of a prosecution. The stages of prosecution-related events for which a defendant is entitled to counsel are presented in Box 10.2.

Box 10.2 Proceedings and the Right to Counsel

Critical Stage	Non-Critical Stage
Custodial interrogation (*Miranda v. Arizona*)	Noncustodial interrogation
Preliminary hearing	Pre-arrest probable cause hearing
Lineup (post-indictment)	Initial appearance
Post-indictment court proceedings	Lineup (preindictment)
Plea bargaining negotiations	Photographic line-up
Trial	Show up
Sentencing	Grand jury
Motion for new trial	Probation/parole revocation
First appeal	Discretionary appeals
Probation/parole revocation (incarceration)	Habeas corpus petitions (non–death penalty)

Right of Self-Representation

If a criminal defendant has a constitutional right to be represented by a lawyer at his or her trial, can that right be transformed into a requirement that counsel must be appointed to represent a defendant? That is, must a criminal defendant out on trial be represented by an attorney, even over their objection, or may they instead reject a lawyer's help and represent themselves? Would it matter if the accused were not likely to do as good a job as a lawyer would in defending against the charges? If there is a right to **self-representation**, what assurance must there be that the accused is forgoing the assistance of counsel with a full understanding that such action may not be in his or her best interests?

Faretta v. California

422 U.S. 806 (1975)

MR. JUSTICE STEWART delivered the opinion of the Court.

Anthony Faretta was charged with grand theft in an information filed in the Superior Court of Los Angeles County, Cal. At the arraignment, the Superior Court Judge assigned to preside at the trial appointed the public defender to represent Faretta. Well before the date of trial, however, Faretta requested that he be permitted to represent himself. Questioning by the judge revealed that Faretta had once represented himself in a criminal prosecution, that he had a high school education, and that he did not want to be represented by the public defender because he believed that that office was "very loaded down with a heavy case load." The judge responded that he believed Faretta was "making a mistake" and emphasized that in further proceedings Faretta would receive no special favors. Nevertheless, after establishing that Faretta wanted to represent himself and did not want a lawyer, the judge, in a "preliminary ruling," accepted Faretta's waiver of the assistance of counsel. The judge indicated, however, that he might reverse this ruling if it later appeared that Faretta was unable to adequately represent himself.

Several weeks thereafter, but still prior to trial, the judge held a hearing to inquire into Faretta's ability to conduct his own defense, and questioned him specifically about both the hearsay rule and the state law governing the challenge of potential jurors. After consideration of Faretta's answers, and observation of his demeanor, the judge ruled that Faretta had not made an intelligent and knowing waiver of his right to the assistance of counsel, and also ruled that Faretta had no constitutional right to conduct his own defense. The judge, accordingly, reversed his earlier ruling permitting self-representation and again appointed the public defender to represent Faretta. Throughout the subsequent trial, the judge required that Faretta's defense be conducted only through the appointed lawyer from the public defender's office. At the conclusion of the trial, the jury found Faretta guilty as charged, and the judge sentenced him to prison. The California Court of Appeal affirmed the trial judge's ruling that Faretta had no federal or state constitutional right to represent himself and the California Supreme Court denied review. We granted certiorari.

II

In the federal courts, the right of self-representation has been protected by statute since the beginnings of our Nation. With few exceptions, each of the several States also accords a defendant the right to represent himself in any criminal case. The Constitutions of 36 States explicitly confer that right.

This Court's past recognition of the right of self-representation, the federal court authority holding the right to be of constitutional dimension, and the state constitutions pointing to the right's fundamental nature form a consensus not easily ignored.

The mere fact that a path is a beaten one," Mr. Justice Jackson once observed, "is a persuasive reason for following it. We confront here a nearly universal conviction, on the part of our people as well as our courts, that forcing a lawyer upon an unwilling defendant is contrary to his basic right to defend himself if he truly wants to do so.

III

This consensus is soundly premised. The right of self-representation finds support in the structure of the Sixth Amendment, as well as in the English and colonial jurisprudence from which the Amendment emerged.

The Sixth Amendment does not provide merely that a defense shall be made for the accused; it grants to the accused personally the right to make his defense. It is the accused, not counsel, who must be informed of the nature and cause of the accusation, who must be confronted with the witnesses against him, and who must be accorded compulsory process for obtaining witnesses in his favor. Although not stated in the Amendment in so many words, the right to self-representation — to make one's own defense personally — is thus necessarily implied by the structure of the Amendment. The right to defend is given directly to the accused; for it is he who suffers the consequences if the defense fails.

The counsel provision supplements this design. It speaks of the "assistance" of counsel, and an assistant, however expert, is still an assistant. The language and spirit of the Sixth Amendment contemplate that counsel, like the other defense tools guaranteed by the Amendment, shall be an aid to a willing defendant — not an organ of the State interposed between an unwilling defendant and his right to defend himself personally. To thrust counsel upon the accused, against his considered wish, thus violates the logic of the Amendment. In such a case, counsel is not an assistant, but a master; and the right to make a defense is stripped of the personal character upon which the Amendment insists. It is true that when a defendant chooses to have a lawyer manage and present his case, law and tradition may allocate to the counsel the power to make binding decisions of trial strategy in many areas. This allocation can only be justified, however, by the defendant's consent, at the outset, to accept counsel as his representative. Unless the accused has acquiesced in such representation, the defense presented is not the defense guaranteed him by the Constitution, for, in a very real sense, it is not his defense.

The Sixth Amendment, when naturally read, thus implies a right of self-representation. This reading is reinforced by the Amendment's roots in English legal history. In the American Colonies, the insistence upon a right of self-representation was, if anything, more fervent than in England.

In sum, there is no evidence that the colonists and the Framers ever doubted the right of self-representation, or imagined that this right might be considered inferior to the right of assistance of counsel. To the contrary, the colonists and the Framers, as well as their English ancestors, always conceived of the right to counsel as an "assistance" for the accused, to be used at his option, in defending himself. The Framers selected in the Sixth Amendment a form of words that necessarily implies the right of self-representation. That conclusion is supported by centuries of consistent history.

IV

There can be no blinking the fact that the right of an accused to conduct his own defense seems to cut against the grain of this Court's decisions holding that the Constitution requires that no accused can be convicted and imprisoned unless he has been accorded the right to the assistance of counsel. See *Powell v. Alabama; Johnson v. Zerbst; Gideon v. Wainwright; Argersinger v. Hamlin*. For it is surely true that the basic thesis of those decisions is that the help of a lawyer is essential to assure the defendant a fair trial. And a strong argument can surely be made that the whole thrust of those decisions must inevitably lead to the conclusion that a State may constitutionally impose a lawyer upon even an unwilling defendant.

But it is one thing to hold that every defendant, rich or poor, has the right to the assistance of counsel, and quite another to say that a State may compel a defendant to accept a lawyer he does not want.

It is undeniable that in most criminal prosecutions defendants could better defend with counsel's guidance than by their own unskilled efforts. But where the defendant will not voluntarily accept representation by counsel, the potential advantage of a lawyer's training and experience can be realized, if at all, only imperfectly. To force a lawyer on a defendant can only lead him to believe that the law contrives against him. Moreover, it is not inconceivable that in some rare instances, the defendant might in fact present his case more effectively by conducting his own defense. Personal liberties are not rooted in the law of averages. The right to defend is personal. The defendant, and not his lawyer or the State, will bear the personal consequences of a conviction. It is the defendant, therefore, who must be free personally to decide whether in his particular case counsel is to his advantage. And although he may conduct his own defense ultimately to his own detriment, his choice must be honored out of "that respect for the individual which is the life-blood of the law."

V

When an accused manages his own defense, he relinquishes, as a purely factual matter, many of the traditional benefits associated with the right to counsel. For this reason, in order to represent himself, the accused must "knowingly and intelligently" forgo those relinquished benefits. *Johnson v. Zerbst*. Although a defendant need not himself have the skill and experience of a lawyer in order competently and intelligently to choose self-representation, he should be made aware of the dangers and disadvantages of self-representation, so that the record will establish that he knows what he is doing and his choice is made with eyes open.

Here, weeks before trial, Faretta clearly and unequivocally declared to the trial judge that he wanted to represent himself and did not want counsel. The record affirmatively shows that Faretta was literate, competent, and understanding, and that he was voluntarily exercising his informed free will. The trial judge had warned Faretta that he thought it was a mistake not to accept the assistance of counsel, and that Faretta would be required to follow all the "ground rules" of trial procedure. We need make no assessment of how well or poorly Faretta had mastered the intricacies of the hearsay rule and the California code provisions that govern challenges of potential jurors on *voir dire*. For his technical legal knowledge, as such, was not relevant to an assessment of his knowing exercise of the right to defend himself.

In forcing Faretta, under these circumstances, to accept against his will a state-appointed public defender, the California courts deprived him of his constitutional right to conduct his own defense. Accordingly, the judgment before us is vacated, and the case is remanded for further proceedings not inconsistent with this opinion.

FURTHER CASE LAW, REFLECTIONS, AND QUESTIONS

1. Which interest seems more critical: the accused's freedom of choice or society's interest in ensuring that all persons charged with a crime receive at least a minimally fair trial designed to produce reliable results? Does the decision in Faretta serve both interests? Can they be?
2. What are the requirements for an effective waiver of the right to counsel? Note the majority opinion's insistence that Faretta's "technical legal knowledge, as such, was not relevant to an assessment of his knowing exercise of the right to defend himself." The Court reaffirmed this point in *Godinez v. Moran*, 509 U.S. 389 (1993).

   In 1984 Moran was charged with three counts of murder. Moran pleaded not guilty to the charges. At the trial judge's request, two psychiatrists examined Moran and concluded that he was competent to stand trial. Moran subsequently told the trial court that he wished to discharge his attorneys, represent himself, and change his pleas to guilty. The court found that Moran understood "the nature of the criminal charges against him" and was "able to assist in his defense", that he was "knowingly and intelligently" waiving his right to the assistance of counsel, and that his guilty pleas were "freely and voluntarily" given. He was ultimately sentenced to death. The appellate court vacated the conviction, reasoning that while a defendant is competent to stand trial if he has a rational and factual understanding of the proceedings and can assist his counsel, he is competent to waive counsel or plead guilty only if he has the capacity for reasoned choice among the available alternatives.

The United States Supreme Court granted certiorari to consider whether a defendant who is competent to stand trial is also competent to waive counsel and plead guilty. The Court, in a 7–2 decision, answered yes to this question. The Court held that "the competency standard for pleading guilty or waiving the right to counsel is the same as the competency standard for standing trial: whether the defendant has "sufficient present ability to consult with his lawyer with a reasonable degree of rational understanding" and a rational as well as factual understanding of the proceedings against him." It reached this conclusion "there is no reason for the competency standard for either of those decisions to be higher than that for standing trial." The Court concluded that "A higher standard is not necessary in order to ensure that a defendant is competent to represent himself, because the ability to do so has no bearing upon his competence to choose self-representation."

3. In *Indiana v. Edwards,* 554 U.S. 164 (2008), the Supreme Court considered whether a state can deny a defendant who is mentally ill but has been determined to be competent to stand trial the *Faretta* right of self-representation. *Edwards* differs from *Moran* in that *Edwards* involved the right to self-representation at trial, not to plead guilty. Retreating from the standard set in *Moran*, the Court accepted the practicality of having a seriously mentally ill defendant represent themselves at trial. Retreating from the standard set in *Moran*, the Court granted the trial court extensive discretion in such situations.

> [T]he Constitution permits judges to take realistic account of the particular defendant's mental capacities by asking whether a defendant who seeks to conduct his own defense at trial is mentally competent to do so. That is to say, the Constitution permits States to insist upon representation by counsel for those competent enough to stand trial under *Dusky v. United States,* 362 U.S. 402 (1960), but who still suffer from severe mental illness to the point where they are not competent to conduct trial proceedings by themselves. 554 U.S. at 178,

4. Even if counsel represents a defendant, the client has the final say so regarding specific *fundamental* decisions. These are generally items that directly implicate a constitutional right. On the other hand, attorneys have the discretion to make decisions involving strategy and tactics. Examples of these decisions are presented in Box 10.3.

Box 10.3 Attorney-Client Decision-Making Authority

Defendant's Decisions to Make *Fundamental Decisions*	Attorney's Decision *Strategic and Tactical Decisions*
Whether to proceed without counsel	How to pursue plea negotiations
What plea to enter	How to craft and respond to motions
Whether to accept a plea offer	Trial strategy
Whether to waive jury trial	What witnesses to call
Whether to testify in his or her own behalf	Conduct of cross-examination
Whether to speak at sentencing	Jury selection
Whether to appeal	What motions and objections to make
	What evidence to introduce

Box 10.4 You Be The Judge

Walt was charged with conspiracy to distribute more than 100 kilograms of marijuana. His family initially hired local attorney Harry to represent him. Walt, however, contacted and hired a famous California attorney, Saul, to represent him. Walt and his family agreed that Harry and Saul would work together on his case.

At an evidentiary hearing shortly after the arraignment, where both lawyers represented Walt, Saul violated a local court rule restricting the cross-examination of a witness to one attorney by passing notes to Harry. A brief time later, Walt told the court he wanted Saul to be his only attorney. The judge denied this request because of the note passing and unethical conduct in an unrelated case. Walt ended up being represented by Perry. Perry requested that Saul be allowed to sit at the counsel table during the trial. The judge denied the request and made Saul sit in the audience. Even though everyone agreed Perry did an excellent job at trial, Walt was found guilty. Walt appealed, arguing his Sixth Amendment right to counsel had been violated.

Should Walt win his appeal? Explain why or why not.

See *United States v. Gonzalez-Lopez*, 548 U.S. 140 (2006).

Ineffective Assistance of Counsel

The Sixth Amendment right to the "Assistance of Counsel" requires more than simply assigning a lawyer to a criminal defendant. Implicit in this guarantee is that the lawyer fulfills the role of trained legal counsel in representing the accused. The defendant has a right, usually stated in the negative, not to be saddled with **ineffective assistance of counsel**. Whether an attorney's representation of an accused crosses the threshold of constitutionally ineffective assistance of counsel depends on a two-part inquiry, as the Supreme Court explained in *Strickland v. Washington*, below. This case involved an allegation that the defendant's attorney had failed to provide minimally adequate representation during a capital sentencing hearing.

Strickland v. Washington

466 U.S. 668 (1984)

JUSTICE O'CONNOR delivered the opinion of the Court.

A convicted defendant's claim that counsel's assistance was so defective as to require reversal of a conviction or death sentence has two components. First, the defendant must show that counsel's performance was deficient. This requires showing that counsel made errors so serious that counsel was not functioning as the "counsel" guaranteed the defendant by the Sixth Amendment. Second, the defendant must show that the deficient performance prejudiced the defense. This requires showing that counsel's errors were so serious as to deprive the defendant of a fair trial, a trial whose result is reliable. Unless a defendant makes both showings, it cannot be said that the conviction or death sentence resulted from a breakdown in the adversary process that renders the result unreliable.

The proper standard for attorney performance is that of reasonably effective assistance. When a convicted defendant complains of the ineffectiveness of counsel's assistance, the defendant must show that counsel's representation fell below an objective standard of reasonableness.

More specific guidelines are not appropriate. The Sixth Amendment refers simply to "counsel," not specifying particular requirements of effective assistance. It relies instead on the legal profession's maintenance of standards sufficient to justify the law's presumption that counsel will fulfill the role in the adversary process that the Amendment envisions. The proper measure of attorney performance remains simply reasonableness under prevailing professional norms.

Representation of a criminal defendant entails certain basic duties. Counsel's function is to assist the defendant, and hence counsel owes the client a duty of loyalty, a duty to avoid conflicts of interest. From counsel's function as assistant to the defendant derive the overarching duty to advocate the defendant's cause and the more particular duties to consult with the defendant on important decisions and to keep the defendant informed of important developments in the course of the prosecution. Counsel also has a duty to bring to bear such skill and knowledge as will render the trial a reliable adversarial testing process.

These basic duties neither exhaustively define the obligations of counsel nor form a checklist for judicial evaluation of attorney performance. In any case presenting an ineffectiveness claim, the performance inquiry must be whether counsel's assistance was reasonable considering all the circumstances. Prevailing norms of practice as reflected in American Bar Association standards and the like, e.g., ABA Standards for Criminal Justice 4-1.1 to 4-8.6 (2d ed 1980) ("The Defense Function"), are guides to determining what is reasonable, but they are only guides. No particular set of detailed rules for counsel's conduct can satisfactorily take account of the variety of circumstances faced by defense counsel or the range of legitimate decisions regarding how best to represent a criminal defendant. Any such set of rules would interfere with the constitutionally protected independence of counsel and restrict the wide latitude counsel must have in making tactical decisions.

Indeed, the existence of detailed guidelines for representation could distract counsel from the overriding mission of vigorous advocacy of the defendant's cause. Moreover, the purpose of the effective assistance guarantee of the Sixth Amendment is not to improve the quality of legal representation, although that is a goal of considerable importance to the legal system. The purpose is simply to ensure that criminal defendants receive a fair trial.

Judicial scrutiny of counsel's performance must be highly deferential. It is all too tempting for a defendant to second guess counsel's assistance after conviction or adverse sentence, and it is all too easy for a court, examining counsel's defense after it has proved unsuccessful, to conclude that a particular act or omission of counsel was unreasonable. A fair assessment of attorney performance requires that every effort be made to eliminate the distorting effects of hindsight, to reconstruct the circumstances of counsel's challenged conduct, and to evaluate the conduct from counsel's perspective at the time. Because of the difficulties inherent in making the evaluation, a court must indulge a strong presumption that counsel's conduct falls within the wide range of reasonable professional assistance; that is, the defendant must overcome the presumption that, under the circumstances, the challenged action "might be considered sound trial strategy."

The availability of intrusive post-trial inquiry into attorney performance or of detailed guidelines for its evaluation would encourage the proliferation of ineffectiveness challenges. Intensive scrutiny of counsel and rigid requirements for acceptable assistance could dampen the ardor and impair the independence of defense counsel, discourage the acceptance of assigned cases, and undermine the trust between attorney and client.

Thus, a court deciding an actual ineffectiveness claim must judge the reasonableness of counsel's challenged conduct on the facts of the particular case, viewed as of the time of counsel's conduct. A convicted defendant making a claim of ineffective assistance must identify the acts or omissions of counsel that are alleged not to have been the result of reasonable professional judgment. The court must then determine whether, in light of all the circumstances, the identified acts or omissions were outside the wide range of professionally competent assistance. In making that determination, the court should keep in mind that counsel's function, as elaborated in prevailing professional norms, is to make the adversarial testing process work in the particular case. At the same time, the court should recognize that counsel is strongly presumed to have rendered adequate assistance and made all significant decisions in the exercise of reasonable professional judgment.

An error by counsel, even if professionally unreasonable, does not warrant setting aside the judgment of a criminal proceeding if the error had no effect on the judgment. The purpose of the Sixth Amendment guarantee of counsel is to ensure that a defendant has the assistance necessary to justify reliance on the outcome of the proceeding. Accordingly, any deficiencies in counsel's performance must be prejudicial to the defense in order to constitute ineffective assistance under the Constitution.

In certain Sixth Amendment contexts, prejudice is presumed. Actual or constructive denial of the assistance of counsel altogether is legally presumed to result in prejudice. So are various kinds of state interference with counsel's assistance. See *United States v. Cronic*, 466 US 648 (1984). Prejudice in these circumstances is so likely that case by case inquiry into prejudice is not worth the cost. Moreover, such circumstances involve impairments of the Sixth Amendment right that are easy to identify and, for that reason and because the prosecution is directly responsible, easy for the government to prevent.

One type of actual ineffectiveness claim warrants a similar, though more limited, presumption of prejudice. In *Cuyler v. Sullivan*, 446 U.S. 335, at 345–350, the Court held that prejudice is presumed when counsel is burdened by an actual conflict of interest. In those circumstances counsel breaches the duty of loyalty, perhaps the most basic of counsel's duties. Even so, the rule is not quite the per se rule of prejudice that exists for the Sixth Amendment claims mentioned above. Prejudice is presumed only if the defendant demonstrates that counsel "actively represented conflicting interests" and that "an actual conflict of interest adversely affected his lawyer's performance."

Conflict of interest claims aside, actual ineffectiveness claims alleging a deficiency in attorney performance are subject to a general requirement that the defendant affirmatively prove prejudice. The government is not responsible for, and hence not able to prevent, attorney errors that will result in reversal of a conviction or sentence. Attorney errors come in an infinite variety and are as likely to be utterly harmless in a particular case as they are to be prejudicial. They cannot be classified according to likelihood of causing prejudice. Nor can they be defined with sufficient precision to inform defense attorneys correctly just what conduct to avoid. Representation is an art, and an act or omission that is unprofessional in one case may be sound or even brilliant in another. Even if a defendant shows that particular errors of counsel were unreasonable, therefore, the defendant must show that they actually had an adverse effect on the defense.

It is not enough for the defendant to show that the errors had some conceivable effect on the outcome of the proceeding. Virtually every act or omission of counsel would meet that test, and not every error that conceivably could have influenced the outcome undermines the reliability of the result of the proceeding. Respondent suggests requiring a showing that the errors "impaired the presentation of the defense." That standard, however, provides no workable principle. Since any error, if it is indeed an error, "impairs" the presentation of the defense, the proposed standard is inadequate because it provides no way of deciding what impairments are sufficiently serious to warrant setting aside the outcome of the proceeding.

On the other hand, we believe that a defendant need not show that counsel's deficient conduct more likely than not altered the outcome in the case. The appropriate test for prejudice finds its roots in the test for materiality of exculpatory information not disclosed to the defense by the prosecution. The defendant must show that there is a reasonable probability that, but for counsel's unprofessional errors, the result of the proceeding would have been different. A reasonable probability is a probability sufficient to undermine confidence in the outcome.

A number of practical considerations are important for the application of the standards we have outlined. Most important, in adjudicating a claim of actual ineffectiveness of counsel, a court should keep in mind that the principles we have stated do not establish mechanical rules. Although those principles should guide the process of decision, the ultimate focus of inquiry must be on the fundamental fairness of the proceeding whose result is being challenged. In every case the court should be concerned with whether, despite the strong presumption of reliability, the result of the particular proceeding is unreliable because of a breakdown in the adversarial process that our system counts on to produce just results.

FURTHER CASE LAW, REFLECTIONS, AND QUESTIONS

1. *Strickland's* test for ineffective assistance of counsel requires the defendant to demonstrate that the lawyer's performance was deficient and that the trial's outcome was prejudiced or adversely affected due to that performance. In other words, even if an attorney provided a woefully inadequate defense of a client, a conviction or sentence will not be disturbed unless the defendant also can show "a reasonable

probability that, but for counsel's unprofessional errors, the result of the proceeding would have been different." How would a defendant make such a showing? Moreover, what constitutes constitutionally deficient performance by counsel? What does the Court mean when it requires that "in light of all the circumstances, the identified acts or omissions were outside the wide range of professionally competent assistance"? In *Strickland*, the Court concluded (7–2) that the defendant had not been afforded constitutionally ineffective assistance of counsel.

2. Ineffective assistance of counsel may be found by an attorney's actions outside the court setting. One prominent area where this occurs involves attorneys giving their clients incorrect legal information and advice. The leading case in this area is *Padilla v. Kentucky*, 559 U.S. 356 (2010). Jose Padilla was indicted by a Kentucky grand jury on multiple felony charges. His lawyer told him he "did not have to worry" about a conviction affecting his immigration status. Based on this advice, he pleaded guilty. Unfortunately, this advice was incorrect, as Padilla's deportation was virtually automatic following a felony conviction under federal law.

    Padilla filed for post-conviction relief, arguing that had it not been for the erroneous advice given by his attorney, he would not have pleaded guilty. While the Kentucky Court of Appeals reversed his conviction, the Kentucky Supreme Court reversed the court of appeals and denied Padilla post-conviction relief on the ground that the Sixth Amendment's effective-assistance-of-counsel guarantee does not protect defendants from erroneous deportation advice because deportation is merely a "collateral" consequence of a conviction.

    The U.S. Supreme Court reversed. The Court held that the failure to warn Padilla of the consequences of a conviction fell below Strickland's standard of reasonableness. A reasonable attorney would have known or at least looked up the law regarding the immigration impact of a non-citizen's conviction. Given the dire ramifications of a guilty plea, the Court found Padilla was also prejudiced by counsel's ineffectiveness since he would have demanded a trial had he known of the automatic deportation statute.

3. A second area where an attorney's out-of-court actions may give rise to a *Strickland* violation involves the failure to conduct an adequate investigation. In *Wiggins v. Smith*, 539 U.S. 510 (2003), counsel at the petitioner's capital trial in Maryland elected to have a judge determine guilt or innocence. The judge found the petitioner guilty of capital murder. A jury was then impaneled to decide whether the petitioner should be sentenced to death. Defense counsel was aware of at least some aspects of the petitioner's disadvantaged social background and upbringing, but instead of conducting a more extensive background investigation or presenting such evidence, the defense elected to argue before the sentencing jury that the evidence supporting the petitioner's conviction for murder was weak. The jury sentenced the petitioner to death, and the state appeals court affirmed.

The U.S. District Court granted Wiggins' habeas corpus petition, finding that the evidence was insufficient to support his conviction and also that he had received constitutionally ineffective assistance of counsel at the capital sentencing hearing. The Fourth Circuit Court of Appeals reversed and reinstated the conviction and sentence. The U.S. Supreme Court vacated the capital sentence, ruling that the decision of defense counsel not to investigate further for potential mitigation evidence fell short of prevailing professional standards and prejudiced the sentencing outcome, thereby violating Wiggins' Sixth Amendment right.

4. The Supreme Court has held that the prejudice associated with an attorney's deficient performance is presumed in several instances. These cases generally fall into four categories.

The first category is when a defense attorney has an actual conflict of interest. Conflicts exist when an attorney simultaneously represents multiple people with potentially adverse interests, an attorney shares a prior client's confidential information that is relevant to the current client's interests, or an attorney has a personal or financial interest that is adverse to a client. Such conflicts are considered "inherently prejudicial." As noted in *Strickland,* conflict claims arise under the *Cuyler* doctrine, which makes prejudice significantly easier to demonstrate than ordinary *Strickland* claims. To prevail, a defendant must show that an actual conflict existed and that the conflict had an "adverse effect" on the defendant during trial, regardless of whether there would not have been a reasonable probability the outcome would have differed.

The second area where prejudice is presumed is when counsel's performance is so lacking it makes a mockery of the adversary process. In *United States v. Chronic*, 466 U.S. 648 (1984), decided the same day as Strickland, the Supreme Court held that if a defense attorney "entirely fails to subject the prosecution's case to a meaningful adversarial testing," prejudice will be presumed. An example of such a case is *Miller v. Martin*, 481 F.3d 468 (7th Cir. 2007). In *Miller*, the defense attorney did not conduct an investigation, give an opening statement, present any evidence during the sentencing hearing, or argue for a sentence different than what was requested by the state in a death penalty prosecution. The court found that counsel's performance was akin to nonperformance and was nonadversarial. Accordingly, it met the criteria presented in *Cronic* for the court to presume the defendant was prejudiced.

The third category where prejudice is presumed occurs when a defendant is actually or constructively denied counsel during a critical stage of a prosecution. *United States v. Chronic*, 466 U.S. 648 (1984). Actual denial of counsel involves situations where an attorney fails to appear in court during a critical stage of a trial, *Cronic*; *Coleman v. Alabama,* 399 U.S. 1 (1970) (defendant denied counsel at a preliminary hearing); *United States v. Mateo,* 950 F.2d 44 (1st Cir. 1991);

Green v. Arn, 809 F.2d 1257 (6th Cir. 1987). Constructive denial of counsel involves situations akin to *Powell v. Alabama* where defense counsel was forced to proceed with trial without a reasonable time to prepare a defense or consult with their client.

The final area under which prejudice is presumed involves instances whereby the government interferes with a defendant's access to their attorney. For example, prejudice was presumed in *United States v. Johnson,* 267 F.3d 376 (5th Cir. 2001) where the trial judge refused to allow counsel to consult with his client during recesses while the defendant was testifying. Such interference violated the defendant's access to and assistance of counsel.

5. If a defense lawyer were to sleep through portions of a capital murder trial, should it be presumed that he provided his client constitutionally ineffective assistance of counsel? It depends. Although the Texas state courts and a panel of the U.S. Court of Appeals for the Fifth Circuit upheld the conviction and death sentence of Calvin Burdine, whose attorney repeatedly dozed off during witness testimony at his trial, the Court of Appeals, sitting *en banc*, concluded that Burdine had been denied his right to the effective assistance of counsel under *Strickland*, and ordered that he be granted a new trial. *Burdine v. Johnson*, 262 F.3d 336 (5th Cir. 2001) (*en banc*). On what basis could the prosecution argue and a court find that a defendant whose lawyer fell asleep during trial was not denied effective assistance of counsel? How does this relate to a presumption of prejudice as discussed above?

Suppose a defendant informs his attorney that they committed the crime for which they are charged but wants to testify that they are actually innocent. Should the attorney accede to the client's wishes and allow them to lie to the jury? Should the attorney violate attorney-client privilege and tell the judge what the client intends to do? This was the situation faced by counsel in the case of *Nix v. Whiteside*, 475 U.S. 157 (1986).

Nix v. Whiteside

475 U.S. 157 (1986)

CHIEF JUSTICE BURGER delivered the opinion of the Court.

Carl Whiteside was convicted of second degree murder by a jury verdict which was affirmed by the Iowa courts. The killing took place on February 8, 1977 in Cedar Rapids, Iowa. Whiteside and two others went to one Calvin Love's apartment late that night, seeking marihuana. Love was in bed when Whiteside and his companions arrived; an argument between Whiteside and Love over the marihuana ensued. At one point, Love directed his girlfriend to get his "piece," and at another point got up, then returned to his bed. According to Whiteside's testimony, Love then started to reach under his pillow and moved toward Whiteside. Whiteside stabbed Love in the chest, inflicting a fatal wound.

Whiteside was charged with murder. Gary L. Robinson was appointed [as counsel] and immediately began investigation. Whiteside gave him a statement that he had stabbed Love as the latter "was pulling a pistol from underneath the pillow on the bed." Upon questioning by Robinson, however, Whiteside indicated that he had not actually seen a gun, but that he was convinced that Love had a gun. No pistol was found on the premises. Robinson interviewed Whiteside's companions who were present during the stabbing and none had seen a gun during the incident. Robinson advised Whiteside that the existence of a gun was not necessary to establish the claim of self defense, and that only a reasonable belief that the victim had a gun nearby was necessary even though no gun was actually present.

Until shortly before trial, Whiteside consistently stated to Robinson that he had not actually seen a gun, but that he was convinced that Love had a gun in his hand. About a week before trial, during preparation for direct examination, Whiteside for the first time told Robinson and his associate Donna Paulsen that he had seen something "metallic" in Love's hand. When asked about this, Whiteside responded that, "in Howard Cook's case there was a gun. If I don't say I saw a gun, I'm dead."

Robinson told Whiteside that such testimony would be perjury and repeated that it was not necessary to prove that a gun was available but only that Whiteside reasonably believed that he was in danger. On Whiteside's insisting that he would testify that he saw "something metallic" Robinson told him, according to Robinson's testimony,

> We could not allow him to [testify falsely] because that would be perjury, and as officers of the court we would be suborning perjury if we allowed him to do it; . . . I advised him that if he did do that it would be my duty to advise the Court of what he was doing and that I felt he was committing perjury; also, that I probably would be allowed to attempt to impeach that particular testimony.

Robinson also indicated he would seek to withdraw from the representation if Whiteside insisted on committing perjury.

Whiteside testified in his own defense at trial and stated that he "knew" that Love had a gun and that he believed Love was reaching for a gun and he had acted swiftly in self defense. On cross examination, he admitted that he had not actually seen a gun in Love's hand. . . .

The jury returned a verdict of second-degree murder and Whiteside moved for a new trial, claiming that he had been deprived of a fair trial by Robinson's admonitions not to state that he saw a gun or "something metallic." The trial court held a hearing, heard testimony by Whiteside and Robinson, and denied the motion. The trial court made specific findings that the facts were as related by Robinson.

The Supreme Court of Iowa affirmed respondent's conviction. . . .

B

Whiteside then petitioned for a writ of habeas corpus in the United States District Court for the Southern District of Iowa. In that petition Whiteside alleged that he had been denied effective assistance of counsel and of his right to present a defense by Robinson's refusal to allow him to testify as he had proposed. The District Court denied the writ. . . .

The United States Court of Appeals for the Eighth Circuit reversed and directed that the writ of habeas corpus be granted. The Court of Appeals accepted the findings of the trial judge, affirmed by the Iowa Supreme Court, that trial counsel believed with good cause that Whiteside would testify falsely and acknowledged that under *Harris v. New York*, 401 US 222 (1971), a criminal defendant's privilege to testify in his own behalf does not include a right to commit perjury. Nevertheless, the court reasoned that an intent to commit perjury, communicated to counsel, does not alter a defendant's right to effective assistance of counsel and that Robinson's admonition to Whiteside that he would inform the court of Whiteside's perjury constituted a threat to violate the attorney's duty to preserve client confidences. According to the Court of Appeals, this threatened violation of client confidences breached the standards of effective representation set down in *Strickland v. Washington*, 466 US 668 (1984). The court also concluded that *Strickland's* prejudice requirement was satisfied by an implication of prejudice from the conflict between Robinson's duty of loyalty to his client and his ethical duties. . . .

II . . .

B

In *Strickland v. Washington*, we held that to obtain relief by way of federal habeas corpus on a claim of a deprivation of effective assistance of counsel under the Sixth Amendment, the movant must establish both serious attorney error and prejudice. To show such error, it must be established that the assistance rendered by counsel was constitutionally deficient in that "counsel made errors so serious that counsel was not functioning as 'counsel' guaranteed the defendant by the Sixth Amendment." To show prejudice, it must be established that the claimed lapses in counsel's performance rendered the trial unfair so as to "undermine confidence in the outcome" of the trial. . . .

C

We turn next to the question presented: the definition of the range of "reasonable professional" responses to a criminal defendant client who informs counsel that he will perjure himself on the stand. We must determine whether, in this setting, Robinson's conduct fell within the wide range of professional responses to threatened client perjury acceptable under the Sixth Amendment.

In *Strickland*, we recognized counsel's duty of loyalty and his "overarching duty to advocate the defendant's case." Plainly, that duty is limited to legitimate, lawful conduct compatible with the very nature of a trial as a search for truth. Although counsel must take all reasonable lawful means to attain the objectives of the client, counsel is precluded from taking steps or in any way assisting the client in presenting false evidence or otherwise violating the law. . . .

These principles have been carried through to contemporary codifications of an attorney's professional responsibility. Disciplinary Rule 7-102 of the Model Code of Professional Responsibility (1980), entitled "Representing a Client within the Bounds of the Law," provides that

> "(A) In his representation of a client, a lawyer shall not:. . .
>
> "(4) Knowingly use perjured testimony or false evidence. . . .
>
> "(7) Counsel or assist his client in conduct that the lawyer knows to be illegal or fraudulent."

The more recent Model Rules of Professional Conduct (1983) similarly admonish attorneys to obey all laws in the course of representing a client:

> "RULE 1.2 Scope of Representation. . .
>
> "(d) A lawyer shall not counsel a client to engage, or assist a client, in conduct that the lawyer knows is criminal or fraudulent. . . ."

Both the Model Code of Professional Conduct and the Model Rules of Professional Conduct also adopt the specific exception from the attorney-client privilege for disclosure of perjury that his client intends to commit or has committed. DR 4-101(C)(3) (intention of client to commit a crime); Rule 3.3 (lawyer has duty to disclose falsity of evidence even if disclosure compromises client confidences). Indeed, both the Model Code and the Model Rules do not merely *authorize* disclosure by counsel of client perjury; they *require* such disclosure. See Rule 3.3(a)(4); DR 7-102(B)(1).

These standards confirm that the legal profession has accepted that an attorney's ethical duty to advance the interests of his client is limited by an equally solemn duty to comply with the law and standards of professional conduct; it specifically ensures that the client may not use false evidence. This special duty of an attorney to prevent and disclose frauds upon the court derives from the recognition that perjury is as much a crime as tampering with witnesses or jurors by way of promises and threats, and undermines the administration of justice. . . . An attorney who aids false testimony by questioning a witness when perjurious responses can be anticipated, risks prosecution for subornation of perjury under Iowa Code §720.3 (1985).

D

Considering Robinson's representation of respondent in light of these accepted norms of professional conduct, we discern no failure to adhere to reasonable professional standards that would in any sense make out a deprivation of the Sixth Amendment right to counsel. Whether Robinson's conduct is seen as a successful attempt to dissuade his client from committing the crime of perjury, or whether seen as a "threat" to withdraw from representation and disclose the illegal scheme, Robinson's representation of Whiteside falls well within accepted standards of professional conduct and the range of reasonable professional conduct acceptable under *Strickland*. . . .

The Court of Appeals' holding that Robinson's "action deprived [Whiteside] of due process and effective assistance of counsel" is not supported by the record since Robinson's action, at most, deprived Whiteside of his contemplated perjury. Nothing counsel did in any way undermined Whiteside's claim that he believed the victim was reaching for a gun. . . . Robinson divulged no client communications until he was compelled to do so in response to Whiteside's post-trial challenge to the quality of his performance. We see this as a case in which the attorney successfully dissuaded the client from committing the crime of perjury.

Robinson's admonitions to his client can in no sense be said to have forced respondent into an impermissible choice between his right to counsel and his right to testify as he proposed for there was no permissible choice to testify falsely. For defense counsel to take steps to persuade a criminal defendant to testify truthfully, or to withdraw, deprives the defendant of neither his right to counsel nor the right to testify truthfully. . . .When an accused proposes to resort to perjury or to produce false evidence, one consequence is the risk of withdrawal of counsel.

On this record, the accused enjoyed continued representation within the bounds of reasonable professional conduct and did in fact exercise his right to testify; at most he was denied the right to have the assistance of counsel in the presentation of false testimony. Similarly, we can discern no breach of professional duty in Robinson's admonition to respondent that he would disclose respondent's perjury to the court. The crime of perjury in this setting is indistinguishable in substance from the crime of threatening or tampering with a witness or a juror. A defendant who informed his counsel that he was arranging to bribe or threaten witnesses or members of the jury would have no "right" to insist on counsel's assistance or silence. Counsel would not be limited to advising against that conduct. An attorney's duty of confidentiality, which totally covers the client's admission of guilt, does not extend to a client's announced plans to engage in future criminal conduct. In short, the responsibility of an ethical lawyer, as an officer of the court and a key component of a system of justice, dedicated to a search for truth, is essentially the same whether the client announces an intention to bribe or threaten witnesses or jurors or to commit or procure perjury. No system of justice worthy of the name can tolerate a lesser standard. . . . Since there has been no breach of any recognized professional duty, it follows that there can be no deprivation of the right to assistance of counsel under the Strickland standard.

E

We hold that, as a matter of law, counsel's conduct complained of here cannot establish the prejudice required for relief under the second strand of the *Strickland* inquiry. Although a defendant need not establish that the attorney's deficient performance more likely than not altered the outcome in order to establish prejudice under *Strickland*, a defendant must show "that there is a reasonable probability that, but for counsel's unprofessional errors, the result of the proceeding would have been different." According to *Strickland*, "[a] reasonable probability is a probability sufficient to undermine confidence in the outcome." The *Strickland* Court noted that the "benchmark" of an ineffective assistance claim is the fairness of the adversary proceeding, and that in judging prejudice and the likelihood of a different outcome, "[a] defendant has no entitlement to the luck of a lawless decision maker."

Whether he was persuaded or compelled to desist from perjury, Whiteside has no valid claim that confidence in the result of his trial has been diminished by his desisting from the contemplated perjury. Even if we were to assume that the jury might have believed his perjury, it does not follow that Whiteside was prejudiced. . . .

Whiteside's attorney treated Whiteside's proposed perjury in accord with professional standards, and since Whiteside's truthful testimony could not have prejudiced the result of his trial, the Court of Appeals was in error to direct the issuance of a writ of habeas corpus and must be reversed. . . .

Justice Stevens, concurring in the judgment. . . .

As we view this case, it appears perfectly clear that respondent intended to commit perjury, that his lawyer knew it, and that the lawyer had a duty — both to the court and to his client, for perjured testimony can ruin an otherwise meritorious case — to take extreme measures to prevent the perjury from occurring. The lawyer was successful and, from our unanimous and remote perspective, it is now pellucidly clear that the client suffered no "legally cognizable prejudice."

Nevertheless, beneath the surface of this case there are areas of uncertainty that cannot be resolved today. A lawyer's certainty that a change in his client's recollection is a harbinger of intended perjury — as well as judicial review of such apparent certainty — should be tempered by the realization that, after reflection, the most honest witness may recall (or sincerely believe he recalls) details that he previously overlooked. Similarly, the post-trial review of a lawyer's pretrial threat to expose perjury that had not yet been committed — and, indeed, may have been prevented by the threat — is by no means the same as review of the way in which such a threat may actually have been carried out. Thus, one can be convinced — as I am — that this lawyer's actions were a proper way to provide his client with effective representation without confronting the much more difficult questions of what a lawyer must, should, or may do after his client has given testimony that the lawyer does not believe. The answer to such questions may well be colored by the particular circumstances attending the actual event and its aftermath. . . .

FURTHER CASE LAW, REFLECTIONS, AND QUESTIONS

1. Was Whiteside's attorney justified in threatening to disclose perjury? Should loyalty to a client ever take precedence over truthfulness in court?
2. If Whiteside had testified that he had seen a metallic object in Calvin Love's hand, might such testimony have bolstered his claim that he believed that his own life was in jeopardy and that he killed Love in self-defense? If so, why does the Court conclude that Whiteside suffered no "prejudice," under *Strickland*, when his lawyer's actions precluded him from offering such testimony?

Box 10.5 You Be the Judge

Lee moved to the United States from South Korea with his parents in 1982 when he was 13 years old. Lee never became a U.S. citizen but lived as a lawful permanent resident. In 2008, Lee was arrested and prosecuted for drug possession with the intent to distribute. Lee's counsel held plea discussions with the government. Lee repeatedly asked his attorney whether he would face deportation. Lee's attorney assured him that he would not be deported as a consequence of pleading guilty. Based on this assurance and given the strong case against him, including a confession, Lee accepted a plea bargain and was sentenced to a year and a day in prison.

Contrary to what his attorney told him, since his conviction qualified as an "aggravated felony," Lee was subject to mandatory deportation under the Immigration and Nationality Act. When Lee learned this, he filed a motion to vacate his conviction and sentence, arguing that his attorney had provided constitutionally ineffective assistance. At an evidentiary hearing, Lee and his counsel testified that "deportation was the determinative issue" to Lee in deciding whether to accept a plea. Lee's counsel testified that if he had known Lee would be deported upon pleading guilty, he would have advised him to go to trial. The District Court denied this motion, and the Sixth Circuit Court of Appeals affirmed. The U.S. Supreme Court granted a writ of certiorari.

1. Was Lee denied effective assistance of counsel?
2. Does the strength of the government's case impact whether or not he was prejudiced?

See how the Court decided *Lee v. United States*, 137 S.Ct. 1958 (2017).

Conclusion

Criminal defense lawyers play a vital role in the adversarial system. They are expected to advocate with skill and vigor on behalf of their clients, even those who are accused and may in fact be guilty of the most serious and reprehensible crimes. At the same time, they must be mindful of the boundaries that define ethical and lawful conduct.

In this chapter, we have examined a number of issues related to the accused's right to counsel, including whether poor people have a constitutional entitlement to court-appointed attorneys, whether a constitutional right of self-representation exists, and the sometimes conflicting obligations of defense lawyers to their clients and the court within the adversarial system of justice. Defense attorneys are expected to champion the criminally accused's interests and insist that the entire constellation of rights owed to criminal defendants be respected. The issues confronting defense counsel, which can be both intriguing and complex, must be resolved if reliable and just results can be achieved in criminal cases.

KEY TERMS

critical stage

indigent

ineffective assistance of counsel

self-representation

REVIEW QUESTIONS

1. What was the significance of *Powell v. Alabama* in the evolution of the right to counsel?
2. What rule was announced in *Betts v. Brady* regarding the appointment of trial counsel for indigent defendants? What was the "special circumstance" rule derived from the case?
3. What rule was established by *Gideon v. Wainwright*? What was the Court's rationale for the decision?
4. Does the right to counsel apply to all criminal prosecutions, as stated in the Sixth Amendment? If not, what are the restrictions?
5. What is the general rule regarding the right to court-appointed counsel in criminal appeals for indigents?
6. What is required to waive the right to counsel effectively?
7. What are the requirements for a defendant to proceed *pro se* at trial? According to the Court, why do people have this right?

8. What are the fundamental trial decisions that are left up to the defendant to make?
9. Under what circumstances is ineffective counsel presumed? What are the implications of this presumption?
10. When does the right to counsel apply?

APPLYING THE LAW

Below are five hypothetical fact scenarios. To practice your understanding of the law that you learned in this chapter and ability to apply it, answer each question posed by applying that law to hypothetical scenarios. Your answers should be supported by relevant caselaw and judicially created rules and tests.

1. Mark, an indigent Criminal Justice major at State U, was arrested for reckless driving and misdemeanor resisting arrest. At his initial appearance, Mark requested that an attorney be appointed to represent him. Due to budget cuts, the prosecutor and the judge agreed that indigent defendants charged with such crimes would not be given counsel. After telling Mark this, the judge released Mark on his own recognizance. Rather than accepting a plea bargain, Mark demanded a trial. Sadly, Mark lost at trial. After renewing his demand for a lawyer, the judge said he had no right to a lawyer and sentenced him to probation and a $5,000 fine.

   If Mark appeals on the grounds that he was denied counsel, how should the court rule?

2. Dennis is charged with first-degree murder for killing his wife. He has never trusted the criminal justice system, and especially doesn't trust attorneys. Dennis decides he is going to represent himself. He'd rather put his fate in his own hands than some attorney in a poor-fitting suit. Dennis notifies the court of his intent to represent himself. The judge informs Dennis of the possible consequences of waiving counsel and asks him questions to ensure he is competent. The judge begins by asking him what hearsay evidence is. Dennis does not know. The judge also asks him if he knows what it means for evidence to be relevant and reliable. Dennis doesn't know this either. Based on these responses, the judge denies Dennis' request to represent himself.

   Was the judge correct in denying Dennis the right to represent himself?

3. Carl and Junior were arrested for armed robbery. During the robbery, they stole jewelry, a flip phone, and assorted other items from an 85-year-old woman. Moreover, they videotaped the robbery and posted it along with their commentary on Instagram. Police also uncovered text messages between the two relishing in their experience. In short, the evidence is overwhelming. Prosecutors offered

a sentence of 10 years in prison for a guilty plea. While Junior accepted the offer, against his attorney Jack's advice, Carl demanded a trial. Fed up with his job, Jack decided to show his disgust by doing as little as possible in defending Carl. During the trial, Jack did not give an opening statement or closing argument, rarely objected, and conducted no cross-examination. When Carl complained about this, Jack explained that it was his strategy. Carl was convicted by the jury and sentenced to 25 years in prison.

Carl appealed his conviction based on ineffective assistance of counsel. What should the outcome of the appeal be?

4. Taylor, a college junior, was arrested for assaulting his roommate after he discovered that the roommate had smoked all of his crack. Hoping to learn the name of Taylor's supplier, the arresting officer, Perry, brought him into an interrogation room and read him the Miranda warnings. Taylor agreed to waive his rights and signed a waiver form. Taylor then gave Perry the name and phone number of his supplier and confessed that he regularly sold cocaine to members of the football team.

   What Taylor didn't know was that minutes after he was arrested and before he confessed, his criminal law professor, who is also a licensed attorney, called the police station and identified himself as Taylor's attorney. He explained that he did not want Taylor to be interrogated unless he was present. The officer who spoke with the professor agreed to these conditions and reassured him that she would relay the message to the interrogating officer. She did not do so.

   Taylor has been charged with various drug-related crimes. He has moved to suppress his statements to Perry on the grounds that he was denied his right to counsel. How should the court rule?

5. Charles was arrested and charged with aggravated assault for stabbing his neighbor with a knife. The prosecutor disclosed to Charles' court-appointed attorney, Diana, the following evidence that would be used against him at trial: A video of the assault that shows Charles was not provoked, a video of the interrogation where Charles waived his Miranda rights and confessed to the crime, a signed confession, and the knife which had Charles' fingerprints on it. Diana told Charles about the evidence and advised him to cut his losses and accept a plea bargain. Charles refused, telling her he was innocent. Being very busy, Diana spent less than one hour preparing for trial. At trial, Diana called only one witness, didn't ask more than 10 questions during cross-examination, raised only a few objections, and made only brief opening and closing statements. Charles was found guilty.

   On appeal, Charles argues Diana provided ineffective assistance of counsel. How should the appellate court rule?

ORAL ARGUMENTS

Ake v. Oklahoma: www.oyez.org/cases/1984/83-5424
Douglas v. California: www.oyez.org/cases/1961/34
Faretta v. California: www.oyez.org/cases/1970-1979/1974/1974_73_5772/argument
Gideon v. Wainwright: www.oyez.org/cases/1962/155
Lee v. United States: www.oyez.org/cases/2016/16-327
McWilliams v. Dunn: www.oyez.org/cases/2016/16-5294
Nix v. Whiteside: www.oyez.org/cases/1980-1989/1985/1985_84_1321/argument
Scott v. Illinois: www.oyez.org/cases/1978/77-1177
Strickland v. Washington: www.oyez.org/cases/1980-1989/1983/1983_82_1554/argument
United States v. Cronic: www.oyez.org/cases/1983/82-660
United States v. Gonzalez-Lopez: www.oyez.org/cases/2005/05-352

CHAPTER 11

The Pretrial Process

LEARNING OBJECTIVES

After reading this chapter, students should be able to:

- Appreciate the prosecutor's function and duty in the criminal justice system
- Understand the process of charging defendants
- Recognize the function and significance of bail and pretrial release decisions
- Explain the concepts of vindictive and selective prosecution
- Understand the method by which preliminary hearings occur
- Comprehend the intricacies of grand jury proceedings
- Understand a prosecutor's duty to disclose exculpatory material evidence
- Recognize a prosecutor's discretion in the plea-bargaining process
- Understand when a defendant may back out of a plea bargain

Introduction

Several subtle yet significant changes occur once a person has been charged with a crime. The arrestee is no longer a suspect but is now a defendant. Additionally, the process no longer focuses on the investigation but has moved to the prosecutorial phase. As we shall see in forthcoming chapters, this shift calls into play a plethora of rights afforded to the defendant and simultaneously places numerous obligations on the prosecution. In this chapter, we look at the rights and burdens involved in the pretrial process — that is, the events that occur after a defendant is arrested and before he or she is brought to trial.

The Initial Appearance

In Chapter 3, we learned that the police typically have the authority to arrest a suspect without first obtaining a warrant. *United States v. Watson*, 423 U.S. 411 (1976). Although this authority is necessary to facilitate the apprehension of suspects caught at the scene of a crime or in a situation where obtaining an arrest warrant is impractical, it does present the criminal justice system with a dilemma. Although there is a need for effective law enforcement, by permitting warrantless arrests, the justice system replaces a judge's detached, neutral assessment of whether probable cause to arrest exists with the on-the-spot, heat-of-the-moment determination of a non-neutral law enforcement officer.

To limit the damage that an erroneous warrantless arrest can cause, courts have set various procedures to ensure that a prompt judicial determination of probable cause to arrest a person is made. Although it is not disputed that such a procedure is necessary to protect the rights of arrested persons, exactly what such a right entails has been the subject of much debate. Should a suspect have a right to a judicial determination as to whether there is probable cause to detain him at the first practicable opportunity? Within 24 hours? Within 8 hours? What if the arrest is on a weekend or holiday?

In *Gerstein v. Pugh*, 420 U.S. 103 (1975), the U.S. Supreme Court held that "a State must provide a fair and reliable determination of probable cause as a condition for any significant pretrial restraint of liberty." The Court further held that this determination must be made "promptly." Following Gerstein, state and lower federal courts disagreed about how "promptly" this probable-cause determination had to be made. In *County of Riverside v. McLaughlin*, the Supreme Court sought to clarify what was constitutionally required.

County of Riverside v. McLaughlin

500 U.S. 44 (1991)

JUSTICE O'CONNOR delivered the opinion of the Court.

In *Gerstein v. Pugh*, 420 U.S. 103 (1975), this Court held that the Fourth Amendment requires a prompt judicial determination of probable cause as a prerequisite to an extended pretrial detention following a warrantless arrest. This case requires us to define what is "prompt" under *Gerstein.*

I

This is a class action brought under 42 U.S.C. §1983 challenging the manner in which the County of Riverside, California, provides probable cause determinations to persons arrested without a warrant. At issue is the County's policy of combining probable cause determinations with its arraignment procedures. Under County policy, which tracks closely the provisions of Cal. Penal Code Ann. §825 (West 1985), arraignments must be conducted without unnecessary delay and, in any event, within two days of arrest. This 2-day requirement excludes from computation weekends and holidays. Thus, an individual arrested without a warrant late in the week may in some cases be held for as long as five days before receiving a probable cause determination. Over the Thanksgiving holiday, a 7-day delay is possible.

III

In *Gerstein*, this Court held unconstitutional Florida procedures under which persons arrested without a warrant could remain in police custody for 30 days or more without a judicial determination of probable cause. In reaching this conclusion we attempted to reconcile important competing interests. On the one hand, States have a strong interest in protecting public safety by taking into custody those persons who are reasonably suspected of having engaged in criminal activity, even where there has been no opportunity for a prior judicial determination of probable cause. On the other hand, prolonged detention based on incorrect or unfounded suspicion may unjustly "imperil [a] suspect's job, interrupt his source of income, and impair his family relationships." We sought to balance these competing concerns by holding that States "must provide a fair and reliable determination of probable cause as a condition for any significant pretrial restraint of liberty, and this determination must be made by a judicial officer either before or promptly after arrest."

The Court thus established a "practical compromise" between the rights of individuals and the realities of law enforcement. Under Gerstein, warrantless arrests are permitted but persons arrested without a warrant must promptly be brought before a neutral magistrate for a judicial determination of probable cause. Significantly, the Court stopped short of holding that jurisdictions were constitutionally compelled to provide a **probable cause hearing** immediately upon taking a suspect into custody and completing booking procedures. We acknowledged the burden that proliferation of pretrial proceedings places on the criminal justice system and recognized that the interests of everyone involved, including those persons who are arrested, might be disserved by introducing further procedural complexity into an already intricate system. Accordingly, we left it to the individual States to integrate prompt probable cause determinations into their differing systems of pretrial procedures.

In so doing, we gave proper deference to the demands of federalism. We recognized that "state systems of criminal procedure vary widely" in the nature and number of pretrial procedures they provide, and we noted that there is no single "preferred" approach. We explained further that "flexibility and experimentation by the States" with respect to integrating probable cause determinations was desirable and that each State should settle upon an approach "to accord with [the] State's pretrial procedure viewed as a whole." Our purpose in *Gerstein* was to make clear that the Fourth Amendment requires every State to provide prompt determinations of probable cause, but that the Constitution does not impose on the States a rigid procedural framework. Rather, individual States may choose to comply in different ways.

Inherent in *Gerstein's* invitation to the States to experiment and adapt was the recognition that the Fourth Amendment does not compel an immediate determination of probable cause upon completing the administrative steps incident to arrest. Plainly, if a probable cause hearing is constitutionally compelled the moment a suspect is finished being "booked," there is no room whatsoever for "flexibility and experimentation by the States." Incorporating probable cause determinations "into the procedure for setting **bail** or fixing other conditions of pretrial release" — which *Gerstein* explicitly contemplated — would be impossible. Waiting even a few hours so that a bail hearing or arraignment could take place at the same time as the probable cause determination would amount to a constitutional violation. Clearly, *Gerstein* is not that inflexible.

Notwithstanding *Gerstein's* discussion of flexibility, the Court of Appeals for the Ninth Circuit held that no flexibility was permitted. It construed *Gerstein* as "requir[ing] a probable cause determination to be made as soon as the administrative steps incident to arrest were completed, and that such steps should require only a brief period." 888 F.2d, at 1278. This same reading is advanced by the dissents. The foregoing discussion readily demonstrates the error of this approach. *Gerstein* held that probable cause determinations must be prompt — not immediate. The Court explained that "flexibility and experimentation" were "desirab[le]"; that "[t]here is no single preferred pretrial procedure"; and that "the nature of the probable cause determination usually will be shaped to accord with a State's pretrial procedure viewed as a whole." The Court of Appeals and Justice Scalia disregard these statements, relying instead on selective quotations from the Court's opinion. As we have explained, *Gerstein* struck a balance between competing interests; a proper understanding of the decision is possible only if one takes into account both sides of the equation.

Justice Scalia claims to find support for his approach in the common law. He points to several statements from the early 1800's to the effect that an arresting officer must bring a person arrested without a warrant before a judicial officer "'as soon as he reasonably can.'" This vague admonition offers no more support for the dissent's inflexible standard than does *Gerstein's* statement that a hearing follow "promptly after arrest." As mentioned at the outset, the question before us today is what is "prompt" under *Gerstein*. We answer that question by recognizing that *Gerstein* struck a balance between competing interests.

B

Given that *Gerstein* permits jurisdictions to incorporate probable cause determinations into other pretrial procedures, some delays are inevitable. For example, where, as in Riverside County, the probable cause determination is combined with arraignment, there will be delays caused by paperwork and logistical problems. Records will have to be reviewed, charging documents drafted, appearance of counsel arranged, and appropriate bail determined. On weekends, when the number of arrests is often higher and available resources tend to be limited, arraignments may get pushed back even further. In our view, the Fourth Amendment permits a reasonable postponement of a probable cause determination while the police cope with the everyday problems of processing suspects through an overly burdened criminal justice system.

But flexibility has its limits; *Gerstein* is not a blank check. A State has no legitimate interest in detaining for extended periods individuals who have been arrested without probable cause. The Court recognized in *Gerstein* that a person arrested without a warrant is entitled to a fair and reliable determination of probable cause and that this determination must be made promptly.

Unfortunately, as lower court decisions applying *Gerstein* have demonstrated, it is not enough to say that probable cause determinations must be "prompt." This vague standard simply has not provided sufficient guidance. Instead, it has led to a flurry of systemic challenges to city and county practices, putting federal judges in the role of making legislative judgments and over-seeing local jailhouse operations.

Our task in this case is to articulate more clearly the boundaries of what is permissible under the Fourth Amendment. Although we hesitate to announce that the Constitution compels a specific time limit, it is important to provide some degree of certainty so that States and counties may establish procedures with confidence that they fall within constitutional bounds. Taking into account the competing interests articulated in Gerstein, we believe that a jurisdiction that provides judicial determinations of probable cause within 48 hours of arrest will, as a general matter, comply with the promptness requirement of Gerstein. For this reason, such jurisdictions will be immune from systemic challenges.

This is not to say that the probable cause determination in a particular case passes constitutional muster simply because it is provided within 48 hours. Such a hearing may nonetheless violate *Gerstein* if the arrested individual can prove that his or her probable cause determination was delayed unreasonably. Examples of unreasonable delay are delays for the purpose of gathering additional evidence to justify the arrest, a delay motivated by ill will against the arrested individual, or delay for delay's sake. In evaluating whether the delay in a particular case is unreasonable, however, courts must allow a substantial degree of flexibility. Courts cannot ignore the often unavoidable delays in transporting arrested persons from one facility to another, handling late-night bookings where no magistrate is readily available, obtaining the presence of an arresting officer who may be busy processing other suspects or securing the premises of an arrest, and other practical realities.

Where an arrested individual does not receive a probable cause determination within 48 hours, the calculus changes. In such a case, the arrested individual does not bear the burden of proving an unreasonable delay. Rather, the burden shifts to the government to demonstrate the existence of a bona fide emergency or other extraordinary circumstance. The fact that in a particular case it may take longer than 48 hours to consolidate pretrial proceedings does not qualify as an extraordinary circumstance. Nor, for that matter, do intervening weekends. A jurisdiction that chooses to offer combined proceedings must do so as soon as is reasonably feasible, but in no event later than 48 hours after arrest.

Justice Scalia urges that 24 hours is a more appropriate outer boundary for providing probable cause determinations. In arguing that any delay in probable cause hearings beyond completing the administrative steps incident to arrest and arranging for a magistrate is unconstitutional, Justice Scalia, in effect, adopts the view of the Court of Appeals. Yet he ignores entirely the Court of Appeals' determination of the time required to complete those procedures. That court, better situated than this one, concluded that it takes 36 hours to process arrested persons in Riverside County. In advocating a 24-hour rule, Justice Scalia would compel Riverside County — and countless others across the Nation — to speed up its criminal justice mechanisms substantially, presumably by allotting local tax dollars to hire additional police officers and magistrates. There may be times when the Constitution compels such direct interference with local control, but this is not one. As we have explained, *Gerstein* clearly contemplated a reasonable accommodation between legitimate competing concerns. We do no more than recognize that such accommodation can take place without running afoul of the Fourth Amendment.

IV

For the reasons we have articulated, we conclude that Riverside County is entitled to combine probable cause determinations with arraignments. The record indicates, however, that the County's current policy and practice do not comport fully with the principles we have outlined. The County's current policy is to offer combined proceedings within two days, exclusive of Saturdays, Sundays, or holidays. As a result, persons arrested on Thursdays may have to wait until the following Monday before they receive a probable cause determination. The delay is even longer if there is an intervening holiday. Thus, the County's regular practice exceeds the 48-hour period we deem constitutionally permissible, meaning that the County is not immune from systemic challenges, such as this class action.

As to arrests that occur early in the week, the County's practice is that "arraignment[s] usually tak[e] place on the last day" possible. There may well be legitimate reasons for this practice; alternatively, this may constitute delay for delay's sake. We leave it to the Court of Appeals and the District Court, on remand, to make this determination.

The judgment of the Court of Appeals is vacated, and the case is remanded for further proceedings consistent with this opinion.

Justice Scalia, dissenting.

The Court views the task before it as one of "balanc[ing] [the] competing concerns" of "protecting public safety," on the one hand, and avoiding "prolonged detention based on incorrect or unfounded suspicion," on the other hand. It purports to reaffirm the " 'practical compromise' " between these concerns struck in *Gerstein v. Pugh*, 420 U.S. 103 (1975). There is assuredly room for such an approach in resolving novel questions of search and seizure under the "reasonableness" standard that the Fourth Amendment sets forth. But not, I think, in resolving those questions on which a clear answer already existed in 1791 and has been generally adhered to by the traditions of our society ever since. As to those matters, the "balance" has already been struck, the "practical compromise" reached — and it is the function of the Bill of Rights to preserve that judgment, not only against the changing views of Presidents and Members of Congress, but also against the changing views of Justices whom Presidents appoint and Members of Congress confirm to this Court.

In my view, absent extraordinary circumstances, it is an "unreasonable seizure" within the meaning of the Fourth Amendment for the police, having arrested a suspect without a warrant, to delay a determination of probable cause for the arrest either (1) for reasons unrelated to arrangement of the probable-cause determination or completion of the steps incident to arrest, or (2) beyond 24 hours after the arrest. Like the Court, I would treat the time limit as a presumption; when the 24 hours are exceeded the burden shifts to the police to adduce unforeseeable circumstances justifying the additional delay.

FURTHER CASE LAW, REFLECTIONS, AND QUESTIONS

1. In reaching its decision in *McLaughlin*, what interests did the Court balance?
2. The Court based its decision in *McLaughlin* on the Fourth Amendment. What do you suppose the result might have been if the Court considered whether due process rights were violated?
3. It is important to remember that the probable-cause determination made in *McLaughlin* deals with probable cause to detain a suspect. This differs from the probable-cause determination made at the preliminary hearing or grand jury, discussed later in this chapter.

Bail and Prevention Detention

After a person is arrested, a decision must be made whether the arrestee should be (1) released from custody on their own recognizance with no conditions other than the arrestee's promise to appear in court attached; (2) released under certain conditions, such as to avoid contact with the alleged victim or to report periodically to a pretrial release supervisor; (3) held pending the payment of bail, or (4) held without bail. A judge or magistrate normally decides which conditions of release are appropriate at the defendant's **initial appearance.**

While individuals arrested do not invariably have a right to be released from custody on bail, the Eighth Amendment to the United States Constitution provides that "excessive bail shall not be required." This provision raises the obvious question: What is excessive bail? In *Stack v. Boyle*, the Supreme Court set forth guidelines to be used by lower courts in deciding what conditions of release or bail should be considered in a given case.

Stack v. Boyle

342 U.S. 1 (1951)

MR. CHIEF JUSTICE VINSON delivered the opinion of the Court.

Indictments have been returned in the Southern District of California charging the twelve petitioners with conspiring to violate the Smith Act. Upon their arrest, bail was fixed for each petitioner in the widely varying amounts of $2,500, $7,500, $75,000, and $100,000. On motion of petitioner Schneiderman following arrest in the Southern District of New York, his bail was reduced to $50,000 before his removal to California. On motion of the Government to increase bail in the case of other petitioners, and after several intermediate procedural steps not material to the issues presented here, bail was fixed in the District Court for the Southern District of California in the uniform amount of $50,000 for each petitioner.

Petitioners moved to reduce bail on the ground that bail as fixed was excessive under the Eighth Amendment. In support of their motion, petitioners submitted statements as to their financial resources, family relationships, health, prior criminal records, and other information. The only evidence offered by the Government was a certified record showing that four persons previously convicted under the Smith Act in the Southern District of New York had forfeited bail. No evidence was produced relating those four persons to the petitioners in this case. At a hearing on the motion, petitioners were examined by the District Judge and cross-examined by an attorney for the Government. Petitioners' factual statements stand uncontroverted.

From the passage of the Judiciary Act of 1789 to the present Federal Rules of Criminal Procedure, Rule 46(a)(1), federal law has unequivocally provided that a person arrested for a non-capital offense shall be admitted to bail. This traditional right to freedom before conviction permits the unhampered preparation of a defense and serves to prevent the infliction of punishment prior to conviction. Unless this right to bail before trial is preserved, the presumption of innocence, secured only after centuries of struggle, would lose its meaning.

The right to release before trial is conditioned upon the accused's giving adequate assurance that he will stand trial and submit to sentence if found guilty. Like the ancient practice of securing the oaths of responsible persons to stand as sureties for the accused, the modern practice of requiring a bail bond or the deposit of a sum of money subject to forfeiture serves as additional assurance of the presence of an accused. Bail set at a figure higher than an amount reasonably calculated to fulfill this purpose is "excessive" under the Eighth Amendment.

Since the function of bail is limited, the fixing of bail for any individual defendant must be based upon standards relevant to the purpose of assuring the presence of that defendant. The traditional standards as expressed in the Federal Rules of Criminal Procedure are to be applied in each case to each defendant. In this case petitioners are charged with offenses under the Smith Act and, if found guilty, their convictions are subject to review with the scrupulous care demanded by our Constitution. Upon final judgment of conviction, petitioners face imprisonment of not more than five years and a fine of not more than $10,000. It is not denied that bail for each petitioner has been fixed in a sum much higher than that usually imposed for offenses with like penalties and yet there has been no factual showing to justify such action in this case. The Government asks the courts to depart from the norm by assuming, without the introduction of evidence, that each petitioner is a pawn in a conspiracy and will, in obedience to a superior, flee the jurisdiction. To infer from the fact of indictment alone a need for bail in an unusually high amount is an arbitrary act. Such conduct would inject into our own system of government the very principles of totalitarianism which Congress was seeking to guard against in passing the statute under which petitioners have been indicted.

If bail in an amount greater than that usually fixed for serious charges of crimes is required in the case of any of the petitioners, that is a matter to which evidence should be directed in a hearing so that the constitutional rights of each petitioner may be preserved. In the absence of such a showing, we are of the opinion that the fixing of bail before trial in these cases cannot be squared with the statutory and constitutional standards for admission to bail.

Judgment of Court of Appeals vacated and case remanded to District Court with directions.

FURTHER CASE LAW, REFLECTIONS, AND QUESTIONS

1. Does it surprise you that bail is to be set at an amount to ensure the defendant's presence at trial? Should bail serve other purposes for the good of the justice system and society?

2. In your opinion, what factors should be considered in setting bail? Should such factors apply equally, or are some deserving of greater weight than others?

In the years since *Stack*, the crime rate has increased. One response to this increase in crime has been legislative actions to get tougher on criminals. *United States v. Salerno* discusses the constitutionality of one such action taken by Congress: the **Bail Reform Act of 1984**. As you read *Salerno*, ask yourself whether its holding can be reconciled with *Stack v. Boyle*.

United States v. Salerno

481 U.S. 739 (1987)

Chief Justice Rehnquist delivered the opinion of the Court.

Responding to "the alarming problem of crimes committed by persons on release," Congress formulated the Bail Reform Act of 1984, as the solution to a bail crisis in the federal courts. The Act represents the National Legislature's considered response to numerous perceived deficiencies in the federal bail process. By providing for sweeping changes in both the way federal courts consider bail applications and the circumstances under which bail is granted, Congress hoped to "give the courts adequate authority to make release decisions that give appropriate recognition to the danger a person may pose to others if released." Section 3142(e) provides that "[i]f, after a hearing pursuant to the provisions of subsection (f), the judicial officer finds that no condition or combination of conditions will reasonably assure the appearance of the person as required and the safety of any other person and the community, he shall order the detention of the person prior to trial." Section 3142(f) provides the arrestee with a number of procedural safeguards. He may request the presence of counsel at the detention hearing, he may testify and present witnesses on his behalf, as well as proffer evidence, and he may cross-examine other witnesses appearing at the hearing. If the judicial officer finds that no conditions of pretrial release can reasonably assure the safety of other persons and the community, he must state his findings of fact in writing, and support his conclusion with "clear and convincing evidence."

The judicial officer is not given unbridled discretion in making the detention determination. Congress has specified the considerations relevant to that decision. These factors include the nature and seriousness of the charges, the substantiality of the Government's evidence against the arrestee, the arrestee's background and characteristics, and the nature and seriousness of the danger posed by the suspect's release. Should a judicial officer order detention, the detainee is entitled to expedited appellate review of the detention order.

Respondents Anthony Salerno and Vincent Cafaro were arrested on March 21, 1986, after being charged in a 29-count indictment alleging various Racketeer Influenced and Corrupt Organizations Act (RICO) violations, mail and wire fraud offenses, extortion, and various criminal gambling violations. The RICO counts alleged 35 acts of racketeering activity, including fraud, extortion, gambling, and conspiracy to commit murder. At respondents' arraignment, the Government moved to have Salerno and Cafaro detained on the ground that no condition of release would assure the safety of the community or any person. The District Court held a hearing at which the Government made a detailed proffer of evidence. The Government's case showed that Salerno was the "boss" of the Genovese crime family of La Cosa Nostra and that Cafaro was a "captain" in the Genovese family. According to the Government's proffer, based in large part on conversations intercepted by a court-ordered wiretap, the two respondents had participated in wide-ranging conspiracies to aid their illegitimate enterprises through violent means. The Government also offered the testimony of two of its trial witnesses, who would assert that Salerno personally participated in two murder conspiracies. Salerno opposed the motion for detention, challenging the credibility of the Government's witnesses. He offered the testimony of several character witnesses as well as a letter from his doctor stating that he was suffering from a serious medical condition. Cafaro presented no evidence at the hearing, but instead characterized the wiretap conversations as merely "tough talk."

The District Court granted the Government's detention motion, concluding that the Government had established by clear and convincing evidence that no condition or combination of conditions of release would ensure the safety of the community or any person.

Respondents present two grounds for invalidating the Bail Reform Act's provisions permitting pretrial detention on the basis of future dangerousness. First, they rely upon the Court of Appeal's conclusion that the Act exceeds the limitations placed upon the Federal Government by the Due Process Clause of the Fifth Amendment. Second, they contend that the Act contravenes the Eighth Amendment's proscription against excessive bail. We treat these contentions in turn.

A

The Due Process Clause of the Fifth Amendment provides that "No person shall... be deprived of life, liberty, or property, without due process of law." This Court has held that the Due Process Clause protects individuals against two types of government action. So-called "substantive due process" prevents the government from engaging in conduct that "shocks the conscience," or interferes with rights "implicit in the concept of ordered liberty." When government action depriving a person of life, liberty, or property survives substantive due process scrutiny, it must still be implemented in a fair manner. This requirement has traditionally been referred to as "procedural" due process.

Respondents first argue that the Act violates substantive due process because the pretrial detention it authorizes constitutes impermissible punishment before trial. The Government however, has never argued that pretrial detention could be upheld if it were "punishment." The Court of Appeals assumed that pretrial detention under the Bail Reform Act is regulatory, not penal, and we agree that it is.

As an initial matter, the mere fact that a person is detained does not inexorably lead to the conclusion that the government has imposed punishment. To determine whether a restriction on liberty constitutes impermissible punishment or permissible regulation, we first look to legislative intent. Unless Congress expressly intended to impose punitive restrictions, the punitive/regulatory distinction turns on "'whether an alternative purpose to which [the restriction] may rationally be connected is assignable for it, and whether it appears excessive in relation to the alternative purpose assigned [to it].'"

We conclude that the detention imposed by the Act falls on the regulatory side of the dichotomy. The legislative history of the Bail Reform Act clearly indicates that Congress did not formulate the pretrial detention provisions as punishment for dangerous individuals. Congress instead perceived pretrial detention as a potential solution to a pressing societal problem. There is no doubt that preventing danger to the community is a legitimate regulatory goal.

Respondents characterize the Due Process Clause as erecting an impenetrable "wall" in this area that "no governmental interest — rational, important, compelling or otherwise — may surmount."

We do not think the Clause lays down any such categorical imperative. We have repeatedly held that the Government's regulatory interest in community safety can, in appropriate circumstances, outweigh an individual's liberty interest. For example, in times of war or insurrection, when society's interest is at its peak, the Government may detain individuals whom the government believes to be dangerous. Even outside the exigencies of war, we have found that sufficiently compelling governmental interests can justify detention of dangerous persons. Thus, we have found no absolute constitutional barrier to detention of potentially dangerous resident aliens pending deportation proceedings. We have also held that the government may detain mentally unstable individuals who present a danger to the public, *Addington v. Texas*, and dangerous defendants who become incompetent to stand trial, *Jackson v. Indiana*.

Respondents characterize all of these cases as exceptions to the "general rule" of substantive due process that the government may not detain a person prior to a judgment of guilt in a criminal trial. Such a "general rule" may freely be conceded, but we think that these cases show a sufficient number of exceptions to the rule that the congressional action challenged here can hardly be characterized as totally novel.

Given the well-established authority of the government, in special circumstances, to restrain individuals' liberty prior to or even without criminal trial and conviction, we think that the present statute providing for pretrial detention on the basis of dangerousness must be evaluated in precisely the same manner that we evaluated the laws in the cases discussed above.

The government's interest in preventing crime by arrestees is both legitimate and compelling. In *Schall*, we recognized the strength of the State's interest in preventing juvenile crime. This general concern with crime prevention is no less compelling when the suspects are adults. Indeed, "[t]he harm suffered by the victim of a crime is not dependent upon the age of the perpetrator." The Bail Reform Act of 1984 responds to an even more particularized governmental interest than the interest we sustained in *Schall*. The statute we upheld in *Schall* permitted pre-trial detention of any juvenile arrested on any charge after a showing that the individual might commit some undefined further crimes. The Bail Reform Act, in contrast, narrowly focuses on a particularly acute problem in which the Government interests are overwhelming. The Act operates only on individuals who have been arrested for a specific category of extremely serious offenses. Congress specifically found that these individuals are far more likely to be responsible for dangerous acts in the community after arrest. Nor is the Act by any means a scattershot attempt to incapacitate those who are merely suspected of these serious crimes. The Government must first of all demonstrate probable cause to believe that the charged crime has been committed by the arrestee, but that is not enough. In a full-blown adversary hearing, the Government must convince a neutral decision maker by clear and convincing evidence that no conditions of release can reasonably assure the safety of the community or any person. While the Government's general interest in preventing crime is compelling, even this interest is heightened when the Government musters convincing proof that the arrestee, already indicted or held to answer for a serious crime, presents a demonstrable danger to the community. Under these narrow circumstances, society's interest in crime prevention is at its greatest.

On the other side of the scale, of course, is the individual's strong interest in liberty. We do not minimize the importance and fundamental nature of this right. But, as our cases hold, this right may, in circumstances where the government's interest is sufficiently weighty, be subordinated to the greater needs of society. We think that Congress' careful delineation of the circumstances under which detention will be permitted satisfies this standard. When the Government proves by clear and convincing evidence that an arrestee presents an identified and articulable threat to an individual or the community, we believe that, consistent with the Due Process Clause, a court may disable the arrestee from executing that threat.

B

Respondents also contend that the Bail Reform Act violates the Excessive Bail Clause of the Eighth Amendment. The Court of Appeals did not address this issue because it found that the Act violates the Due Process Clause. We think that the Act survives a challenge founded upon the Eighth Amendment.

While we agree that a primary function of bail is to safeguard the courts' role in adjudicating the guilt or innocence of defendants, we reject the proposition that the Eighth Amendment categorically prohibits the government from pursuing other admittedly compelling interests through regulation of pretrial release.

Of course, to determine whether the Government's response is excessive, we must compare that response against the interest the Government seeks to protect by means of that response. Thus, when the Government has admitted that its only interest is in preventing flight, bail must be set by a court at a sum designed to ensure that goal, and no more. We believe that when Congress has mandated detention on the basis of a compelling interest other than prevention of flight, as it has here, the Eighth Amendment does not require release on bail.

III

In our society liberty is the norm, and detention prior to trial or without trial is the carefully limited exception. We hold that the provisions for pretrial detention in the Bail Reform Act of 1984 fall within that carefully limited exception. The Act authorizes the detention prior to trial of arrestees charged with serious felonies who are found after an adversary hearing to pose a threat to the safety of individuals or to the community which no condition of release can dispel. The numerous procedural safeguards detailed above must attend this adversary hearing. We are unwilling to say that this congressional determination, based as it is upon that primary concern of every government — a concern for the safety and indeed the lives of its citizens — on its face violates either the Due Process Clause of the Fifth Amendment or the Excessive Bail Clause of the Eighth Amendment.

The judgment of the Court of Appeals is therefore, Reversed.

JUSTICE MARSHALL, with whom JUSTICE BRENNAN joins, dissenting.

This case brings before the Court for the first time a statute in which Congress declares that a person innocent of any crime may be jailed indefinitely, pending the trial of allegations which are legally presumed to be untrue, if the Government shows to the satisfaction of a judge that the accused is likely to commit crimes, unrelated to the pending charges, at any time in the future. Such statutes, consistent with the usages of tyranny and the excesses of what bitter experience teaches us to call the police state, have long been thought incompatible with the fundamental human rights protected by our Constitution. Today a majority of this Court holds otherwise. Its decision disregards basic principles of justice established centuries ago and enshrined beyond the reach of governmental interference in the Bill of Rights.

IV

There is a connection between the peculiar facts of this case and the evident constitutional defects in the statute which the Court upholds today. Respondent Cafaro was originally incarcerated for an indeterminate period at the request of the Government, which believed (or professed to believe) that his release imminently threatened the safety of the community. That threat apparently vanished, from the Government's point of view, when Cafaro agreed to act as a covert agent of the Government. There could be no more eloquent demonstration of the coercive power of authority to imprison upon prediction, or of the dangers which the almost inevitable abuses pose to the cherished liberties of a free society.

I dissent.

FURTHER CASE LAW, REFLECTIONS, AND QUESTIONS

1. According to the Court, which factors should a magistrate consider in deciding about pretrial detention? Are these factors appropriate? Do they limit the discretion given to the magistrate? How so?
2. Is **preventive detention** a form of punishment?
3. In his dissent, Justice Marshall raises the fact that defendant Cafaro was released on $1-million bail to allow him to work as a government informant. Do you agree with Justice Marshall's argument that this evidence shows the coercive nature of preventive detention? Do you agree with his statement that the threat posed by Cafaro to society, as previously argued by the government, vanished once he agreed to be an informant?

The Decision to Charge a Suspect

In a perfect world, all suspects arrested would face prosecution. In reality, all prosecutors' offices lack the capacity to do so. Due to these resource limitations, prosecutors must decide which cases to pursue and which to dismiss.

The American Bar Association has published recommended standards regarding prosecutorial discretion in the charging decision. Standard 3-3.9 of the Criminal Justice Standards for the Prosecution Function, 4th Ed (American Bar Association, 2017) states:

> a. A prosecutor should not institute, or cause to be instituted, or permit the continued pendency of criminal charges when the prosecutor knows that

> the charges are not supported by probable cause. A prosecutor should not institute, cause to be instituted, or permit the continued pendency of criminal charges in the absence of sufficient admissible evidence to support a conviction.
>
> b. The prosecutor is not obliged to present all charges which the evidence might support. The prosecutor may in some circumstances and for good cause consistent with the public interest decline to prosecute, notwithstanding that sufficient evidence may exist which would support a conviction.

Factors which are appropriate for prosecutors to consider in exercising their charging discretion include:

- A reasonable doubt on the part of the prosecutor regarding the accused's actual guilt
- The seriousness and extent of harm caused by the alleged offense
- A disproportionate punishment in relation to the offense or the offender's circumstances
- Suspected improper motives of the complainant
- The victim's reluctance or refusal to testify
- The accused's cooperation in investigating or prosecuting other offenders
- The availability and likelihood of prosecution by another jurisdiction

While these items may be considered in charging decisions, they are not mandatory but merely advisory. In fact, the Supreme Court has repeatedly held that prosecutors have near limitless discretion in deciding what cases to pursue.

There are, however, two general and narrowly defined limitations on who prosecutors decide to file criminal charges against: "selective" and "vindictive" prosecutions. While every decision to prosecute is "selective," selective prosecution refers to targeting individuals for prosecution with a discriminatory intent in such a way that has a discriminatory impact. The Supreme Court discussed **selective prosecution** in *Wayte v. United States.*

Selective Prosecution

Wayte v. United States

470 U.S. 598 (1985)

JUSTICE POWELL delivered the opinion of the Court.

[A Presidential Proclamation issued in July 1980 directed males born during 1960 to register with the Selective Service System. Registrants' names and other relevant information were collected so that Selective Service would be able to identify men eligible for military duty in case a need later arose to draft them. The knowing and willful failure to register was a crime punishable by fine and imprisonment.

[The defendant, David Wayte, was a member of the cohort of young men who were required to register, but he declined to do so. "Instead, he wrote several letters to Government officials, including the President, stating that he had not registered and did not intend to do so." Wayte's name thus was included in a Selective Service file of men who personally reported that they would not register or who were reported by others as having failed to register. Selective Service adopted a "passive enforcement" policy, under which only men in this file would be investigated or prosecuted for nonregistration. Pursuant to this policy, Selective Service mailed a letter in June 1981 to each reported violator, explaining that he was delinquent, requesting that he register, and advising him that he faced possible prosecution for noncompliance. Wayte received such a letter and ignored it.

[Thereafter, Wayte was one of approximately 285 men whose names were referred to the FBI and to U.S. Attorneys in the districts where the nonregistrants lived. Pursuant to the Justice Department's so-called "beg" policy, nonregistrants were not immediately prosecuted. Instead, U.S. Attorneys wrote the men letters warning that prosecution would be considered unless registration was completed by a designated date, and FBI agents attempted to interview nonregistrants before a prosecution was started. Finally, the President announced a "grace period" until the end of February 1982, throughout which nonregistrants could comply without penalty. Wayte still refused to register.]

Over the next few months, the Department decided to begin prosecuting those young men who, despite the grace period and "beg" policy, continued to refuse to register. It recognized that under the passive enforcement system those prosecuted were "liable to be vocal proponents of nonregistration" or persons "with religious or moral objections." It also recognized that prosecutions would "undoubtedly result in allegations that the [case was] brought in retribution for the nonregistrant's exercise of his first amendment rights." The Department was advised, however, that Selective Service could not develop a more "active" enforcement system for quite some time. Because of this, the Department decided to begin seeking indictments under the passive system without further delay. On May 21, 1982, United States Attorneys were notified to begin prosecution of nonregistrants. On June 28, 1982, FBI agents interviewed petitioner, and he continued to refuse to register. Accordingly, on July 22, 1982, an indictment was returned against him for knowingly and willfully failing to register with the Selective Service.

Petitioner moved to dismiss the indictment on the ground of selective prosecution. He contended that he and the other indicted nonregistrants were "vocal" opponents of the registration program who had been impermissibly targeted (out of an estimated 674,000 nonregistrants) for prosecution on the basis of their exercise of First Amendment rights. After a hearing, the District Court for the Central District of California granted petitioner's broad request for discovery and directed the Government to produce certain documents and make certain officials available to testify. The Government produced some documents and agreed to make some Government officials available but, citing executive privilege, it withheld other documents and testimony.

On November 15, 1982, the District Court dismissed the indictment on the ground that the Government had failed to rebut petitioner's prima facie case of selective prosecution. The Court of Appeals reversed. We granted certiorari on the question of selective prosecution.

In our criminal justice system, the Government retains "broad discretion" as to whom to prosecute. "[S]o long as the prosecutor has probable cause to believe that the accused committed an offense defined by statute, the decision whether or not to prosecute, and what charge to file or bring before a grand jury, generally rests entirely in his discretion." This broad discretion rests largely on the recognition that the decision to prosecute is particularly ill-suited to judicial review. Such factors as the strength of the case, the prosecution's general deterrence value, the Government's enforcement priorities, and the case's relationship to the Government's overall enforcement plan are not readily susceptible to the kind of analysis the courts are competent to undertake. Judicial supervision in this area, moreover, entails systemic costs of particular concern. Examining the basis of a prosecution delays the criminal proceeding, threatens to chill law enforcement by subjecting the prosecutor's motives and decision making to outside inquiry, and may undermine prosecutorial effectiveness by revealing the Government's enforcement policy. All these are substantial concerns that make the courts properly hesitant to examine the decision whether to prosecute.

As we have noted in a slightly different context, however, although prosecutorial discretion is broad, it is not "'unfettered.' Selectivity in the enforcement of criminal laws is subject to constitutional constraints." In particular, the decision to prosecute may not be "deliberately based upon an unjustifiable standard such as race, religion, or other arbitrary classification," including the exercise of protected statutory and constitutional rights.

It is appropriate to judge selective prosecution claims according to ordinary equal protection standards. Under our prior cases, these standards require petitioner to show both that the passive enforcement system had a discriminatory effect and that it was motivated by a discriminatory purpose. All petitioner has shown here is that those eventually prosecuted, along with many not prosecuted, reported themselves as having violated the law. He has not shown that the enforcement policy selected nonregistrants for prosecution on the basis of their speech. Indeed, he could not have done so given the way the "beg" policy was carried out. The Government did not prosecute those who reported themselves but later registered. Nor did it prosecute those who protested registration but did not report themselves or were not reported by others. In fact, the Government did not even investigate those who wrote letters to Selective Service criticizing registration unless their letters stated affirmatively that they had refused to comply with the law. The Government, on the other hand, did prosecute people who reported themselves or were reported by others but who did not publicly protest. These facts demonstrate that the Government treated all reported nonregistrants similarly. It did not subject vocal nonregistrants to any special burden. Indeed, those prosecuted in effect selected themselves for prosecution by refusing to register after being reported and warned by the Government.

Even if the passive policy had a discriminatory effect, petitioner has not shown that the Government intended such a result. The evidence he presented demonstrated only that the Government was aware that the passive enforcement policy would result in prosecution of vocal objectors and that they would probably make selective prosecution claims. As we have noted, however: "'Discriminatory purpose' implies more than intent as awareness of consequences. It implies that the decisionmaker selected or reaffirmed a particular course of action at least in part 'because of,' not merely 'in spite of,' its adverse effects upon an identifiable group." In the present case, petitioner has not shown that the Government prosecuted him because of his protest activities. Absent such a showing, his claim of selective prosecution fails.

FURTHER CASE LAW, REFLECTIONS, AND QUESTIONS

1. Wasn't the effect of the Justice Department's prosecution policy to concentrate on vocal opponents of the Selective Service registration system? If, in practice, prosecutions disproportionately were initiated against those nonregistrants who aggressively criticized the registration system, does this represent a threat to First Amendment values? Under the Court's ruling in Wayte, is it enough for a defendant to demonstrate an unequal pattern of prosecution to prove unlawful selective prosecution, or must something more be shown?

2. The Court holds in *Wayte* that prosecutors must be given broad latitude in making their charging decisions. What reasons are offered in support of this policy of judicial deference? Are they convincing?

3. The Justice Department seemed almost to bend over backward not to prosecute Wayte and others like him who had failed to register with the Selective Service. What if a prosecution had commenced immediately after government officials received Wayte's initial critical letter? Would Wayte have prevailed if he could establish that only nonregistrants like himself, who criticized the registration requirements, were subject to criminal charges? Under what circumstances can you envision a claim of illegal selective prosecution succeeding?

Vindictive Prosecutions

Vindictive **prosecution** refers to a prosecutor's decision to retaliate against a defendant for exercising a right conferred by law within the criminal justice system. The "selective" prosecution issues that we considered in the previous section concerned allegations that defendants were singled out for prosecution for constitutionally impermissible reasons extrinsic to the criminal justice system, such as the exercise of First Amendment rights or their race.

Under the general subject of vindictive prosecutions, we consider, for example, whether a defendant who exercises his constitutional right to plead not guilty and have a trial by jury can, for that reason, be charged with a more serious crime than a similarly situated defendant who agrees to plead guilty. Similarly, assume that a court nullifies a defendant's conviction after exercising her right to appeal. If the defendant is given a new trial, can she be prosecuted on a more serious charge? Can a harsher sentence be given if she is convicted at the new trial than the one originally given before the appeal?

We begin our examination of vindictive prosecution with *Bordenkircher v. Hayes.*

Bordenkircher v. Hayes

434 U.S. 357 (1978)

MR. JUSTICE STEWART delivered the opinion of the Court.

The question in this case is whether the Due Process Clause of the Fourteenth Amendment is violated when a state prosecutor carries out a threat made during plea negotiations to reindict the accused on more serious charges if he does not plead guilty to the offense with which he was originally charged.

The respondent, Paul Lewis Hayes, was indicted by a Fayette County, Ky., grand jury on a charge of uttering a forged instrument in the amount of $88.30, an offense then punishable by a term of 2 to 10 years in prison. After arraignment, Hayes, his retained counsel, and the Commonwealth's Attorney met in the presence of the Clerk of the Court to discuss a possible plea agreement. During these conferences, the prosecutor offered to recommend a sentence of five years in prison if Hayes would plead guilty to the indictment. He also said that if Hayes did not plead guilty and "save the court the inconvenience and necessity of a trial," he would return to the grand jury to seek an indictment under the Kentucky Habitual Criminal Act,[1] which would subject Hayes to a mandatory sentence of life imprisonment by reason of his two prior felony convictions. Hayes chose not to plead guilty, and the prosecutor did obtain an indictment charging him under the Habitual Criminal Act. It is not disputed that the recidivist charge was fully justified by the evidence, that the prosecutor was in possession of this evidence at the time of the original indictment, and that Hayes' refusal to plead guilty to the original charge was what led to his indictment under the habitual criminal statute.

A jury found Hayes guilty on the principal charge of uttering a forged instrument and, in a separate proceeding, further found that he had twice before been convicted of felonies. As required by the habitual offender statute, he was sentenced to a life term in the penitentiary. The Kentucky Court of Appeals rejected Hayes' constitutional objections to the enhanced sentence, holding in an unpublished opinion that imprisonment for life with the possibility of parole was constitutionally permissible in light of the previous felonies of which Hayes had been convicted, and that the prosecutor's decision to indict him as a habitual offender was a legitimate use of available leverage in the plea bargaining process.

On Hayes' petition for a federal writ of habeas corpus, the United States District Court for the Eastern District of Kentucky agreed that there had been no constitutional violation in the sentence or the indictment procedure, and denied the writ. The Court of Appeals for the Sixth Circuit reversed the District Court's judgment.

It may be helpful to clarify at the outset the nature of the issue in this case. While the prosecutor did not actually obtain the recidivist indictment until after the plea conferences had ended, his intention to do so was clearly expressed at the outset of the plea negotiations. Hayes was thus fully informed of the true terms of the offer when he made his decision to plead not guilty. This is not a situation, therefore, where the prosecutor without notice brought an additional and more serious charge after plea negotiations relating only to the original indictment had ended with the defendant's insistence on pleading not guilty. As a practical matter, in short, this case would be no different if the grand jury had indicted Hayes as a recidivist from the outset, and the prosecutor had offered to drop that charge as part of the plea bargain.

The Court of Appeals nonetheless drew a distinction between "concessions relating to prosecution under an existing indictment," and threats to bring more severe charges not contained in the original indictment — a line it thought necessary in order to establish a prophylactic rule to guard against the evil of prosecutorial vindictiveness. Quite apart from this chronological distinction, however, the Court of Appeals found that the prosecutor had acted vindictively in the present case since he had conceded that the indictment was influenced by his desire to induce a guilty plea.

This Court held in *North Carolina v. Pearce*, 395 U.S. 711, 725 (1969), that the Due Process Clause of the Fourteenth Amendment "requires that vindictiveness against a defendant for having successfully attacked his first conviction must play no part in the sentence he receives after a new trial." The same principle was later applied to prohibit a prosecutor from reindicting a convicted misdemeanant on a felony charge after the defendant had invoked an appellate remedy, since in this situation there was also a "realistic likelihood of 'vindictiveness.'" *Blackledge v. Perry,* 417 U.S. 21, 27 (1974).

In those cases the Court was dealing with the State's unilateral imposition of a penalty upon a defendant who had chosen to exercise a legal right to attack his original conviction — a situation "very different from the give-and-take negotiation common in plea bargaining between the prosecution and defense, which arguably possess relatively equal bargaining power." *Parker v. North Carolina*, 397 U.S. 790 (1970). The Court has emphasized that the due process violation in cases such as *Pearce* and *Perry* lay not in the possibility that a defendant might be deterred from the exercise of a legal right, but rather in the danger that the State might be retaliating against the accused for lawfully attacking his conviction.

To punish a person because he has done what the law plainly allows him to do is a due process violation of the most basic sort, and for an agent of the State to pursue a course of action whose objective is to penalize a person's reliance on his legal rights is "patently unconstitutional." But in the "give-and-take" of plea bargaining, there is no such element of punishment or retaliation so long as the accused is free to accept or reject the prosecution's offer.

Plea bargaining flows from "the mutuality of advantage" to defendants and prosecutors, each with his own reasons for wanting to avoid trial. Defendants advised by competent counsel and protected by other procedural safeguards are presumptively capable of intelligent choice in response to prosecutorial persuasion, and unlikely to be driven to false self-condemnation. Indeed, acceptance of the basic legitimacy of plea bargaining necessarily implies rejection of any notion that a guilty plea is involuntary in a constitutional sense simply because it is the end result of the bargaining process. By hypothesis, the plea may have been induced by promises of a recommendation of a lenient sentence or a reduction of charges, and thus by fear of the possibility of a greater penalty upon conviction after a trial.

While confronting a defendant with the risk of more severe punishment clearly may have a "discouraging effect on the defendant's assertion of his trial rights, the imposition of these difficult choices [is] an inevitable" — and permissible — "attribute of any legitimate system which tolerates and encourages the negotiation of pleas." It follows that, by tolerating and encouraging the negotiation of pleas, this Court has necessarily accepted as constitutionally legitimate the simple reality that the prosecutor's interest at the bargaining table is to persuade the defendant to forgo his right to plead not guilty.

It is not disputed here that Hayes was properly chargeable under the recidivist statute, since he had in fact been convicted of two previous felonies. In our system, so long as the prosecutor has probable cause to believe that the accused committed an offense defined by statute, the decision whether or not to prosecute, and what charge to file or bring before a grand jury, generally rests entirely in his discretion. Within the limits set by the legislature's constitutionally valid definition of chargeable offenses, "the conscious exercise of some selectivity in enforcement is not in itself a federal constitutional violation" so long as "the selection was [not] deliberately based upon an unjustifiable standard such as race, religion, or other arbitrary classification." *Oyler v. Boles*, 368 U.S. 448 (1962). To hold that the prosecutor's desire to induce a guilty plea is an "unjustifiable standard," which, like race or religion, may play no part in his charging decision, would contradict the very premises that underlie the concept of plea bargaining itself. Moreover, a rigid constitutional rule that would prohibit a prosecutor from acting forthrightly in his dealings with the defense could only invite unhealthy subterfuge that would drive the practice of plea bargaining back into the shadows from which it has so recently emerged. There is no doubt that the breadth of discretion that our country's legal system vests in prosecuting attorneys carries with it the potential for both individual and institutional abuse. And broad though that discretion may be, there are undoubtedly constitutional limits upon its exercise. We hold only that the course of conduct engaged in by the prosecutor in this case, which no more than openly presented the defendant with the unpleasant alternatives of forgoing trial or facing charges on which he was plainly subject to prosecution, did not violate the Due Process Clause of the Fourteenth Amendment.

FURTHER CASE LAW, REFLECTIONS, AND QUESTIONS

1. Justice Stewart's opinion for the Court in *Bordenkircher v. Hayes* distinguishes between "the State's unilateral imposition of a penalty upon a defendant who had chosen to exercise a legal right" and the "very different" situation involving "the give-and-take negotiation in plea bargaining between the prosecution and defense." It characterizes the circumstances in *Hayes* as falling within the latter category. Is this an apt characterization? What "give and take" do you envision having occurred during the plea negotiations? Must more be involved than the prosecutor instructing the defendant that if he does not "take" what the prosecutor offers to "give," he must accept the consequences? Is there roughly equal bargaining leverage between the parties, or is the prosecutor essentially in a position "unilaterally" to stipulate the plea-bargaining conditions? We consider plea bargaining at greater length later in this chapter.

2. What if the prosecutor originally had obtained an indictment against Hayes under the Habitual Criminal Act and thereafter had offered to dismiss that indictment and allow Hayes to plead guilty to uttering a forged instrument with a recommendation for a five-year sentence? Would his offer then be perceived as a more generous one, indeed, even as a gracious one, in contrast to the actual circumstances of the case? Should the timing of the prosecutor's decision to pursue the indictment under the Habitual Criminal Act make a difference, either in fact or in law? What are Justice Powell's views about the timing issue?

Box 11.1 You Be the Judge

While serving time in prison, Perry got into a fight with another inmate who was seriously injured. Perry was charged with the misdemeanor of assault with a deadly weapon. He was convicted in the district court and sentenced to six months in prison. Under North Carolina law, a defendant convicted in the district court has a right to a *trial de novo* (new trial) in the superior court. Perry availed himself of this option and filed notice of appeal. Shortly thereafter, the prosecutor obtained an indictment charging Perry with felony assault with a deadly weapon with intent to kill or cause serious injury. Perry entered a guilty plea and was sentenced to five years in prison. Perry appealed on the grounds of vindictive prosecution. He argued that his felony indictment was a penalty for exercising his right to a trial de novo and violated the Due Process Clause of the Fourteenth Amendment.

Should Perry succeed in his appeal? Why or why not?

See *Blackledge v. Perry*, 417 U.S. 21 (1974).

Formally Charging a Defendant

Once a prosecutor decides to pursue criminal charges against a defendant, they must take the required steps to obtain a formal charging document. The two types of documents are an **information** or an **indictment**. Both contain the actual charges against a defendant. Informations and indictments require the state to present probable cause that the defendant committed the specific crimes to a neutral body. Informations are issued by a judge at a preliminary hearing, whereas indictments are issued by a grand jury. The following sections examine the law surrounding these processes.

The Preliminary Hearing

The **preliminary hearing** is a formal adversarial proceeding. Although the Constitution does not guarantee it, it is a statutory right in the federal and many state criminal justice systems. The primary function of a preliminary hearing is to provide a court officer (judge or magistrate) with an opportunity to determine whether there is sufficient evidence to bind a defendant over for trial. If the judge finds probable cause to believe that the defendant committed the crime(s) for which he or she is charged, an information is filed that lists the specific crimes for which probable cause was found. At this point, the defendant is bound over to the trial court for further proceedings. If the judge determines probable cause does not exist, the case is dismissed, although charges may be refiled by the prosecution at a future time.

Many procedural aspects of a preliminary hearing are similar to a trial. Both proceedings are held in open court before a judge or magistrate. The defendant has a right to be present and, as we shall see, to be represented by counsel. Witnesses are called to testify, and the defendant has the right to cross-examination. Despite these procedural similarities, many differences exist between a preliminary hearing and a criminal trial.

One difference involves the type of evidence the parties are permitted to introduce. In most jurisdictions, hearsay evidence — that is, out-of-court statements made by a non-testifying person — is permitted in preliminary hearings. Absent a legally approved exception, hearsay evidence is not permitted at a trial. Additionally, in most jurisdictions, illegally obtained evidence is admissible at a preliminary hearing but not at a trial.

As noted above, the formal purpose of a preliminary hearing is to provide a court officer an opportunity to determine whether there is probable cause to believe the defendant committed the crimes of which he or she has been accused. In reality, probable cause is rarely found to be lacking at a preliminary hearing. Despite this fact, defendants seldom waive their right to a preliminary hearing because they often recognize other benefits. These benefits and the ramifications of being bound over for trial are explained in *Coleman v. Alabama*.

Coleman v. Alabama

399 U.S. 1 (1970)

MR. JUSTICE BRENNAN announced the judgment of the Court.

Petitioners were convicted in an Alabama Circuit Court of assault with intent to murder in the shooting of one Reynolds after he and his wife parked their car on an Alabama highway to change a flat tire. The Alabama Court of Appeals affirmed and the Alabama Supreme Court denied review. We granted certiorari. We vacate and remand.

[In their petition] petitioners argue that the preliminary hearing prior to their indictment was a "critical stage" of the prosecution and that Alabama's failure to provide them with appointed counsel at the hearing therefore unconstitutionally denied them the assistance of counsel.

II

This Court has held that a person accused of crime "requires the guiding hand of counsel at every step in the proceedings against him," *Powell v. Alabama*, 287 U.S. 45 and that that constitutional principle is not limited to the presence of counsel at trial. "It is central to that principle that in addition to counsel's presence at trial, the accused is guaranteed that he need not stand alone against the State at any stage of the prosecution, formal or informal, in court or out, where counsel's absence might derogate from the accused's right to a fair trial." *United States v.* Wade, 388 U.S. 218, 226 (1967).

> The principle of *Powell v. Alabama* and succeeding cases requires that we scrutinize any pretrial confrontation of the accused to determine whether the presence of his counsel is necessary to preserve the defendant's basic right to a fair trial as affected by his right meaningfully to cross-examine the witnesses against him and to have effective assistance of counsel at the trial itself. It calls upon us to analyze whether potential substantial prejudice to defendant's rights inheres in the particular confrontation and the ability of counsel to help avoid that prejudice. *Id.* at 227.

Applying this test, the Court has held that "critical stages" include the pretrial type of arraignment where certain rights may be sacrificed or lost, and the pretrial lineup.

The preliminary hearing is not a required step in an Alabama prosecution. The prosecutor may seek an indictment directly from the grand jury without a preliminary hearing. The opinion of the Alabama Court of Appeals in this case instructs us that under Alabama law the sole purposes of a preliminary hearing are to determine whether there is sufficient evidence against the accused to warrant presenting his case to the grand jury and, if so, to fix bail if the offense is bailable. The court continued:

> At the preliminary hearing, the accused is not required to advance any defenses, and failure to do so does not preclude him from availing himself of every defense he may have upon the trial of the case. Also, *Pointer v. Texas* 380 U.S. 400, (1965) bars the admission of testimony given at a pretrial proceeding where the accused did not have the benefit of cross-examination by and through counsel. Thus, nothing occurring at the preliminary hearing in absence of counsel can substantially prejudice the rights of the accused on trial. 211 So.2d, at 921.

This Court is of course bound by this construction of the governing Alabama law. However, from the fact that in cases where the accused has no lawyer at the hearing the Alabama courts prohibit the State's use at trial of anything that occurred at the hearing, it does not follow that the Alabama preliminary hearing is not a "critical stage" of the State's criminal process. The determination whether the hearing is a "critical stage" requiring the provision of counsel depends, as noted, upon an analysis "whether potential substantial prejudice to defendant's rights inheres in the confrontation and the ability of counsel to help avoid that prejudice." Plainly the guiding hand of counsel at the preliminary hearing is essential to protect the indigent accused against an erroneous or improper prosecution. First, the lawyer's skilled examination and cross-examination of witnesses may expose fatal weaknesses in the State's case that may lead the magistrate to refuse to bind the accused over. Second, in any event, the skilled interrogation of witnesses by an experienced lawyer can fashion a vital impeachment tool for use in cross-examination of the State's witnesses at the trial, or preserve testimony favorable to the accused of a witness who does not appear at the trial. Third, trained counsel can more effectively discover the case the State has against his client and make possible the preparation of a proper defense to meet that case at the trial. Fourth, counsel can also be influential at the preliminary hearing in making effective arguments for the accused on such matters as the necessity for an early psychiatric examination or bail.

The inability of the indigent accused on his own to realize these advantages of a lawyer's assistance compels the conclusion that the Alabama preliminary hearing is a "critical stage" of the State's criminal process at which the accused is as much entitled to such aid (of counsel) as at the trial itself.

III

There remains, then, the question of the relief to which petitioners are entitled. The trial transcript indicates that the prohibition against use by the State at trial of anything that occurred at the preliminary hearing was scrupulously observed. But on the record it cannot be said whether or not petitioners were otherwise prejudiced by the absence of counsel at the preliminary hearing. That inquiry in the first instance should more properly be made by the Alabama courts. The test to be applied is whether the denial of counsel at the preliminary hearing was harmless error under *Chapman v. California*, 386 U.S. 18 (1967).

We accordingly vacate the petitioners' convictions and remand the case to the Alabama courts for such proceedings not inconsistent with this opinion as they may deem appropriate to determine whether such denial of counsel was harmless error, and therefore whether the convictions should be reinstated or a new trial ordered.

FURTHER CASE LAW, REFLECTIONS, AND QUESTIONS

1. In *Holmes v. South Carolina*, 547 U.S. 319 (2006) (discussed in the next chapter), the Supreme Court ruled that excluding third-party guilt evidence violated the defendant's right to present a complete defense. What is the significance of this ruling in the context of a defendant's due process rights and the potential consequences for the criminal justice system?

2. What benefits did the court identify in having an attorney represent the accused at a preliminary hearing? Do you think the Court justifies the added burden on the criminal justice system of having attorneys represent defendants at this early stage in the adjudication process?

Grand Jury Proceedings

In the federal and criminal justice systems of more than one-third of the states, a grand jury must bring formal charges against a defendant. A **grand jury** is a group of citizens (12 or more, depending on the state) who review evidence of alleged wrongdoing and determine whether there is sufficient evidence to bring criminal charges against an individual. Evidence is presented to the grand jury through the testimony of witnesses in response to questions posed by a prosecutor. If the grand jury determines (usually by a majority vote) that there is probable cause to believe that a person committed a crime, it returns a **true bill** of indictment. An indictment is a formal charging instrument that specifies the defendant's name, the alleged crime, the date of the crime, and the acts that constitute the crime. The specific crimes that a defendant is alleged to have committed are listed in separate counts in the indictment.

Although indictment by grand jury is currently not the predominant method of initiating state criminal charges against a defendant, this was not always the case. When the Bill of Rights was adopted, all states required that felony prosecutions be initiated by indictment. Unsurprisingly, the Bill of Rights contained a similar requirement for federal prosecutions. The Fifth Amendment provides that "no person shall be held to answer for a capital, or otherwise infamous crime, unless on a presentment or indictment of a Grand Jury."

Michigan became the first state to permit felony prosecutions without a grand jury indictment in 1859. Several states thereafter followed Michigan's lead. The constitutionality of state felony prosecutions being commenced by a prosecutor's information and preliminary hearing, without grand jury indictment, was considered by the United States Supreme Court well over a century ago in *Hurtado v. California*, 110 U.S. 516 (1884). The Court held that states are not required to present charges to a grand jury in order to prosecute an individual. The justices reasoned that the process of "examination and commitment by a magistrate, certifying to the probable guilt of the defendant, with the right on his part to the aid of counsel, and to the cross-examination of the witnesses produced for the prosecution," was a reasonable alternative to the grand jury and did not violate the Fourteenth Amendment's due-process clause. The Court also confirmed that the Fifth Amendment's grand jury provisions do not directly apply to the states. Accordingly, states are permitted to initiate prosecutions through informations or preliminary hearings.

When a grand jury is used to initiate a prosecution, the federal Constitution and state constitutions require that certain procedural safeguards and substantive requirements be observed. These requirements concern (1) the composition of the grand jury, which will be discussed in chapter 12 when the selection of jurors is examined, and (2) the evidence that may be presented to and considered by the grand jury.

Evidence Presented to the Grand Jury

Evidence is presented to the grand jury in a nonadversarial proceeding. Only the grand jurors, the prosecutor, the testifying witness, and a court stenographer are present when testimony is offered. The accused is not entitled to question witnesses or be present when they testify.

The Supreme Court has ruled that testimony that would not be admissible at trial may be presented to the grand jury. In *Costello v. United States*, the Court discussed the rationale behind this policy.

Costello v. United States

350 U.S. 359 (1956)

MR. JUSTICE BLACK delivered the opinion of the Court.

We granted certiorari in this case to consider a single question: "May a defendant be required to stand trial and a conviction be sustained where only hearsay evidence was presented to the grand jury which indicted him?"

Petitioner, Frank Costello, was indicted for willfully attempting to evade payment of income taxes due the United States for the years 1947, 1948 and 1949. The charge was that petitioner falsely and fraudulently reported less income than he and his wife actually received during the taxable years in question. At trial the Government offered evidence designed to show increases in Costello's net worth in an attempt to prove that he had received more income during the years in question than he had reported. To establish its case the Government called and examined 144 witnesses and introduced 368 exhibits. All of the testimony and documents related to business transactions and expenditures by petitioner and his wife.

The prosecution concluded its case by calling three government agents. Their investigations had produced the evidence used against petitioner at the trial. They were allowed to summarize the vast amount of evidence already heard and to introduce computations showing, if correct, that petitioner and his wife had received far greater income than they had reported.

Counsel for petitioner asked each government witness at the trial whether he had appeared before the grand jury which returned the indictment. This cross-examination developed the fact that the three investigating officers had been the only witnesses before the grand jury. After the Government concluded its case, petitioner moved to dismiss the indictment on the ground that the only evidence before the grand jury was "hearsay," since the three officers had no firsthand knowledge of the transactions upon which their computations were based. Nevertheless the trial court again refused to dismiss the indictment, and petitioner was convicted. The Court of Appeals affirmed, holding that the indictment was valid even though the sole evidence before the grand jury was hearsay. Petitioner here urges: (1) that an indictment based solely on hearsay evidence violates that part of the Fifth Amendment providing that "No person shall be held to answer for a capital, or otherwise infamous crime, unless on a presentment or indictment of a Grand Jury" and (2) that if the Fifth Amendment does not invalidate an indictment based solely on hearsay we should now lay down such a rule for the guidance of federal courts.

The Fifth Amendment provides that federal prosecutions for capital or otherwise infamous crimes must be instituted by presentments or indictments of grand juries. But neither the Fifth Amendment nor any other constitutional provision prescribes the kind of evidence upon which grand juries must act. The grand jury is an English institution, brought to this country by the early colonists and incorporated in the Constitution by the Founders. There is every reason to believe that our constitutional grand jury was intended to operate substantially like its English progenitor. The basic purpose of the English grand jury was to provide a fair method for instituting criminal proceedings against persons believed to have committed crimes. Grand jurors were selected from the body of the people and their work was not hampered by rigid procedural or evidential rules. In fact, grand jurors could act on their own knowledge and were free to make their presentments or indictments on such information as they deemed satisfactory. Despite its broad power to institute criminal proceedings the grand jury grew in popular favor with the years. It acquired an independence in England free from control by the Crown or judges. Its adoption in our Constitution as the sole method for preferring charges in serious criminal cases shows the high place it held as an instrument of justice. And in this country as in England of old the grand jury has convened as a body of laymen, free from technical rules, acting in secret, pledged to indict no one because of prejudice and to free no one because of special favor.

In *Holt v. United States*, 218 U.S. 245, this Court had to decide whether an indictment should be quashed because it was supported in part by incompetent evidence. Aside from the incompetent evidence "there was very little evidence against the accused." The Court refused to hold that such an indictment should be quashed, pointing out that "The abuses of criminal practice would be enhanced if indictments could be upset on such a ground." The same thing is true whereas here all the evidence before the grand jury was in the nature of "hearsay." If indictments were to be held open to challenge on the ground that there was inadequate or incompetent evidence before the grand jury, the resulting delay would be great indeed. The result of such a rule would be that before trial on the merits a defendant could always insist on a kind of preliminary trial to determine the competency and adequacy of the evidence before the grand jury. This is not required by the Fifth Amendment.

An indictment returned by a legally constituted and unbiased grand jury, like an information drawn by the prosecutor, if valid on its face, is enough to call for trial of the charge on the merits. The Fifth Amendment requires nothing more.

Petitioner urges that this Court should exercise its power to supervise the administration of justice in federal courts and establish a rule permitting defendants to challenge indictments on the ground that they are not supported by adequate or competent evidence. No persuasive reasons are advanced for establishing such a rule. It would run counter to the whole history of the grand jury institution, in which laymen conduct their inquiries unfettered by technical rules. Neither justice nor the concept of a fair trial requires such a change. In a trial on the merits, defendants are entitled to a strict observance of all the rules designed to bring about a fair verdict. Defendants are not entitled, however, to a rule which would result in interminable delay but add nothing to the assurance of a fair trial.

Affirmed.

FURTHER CASE LAW, REFLECTIONS, AND QUESTIONS

1. Does the decision in *Costello* seem more concerned with the threat of "interminable delay" than protecting the rights of a suspected felon? Is there anything wrong with this? Is there a better way to strike an appropriate balance between these interests?

2. Should all evidence be permitted to be presented to a grand jury? What about evidence obtained through coercion? Through an illegal search? Through an illegal lineup? In *United States v. Calandra*, 414 U.S. 338 (1974), the Supreme Court considered whether it was permissible to present evidence seized in violation of a suspect's Fourth Amendment rights to a grand jury. Writing for a six-member majority, Justice Powell stated:

   > In deciding whether to extend the exclusionary rule to grand jury proceedings, we must weigh the potential injury to the historic role and functions of the grand jury against the potential benefits of the rule as applied in this context. It is evident that this extension of the exclusionary rule would seriously impede the grand jury. Because the grand jury does not finally adjudicate guilt or innocence, it has traditionally been allowed to pursue its investigative and accusatorial functions unimpeded by the evidentiary and procedural restrictions applicable to a criminal trial. Permitting [the invocation] of the exclusionary rule before a grand jury would precipitate adjudication of issues hitherto reserved for the trial on the merits and would delay and disrupt grand jury proceedings. *Id.* at 349.

3. What if the prosecution has in its possession evidence that suggests the defendant may not have committed the crimes that the grand jury is considering? Can the prosecution keep this evidence from the grand jury? Would doing so violate the

defendant's rights? In *United States v. Williams*, 504 U.S. 36 (1992), the Supreme Court held that prosecutors had no constitutional obligation to present exculpatory evidence (evidence that was favorable to a defendant) to a grand jury. The Court held that a court could not require a grand jury to consider any specific evidence because it was an institution over whose functioning the courts did not preside. Additionally, the Court found that requiring evidence beneficial to a defendant be presented to a grand jury was inconsistent with its traditional function, which was to determine whether enough evidence existed to prosecute, not to allow the accused to put on a defense.

` It should be noted that a number of states have departed from *Williams* on state constitutional grounds and require prosecutors to present exculpatory evidence to a grand jury to use in deciding whether to issue an indictment.

4. The limited amount of Supreme Court precedent related to grand juries has consistently limited the ability of a defendant to challenge an indictment based on the evidence that was considered. For these reasons, the belief that a prosecutor could indict a ham sandwich is largely accurate.
5. Arguably, a great deal of time, money, and judicial resources would be saved if prosecutors presented exculpatory evidence to a grand jury instead of waiting until a person is indicted. Why do you suppose a prosecutor would be averse to presenting all of the evidence to a grand jury in light of these considerations?
6. Box 11.2 compares aspects of grand juries to preliminary hearings.

Box 11.2 Comparing Grand Juries v. Preliminary Hearings

	Grand Jury	Preliminary Hearing
Defendant present	N	Y
Represented by counsel	N	Y
Public hearing	N	Y
Right to testify	N	Y
Right to present evidence	N	Y
Right to cross-examination	N	Y
Decision maker	Jurors	Judge/Magistrate
Charging Document	Indictment	Information
Presiding officer	Foreperson	Judge/Magistrate
Adversarial	N	Y
Critical stage	N	Y

The Indictment

If a grand jury finds that there is probable cause to believe that an individual violated one or more criminal statutes, it will issue an **indictment**. The indictment is a formal charging document, prepared by the prosecutor, and found to be true by the grand jury. An indictment must contain a concise statement of the essential facts constituting the elements of the offense charged. It need not be overly specific but must contain sufficient detail to inform the defendant what he or she is charged with and what actions gave rise to the offense. In the following case, the Supreme Court addressed whether the omission from an indictment of an essential element of a criminal offense requires reversal of a conviction.

United States v. Resendiz-Ponce

549 U.S. 102 (2007)

JUSTICE STEVENS delivered the opinion of the Court.

A jury convicted respondent Juan Resendiz-Ponce, a Mexican citizen, of illegally attempting to reenter the United States. Because the indictment failed to allege a specific overt act that he committed in seeking reentry, the Court of Appeals set aside his conviction and remanded for dismissal of the indictment.

I

Respondent was deported twice, once in 1988 and again in 2002, before his attempted reentry on June 1, 2003. On that day, respondent walked up to a port of entry and displayed a photo identification of his cousin to the border agent. Respondent told the agent that he was a legal resident and that he was traveling to Calexico, California. Because he did not resemble his cousin, respondent was questioned, taken into custody, and ultimately charged with a violation of 8 U.S.C. §1326(a).[1] The indictment alleged:

"On or about June 1, 2003, JUAN RESENDIZ-PONCE, an alien, knowingly and intentionally attempted to enter the United States of America at or near San Luis in

---

1. Title 8 U.S.C. §1326 provides, in part:

"Reentry of removed aliens

"(a) In general

"Subject to subsection (b) of this section, any alien who-

"(1) has been denied admission, excluded, deported, or removed or has departed the United States while an order of exclusion, deportation, or removal is outstanding, and thereafter

"(2) enters, attempts to enter, or is at any time found in, the United States, unless (A) prior to his reembarkation at a place outside the United States or his application for admission from foreign contiguous territory, the Attorney General has expressly consented to such alien's reapplying for admission; or (B) with respect to an alien previously denied admission and removed, unless such alien shall establish that he was not required to obtain such advance consent under this chapter or any prior Act, "shall be fined under title 18, or imprisoned not more than 2 years, or both."

the District of Arizona, after having been previously denied admission, excluded, deported, and removed from the United States at or near Nogales, Arizona, on or about October 15, 2002, and not having obtained the express consent of the Secretary of the Department of Homeland Security to reapply for admission.

"In violation of Title 8, United States Code, Sections 1326(a) and enhanced by (b)(2)."

Respondent moved to dismiss the indictment, contending that it "fail[ed] to allege an essential element, an overt act, or to state the essential facts of such overt act." The District Court denied the motion and, after the jury found him guilty, sentenced respondent to a 63-month term of imprisonment.

The Ninth Circuit reversed, reasoning that an indictment's omission of "an essential element of the offense is a fatal flaw not subject to mere harmless error analysis." In the court's view, respondent's indictment was fatally flawed because it nowhere alleged "any specific overt act that is a substantial step" toward the completion of the unlawful reentry. The panel majority explained:

> The defendant has a right to be apprised of what overt act the government will try to prove at trial, and he has a right to have a grand jury consider whether to charge that specific overt act. Physical crossing into a government inspection area is but one of a number of other acts that the government might have alleged as a substantial step toward entry into the United States. The indictment might have alleged the tendering a bogus identification card; it might have alleged successful clearance of the inspection area; or it might have alleged lying to an inspection officer with the purpose of being admitted. A grand jury never passed on a specific overt act, and Resendiz was never given notice of what specific overt act would be proved at trial.

II

The Government does not disagree with respondent's submission that he cannot be guilty of attempted reentry unless he committed an overt act qualifying as a substantial step toward completion of his goal. Nor does it dispute that "[a]n indictment must set forth each element of the crime that it charges." It instead contends that the indictment at bar implicitly alleged that respondent engaged in the necessary overt act "simply by alleging that he 'attempted to enter the United States.'" We agree.

Not only does the word "attempt" as used in common parlance connote action rather than mere intent, but more importantly, as used in the law for centuries, it encompasses both the overt act and intent elements. Consequently, an indictment alleging attempted illegal reentry need not specifically allege a particular overt act or any other "component par[t]" of the offense. See *Hamling v. United States*, 418 U.S. 87, 119 (1974). Just as it was enough for the indictment in Hamling to allege that the defendant mailed "obscene" material it was enough for the indictment in this case to point to the relevant criminal statute and allege that "[o]n or about June 1, 2003," respondent "attempted to enter the United States of America at or near San Luis in the District of Arizona,"

In Hamling, we identified two constitutional requirements for an indictment: "first, [that it] contains the elements of the offense charged and fairly informs a defendant of the charge against which he must defend, and, second, [that it] enables him to plead an acquittal or conviction in bar of future prosecutions for the same offense." In this case, the use of the word "attempt," coupled with the specification of the time and place of respondent's attempted illegal reentry, satisfied both. Indeed, the time-and-place information provided respondent with more adequate notice than would an indictment describing particular overt acts. After all, a given defendant may have approached the border or lied to a border-patrol agent in the course of countless attempts on innumerable occasions. For the same reason, the time-and-date specification in respondent's indictment provided ample protection against the risk of multiple prosecutions for the same crime.

Respondent nonetheless maintains that the indictment would have been sufficient only if it had alleged any of three overt acts performed during his attempted reentry: that he walked into an inspection area; that he presented a misleading identification card; or that he lied to the inspector. Individually and cumulatively, those acts tend to prove the charged attempt-but none was essential to the finding of guilt in this case. All three acts were rather part of a single course of conduct culminating in the charged "attempt."

Respondent is of course correct that while an indictment parroting the language of a federal criminal statute is often sufficient, there are crimes that must be charged with greater specificity. A clear example is the statute making it a crime for a witness summoned before a congressional committee to refuse to answer any question "pertinent to the question under inquiry." 2 U.S.C. §192. As we explained at length in our opinion in *Russell v. United States,* 369 U.S. 749 (1962), a valid indictment for such a refusal to testify must go beyond the words of §192 and allege the subject of the congressional hearing in order to determine whether the defendant's refusal was "pertinent." Based on a number of cases arising out of congressional investigations, we recognized that the relevant hearing's subject was frequently uncertain but invariably "central to every prosecution under the statute." Both to provide fair notice to defendants and to ensure that any conviction would arise out of the theory of guilt presented to the grand jury, we held that indictments under §192 must do more than restate the language of the statute.

Our reasoning in *Russell* suggests that there was no infirmity in the present indictment. First, unlike the statute at issue in *Russell,* guilt under 8 U.S.C. §1326(a) does not "depen[d] so crucially upon such a specific identification of fact. Second, before explaining the special need for particularity in charges brought under 2 U.S.C. §192, Justice Stewart noted that, in 1872, Congress had enacted a statute reflecting "the drift of the law away from the rules of technical and formalized pleading which had characterized an earlier era." Other than that statute, which was repealed in 1948, there was no other legislation dealing generally with the subject of indictments until the promulgation of Federal Rule of Criminal Procedure 7(c)(1). As we have said, the Federal Rules "were designed to eliminate technicalities in criminal pleadings and are to be construed to secure simplicity in procedure." While detailed allegations might well have been required under common-law pleading rules, they surely are not contemplated by Rule 7(c)(1), which provides that an indictment "shall be a plain, concise, and definite written statement of the essential facts constituting the offense charged."

Because we are satisfied that respondent's indictment fully complied with that Rule and did not deprive him of any significant protection that the constitutional guarantee of a grand jury was intended to confer, we reverse the judgment of the Court of Appeals and remand the case for further proceedings consistent with this opinion.

FURTHER CASE LAW, REFLECTIONS, AND QUESTIONS

1. What are the potential long-term impacts of the United States v. Resendiz-Ponce decision on the functioning of the criminal justice system? How might this ruling influence how indictments are drafted and challenged, and the role of appellate review in addressing errors in criminal proceedings?
2. Note that faulty indictments do not mean the defendant walks free. Instead, the case will be dismissed without prejudice, and the prosecution will be permitted to refile the charges with an appropriate indictment.

Pretrial Discovery

In modern times, following the formal charging of a defendant at the arraignment, the parties participate in pretrial **discovery**. Under the common law, courts did not have the authority to require pretrial discovery. Instead, it was up to state legislatures to establish rules of discovery. Before the 20th century, states had refrained from doing so. Accordingly, limited disclosure of information took place prior to trial. This forced both parties to guess what evidence the other side had at its disposal. The result was often "trial by ambush."

In the early 1900s, states began establishing rules for discovery in criminal prosecutions. The materials and processes involved in discovery varied significantly from state to state. As time passed, states took steps to limit trial by ambush and standardize the role of courts in overseeing the discovery process through legislation and court rules.

In the modern era, in most jurisdictions, there are three general classes of evidence prosecutors must disclose to a defendant before trial. The first involves testimony and physical evidence that the prosecutor intends to use at trial. This includes police reports, witness interviews, lab reports, and reports prepared by expert witnesses. The disclosure of these items is generally required by court rule, and failure to provide proper disclosure is likely to lead to their exclusion from use during a trial. This is necessary to allow the defense to employ their own experts and intelligently rebut the prosecution's case as well as prepare a defense. The other two types of evidence that prosecutors are required to disclose to a defendant, exculpatory material evidence and impeachment evidence, are far less simple to identify.

Exculpatory evidence is evidence favorable to the defendant. While granting the states great autonomy in the pretrial discovery practices they employ, the Supreme Court has addressed whether state prosecutors must disclose exculpatory evidence to the defense and, if so, what limits may be placed on what is disclosed.

The foundational case in the modern era of discovery law is *Brady v. Maryland*, 373 U.S. 83 (1963). The Supreme Court held that withholding exculpatory evidence specifically requested by the defense violates due process where the evidence is material either to guilt or punishment. The exclusion of evidence is required regardless of the State's good or bad faith. The Court stated that evidence is material if there is a reasonable probability that the result of the proceeding would have been different had the evidence been disclosed. Brady does not require that non-material evidence be disclosed.

The **Brady rule** applies to exculpatory evidence as well as evidence that may be used to impeach government witnesses. Impeachment evidence, such as whether a witness is receiving a benefit from the government for their testimony, whether they have prior criminal convictions, or any other information that may be used to call the witness's credibility into doubt, must be disclosed if it meets the test of **materiality**.

Even though *Brady* appears clear about the obligation to disclose exculpatory evidence, questions have arisen since it was decided. Who should determine the exculpatory nature or the relevance of the evidence? Must evidence possessed by police but not by the prosecutor be revealed? Does evidence not intended by the prosecution to be used at trial need to be disclosed? Must the defense request specific evidence for the *Brady* rule to apply? These issues have caused sharp disagreement among the Supreme Court Justices. In *Kyles v. Whitley*, the Supreme Court looked at these and related issues.

Kyles v. Whitley

514 U.S. 419 (1995)

MR. JUSTICE SOUTER delivered the opinion of the Court.

The record indicates that, at about 2:20 p.m. on Thursday, September 20, 1984, 60-year-old Dolores Dye left the Schwegmann Brothers' store (Schwegmann's) in New Orleans after doing some food shopping. As she put her grocery bags into the trunk of her red Ford LTD, a man accosted her and after a short struggle drew a revolver, fired into her left temple, and killed her. The gunman took Dye's keys and drove away in the LTD.

New Orleans police took statements from six eyewitnesses, who offered various descriptions of the gunman. They agreed that he was a black man, and four of them said that he had braided hair. The witnesses differed significantly, however, in their descriptions of height, age, weight, build, and hair length. Two reported seeing a man of 17 or 18, while another described the gunman as looking as old as 28. One witness described him as 5'4" or 5'5" , medium build, 140-150 pounds; another described the man as slim and close to six feet. One witness said he had a mustache; none of the others spoke of any facial hair at all. One witness said the murderer had shoulder-length hair; another described the hair as "short."

At 5:30 p.m., on September 22, a man identifying himself as James Joseph called the police and reported that on the day of the murder he had bought a red Thunderbird from a friend named Curtis, whom he later identified as petitioner, Curtis Kyles. He said that he had subsequently read about Dye's murder in the newspapers and feared that the car he purchased was the victim's. He agreed to meet with the police.

A few hours later, the informant met New Orleans Detective John Miller, who was wired with a hidden body microphone, through which the ensuing conversation was recorded. The informant now said his name was Joseph Banks and that he was called Beanie. His actual name was Joseph Wallace. (Because the informant had so many aliases, we will follow the convention of the court below and refer to him throughout this opinion as Beanie.)

His story, as well as his name, had changed since his earlier call. In place of his original account of buying a Thunderbird from Kyles on Thursday, Beanie told Miller that he had not seen Kyles at all on Thursday, and had bought a red LTD the previous day, Friday. Beanie led Miller to the parking lot of a nearby bar, where he had left the red LTD, later identified as Dye's.

Beanie told Miller that he lived with Kyles's brother-in-law (later identified as Johnny Burns), whom Beanie repeatedly called his "partner." Beanie described Kyles as slim, about 6-feet tall, 24 or 25 years old, with a "bush" hairstyle. When asked if Kyles ever wore his hair in plaits, Beanie said that he did but that he "had a bush" when Beanie bought the car.

During the conversation, Beanie repeatedly expressed concern that he might himself be a suspect in the murder. He explained that he had been seen driving Dye's car on Friday evening in the French Quarter, admitted that he had changed its license plates, and worried that he "could have been charged" with the murder on the basis of his possession of the LTD. He asked if he would be put in jail. Miller acknowledged that Beanie's possession of the car would have looked suspicious, but reassured him that he "didn't do anything wrong."

Beanie seemed eager to cast suspicion on Kyles, who allegedly made his living by "robbing people," and had tried to kill Beanie at some prior time. Beanie said that Kyles regularly carried two pistols, a .38 and a .32, and that if the police could "set him up good," they could "get that same gun" used to kill Dye. Beanie rode with Miller and Miller's supervisor, Sgt. James Eaton, in an unmarked squad car to Desire Street, where he pointed out the building containing Kyles's apartment.

Beanie told the officers that after he bought the car, he, and his "partner" (Burns) drove Kyles to Schwegmann's about 9 p.m. on Friday evening to pick up Kyles's car, described as an orange four-door Ford. When asked where Kyles's car had been parked, Beanie replied that it had been "[o]n the same side [of the lot] where the woman was killed at." The officers later drove Beanie to Schwegmann's, where he indicated the space where he claimed Kyles's car had been parked. Beanie went on to say that when he and Burns had brought Kyles to pick up the car, Kyles had gone to some nearby bushes to retrieve a brown purse, which Kyles subsequently hid in a wardrobe at his apartment. Beanie said that Kyles had "a lot of groceries" in Schwegmann's bags and a new baby's potty "in the car." Beanie told Eaton that Kyles's garbage would go out the next day and that if Kyles was "smart" he would "put [the purse] in [the] garbage." Beanie made it clear that he expected some reward for his help, saying at one point that he was not "doing all of this for nothing." The police repeatedly assured Beanie that he would not lose the $400 he paid for the car.

After the visit to Schwegmann's, Eaton and Miller took Beanie to a police station where Miller interviewed him again on the record, which was transcribed and signed by Beanie, using his alias "Joseph Banks." This statement, Beanie's third (the telephone call being the first, then the recorded conversation), repeats some of the essentials of the second one: that Beanie had purchased a red Ford LTD from Kyles for $400 on Friday evening; that Kyles had his hair "combed out" at the time of the sale; and that Kyles carried a .32 and a .38 with him "all the time."

Portions of the third statement, however, embellished, or contradicted Beanie's preceding story and were even internally inconsistent. Beanie reported that after the sale, he and Kyles unloaded Schwegmann's grocery bags from the trunk and back seat of the LTD and placed them in Kyles's own car. Beanie said that Kyles took a brown purse from the front seat of the LTD and that they then drove in separate cars to Kyles's apartment, where they unloaded the groceries. Beanie also claimed that, a few hours later, he and his "partner" Burns went with Kyles to Schwegmann's, where they recovered Kyles's car and a "big brown pocketbook" from "next to a building." Beanie did not explain how Kyles could have picked up his car and recovered the purse at Schwegmann's, after Beanie had seen Kyles with both just a few hours earlier. The police neither noted the inconsistencies nor questioned Beanie about them.

Although the police did not thereafter put Kyles under surveillance, they learned about events at his apartment from Beanie, who went there twice on Sunday. According to a fourth statement by Beanie, this one given to the chief prosecutor in November (between the first and second trials), he first went to the apartment about 2 p.m., after a telephone conversation with a police officer who asked whether Kyles had the gun that was used to kill Dye. Beanie stayed in Kyles's apartment until about 5 p.m., when he left to call Detective John Miller. Then he returned about 7 p.m. and stayed until about 9:30 p.m., when he left to meet Miller, who also asked about the gun. According to this fourth statement, Beanie "rode around" with Miller until 3 a.m. on Monday, September 24. Sometime during those same early morning hours, detectives were sent at Sgt. Eaton's behest to pick up the rubbish outside Kyles's building. As Sgt. Eaton wrote in an interoffice memorandum, he had "reason to believe the victims personal papers and the Schwegmann's bags will be in the trash."

At 10:40 a.m., Kyles was arrested as he left the apartment, which was then searched under a warrant. Behind the kitchen stove, the police found a .32-caliber revolver containing five live rounds and one spent cartridge. Ballistics tests later showed that this pistol was used to murder Dye. In a wardrobe in a hallway leading to the kitchen, the officers found a homemade shoulder holster that fit the murder weapon. In a bedroom dresser drawer, they discovered two boxes of ammunition, one containing several .32-caliber rounds of the same brand as those found in the pistol. Back in the kitchen, various cans of cat and dog food, some of them of the brands Dye typically purchased, were found in Schwegmann's sacks. No other groceries were identified as possibly being Dye's, and no potty was found. Later that afternoon at the police station, police opened the rubbish bags and found the victim's purse, identification, and other personal belongings wrapped in a Schwegmann's sack.

The gun, the LTD, the purse, and the cans of pet food were dusted for fingerprints. The gun had been wiped clean. Several prints were found on the purse and on the LTD, but none was identified as Kyles's. Dye's prints were not found on any of the cans of pet food. Kyles's prints were found, however, on a small piece of paper taken from the front passenger-side floorboard of the LTD. The crime laboratory recorded the paper as a Schwegmann's sales slip, but without noting what had been printed on it, which was obliterated in the chemical process of lifting the fingerprints. A second Schwegmann's receipt was found in the trunk of the LTD, but Kyles's prints were not found on it. Beanie's fingerprints were not compared to any of the fingerprints found.

The lead detective on the case, John Dillman, put together a photo lineup that included a photograph of Kyles (but not of Beanie) and showed the array to five of the six eyewitnesses who had given statements. Three of them picked the photograph of Kyles; the other two could not confidently identify Kyles as Dye's assailant.

B

Kyles was indicted for first-degree murder. Before trial, his counsel filed a lengthy motion for disclosure by the State of any exculpatory or impeachment evidence. The prosecution responded that there was "no exculpatory evidence of any nature," despite the government's knowledge of the following evidentiary items: (1) the six contemporaneous eyewitness statements taken by police following the murder; (2) records of Beanie's initial call to the police; (3) the tape recording of the Saturday conversation between Beanie and officers Eaton and Miller; (4) the typed and signed statement given by Beanie on Sunday morning; (5) the computer print-out of license numbers of cars parked at Schwegmann's on the night of the murder, which did not list the number of Kyles's car; (6) the internal police memorandum calling for the seizure of the rubbish after Beanie had suggested that the purse might be found there; and (7) evidence linking Beanie to other crimes at Schwegmann's and to an unrelated murder committed in January before the Dye murder.

At the first trial, in November, the heart of the State's case was eyewitness testimony from four people who were at the scene of the crime (three of whom had previously picked Kyles from the photo lineup). Kyles maintained his innocence, offered supporting witnesses, and supplied an alibi that he had been picking up his children from school at the time of the murder. The theory of the defense was that Kyles had been framed by Beanie, who had planted evidence in Kyles's apartment and his rubbish for the purposes of shifting suspicion away from himself and obtaining reward money. Beanie did not testify as a witness for either the defense or the prosecution.

Because the State withheld evidence, its case was much stronger, and the defense case much weaker, than the full facts would have suggested. Even so, the jury deadlocked on the issue of guilt, and a mistrial was declared.

After the mistrial, the chief trial prosecutor, Cliff Strider, interviewed Beanie. Strider's notes show that Beanie again changed important elements of his story. He said that he went with Kyles to retrieve Kyles's car from the Schwegmann's lot on Thursday, the day of the murder, at some time between 5 and 7:30 p.m., not on Friday, at 9 p.m., as he had said in his second and third statements. (Indeed, in his second statement, Beanie said that he had not seen Kyles at all on Thursday. He also said, for the first time, that when they had picked up the car they were accompanied not only by Johnny Burns but also by Kevin Black, who had testified for the defense at the first trial. Beanie now claimed that after getting Kyles's car they went to Black's house, retrieved a number of bags of groceries, a child's potty, and a brown purse, all of which they took to Kyles's apartment. Beanie also stated that on the Sunday after the murder he had been at Kyles's apartment two separate times. Notwithstanding the many inconsistencies and variations among Beanie's statements, neither Strider's notes nor any of the other notes and transcripts were given to the defense.

In December 1984, Kyles was tried a second time. Again, the heart of the State's case was the testimony of four eyewitnesses who positively identified Kyles in front of the jury. Once again, Beanie did not testify. Kyles was convicted of first-degree murder and sentenced to death. Beanie received a total of $1,600 in reward money.

Following direct appeal, it was revealed in the course of state collateral review that the State had failed to disclose evidence favorable to the defense. After exhausting state remedies, Kyles sought relief on federal habeas, claiming, among other things, that the evidence withheld was material to his defense and that his conviction was thus obtained in violation of *Brady* Although the District Court denied relief and the Fifth Circuit affirmed, Judge King dissented, writing that "[f]or the first time in my fourteen years on this court.... I have serious reservations about whether the State has sentenced to death the right man."

III

The prosecution's affirmative duty to disclose evidence favorable to a defendant can trace its origins to early 20th-century strictures against misrepresentation and is of course most prominently associated with this Court's decision in *Brady v. Maryland,* 373 U.S. 83 (1963). *Brady* held "that the suppression by the prosecution of evidence favorable to an accused upon request violates due process where the evidence is material either to guilt or to punishment, irrespective of the good faith or bad faith of the prosecution."

In *United States v. Bagley,* 473 U.S. 667 (1985), the Court disavowed any difference between exculpatory and impeachment evidence for *Brady* purposes. *Bagley* held that regardless of request, favorable evidence is material, and constitutional error results from its suppression by the government, "if there is a reasonable probability that, had the evidence been disclosed to the defense, the result of the proceeding would have been different."

[Several] aspects of materiality under *Bagley* bear emphasis. Although the constitutional duty is triggered by the potential impact of favorable but undisclosed evidence, a showing of materiality does not require demonstration by a preponderance that disclosure of the suppressed evidence would have resulted ultimately in the defendant's acquittal. *Bagley's* touchstone of materiality is a "reasonable probability" of a different result, and the adjective is important. The question is not whether the defendant would more likely than not have received a different verdict with the evidence, but whether in its absence he received a fair trial, understood as a trial resulting in a verdict worthy of confidence. A "reasonable probability" of a different result is accordingly shown when the government's evidentiary suppression "undermines confidence in the outcome of the trial."

The second aspect of *Bagley* materiality bearing emphasis here is that it is not a sufficiency of evidence test. A defendant need not demonstrate that after discounting the inculpatory evidence in light of the undisclosed evidence, there would not have been enough left to convict. The possibility of an acquittal on a criminal charge does not imply an insufficient evidentiary basis to convict. One does not show a *Brady* violation by demonstrating that some of the inculpatory evidence should have been excluded, but by showing that the favorable evidence could reasonably be taken to put the whole case in such a different light as to undermine confidence in the verdict.

The final aspect of *Bagley* materiality to be stressed here is its definition in terms of suppressed evidence considered collectively, not item by item.

While the definition of *Bagley* materiality in terms of the cumulative effect of suppression must be seen as leaving the government with a degree of discretion, it must also be understood as imposing a corresponding burden. On the one hand, showing that the prosecution knew of an item of favorable evidence unknown to the defense does not amount to a *Brady* violation, without more. But the prosecution, which alone can know what is undisclosed, must be assigned the consequent responsibility to gauge the likely net effect of all such evidence and make disclosure when the point of "reasonable probability" is reached. This in turn means that the individual prosecutor has a duty to learn of any favorable evidence known to the others acting on the government's behalf in the case, including the police. But whether the prosecutor succeeds or fails in meeting this obligation (whether, that is, a failure to disclose is in good faith or bad faith,) the prosecution's responsibility for failing to disclose known, favorable evidence rising to a material level of importance is inescapable.

The State of Louisiana would prefer an even more lenient rule. It pleads that some of the favorable evidence in issue here was not disclosed even to the prosecutor until after trial, and it suggested below that it should not be held accountable under *Bagley* and *Brady* for evidence known only to police investigators and not to the prosecutor. To accommodate the State in this manner would, however, amount to a serious change of course from the *Brady* line of cases. In the State's favor it may be said that no one doubts that police investigators sometimes fail to inform a prosecutor of all they know. But neither is there any serious doubt that "procedures and regulations can be established to carry [the prosecutor's] burden and to insure communication of all relevant information on each case to every lawyer who deals with it." Since, then, the prosecutor has the means to discharge the government's *Brady* responsibility if he will, any argument for excusing a prosecutor from disclosing what he does not happen to know about boils down to a plea to substitute the police for the prosecutor, and even for the courts themselves, as the final arbiters of the government's obligation to ensure fair trials.

Short of doing that, we were asked at oral argument to raise the threshold of materiality because the *Bagley* standard "makes it difficult. . . .to know" from the "perspective [of the prosecutor at] trial exactly what might become important later on." The State asks for "a certain amount of leeway in making a judgment call" as to the disclosure of any given piece of evidence.

Uncertainty about the degree of further "leeway" that might satisfy the State's request for a "certain amount" of it is the least of the reasons to deny the request. At bottom, what the State fails to recognize is that, with or without more leeway, the prosecution cannot be subject to any disclosure obligation without at some point having the responsibility to determine when it must act. Indeed, even if due process were thought to be violated by every failure to disclose an item of exculpatory or impeachment evidence (leaving harmless error as the government's only fallback), the prosecutor would still be forced to make judgment calls about what would count as favorable evidence, owing to the very fact that the character of a piece of evidence as favorable will often turn on the context of the existing or potential evidentiary record. Since the prosecutor would have to exercise some judgment even if the State were subject to this most stringent disclosure obligation, it is hard to find merit in the State's complaint over the responsibility for judgment under the existing system, which does not tax the prosecutor with error for any failure to disclose, absent a further showing of materiality. Unless, indeed, the adversary system of prosecution is to descend to a gladiatorial level unmitigated by any prosecutorial obligation for the sake of truth, the government simply cannot avoid responsibility for knowing when the suppression of evidence has come to portend such an effect on a trial's outcome as to destroy confidence in its result.

This means, naturally, that a prosecutor anxious about tacking too close to the wind will disclose a favorable piece of evidence. See *Agurs*, 427 U.S., at 108 ("The prudent prosecutor will resolve doubtful questions in favor of disclosure"). This is as it should be. Such disclosure will serve to justify trust in the prosecutor as "the representative. . . .of a sovereignty. . . .whose interest. . . .in a criminal prosecution is not that it shall win a case, but that justice shall be done. And it will tend to preserve the criminal trial, as distinct from the prosecutor's private deliberations, as the chosen forum for ascertaining the truth about criminal accusations. The prudence of the careful prosecutor should not therefore be discouraged.

IV

In this case, disclosure of the suppressed evidence to competent counsel would have made a different result reasonably probable. As the District Court put it, "the essence of the State's case" was the testimony of eyewitnesses, who identified Kyles as Dye's killer. Disclosure of their statements would have resulted in a markedly weaker case for the prosecution and a markedly stronger one for the defense. To begin with, the value of two of those witnesses would have been substantially reduced or destroyed.

The State rated Henry Williams as its best witness, who testified that he had seen the struggle and the actual shooting by Kyles. The jury would have found it helpful to probe this conclusion in the light of Williams's contemporaneous statement, in which he told the police that the assailant was "a black male, about 19 or 20 years old, about 5'4" or 5'5" , 140 to 150 pounds, medium build" and that "his hair looked like it was platted." If cross-examined on this description, Williams would have had trouble explaining how he could have described Kyles, 6-feet tall and thin, as a man more than half a foot shorter with a medium build. Indeed, since Beanie was 22 years old, 5' 5" tall, and 159 pounds, the defense would have had a compelling argument that Williams's description pointed to Beanie but not to Kyles.

The trial testimony of a second eyewitness, Isaac Smallwood, was equally damning to Kyles. He testified that Kyles was the assailant, and that he saw him struggle with Dye. He said he saw Kyles take a ".32, a small black gun" out of his right pocket, shoot Dye in the head, and drive off in her LTD. When the prosecutor asked him whether he actually saw Kyles shoot Dye, Smallwood answered "Yeah."

Smallwood's statement taken at the parking lot, however, was vastly different. Immediately after the crime, Smallwood claimed that he had not seen the actual murder and had not seen the assailant outside the vehicle. "I heard a loud pop," he said. "When I looked around I saw a lady laying on the ground, and there was a red car coming toward me." Smallwood said that he got a look at the culprit, a black teenage male with a mustache and shoulder-length braided hair, as the victim's red Thunderbird passed where he was standing. When a police investigator specifically asked him whether he had seen the assailant outside the car, Smallwood answered that he had not; the gunman "was already in the car and coming toward me."

A jury would reasonably have been troubled by the adjustments to Smallwood's original story by the time of the second trial. The struggle and shooting, which earlier he had not seen, he was able to describe with such detailed clarity as to identify the murder weapon as a small black .32-caliber pistol, which, of course, was the type of weapon used. His description of the victim's car had gone from a "Thunderbird" to an "LTD"; and he saw fit to say nothing about the assailant's shoulder-length hair and moustache, details noted by no other eyewitness. These developments would have fueled a withering cross-examination, destroying confidence in Smallwood's story and raising a substantial implication that the prosecutor had coached him to give it.

Since the evolution over time of a given eyewitness's description can be fatal to its reliability, the Smallwood and Williams identifications would have been severely undermined by use of their suppressed statements. The likely damage is best understood by taking the word of the prosecutor, who contended during closing arguments that Smallwood and Williams were the State's two best witnesses. Nor, of course, would the harm to the State's case on identity have been confined to their testimony alone. The fact that neither Williams nor Smallwood could have provided a consistent eyewitness description pointing to Kyles would have undercut the prosecution all the more because the remaining eyewitnesses called to testify had their best views of the gunman only as he fled the scene with his body partly concealed in Dye's car. And even aside from such important details, the effective impeachment of one eyewitness can call for a new trial even though the attack does not extend directly to others, as we have said before.

B

Damage to the prosecution's case would not have been confined to evidence of the eyewitnesses, for Beanie's various statements would have raised opportunities to attack not only the probative value of crucial physical evidence and the circumstances in which it was found, but the thoroughness and even the good faith of the investigation, as well. By the State's own admission, Beanie was essential to its investigation and, indeed, "made the case" against Kyles. Contrary to what one might hope for from such a source, however, Beanie's statements to the police were replete with inconsistencies and would have allowed the jury to infer that Beanie was anxious to see Kyles arrested for Dye's murder. Their disclosure would have revealed a remarkably uncritical attitude on the part of the police.

If the defense had called Beanie as an adverse witness, he could not have said anything of any significance without being trapped by his inconsistencies. A short recapitulation of some of them will make the point. In Beanie's initial meeting with the police, and in his signed statement, he said he bought Dye's LTD and helped Kyles retrieve his car from the Schwegmann's lot on Friday. In his first call to the police, he said he bought the LTD on Thursday, and in his conversation with the prosecutor between trials it was again on Thursday that he said he helped Kyles retrieve Kyles's car. Although none of the first three versions of this story mentioned Kevin Black as taking part in the retrieval of the car and transfer of groceries, after Black implicated Beanie by his testimony for the defense at the first trial, Beanie changed his story to include Black as a participant. In Beanie's several accounts, Dye's purse first shows up variously next to a building, in some bushes, in Kyles's car, and at Black's house.

Even if Kyles's lawyer had followed the more conservative course of leaving Beanie off the stand, though, the defense could have examined the police to good effect on their knowledge of Beanie's statements and so have attacked the reliability of the investigation in failing even to consider Beanie's possible guilt and in tolerating (if not countenancing) serious possibilities that incriminating evidence had been planted.

By demonstrating the detectives' knowledge of Beanie's affirmatively self-incriminating statements, the defense could have laid the foundation for a vigorous argument that the police had been guilty of negligence. In his initial meeting with police, Beanie admitted twice that he changed the license plates on the LTD. This admission enhanced the suspiciousness of his possession of the car; the defense could have argued persuasively that he was no bona fide purchaser. And when combined with his police record, evidence of prior criminal activity near Schwegmann's, and his status as a suspect in another murder, his devious behavior gave reason to believe that he had done more than buy a stolen car. There was further self-incrimination in Beanie's statement that Kyles's car was parked in the same part of the Schwegmann's lot where Dye was killed. Beanie's apparent awareness of the specific location of the murder could have been based, as the State contends, on television or newspaper reports, but perhaps it was not. (Beanie saying that he knew about the murder because his brother-in-law had seen it "on T.V. and in the paper" and had told Beanie). Since the police admittedly never treated Beanie as a suspect, the defense could thus have used his statements to throw the reliability of the investigation into doubt and to sully the credibility of Detective Dillman, who testified that Beanie was never a suspect, and that he had "no knowledge" that Beanie had changed the license plate.

The admitted failure of the police to pursue these pointers toward Beanie's possible guilt could only have magnified the effect on the jury of explaining how the purse and the gun happened to be recovered. In Beanie's original recorded statement, he told the police that "[Kyles's] garbage goes out tomorrow," and that "if he's smart he'll put [the purse] in [the] garbage." These statements, along with the internal memorandum stating that the police had "reason to believe" Dye's personal effects and Schwegmann's bags would be in the garbage, would have supported the defense's theory that Beanie was no mere observer, but was determining the investigation's direction and success. The potential for damage from using Beanie's statement to undermine the ostensible integrity of the investigation is only confirmed by the prosecutor's admission at one of Kyles's postconviction hearings, that he did not recall a single instance before this case when police had searched and seized garbage on the street in front of a residence, and by Detective Miller's admission at the same hearing that he thought at the time that it "was a possibility" that Beanie had planted the incriminating evidence in the garbage. If a police officer thought so, a juror would have, too.

To the same effect would have been an enquiry based on Beanie's apparently revealing remark to police that "if you can set [Kyles] up good, you can get that same gun." While the jury might have understood that Beanie meant simply that if the police investigated Kyles, they would probably find the murder weapon, the jury could also have taken Beanie to have been making the more sinister suggestion that the police "set up" Kyles, and the defense could have argued that the police accepted the invitation. The prosecutor's notes of his interview with Beanie would have shown that police officers were asking Beanie the whereabouts of the gun all day Sunday, the very day when he was twice at Kyles's apartment and was allegedly seen by Johnny Burns lurking near the stove, where the gun was later found. Beanie's same statement, indeed, could have been used to cap an attack on the integrity of the investigation and on the reliability of Detective Dillman, who testified on cross-examination that he did not know if Beanie had been at Kyles's apartment on Sunday.

D

In assessing the significance of the evidence withheld, one must of course bear in mind that not every item of the State's case would have been directly undercut if the *Brady* evidence had been disclosed. It is significant, however, that the physical evidence remaining unscathed would, by the State's own admission, hardly have amounted to overwhelming proof that Kyles was the murderer. Ammunition and a holster were found in Kyles's apartment, but if the jury had suspected the gun had been planted the significance of these items might have been left in doubt. The fact that pet food was found in Kyles's apartment was consistent with the testimony of several defense witnesses that Kyles owned a dog and that his children fed stray cats. The brands of pet food found were only two of the brands that Dye typically bought, and these two were common, whereas the one specialty brand that was found in Dye's apartment after her murder, was not found in Kyles's apartment. Although Kyles was wrong in describing the cat food as being on sale the day he said he bought it, he was right in describing the way it was priced at Schwegmann's market, where he commonly shopped.

Similarly un-dispositive is the small Schwegmann's receipt on the front passenger floorboard of the LTD, the only physical evidence that bore a fingerprint identified as Kyles's. Kyles explained that Beanie had driven him to Schwegmann's on Friday to buy cigarettes and transmission fluid, and he theorized that the slip must have fallen out of the bag when he removed the cigarettes. This explanation is consistent with the location of the slip when found and with its small size. The State cannot very well argue that the fingerprint ties Kyles to the killing without also explaining how the 2-inch-long register slip could have been the receipt for a week's worth of groceries, which Dye had gone to Schwegmann's to purchase.

The inconclusiveness of the physical evidence does not, to be sure, prove Kyles's innocence, and the jury might have found the eyewitness testimony of Territo and Kersh sufficient to convict, even though less damning to Kyles than that of Smallwood and Williams. But the question is not whether the State would have had a case to go to the jury if it had disclosed the favorable evidence, but whether we can be confident that the jury's verdict would have been the same. Confidence that it would have been cannot survive a recap of the suppressed evidence and its significance for the prosecution. The jury would have been entitled to find

(a) that the investigation was limited by the police's uncritical readiness to accept the story and suggestions of an informant whose accounts were inconsistent to the point, for example, of including four different versions of the discovery of the victim's purse, and whose own behavior was enough to raise suspicions of guilt;

(b) that the lead police detective who testified was either less than wholly candid or less than fully informed;

(c) that the informant's behavior raised suspicions that he had planted both the murder weapon and the victim's purse in the places they were found;

(d) that one of the four eyewitnesses crucial to the State's case had given a description that did not match the defendant and better described the informant;

(e) that another eyewitness had been coached, since he had first stated that he had not seen the killer outside the getaway car, or the killing itself, whereas at trial he claimed to have seen the shooting, described the murder weapon exactly, and omitted portions of his initial description that would have been troublesome for the case;

(f) that there was no consistency to eyewitness descriptions of the killer's height, build, age, facial hair, or hair length.

Since all of these possible findings were precluded by the prosecution's failure to disclose the evidence that would have supported them, "fairness" cannot be stretched to the point of calling this a fair trial. Perhaps, confidence that the verdict would have been the same could survive the evidence impeaching even two eyewitnesses if the discoveries of gun and purse were above suspicion. Perhaps those suspicious circumstances would not defeat confidence in the verdict if the eyewitnesses had generally agreed on a description and were free of impeachment. But confidence that the verdict would have been unaffected cannot survive when suppressed evidence would have entitled a jury to find that the eyewitnesses were not consistent in describing the killer, that two out of the four eyewitnesses testifying were unreliable, that the most damning physical evidence was subject to suspicion, that the investigation that produced it was insufficiently probing, and that the principal police witness was insufficiently informed or candid. This is not the "massive" case envisioned by the dissent, it is a significantly weaker case than the one heard by the first jury, which could not even reach a verdict.

The judgment of the Court of Appeals is reversed, and the case is remanded for further proceedings consistent with this opinion.

Justice Scalia, with whom the Chief Justice, Justice Kennedy, and Justice Thomas join, dissenting.

It is fundamental to the discovery rule of *Brady v. Maryland*, 373 U.S. 83 (1963), that the materiality of a failure to disclose favorable evidence "must be evaluated in the context of the entire record." It is simply not enough to show that the undisclosed evidence would have allowed the defense to weaken, or even to "destroy," the *particular* prosecution witnesses or items of prosecution evidence to which the undisclosed evidence relates. It is petitioner's burden to show that in light of all the evidence, including that untainted by the *Brady* violation, it is reasonably probable that a jury would have entertained a reasonable doubt regarding petitioner's guilt. The Court's opinion fails almost entirely to take this principle into account. Having spent many pages assessing the effect of the *Brady* material on two prosecution witnesses and a few items of prosecution evidence, it dismisses the remainder of the evidence against Kyles in a quick page-and-a-half.

In any analysis of this case, the desperate implausibility of the theory that petitioner put before the jury must be kept firmly in mind. The first half of that theory-designed to neutralize the physical evidence (Mrs. Dye's purse in his garbage, the murder weapon behind his stove)-was that petitioner was the victim of a "frame-up" by the police informer and evil genius, Beanie. Now it is not unusual for a guilty person who knows that he is suspected of a crime to try to shift blame to someone else; and it is less common, but not unheard of, for a guilty person who is neither suspected nor subject to suspicion (because he has established a perfect alibi), to call attention to himself by coming forward to point the finger at an innocent person. But petitioner's theory is that the guilty Beanie, who *could* plausibly be accused of the crime (as petitioner's brief amply demonstrates), but who was *not* a suspect any more than Kyles was (the police as yet had no leads,), injected both Kyles and himself into the investigation in order to get the innocent Kyles convicted. If this were not stupid enough, the wicked Beanie is supposed to have suggested that the police search his victim's premises *a full day before he got around to planting the incriminating evidence on the premises.*

The second half of petitioner's theory was that he was the victim of a quadruple coincidence, in which four eyewitnesses to the crime mistakenly identified him as the murderer-three picking him out of a photo array without hesitation, and all four affirming their identification in open court after comparing him with Beanie. The extraordinary mistake petitioner had to persuade the jury these four witnesses made was not simply to mistake the real killer, Beanie, for the very same innocent third party (hard enough to believe), but in addition to mistake him *for the very man Beanie had chosen to frame*-the last and most incredible level of coincidence. However small the chance that the jury would believe any one of those improbable scenarios, the likelihood that it would believe them all together is far smaller. The Court concludes that it is "reasonably probable" the undisclosed witness interviews would have persuaded the jury of petitioner's implausible theory of mistaken eyewitness testimony, and then argues that it is "reasonably probable" the undisclosed information regarding Beanie would have persuaded the jury of petitioner's implausible theory regarding the incriminating physical evidence. I think neither of those conclusions is remotely true, but even if they were the Court would still be guilty of a fallacy in declaring victory on each implausibility in turn, and thus victory on the whole, without considering the infinitesimal probability of the jury's swallowing the entire concoction of implausibility squared.

This basic error of approaching the evidence piecemeal is also what accounts for the Court's obsessive focus on the credibility or culpability of Beanie, who did not even testify at trial and whose credibility or innocence the State has never once avowed. The

Court's opinion reads as if either petitioner or Beanie must be telling the truth, and any evidence tending to inculpate or undermine the credibility of the one would exculpate or enhance the credibility of the other. But the jury verdict in this case said only that petitioner was guilty of the murder. That is perfectly consistent with the possibilities that Beanie repeatedly lied, that he was an accessory after the fact, or even that he planted evidence against petitioner. Even if the undisclosed evidence would have allowed the defense to thoroughly impeach Beanie and to suggest the above possibilities, the jury could well have believed *all* of those things and yet have condemned petitioner because it could not believe that *all four* of the eyewitnesses were similarly mistaken.

II

The undisclosed evidence does not create a "'reasonable probability' of a different result." The physical evidence confirms the immateriality of the nondisclosures. In a garbage bag outside petitioner's home the police found Mrs. Dye's purse and other belongings. Inside his home they found, behind the kitchen stove, the .32-caliber revolver used to kill Mrs. Dye; hanging in a wardrobe, a homemade shoulder holster that was "a perfect fit" for the revolver); in a dresser drawer in the bedroom, two boxes of gun cartridges, one containing only .32-caliber rounds of the same brand found in the murder weapon, another containing .22, .32, and .38-caliber rounds; in a kitchen cabinet, eight empty Schwegmann's bags; and in a cupboard underneath that cabinet, one Schwegmann's bag containing 15 cans of pet food. Petitioner's account at trial was that Beanie planted the purse, gun, and holster, that petitioner received the ammunition from Beanie as collateral for a loan, and that petitioner had bought the pet food the day of the murder. That account strains credulity to the breaking point.

The State presented to the jury a massive core of evidence showing that petitioner was guilty of murder, and that he lied about his guilt. The effect that the *Brady* materials would have had in chipping away at the edges of the State's case can only be called immaterial. For the same reasons I reject petitioner's claim that the *Brady* materials would have created a "residual doubt" sufficient to cause the sentencing jury to withhold capital punishment.

I respectfully dissent.

FURTHER CASE LAW, REFLECTIONS, AND QUESTIONS

1. Following the Supreme Court's reversal, Curtis Kyles was brought to trial on the murder charge on three subsequent occasions. Each trial resulted in a hung jury. Deciding against pursuing yet another trial, prosecutors dropped the charge, and Kyles was released from prison in February 1998. *See* Death Penalty Information Center, "Curtis Kyles," available at: www.deathpenaltyinfo.org/innocence-cases-1994-2003 (last visited March 29, 2021).

2. In your opinion, should each piece of exculpatory evidence be weighed individually or cumulatively in determining materiality?
3. How does the Court define materiality? Why is this critical in determining if evidence must be disclosed to the defense?
4. Are there problems with the prosecution deciding whether evidence is exculpatory or material? If evidence is not exculpatory and material, the prosecutor need not disclose its existence to anybody, including the defense or the judge. What happens if a prosecutor does not disclose potentially exculpatory evidence to the defense and the defense never learns of its existence? How might you address this dilemma?
5. The Supreme Court applied the standard espoused in *Kyles v. Whitley* in the case of *Glossip v. Oklahoma,* 604 US __ (2025). In 1997, Barry Van Treese, a motel owner, was murdered by Justin Sneed, a maintenance worker at the motel. Sneed confessed to the crime and, in exchange for avoiding the death penalty, testified that the motel manager, Richard Glossip, had hired him to carry out the killing. Sneed's testimony formed the central evidence against Glossip, who has always maintained his innocence.

Glossip was convicted and sentenced to death in 1998. That conviction was overturned in 2001 due to ineffective assistance of counsel, but he was retried in 2004 and again sentenced to death. Over the years, Glossip faced numerous execution dates, many postponed due to legal challenges and concerns over Oklahoma's lethal injection protocol.

In 2022, Glossip's attorneys uncovered previously undisclosed evidence that Sneed was under psychiatric care and prescribed lithium at the time of his testimony — facts he denied at trial. The prosecution failed to correct this lie, despite knowing it was untrue. Additional evidence showed that prosecutors may have coached Sneed to alter his testimony. After an independent review, Oklahoma Attorney General Gentner Drummond acknowledged the prosecutorial misconduct and supported a new trial. Nonetheless, the Oklahoma Court of Criminal Appeals denied relief, prompting Glossip to seek intervention from the U.S. Supreme Court.

On February 25, 2025, the Supreme Court, in a 5–3 decision, overturned Glossip's conviction and ordered a new trial. Writing for the majority, Justice Sonia Sotomayor held that the prosecution's failure to correct false testimony violated Glossip's due process rights, citing *Napue v. Illinois,* 360 U.S. 264 (1959). The Court ruled that correcting this false testimony would likely have changed the jury's assessment of Sneed's reliability. Additionally, the prosecution's misconduct extended beyond *Napue.* It suppressed exculpatory evidence, interfered with witness testimony, and allowed destruction of key physical evidence. Given these cumulative errors and their impact on the fairness of the trial, the Court held that Glossip is entitled to a new trial.

Is There a Duty for the Police to Preserve Potentially Exculpatory Evidence?

The police function in investigating crimes is crucial to successful prosecutions. How the police perform their jobs can affect a criminal prosecution in several ways. For example, an unreasonable search or seizure may result in suppressing evidence that would be useful or even essential to prove guilt. The violation of a suspect's *Miranda* rights may cause a confession to be inadmissible at trial. And, as the Court has made clear in *Kyles v. Whitley*, the failure by the police to share potentially exculpatory evidence with a prosecutor does not insulate the prosecutor from his or her duty under *Brady* and *Bagley* to make that evidence available to the defense.

We now consider an issue that generally relates to *Brady* and the prosecution's obligation to provide material exculpatory evidence to the defense. Do the police, because they serve as a vital link in the chain of a prosecution, have a duty analogous to the prosecutor's to preserve evidence that could be useful to the accused in defending against criminal charges?

Arizona v. Youngblood

488 U.S. 51 (1988)

Chief Justice Rehnquist delivered the opinion of the Court.

[On October 29, 1983 a 10-year-old boy was abducted from a church carnival by a man who drove the boy to a secluded location and repeatedly sodomized him. The man thereafter released the boy, who made his way home and was taken to a hospital and treated for rectal injuries. A physician used a "sexual assault kit" to collect evidence of the attack, including swabs of the boy's rectum and mouth and samples of the boy's saliva, blood, and hair. The police placed the kit in a secure refrigerator at the police station, and also collected the boy's T-shirt and underwear. These items of clothing were not refrigerated or frozen.

[Nine days after the attack, the boy identified Youngblood as his assailant from a photograph array. The following day, a police criminologist examined the sexual assault kit and determined that sexual contact had occurred but performed no other tests and did not test the boy's clothing. He returned the sexual assault kit to the refrigerator. Youngblood was located and arrested approximately four weeks later, on December 9, 1983. He subsequently was indicted on charges of child molestation, sexual assault, and kidnapping.

[An ABO blood group test later was performed on the rectal swab sample, but it failed to detect any blood group substances. The police criminologist examined the boy's clothing for the first time in January 1985. He located semen stains on both the T-shirt and the underwear, but was unsuccessful in obtaining blood group substances from the stains using the ABO technique. "He also performed a P-30 protein molecule test on the stains, which indicated that only a small quantity of semen was present on the clothing; it was inconclusive as to the assailant's identity."

[At his trial, Youngblood contended that the boy had erroneously identified him as his assailant. "[B]oth a criminologist for the State and an expert witness for respondent testified as to what might have been shown by tests performed on the samples shortly after they were gathered, or by later tests performed on the samples from the boy's clothing had the clothing been properly refrigerated. The court instructed the jury that if they found that the State had destroyed or lost evidence, they might "infer that the true fact is against the State's interest." The jury found Youngblood guilty as charged.

[The Arizona Court of Appeals reversed. It held that "when identity is an issue at trial and the police permit the destruction of evidence that could eliminate the defendant as the perpetrator, such loss is material to the defense and is a denial of due process." The Court of Appeals concluded on the basis of the expert testimony at trial that timely performance of tests with properly preserved semen samples could have produced results that might have completely exonerated respondent. The Court of Appeals reached this conclusion even though it did "not imply any bad faith on the part of the State."

[The Supreme Court granted certiorari "to consider the extent to which the Due Process Clause of the Federal Constitution requires the State to preserve evidentiary material that might be useful to a criminal defendant."]

Decision of this case requires us to consider what might loosely be called the area of constitutionally guaranteed access to evidence. In *Brady v. Maryland*, we held "that the suppression by the prosecution of evidence favorable to the accused upon request violates due process where the evidence is material either to guilt or to punishment, irrespective of the good faith or bad faith of the prosecution." In *United States v. Agurs*, we held that the prosecution had a duty to disclose some evidence of this description even though no requests were made for it, but at the same time we rejected the notion that a "prosecutor has a constitutional duty routinely to deliver his entire file to defense counsel."

There is no question but that the State complied with *Brady* and *Agurs* here. The State disclosed relevant police reports to respondent, which contained information about the existence of the swab and the clothing, and the boy's examination at the hospital. The State provided respondent's expert with the laboratory reports and notes prepared by the police criminologist, and respondent's expert had access to the swab and to the clothing.

If respondent is to prevail on federal constitutional grounds, then, it must be because of some constitutional duty over and above that imposed by cases such as *Brady* and *Agurs*. Our most recent decision in this area of the law, *California v. Trombetta*,

467 US 479 (1984), arose out of a drunk driving prosecution in which the State had introduced test results indicating the concentration of alcohol in the blood of two motorists. The defendants sought to suppress the test results on the ground that the State had failed to preserve the breath samples used in the test. We rejected this argument for several reasons: first, "the officers here were acting in 'good faith and in accord with their normal practice,'" second, in the light of the procedures actually used the chances that preserved samples would have exculpated the defendants were slim, and, third, even if the samples might have shown inaccuracy in the tests, the defendants had "alternative means of demonstrating their innocence." In the present case, the likelihood that the preserved materials would have enabled the defendant to exonerate himself appears to be greater than it was in *Trombetta*, but here, unlike in *Trombetta*, the State did not attempt to make any use of the materials in its own case in chief.

Our decisions in related areas have stressed the importance for constitutional purposes of good or bad faith on the part of the Government when the claim is based on loss of evidence attributable to the Government. In *United States v. Marion*, 404 US 307 (1971), we said that "[n]o actual prejudice to the conduct of the defense is alleged or proved, and there is no showing that the Government intentionally delayed to gain some tactical advantage over appellees or to harass them." Similarly, in *United States v. Valenzuela-Bernal*, we considered whether the Government's deportation of two witnesses who were illegal aliens violated due process. We held that the prompt deportation of the witnesses was justified "upon the Executive's good-faith determination that they possess no evidence favorable to the defendant in a criminal prosecution."

The Due Process Clause of the Fourteenth Amendment, as interpreted in *Brady*, makes the good or bad faith of the State irrelevant when the State fails to disclose to the defendant material exculpatory evidence. But we think the Due Process Clause requires a different result when we deal with the failure of the State to preserve evidentiary material of which no more can be said than that it could have been subjected to tests, the results of which might have exonerated the defendant. Part of the reason for the difference in treatment is found in the observation made by the Court in *Trombetta*, that "whenever potentially exculpatory evidence is permanently lost, courts face the treacherous task of divining the import of materials whose contents are unknown and, very often, disputed." Part of it stems from our unwillingness to read the "fundamental fairness" requirement of the Due Process Clause as imposing on the police an undifferentiated and absolute duty to retain and to preserve all material that might be of conceivable evidentiary significance in a particular prosecution. We think that requiring a defendant to show bad faith on the part of the police both limits the extent of the police's obligation to preserve evidence to reasonable bounds and confines it to that class of cases where the interests of justice most clearly require it, *i.e.*, those cases in which the police themselves by their conduct indicate that the evidence could form a basis for exonerating the defendant. We therefore hold that unless a criminal defendant can show bad faith on the part of the police, failure to preserve potentially useful evidence does not constitute a denial of due process of law.

In this case, the police collected the rectal swab and clothing on the night of the crime: respondent was not taken into custody until six weeks later. The failure of the police to refrigerate the clothing and to perform tests on the semen samples can at worst be described as negligent. None of this information was concealed from respondent at trial, and the evidence — such as it was — was made available to respondent's expert who declined to perform any tests on the samples. The Arizona Court of Appeals noted in its opinion — and we agree — that there was no suggestion of bad faith on the part of the police. It follows, therefore, from what we have said, that there was no violation of the Due Process Clause.

The Arizona Court of Appeals also referred somewhat obliquely to the State's "inability to quantitatively test" certain semen samples with the newer P-30 test. If the court means by this statement that the Due Process Clause is violated when the police fail to use a particular investigatory tool, we strongly disagree. The situation here is no different than a prosecution for drunk driving that rests on police observation alone; the defendant is free to argue to the finder of fact that a breathalyzer test might have been exculpatory, but the police do not have a constitutional duty to perform any particular tests.

The judgment of the Arizona Court of Appeals is reversed, and the case is remanded for further proceedings not inconsistent with this opinion.

JUSTICE STEVENS, concurring in the judgment.

Three factors are of critical importance to my evaluation of this case. First, at the time the police failed to refrigerate the victim's clothing, and thus negligently lost potentially valuable evidence, they had at least as great an interest in preserving the evidence as did the person later accused of the crime. In cases such as this, even without a prophylactic sanction such as dismissal of the indictment, the State has a strong incentive to preserve the evidence.

Second, although it is not possible to know whether the lost evidence would have revealed any relevant information, it is unlikely that the defendant was prejudiced by the State's omission. In examining witnesses and in her summation, defense counsel impressed upon the jury the fact that the State failed to preserve the evidence and that the State could have conducted tests that might well have exonerated the defendant. More significantly, the trial judge instructed the jury: "If you find that the State has allowed to be destroyed or lost any evidence whose content or quality are in issue, you may infer that the true fact is against the State's interest." As a result, the uncertainty as to what the evidence might have proved was turned to the defendant's advantage.

Third, the fact that no juror chose to draw the permissive inference that proper preservation of the evidence would have demonstrated that the defendant was not the assailant suggests that the lost evidence was "immaterial." In declining defense counsel's and the court's invitations to draw the permissive inference, the jurors in effect indicated that, in their view, the other evidence at trial was so overwhelming that it was highly improbable that the lost evidence was exculpatory. Presumably, in a case involving a closer question as to guilt or innocence, the jurors would have been more ready to infer that the lost evidence was exculpatory.

With these factors in mind, I concur in the Court's judgment. I do not, however, join the Court's opinion because it announces a proposition of law that is much broader than necessary to decide this case. It states, "that unless a criminal defendant can show bad faith on the part of the police, failure to preserve potentially useful evidence does not constitute a denial of due process of law." In my opinion, there may well be cases in which the defendant is unable to prove that the State acted in bad faith but in which the loss or destruction of evidence is nonetheless so critical to the defense as to make a criminal trial fundamentally unfair. This, however, is not such a case.

FURTHER CASE LAW, REFLECTIONS, AND QUESTIONS

1. If the prosecutor's good or bad faith is irrelevant to a claimed *Brady* violation, why is a showing of bad faith necessary for the defendant to prevail when the police fail to preserve potentially exculpatory evidence?
2. Assume that Youngblood had a codefendant, Oldblood, against whom a police officer held a personal grudge. Further, assume that the officer intentionally and in bad faith destroyed physical evidence that may have been useful to Oldblood's defense. In contrast, potentially exculpatory evidence relevant to Youngblood became unavailable through no apparent bad faith on the part of the police. Would you expect different results in resolving Oldblood's and Youngblood's cases? Would the basic fairness of their respective trials — defined in terms of confidence that a just result had been produced based on all potentially relevant evidence — be affected by whether the police acted in bad faith? On the other hand, what inferences does Chief Justice Rehnquist suggest might be supported by the bad-faith destruction of evidence?
3. What exactly does bad faith mean in this context? Does the Court provide examples or suggest how this term should be defined?

Box 11.3 You Be the Judge

One Monday evening, Dwayne robbed a laundromat. During the robbery, a laundromat attendant was shot and killed. From the beginning, Dwayne admitted that he committed the robbery and that the shots came from his gun, but claimed the attendant was shot accidentally.

At trial, the only issue was whether Dwayne was guilty of aggravated first-degree murder, which requires proof of premeditation; or of first-degree (felony) murder, which does not. The state presented the testimony of Dwayne's brother, Rodney, who was at the laundromat. Rodney testified that Dwayne told him that he intended to rob the laundromat and "leave no witnesses."

Before trial, the police administered a polygraph test to Rodney. Although inadmissible at trial, polygraphs can help the prosecution clarify important issues. The test indicated that Rodney was lying. The prosecutor never disclosed the test to the defense because he believed he was not required to do so under *Brady*.

Dwayne was found guilty of aggravated first-degree murder and sentenced to death. After the trial, Dwayne learned of the polygraph test. He filed an appeal on the grounds that the prosecution had failed to disclose the test results in violation of *Brady*.

Were Dwayne's rights violated? Explain in detail.

See *Wood v. Bartholomew*, 516 U.S. 1 (1995)

The Plea Bargain

Plea bargaining is the process whereby the accused and prosecutor in a criminal case work out a mutually satisfactory disposition of the case, subject to court approval. Using plea bargaining helps courts operate more efficiently by facilitating the disposition of cases without the time and expense associated with a jury trial. It is also beneficial to the prosecution and the defendant. For a defendant, a **plea bargain** reduces the risk associated with multiple convictions or a mandatory minimum sentence. For the prosecution, the benefits include obtaining a conviction without running the risk and uncertainty of a jury trial, ensuring the defendant receives an acceptable level of punishment, and freeing up prosecutorial resources to work on other matters.

There are four common categories of plea bargains.

1. Charge bargain (a). As part of a plea bargain, a defendant may be allowed to plead guilty to a lesser charge than the one presented in the indictment. For example, a defendant charged with aggravated assault may be permitted to

plead guilty to simple assault in exchange for waiving their rights associated with a trial.

2. Charge bargain (b). As part of a plea bargain, a defendant may be allowed to plead guilty to some offenses charged in an indictment and have other charged offenses dismissed.
3. Sentence bargain. The defendant may plead guilty to the crimes charged in an indictment on the condition that the defendant would receive an agreed-upon sentence lighter than expected following a conviction obtained at trial. However, it is important to note that a prosecutor cannot guarantee a lighter sentence will be given; the judge has the discretion to impose any legally authorized sentence. While this rarely occurs, should the judge reject the bargained-for sentence, the defendant has the right to withdraw from the plea bargain and stand trial.
4. Enhancement waivers. While beyond the scope of this text, there are a number of items that can serve to increase a sentence beyond what is authorized for an offense by itself. The ability of a court to impose increased sentences based on prior convictions, using a firearm, hate-based crimes, and crimes against a vulnerable person (child, the elderly, or disabled) can be waived by the prosecution in exchange for a guilty plea.

Constitutional Requirements for a Plea Bargain

Regardless of which of the four types of plea bargains are involved, the United States Supreme Court has held that guilty pleas and plea bargains are constitutional so long as several requirements are met. Specifically, for a plea bargain to be valid, it must be shown that it was entered into knowingly, intelligently, and voluntarily. The standards for these items were discussed by the Supreme Court in *Brady v. United States*.

Brady v. United States

397 U.S. 742 (1970)

MR. JUSTICE WHITE delivered the opinion of the Court.

In 1959, petitioner was charged with kidnapping in violation of 18 U.S.C.§1201(a). Since the indictment charged that the victim of the kidnapping was not liberated unharmed, petitioner faced a maximum penalty of death if the verdict of the jury should so recommend. Petitioner, represented by competent counsel throughout, first elected to plead not guilty. Apparently because the trial judge was unwilling to try the case without a jury, petitioner made no serious attempt to reduce the possibility of a death penalty by waiving a jury trial. Upon learning that his codefendant, who had confessed to the authorities, would plead guilty and be available to testify against him, petitioner changed his plea to guilty. His plea was accepted after the trial judge twice questioned him as to the voluntariness of his plea. Petitioner was sentenced to 50 years imprisonment, later reduced to 30.

II

The trial judge in 1959 found the plea voluntary before accepting it; the District Court in 1968, after an evidentiary hearing, found that the plea was voluntarily made; the Court of Appeals specifically approved the finding of voluntariness. We see no reason on this record to disturb the judgment of those courts. Petitioner, advised by competent counsel, tendered his plea after his codefendant, who had already given a confession, determined to plead guilty and became available to testify against petitioner. It was this development that the District Court found to have triggered Brady's guilty plea.

The voluntariness of Brady's plea can be determined only by considering all of the relevant circumstances surrounding it. One of these circumstances was the possibility of a heavier sentence following a guilty verdict after a trial. It may be that Brady, faced with a strong case against him and recognizing that his chances for acquittal were slight, preferred to plead guilty and thus limit the penalty to life imprisonment rather than to elect a jury trial which could result in a death penalty. But even if we assume that Brady would not have pleaded guilty except for the death penalty provision of §1201(a), this assumption merely identifies the penalty provision as a "but for" cause of his plea. That the statute caused the plea in this sense does not necessarily prove that the plea was coerced and invalid as an involuntary act.

The State to some degree encourages pleas of guilty at every important step in the criminal process. For some people, their breach of a State's law is alone sufficient reason for surrendering themselves and accepting punishment. For others, apprehension and charge, both threatening acts by the Government, jar them into admitting their guilt. In still other cases, the post-indictment accumulation of evidence may convince the defendant and his counsel that a trial is not worth the agony and expense to the defendant and his family. All these pleas of guilty are valid in spite of the State's responsibility for some of the factors motivating the pleas; the pleas are no more improperly compelled than is the decision by a defendant at the close of the State's evidence at trial that he must take the stand or face certain conviction.

Of course, the agents of the State may not produce a plea by actual or threatened physical harm or by mental coercion overbearing the will of the defendant. But nothing of the sort is claimed in this case; nor is there evidence that Brady was so gripped by fear of the death penalty or hope of leniency that he did not or could not, with the help of counsel, rationally weigh the advantages of going to trial against the advantages of pleading guilty. Brady's claim is of a different sort: that it violates the Fifth Amendment to influence or encourage a guilty plea by opportunity or promise of leniency and that a guilty plea is coerced and invalid if influenced by the fear of a possibly higher penalty for the crime charged if a conviction is obtained after the State is put to its proof.

Insofar as the voluntariness of his plea is concerned, there is little to differentiate Brady from (1) the defendant, in a jurisdiction where the judge and jury have the same range of sentencing power, who pleads guilty because his lawyer advises him that the judge will very probably be more lenient than the jury; (2) the defendant, in a jurisdiction where the judge alone has sentencing power, who is advised by counsel that the judge is normally more lenient with defendants who plead guilty than with those who go to trial; (3) the defendant who is permitted by prosecutor and judge to plead guilty to a lesser offense included in the offense charged; and (4) the defendant who pleads guilty to certain counts with the understanding that other charges will be dropped. In each of these situations, as in Brady's case, the defendant might never plead guilty absent the possibility or certainty that the plea will result in a lesser penalty than the sentence that could be imposed after a trial and a verdict of guilty. We decline to hold, however, that a guilty plea is compelled and invalid under the Fifth Amendment whenever motivated by the defendant's desire to accept the certainty or probability of a lesser penalty rather than face a wider range of possibilities extending from acquittal to conviction and a higher penalty authorized by law for the crime charged.

The issue we deal with is inherent in the criminal law and its administration because guilty pleas are not constitutionally forbidden, because the criminal law characteristically extends to judge or jury a range of choice in setting the sentence in individual cases, and because both the State and the defendant often find it advantageous to preclude the possibility of the maximum penalty authorized by law. For a defendant who sees slight possibility of acquittal, the advantages of pleading guilty and limiting the probable penalty are obvious — his exposure is reduced, the correctional processes can begin immediately, and the practical burdens of a trial are eliminated. For the State there are also advantages — the more promptly imposed punishment after an admission of guilt may more effectively attain the objectives of punishment; and with the avoidance of trial, scarce judicial and prosecutorial resources are conserved for those cases in which there is a substantial issue of the defendant's guilt or in which there is substantial doubt that the State can sustain its burden of proof. It is this mutuality of advantage that perhaps explains the fact that at present well over three-fourths of the criminal convictions in this country rest on pleas of guilty, a great many of them no doubt motivated at least in part by the hope or assurance of a lesser penalty than might be imposed if there were a guilty verdict after a trial to judge or jury.

Of course, that the prevalence of guilty pleas is explainable does not necessarily validate those pleas or the system which produces them. But we cannot hold that it is unconstitutional for the State to extend a benefit to a defendant who in turn extends a substantial benefit to the State and who demonstrates by his plea that he is ready and willing to admit his crime and to enter the correctional system in a frame of mind that affords hope for success in rehabilitation over a shorter period of time than might otherwise be necessary.

A contrary holding would require the States and Federal Government to forbid guilty pleas altogether, to provide a single invariable penalty for each crime defined by the statutes, or to place the sentencing function in a separate authority having no knowledge of the manner in which the conviction in each case was obtained. In any event, it would be necessary to forbid prosecutors and judges to accept guilty pleas to selected counts, to lesser included offenses, or to reduced charges. The Fifth Amendment does not reach so far.

The standard as to the voluntariness of guilty pleas must be essentially that defined by Judge Tuttle of the Court of Appeals for the Fifth Circuit:

A plea of guilty entered by one fully aware of the direct consequences, including the actual value of any commitments made to him by the court, prosecutor, or his own counsel, must stand unless induced by threats (or promises to discontinue improper harassment), misrepresentation (including unfulfilled or unfulfillable promises), or perhaps by promises that are by their nature improper as having no proper relationship to the prosecutor's business (e.g., bribes).

Under this standard, a plea of guilty is not invalid merely because entered to avoid the possibility of a death penalty.

III

The record before us also supports the conclusion that Brady's plea was intelligently made. He was advised by competent counsel, he was made aware of the nature of the charge against him, and there was nothing to indicate that he was incompetent or otherwise not in control of his mental faculties; once his confederate had pleaded guilty and became available to testify, he chose to plead guilty, perhaps to ensure that he would face no more than life imprisonment or a term of years. Brady was aware of precisely what he was doing when he admitted that he had kidnapped the victim and had not released her unharmed.

Often the decision to plead guilty is heavily influenced by the defendant's appraisal of the prosecution's case against him and by the apparent likelihood of securing leniency should a guilty plea be offered and accepted. Considerations like these frequently present imponderable questions for which there are no certain answers; judgments may be made that in the light of later events seem improvident, although they were perfectly sensible at the time. The rule that a plea must be intelligently made to be valid does not require that a plea be vulnerable to later attack if the defendant did not correctly assess every relevant factor entering into his decision. A defendant is not entitled to withdraw his plea merely because he discovers long after the plea has been accepted that his calculus misapprehended the quality of the State's case or the likely penalties attached to alternative courses of action. More particularly, absent misrepresentation or other impermissible conduct by state agents, a voluntary plea of guilty intelligently made in the light of the then applicable law does not become vulnerable because later judicial decisions indicate that the plea rested on a faulty premise. A plea of guilty triggered by the expectations of a competently counseled defendant that the State will have a strong case against him is not subject to later attack because the defendant's lawyer correctly advised him with respect to the then existing law as to possible penalties but later pronouncements of the courts, as in this case, hold that the maximum penalty for the crime in question was less than was reasonably assumed at the time the plea was entered.

This is not to say that guilty plea convictions hold no hazards for the innocent or that the methods of taking guilty pleas presently employed in this country are necessarily valid in all respects. This mode of conviction is no more foolproof than full trials to the court or to the jury. Accordingly, we take great precautions against unsound results, and we should continue to do so, whether conviction is by plea or by trial. We would have serious doubts about this case if the encouragement of guilty pleas by offers of leniency substantially increased the likelihood that defendants, advised by competent counsel, would falsely condemn themselves. But our view is to the contrary and is based on our expectations that courts will satisfy themselves that pleas of guilty are voluntarily and intelligently made by competent defendants with adequate advice of counsel and that there is nothing to question the accuracy and reliability of the defendants' admissions that they committed the crimes with which they are charged. In the case before us, nothing in the record impeaches Brady's plea or suggests that his admissions in open court were anything but the truth.

Although Brady's plea of guilty may well have been motivated in part by a desire to avoid a possible death penalty, we are convinced that his plea was voluntarily and intelligently made and we have no reason to doubt that his solemn admission of guilt was truthful.

FURTHER CASE LAW, REFLECTIONS, AND QUESTIONS

1. Is there a meaningful distinction between providing an "incentive" to forgo the rights to a trial by jury and to plead not guilty to a criminal charge and "punishing" a defendant for exercising those constitutional rights by "increasing" his or her risk of punishment if he or she insists on pleading not guilty?
2. In *Brady*, the defendant's plea was not deprived of its "intelligent" nature because defense counsel did not anticipate, at the time that the guilty plea was entered, that the law on the books would subsequently be ruled unconstitutional. What, however, of counsel's failure to advise the accused of the present availability of existing defenses to the charge, such as the possibility that a confession might be suppressed from evidence? Would such an oversight render the accused's plea of guilty uninformed, or make it "unintelligent" in nature? In *McMann v.*

Richardson, 397 U.S. 759 (1970), the Supreme Court held that so long as counsel's advice was "within the range of competence demanded of attorneys in a criminal case," the intelligence of the guilty plea was not undermined. Recall in the previous chapter, we read in *Padilla v. Kentucky* that an attorney's failure to inform a client of the immigration consequences of a conviction fell below the range of competence demanded of defense counsel.

3. Judges are careful to ensure that the record of the change of plea hearing contains evidence of the requirements described in *Brady*. The elements of a typical hearing are presented in Box 11.4.

Box 11.4 The Change of Plea Hearing

Trial court judges are required to ensure that a guilty plea was entered into knowingly, intelligently, and voluntarily. To do this during the change of plea hearing, the judge will ask the defendant whether he or she:

1. Understands the charges against them.
2. Understands the range of possible sentences for the offenses charged.
3. Understands the terms of any plea agreement.
4. Has had the opportunity to consult with counsel regarding the plea agreement.
5. Understands that they are waiving the following constitutional rights:
   a. The right to trial by jury.
   b. The assistance of counsel during the jury trial.
   c. The right to confront and cross-examine witnesses against them.
   d. The right to present evidence and to have the state compel witnesses of their choosing to testify.
   e. The right to remain silent and be presumed innocent until proven guilty beyond a reasonable doubt.

The judge will also question the defendant regarding the voluntariness of the plea. The judge will ask whether the defendant was coerced into pleading guilty, and whether any physical threats or promises not contained in the plea agreement were made. The judge will also ask the defendant if they have reviewed the written plea agreement with their attorney, whether they have any questions about its contents, and whether they wish to enter into it.

After establishing that the constitutional requirements are met, the judge typically asks the prosecutor or defendant to briefly state on the record what acts the defendant committed. This statement must state facts that establish the elements of the criminal offense were present.

By placing the defendant's knowledge of these items on the record the court preempts any future attempt by a defendant to argue that the plea was unintelligently or involuntarily made.

For an example of what a change of plea hearing looks like, the link below connects to a video of Nikolas Cruz's (the Parkland shooter) change of plea hearing. youtu.be/YiwgDksYw_c?t=574

Broken Promises

A plea agreement is somewhat like a contract. Each party gives a benefit to the other party and in return receives a benefit. In the case of plea bargaining, the defendant provides the prosecution with a plea of guilty to a charge, and the prosecution gives the defendant items such as a lesser punishment, dismissal of additional charges, or a promise to make a recommendation or refrain from making a recommendation to the judge regarding the sentence to be imposed. What happens if one party performs its end of the bargain, but the other party does not? Consider the following case.

Santobello v. New York

404 U.S. 257 (1971)

MR. CHIEF JUSTICE BURGER delivered the opinion of the Court.

The facts are not in dispute. The State of New York indicted petitioner in 1969 on two felony counts, Promoting Gambling in the First Degree, and Possession of Gambling Records in the First Degree. Petitioner first entered a plea of not guilty to both counts. After negotiations, the Assistant District Attorney in charge of the case agreed to permit petitioner to plead guilty to a lesser-included offense, Possession of Gambling Records in the Second Degree, N.Y. Penal Law §225.15, conviction of which would carry a maximum prison sentence of one year. The prosecutor agreed to make no recommendation as to the sentence.

On June 16, 1969, petitioner accordingly withdrew his plea of not guilty and entered a plea of guilty to the lesser charge. Petitioner represented to the sentencing judge that the plea was voluntary and that the facts of the case, as described by the Assistant District Attorney, were true. The court accepted the plea and set a date for sentencing. A series of delays followed, owing primarily to the absence of a pre-sentence report, so that by September 23, 1969, petitioner had still not been sentenced. By that date petitioner acquired new defense counsel.

On January 9 petitioner appeared before a different judge, the judge who had presided over the case to this juncture having retired.. . . At this appearance, another prosecutor had replaced the prosecutor who had negotiated the plea. The new prosecutor recommended the maximum one-year sentence. In making this recommendation, he cited petitioner's criminal record and alleged links with organized crime. Defense counsel immediately objected on the ground that the State had promised petitioner before the plea was entered that there would be no sentence recommendation by the prosecution. He sought to adjourn the sentence hearing in order to have time to prepare proof of the first prosecutor's promise. The second prosecutor, apparently ignorant of his colleague's commitment, argued that there was nothing in the record to support petitioner's claim of a promise, but the State, in subsequent proceedings, has not contested that such a promise was made.

The sentencing judge ended discussion, with the following statement, quoting extensively from the pre-sentence report:

> Mr. Aronstein [Defense Counsel], I am not at all influenced by what the District Attorney says, so that there is no need to adjourn the sentence, and there is no need to have any testimony. It doesn't make a particle of difference what the District Attorney says he will do, or what he doesn't do.
>
> I have here, Mr. Aronstein, a probation report. I have here a history of a long, long serious criminal record. I have here a picture of the life history of this man." The judge then imposed the maximum sentence of one year.

This record represents another example of an unfortunate lapse in orderly prosecutorial procedures, in part, no doubt, because of the enormous increase in the workload of the often understaffed prosecutor's offices. The heavy workload may well explain these episodes, but it does not excuse them. The disposition of criminal charges by agreement between the prosecutor and the accused, sometimes loosely called "plea bargaining," is an essential component of the administration of justice. Properly administered, it is to be encouraged. If every criminal charge were subjected to a full-scale trial, the States and the Federal Government would need to multiply by many times the number of judges and court facilities.

Disposition of charges after plea discussions is not only an essential part of the process but a highly desirable part for many reasons. It leads to prompt and largely final disposition of most criminal cases; it avoids much of the corrosive impact of enforced idleness during pre-trial confinement for those who are denied release pending trial; it protects the public from those accused persons who are prone to continue criminal conduct even while on pre-trial release; and, by shortening the time between charge and disposition, it enhances whatever may be the rehabilitative prospects of the guilty when they are ultimately imprisoned.

However, all of these considerations presuppose fairness in securing agreement between an accused and a prosecutor. It is now clear, for example, that the accused pleading guilty must be counseled, absent a waiver. Fed.Rule Crim.Proc. 11, governing pleas in federal courts, now makes clear that the sentencing judge must develop, on the record, the factual basis for the plea, as, for example, by having the accused describe the conduct that gave rise to the charge. The plea must, of course, be voluntary and knowing and if it was induced by promises, the essence of those promises must in some way be made known. There is, of course, no absolute right to have a guilty plea accepted. A court may reject a plea in exercise of sound judicial discretion.

This phase of the process of criminal justice, and the adjudicative element inherent in accepting a plea of guilty, must be attended by safeguards to insure the defendant what is reasonably due in the circumstances. Those circumstances will vary, but a constant factor is that when a plea rests in any significant degree on a promise or agreement of the prosecutor, so that it can be said to be part of the induce mentor consideration, such promise must be fulfilled.

On this record, petitioner "bargained" and negotiated for a particular plea in order to secure dismissal of more serious charges, but also on condition that no sentence recommendation would be made by the prosecutor. It is now conceded that the promise to abstain from a recommendation was made, and at this stage the prosecution is not in a good position to argue that its inadvertent breach of agreement is immaterial. The staff lawyers in a prosecutor's office have the burden of "letting the left hand know what the right hand is doing" or has done. That the breach of agreement was inadvertent does not lessen its impact.

We need not reach the question whether the sentencing judge would or would not have been influenced had he known all the details of the negotiations for the plea. He stated that the prosecutor's recommendation did not influence him and we have no reason to doubt that. Nevertheless, we conclude that the interests of justice and appropriate recognition of the duties of the prosecution in relation to promises made in the negotiation of pleas of guilty will be best served by remanding the case to the state courts for further consideration. The ultimate relief to which petitioner is entitled we leave to the discretion of the state court, which is in a better position to decide whether the circumstances of this case require only that there be specific performance of the agreement on the plea, in which case petitioner should be resentenced by a different judge, or whether, in the view of the state court, the circumstances require granting the relief sought by petitioner, i.e., the opportunity to withdraw his plea of guilty. We emphasize that this is in no sense to question the fairness of the sentencing judge; the fault here rests on the prosecutor, not on the sentencing judge.

The judgment is vacated and the case is remanded for reconsideration not inconsistent with this opinion.

Mr. Justice Douglas, concurring.

I join the opinion of the Court and add only a word. I agree that New York did not keep its "plea bargain" with petitioner and that it is no excuse for the default merely because a member of the prosecutor's staff who was not a party to the "plea bargain" was in charge of the case when it came before the New York court. The staff of the prosecution is a unit, and each member must be presumed to know the commitments made by any other member. If responsibility could be evaded that way, the prosecution would have designed another deceptive "contrivance."

FURTHER CASE LAW, REFLECTIONS, AND QUESTIONS

1. Although the Court unanimously agreed that the plea bargain in *Santobello* was broken, there was disagreement about the proper remedy. What possible remedies are there, and what did the Court choose? Do you think this remedy is fair?
2. A plea agreement is a contract. Both parties are required to fulfill their obligations under it. Additionally, once a plea offer is made, accepted, and entered into before a judge, it is very difficult for either side to withdraw from the agreement.

Box 11.5 You Be the Judge

John was charged with first-degree murder, punishable by life imprisonment or death. Before the trial, he entered a plea bargain whereby John would plead guilty to second-degree murder and receive a sentence of 25 years. Additionally, John would testify against two other suspects who were allegedly involved in the murder. The parties agreed to the following as part of the plea bargain.

> The defendant hereby agrees to testify fully and completely in any Court, State, or Federal, when requested by proper authorities against any and all parties involved in the murder.
>
> All parties agree that the defendant shall testify truthfully and completely at all times, whether under oath or not, to the crimes mentioned in this agreement. Should the defendant refuse to testify, should he at any time testify untruthfully, or if any material fact in the defendant's transcribed statements given to the State prior to this agreement is false, then this entire agreement is null and void, and the original charges will be automatically reinstated.

John testified at a trial of the two suspects who were found guilty; however, the convictions were reversed on appeal. When asked to testify at the retrial of the suspects, John refused. In response to this refusal, the prosecution moved to nullify the plea agreement and reinstate the first-degree murder charge.

Did John violate the agreement?

Did the prosecution operate in bad faith?

Should the judge grant the prosecution's motion to reinstate the charge of first-degree murder?

See *Ricketts v. Adamson*, 483 U.S. 1 (1987).

The Innocent Defendant

Before a court can accept a defendant's guilty plea, either alone or as part of a plea agreement, the judge must find that there is a factual basis for the guilty plea. In finding a factual basis, the judge may consider many items, including a defendant's statements, police and scientific reports, grand jury or preliminary hearing transcripts, or other credible information. The purpose behind the judge finding a factual basis exists is to ensure only guilty defendants are convicted of crimes.

What if a defendant wants to plead guilty yet still maintain their innocence? While it might seem crazy for an innocent person to plead guilty, it happens quite often. There are several reasons for this. Consider the plight of Joe, a homeless person arrested for a misdemeanor. He is actually innocent. As Joe has no money to put up for bail, he will likely be held in jail pending trial. At the initial appearance, the prosecutor tells Joe that if he pleads guilty, he will receive a sentence of time served and be given his freedom immediately. Should Joe maintain his innocence and stay in jail for a few weeks to a month awaiting trial? Should he plead guilty to a crime he did not commit to get out of jail?

While Joe's dilemma might not seem very important, it raises an important philosophical question. Should an innocent person be allowed to plead guilty? Should a court facilitate such an act? This was what the Court considered in the following case.

North Carolina v. Alford

400 U.S. 25 (1970)

Mr. Justice White delivered the opinion of the Court.

On December 2, 1963, Alford was indicted for first-degree murder, a capital offense under North Carolina law. The court appointed an attorney to represent him, and this attorney questioned all but one of the various witnesses who appellee said would substantiate his claim of innocence. The witnesses, however, did not support Alford's story but gave statements that strongly indicated his guilt. Faced with strong evidence of guilt and no substantial evidentiary support for the claim of innocence, Alford's attorney recommended that he plead guilty, but left the ultimate decision to Alford himself. The prosecutor agreed to accept a plea of guilty to a charge of second-degree murder, and on December 10, 1963, Alford pleaded guilty to the reduced charge.

Before the plea was finally accepted by the trial court, the court heard the sworn testimony of a police officer who summarized the State's case. Two other witnesses besides Alford were also heard. Although there was no eyewitness to the crime, the testimony indicated that shortly before the killing Alford took his gun from his house, stated his intention to kill the victim, and returned home with the declaration that he had carried out the killing. After the summary presentation of the State's case, Alford took the stand and testified that he had not committed the murder but that he was pleading guilty because he faced the threat of the death penalty if he did not do so. In response to the questions of his counsel, he acknowledged that his counsel had informed him of the difference between second- and first-degree murder and of his rights in case he chose to go to trial. The trial court then asked appellee if, in light of his denial of guilt, he still desired to plead guilty to second-degree murder and appellee answered, "Yes, sir. I plead guilty on — from the circumstances that he [Alford's attorney] told me." After eliciting information about Alford's prior criminal record, which was a long one, the trial court sentenced him to 30 years' imprisonment, the maximum penalty for second-degree murder.

We held in *Brady v. United States*, 397 U.S.742 (1970), that a plea of guilty which would not have been entered except for the defendant's desire to avoid a possible death penalty and to limit the maximum penalty to life imprisonment or a term of years was not for that reason compelled within the meaning of the Fifth Amendment. The standard was and remains whether the plea represents a voluntary and intelligent choice among the alternative courses of action open to the defendant. That he would not have pleaded except for the opportunity to limit the possible penalty does not necessarily demonstrate that the plea of guilty was not the product of a free and rational choice, especially where the defendant was represented by competent counsel whose advice was that the plea would be to the defendant's advantage.

As previously recounted after Alford's plea of guilty was offered and the State's case was placed before the judge, Alford denied that he had committed the murder but reaffirmed his desire to plead guilty to avoid a possible death sentence and to limit the penalty to the 30-year maximum provided for second-degree murder. Ordinarily, a judgment of conviction resting on a plea of guilty is justified by the defendant's admission that he committed the crime charged against him and his consent that judgment be entered without a trial of any kind. The plea usually subsumes both elements, and justifiably so, even though there is no separate, express admission by the defendant that he committed the particular acts claimed to constitute the crime charged in the indictment. Here Alford entered his plea but accompanied it with the statement that he had not shot the victim.

If Alford's statements were to be credited as sincere assertions of his innocence, there obviously existed a factual and legal dispute between him and the State. Without more, it might be argued that the conviction entered on his guilty plea was invalid, since his assertion of innocence negated any admission of guilt, which, as we observed last Term in Brady, is normally central to the plea and the foundation for entering judgment against the defendant.

In addition to Alford's statement, however, the court had heard an account of the events on the night of the murder, including information from Alford's acquaintances that he had departed from his home with his gun stating his intention to kill and that he had later declared that he had carried out his intention. Nor had Alford wavered in his desire to have the trial court determine his guilt without a jury trial. Although denying the charge against him, he nevertheless preferred the dispute between him and the State to be settled by the judge in the context of a guilty plea proceeding rather than by a formal trial. Thereupon, with the State's telling evidence and Alford's denial before it, the trial court proceeded to convict and sentence Alford for second-degree murder.

State and lower federal courts are divided upon whether a guilty plea can be accepted when it is accompanied by protestations of innocence and hence contains only a waiver of trial but no admission of guilt. Some courts, giving expression to the principle that our law only authorizes a conviction where guilt is shown, require that trial judges reject such pleas. But others have concluded that they should not force any defense on a defendant in a criminal case, particularly when advancement of the defense might end in disaster. They have argued that, since guilt, or the degree of guilt, is at times uncertain and elusive an accused, though believing in or entertaining doubts respecting his innocence, might reasonably conclude a jury would be convinced of his guilt and that he would fare better in the sentence by pleading guilty.

The issue in *Hudson v. United States*, 272 U.S. 451 (1926), was whether a federal court has power to impose a prison sentence after accepting a plea of **nolo contendere**, a plea by which a defendant does not expressly admit his guilt, but nonetheless waives his right to a trial and authorizes the court for purposes of the case to treat him as if he were guilty. The Court held that a trial court does have such power. The federal courts have uniformly followed this rule, even in cases involving moral turpitude.

Implicit in the nolo contendere cases is a recognition that the Constitution does not bar imposition of a prison sentence upon an accused who is unwilling expressly to admit his guilt but who, faced with grim alternatives, is willing to waive his trial and accept the sentence.

These cases would be directly in point if Alford had simply insisted on his plea but refused to admit the crime. The fact that his plea was denominated a plea of guilty rather than a plea of nolo contendere is of no constitutional significance with respect to the issue now before us, for the Constitution is concerned with the practical consequences, not the formal categorizations, of state law. Thus, while most pleas of guilty consist of both a waiver of trial and an express admission of guilt, the latter element is not a constitutional requisite to the imposition of criminal penalty. An individual accused of crime may voluntarily, knowingly, and understandingly consent to the imposition of a prison sentence even if he is unwilling or unable to admit his participation in the acts constituting the crime.

Nor can we perceive any material difference between a plea that refuses to admit commission of the criminal act and a plea containing a protestation of innocence when, as in the instant case, a defendant intelligently concludes that his interests require entry of a guilty plea and the record before the judge contains strong evidence of actual guilt. Here the State had a strong case of first-degree murder against Alford. Whether he realized or disbelieved his guilt, he insisted on his plea because in his view he had absolutely nothing to gain by a trial and much to gain by pleading. Because of the overwhelming evidence against him, a trial was precisely what neither Alford nor his attorney desired. Confronted with the choice between a trial for first-degree murder, on the one hand, and a plea of guilty to second-degree murder, on the other, Alford quite reasonably chose the latter and thereby limited the maximum penalty to a 30-year term. When his plea is viewed in light of the evidence against him, which substantially negated his claim of innocence and which further provided a means by which the judge could test whether the plea was being intelligently entered, its validity cannot be seriously questioned. In view of the strong factual basis for the plea demonstrated by the State and Alford's clearly expressed desire to enter it despite his professed belief in his innocence, we hold that the trial judge did not commit constitutional error in accepting it.

Alford now argues in effect that the State should not have allowed him this choice but should have insisted on proving him guilty of murder in the first degree. The States in their wisdom may take this course by statute or otherwise and may prohibit the practice of accepting pleas to lesser included offenses under any circumstances. But this is not the mandate of the Fourteenth Amendment and the Bill of Rights. The prohibitions against involuntary or unintelligent pleas should not be relaxed, but neither should an exercise in arid logic render those constitutional guarantees counterproductive and put in jeopardy the very human values they were meant to preserve.

MR. JUSTICE BRENNAN, with whom MR. JUSTICE DOUGLAS and MR. JUSTICE MARSHALL join, dissenting.

Last Term, this Court held, over my dissent, that a plea of guilty may validly be induced by an unconstitutional threat to subject the defendant to the risk of death, so long as the plea is entered in open court and the defendant is represented by competent counsel who is aware of the threat, albeit not of its unconstitutionality. *Brady v. United States*, 397 U.S. 742 (1970); *Parker v. North Carolina*, 397 U.S. 790 (1970). Today the Court makes clear that its previous holding was intended to apply even when the record demonstrates that the actual effect of the unconstitutional threat was to induce a guilty plea from a defendant who was unwilling to admit his guilt.

I adhere to the view that, in any given case, the influence of such an unconstitutional threat must necessarily be given weight in determining the voluntariness of a plea. And, without reaching the question whether due process permits the entry of judgment upon a plea of guilty accompanied by a contemporaneous denial of acts constituting the crime, I believe that at the very least such a denial of guilt is also a relevant factor in determining whether the plea was voluntarily and intelligently made. With these factors in mind, it is sufficient in my view to state that the facts set out in the majority opinion demonstrate that Alford was so gripped by fear of the death penalty that his decision to plead guilty was not voluntary but was "the product of duress as much so as choice reflecting physical constraint.

FURTHER CASE LAW, REFLECTIONS, AND QUESTIONS

1. Are you troubled at all by the Court's seeming indifference regarding whether Alford was actually guilty of committing the crime?
2. While all jurisdictions require a factual basis for a guilty plea, courts usually require only a general nexus between the original offense and the charge to which a defendant pleads guilty. Should such a nexus be required, or so long as all parties agree, should they be permitted to enter into a plea agreement covering a nonexistent crime?

Conclusion

In this chapter, we examined a number of steps in the post-arrest pretrial process. Throughout, we saw the prosecutor's central role in the process's operation. From examining arrests to determine which case to formally prosecute, to determining what evidence to disclose to the defense, and deciding whether to offer the defendant a plea bargain and what such a bargain should entail, the prosecutor is the lynchpin to the adjudication process.

The decisions made by prosecutors as well as other procedural and substantive items, however, are limited by the Constitution and ultimately the Supreme Court. The balance imposed by the Supreme Court is essential to the effective operation of the pretrial process. In the next chapter, we will examine how this balance continues through the criminal trial.

KEY TERMS

Bail Reform Act of 1984	nolo contendre
Brady rule	plea bargain
discovery	preliminary hearing
grand jury	preventive detention
indictment	probable cause hearing
information	selective prosecution
initial appearance	true bill
materiality	vindictive prosecution

REVIEW QUESTIONS

1. What is the primary purpose of the initial appearance? How soon must the initial appearance happen after arrest? What other essential things occur during the initial appearance?
2. What are a judge's or magistrate's options concerning bail? What does it mean for bail to be excessive? Why is preventative detention legal in certain circumstances when there is a presumption of innocence? Is this antithetical to the presumption of innocence?
3. What is the purpose of a grand jury? Is a grand jury proceeding adversarial? What exactly does a grand jury proceeding look like?
4. What is the purpose of a preliminary hearing? Is a preliminary hearing adversarial? What exactly goes on during a preliminary hearing?
5. What is the purpose of discovery? What evidence does the prosecution of a legal obligation to disclose? How does the Court define this type of evidence?
6. What are the requirements for a defendant to enter a guilty plea? How does a judge ensure this happens?
7. What must be shown to prove vindictive prosecution?
8. In the case of *Wayte v. United States,* what was the rationale behind the Court's decision regarding selective prosecution? What must a defendant prove to establish selective prosecution?
9. What happens if evidence in the possession of the police is destroyed prior to trial? Does it matter how it was destroyed?
10. What is a no-contest plea?

APPLYING THE LAW

Below are five hypothetical fact scenarios. To practice your understanding of the law that you learned in this chapter and your ability to apply it, answer each question posed by applying that law to the hypothetical scenarios. Your answers should be supported by relevant caselaw and judicially created rules and tests.

1. A wealthy couple has hired a nanny to watch their 6-month-old daughter while they are both at work. The nanny not only babysits but also takes care of household chores and does the grocery shopping. While grocery shopping on a hot and sunny day, the new nanny forgets that the 6-month-old is asleep in her car seat in the back of the car. After an hour of shopping, when the nanny returns, she sees the baby in the backseat. Terrified, she opens the car and calls 911. Unfortunately,

the baby died from the heat. The district attorney gets the case and declines to file charges. The parents speak to the DA, and he tells them that it was just an accident and that the former nanny has "created her own prison," and he doesn't need to put her in one. The parents hire a law firm to represent them and force the district attorney to file charges.

What should the court do about the lawsuit to force the district attorney to file charges?

2. John is implicated and arrested for several white-collar crimes. The prosecution makes a deal with him that if he agrees to testify against several other defendants, she will recommend a sentence of five years in prison rather than the 50 years he is facing. John testifies against each of the defendants, and they are all convicted; however, according to the prosecution, she didn't get the sentences she had hoped for in most of the cases, and she thinks it's because John may have held back some information and wasn't as convincing on the stand. Because of this, the prosecution does not recommend a lighter sentence for John.

   John's attorney files a motion with the court to enforce the original plea deal and impose a five-year sentence. The prosecution counters that it wants to withdraw all plea offers and take the case to trial. How should the court decide?

3. A State County grand jury indicted Dillon on a charge of uttering a forged instrument in the amount of $88.30, an offense punishable by a term of 2 to 10 years in prison. Dillon's attorney and the prosecutor met to discuss a possible plea agreement. The prosecutor offered to recommend a sentence of five years in prison if Dillon would plead guilty to the indictment. The prosecutor also said that if Dillon did not plead guilty and "save the court the inconvenience and necessity of a trial," he would return to the grand jury to seek an indictment under the State Habitual Criminal Act, which would subject Dillon to a mandatory sentence of life imprisonment because of his two prior felony convictions. Dillon chose to plead not guilty, and the prosecutor obtained an indictment charging him under the Habitual Criminal Act. A jury found Dillon guilty of all charges, and as required by the habitual offender statute, he was sentenced to a life term in prison.

   Were Dillon's Due Process rights violated?

4. Jay was arrested for hijacking a truck and stealing its contents. Police found 10 tablet computers on the truck's manifest, still in their boxes, in his garage. The evidence against him was substantial. Jay's fingerprints were also all over the truck. Video surveillance showed a person who looked like Jay robbing the store. The truck driver identified Jay as the robber. On the other hand, the passenger did not identify Jay.

   Prior to trial the prosecutor disclosed to Jay's lawyer evidence related to the tablets being found in his garage, his fingerprints being on the truck, and the interview of the truck driver where he identified Jay. After much discussion, the prosecutor did not disclose the interview of the passenger, where he identified another individual as the robber. Jay is convicted at trial.

A week after the conviction, Jay's lawyer discovers that the passenger was interviewed and failed to identify Jay as the robber. Jay's lawyer has filed a motion for a new trial, arguing that the prosecution violated Jay's due process rights by failing to disclose the passenger's statement. Did the prosecution violate Jay's rights?

5. Don, a WSU sophomore, and his fraternity brothers were legally required to register for the draft. Like millions of Americans who thought the draft was discriminatory and not needed, Don's entire fraternity decided they would not register as required. Don, being opposed to the wars in the Middle East, took this a step further. To voice his dissent, he wrote letters to various government officials stating that he had not registered and did not intend to do so. The following week, Don was arrested by the FBI and charged criminally for failing to register for the draft.

   Does the prosecution of Don violate the Constitution? Explain why or why not, citing appropriate cases.

ORAL ARGUMENTS

Arizona v. Youngblood: www.oyez.org/cases/1980-1989/1988/1988_86_1904/argument
Blackledge v. Perry: www.oyez.org/cases/1973/72-1660
Bordenkircher v. Hayes: www.oyez.org/cases/1970-1979/1977/1977_76_1334/argument
Brady v. United States: www.oyez.org/cases/1960-1969/1969/1969_270/argument
Coleman v. Alabama: www.oyez.org/cases/1969/72
Costello v. United States: www.oyez.org/cases/1955/72
County of Riverside v. McLaughlin: www.oyez.org/cases/1990/89-1817
Kyles v. Whitley: www.oyez.org/cases/1990-1999/1994/1994_93_7927/argument
North Carolina v. Alford: www.oyez.org/cases/1960-1969/1969/1969_14_2/argument
Santobello v. New York: www.oyez.org/cases/1970-1979/1971/1971_70_98/argument
United States v. Resendiz-Ponce: www.oyez.org/cases/2006/05-998
United States v. Salerno: www.oyez.org/cases/1980-1989/1986/1986_86_87/argument
United States v. Williams: www.oyez.org/cases/2000-2009/2007/2007_06_694/argument
Wayte v. United States: www.oyez.org/cases/1980-1989/1984/1984_83_1292/argument

REFERENCES

American Bar Association. (2017). *Criminal justice standards for the prosecution function* (4th ed.). American Bar Association.

CHAPTER 12

The Trial Process

LEARNING OBJECTIVES

After reading this chapter, students should be able to:

- Understand the right to a speedy trial
- Comprehend the jury selection process and the right to a fair and impartial jury
- Explain the difference between a challenge for cause and a peremptory challenge
- Understand what a Batson violation is and how it is determined
- Comprehend a defendant's right to or not to testify
- Understand the components of the Confrontation Clause and how it has evolved

Introduction

Once an individual has been formally charged with a crime, it is still necessary to determine whether he or she in fact committed the crime. The formal charging of a defendant is merely an accusation. Unless the accusation is dismissed, the accused is entitled to a formal determination of his or her guilt or innocence regarding the charges.

The vast majority of individuals charged with crimes have their cases resolved by plea bargaining and guilty pleas, and only a tiny fraction of people arrested for crimes ever have their cases decided at a trial. While only a comparatively small number of cases ever result in a trial, these cases are essential to the criminal justice system's goals of safeguarding the innocent from conviction and ensuring that the prosecution acts fairly whenever it attempts to prove that an accused offender is, in fact, guilty. With the other means of arriving at a conviction, the guilty plea, the defendant admits to committing the crime and thereby waives several important constitutional protections related to the proof of his or her guilt. On the other hand, a criminal trial is triggered by the defendant's plea of not guilty or denial that he or she committed the alleged crime. As a result of this plea, the government must prove, within the strictures and confines of the Constitution and Bill of Rights, that the defendant is guilty of the crime.

The trial of individuals accused of crimes dates back thousands of years. Although trials took many different forms throughout history, they served the same essential function: to resolve disputes between two or more parties. In Biblical times, it was not uncommon to appeal to divine intervention to resolve controversies through trial by ordeal. During medieval times, men would joust and duel to determine which party to a dispute was in the right. In colonial America, people suspected of being witches were weighted with rocks and thrown into water to see whether they floated, thus evidencing their innocence (or lack thereof).

The modern trial system, as we conceive it, has its roots in thirteenth-century England. Article 39 of the Magna Carta, signed in 1215, stated, "No freeman shall be taken or imprisoned nor will we go upon him nor will we send upon him, unless by the lawful judgement of his peers, or by the law of the land." While the judgment of one's peers guaranteed by the Magna Carta had a much different meaning in 1215 than it does now, this right evolved to become one of the cornerstones of the English justice system.

When the American colonies were settled, the colonists brought the English trial system with them. In the seventeenth and eighteenth centuries, colonial charters guaranteed individuals the right to be tried by a jury of their peers. King George's abuse of this right angered the colonists and formed one of the grievances set forth in the Declaration of Independence. At the time of the American Revolution, the right to trial by jury was recognized throughout the colonies.

This practice was perpetuated under the U.S. Constitution. At the time of the Constitutional Convention in the 1780s, many Americans remained leery of the power of a centralized government reminiscent of the English monarchy from which they had recently obtained their freedom. A jury of lay citizens, to stand between the government and individuals accused of crime, was one of the bedrock protections guaranteed by the new Constitution. Article III, Section 2, of the U.S. Constitution provided, "The Trial of all Crimes. . . shall be by Jury." When the Sixth Amendment to the Constitution was ratified in 1791, an individual's right to a jury trial in criminal cases was again explicitly recognized, along with other rights considered essential to the trial process:

> In all criminal prosecutions, the accused shall enjoy the right to a speedy and public trial, by an impartial jury of the State and district wherein the crime shall have been committed, . . . to be confronted with the witnesses against him; [and] to have compulsory process for obtaining witnesses in his favor.

The Fifth Amendment recognized other procedural safeguards important to the guilt determination process, including the right against compelled self-incrimination ("nor shall be compelled in any criminal case to be a witness against himself"), and due-process protections ("nor be deprived of life, liberty, or property, without due process of law"). As we have seen, the Fourteenth Amendment bound the states to observe due process of law and also prohibited the states from denying "to any person within [their] jurisdiction the equal protection of the laws."

In this chapter, we examine several aspects of the trial process. We begin by considering the right to a **"speedy" trial**. We next explore the requirement that an individual be "competent" to stand trial for the crime he or she has been accused of committing. The inquiry next shifts to the burden of proof required to convict a defendant of a crime.

Several issues related to trial by jury are then addressed, including whether that right literally attaches "in all criminal prosecutions" or applies only to certain charges, the meaning of the right to an "impartial" jury, the composition and selection of trial juries, and whether criminal trial verdicts must be returned by 12-member unanimous juries. We then consider the accused's testimonial rights at a criminal trial. For example, may the defendant be penalized for not testifying at trial? Conversely, may the defendant be prevented from testifying? The rights of confrontation and cross-examination, including the defendant's right to be physically present during his or her trial, are then discussed.

Like the other constitutional provisions we have considered, the precise scope and meaning of the rights that we examine in this chapter cannot be gleaned from the text of the Sixth, Fifth, and Fourteenth Amendments. We thus consider how the courts have interpreted the basic constitutional protections relevant to the trial of criminal cases.

Box 12.1: Defendant's Right at Trial

Speedy Trial	*Barker v. Wingo* (1972)
Public Trial	*Waller v. Georgia* (1984)
Trial by Jury	*Duncan v. Louisiana* (1968)
Jury of the Vicinage	*Beavers v. Henkel* (1904)
Notice	*In re Oliver* (1948)
Unanimous Verdict	*Ramos v. Louisiana* (2020)
Remain Silent	*Griffin v. California* (1965)
Testify	*Rock v. Arkansas* (1987)
Compulsory Process	*Washington v. Texas* (1967)
Present at Trial	*Illinois v. Allen* (1970)
Confrontation	*Pointer v. Texas* (1965) & *Davis v. Alaska* (1974)

The Right to a Speedy Trial

One basic principle of the American criminal justice system is that a person is considered innocent until proven guilty. It is therefore logical, if not essential, that a person accused of a crime should have the opportunity to have the cloud of accusation lifted promptly through a timely disposition of his or her case. Based largely on this premise, the Sixth Amendment explicitly guarantees the right to a speedy trial in all criminal prosecutions. While this general maxim is not controversial, it has been difficult, if not impossible, to quantify what constitutes a denial of a defendant's speedy-trial rights.

The Supreme Court has held that a delay between the time law enforcement uncovers illegal activity and the time formal charges are filed will seldom support a claim that the right to a speedy trial was violated. In *United States v. Marion,* 404 U.S. 307 (1971), the Court held that before a constitutional violation can be established, a defendant must demonstrate that the government engaged in deliberate inaction to gain a tactical advantage or that he or she suffered actual prejudice from the delay.

What was left unaddressed in *Marion* was what if the delay is (a) after the defendant is indicted and (b) deliberately caused by the government in an effort to gain a tactical advantage? These questions were addressed in the following case.

Barker v. Wingo

407 U.S. 514 (1972)

MR. JUSTICE POWELL delivered the opinion of the Court.

On July 20, 1958, in Christian County, Kentucky, an elderly couple was beaten to death by intruders wielding an iron tire tool. Two suspects, Silas Manning and Willie Barker, the petitioner, were arrested shortly thereafter. The grand jury indicted them on September 15. Counsel was appointed on September 17, and Barker's trial was set for October 21. The Commonwealth had a stronger case against Manning, and it believed that Barker could not be convicted unless Manning testified against him. Manning was naturally unwilling to incriminate himself. Accordingly, on October 23, the day Silas Manning was brought to trial, the Commonwealth sought and obtained the first of what was to be a series of 16 continuances of Barker's trial. Barker made no objection. By first convicting Manning, the Commonwealth would remove possible problems of self-incrimination and would be able to assure his testimony against Barker.

The Commonwealth encountered more than a few difficulties in its prosecution of Manning. The first trial ended in a **hung jury**. A second trial resulted in a conviction, but the Kentucky Court of Appeals reversed because of the admission of evidence obtained by an illegal search. At his third trial, Manning was again convicted, and the Court of Appeals again reversed because the trial court had not granted a change of **venue**. A fourth trial resulted in a hung jury. Finally, after five trials, Manning was convicted, in March 1962, of murdering one victim, and after a sixth trial, in December 1962, he was convicted of murdering the other.

[Barker's trial was continued 14 times while the State was securing its conviction of Manning. Subsequent to the final conviction of Manning, Barker's trial was continued several times due to the illness of the chief investigating officer in the case. These continuances were made over Barker's objections. Barker's trial began on October 9, 1963. With Manning testifying as the chief prosecution witness, Barker was convicted and given a life sentence.]

II

The right to a speedy trial is generically different from any of the other rights enshrined in the Constitution for the protection of the accused. In addition to the general concern that all accused persons be treated according to decent and fair procedures, there is a societal interest in providing a speedy trial which exists separate from, and at times in opposition to, the interests of the accused. The inability of courts to provide a prompt trial has contributed to a large backlog of cases in urban courts which, among other things, enables defendants to negotiate more effectively for pleas of guilty to lesser offenses and otherwise manipulate the system. In addition, persons released on bond for lengthy periods awaiting trial have an opportunity to commit other crimes. Moreover, the longer an accused is free awaiting trial, the more tempting becomes his opportunity to jump bail and escape. Finally, delay between arrest and punishment may have a detrimental effect on rehabilitation.

If an accused cannot make bail, he is generally confined, as was Barker for 10 months, in a local jail. This contributes to the overcrowding and generally deplorable state of those institutions. Lengthy exposure to these conditions "has a destructive effect on human character and makes the rehabilitation of the individual offender much more difficult." At times the result may even be violent rioting. Finally, lengthy pre-trial detention is costly. The cost of maintaining a prisoner in jail varies from $3 to $9 per day, and this amounts to millions across the Nation. In addition, society loses wages which might have been earned, and it must often support families of incarcerated breadwinners.

A second difference between the right to speedy trial and the accused's other constitutional rights is that deprivation of the right may work to the accused's advantage. Delay is not an uncommon defense tactic. As the time between the commission of the crime and trial lengthens, witnesses may become unavailable or their memories may fade. If the witnesses support the prosecution, its case will be weakened, sometimes seriously so. And it is the prosecution which carries the burden of proof. Thus, unlike the right to counsel or the right to be free from compelled self-incrimination, deprivation of the right to speedy trial does not per se prejudice the accused's ability to defend himself.

Finally, and perhaps most importantly, the right to speedy trial is a more vague concept than other procedural rights. It is, for example, impossible to determine with precision when the right has been denied. We cannot definitely say how long is too long in a system where justice is supposed to be swift but deliberate. As a consequence, there is no fixed point in the criminal process when the State can put the defendant to the choice of either exercising or waiving the right to a speedy trial.

The amorphous quality of the right also leads to the unsatisfactorily severe remedy of dismissal of the indictment when the right has been deprived. This is indeed a serious consequence because it means that a defendant who may be guilty of a serious crime will go free, without having been tried. Such a remedy is more serious than an exclusionary rule or a reversal for a new trial, but it is the only possible remedy.

III

Perhaps because the speedy trial right is so slippery, two rigid approaches are urged upon us as ways of eliminating some of the uncertainty which courts experience in protecting the right. The first suggestion is that we hold that the Constitution requires a criminal defendant to be offered a trial within a specified time period. The result of such a ruling would have the virtue of clarifying when the right is infringed and of simplifying courts' application of it.

But such a result would require this Court to engage in legislative or rulemaking activity, rather than in the adjudicative process to which we should confine our efforts. We do not establish procedural rules for the States, except when mandated by the Constitution. We find no constitutional basis for holding that the speedy trial right can be quantified into a specified number of days or months. The States, of course, are free to prescribe a reasonable period consistent with constitutional standards but our approach must be less precise.

The second suggested alternative would restrict consideration of the right to those cases in which the accused has demanded a speedy trial. The demand-waiver doctrine provides that a defendant waives any consideration of his right to speedy trial for any period prior to which he has not demanded a trial. Under this rigid approach, a prior demand is a necessary condition to the consideration of the speedy trial right. This essentially was the approach the Sixth Circuit took below.

Such an approach, by presuming waiver of a fundamental right from inaction, is inconsistent with this Court's pronouncements on waiver of constitutional rights. The Court has defined waiver as "an intentional relinquishment or abandonment of a known right or privilege." *Johnson v. Zerbst*, 304 U.S. 458, 464 (1938). Courts should "indulge every reasonable presumption against waiver," and they should "not presume acquiescence in the loss of fundamental rights."

The nature of the speedy trial right does make it impossible to pinpoint a precise time in the process when the right must be asserted or waived, but that fact does not argue for placing the burden of protecting the right solely on defendants. A defendant has no duty to bring himself to trial; the State has that duty as well as the duty of insuring that the trial is consistent with due process. Moreover, for the reasons earlier expressed, society has a particular interest in bringing swift prosecutions, and society's representatives are the ones who should protect that interest.

It is also noteworthy that such a rigid view of the demand-waiver rule places defense counsel in an awkward position. Unless he demands a trial early and often, he is in danger of frustrating his client's right. If counsel is willing to tolerate some delay because he finds it reasonable and helpful in preparing his own case, he may be unable to obtain a speedy trial for his client at the end of that time. Since under the demand-waiver rule no time runs until the demand is made, the government will have whatever time is otherwise reasonable to bring the defendant to trial after a demand has been made. Thus, if the first demand is made three months after arrest in a jurisdiction which prescribes a six-month rule, the prosecution will have a total of nine months — which may be wholly unreasonable under the circumstances. The result in practice is likely to be either an automatic, pro forma demand made immediately after appointment of counsel or delays which, but for the demand-waiver rule, would not be tolerated. Such a result is not consistent with the interests of defendants, society, or the Constitution.

We reject, therefore, the rule that a defendant who fails to demand a speedy trial forever waives his right. We think the better rule is that the defendant's assertion of or failure to assert his right to a speedy trial is one of the factors to be considered in an inquiry into the deprivation of the right. Such a formulation avoids the rigidities of the demand-waiver rule and the resulting possible unfairness in its application. It allows the trial court to exercise a judicial discretion based on the circumstances, including due consideration of any applicable formal procedural rule. It would permit, for example, a court to attach a different weight to a situation in which the defendant knowingly fails to object from a situation in which his attorney acquiesces in long delay without adequately informing his client, or from a situation in which no counsel is appointed. It would also allow a court to weigh the frequency and force of the objections as opposed to attaching significant weight to a purely pro forma objection.

We, therefore, reject both of the inflexible approaches — the fixed-time period because it goes further than the Constitution requires; the demand-waiver rule because it is insensitive to a right which we have deemed fundamental. The approach we accept is a balancing test, in which the conduct of both the prosecution and the defendant are weighed.

IV

A balancing test necessarily compels courts to approach speedy trial cases on an ad hoc basis. We can do little more than identify some of the factors which courts should assess in determining whether a particular defendant has been deprived of his right. Though some might express them in different ways, we identify four such factors: Length of delay, the reason for the delay, the defendant's assertion of his right, and prejudice to the defendant.

The length of the delay is to some extent a triggering mechanism. Until there is some delay which is presumptively prejudicial, there is no necessity for inquiry into the other factors that go into the balance. Nevertheless, because of the imprecision of the right to speedy trial, the length of delay that will provoke such an inquiry is necessarily dependent upon the peculiar circumstances of the case. To take but one example, the delay that can be tolerated for an ordinary street crime is considerably less than for a serious, complex conspiracy charge.

Closely related to length of delay is the reason the government assigns to justify the delay. Here, too, different weights should be assigned to different reasons. A deliberate attempt to delay the trial in order to hamper the defense should be weighed heavily against the government. A more neutral reason such as negligence or overcrowded courts should be weighed less heavily but nevertheless should be considered since the ultimate responsibility for such circumstances must rest with the government rather than with the defendant. Finally, a valid reason, such as a missing witness, should serve to justify appropriate delay.

We have already discussed the third factor, the defendant's responsibility to assert his right. Whether and how a defendant asserts his right is closely related to the other factors we have mentioned. The strength of his efforts will be affected by the length of the delay, to some extent by the reason for the delay, and most particularly by the personal prejudice, which is not always readily identifiable, that he experiences. The more serious the deprivation, the more likely a defendant is to complain. The defendant's assertion of his speedy trial right, then, is entitled to strong evidentiary weight in determining whether the defendant is being deprived of the right. We emphasize that failure to assert the right will make it difficult for a defendant to prove that he was denied a speedy trial.

A fourth factor is prejudice to the defendant. Prejudice, of course, should be assessed in the light of the interests of defendants which the speedy trial right was designed to protect. This Court has identified three such interests: (i) to prevent oppressive pretrial incarceration; (ii) to minimize anxiety and concern of the accused; and (iii) to limit the possibility that the defense will be impaired. Of these, the most serious is the last, because the inability of a defendant adequately to prepare his case skews the fairness of the entire system. If witnesses die or disappear during a delay, the prejudice is obvious. There is also prejudice if defense witnesses are unable to recall accurately events of the distant past. Loss of memory, however, is not always reflected in the record because what has been forgotten can rarely be shown.

We regard none of the four factors identified above as either a necessary or sufficient condition to the finding of a deprivation of the right of speedy trial. Rather, they are related factors and must be considered together with such other circumstances as may be relevant. In sum, these factors have no talismanic qualities; courts must still engage in a difficult and sensitive balancing process. But, because we are dealing with a fundamental right of the accused, this process must be carried out with full recognition that the accused's interest in a speedy trial is specifically affirmed in the Constitution.

V

The difficulty of the task of balancing these factors is illustrated by this case, which we consider to be close. It is clear that the length of delay between arrest and trial — well over five years — was extraordinary. Only seven months of that period can be attributed to a strong excuse, the illness of the ex-sheriff who was in charge of the investigation. Perhaps some delay would have been permissible under ordinary circumstances, so that Manning could be utilized as a witness in Barker's trial, but more than four years was too long a period, particularly since a good part of that period was attributable to the Commonwealth's failure or inability to try Manning under circumstances that comported with due process.

Two counterbalancing factors, however, outweigh these deficiencies. The first is that prejudice was minimal. Of course, Barker was prejudiced to some extent by living for over four years under a cloud of suspicion and anxiety. Moreover, although he was released on bond for most of the period, he did spend 10 months in jail before trial. But there is no claim that any of Barker's witnesses died or otherwise became unavailable owing to the delay. The trial transcript indicates only two very minor lapses of memory — one on the part of a prosecution witness — which were in no way significant to the outcome.

More important than the absence of serious prejudice, is the fact that Barker did not want a speedy trial. Counsel was appointed for Barker immediately after his indictment and represented him throughout the period. No question is raised as to the competency of such counsel. Despite the fact that counsel had notice of the motions for continuances, the record shows no action whatever taken between October 21, 1958, and February 12, 1962, that could be construed as the assertion of the speedy trial right. On the latter date, in response to another motion for continuance, Barker moved to dismiss the indictment. The record does not show on what ground this motion was based, although it is clear that no alternative motion was made for an immediate trial. Instead the record strongly suggests that while he hoped to take advantage of the delay in which he had acquiesced, and thereby obtain a dismissal of the charges, he definitely did not want to be tried. Counsel conceded as much at oral argument:

> "Your honor, I would concede that Willie Mae Barker probably — I don't know this for a fact — probably did not want to be tried. I don't think any man wants to be tried. And I don't consider this a liability on his behalf. I don't blame him."

The probable reason for Barker's attitude was that he was gambling on Manning's acquittal. The evidence was not very strong against Manning, as the reversals and hung juries suggest, and Barker undoubtedly thought that if Manning were acquitted, he would never be tried. Counsel also conceded this:

> "Now, it's true that the reason for this delay was the Commonwealth of Kentucky's desire to secure the testimony of the accomplice, Silas Manning. And it's true that if Silas Manning were never convicted, Willie Mae Barker would never have been convicted. We concede this."

That Barker was gambling on Manning's acquittal is also suggested by his failure, following the pro forma motion to dismiss filed in February 1962, to object to the Commonwealth's next two motions for continuances. Indeed, it was not until March 1963, after Manning's convictions were final, that Barker, having lost his gamble, began to object to further continuances. At that time, the Commonwealth's excuse was the illness of the ex-sheriff, which Barker has conceded justified the further delay.

We do not hold that there may never be a situation in which an indictment may be dismissed on speedy trial grounds where the defendant has failed to object to continuances. There may be a situation in which the defendant was represented by incompetent counsel, was severely prejudiced, or even cases in which the continuances were granted *ex parte*. But barring extraordinary circumstances, we would be reluctant indeed to rule that a defendant was denied this constitutional rule on a record that strongly indicates, as does this one, that the defendant did not want a speedy trial. We hold, therefore, that Barker was not deprived of his due process right to a speedy trial.

The judgment of the Court of Appeals is Affirmed.

FURTHER CASE LAW, REFLECTIONS, AND QUESTIONS

1. Do the four factors considered in determining whether a speedy-trial violation occurred seem reasonable? Which factor, if any, do you think should be given the greatest weight?
2. If a defendant's right to a speedy trial is violated, what remedy should he or she have?
3. The *Barker* Court emphasized the lack of prejudice against the defendant caused by the delay. The Court went so far as to imply that Barker accepted and even wanted the delay, hoping it would weaken the prosecution's case against him. Does this mean that no matter how egregious the prosecution's action in causing the delay, absent a showing that the defendant was harmed, there can be no violation of the right to a speedy trial?

Box 12.2 You Be the Judge

In 1980, Marc Doggett was indicted on federal drug charges. When Drug Enforcement Administration (DEA) agents went to his home to arrest him, they found he had gone to Colombia several days earlier. The DEA later found out that Doggett was in prison in Panama on unrelated charges. While the Panamanian government promised to expel Doggett back to the United States when he was no longer in custody, the DEA agent in charge did not follow up on the case, and he was not deported. Doggett reentered the United States legally in 1982 and lived openly under his own name. No one looked into Doggett's whereabouts, but in 1988, a random credit check of individuals with outstanding warrants conducted by the Marshal's Service revealed his place of residence. He was arrested in September 1988, 8 1/2 years after his indictment. Doggett moved to dismiss the indictment, arguing that the government's failure to prosecute him earlier violated his Sixth Amendment right to a speedy trial.

Should the motion be granted?

See *Doggett v. United States*, 505 U.S. 647 (1992).

Trial by Jury

As we have already seen, both Article III, Section 2, of the U.S. Constitution and the Sixth Amendment unequivocally seem to guarantee an individual charged with a crime the right to be tried by a jury. A jury is a body of people (between six and twelve) sworn to give a verdict in a legal case on the basis of evidence submitted to them in court. However, this language is not to be taken at face value. Prior to the 1968 case of *Duncan v. Louisiana*, the Sixth Amendment right to a trial by jury in criminal cases did not apply to the states (see Chapter 2). Of course, this does not mean that jury trials were not provided in state criminal cases before 1968; they clearly were, but they could be limited according to peculiar rules of state law. In *Duncan*, the Court provided guidance concerning when a criminal defendant in a state case is entitled to a jury trial under the federal Constitution. As you read Duncan and consider its holding, contemplate what the Court actually said and, just as importantly, what the Court did not say concerning the scope of the Sixth Amendment's right to trial by jury in state criminal cases.

Duncan v. Louisiana

391 U.S. 145 (1968)

MR. JUSTICE WHITE delivered the opinion of the Court.

Appellant, Gary Duncan, was convicted of simple battery in the Twenty-fifth Judicial District Court of Louisiana. Under Louisiana law, simple battery is a misdemeanor, punishable by a maximum of two years imprisonment and a $300 fine. Appellant sought trial by jury, but because the Louisiana Constitution grants jury trials only in cases in which capital punishment or imprisonment at hard labor may be imposed, the trial judge denied the request. Appellant was convicted and sentenced to serve 60 days in the parish prison and pay a fine of $150. Appellant sought review in the Supreme Court of Louisiana, asserting that the denial of jury trial violated rights guaranteed to him by the United States Constitution. The Supreme Court, finding "[n]o error of law in the ruling complained of," denied appellant a writ of certiorari. Pursuant to 28 U.S.C. §1257 (2) appellant sought review in this Court, alleging that the Sixth and Fourteenth Amendments to the United States Constitution secure the right to jury trial in state criminal prosecutions where a sentence as long as two years may be imposed.

Appellant was 19 years of age when tried. While driving on Highway 23 in Plaquemines Parish on October 18, 1966, he saw two younger cousins engaged in a conversation by the side of the road with four white boys. Knowing his cousins, Negroes who had recently transferred to a formerly all-white high school, had reported the occurrence of racial incidents at the school, Duncan stopped the car, got out, and approached the six boys. At trial, the white boys and a white onlooker testified, as did appellant and his cousins. The testimony was in dispute on many points, but the witnesses agreed that appellant and the white boys spoke to each other, that appellant encouraged his cousins to break off the encounter and enter his car, and that appellant was about to enter the car himself for the purpose of driving away with his cousins. The whites testified that just before getting in the car appellant slapped Herman Landry, one of the white boys, on the elbow. The Negroes testified that appellant had not slapped Landry, but had merely touched him. The trial judge concluded that the State had proved beyond a reasonable doubt that Duncan had committed simple battery, and found him guilty.

I

The Fourteenth Amendment denies the States the power to "deprive any person of life, liberty, or property, without due process of law." In resolving conflicting claims concerning the meaning of this spacious language, the Court has looked increasingly to the Bill of Rights for guidance; many of the rights guaranteed by the first eight Amendments to the Constitution have been held to be protected against state action by the Due Process Clause of the Fourteenth Amendment. That clause now protects the right to compensation for property taken by the State; the rights of speech, press, and religion covered by the First Amendment; the Fourth Amendment rights to be free from unreasonable searches and seizures and to have excluded from criminal trials any evidence illegally seized; the right guaranteed by the Fifth Amendment to be free of compelled self-incrimination; and the Sixth Amendment rights to counsel, to a speedy and public trial, to confrontation of opposing witnesses, and to compulsory process for obtaining witnesses.

The test for determining whether a right extended by the Fifth and Sixth Amendments with respect to federal criminal proceedings is also protected against state action by the Fourteenth Amendment has been phrased in a variety of ways in the opinions of this Court. The question has been asked whether a right is among those "'fundamental principles of liberty and justice which lie at the base of all our civil and political institutions,' " *Powell v. Alabama*, 287 U.S. 45, 67 (1932); whether it is "basic in our system of jurisprudence"; and whether it is "a fundamental right, essential to a fair trial," *Gideon v. Wainwright*, 372 U.S. 335, 343–344 (1963). The claim before us is that the right to trial by jury guaranteed by the Sixth Amendment meets these tests. The position of Louisiana, on the other hand, is that the Constitution imposes upon the States no duty to give a jury trial in any criminal case, regardless of the seriousness of the crime or the size of the punishment which may be imposed. Because we believe that trial by jury in criminal cases is fundamental to the American scheme of justice, we hold that the Fourteenth Amendment guarantees a right of jury trial in all criminal cases which — were they to be tried in a federal court — would come within the Sixth Amendment's guarantee. Since we consider the appeal before us to be such a case, we hold that the Constitution was violated when appellant's demand for jury trial was refused.

Jury trial came to America with English colonists, and received strong support from them. Royal interference with the jury trial was deeply resented. Among the resolutions adopted by the First Congress of the American Colonies (the Stamp Act Congress) on October 19, 1765 — resolutions deemed by their authors to state "the most essential rights and liberties of the colonists" — was the declaration:

"That trial by jury is the inherent and invaluable right of every British subject in these colonies."

The Declaration of Independence stated solemn objections to the King's making "judges dependent on his will alone, for the tenure of their offices, and the amount and payment of their salaries," to his "depriving us in many cases, of the benefits of Trial by Jury," and to his "transporting us beyond Seas to be tried for pretended offenses." The Constitution itself, in art. III, §2 commanded: "The Trial of all Crimes, except in Cases of Impeachment, shall be by Jury; and such Trial shall be held in the State where the said Crimes shall have been committed."

Objections to the Constitution because of the absence of a bill of rights were met by the immediate submission and adoption of the Bill of Rights. Included was the Sixth Amendment which, among other things, provided: "In all criminal prosecutions, the accused shall enjoy the right to a speedy and public trial, by an impartial jury of the State and district wherein the crime shall have been committed."

The constitutions adopted by the original States guaranteed jury trial. Also, the constitution of every State entering the Union thereafter in one form or another protected the right to jury trial in criminal cases.

The guarantees of jury trial in the Federal and State Constitutions reflect a profound judgment about the way in which law should be enforced and justice administered. A right to jury trial is granted to criminal defendants in order to prevent oppression by the Government. Those who wrote our constitutions knew from history and experience that it was necessary to protect against unfounded criminal charges brought to eliminate enemies and against judges too responsive to the voice of higher authority. The framers of the constitutions strove to create an independent judiciary but insisted upon further protection against arbitrary action. Providing an accused with the right to be tried by a jury of his peers gave him an inestimable safeguard against the corrupt or overzealous prosecutor and against the compliant, biased, or eccentric judge. If the defendant preferred the common-sense judgment of a jury to the more tutored but perhaps less sympathetic reaction of the single judge, he was to have it. Beyond this, the jury trial provisions in the Federal and State Constitutions reflect a fundamental decision about the exercise of official power — a reluctance to entrust plenary powers over the life and liberty of the citizen to one judge or to a group of judges. Fear of unchecked power, so typical of our State and Federal Governments in other respects, found expression in the criminal law in this insistence upon community participation in the determination of guilt or innocence. The deep commitment of the Nation to the right of jury trial in serious criminal cases as a defense against arbitrary law enforcement qualifies for protection under the Due Process Clause of the Fourteenth Amendment, and must therefore be respected by the States.

Of course jury trial has "its weaknesses and the potential for misuse," *Singer v. United States*, 380 U.S. 24, 35 (1965). We are aware of the long debate, especially in this century, among those who write about the administration of justice, as to the wisdom of permitting untrained laymen to determine the facts in civil and criminal proceedings. Although the debate has been intense, with powerful voices on either side, most of the controversy has centered on the jury in civil cases. Indeed, some of the severest critics of civil juries acknowledge that the arguments for criminal juries are much stronger. In addition, at the heart of the dispute have been express or implicit assertions that juries are incapable of adequately understanding evidence or determining issues of fact, and that they are unpredictable, quixotic, and little better than a roll of dice. Yet, the most recent and exhaustive study of the jury in criminal cases concluded that juries do understand the evidence and come to sound conclusions in most of the cases presented to them and that when juries differ with the result at which the judge would have arrived, it is usually because they are serving some of the very purposes for which they were created and for which they are now employed.

The State of Louisiana urges that holding that the Fourteenth Amendment assures a right to jury trial will cast doubt on the integrity of every trial conducted without a jury. Plainly, this is not the import of our holding. Our conclusion is that in the American States, as in the federal judicial system, a general grant of jury trial for serious offenses is a fundamental right, essential for preventing miscarriages of justice and for assuring that fair trials are provided for all defendants. We would not assert, however, that every criminal trial — or any particular trial — held before a judge alone is unfair or that a defendant may never be as fairly treated by a judge as he would be by a jury. Thus we hold no constitutional doubts about the practices, common in both federal and state courts, of accepting waivers of jury trial and prosecuting petty crimes without extending a right to jury trial. However, the fact is that in most places more trials for serious crimes are to juries than to a court alone; a great many defendants prefer the judgment of a jury to that of a court. Even where defendants are satisfied with bench trials, the right to a jury trial very likely serves its intended purpose of making judicial or prosecutorial unfairness less likely.

Louisiana's final contention is that even if it must grant jury trials in serious criminal cases, the conviction before us is valid and constitutional because here the petitioner was tried for simple battery and was sentenced to only 60 days in the parish prison. We are not persuaded. It is doubtless true that there is a category of petty crimes or offenses which is not subject to the Sixth Amendment jury trial provision and should not be subject to the Fourteenth Amendment jury trial requirement here applied to the States. Crimes carrying possible penalties up to six months do not require a jury trial if they otherwise qualify as petty offenses. But the penalty authorized for a particular crime is of major relevance in determining whether it is serious or not and may in itself, if severe enough, subject the trial to the mandates of the Sixth Amendment. The penalty authorized by the law of the locality may be taken "as a gauge of its social and ethical judgments" of the crime in question. In the case before us the Legislature of Louisiana has made simple battery a criminal offense punishable by imprisonment for up to two years and a fine. The question, then, is whether a crime carrying such a penalty is an offense which Louisiana may insist on trying without a jury.

We think not. So-called petty offenses were tried without juries both in England and in the Colonies and have always been held to be exempt from the otherwise comprehensive language of the Sixth Amendment's jury trial provisions. There is no substantial evidence that the Framers intended to depart from this established common-law practice, and the possible consequences to defendants from convictions for petty offenses have been thought insufficient to outweigh the benefits to efficient law enforcement and simplified judicial administration resulting from the availability of speedy and inexpensive nonjury adjudications. These same considerations compel the same result under the Fourteenth Amendment. Of course the boundaries of the petty offense category have always been ill-defined, if not ambulatory. In the absence of an explicit constitutional provision, the definitional task necessarily falls on the courts, which must either pass upon the validity of legislative attempts to identify those petty offenses which are exempt from jury trial or, where the legislature has not addressed itself to the problem, themselves face the question in the first instance. In either case it is necessary to draw a line in the spectrum of crime, separating petty from serious infractions. This process, although essential, cannot be wholly satisfactory, for it requires attaching different consequences to events which, when they lie near the line, actually differ very little.

In determining whether the length of the authorized prison term or the seriousness of other punishment is enough in itself to require a jury trial, we are counseled by *District of Columbia v. Clawans*, 300 U.S. 617(1937), to refer to objective criteria, chiefly the existing laws and practices in the Nation. In the federal system, petty offenses are defined as those punishable by no more than six months in prison and a $500 fine. In 49 of the 50 States crimes subject to trial without a jury, which occasionally include simple battery, are punishable by no more than one year in jail. Moreover, in the late 18th century in America crimes triable without a jury were for the most part punishable by no more than a six-month prison term, although there appear to have been exceptions to this rule. We need not settle in this case the exact location of the line between petty offenses and serious crimes. It is sufficient for our purposes to hold that a crime punishable by two years in prison is, based on past and contemporary standards in this country, a serious crime and not a petty offense. Consequently, appellant was entitled to a jury trial and it was an error to deny it.

The judgment below is reversed and the case is remanded for proceedings not inconsistent with this opinion.

FURTHER CASE LAW, REFLECTIONS, AND QUESTIONS

1. Do the same circumstances and reasons that gave rise to the inclusion of a right to a jury trial in the Constitution in the 18th century seem persuasive or valid today?
2. The Duncan Court states, "If the defendant preferred the common-sense judgment of a jury to the more tutored but perhaps less sympathetic reaction of a single judge, he was to have it." Does this language mean that a defendant is guaranteed the right to trial by jury because the jury might find him or her sympathetic and show him or her mercy? Is this fair?

Duncan tells us that a defendant charged with a serious crime is entitled to a jury trial and that one accused of a petty crime is not. The *Duncan* Court, however, did not define when a crime is serious, petty, or somewhere in between. The Court addressed this issue two years later in *Baldwin v. New York.*

Baldwin v. New York

399 U.S. 117 (1970)

Mr. Justice White announced the judgment of the Court.

Appellant was arrested and charged with "jostling" — a Class A misdemeanor in New York, punishable by a maximum term of imprisonment of one year. He was brought to trial in the New York City Criminal Court. Section 40 of the New York City Criminal Court Act declares that all trials in that court shall be without a jury. Appellant's pretrial motion for jury trial was accordingly denied. He was convicted and sentenced to imprisonment for the maximum term. The New York Court of Appeals affirmed the conviction, rejecting appellant's argument that §40 was unconstitutional insofar as it denied him an opportunity for jury trial. We noted probable jurisdiction. We reverse.

In *Duncan v. Louisiana,* 391 U.S. 145 (1968), we held that the Sixth Amendment, as applied to the States through the Fourteenth, requires that defendants accused of serious crimes be afforded the right to trial by jury. We also reaffirmed the long established view that so-called "petty offenses" may be tried without a jury. Thus the task before us in this case is the essential if not wholly satisfactory one, of determining the line between "petty" and "serious" for purposes of the Sixth Amendment right to jury trial.

Prior cases in this Court narrow our inquiry and furnish us with the standard to be used in resolving this issue. In deciding whether an offense is "petty," we have sought objective criteria reflecting the seriousness with which society regards the offense, and we have found the most relevant such criteria in the severity of the maximum authorized penalty. Applying these guidelines, we have held that a possible six-month penalty is short enough to permit classification of the offense as "petty," but that a two-year maximum is sufficiently "serious" to require an opportunity for jury trial. The question in this case is whether the possibility of a one-year sentence is enough in itself to require the opportunity for a jury trial. We hold that it is. More specifically, we have concluded that no offense can be deemed "petty" for purposes of the right to trial by jury where imprisonment for more than six months is authorized.

New York has urged us to draw the line between "petty" and "serious" to coincide with the line between misdemeanor and felony. As in most States, the maximum sentence of imprisonment for a misdemeanor in New York is one year, for a felony considerably longer. It is also true that the collateral consequences attaching to a felony conviction are more severe than those attaching to a conviction for a misdemeanor. And, like other States, New York distinguishes between misdemeanors and felonies in determining such things as whether confinement shall be in county or regional jails, rather than state prison, and whether prosecution may proceed by information or complaint, rather than by grand jury indictment. But while these considerations reflect what may readily be admitted — that a felony conviction is more serious than a misdemeanor conviction — they in no way detract from appellant's contention that some misdemeanors are also "serious" offenses. Indeed we long ago declared that the Sixth Amendment right to jury trial is not to be construed as relating only to felonies, or offences punishable by confinement in the penitentiary. It embraces as well some classes of misdemeanors, the punishment of which involves or may involve the deprivation of the liberty of the citizen.

A better guide in determining whether the length of the authorized prison term or the seriousness of other punishment is enough in itself to require a jury trial" is disclosed by "the existing laws and practices in the Nation. In the federal system, as we noted in *Duncan*, petty offenses have been defined as those punishable by no more than six months in prison and a $500 fine. And, with a few exceptions, crimes triable without a jury in the American States since the late 18th century were also generally punishable by no more than a six-month prison term. Indeed, when *Duncan* was decided two Terms ago, we could discover only three instances in which a State denied jury trial for a crime punishable by imprisonment for longer than six months: the Louisiana scheme at issue in *Duncan*, a New Jersey statute punishing disorderly conduct, and the New York City statute at issue in this case. These three instances have since been reduced to one. In response to the decision in *Duncan*, Louisiana has lowered the penalty for certain misdemeanors to six months, and has provided for a jury trial where the penalty still exceeds six months. New Jersey has amended its disorderly persons statute by reducing the maximum penalty to six months' imprisonment and a $500 fine. Even New York State would have provided appellant with a six-man jury trial for this offense if he had been tried outside the City of New York. In the entire Nation, New York City alone denies an accused the right to interpose between himself and a possible prison term of over six months, the commonsense judgment of a jury of his peers. This near-uniform judgment of the Nation furnishes us with the only objective criterion by which a line could ever be drawn — on the basis of the possible penalty alone — between offenses that are and that are not regarded as "serious" for purposes of trial by jury.

Of necessity, the task of drawing a line "requires attaching different consequences to events which, when they lie near the line, actually differ very little." One who is threatened with the possibility of imprisonment for six months may find little difference between the potential consequences that face him, and the consequences that faced appellant here. Indeed, the prospect of imprisonment for however short a time will seldom be viewed by the accused as a trivial or "petty" matter and may well result in quite serious repercussions affecting his career and his reputation. Where the accused cannot possibly face more than six months' imprisonment, we have held that these disadvantages, onerous though they may be, may be outweighed by the benefits that result from speedy and inexpensive nonjury adjudications. We cannot, however, conclude that these administrative conveniences, in light of the practices that now exist in every one of the 50 States as well as in the federal courts, can similarly justify denying an accused the important right to trial by jury where the possible penalty exceeds six months' imprisonment. The conviction is Reversed.

FURTHER CASE LAW, REFLECTIONS, AND QUESTIONS

1. The length of the maximum possible term of imprisonment for a crime is not the sole factor in determining whether the offense is "petty" or "serious." In *Blanton v. City of North Las Vegas*, 489 U.S. 538, 544 (1989), the Court stated, "A defendant is entitled to a jury trial if he can demonstrate that any additional statutory penalties, viewed in conjunction with the maximum authorized period of incarceration, are so severe that they reflect a legislative determination that the offense in question is a 'serious' one." The *Blanton* Court went on to hold that automatic driver's license suspension, coupled with a maximum period of incarceration of six months for a first-time DUI conviction, is not sufficiently severe to make the crime "serious."

2. Does a defendant have a right to a jury trial if he is being prosecuted in a single proceeding for multiple petty offenses whose aggregate maximum period of incarceration exceeds six months? In *Lewis v. United States*, 518 U.S. 322 (1996), the Supreme Court held that a defendant in such a situation does not have a Sixth Amendment right to a jury trial. The Court held that the right to a jury trial applies only to serious offenses and that the accumulation of two or more petty offenses does not entitle the accused to a trial by jury.

3. If a person has a right to a jury trial for a crime punishable by over six months in jail, does she have the corollary right to decline to have a jury hear her case and instead opt for a trial before a judge, sitting without a jury? In *Singer v. United States*, 380 U.S. 24 (1965), the Supreme Court unanimously held that a defendant had no right to have his or her case tried before a judge alone. Do you think a defendant should be allowed to be tried without a jury over the prosecution's objections? Which factors affect your decision?

A NOTE ON JURY NULLIFICATION

As touched on briefly in *Duncan*, juries and judges have different roles in deciding the outcome of a criminal trial. Juries decide the facts of a case. If there are differing accounts or conflicting testimony, it is for the jury to determine what evidence and testimony to believe. On the other hand, the judge determines the law of the case. The judge tells the jury what law to apply to the facts. Jurors are not to question the legal standards given to them by the judge in **jury instructions**. Instead, they only decide what the facts are and apply those facts to the law as stated in the jury instructions.

Although jurors are instructed to follow the law as given to them by the judge, at times, jurors are faced with situations involving a particular case in which they believe strictly applying the law would bring about an injustice. In such circumstances, what can and should jurors do? For example, if a doctor performs an abortion on a woman to save the woman's life, and a state law considers such an act to be murder, must a juror vote to find the doctor guilty even though they believe the law is morally repugnant? If one or more jurors vote to acquit, despite there being no factual dispute or question as to what the law says, the jurors have partaken in jury nullification.

The reason jurors have this power rests in the purpose of trial by jury. As Justice White wrote in *Duncan v. Louisiana,* the jury in a criminal trial serves as the conscience of the community. Rather than the government having the final say regarding whether a person has violated a criminal law, it is the jury, made up of typical citizens, that has the job of finding a defendant guilty of a criminal act. "If the defendant preferred the common-sense judgment of a jury to the more tutored but perhaps less sympathetic reaction of the single judge, he was to have it" (*Duncan v. Louisiana,* 1968). The use of ordinary people, who, rather than strictly applying the law as provided, may allow sympathy and common sense to enter into their deliberations and verdict, is a foundation of the jury system. It has also caused problems for the courts in the form of jury nullification.

Jury nullification occurs when a jury, based on its sense of justice and fairness, refuses to abide by the law and convict in a particular case even though the defendant is unquestionably guilty under the law. It occurs when a jury refuses "to apply a law in situations where strict application of the law would lead to an unjust or inequitable result" (Scheflin & Van Dyke, 1980, p. 54). Jury nullification is vexing for courts because the exercise of this authority is unreviewable due to the constitutional prohibition against "double jeopardy" — the retrying of an acquitted defendant for the same offense. Once a jury acquits a defendant, for whatever reason, the defendant cannot be retried for the same act.

It is important to note that jury nullification can only be used to acquit a defendant. It cannot be used to convict a person despite a lack of evidence. Suppose there is insufficient evidence to sustain a conviction beyond a reasonable doubt, and a jury returns a guilty verdict. In that case, the judge has to override the verdict and enter a judgment of acquittal. The failure of the trial judge to do so is subject to appellate review. Acts of jury nullification to acquit defendants are unreviewable.

Although jury nullification is often viewed negatively, there are times when a jury's exercise of its nullification power is desirable. Examples include juries refusing to convict in cases involving Northerners violating fugitive slave laws by harboring runaway slaves in the 1800s, Vietnam War protesters who refused to register for the draft, and battered women who kill their batterer in a situation not falling under the doctrine of self-defense. The use of nullification by a jury is rare, but it does occur. The types of cases giving rise to jury nullification today are likely to involve the medical use of marijuana, mercy killings or euthanasia, and instances when the jury knows or senses that a defendant will face an unfairly long prison sentence if convicted because of "three strikes and you're out" laws and other offenses involving mandatory sentences.

Despite its occasional benevolent and appropriate use, American courts view jury nullification harshly. Jurors are told they must apply the law as contained in the jury instructions. In fact, if a juror or jury asks the judge about jury nullification and their right to go beyond the letter of the law in reaching a verdict, judges tell the jury that jury nullification is not allowed and that they must follow the law. Moreover, jurors who refuse to apply the law may be removed from the jury if this fact is uncovered prior to a verdict being reached (*United States v. Thomas,* 116 F.3d 606 (2d Cir. 1997).

Although a legal argument can be made as to why jurors should be instructed about their right and power to partake in jury nullification, nearly all federal and state courts that have considered the issue have held that such an instruction is not required by the Constitution (Brody, 1995; Conrad, 1998). Whereas it is acknowledged that jury nullification is appropriate in rare instances, courts are loath to encourage it and are willing to accept its occurrence when juries come to such a result on their own. For an excellent depiction of jury nullification in action, the 1986 episode of the PBS series *Frontline* titled "Inside the Jury Room" is highly recommended. The report presents the deliberations of an actual jury in which jury nullification becomes a central issue.

Selecting a Jury

It is often said and widely believed that a jury trial can be won or lost during jury selection. Consequently, actions and rules that affect the composition of juries have been highly litigated. The litigation has focused on actions taken during two stages of the adjudication process: calling potential jurors to court from the general population, referred to as a **jury pool**, and excluding potential jurors who appear in court from serving on juries as a result of selection procedures.

Names of potential jurors who might be called to court can be chosen from several different sources. Some jurisdictions identify potential jurors solely from voter registration lists and/or property tax registries. Others also get names from driver's license records, public assistance lists, and other sources. Which sources seem most likely to include the greatest number of names of persons eligible for jury service? Are there any drawbacks to using less inclusive lists? Do any of the lists exclude a recognizable class of individuals?

Whatever the source, and however the lists used to identify potential jurors are compiled, the selection system used must pass constitutional muster. Specifically, it must not discriminate against a discrete or "cognizable" class of individuals and must represent a **fair cross-section of the community**. Of course, invidious discrimination would be easy to detect if a jurisdiction had laws or court rules prohibiting a class of people from serving as jurors. *Strauder v. West Virginia*, 100 U.S. 303 (1880). However, what if instead of explicitly precluding certain members of society from jury service, a state permitted members of a group to be jurors, but only if they individually petitioned to serve? Such was the system the Supreme Court considered in *Taylor v. Louisiana*, discussed in the following case.

Duren v. Missouri

439 U.S. 357 (1979)

MR. JUSTICE WHITE delivered the opinion of the Court.

In *Taylor v. Louisiana*, 419 U.S. 522 (1975), this Court held that systematic exclusion of women during the jury-selection process, resulting in **jury pools** not "reasonably representative" of the community, denies a criminal defendant his right, under the Sixth and Fourteenth Amendments, to a **petit jury** selected from a fair cross section of the community. Under the system invalidated in *Taylor*, a woman could not serve on a jury unless she filed a written declaration of her willingness to do so. As a result, although 53% of the persons eligible for jury service were women, less than 1% of the 1,800 persons whose names were drawn from the jury wheel during the year in which appellant Taylor's jury was chosen were female.

At the time of our decision in *Taylor*, no other State provided that women could not serve on a jury unless they volunteered to serve. However, five States, including

Missouri, provided an automatic exemption from jury service for any women requesting not to serve. Subsequent to *Taylor*, three of these States eliminated this exemption. Only Missouri and Tennessee continue to exempt women from jury service upon request. Today we hold that such systematic exclusion of women that results in jury venires averaging less than 15% female violates the Constitution's fair-cross-section requirement.

I

Petitioner Duren was indicted in 1975 in the Circuit Court of Jackson County, Mo., for first-degree murder and first-degree robbery. In a pretrial motion to quash his petit jury panel, and again in a post-conviction motion for a new trial, he contended that his right to trial by a jury chosen from a fair cross section of his community was denied by provisions of Missouri law granting women who so request an automatic exemption from jury service. Both motions were denied.

At hearings on these motions, petitioner established that the jury-selection process in Jackson County begins with the annual mailing of a questionnaire to persons randomly selected from the Jackson County voter registration list. Approximately 70,000 questionnaires were mailed in 1975. The questionnaire contains a list of occupations and other categories which are the basis under Missouri law for either disqualification or exemption from jury service. Included on the questionnaire is a paragraph prominently addressed "TO WOMEN" that states in part, "[A]ny woman who elects not to serve will fill out this paragraph and mail this questionnaire to the jury commissioner at once." A similar paragraph is addressed "TO MEN OVER 65 YEARS OF AGE," who are also statutorily exempt upon request.

The names of those sent questionnaires are placed in the master jury wheel for Jackson County, except for those returning the questionnaire who indicate disqualification or claim an applicable exemption. Summonses are mailed on a weekly basis to prospective jurors randomly drawn from the jury wheel. The summons, like the questionnaire, contains special directions to men over 65 and to women, this time advising them to return the summons by mail if they desire not to serve. The practice also is that even those women who do not return the summons are treated as having claimed exemption if they fail to appear for jury service on the appointed day. Other persons seeking to claim an exemption at this stage must make written or personal application to the court.

Petitioner established that according to the 1970 census, 54% of the adult inhabitants of Jackson County were women. He also showed that for the periods June-October 1975 and January-March 1976, 11,197 persons were summoned and that 2,992 of these, or 26.7%, were women. Of those summoned, 741 women and 4,378 men appeared for service. Thus, 14.5% (741 of 5,119) of the persons on the postsummons weekly venires during the period in which petitioner's jury was chosen were female. In March 1976, when petitioner's trial began, 15.5% of those on the weekly venires were women (110 of 707). Petitioner's jury was selected from a 53-person panel on which there were 5 women; all 12 jurors chosen were men. None of the foregoing statistical evidence was disputed.

In affirming petitioner's conviction, the Missouri Supreme Court questioned two aspects of his statistical presentation. First, it considered the census figures inadequate because they were six years old and might not precisely mirror the percentage of women registered to vote. Second, petitioner had not unequivocally demonstrated the extent to which the low percentage of women appearing for jury service was due to the automatic exemption for women, rather than to sex-neutral exemptions such as that for persons over age 65.

The court went on to hold, however, that even accepting petitioner's statistical proof, "the number of female names in the wheel, those summoned and those appearing were well above acceptable constitutional standards."

II

We think that in certain crucial respects the Missouri Supreme Court misconceived the nature of the fair-cross-section inquiry set forth in *Taylor*. In holding that petit juries must be drawn from a source fairly representative of the community, we explained that jury wheels, pools of names, panels, or venires from which juries are drawn must not systematically exclude distinctive groups in the community and thereby fail to be reasonably representative thereof.

In order to establish a prima facie violation of the fair-cross-section requirement, the defendant must show (1) that the group alleged to be excluded is a "distinctive" group in the community; (2) that the representation of this group in venires from which juries are selected is not fair and reasonable in relation to the number of such persons in the community; and (3) that this underrepresentation is due to systematic exclusion of the group in the jury-selection process.

With respect to the first part of the prima facie test, *Taylor* without doubt established that women are sufficiently numerous and distinct from men so that if they are systematically eliminated from jury panels, the Sixth Amendment's fair-cross-section requirement cannot be satisfied.

B

The second prong of the prima facie case was established by petitioner's statistical presentation. Initially, the defendant must demonstrate the percentage of the community made up of the group alleged to be underrepresented, for this is the conceptual benchmark for the Sixth Amendment fair-cross-section requirement. In *Taylor*, the State had stipulated that 53% of the population eligible for jury service was female, while petitioner Duren has relied upon a census measurement of the actual percentage of women in the community (54%). In the trial court, the State of Missouri never challenged these data. Petitioner's presentation was clearly adequate prima facie evidence of population characteristics for the purpose of making a fair-cross-section violation.

Given petitioner's proof that in the relevant community slightly over half of the adults are women, we must disagree with the conclusion of the court below that jury venires containing approximately 15% women are "reasonably representative" of this community. If the percentage of women appearing on jury pools in Jackson County had precisely mirrored the percentage of women in the population, more than one of every two prospective jurors would have been female. In fact, less than one of every six prospective jurors was female; 85% of the average jury was male. Such a gross discrepancy between the percentage of women in jury venires and the percentage of women in the community requires the conclusion that women were not fairly represented in the source from which petit juries were drawn in Jackson County.

C

Finally, in order to establish a prima facie case, it was necessary for petitioner to show that the underrepresentation of women, generally and on his venire, was due to their systematic exclusion in the jury-selection process. Petitioner's proof met this requirement. His undisputed demonstration that a large discrepancy occurred not just occasionally, but in every weekly venire for a period of nearly a year manifestly indicates that the cause of the underrepresentation was systematic - that is, inherent in the particular jury-selection process utilized.

Petitioner Duren's statistics and other evidence also established when in the selection process the systematic exclusion took place. There was no indication that underrepresentation of women occurred at the first stage of the selection process — the questionnaire canvass of persons randomly selected from the relevant voter registration list. The first sign of a systematic discrepancy is at the next stage — the construction of the jury wheel from which persons are randomly summoned for service. Less than 30% of those summoned were female, demonstrating that a substantially larger number of women answering the questionnaire claimed either ineligibility or exemption from jury service. Moreover, at the summons stage women were not only given another opportunity to claim exemption, but also were presumed to have claimed exemption when they did not respond to the summons. Thus, the percentage of women at the final, venire, stage (14.5%) was much lower than the percentage of women who were summoned for service (26.7%).

The resulting disproportionate and consistent exclusion of women from the jury wheel and at the venire stage was quite obviously due to the system by which juries were selected. Petitioner demonstrated that the underrepresentation of women in the final pool of prospective jurors was due to the operation of Missouri's exemption criteria — whether the automatic exemption for women or other statutory exemptions — as implemented in Jackson County. Women were therefore systematically underrepresented within the meaning of *Taylor*.

III

The demonstration of a prima facie fair-cross-section violation by the defendant is not the end of the inquiry into whether a constitutional violation has occurred. We have explained that States remain free to prescribe relevant qualifications for their jurors and to provide reasonable exemptions so long as it may be fairly said that the jury lists or panels are representative of the community. However, we cautioned that the right to a proper jury cannot be overcome on merely rational grounds. Rather, it requires that a significant state interest be manifestly and primarily advanced by those aspects of the jury-selection process, such as exemption criteria, that result in the disproportionate exclusion of a distinctive group.

The Supreme Court of Missouri suggested that the low percentage of women on jury venires in Jackson County may have been due to a greater number of women than of men qualifying for or claiming permissible exemptions, such as those for persons over 65, teachers, and government workers. Respondent further argues that petitioner has not proved that the exemption for women had "any effect" on or was responsible for the underrepresentation of women on venires.

However, once the defendant has made a *prima facie* showing of an infringement of his constitutional right to a jury drawn from a fair cross section of the community, it is the State that bears the burden of justifying this infringement by showing attainment of a fair cross section to be incompatible with a significant state interest. Assuming, arguendo, that the exemptions mentioned by the court below would justify failure to achieve a fair community cross section on jury venires, the State must demonstrate that these exemptions caused the underrepresentation complained of. The record contains no such proof, and mere suggestions or assertions to that effect are insufficient.

The other possible cause of the disproportionate exclusion of women on Jackson County jury venires is, of course, the automatic exemption for women. Neither the Missouri Supreme Court nor respondent in its brief has offered any substantial justification for this exemption. In response to questioning at oral argument, counsel for respondent ventured that the only state interest advanced by the exemption is safeguarding the important role played by women in home and family life. But exempting all women because of the preclusive domestic responsibilities of some women is insufficient justification for their disproportionate exclusion on jury venires. What we stated in *Taylor* with respect to the system there challenged under which women could "opt in" for jury service is equally applicable to Missouri's "opt out" exemption:

> It is untenable to suggest these days that it would be a special hardship for each and every woman to perform jury service or that society cannot spare any women from their present duties. This may be the case with many, and it may be burdensome to sort out those who should be exempted from those who should serve. But that task is performed in the case of men, and the administrative convenience in dealing with women as a class is insuf-

> ficient justification for diluting the quality of community judgment represented by the jury in criminal trials.
>
> If it was ever the case that women were unqualified to sit on juries or were so situated that none of them should be required to perform jury service, that time has long since passed. 419 U.S., at 534-535, 537 (footnote omitted).

The judgment of the Missouri Supreme Court is reversed, and the case is remanded for further proceedings not inconsistent with this opinion.

FURTHER CASE LAW, REFLECTIONS, AND QUESTIONS

1. The fair cross-section of the community requirement of the Sixth Amendment has been limited to disproportionate representation related to gender and race. Why might this be? Are there other identifiable groups you believe should also be protected?

2. The make-up of a jury pool may also be challenged under the Equal Protection Clause of the Fourteenth Amendment. To succeed under a theory of equal protection, a defendant must establish that a cognizable group of people was intentionally excluded from the jury pool. How does this differ from the standard discussed in *Duren*?

3. Box 12.3 lists the number of states that provide specific exemptions from serving on a jury. Do you believe these exemptions are appropriate? Are there other professions that should be exempt?

Box 12.3 Exemptions from Jury Service

Exemption	States With Exemption
Political officeholders	16
Law enforcement	12
Judicial officers	9
Health care professionals (including dentists and veterinarians)	7
Sole caregivers	7
Attorneys	6
Active military	5
Other exemptions, including clergy, teachers, journalists, mariners, accountants, and individuals with specific religious designations	12

Voir Dire and Challenges to Potential Jurors

Individuals who report for jury duty typically assemble for preliminary instructions and then are assigned to different courtrooms where trials occur. The individuals assigned to report to a given courtroom is called the **venire**, or **jury panel**. A venire may range anywhere from 25 people or fewer to 250 or more, depending on the notoriety of the case, the offense charged, and how many jurors must be seated. The trial jury is selected from this group of people.

The members of the jury panel are given an oath binding them to give honest answers to questions asked during the jury selection process. The venire members are then asked questions, either individually or collectively, by the judge and/or the lawyers in the case. This questioning process is known as **voir dire**.

Attorneys use voir dire to identify jurors with a bias that prevents them from being fair and impartial, as well as to identify people who are believed to be predisposed to their client's position in a case. Based on the information obtained during the voir dire, there are two means by which potential jurors can be removed from the jury panel: a challenge for cause or a peremptory challenge.

Challenges for Cause

If an attorney believes a potential juror is biased and cannot be fair and impartial, the attorney may make a **challenge for cause**. In making such a challenge, the attorney must provide the judge with a legal reason why the potential juror is unfit to serve on the jury. A judge will uphold a challenge for cause if she is convinced that the juror is biased and will not be fair or impartial. This may involve items such as being a victim, having a family member who was the victim of the type of crime involved in the trial, being strongly opposed to the law that is the basis for the criminal charge, having a close family member in law enforcement, being a member of an organization whose purpose involves advocating for issues related to the crimes under consideration (e.g., Mothers Against Drunk Drivers, the National Rifle Association, or the National Organization for the Reform of Marijuana Laws), or an explicitly stated racial, gender, or other forms of bias.

The prosecution and defense have unlimited challenges for cause they can make. Because voir dire is used to identify jurors who cannot be fair and impartial, it makes sense that there should be no limit on the number of potential jurors who may be removed from the case. That being said, challenges for cause are typically denied by the trial judge. Because potential jurors rarely make an explicit statement about bias, if the judge does not think there is sufficient evidence of bias present, the challenge will be denied. That does not, however, mean the person will be seated on the jury, as they can still be removed via a peremptory challenge, discussed below.

A special category of cases where challenges for cause have been controversial involves cases involving capital punishment. The ability of jurors to set aside their personal views and judge a case on its own merits has been a key issue in death penalty cases. Given the strong opinions jurors may hold for or against capital punishment, the Supreme Court has held that states may require jurors hearing cases where the death penalty is a possible sentence to be "death-qualified." During jury selection, potential jurors will be questioned regarding their attitude toward the death penalty. A potential juror may be challenged for cause if their views about the death penalty "would prevent or substantially impair the performance of his duties as a juror in accordance with his instructions and his oath." Wainwright v. Witt, 469 U.S. 412, 420 (1985). Does this seem appropriate? Do you think a different standard for death qualification should be used? If so, what would be more appropriate?

Peremptory Challenges

After challenges for cause have been resolved and the voir dire has been completed, the attorneys are given the opportunity to have a certain number of potential jurors removed from the panel without having to state a reason. These are known as **peremptory challenges**. Peremptory challenges allow each side to remove a limited number of potential jurors (normally between 4 and 8) who the attorney believes will have a negative view toward their case or client, or a positive predisposition toward the other party. They are often used to remove a potential juror with a perceived predisposition but whose biases cannot be shown with enough certainty to warrant a challenge for cause. By allowing each side to remove a fixed number of jurors, peremptory challenges allow for a fairer, more balanced jury.

Peremptory challenges are often based on a lawyer's hunches, experience, and instinct based on information heard during the voir dire. This may be based on pure intuition or on the juror's background, education level, or life experiences made known during voir dire. A defendant may not want a person whose husband is a police officer to be on the jury out of fear that the juror will be predisposed to believe the testimony of law enforcement officers. Conversely, a prosecutor may not want a social worker who works with individuals and families on a daily basis for fear that compassion for people such as the defendant will impact the potential juror's decision-making.

Historically, attorneys enjoyed virtually unlimited discretion in exercising their peremptory challenges. This license came abruptly to a halt when the Supreme Court recognized other values, reflected in the equal protection of the law, that conflicted with the lawyers' quest to exclude potential jurors from participating in trials by exercising peremptory challenges. The leading case in this area is *Batson v. Kentucky*.

Batson v. Kentucky

476 U.S. 79 (1986)

JUSTICE POWELL delivered the opinion of the Court.

Petitioner, a black man, was indicted in Kentucky on charges of second-degree burglary and receipt of stolen goods. On the first day of trial in Jefferson Circuit Court, the judge conducted voir dire examination of the venire, excused certain jurors for cause, and permitted the parties to exercise peremptory challenges. The prosecutor used his peremptory challenges to strike all four black persons on the venire, and a jury composed only of white persons was selected. Defense counsel moved to discharge the jury before it was sworn on the ground that the prosecutor's removal of the black veniremen violated petitioner's rights under the Sixth and Fourteenth Amendments to a jury drawn from a cross section of the community, and under the Fourteenth Amendment to equal protection of the laws. Counsel requested a hearing on his motion. Without expressly ruling on the request for a hearing, the trial judge observed that the parties were entitled to use their peremptory challenges to "strike anybody they want to." The judge then denied petitioner's motion, reasoning that the cross-section requirement applies only to selection of the venire and not to selection of the petit jury itself.

II

In *Swain v. Alabama*, this Court recognized that a State's purposeful or deliberate denial to Negroes on account of race of participation as jurors in the administration of justice violates the Equal Protection Clause. This principle has been consistently and repeatedly reaffirmed, in numerous decisions of this Court both preceding and following Swain. We reaffirm the principle today.

A

More than a century ago, the Court decided that the State denies a black defendant equal protection of the laws when it puts him on trial before a jury from which members of his race have been purposefully excluded. *Strauder v. West Virginia*, 100 U.S. 303 (1880). That decision laid the foundation for the Court's unceasing efforts to eradicate racial discrimination in the procedures used to select the venire from which individual jurors are drawn. In Strauder, the Court explained that the central concern of the recently ratified Fourteenth Amendment was to put an end to governmental discrimination on account of race. Exclusion of black citizens from service as jurors constitutes a primary example of the evil the Fourteenth Amendment was designed to cure.

In holding that racial discrimination in jury selection offends the Equal Protection Clause, the Court in *Strauder* recognized, however, that a defendant has no right to a petit jury composed in whole or in part of persons of his own race. The number of our races and nationalities stands in the way of evolution of such a conception of the demand of equal protection. But the defendant does have the right to be tried by a jury whose members are selected pursuant to nondiscriminatory criteria. The Equal Protection Clause guarantees the defendant that the State will not exclude members of his race from the jury venire on account of race, or on the false assumption that members of his race as a group are not qualified to serve as jurors.

Purposeful racial discrimination in selection of the venire violates a defendant's right to equal protection because it denies him the protection that a trial by jury is intended to secure. The very idea of a jury is a body composed of the peers or equals of the person whose rights it is selected or summoned to determine; that is, of his neighbors, fellows, associates, persons having the same legal status in society as that which he holds. The petit jury has occupied a central position in our system of justice by safeguarding a person accused of crime against the arbitrary exercise of power by prosecutor or judge. Those on the venire must be indifferently chosen, to secure the defendant's right under the Fourteenth Amendment to protection of life and liberty against race or color prejudice.

B

As in any equal protection case, the "burden is, of course," on the defendant who alleges discriminatory selection of the venire "to prove the existence of purposeful discrimination." In deciding if the defendant has carried his burden of persuasion, a court must undertake "a sensitive inquiry into such circumstantial and direct evidence of intent as may be available."

Circumstantial evidence of invidious intent may include proof of disproportionate impact. We have observed that under some circumstances proof of discriminatory impact may for all practical purposes demonstrate unconstitutionality because in various circumstances the discrimination is very difficult to explain on nonracial grounds. For example, "total or seriously disproportionate exclusion of Negroes from jury venires, is itself such an unequal application of the law as to show intentional discrimination.

Moreover, since *Swain*, we have recognized that a black defendant alleging that members of his race have been impermissibly excluded from the venire may make out a prima facie case of purposeful discrimination by showing that the totality of the relevant facts gives rise to an inference of discriminatory purpose. Once the defendant makes the requisite showing, the burden shifts to the State to explain adequately the racial exclusion. The State cannot meet this burden on mere general assertions that its officials did not discriminate or that they properly performed their official duties. Rather, the State must demonstrate that "permissible racially neutral selection criteria and procedures have produced the monochromatic result."

The showing necessary to establish a prima facie case of purposeful discrimination in selection of the venire may be discerned in this Court's decisions. The defendant initially must show that he is a member of a racial group capable of being singled out for differential treatment. In combination with the evidence, a defendant may then make a prima facie case by proving that in the particular jurisdiction members of his race have not been summoned for jury service over an extended period of time. Proof of systematic exclusion from the venire raises an inference of purposeful discrimination because the "result bespeaks discrimination."

Since the ultimate issue is whether the State has discriminated in selecting the defendant's venire, however, the defendant may establish a prima facie case in other ways than by evidence of long-continued unexplained absence of members of his race from many panels. In cases involving the venire, this Court has found a prima facie case on proof that members of the defendant's race were substantially underrepresented on the venire from which his jury was drawn, and that the venire was selected under a practice providing "the opportunity for discrimination." This combination of factors raises the necessary inference of purposeful discrimination because the Court has declined to attribute to chance the absence of black citizens on a particular jury array where the selection mechanism is subject to abuse. When circumstances suggest the need, the trial court must undertake a "factual inquiry" that "takes into account all possible explanatory factors" in the particular case.

C

The standards for assessing a prima facie case in the context of discriminatory selection of the venire have been fully articulated since Swain. These principles support our conclusion that a defendant may establish a prima facie case of purposeful discrimination in selection of the petit jury solely on evidence concerning the prosecutor's exercise of peremptory challenges at the defendant's trial. To establish such a case, the defendant first must show that he is a member of a cognizable racial group, and that the prosecutor has exercised peremptory challenges to remove from the venire members of the defendant's race. Second, the defendant is entitled to rely on the fact, as to which there can be no dispute, that peremptory challenges constitute a jury selection practice that permits "those to discriminate who are of a mind to discriminate." Finally, the defendant must show that these facts and any other relevant circumstances raise an inference that the prosecutor used that practice to exclude the veniremen from the petit jury on account of their race. This combination of factors in the empaneling of the petit jury, as in the selection of the venire, raises the necessary inference of purposeful discrimination.

In deciding whether the defendant has made the requisite showing, the trial court should consider all relevant circumstances. For example, a "pattern" of strikes against black jurors included in the particular venire might give rise to an inference of discrimination. Similarly, the prosecutor's questions and statements during voir dire examination and in exercising his challenges may support or refute an inference of discriminatory purpose. These examples are merely illustrative. We have confidence that trial judges, experienced in supervising voir dire, will be able to decide if the circumstances concerning the prosecutor's use of peremptory challenges creates a prima facie case of discrimination against black jurors.

Once the defendant makes a prima facie showing, the burden shifts to the State to come forward with a neutral explanation for challenging black jurors. Though this requirement imposes a limitation in some cases on the full peremptory character of the historic challenge, we emphasize that the prosecutor's explanation need not rise to the level justifying exercise of a challenge for cause. But the prosecutor may not rebut the defendant's prima facie case of discrimination by stating merely that he challenged jurors of the defendant's race on the assumption — or his intuitive judgment — that they would be partial to the defendant because of their shared race.

Just as the Equal Protection Clause forbids the States to exclude black persons from the venire on the assumption that blacks as a group are unqualified to serve as jurors, so it forbids the States to strike black veniremen on the assumption that they will be biased in a particular case simply because the defendant is black. The core guarantee of equal protection, ensuring citizens that their State will not discriminate on account of race, would be meaningless were we to approve the exclusion of jurors on the basis of such assumptions, which arise solely from the jurors' race. Nor may the prosecutor rebut the defendant's case merely by denying that he had a discriminatory motive or "affirm[ing] [his] good faith in making individual selections." If these general assertions were accepted as rebutting a defendant's prima facie case, the Equal Protection Clause "would be but a vain and illusory requirement." The prosecutor therefore must articulate a neutral explanation related to the particular case to be tried. The trial court then will have the duty to determine if the defendant has established purposeful discrimination.

IV

The State contends that our holding will eviscerate the fair trial values served by the peremptory challenge. Conceding that the Constitution does not guarantee a right to peremptory challenges and that Swain did state that their use ultimately is subject to the strictures of equal protection, the State argues that the privilege of unfettered exercise of the challenge is of vital importance to the criminal justice system.

While we recognize, of course, that the peremptory challenge occupies an important position in our trial procedures, we do not agree that our decision today will undermine the contribution the challenge generally makes to the administration of justice. The reality of practice, amply reflected in many state and federal court opinions, shows that the challenge may be, and unfortunately at times has been, used to discriminate against black jurors. By requiring trial courts to be sensitive to the racially discriminatory use of peremptory challenges, our decision enforces the mandate of equal protection and furthers the ends of justice. In view of the heterogeneous population of our Nation, public respect for our criminal justice system and the rule of law will be strengthened if we ensure that no citizen is disqualified from jury service because of his race.

V

In this case, petitioner made a timely objection to the prosecutor's removal of all black persons on the venire. Because the trial court flatly rejected the objection without requiring the prosecutor to give an explanation for his action, we remand this case for further proceedings. If the trial court decides that the facts establish, prima facie, purposeful discrimination and the prosecutor does not come forward with a neutral explanation for his action, our precedents require that petitioner's conviction be reversed.

FURTHER CASE LAW, REFLECTIONS, AND QUESTIONS

1. Must a prosecutor always explain his or her reason for using a peremptory challenge against an African American venire member? What do you understand a "prima facie" case of race discrimination to be? How can it be demonstrated?
2. Which of the following would be race-neutral reasons a lawyer could base peremptory challenges on? (a) The juror was not paying attention. (b) The juror smiled at the defendant. (c) The juror glared at the prosecutor. Can any of these reasons be proven or disproven? How does this affect the use of the Batson test? If you were a judge, and the prosecutor explained that she excused a potential juror because he smiled at the defendant, would you accept this as a race-neutral reason under the Batson rules? See Box 12.4 for how one state is addressing this problem.
3. Note that the defendant in *Batson*, like the excluded jurors, was African American. Should a white defendant be able to raise a Batson objection to a prosecutor striking black jurors? In *Powers v. Ohio*, 499 U.S. 400 (1991), the Supreme Court answered this question affirmatively. The Court explained that the Equal Protection Clause prohibits a prosecutor from using the State's peremptory challenges to exclude otherwise qualified and unbiased persons from the petit jury solely because of their race, a practice that forecloses a significant opportunity to participate in civic life. An individual juror does not have a right to sit in on any particular petit jury, but he or she does possess the right not to be excluded from one on account of race. The Court held that since the excused juror cannot redress the improper exclusion, the defendant has the right to object to an inappropriate exercise of a peremptory challenge.
4. *Batson* and *Powers* held that the prosecution cannot exclude potential jurors because of their race. Should the defendant face the same restrictions? The Court

said yes in Georgia v. McCollum, 505 U.S. 42 (1992). For the same reasons stated in Batson and Powers, the Court held that the prosecution has the right to object to defense counsel's peremptory challenges that violate the Batson rule.

5. Can a party use peremptory challenges to remove potential jurors because they are men or women? In *J.E.B. v. Alabama*, 511 U.S. 127 (1994), the Supreme Court said no. J.E.B. involved a trial to determine paternity and child support. During jury selection, the State, on behalf of the mother of the child, used 9 of its 10 peremptory challenges to strike male jurors. As a result, an all-female jury was seated. J.E.B., the alleged father, objected and argued that the State had unconstitutionally struck male jurors solely because of their gender. The trial court overruled the objection, and the jury found J.E.B. to be the child's father. The Supreme Court held that it is unconstitutional to use peremptory challenges to remove potential jurors from the panel based solely on gender. The Court stated that it is improper to assume that a person would be biased in a particular case solely because of gender stereotypes and ruled that J.E.B.'s equal-protection rights had been violated.

Box 12.4 Putting Teeth into *Batson* to Reduce Race-based Peremptory Challenges

The ease with which parties can meet the requirements to sustain individual or systemic racially or ethnically motivated challenges has led to a reexamination of Batson. In 2018, the Washington State Supreme Court used its rule-making authority to "eliminate the unfair exclusion of potential jurors based on race or ethnicity" (GR-37 [a]). GR-37 does this by addressing four historically troubling aspects of Batson challenges.

1. Unlike *Batson*, the rule does not require proof of purposeful discrimination for a peremptory challenge to be denied. Instead, it provides that the challenge should be denied if an objective observer could view race or ethnicity as one factor behind a challenge. Critically, in making this determination, the court should consider the existence of "implicit, institutional, and unconscious biases" that have previously led to the unfair exclusion of potential jurors.

2. The rule provides case-specific circumstances that a court should consider. These include the nature of questioning of prospective jurors during voir dire; whether jurors who provided similar answers to questions were treated differently based on race or ethnicity; whether a specific justification for a challenge is disproportionately associated with a given race or ethnicity; and whether the party making the challenge has disproportionately challenged jurors based on race or ethnicity in the present case or past cases.

3. The rule lists presumptively invalid justifications put forth to support a peremptory challenge. Reasons listed, that have been historically associated with improper discrimination in jury selection, include having prior contact with law

enforcement officers; expressing a distrust of law enforcement officers or a belief that they engage in racial profiling; having close relationships with people who have had negative experiences with law enforcement; living in a high crime neighborhood; receiving state benefits; and not being a native English speaker.

4. The rule prohibits the reliance on uncorroborated conduct by a prospective juror during jury selection. Due to the frequent use of conduct-based justifications that are often unverifiable, the rule requires any party that intends to use such conduct as a justification for a peremptory challenge to provide notice to the court and opposing party of the conduct to allow the behavior to be explored and addressed in a timely manner. Conduct listed explicitly in the rule includes "allegations that the prospective juror was sleeping, inattentive, or staring or failing to make eye contact; exhibited a problematic attitude, body language, or demeanor; or provided unintelligent or confused answers."

In your opinion, what impact will the changes enacted by GR-37 have on the use of race and ethnically-based peremptory challenges?

Box 12.5 You Be the Judge

Jimmy, a Black man, was on trial for armed robbery. During jury selection, he objected to the prosecutor's use of peremptory challenges to strike two black men from the jury panel based on *Batson v. Kentucky*. In response, the prosecutor stated:

> I struck [juror] number twenty-two because of his long hair. He had long curly hair. He had the longest hair of anybody on the panel by far. He appeared to me to not be a good juror for that fact, the fact that he had long hair hanging down shoulder length, curly, unkempt hair. Also, he had a mustache and a goatee-type beard. And juror number twenty-four also has a mustache and goatee-type beard. Those are the only two people on the jury. . . with the facial hair. And I don't like the way they looked, with the way the hair is cut, both of them. And the mustaches and the beards look suspicious to me.

How should the court rule on the Batson motion?

Had the case occurred in Washington state, would the result have been different?

See *Purkett v. Elem*, 514 U.S. 765 (1995).

Jury selection requires the court and attorneys to consider challenges for cause and peremptory challenges. One could view the availability of peremptory challenges as a safety net to remove a juror perceived as biased but successfully challenged for cause. Is this fair? What if the trial court judge erroneously denies a challenge for cause, and a defendant feels it necessary to exercise a peremptory challenge to remove the "biased" juror? This is the situation before the Court in *United States v. Martinez-Salazar*, 528 U.S. 304 (2000).

Abel Martinez-Salazar was charged with multiple federal narcotics and weapons offenses. The District Court allotted each party ten peremptory challenges. Prospective juror Don Gilbert indicated several times that he would favor the prosecution. Martinez-Salazar's counsel challenged him for cause several times; however, the court declined to excuse Gilbert. Eventually, Martinez-Salazar used a peremptory challenge to have Gilbert removed. Subsequently, Martinez-Salazar used up all of his peremptory challenges, and he did not object to the final seating of the jurors. Martinez-Salazar was then convicted on all counts. On appeal, he argued that the District Court abused its discretion in refusing to strike Gilbert for cause and that this error misused one of his peremptory challenges. The Court of Appeals agreed. The court found that the District Court's error violated Martinez-Salazar's Fifth Amendment due process rights because it forced him to use a peremptory challenge curatively, which impaired his right to a full complement of peremptory challenges. The Court of Appeals held that the error required an automatic reversal.

The Supreme Court disagreed. In a unanimous decision, the Court held that a defendant's exercise of peremptory challenges is not denied or impaired when the defendant chooses to use such a challenge to remove a juror who should have been excused for cause. The Court held that "if the defendant elects to cure such an error by exercising a peremptory challenge and is subsequently convicted by a jury on which no biased juror sat, he has not been deprived of any rule-based or constitutional right." The Court also concluded that losing a peremptory challenge did not violate the Sixth Amendment right to an impartial jury.

Undoubtedly, this places a defendant in a very difficult position, having to either (a) use a peremptory challenge to remove a juror whom they perceive to be biased from the jury and thereby waiving the right to raise on appeal the improper denial of a challenge for cause, or (b) leave the perceived biased juror on the jury and hope to obtain relief on appeal. As it is very rare for an appellate court to reverse a conviction based on a trial judge's decision during jury selection, the defendant is caught between a rock and a hard place. If you were advising a defendant in this position, what would you advise her to do? Why?

Size of the Trial Jury

Duncan and *Baldwin* held that a person charged with a nonpetty offense is entitled to a jury trial. They did not, however, say what constitutes a jury. Do three people make a jury? How about six or eight? Under the common law, and when the Sixth Amendment was adopted, juries comprised 12 people. Does this historical fact mean that contemporary criminal trial juries must continue to have 12 members? The Supreme

Court confronted this question in *Williams v. Florida*, which was decided the same day as *Baldwin*, when it was asked to give its stamp of approval to six-person juries.

Williams v. Florida

399 U.S. 78 (1970)

MR. JUSTICE WHITE delivered the opinion of the Court.

Prior to his trial for robbery in the State of Florida, petitioner filed a motion to impanel a 12-man jury instead of the six-man jury provided by Florida law in all but capital cases. That motion was denied. Petitioner was convicted as charged and was sentenced to life imprisonment.

II

In *Duncan v. Louisiana*, 391 U.S. 145 (1968), we held that the Fourteenth Amendment guarantees a right to trial by jury in all criminal cases that — were they to be tried in a federal court — would come within the Sixth Amendment's guarantee. Petitioner's trial for robbery on July 3, 1968, clearly falls within the scope of that holding.

The question in this case then is whether the constitutional guarantee of a trial by "jury" necessarily requires trial by exactly 12 persons, rather than some lesser number — in this case six. We hold that the 12-man panel is not a necessary ingredient of "trial by jury," and that respondent's refusal to impanel more than the six members provided for by Florida law did not violate petitioner's Sixth Amendment rights as applied to the States through the Fourteenth.

We had occasion in *Duncan v. Louisiana*, supra, to review briefly the oft-told history of the development of trial by jury in criminal cases. That history revealed a long tradition attaching great importance to the concept of relying on a body of one's peers to determine guilt or innocence as a safeguard against arbitrary law enforcement. That same history, however, affords little insight into the considerations that gradually led the size of that body to be generally fixed at 12. Some have suggested that the number 12 was fixed upon simply because that was the number of the presentment jury from the hundred, from which the petit jury developed.

Other, less circular but more fanciful reasons for the number 12 have been given, "but they were all brought forward after the number was fixed," and rest on little more than mystical or superstitious insights into the significance of "12." Lord Coke's explanation that the "number of twelve is much respected in holy writ, as 12 apostles, 12 stones, 12 tribes, etc." is typical. In short, while sometime in the 14th century the size of the jury at common law came to be fixed generally at 12, that particular feature of the jury system appears to have been a historical accident, unrelated to the great purposes which gave rise to the jury in the first place. The question before us is whether this accidental feature of the jury has been immutably codified into our Constitution.

The purpose of the jury trial, as we noted in *Duncan*, is to prevent oppression by the Government. "Providing an accused with the right to be tried by a jury of his peers gave him an inestimable safeguard against the corrupt or overzealous prosecutor and against the compliant, biased, or eccentric judge." Given this purpose, the essential feature of a jury obviously lies in the interposition between the accused and his accuser of the commonsense judgment of a group of laymen, and in the community participation and shared responsibility that results from that group's determination of guilt or innocence. The performance of this role is not a function of the particular number of the body that makes up the jury. To be sure, the number should probably be large enough to promote group deliberation, free from outside attempts at intimidation, and to provide a fair possibility for obtaining a representative cross-section of the community. But we find little reason to think that these goals are in any meaningful sense less likely to be achieved when the jury numbers six, than when it numbers 12 — particularly if the requirement of unanimity is retained. And, certainly the reliability of the jury as a fact finder hardly seems likely to be a function of its size.

It might be suggested that the 12-man jury gives a defendant a greater advantage since he has more "chances" of finding a juror who will insist on acquittal and thus prevent conviction. But the advantage might just as easily belong to the State, which also needs only one juror out of twelve insisting on guilt to prevent acquittal. What few experiments have occurred — usually in the civil area — indicate that there is no discernible difference between the results reached by the two different-sized juries. In short, neither currently available evidence nor theory suggests that the 12-man jury is necessarily more advantageous to the defendant than a jury composed of fewer members.

Similarly, while in theory the number of viewpoints represented on a randomly selected jury ought to increase as the size of the jury increases, in practice the difference between the 12-man and the six-man jury in terms of the cross-section of the community represented seems likely to be negligible. Even the 12-man jury cannot insure representation of every distinct voice in the community, particularly given the use of the peremptory challenge. As long as arbitrary exclusions of a particular class from the jury rolls are forbidden, the concern that the cross-section will be significantly diminished if the jury is decreased in size from 12 to six seems an unrealistic one.

We conclude, in short, as we began: the fact that the jury at common law was composed of precisely 12 is a historical accident, unnecessary to effect the purposes of the jury system and wholly without significance "except to mystics." To read the Sixth Amendment as forever codifying a feature so incidental to the real purpose of the Amendment is to ascribe a blind formalism to the Framers which would require considerably more evidence than we have been able to discover in the history and language of the Constitution or in the reasoning of our past decisions.

Legislatures may well have their own views about the relative value of the larger and smaller juries, and may conclude that, wholly apart from the jury's primary function, it is desirable to spread the collective responsibility for the determination of guilt among the larger group. In capital cases, for example, it appears that no State provides for less than 12 jurors — a fact that suggests implicit recognition of the value of the larger body as a means of legitimating society's decision to impose the death penalty. Our holding does no more than leave these considerations to Congress and the States, unrestrained by an interpretation of the Sixth Amendment that would forever dictate the precise number that can constitute a jury. Consistent with this holding, we conclude that petitioner's Sixth Amendment rights, as applied to the States through the Fourteenth Amendment, were not violated by Florida's decision to provide a six-man rather than a 12-man jury. The judgment of the Florida District Court of Appeal is Affirmed.

FURTHER CASE LAW, REFLECTIONS, AND QUESTIONS

1. Eight years after Williams was decided, the Court ruled that criminal trial juries cannot shrink below six members. In *Ballew v. Georgia*, 435 U.S. 223 (1978), the justices invalidated Georgia's use of five-person juries in misdemeanor trials. The Court found that juries of fewer than six members are less likely to recall evidence, to conduct effective deliberations, and to reflect a representative cross-section of the community. The Court went so far as to say that the use of such juries "calls into doubt the results achieved." Justice Blackmun's lead opinion in *Ballew*, which was joined by only one other justice, relied heavily on social science evidence about jury decision-making. Not surprisingly, most studies concerning the consequences of reducing the size of juries from 12 members to six members found that the larger jury conducts "higher quality" deliberations than the smaller jury. Nevertheless, the Court in *Ballew* expressly reaffirmed Williams' holding that six-person juries are constitutionally permissible.

2. If you were being tried for a crime, would you prefer to have your fate determined by a jury of twelve or six citizens? What are the state's interests in impaneling a jury of only six members?

3. The Court's decisions in *Williams* and *Ballew* state that juries in criminal trials with as few as six jurors are constitutional. What about juries in federal trials? Since the Sixth Amendment, standing alone, governs Federal trials, its explicit language mandating that juries consist of 12 people remains the standard for jury trials in the federal system. Two items relating to this are worth noting.

   While Federal Rule of Criminal Procedure 23(b) permits the parties in a trial to stipulate to having a trial of fewer than 12 people, the court in *United*

States v. Ullah, 976 F.2d 509 (9th Cir. 1992) held that juries of greater than 12 people are never permitted under the Constitution.

Rule 23(b) of the Federal Rules of Criminal Procedure also provides that if the trial court determines that there is "just cause" to dismiss a juror (even during deliberations), the court may excuse that juror if it concludes that the remaining eleven jurors may return a valid verdict. Just cause has been found to exist when a juror became ill during deliberations.

Is a Unanimous Verdict Required?

As with the use of 12-person juries, the requirement that a jury reach a unanimous verdict was also firmly established in England and the United States. Having all jurors agree on a verdict legitimizes the decision, thereby providing society with a sense that the verdict must be correct. Despite the general sense that unanimous verdicts are a necessary component of the jury system, by the 20th century, several states permitted nonunanimous verdicts in criminal prosecutions.

In 1972, the Supreme Court decided two cases that held that there was no constitutional requirement that jury verdicts in criminal trials be unanimous. In *Apodaca v. Oregon* (1972), the Court held that Oregon's law permitting 10–2 verdicts in noncapital cases did not diminish the jury's function as it articulated in Williams 2 years before. Similarly, in *Johnson v. Louisiana* (1972), the Court held that Louisiana's statute permitting 9–3 verdicts in noncapital cases did not diminish the validity or reliability of the decision. Interestingly, since Johnson and Apodaca were decided, no other states have abandoned the requirement for unanimity. Moreover, the Court has not been asked to consider the constitutionality of verdicts with less than a 75% majority, but in 1979, the Supreme Court held that when a six-person jury is used, the verdict must be unanimous, *Burch v. Louisiana*, 441 U.S. 130 (1979).

The law remained that way for forty years. Notably, in 2019, only two states allowed a defendant to be convicted of a felony by a non-unanimous verdict. In 2019, Evangelisto Ramos was convicted of murder by a 10-2 vote by a Louisiana jury. Ramos petitioned the United States Supreme Court to review his case and overrule the earlier decision in *Apodaca* that permitted nonunanimous verdicts. In *Ramos v. Louisiana*, 590 U.S. 83 (2020), the Court held that the 6th Amendment right to a jury trial requires unanimous verdicts in state felony prosecutions. The Court found that the 6th Amendment right to a jury trial is incorporated to the states under the 14th Amendment, which means that "if the jury trial right requires a unanimous verdict in federal court, it requires no less in state court." The court expressly overruled *Apodaca*, calling it "gravely mistaken." The decision in *Ramos* meant that Oregon was required to amend its criminal procedure to require unanimous verdicts in felony cases.

Testimonial Rights of the Defendant

The Right to Refrain from Testifying

The Fifth Amendment provides that "no person. . . shall be compelled in any criminal case to be a witness against himself." Despite this right, might there not be an appearance or inference of guilt if a defendant does not testify in his or her defense to refute the allegations made against him or her? For example, if you were a juror in a case in which a defendant was accused of committing a brutal murder, what would you think if he did not take the witness stand and maintain his innocence? Is it at least possible that a defendant who does not testify cannot refute the charge because he is in fact guilty of the crime? If that is one possible inference, should a prosecutor or the trial judge be allowed to explain to the jury that they might draw this conclusion from the defendant's failure to testify? This issue is considered in *Griffin v. California*.

Griffin v. California

380 U.S. 609 (1965)

MR. JUSTICE DOUGLAS delivered the opinion of the Court.

Petitioner was convicted of murder in the first degree after a jury trial in a California court. He did not testify at the trial on the issue of guilt, though he did testify at the separate trial on the issue of penalty. The trial court instructed the jury on the issue of guilt, stating that a defendant has a constitutional right not to testify. But it told the jury:

> As to any evidence or facts against him which the defendant can reasonably be expected to deny or explain because of facts within his knowledge, if he does not testify or if, though he does testify, he fails to deny or explain such evidence, the jury may take that failure into consideration as tending to indicate the truth of such evidence and as indicating that among the inferences that may be reasonably drawn there from those unfavorable to the defendant are the more probable.

It added, however, that no such inference could be drawn as to evidence respecting which he had no knowledge. It stated that failure of a defendant to deny or explain the evidence of which he had knowledge does not create a presumption of guilt nor by itself warrant an inference of guilt nor relieve the prosecution of any of its burden of proof.

Petitioner had been seen with the deceased the evening of her death, the evidence placing him with her in the alley where her body was found. The prosecutor made much of the failure of petitioner to testify:

> The defendant certainly knows whether Essie Mae had this beat up appearance at the time he left her apartment and went down the alley with

> her. What kind of man is it that would want to have sex with a woman that beat up if she was beat up at the time he left?
>
> He would know that. He would know how she got down the alley. He would know how the blood got on the bottom of the concrete steps. He would know how long he was with her in that box. He would know how her wig got off. He would know whether he beat her or mistreated her. He would know whether he walked away from that place cool as a cucumber when he saw Mr. Villasenor because he was conscious of his own guilt and wanted to get away from that damaged or injured woman.
>
> These things he has not seen fit to take the stand and deny or explain. And in the whole world, if anybody would know, this defendant would know. Essie Mae is dead, she can't tell you her side of the story. The defendant won't.
>
> The death penalty was imposed and the California Supreme Court affirmed.

The question remains whether, statute or not, the comment rule, approved by California, violates the Fifth Amendment. We think it does. It is in substance a rule of evidence that allows the State the privilege of tendering to the jury for its consideration of the failure of the accused to testify. No formal offer of proof is made as in other situations; but the prosecutor's comment and the court's acquiescence are the equivalent of an offer of evidence and its acceptance. The Court in the Wilson case stated:

> The act was framed with a due regard also to those who might prefer to rely upon the presumption of innocence which the law gives to everyone, and not wish to be witnesses. It is not everyone who can safely venture on the witness stand, though entirely innocent of the charge against him. Excessive timidity, nervousness when facing others and attempting to explain trans-actions of a suspicious character, and offenses charged against him, will often confuse and embarrass him to such a degree as to increase rather than remove prejudices against him. It is not everyone, however honest, who would therefore willingly be placed on the witness stand. The statute, in tenderness to the weakness of those who from the causes mentioned might refuse to ask to be witnesses, particularly when they may have been in some degree compromised by their association with others, declares that the failure of a defendant in a criminal action to request to be a witness shall not create any presumption against him. 149 U.S., p.66.

Comment on the refusal to testify is a remnant of the "inquisitorial system of criminal justice," which the Fifth Amendment outlaws. It is a penalty imposed by courts for exercising a constitutional privilege. It cuts down on the privilege by making its assertion costly. It is said, however, that the inference of guilt for failure to testify as to facts peculiarly within the accused's knowledge is in any event natural and irresistible, and that comment on the failure does not magnify that inference into a penalty for asserting a constitutional privilege. What the jury may infer, given no help from the court, is one thing. What it may infer when the court solemnizes the silence of the accused into evidence against him is quite another.

We said in *Malloy v. Hogan*, that "the same standards must determine whether an accused's silence in either a federal or state proceeding is justified." We take that in its literal sense and hold that the Fifth Amendment, in its direct application to the Federal Government and in its bearing on the States by reason of the Fourteenth Amendment, forbids either comment by the prosecution on the accused's silence or instructions by the court that such silence is evidence of guilt.

Reversed.

FURTHER CASE LAW, REFLECTIONS, AND QUESTIONS

1. Following the reversal of Griffin's conviction, he was tried again for murder, and a **mistrial** was declared when the jury was deadlocked. In his third trial, Griffin was found guilty of first-degree murder and sentenced to death. On appeal, the trial court's judgment of conviction and imposition of the death penalty were reversed, and a life sentence was imposed.

2. If you were on a jury, what, if anything, would you infer if a defendant did not testify?

3. Would a judge's instruction informing you not to consider the defendant's silence make a difference in how you decided the case? Do you think such an instruction would be beneficial to a defendant? In *Carter v. Kentucky*, 450 U.S. 288 (1981), the Court held that to protect a defendant from unjustified speculation by a jury concerning his or her failure to testify, a judge must give such an instruction at the defendant's request. However, some defendants may not want a judge to deliver such an instruction, fearing it may "red-flag" their failure to testify. In *Lakeside v. Oregon*, 435 U.S. 333 (1978), the Court held that it was constitutionally permissible for a judge to give a protective instruction despite the defendant's objection to it. What would explain why an instruction designed to protect the defendant can be given in the face of an objection made by the very person who presumably benefits from the instruction but does not want its "protection"?

Compulsory Process and the Right to Present Evidence

The Sixth Amendment provides that all criminal defendants have the right to "compulsory process for obtaining witnesses in his favor." The **Compulsory Process Clause** has two components. The first guarantees a defendant the right to obtain witnesses, documents, and other evidence necessary to defend himself or herself. This includes the right to have subpoenas issued to compel the attendance of potential witnesses in court. The second component, the Compulsory Process Clause, provides a defendant with the right to present evidence and witnesses at trial.

While seemingly straightforward, the Supreme Court has found that the Compulsory Process Clause does not permit a defendant to present any and all evidence desired at trial. To be used at trial, evidence must be relevant and reliable. While the rules of evidence, which are very complex, govern such items, when evidence sought to be presented by a defendant in a criminal trial is precluded by the trial judge, the Compulsory Process Clause may come into play. Consider the following case and how the Court balances the rights of the defendant with the need to fairly and efficiently administer justice.

Washington v. Texas

388 U.S. 14 (1967)

MR. CHIEF JUSTICE WARREN delivered the opinion of the Court.

We granted certiorari in this case to determine whether the right of a defendant in a criminal case under the Sixth Amendment to have compulsory process for obtaining witnesses in his favor is applicable to the States through the Fourteenth Amendment, and whether that right was violated by a state procedural statute providing that persons charged as principals, accomplices, or accessories in the same crime cannot be introduced as witnesses for each other.

Petitioner, Jackie Washington, was convicted in Dallas County, Texas, of murder with malice and was sentenced by a jury to 50 years in prison. The prosecution's evidence showed that petitioner, an 18-year-old youth, had dated a girl named Jean Carter until her mother had forbidden her to see him. The girl thereafter began dating another boy, the deceased. Evidently motivated by jealousy, petitioner with several other boys began driving around the City of Dallas on the night of August 29, 1964, looking for a gun. The search eventually led to one Charles Fuller, who joined the group with his shotgun. After obtaining some shells from another source, the group of boys proceeded to Jean Carter's home, where Jean, her family and the deceased were having supper. Some of the boys threw bricks at the house and then ran back to the car, leaving petitioner and Fuller alone in front of the house with the shotgun. At the sound of the bricks the deceased and Jean Carter's mother rushed out on the porch to investigate. The shotgun was fired by either petitioner or Fuller, and the deceased was fatally wounded. Shortly afterward petitioner and Fuller came running back to the car where the other boys waited, with Fuller carrying the shotgun.

Petitioner testified on his own behalf. He claimed that Fuller, who was intoxicated, had taken the gun from him, and that he had unsuccessfully tried to persuade Fuller to leave before the shooting. Fuller had insisted that he was going to shoot someone, and petitioner had run back to the automobile. He saw the girl's mother come out of the door as he began running, and he subsequently heard the shot. At the time, he had thought that Fuller had shot the woman. In support of his version of the facts, petitioner offered the testimony of Fuller. The record indicates that Fuller would have testified that petitioner pulled at him and tried to persuade him to leave, and that petitioner ran before Fuller fired the fatal shot.

It is undisputed that Fuller's testimony would have been relevant and material, and that it was vital to the defense. Fuller was the only person other than petitioner who knew exactly who had fired the shotgun and whether petitioner had at the last minute attempted to prevent the shooting. Fuller, however, had been previously convicted of the same murder and sentenced to 50 years in prison, and he was confined in the Dallas County jail. Two Texas statutes provided at the time of the trial in this case that persons charged or convicted as coparticipants in the same crime could not testify for one another, although there was no bar to their testifying for the State. On the basis of these statutes the trial judge sustained the State's objection and refused to allow Fuller to testify. Petitioner's conviction followed, and it was upheld on appeal by the Texas Court of Criminal Appeals. We granted certiorari. We reverse.

I

We have not previously been called upon to decide whether the right of an accused to have compulsory process for obtaining witnesses in his favor, guaranteed in federal trials by the Sixth Amendment, is so fundamental and essential to a fair trial that it is incorporated in the Due Process Clause of the Fourteenth Amendment. At one time, it was thought that the Sixth Amendment had no application to state criminal trials. That view no longer prevails, and in recent years we have increasingly looked to the specific guarantees of the Sixth Amendment to determine whether a state criminal trial was conducted with due process of law. We have held that due process requires that the accused have the assistance of counsel for his defense, that he be confronted with the witnesses against him, and that he have the right to a speedy and public trial.

The right of an accused to have compulsory process for obtaining witnesses in his favor stands on no lesser footing than the other Sixth Amendment rights that we have previously held applicable to the States. This Court had occasion in *In re Oliver*, 333 U.S. 257 (1948), to describe what it regarded as the most basic ingredients of due process of law. It observed that:

> "A person's right to reasonable notice of a charge against him, and an opportunity to be heard in his defense a right to his day in court are basic in

> our system of jurisprudence; and these rights include, as a minimum, a right to examine the witnesses against him, to offer testimony, and to be represented by counsel." 333 U.S., at 273 (footnote omitted).

The right to offer the testimony of witnesses, and to compel their attendance, if necessary, is in plain terms the right to present a defense, the right to present the defendant's version of the facts as well as the prosecution's to the jury so it may decide where the truth lies. Just as an accused has the right to confront the prosecution's witnesses for the purpose of challenging their testimony, he has the right to present his own witnesses to establish a defense. This right is a fundamental element of due process of law.

II

Since the right to compulsory process is applicable in this state proceeding, the question remains whether it was violated in the circumstances of this case. The testimony of Charles Fuller was denied to the defense not because the State refused to compel his attendance, but because a state statute made his testimony inadmissible whether he was present in the courtroom or not. We are thus called upon to decide whether the Sixth Amendment guarantees a defendant the right under any circumstances to put his witnesses on the stand, as well as the right to compel their attendance in court. The resolution of this question requires some discussion of the common-law context in which the Sixth Amendment was adopted.

Joseph Story, in his famous Commentaries on the Constitution of the United States, observed that the right to compulsory process was included in the Bill of Rights in reaction to the notorious common-law rule that in cases of treason or felony the accused was not allowed to introduce witnesses in his defense at all. Although the absolute prohibition of witnesses for the defense had been abolished in England by statute before 1787, the Framers of the Constitution felt it necessary specifically to provide that defendants in criminal cases should be provided the means of obtaining witnesses so that their own evidence, as well as the prosecution's, might be evaluated by the jury.

Despite the abolition of the rule generally disqualifying defense witnesses, the common law retained a number of restrictions on witnesses who were physically and mentally capable of testifying. To the extent that they were applicable, they had the same effect of suppressing the truth that the general proscription had had. Defendants and codefendants were among the large class of witnesses disqualified from testifying on the ground of interest. A party to a civil or criminal case was not allowed to testify on his own behalf for fear that he might be tempted to lie. Although originally the disqualification of a codefendant appears to have been based only on his status as a party to the action, and in some jurisdictions co-indictees were allowed to testify for or against each other if granted separate trials, other jurisdictions came to the view that accomplices or co-indictees were incompetent to testify at least in favor of each other even at separate trials, and in spite of statutes making a defendant competent to testify in his own behalf. It was thought that if two persons charged with the same crime were allowed to testify on behalf of each other, "each would try to swear the other out of the charge." This rule, as well as the other disqualifications for interest, rested on the unstated premises that the right to present witnesses was subordinate to the court's interest in preventing perjury, and that erroneous decisions were best avoided by preventing the jury from hearing any testimony that might be perjured, even if it were the only testimony available on a crucial issue.

The federal courts followed the common-law restrictions for a time, despite the Sixth Amendment. In *United States v. Reid*, 12 How. 361 (1852), the question was whether one of two defendants jointly indicted for murder on the high seas could call the other as a witness. Although this Court expressly recognized that the Sixth Amendment was designed to abolish some of the harsh rules of the common law, particularly including the refusal to allow the defendant in a serious criminal case to present witnesses in his defense, it held that the rules of evidence in the federal courts were those in force in the various States at the time of the passage of the Judiciary Act of 1789, including the disqualification of defendants indicted together. The holding in *United States v. Reid* was not satisfactory to later generations, however, and in 1918 this Court expressly overruled it, refusing to be bound by "the dead hand of the common-law rule of 1789," and taking note of "the conviction of our time that the truth is more likely to be arrived at by hearing the testimony of all persons of competent understanding who may seem to have knowledge of the facts involved in a case, leaving the credit and weight of such testimony to be determined by the jury or by the court." *Rosen v. United States*, 245 U.S. 467, 471 .

Although *Rosen v. United States* rested on nonconstitutional grounds, we believe that its reasoning was required by the Sixth Amendment. In light of the common-law history, and in view of the recognition in the Reid case that the Sixth Amendment was designed in part to make the testimony of a defendant's witnesses admissible on his behalf in court, it could hardly be argued that a State would not violate the clause if it made all defense testimony inadmissible as a matter of procedural law. It is difficult to see how the Constitution is any less violated by arbitrary rules that prevent whole categories of defense witnesses from testifying on the basis of a priori categories that presume them unworthy of belief.

The rule disqualifying an alleged accomplice from testifying on behalf of the defendant cannot even be defended on the ground that it rationally sets apart a group of persons who are particularly likely to commit perjury. The absurdity of the rule is amply demonstrated by the exceptions that have been made to it. For example, the accused accomplice may be called by the prosecution to testify against the defendant. Common sense would suggest that he often has a greater interest in lying in favor of the prosecution rather than against it, especially if he is still awaiting his own trial or sentencing. To think that criminals will lie to save their fellows but not to obtain favors from the prosecution for themselves is indeed to clothe the criminal class with more nobility than one might expect to find in the public at large. Moreover, under the Texas statutes the accused accomplice is no longer disqualified if he is acquitted at his own trial. Presumably, he would then be free to testify on behalf of his comrade, secure in the knowledge that he could incriminate himself as freely as he liked in his testimony, since he could not again be prosecuted for the same offense. The Texas law leaves him free to testify when he has a great incentive to perjury, and bars his testimony in situations where he has a lesser motive to lie.

We hold that the petitioner in this case was denied his right to have compulsory process for obtaining witnesses in his favor because the State arbitrarily denied him the right to put on the stand a witness who was physically and mentally capable of testifying to events that he had personally observed, and whose testimony would have been relevant and material to the defense. The Framers of the Constitution did not intend to commit the futile act of giving to a defendant the right to secure the attendance of witnesses whose testimony he had no right to use. The judgment of conviction must be reversed.

FURTHER CASE LAW, REFLECTIONS, AND QUESTIONS

1. The compulsory process clause guarantees a defendant the right to secure and present the testimony of witnesses on his or her behalf. Should a witness be unwilling to testify, the court will issue a subpoena and compel their testimony.

2. A defendant's right to present evidence is not absolute. Testimony and physical evidence must meet the standards set forth in the jurisdiction's rules of evidence and procedure to be admissible at trial. In *Taylor v. Illinois*, 479 U.S. 1063 (1987), defense counsel deliberately failed to disclose a witness to the prosecution. As a sanction, the trial court precluded the witness from testifying. The Supreme Court affirmed the conviction, finding "[t]he Compulsory Process Clause provides [the defendant] with an effective weapon, but it is a weapon that cannot be used irresponsibly." *Taylor*, 484 U.S. at 411. The Court posited that the adversarial process would be destroyed if either side could simply refuse to follow the basic rules of the Court.

The compulsory process clause grants defendants the right to present evidence and call witnesses in their defense. Logic would seem to indicate that it also allows a defendant to raise whatever defense they desire. As illustrated in the following case, this is not correct.

Holmes v. South Carolina

547 U. S. 319 (2006)

JUSTICE ALITO delivered the opinion of the Court.

This case presents the question whether a criminal defendant's federal constitutional rights are violated by an evidence rule under which the defendant may not introduce proof of third-party guilt if the prosecution has introduced forensic evidence that, if believed, strongly supports a guilty verdict.

I

On the morning of December 31, 1989, 86-year-old Mary Stewart was beaten, raped, and robbed in her home. She later died of complications stemming from her injuries. Petitioner was convicted by a South Carolina jury of murder, first-degree criminal sexual conduct, first-degree burglary, and robbery, and he was sentenced to death. Upon state postconviction review, however, petitioner was granted a new trial.

At the second trial, the prosecution relied heavily on the following forensic evidence:

> (1) [Petitioner's] palm print was found just above the door knob on the interior side of the front door of the victim's house; (2) fibers consistent with a black sweatshirt owned by [petitioner] were found on the victim's bed sheets; (3) matching blue fibers were found on the victim's pink nightgown and on [petitioner's] blue jeans; (4) microscopically consistent fibers were found on the pink nightgown and on [petitioner's] underwear; (5) [petitioner's] underwear contained a mixture of DNA from two individuals, and 99.99% of the population other than [petitioner] and the victim were excluded as contributors to that mixture; and (6) [petitioner's] tank top was found to contain a mixture of [petitioner's] blood and the victim's blood.

In addition, the prosecution introduced evidence that petitioner had been seen near Stewart's home within an hour of the time when, according to the prosecution's evidence, the attack took place.

As a major part of his defense, petitioner attempted to undermine the State's forensic evidence by suggesting that it had been contaminated and that certain law enforcement officers had engaged in a plot to frame him. Petitioner's expert witnesses criticized the procedures used by the police in handling the fiber and DNA evidence and in collecting the fingerprint evidence. Another defense expert provided testimony that petitioner cited as supporting his claim that the palm print had been planted by the police.

Petitioner also sought to introduce proof that another man, Jimmy McCaw White, had attacked Stewart. At a pretrial hearing, petitioner proffered several witnesses who placed White in the victim's neighborhood on the morning of the assault, as well as four other witnesses who testified that White had either acknowledged that petitioner was innocent or had actually admitted to committing the crimes. One witness recounted that when he asked White about the "word. . . on the street" that White was responsible for Stewart's murder, White "put his head down and he raised his head back up and he said, well, you know I like older women." According to this witness, White added that "he did what they say he did" and that he had "no regrets about it at all." Another witness, who had been incarcerated with White, testified that White had admitted to assaulting Stewart, that a police officer had asked the witness to testify falsely against petitioner, and that employees of the prosecutor's office, while soliciting the witness' cooperation, had spoken of manufacturing evidence against petitioner. White testified at the pretrial hearing and denied making the incriminating statements. also provided an alibi for the time of the crime, but another witness refuted his alibi.

The trial court excluded petitioner's third-party guilt evidence citing State v. Gregory, 16 S. E. 2d 532 (1941), which held that such evidence is admissible if it raises a reasonable inference or presumption as to the defendant's own innocence but is not admissible if it merely casts a bare suspicion upon another or raises a conjectural inference as to the commission of the crime by another.

II

State and federal rulemakers have broad latitude under the Constitution to establish rules excluding evidence from criminal trials. This latitude, however, has limits. Whether rooted directly in the Due Process Clause of the Fourteenth Amendment or in the Compulsory Process or Confrontation clauses of the Sixth Amendment, the Constitution guarantees criminal defendants a meaningful opportunity to present a complete defense. This right is abridged by evidence rules that infringe upon a weighty interest of the accused and are arbitrary or 'disproportionate to the purposes they are designed to serve.

This Court's cases contain several illustrations of "arbitrary" rules, *i.e.*, rules that excluded important defense evidence but that did not serve any legitimate interests. In *Washington* v. *Texas* state statutes barred a person who had been charged as a participant in a crime from testifying in defense of another alleged participant unless the witness had been acquitted. As a result, when the defendant in *Washington* was tried for murder, he was precluded from calling as a witness a person who had been charged and previously convicted of committing the same murder.

A similar constitutional violation occurred in *Chambers* v. *Mississippi.* A murder defendant called as a witness a man named McDonald, who had previously confessed to the murder. When McDonald repudiated the confession on the stand, the defendant was denied permission to examine McDonald as an adverse witness based on the State's voucher rule, which barred parties from impeaching their own witnesses.

In addition, because the state hearsay rule did not include an exception for statements against penal interest, the defendant was not permitted to introduce evidence that McDonald had made self-incriminating statements to three other persons.

In *Rock* v. *Arkansas* this Court held that a rule prohibiting hypnotically refreshed testimony was unconstitutional because "[w]holesale inadmissibility of a defendant's testimony is an arbitrary restriction on the right to testify in the absence of clear evidence by the State repudiating the validity of all post-hypnotic recollections."

While the Constitution thus prohibits the exclusion of defense evidence under rules that serve no legitimate purpose or that are disproportionate to the ends that they are asserted to promote, well-established rules of evidence permit trial judges to exclude evidence if its probative value is outweighed by certain other factors such as unfair prejudice, confusion of the issues, or potential to mislead the jury.

In *Gregory*, the South Carolina Supreme Court adopted and applied a rule apparently intended to be of this type, given the court's references to the "applicable rule" from Corpus Juris and American Jurisprudence:

> Evidence offered by accused as to the commission of the crime by another person must be limited to such facts as are inconsistent with his own guilt, and to such facts as raise a reasonable inference or presumption as to his own innocence; evidence which can have (no) other effect than to cast a bare suspicion upon another, or to raise a conjectural inference as to the commission of the crime by another, is not admissible.

Under this rule, the trial judge does not focus on the probative value or the potential adverse effects of admitting the defense evidence of third-party guilt. Instead, the critical inquiry concerns the strength of the prosecution's case: If the prosecution's case is strong enough, the evidence of third-party guilt is excluded even if that evidence, if viewed independently, would have great probative value and even if it would not pose an undue risk of harassment, prejudice, or confusion of the issues.

Interpreted in this way, the rule applied by the State Supreme Court does not rationally serve the end that the *Gregory* rule and its analogues in other jurisdictions were designed to promote, *i.e.*, to focus the trial on the central issues by excluding evidence that has only a very weak logical connection to the central issues. The rule applied in this case appears to be based on the following logic: Where (1) it is clear that only one person was involved in the commission of a particular crime and (2) there is strong evidence that the defendant was the perpetrator, it follows that evidence of third-party guilt must be weak. But this logic depends on an accurate evaluation of the prosecution's proof, and the true strength of the prosecution's proof cannot be assessed without considering challenges to the reliability of the prosecution's evidence. Just because the prosecution's evidence, *if credited*, would provide strong support for a guilty verdict, it does not follow that evidence of third-party guilt has only a weak logical connection to the central issues in the case. And where the credibility of the prosecution's witnesses or the reliability of its evidence is not conceded, the strength of the prosecution's case cannot be assessed without making the sort of factual findings that have traditionally been reserved for the trier of fact and that the South Carolina courts did not purport to make in this case.

The rule applied in this case is no more logical than its converse would be, *i.e.*, a rule barring the prosecution from introducing evidence of a defendant's guilt if the defendant is able to proffer, at a pretrial hearing, evidence that, if believed, strongly supports a verdict of not guilty. In the present case, for example, the petitioner proffered evidence that, if believed, squarely proved that White, not petitioner, was the perpetrator. It would make no sense, however, to hold that this proffer precluded the prosecution from introducing its evidence, including the forensic evidence that, if credited, provided strong proof of the petitioner's guilt.

By evaluating the strength of only one party's evidence, no logical conclusion can be reached regarding the strength of contrary evidence offered by the other side to rebut or cast doubt. Because the rule applied by the State Supreme Court in this case did not heed this point, the rule is "arbitrary" in the sense that it does not rationally serve the end that the *Gregory* rule and other similar third-party guilt rules were designed to further. Nor has the State identified any other legitimate end that the rule serves. It follows that the rule applied in this case by the State Supreme Court violates a criminal defendant's right to have a meaningful opportunity to present a complete defense.

III

For these reasons, we vacate the judgment of the South Carolina Supreme Court and remand the case for further proceedings not inconsistent with this opinion.

FURTHER CASE LAW, REFLECTIONS, AND QUESTIONS

1. How would you summarize the rule established in *Holmes*? Does it make sense to you?
2. What are some implications of the Court's rejection of South Carolina's evidentiary rule that excluded third-party guilt evidence when the prosecution's case was "strong"? How does this ruling affect the discretion of trial courts in managing evidence?
3. Should a defendant's ability to present any evidence or raise any defense they want be unlimited? If not, does *Holmes* strike an appropriate balance?

The Right to Testify

We have seen that the Constitution guarantees criminal defendants the right not to testify when facing trial and the right to present evidence at trial. A third related issue involves whether defendants have a constitutional right to testify in their own defense if they desire.

Notice that the Sixth Amendment does not provide for a right to testify at trial in one's own defense. The following case discusses whether such a right exists, and if so, what limits may be placed on the right.

Rock v. Arkansas

483 U.S. 44 (1987)

JUSTICE BLACKMUN delivered the opinion of the Court.

Petitioner Vickie Lorene Rock was charged with manslaughter in the death of her husband, Frank Rock, on July 2, 1983. That night a fight erupted when Frank refused to let petitioner eat some pizza and prevented her from leaving the apartment to get something else to eat. When police arrived on the scene they found Frank on the floor with a bullet wound in his chest. Petitioner urged the officers to help her husband, and cried to a sergeant, "Please save him" and "Don't let him die."

Because petitioner could not remember the precise details of the shooting, her attorney suggested that she submit to hypnosis in order to refresh her memory. Petitioner was hypnotized twice by Doctor Bettye Back, a licensed neuropsychologist with training in the field of hypnosis. Doctor Back interviewed petitioner for an hour prior to the first hypnosis session, taking notes on petitioner's general history and her recollections of the shooting. Both hypnosis sessions were recorded on tape. Petitioner did not relate any new information during either of the sessions, but, after the hypnosis, she was able to remember that at the time of the incident she had her thumb on the hammer of the gun, but had not held her finger on the trigger. She also recalled that the gun had discharged when her husband grabbed her arm during the scuffle. As a result of the details that petitioner was able to remember about the shooting, her counsel arranged for a gun expert to examine the handgun, a single-action Hawes .22 Deputy Marshal. That inspection revealed that the gun was defective and prone to fire, when hit or dropped, without the trigger's being pulled.

When the prosecutor learned of the hypnosis sessions, he filed a motion to exclude petitioner's testimony. The trial judge held a pretrial hearing on the motion and concluded that no hypnotically refreshed testimony would be admitted. The court issued an order limiting petitioner's testimony to "matters remembered and stated to the examiner prior to being placed under hypnosis." At trial, petitioner introduced testimony by the gun expert, but the court limited petitioner's own description of the events on the day of the shooting to a reiteration of the sketchy information in Doctor

Back's notes. The jury convicted petitioner on the manslaughter charge and she was sentenced to 10 years' imprisonment and a $10,000 fine.

On appeal, the Supreme Court of Arkansas rejected petitioner's claim that the limitations on her testimony violated her right to present her defense. The court concluded that the dangers of admitting this kind of testimony outweigh whatever probative value it may have, and decided to follow the approach of States that have held hypnotically refreshed testimony of witnesses inadmissible per se. Although the court acknowledged that "a defendant's right to testify is fundamental, it ruled that the exclusion of petitioner's testimony did not violate her constitutional rights. Any prejudice or deprivation she suffered was minimal and resulted from her own actions and not by any erroneous ruling of the court.

II

The right to testify on one's own behalf at a criminal trial has sources in several provisions of the Constitution. It is one of the rights that are essential to due process of law in a fair adversary process. The necessary ingredients of the Fourteenth Amendment's guarantee that no one shall be deprived of liberty without due process of law include a right to be heard and to offer testimony: A person's right to reasonable notice of a charge against him, and an opportunity to be heard in his defense — a right to his day in court — are basic in our system of jurisprudence; and these rights include, as a minimum, a right to examine the witnesses against him, to offer testimony, and to be represented by counsel.

The right to testify is also found in the Compulsory Process Clause of the Sixth Amendment, which grants a defendant the right to call "witnesses in his favor," a right that is guaranteed in the criminal courts of the States by the Fourteenth Amendment. Logically included in the accused's right to call witnesses whose testimony is "material and favorable to his defense," is a right to testify himself, should he decide it is in his favor to do so. In fact, the most important witness for the defense in many criminal cases is the defendant himself. There is no justification today for a rule that denies an accused the opportunity to offer his own testimony. Like the truthfulness of other witnesses, the defendant's veracity, which was the concern behind the original common-law rule, can be tested adequately by cross-examination.

Moreover, in *Faretta v. California* the Court recognized that the Sixth Amendment grants to the accused personally the right to make his defense. It is the accused, not counsel, who must be informed of the nature and cause of the accusation, who must be confronted with the witnesses against him, and who must be accorded compulsory process for obtaining witnesses in his favor.

Even more fundamental to a personal defense than the right of self-representation, which was found to be necessarily implied by the structure of the Amendment, is an accused's right to present his own version of events in his own words. A defendant's opportunity to conduct his own defense by calling witnesses is incomplete if he may not present himself as a witness.

The opportunity to testify is also a necessary corollary to the Fifth Amendment's guarantee against compelled testimony. In Harris v. New York, 401 U.S. 222 (1971), the Court stated: "Every criminal defendant is privileged to testify in his own defense, or to refuse to do so." Id., at 225.

III

The question now before the Court is whether a criminal defendant's right to testify may be restricted by a state rule that excludes her post-hypnosis testimony.

Of course, the right to present relevant testimony is not without limitation. The right may, in appropriate cases, bow to accommodate other legitimate interests in the criminal trial process. But restrictions of a defendant's right to testify may not be arbitrary or disproportionate to the purposes they are designed to serve. In applying its evidentiary rules a State must evaluate whether the interests served by a rule justify the limitation imposed on the defendant's constitutional right to testify.

IV

The Arkansas rule enunciated by the state courts does not allow a trial court to consider whether posthypnosis testimony may be admissible in a particular case; it is a per se rule prohibiting the admission at trial of any defendant's hypnotically refreshed testimony on the ground that such testimony is always unreliable. Thus, in Arkansas an accused's testimony is limited to matters that he or she can prove were remembered before hypnosis. This rule operates to the detriment of any defendant who undergoes hypnosis, without regard to the reasons for it, the circumstances under which it took place, or any independent verification of the information it produced.

In this case, the application of that rule had a significant adverse effect on petitioner's ability to testify. It virtually prevented her from describing any of the events that occurred on the day of the shooting, despite corroboration of many of those events by other witnesses. Even more importantly, under the court's rule petitioner was not permitted to describe the actual shooting except in the words contained in Doctor Back's notes. The expert's description of the gun's tendency to misfire would have taken on greater significance if the jury had heard petitioner testify that she did not have her finger on the trigger and that the gun went off when her husband hit her arm.

Although the Arkansas court concluded that any testimony that cannot be proved to be the product of prehypnosis memory is unreliable, many courts have eschewed a per se rule and permit the admission of hypnotically refreshed testimony. Hypnosis by trained physicians or psychologists has been recognized as a valid therapeutic technique since 1958, although there is no generally accepted theory to explain the phenomenon, or even a consensus on a single definition of hypnosis.

The more traditional means of assessing accuracy of testimony also remain applicable in the case of a previously hypnotized defendant. Certain information recalled as a result of hypnosis may be verified as highly accurate by corroborating evidence. Cross-examination, even in the face of a confident defendant, is an effective tool for revealing inconsistencies. Moreover, a jury can be educated to the risks of hypnosis through expert testimony and cautionary instructions. Indeed, it is probably to a defendant's advantage to establish carefully the extent of his memory prior to hypnosis, in order to minimize the decrease in credibility the procedure might introduce.

Arkansas has not justified the exclusion of all of a defendant's testimony that the defendant is unable to prove to be the product of prehypnosis memory. A State's legitimate interest in barring unreliable evidence does not extend to per se exclusions that may be reliable in an individual case. Wholesale inadmissibility of a defendant's testimony is an arbitrary restriction on the right to testify in the absence of clear evidence by the State repudiating the validity of all posthypnosis recollections. The State would be well within its powers if it established guidelines to aid trial courts in the evaluation of posthypnosis testimony and it may be able to show that testimony in a particular case is so unreliable that exclusion is justified. But it has not shown that hypnotically enhanced testimony is always so untrustworthy and so immune to the traditional means of evaluating credibility that it should disable a defendant from presenting her version of the events for which she is on trial.

In this case, the defective condition of the gun corroborated the details petitioner remembered about the shooting. The tape recordings provided some means to evaluate the hypnosis and the trial judge concluded that Doctor Back did not suggest responses with leading questions. Those circumstances present an argument for admissibility of petitioner's testimony in this particular case, an argument that must be considered by the trial court. Arkansas' per se rule excluding all posthypnosis testimony infringes impermissibly on the right of the defendant to testify on his own behalf.

The judgment of the Supreme Court of Arkansas is vacated, and the case is remanded to that court for further proceedings not inconsistent with this opinion.

FURTHER CASE LAW, REFLECTIONS, AND QUESTIONS

1. Notice that a defendant's right to testify is not unlimited. A criminal defendant's testimony is generally governed by the same rules of evidence that apply to the testimony of other witnesses. Does this seem fair?
2. The Court in *Rock* objected to the absolute nature of the Arkansas statute. How could the Arkansas legislature reformulate the rule to have a similar yet constitutional effect?

Confrontation and Cross-Examination

The Sixth Amendment provides that a defendant has a right "to be confronted with the witnesses against him." The **confrontation clause** provides the basis for several rights realized by a criminal defendant. It generally requires that the witnesses who will give testimony against the defendant appear at trial and confront the defendant face to face. As with many other rules, there are exceptions to this policy.

"Face-to-Face" Confrontation

In *Coy v. Iowa*, 487 U.S. 1012 (1988), the Court was asked to recognize an exception to the "face-to-face" testimony contemplated by the confrontation clause in a case involving an Iowa statute that required that children who were the alleged victims of sexual abuse be allowed to testify in criminal trials from behind a screen. Under this arrangement, the defendant would be in the same room as the witness and could hear the witness, but the defendant and the witness could not see each other. The Supreme Court held that the statutory procedure, which applied in all cases of child abuse without regard to the peculiar circumstances of the alleged offense or the particularities of a child witness, violated the defendant's right to a "face-to-face" confrontation with accusing witnesses. While the Court declared the Iowa statute unconstitutional, it stated in dicta that the right to face-to-face confrontation "may give way to other important interests." Two years later, in *Maryland v. Craig*, the Court picked up where it left off in Coy.

Maryland v. Craig

497 U.S. 836 (1990)

JUSTICE O'CONNOR delivered the opinion of the Court.

In October 1986, a Howard County grand jury charged respondent, Sandra Ann Craig, with child abuse, first and second degree sexual offenses, perverted sexual practice, assault, and battery. The named victim in each count was a 6-year-old girl who, from August 1984 to June 1986, had attended a kindergarten and prekindergarten center owned and operated by Craig.

In March 1987, before the case went to trial, the State sought to invoke a Maryland statutory procedure that permits a judge to receive, by one-way closed circuit television, the testimony of a child witness who is alleged to be a victim of child abuse. To invoke the procedure, the trial judge must first "determin[e] that testimony by the child victim in the courtroom will result in the child suffering serious emotional distress such that the child cannot reasonably communicate." Md.Cts. & Jud.Proc. Code Ann. §9–102(a)(1)(ii) (1989). Once the procedure is invoked, the child witness, prosecutor, and defense counsel withdraw to a separate room; the judge, jury, and defendant remain in the courtroom. The child witness is then examined and cross-examined in the separate room, while a video monitor records and displays the witness's testimony to those in the courtroom. During this time, the witness cannot see the defendant. The defendant remains in electronic communication with defense counsel, and objections may be made and ruled on as if the witness were testifying in the courtroom.

In support of its motion invoking the one-way closed circuit television procedure, the State presented expert testimony that the named victim, as well as a number of other children who were alleged to have been sexually abused by Craig, would suffer serious emotional distress such that they could not reasonably communicate if required to testify in the courtroom.

Craig objected to the use of the procedure on Confrontation Clause grounds, but the trial court rejected that contention, concluding that although the statute "take[s] away the right of the defendant to be face to face with his or her accuser," the defendant retains the "essence of the right of confrontation," including the right to observe, cross-examine, and have the jury view the demeanor of the witness. The trial court further found that, "based upon the evidence presented, the testimony of each of these children in a courtroom will result in each child suffering serious emotional distress such that each of these children cannot reasonably communicate." The trial court then found the named victim and three other children competent to testify and accordingly permitted them to testify against Craig via the one-way closed circuit television procedure. The jury convicted Craig on all counts, and the Maryland Court of Special Appeals affirmed the convictions. The Court of Appeals of Maryland reversed and remanded for a new trial.

We granted certiorari to resolve the important Confrontation Clause issues raised by this case.

II

The Confrontation Clause of the Sixth Amendment, made applicable to the States through the Fourteenth Amendment, provides: "In all criminal prosecutions, the accused shall enjoy the right. . . to be confronted with the witnesses against him."

We observed in *Coy v. Iowa* that the Confrontation Clause guarantees the defendant a face-to-face meeting with witnesses appearing before the trier of fact. We have never held, however, that the Confrontation Clause guarantees criminal defendants the absolute right to a face-to-face meeting with witnesses against them at trial. Indeed, in *Coy v. Iowa*, we expressly left for another day the question whether any exceptions exist to the "irreducible literal meaning of the Clause: 'a right to meet face to face all those who appear and give evidence at trial. The procedure challenged in *Coy* involved the placement of a screen that prevented two child witnesses in a child abuse case from seeing the defendant as they testified against him at trial. In holding that the use of this procedure violated the defendant's right to confront witnesses against him, we suggested that any exception to the right would surely be allowed only when necessary to further an important public policy — i.e., only upon a showing of something more than the generalized, "legislatively imposed presumption of trauma" underlying the statute at issue in that case. We concluded that since there had been no individualized findings that these particular witnesses needed special protection, the judgment [in the case before us] could not be sustained by any conceivable exception." Because the trial court in this case made individualized findings that each of the child witnesses needed special protection, this case requires us to decide the question reserved in *Coy*.

The central concern of the Confrontation Clause is to ensure the reliability of the evidence against a criminal defendant by subjecting it to rigorous testing in the context of an adversary proceeding before the trier of fact. The word "confront," after all, also means a clashing of forces or ideas, thus carrying with it the notion of adversariness.

The right guaranteed by the Confrontation Clause includes not only a "personal examination," but also (1) insures that the witness will give his statements under oath — thus impressing him with the seriousness of the matter and guarding against the lie by the possibility of a penalty for perjury; (2) forces the witness to submit to cross-examination, the greatest legal engine ever invented for the discovery of truth; and (3) permits the jury that is to decide the defendant's fate to observe the demeanor of the witness in making his statement, thus aiding the jury in assessing his credibility.

The combined effect of these elements of confrontation — physical presence, oath, cross examination, and observation of demeanor by the trier of fact — serves the purposes of the Confrontation Clause by ensuring that evidence admitted against an accused is reliable and subject to the rigorous adversarial testing that is the norm of Anglo-American criminal proceedings.

For this reason, we have never insisted on an actual face-to-face encounter at trial in every instance in which testimony is admitted against a defendant. Instead, we have repeatedly held that the Clause permits, where necessary, the admission of certain hearsay statements against a defendant despite the defendant's inability to confront the declarant at trial.

In sum, our precedents establish that "the Confrontation Clause reflects a preference for face-to-face confrontation at trial, a preference that must occasionally give way to considerations of public policy and the necessities of the case. We have attempted to harmonize the goal of the Clause — placing limits on the kind of evidence that may be received against a defendant — with a societal interest in accurate fact finding, which may require consideration of out-of-court statements. We have accordingly interpreted the Confrontation Clause in a manner sensitive to its purposes and sensitive to the necessities of trial and the adversary process. Thus, though we reaffirm the importance of face-to-face confrontation with witnesses appearing at trial, we cannot say that such confrontation is an indispensable element of the Sixth Amendment's guarantee of the right to confront one's accusers.

This interpretation of the Confrontation Clause is consistent with our cases holding that other Sixth Amendment rights must also be interpreted in the context of the necessities of trial and the adversary process. We see no reason to treat the face-to-face component of the confrontation right any differently, and indeed we think it would be anomalous to do so.

That the face-to-face confrontation requirement is not absolute does not, of course, mean that it may easily be dispensed with. As we suggested in Coy, our precedents confirm that a defendant's right to confront accusatory witnesses may be satisfied absent a physical, face-to-face confrontation at trial only where denial of such confrontation is necessary to further an important public policy and only where the reliability of the testimony is otherwise assured.

III

Maryland's statutory procedure, when invoked, prevents a child witness from seeing the defendant as he or she testifies against the defendant at trial. We find it significant, however, that Maryland's procedure preserves all of the other elements of the confrontation right: The child witness must be competent to testify and must testify under oath; the defendant retains full opportunity for contemporaneous cross examination; and the judge, jury, and defendant are able to view (albeit by video monitor) the demeanor (and body) of the witness as he or she testifies. Although we are mindful of the many subtle effects face-to-face confrontation may have on an adversary criminal proceeding, the presence of these other elements of confrontation — oath, cross-examination, and observation of the witness's demeanor — adequately ensures that the testimony is both reliable and subject to rigorous adversarial testing in a manner functionally equivalent to that accorded live, in-person testimony. These safeguards of reliability and adversariness render the use of such a procedure a far cry from the undisputed prohibition of the Confrontation Clause. We think these elements of effective confrontation not only permit a defendant to confound and undo the false accuser, or reveal the child coached by a malevolent adult, but may well aid a defendant in eliciting favorable testimony from the child witness. Indeed, to the extent the child witness's testimony may be said to be technically given out of court (though we do not so hold), these assurances of reliability and adversariness are far greater than those required for admission of hearsay testimony under the Confrontation Clause. We are therefore confident that use of the one-way closed circuit television procedure, where necessary to further an important state interest, does not impinge upon the truth-seeking or symbolic purposes of the Confrontation Clause.

The critical inquiry in this case, therefore, is whether use of the procedure is necessary to further an important state interest. The State contends that it has a substantial interest in protecting children who are allegedly victims of child abuse from the trauma of testifying against the alleged perpetrator and that its statutory procedure for receiving testimony from such witnesses is necessary to further that interest.

We conclude today that a State's interest in the physical and psychological well-being of child abuse victims may be sufficiently important to outweigh, at least in some cases, a defendant's right to face his or her accusers in court. That a significant majority of States have enacted statutes to protect child witnesses from the trauma of giving testimony in child abuse cases attests to the widespread belief in the importance of such a public policy.

Given the State's traditional and "'transcendent interest in protecting the welfare of children,'" and buttressed by the growing body of academic literature documenting the psychological trauma suffered by child abuse victims who must testify in court, we will not second-guess the considered judgment of the Maryland Legislature regarding the importance of its interest in protecting child abuse victims from the emotional trauma of testifying. Accordingly, we hold that, if the State makes an adequate showing of necessity, the state interest in protecting child witnesses from the trauma of testifying in a child abuse case is sufficiently important to justify the use of a special procedure that permits a child witness in such cases to testify at trial against a defendant in the absence of face-to-face confrontation with the defendant.

The requisite finding of necessity must of course be a case-specific one: The trial court must hear evidence and determine whether use of the one-way closed circuit television procedure is necessary to protect the welfare of the particular child witness who seeks to testify. The trial court must also find that the child witness would be traumatized, not by the courtroom generally, but by the presence of the defendant. Denial of face-to-face confrontation is not needed to further the state interest in protecting the child witness from trauma unless it is the presence of the defendant that causes the trauma. In other words, if the state interest were merely the interest in protecting child witnesses from courtroom trauma generally, denial of face-to-face confrontation would be unnecessary because the child could be permitted to testify in less intimidating surroundings, albeit with the defendant present. Finally, the trial court must find that the emotional distress suffered by the child witness in the presence of the defendant is more than de minimis, i.e., more than "mere nervousness or excitement or some reluctance to testify."

In sum, we conclude that where necessary to protect a child witness from trauma that would be caused by testifying in the physical presence of the defendant, at least where such trauma would impair the child's ability to communicate, the Confrontation Clause does not prohibit use of a procedure that, despite the absence of face-to-face confrontation, ensures the reliability of the evidence by subjecting it to rigorous adversarial testing and thereby preserves the essence of effective confrontation. Because there is no dispute that the child witnesses in this case testified under oath, were subject to full cross-examination, and were able to be observed by the judge, jury, and defendant as they testified, we conclude that, to the extent that a proper finding of necessity has been made, the admission of such testimony would be consonant with the Confrontation Clause.

IV

The Maryland Court of Appeals held, as we do today, that although face-to-face confrontation is not an absolute constitutional requirement, it may be abridged only where there is a case-specific finding of necessity. Given this latter requirement, the Court of Appeals reasoned that "[t]he question of whether a child is unavailable to testify should not be asked in terms of inability to testify in the ordinary courtroom setting, but in the much narrower terms of the witness's inability to testify in the presence of the accused. "The determinative inquiry required to preclude face-to-face confrontation is the effect of the presence of the defendant on the witness or the witness's testimony." The Court of Appeals accordingly concluded that, as a prerequisite to use of the §9-102 procedure, the Confrontation Clause requires the trial court to make a specific finding that testimony by the child in the courtroom in the presence of the defendant would result in the child suffering serious emotional distress such that the child could not reasonably communicate. This conclusion is consistent with our holding today.

In addition, however, the Court of Appeals interpreted our decision in Coy to impose two subsidiary requirements. First, the court held that §9-102 ordinarily cannot be invoked unless the child witness initially is questioned (either in or outside the courtroom) in the defendant's presence. Second, the court asserted that, before using the one-way television procedure, a trial judge must determine whether a child would suffer "severe emotional distress" if he or she were to testify by two-way closed circuit television.

Reviewing the evidence presented to the trial court in support of the finding required under §9-102(a)(1)(ii), the Court of Appeals determined that "the finding of necessity required to limit the defendant's right of confrontation through invocation of §9-102 was not made here. The Court of Appeals noted that the trial judge "had the benefit only of expert testimony on the ability of the children to communicate; he did not question any of the children himself, nor did he observe any child's behavior on the witness stand before making his ruling. He did not explore any alternatives to the use of one-way closed-circuit television. The Court of Appeals also observed that the testimony in this case was not sharply focused on the effect of the defendant's presence on the child witnesses.

The Court of Appeals appears to have rested its conclusion at least in part on the trial court's failure to observe the children's behavior in the defendant's presence and its failure to explore less restrictive alternatives to the use of the one-way closed circuit television procedure. Although we think such evidentiary requirements could strengthen the grounds for use of protective measures, we decline to establish, as a matter of federal constitutional law, any such categorical evidentiary prerequisites for the use of the one-way television procedure. The trial court in this case, for example, could well have found, on the basis of the expert testimony before it, that testimony by the child witnesses in the courtroom in the defendant's presence "will result in [each] child suffering serious emotional distress such that the child cannot reasonably communicate." So long as a trial court makes such a case-specific finding of necessity, the Confrontation Clause does not prohibit a State from using a one-way closed circuit television procedure for the receipt of testimony by a child witness in a child abuse case. Because the Court of Appeals held that the trial court had not made the requisite finding of necessity under its interpretation of the high threshold required by Coy before §9-102 may be invoked, we cannot be certain whether the Court of Appeals could reach the same conclusion in light of the legal standard we establish today. We therefore vacate the judgment of the Court of Appeals of Maryland and remand the case for further proceedings not inconsistent with this opinion.

FURTHER CASE LAW, REFLECTIONS, AND QUESTIONS

1. What kind of signal about the defendant's guilt or innocence do you think the jury is given by having the child testify in another room while the defendant stays in the courtroom? Do you think such an arrangement adds credibility to the child's claims?
2. Could the Maryland procedure used in *Craig* be applied to other proceedings? Would such a procedure make it easier and less traumatic for adult rape victims to testify? Should the Maryland procedure be limited to child witnesses, or should a court consider each witness on a case-by-case basis?
3. What if a defendant charged with child abuse in Maryland wants to act as his own attorney? Should he be allowed to conduct face-to-face cross-examination of the child victims despite evidence that such a confrontation would be detrimental to the children? See *Fields v. Murray*, 49 F.3d 1024 (4th Cir. 1995), cert. denied, 516 U.S. 884 (1995).

Cross-Examination as a Means of Confrontation

The primary and unquestionably most important purpose behind the confrontation clause is protecting the defendant's right to cross-examine adverse witnesses. **Cross-examination** allows the opposing party to test the reliability and credibility of witnesses and helps assure the "accuracy of the truth-determining process. "It is, indeed, an essential and fundamental requirement for the kind of fair trial which is this country's constitutional goal." *Chambers v. Mississippi*, 410 U.S. 284, 295 (1973).

Despite being of critical importance, the right to confront witnesses through cross-examination is not absolute. The scope and limits of this right was at issue in *Davis v. Alaska*.

Davis v. Alaska

415 U.S. 308 (1974)

MR. CHIEF JUSTICE BURGER delivered the opinion of the Court.

When the Polar Bar in Anchorage closed in the early morning hours of February 16, 1970, well over a thousand dollars in cash and checks was in the bar's Mosler safe. About midday, February 16, it was discovered that the bar had been broken into and the safe, about two feet square and weighing several hundred pounds, had been removed from the premises.

Later that afternoon the Alaska State Troopers received word that a safe had been discovered about 26 miles outside Anchorage near the home of Jess Straight and his family. Richard Green, Jess Straight's stepson, told investigating troopers on the scene that at about noon on February 16 he had seen and spoken with two Negro men standing alongside a late-model metallic blue Chevrolet sedan near where the safe was later discovered. The next day Anchorage police investigators brought him to the police station where Green was given six photographs of adult Negro males. Green identified the photograph of petitioner as that of one of the men he had encountered the day before and described to the police. Petitioner was arrested the next day, February 18. On February 19, Green picked petitioner out of a lineup of seven Negro males.

Green was a crucial witness for the prosecution. He testified at trial that while on an errand for his mother he confronted two men standing beside a late-model metallic blue Chevrolet, parked on a road near his family's house. On his return from the errand Green again passed the two men and he saw the man with whom he had had the conversation standing at the rear of the car with "something like a crowbar" in his hands. Green identified petitioner at the trial as the man with the "crowbar." The safe was discovered later that afternoon at the point, according to Green, where the Chevrolet had been parked.

Before testimony was taken at the trial of petitioner, the prosecutor moved for a protective order to prevent any reference to Green's juvenile record by the defense in the course of cross examination. At the time of the trial and at the time of the events Green testified to, Green was on probation by order of a juvenile court after having been adjudicated a delinquent for burglarizing two cabins. Green was 16 years of age at the time of the Polar Bar burglary but had turned 17 prior to trial.

In opposing the protective order, petitioner's counsel made it clear that he would not introduce Green's juvenile adjudication as a general impeachment of Green's character as a truthful person but, rather, to show specifically that at the same time Green was assisting the police in identifying petitioner he was on probation for burglary. From this petitioner would seek to show — or at least argue — that Green acted out of fear of concern of possible jeopardy to his probation. Not only might Green have made a hasty and faulty identification of petitioner to shift suspicion away from himself as one who robbed the Polar Bar, but Green might have been subject to undue pressure from the police and made his identifications under fear of possible probation revocation. Green's record would be revealed only as necessary to probe Green for bias and prejudice and not generally to call Green's good character into question.

The trial court granted the motion for a protective order, relying on Alaska Rule of Children's Procedure 23, and Alaska Stat. §47.10.080(g) (1971).

Although prevented from revealing that Green had been on probation for the juvenile delinquency adjudication for burglary at the same time that he originally identified petitioner, counsel for petitioner did his best to expose Green's state of mind at the time Green discovered that a stolen safe had been discovered near his home. Green denied that he was upset or uncomfortable about the discovery of the safe. He claimed not to have been worried about any suspicions the police might have been expected to harbor against him, though Green did admit that it crossed his mind that the police might have thought he had something to do with the crime.

Defense counsel cross-examined Green in part as follows:

> "Q. Did that thought ever enter your mind that you — that the police might think that you were somehow connected with this?
>
> "A. No, it didn't really bother me, no.
>
> "Q. Well, but
>
> "A. I mean, you know, it didn't — it didn't come into my mind as worrying me, you know.
>
> "Q. That really wasn't — wasn't my question, Mr. Green. Did you think that — not whether it worried you so much or not, but did you feel that there was a possibility that the police might somehow think that you had something?
>
> "A. That came across my mind, yes sir.
>
> "Q. That did cross your mind?
>
> "A. Yes.
>
> "Q. So as I understand it you went down to the — you drove in with the police in — in their car from mile 25, Glenn Highway down to the city police station?

"A. Yes, sir.

"Q. And then went into the investigators' room with Investigator Gray and Investigator Weaver?

"A. Yeah.

"Q. And they started asking you questions about — about the incident, is that correct?

"A. Yeah.

"Q. Had you ever been questioned like that before by any law enforcement officers?

"A. No.

"MR. RIPLEY: I'm going to object to this, Your Honor, it's a carry-on with rehash of the same thing. He's attempting to raise in the jury's mind.

"THE COURT: I'll sustain the objection."

Since defense counsel was prohibited from making inquiry as to the witness's being on probation under a juvenile court adjudication, Green's protestations of unconcern over possible police suspicion that he might have had a part in the Polar Bar burglary and his categorical denial of ever having been the subject of any similar law-enforcement interrogation went unchallenged. The tension between the right of confrontation and the State's policy of protecting the witness with a juvenile record is particularly evident in the final answer given by the witness. Since it is probable that Green underwent some questioning by police when he was arrested for the burglaries on which his juvenile adjudication of delinquency rested, the answer can be regarded as highly suspect at the very least. The witness was in effect asserting, under protection of the trial court's ruling, a right to give a questionably truthful answer to a cross-examiner pursuing a relevant line of inquiry; it is doubtful whether the bold "No" answer would have been given by Green absent a belief that he was shielded from traditional cross-examination. It would be difficult to conceive of a situation more clearly illustrating the need for cross-examination.

The Alaska Supreme Court affirmed petitioner's conviction, concluding that since "our reading of the trial transcript convinces us that counsel for the defendant was able adequately to question the youth in considerable detail concerning the possibility of bias or motive." 499 P.2d 1025, 1036 (1972). Although the court admitted that Green's denials of any sense of anxiety or apprehension upon the safe's being found close to his home were possibly self-serving, "The suggestion was nonetheless brought to the attention of the jury, and that body was afforded the opportunity to observe the demeanor of the youth and pass on his credibility." The court concluded that, in light of the indirect references permitted, there was no error.

(2)

The Sixth Amendment to the Constitution guarantees the right of an accused in a criminal prosecution "to be confronted with the witnesses against him." This right is secured for defendants in state as well as federal criminal proceedings under *Pointer v. Texas*, 380 U.S. 400 (1965). Confrontation means more than being allowed to confront the witness physically. "Our cases construing the (confrontation) clause hold that a primary interest secured by it is the right of cross-examination." Professor Wigmore stated:

> The main and essential purpose of confrontation is to secure for the opponent the opportunity of cross-examination. The opponent demands confrontation, not for the idle purpose of gazing upon the witness, or of being gazed upon by him, but for the purpose of cross-examination, which cannot be had except by the direct and personal putting of questions and obtaining immediate answers. 5 J. Wigmore, Evidence §1395, p. 123 (3d ed 1940).

Cross-examination is the principal means by which the believability of a witness and the truth of his testimony are tested. Subject always to the broad discretion of a trial judge to preclude repetitive and unduly harassing interrogation, the cross-examiner is not only permitted to delve into the witness's story to test the witness's perceptions and memory, but the cross-examiner has traditionally been allowed to impeach, i.e., discredit, the witness. The partiality of a witness is subject to exploration at trial and is "always relevant as discrediting the witness and affecting the weight of his testimony." 3A J. Wigmore, Evidence §940, p. 775 (Chadbourn rev. 1970).

In the instant case, defense counsel sought to show the existence of possible bias and prejudice of Green, causing him to make a faulty initial identification of petitioner, which in turn could have affected his later in-court identification of petitioner.

We cannot speculate as to whether the jury, as sole judge of the credibility of a witness, would have accepted this line of reasoning had counsel been permitted to fully present it. But we do conclude that the jurors were entitled to have the benefit of the defense theory before them so that they could make an informed judgment as to the weight to place on Green's testimony which provided a crucial link in the proof of petitioner's act. The accuracy and truthfulness of Green's testimony were key elements in the State's case against petitioner. The claim of bias which the defense sought to develop was admissible to afford a basis for an inference of undue pressure because of Green's vulnerable status as a probationer, as well as of Green's possible concern that he might be a suspect in the investigation.

We cannot accept the Alaska Supreme Court's conclusion that the cross-examination that was permitted defense counsel was adequate to develop the issue of bias properly to the jury. While counsel was permitted to ask Green whether he was biased, counsel was unable to make a record from which to argue why Green might have been biased or otherwise lacked that degree of impartiality expected of a witness at trial. On the basis of the limited cross-examination that was permitted, the jury might well have thought that defense counsel was engaged in a speculative and baseless line of attack on the credibility of an apparently blameless witness or, as the prosecutor's objection put it, a "rehash" of prior cross-examination. On these facts it seems clear to us that to make any such inquiry effective, defense counsel should have been permitted to expose to the jury the facts from which jurors, as the sole triers of fact and credibility, could appropriately draw inferences relating to the reliability of the witness. Petitioner was thus denied the right of effective cross-examination which "would be constitutional error of the first magnitude and no amount of showing of want of prejudice would cure it."

(3)

The claim is made that the State has an important interest in protecting the anonymity of juvenile offenders and that this interest outweighs any competing interest this petitioner might have in cross-examining Green about his being on probation.

We do not and need not challenge the State's interest as a matter of its own policy in the administration of criminal justice to seek to preserve the anonymity of a juvenile offender. Here, however, petitioner sought to introduce evidence of Green's probation for the purpose of suggesting that Green was biased and, therefore, that his testimony was either not to be believed in his identification of petitioner or at least very carefully considered in that light. Serious damage to the strength of the State's case would have been a real possibility had petitioner been allowed to pursue this line of inquiry. In this setting we conclude that the right of confrontation is paramount to the State's policy of protecting a juvenile offender. Whatever temporary embarrassment might result to Green or his family by disclosure of his juvenile record — if the prosecution insisted on using him to make its case — is outweighed by petitioner's right to probe into the influence of possible bias in the testimony of a crucial identification witness.

The State's policy interest in protecting the confidentiality of a juvenile offender's record cannot require yielding such a vital constitutional right as the effective cross-examination for bias of an adverse witness. The State could have protected Green from exposure of his juvenile adjudication in these circumstances by refraining from using him to make out its case; the State cannot, consistent with the right of confrontation, require the petitioner to bear the full burden of vindicating the State's interest in the secrecy of juvenile criminal records. The judgment affirming petitioner's convictions of burglary and grand larceny is reversed and the case is remanded for further proceedings not inconsistent with this opinion.

Reversed and remanded.

FURTHER CASE LAW, REFLECTIONS, AND QUESTIONS

1. Cross-examination is a key aspect of the right to confront witnesses. The right to cross-examine helps distinguish the American criminal justice system from many others. An adversarial system assumes that effective cross-examination is the best way to test a witness's veracity and accuracy of recollection. Since this right is designed to help promote the truth-seeking process, attorneys generally are given great latitude in cross-examining witnesses.
2. How does *Davis v. Alaska* address the tension between a fair trial and protecting the privacy of juvenile records? Is the balancing performed by the Court appropriate?
3. In your opinion, are there any circumstances in which the right to confront and cross-examine witnesses should be limited? If so, what might those circumstances be, and how should courts handle such situations?

Hearsay and the Right of Confrontation

Hearsay is an out-of-court statement being introduced to prove the matter asserted. As a rule, hearsay is not admissible as evidence against a defendant in a criminal trial. This is because the defendant has no opportunity to cross-examine (confront) the witness who made the statement. Nor, in most cases, will the hearsay statement have been made under oath. Furthermore, because the witness does not appear in court, the jury cannot observe the witness's demeanor, or the "cut of his jib," and make corresponding judgments about his or her credibility.

The prosecution, however, is not forbidden in all cases from using hearsay statements against a defendant. Numerous exceptions exist to the "hearsay rule." In *Ohio v. Roberts*, 448 U.S. 56 (1980), the Supreme Court adopted the "rule of necessity" for the introduction of hearsay statements against a criminal defendant who challenged the admission of out-of-court statements on Sixth Amendment grounds. Under this rule, hearsay testimony is admissible if there is a showing that the witness is unavailable and that the statement bears adequate "indicia of reliability." Under this standard, victim statements, forensic reports, and many other types of hearsay statements were found to be admissible at trial because the trial judge found them to be reliable.

In 2004, the Supreme Court overruled Roberts and set forth a new standard for protecting a defendant's confrontation rights in matters involving out-of-court statements.

Crawford v. Washington

541 U.S. 36 (2004)

JUSTICE SCALIA delivered the opinion of the Court

On August 5, 1999, Kenneth Lee was stabbed at his apartment. Police arrested petitioner later that night. After giving petitioner and his wife *Miranda* warnings, detectives interrogated each of them twice. Petitioner eventually confessed that he and Sylvia had gone in search of Lee because he was upset over an earlier incident in which Lee had tried to rape her. The two had found Lee at his apartment, and a fight ensued in which Lee was stabbed in the torso and petitioner's hand was cut.

Petitioner gave the following account of the fight:

> "Q. Okay. Did you ever see anything in [Lee's] hands?
>
> "A. I think so, but I'm not positive.
>
> "Q. Okay, when you think so, what do you mean by that?
>
> "A. I coulda swore I seen him goin' for somethin' before, right before everything happened. He was like reachin,' fiddlin' around down here and stuff... and I just... I don't know, I think, this is just a possibility, but I think, I think that he pulled somethin' out and I grabbed for it and that's how I got cut... but I'm not positive. I, I, my mind goes blank when things like this happen. I mean, I just, I remember things wrong, I remember things that just doesn't, don't make sense to me later."

Sylvia generally corroborated petitioner's story about the events leading up to the fight, but her account of the fight itself was arguably different–particularly with respect to whether Lee had drawn a weapon before petitioner assaulted him:

> "Q. Did Kenny do anything to fight back from this assault?
>
> "A. (pausing) I know he reached into his pocket... or somethin'... I don't know what.
>
> "Q. After he was stabbed?
>
> "A. He saw Michael coming up. He lifted his hand... his chest open, he might [have] went to go strike his hand out or something and then (inaudible).
>
> "Q. Okay, you, you gotta speak up.
>
> "A. Okay, he lifted his hand over his head maybe to strike Michael's hand down or something and then he put his hands in his... put his right hand in his right pocket... took a step back... Michael proceeded to stab him... then his hands were like... how do you explain this... open arms... with his hands open and he fell down... and we ran (describing subject holding hands open, palms toward assailant).

"Q. Okay when he's standing there with his open hands, you're talking about Kenny, correct?

"A. Yeah, after, after the fact, yes.

"Q. Did you see anything in his hands at that point?

"A. (pausing) um (no)."

The State charged petitioner with assault and attempted murder. At trial, he claimed self-defense. Sylvia did not testify because of the state marital privilege, which generally bars a spouse from testifying without the other spouse's consent. In Washington, this privilege does not extend to a spouse's out-of-court statements admissible under a hearsay exception, so the State sought to introduce Sylvia's tape-recorded statements to the police as evidence that the stabbing was not in self-defense. Noting that Sylvia had admitted she led petitioner to Lee's apartment and thus had facilitated the assault, the State invoked the hearsay exception for statements against penal interest.

Petitioner countered that, state law notwithstanding, admitting the evidence would violate his federal constitutional right to be "confronted with the witnesses against him." According to our description of that right in *Ohio v. Roberts,* 448 U.S. 56 (1980), it does not bar admission of an unavailable witness's statement against a criminal defendant if the statement bears "adequate 'indicia of reliability.'" To meet that test, evidence must either fall within a "firmly rooted hearsay exception" or bear "particularized guarantees of trustworthiness." The trial court here admitted the statement on the latter ground, offering several reasons why it was trustworthy: Sylvia was not shifting blame but rather corroborating her husband's story that he acted in self-defense or "justified reprisal"; she had direct knowledge as an eyewitness; she was describing recent events; and she was being questioned by a "neutral" law enforcement officer. The prosecution played the tape for the jury and relied on it in **closing [argument]**, arguing that it was "damning evidence" that "completely refutes [petitioner's] claim of self-defense." The jury convicted petitioner of assault.

The Washington Court of Appeals reversed. It applied a nine-factor test to determine whether Sylvia's statement bore particularized guarantees of trustworthiness, and noted several reasons why it did not: The statement contradicted one she had previously given; it was made in response to specific questions; and at one point she admitted she had shut her eyes during the stabbing. The court considered and rejected the State's argument that Sylvia's statement was reliable because it coincided with petitioner's to such a degree that the two "interlocked." The court determined that, although the two statements agreed about the events leading up to the stabbing, they differed on the issue crucial to petitioner's self-defense claim: "[Petitioner's] version asserts that Lee may have had something in his hand when he stabbed him; but Sylvia's version has Lee grabbing for something only after he has been stabbed."

The Washington Supreme Court reinstated the conviction, unanimously concluding that, although Sylvia's statement did not fall under a firmly rooted hearsay exception, it bore guarantees of trustworthiness: " '[W]hen a codefendant's confession is virtually identical [to, *i.e.*, interlocks with,] that of a defendant, it may be deemed reliable.'" The court explained: "Although the Court of Appeals concluded that the statements were contradictory, upon closer inspection they appear to overlap. Both of the Crawfords' statements indicate that Lee was possibly grabbing for a weapon, but they are equally unsure when this event may have taken place. They are also equally unsure how Michael received the cut on his hand, leading the court to question when, if ever, Lee possessed a weapon. In this respect they overlap.

We granted certiorari to determine whether the State's use of Sylvia's statement violated the Confrontation Clause.

The Sixth Amendment's Confrontation Clause provides that, "[i]n all criminal prosecutions, the accused shall enjoy the right to be confronted with the witnesses against him." We have held that this bedrock procedural guarantee applies to both federal and state prosecutions. As noted above, *Roberts* says that an unavailable witness's out-of-court statement may be admitted so long as it has adequate indicia of reliability–*i.e.*, falls within a "firmly rooted hearsay exception" or bears "particularized guarantees of trustworthiness." Petitioner argues that this test strays from the original meaning of the Confrontation Clause and urges us to reconsider it.

This history supports two inferences about the meaning of the Sixth Amendment.

A

First, the principal evil at which the Confrontation Clause was directed was the civil-law mode of criminal procedure, and particularly its use of *ex parte* examinations as evidence against the accused.

Accordingly, we once again reject the view that the Confrontation Clause applies of its own force only to in-court testimony, and that its application to out-of-court statements introduced at trial depends upon "the law of Evidence for the time being." Leaving the regulation of out-of-court statements to the law of evidence would render the Confrontation Clause powerless to prevent even the most flagrant inquisitorial practices.

The text of the Confrontation Clause applies to "witnesses" against the accused–in other words, those who "bear testimony." "Testimony," in turn, is typically "[a] solemn declaration or affirmation made for the purpose of establishing or proving some fact."

Various formulations of this core class of "testimonial" statements exist: "*ex parte* in-court testimony or its functional equivalent–that is, material such as affidavits, custodial examinations, prior testimony that the defendant was unable to cross-examine, or similar pretrial statements that declarants would reasonably expect to be used prosecutorially"; "extrajudicial statements contained in formalized testimonial materials, such as affidavits, depositions, prior testimony, or confessions," *White v. Illinois*, 502 U.S. 346, 365 (1992) (Thomas, J., joined by Scalia, J., concurring in part and concurring in judgment); "statements that were made under circumstances which would lead an objective witness reasonably to believe that the statement would be available for use at a later trial." These formulations all share a common nucleus and then define the Clause's coverage at various levels of abstraction around it. Regardless of the precise articulation, some statements qualify under any definition–for example, *ex parte* testimony at a preliminary hearing.

Statements taken by police officers in the course of interrogations are also testimonial under even a narrow standard.

B

The historical record also supports a second proposition: that the Framers would not have allowed admission of testimonial statements of a witness who did not appear at trial unless he was unavailable to testify, and the defendant had had a prior opportunity for cross-examination. The text of the Sixth Amendment does not suggest any open-ended exceptions from the confrontation requirement to be developed by the courts. Rather, the "right to be confronted with the witnesses against him," is most naturally read as a reference to the right of confrontation at common law, admitting only those exceptions established at the time of the founding.

We do not read the historical sources to say that a prior opportunity to cross-examine was merely a sufficient, rather than a necessary, condition for admissibility of testimonial statements. They suggest that this requirement was dispositive, and not merely one of several ways to establish reliability.

IV

Our case law has been largely consistent with these two principles. Our leading early decision, for example, involved a deceased witness's prior trial testimony. Mattox v. United States, 156 U.S. 237 (1895). In allowing the statement to be admitted, we relied on the fact that the defendant had had, at the first trial, an adequate opportunity to confront the witness: "The substance of the constitutional protection is preserved to the prisoner in the advantage he has once had of seeing the witness face to face, and of subjecting him to the ordeal of a cross-examination. This, the law says, he shall under no circumstances be deprived of."

Our later cases conform to Mattox's holding that prior trial or preliminary hearing testimony is admissible only if the defendant had an adequate opportunity to cross-examine. Even where the defendant had such an opportunity, we excluded the testimony where the government had not established unavailability of the witness. We similarly excluded accomplice confessions where the defendant had no opportunity to cross-examine.

Our cases have remained faithful to the Framers' understanding: Testimonial statements of witnesses absent from trial have been admitted only where the declarant is unavailable, and only where the defendant has had a prior opportunity to cross-examine.

V

A

Where testimonial statements are involved, we do not think the Framers meant to leave the Sixth Amendment's protection to the vagaries of the rules of evidence, much less to amorphous notions of "reliability." Certainly none of the authorities discussed above acknowledges any general reliability exception to the common-law rule. Admitting statements deemed reliable by a judge is fundamentally at odds with the right of confrontation. To be sure, the Clause's ultimate goal is to ensure reliability of evidence, but it is a procedural rather than a substantive guarantee. It commands, not that evidence be reliable, but that reliability be assessed in a particular manner: by testing in the crucible of cross-examination. The Clause thus reflects a judgment, not only about the desirability of reliable evidence (a point on which there could be little dissent), but about how reliability can best be determined.

The *Roberts* test allows a jury to hear evidence, untested by the adversary process, based on a mere judicial determination of reliability. It thus replaces the constitutionally prescribed method of assessing reliability with a wholly foreign one. In this respect, it is very different from exceptions to the Confrontation Clause that make no claim to be a surrogate means of assessing reliability. For example, the rule of forfeiture by wrongdoing (which we accept) extinguishes confrontation claims on essentially equitable grounds; it does not purport to be an alternative means of determining reliability.

Dispensing with confrontation because testimony is obviously reliable is akin to dispensing with jury trial because a defendant is obviously guilty. This is not what the Sixth Amendment prescribes.

B

The legacy of *Roberts* in other courts vindicates the Framers' wisdom in rejecting a general reliability exception. The framework is so unpredictable that it fails to provide meaningful protection from even core confrontation violations.

Reliability is an amorphous, if not entirely subjective, concept. There are countless factors bearing on whether a statement is reliable; the nine-factor balancing test applied by the Court of Appeals below is representative. The unpardonable vice of the *Roberts* test, however, is not its unpredictability, but its demonstrated capacity to admit core testimonial statements that the Confrontation Clause plainly meant to exclude.

C

Roberts' failings were on full display in the proceedings below. Sylvia Crawford made her statement while in police custody, herself a potential suspect in the case. Indeed, she had been told that whether she would be released "depend[ed] on how the investigation continues." In response to often leading questions from police detectives, she implicated her husband in Lee's stabbing and at least arguably undermined his self-defense claim. Despite all this, the trial court admitted her statement, listing several reasons why it was reliable. In its opinion reversing, the Court of Appeals listed several *other* reasons why the statement was *not* reliable. Finally, the State Supreme Court relied exclusively on the interlocking character of the statement and disregarded every other factor the lower courts had considered. The case is thus a self-contained demonstration of *Roberts'* unpredictable and inconsistent application.

Each of the courts also made assumptions that cross-examination might well have undermined. The trial court, for example, stated that Sylvia Crawford's statement was reliable because she was an eyewitness with direct knowledge of the events. But Sylvia at one point told the police that she had "shut [her] eyes and. . . didn't really watch" part of the fight, and that she was "in shock." The trial court also buttressed its reliability finding by claiming that Sylvia was "being questioned by law enforcement, and, thus, the [questioner] is neutral to her and not someone who would be inclined to advance her interests and shade her version of the truth unfavorably toward the defendant." The Framers would be astounded to learn that *ex parte* testimony could be admitted against a criminal defendant because it was elicited by "neutral" government officers. But even if the court's assessment of the officer's motives was accurate, it says nothing about Sylvia's perception of her situation. Only cross-examination could reveal that.

The State Supreme Court gave dispositive weight to the interlocking nature of the two statements–that they were both ambiguous as to when and whether Lee had a weapon. The court's claim that the two statements were *equally* ambiguous is hard to accept. Petitioner's statement is ambiguous only in the sense that he had lingering doubts about his recollection: "A. I coulda swore I seen him goin' for somethin' before, right before everything happened. . . . [B]ut I'm not positive." Sylvia's statement, on the other hand, is truly inscrutable, since the key timing detail was simply assumed in the leading question she was asked: "Q. Did Kenny do anything to fight back from this assault?" Moreover, Sylvia specifically said Lee had nothing in his hands after he was stabbed, while petitioner was not asked about that.

The prosecutor obviously did not share the court's view that Sylvia's statement was ambiguous — he called it "damning evidence" that "completely refutes [petitioner's] claim of self-defense." We have no way of knowing whether the jury agreed with the prosecutor or the court. Far from obviating the need for cross-examination, the "interlocking" ambiguity of the two statements made it all the more imperative that they be tested to tease out the truth.

Where nontestimonial hearsay is at issue, it is wholly consistent with the Framers' design to afford the States flexibility in their development of hearsay law — as does *Roberts*, and as would an approach that exempted such statements from Confrontation Clause scrutiny altogether. Where testimonial evidence is at issue, however, the Sixth Amendment demands what the common law required: unavailability and a prior opportunity for cross-examination. We leave for another day any effort to spell out a comprehensive definition of "testimonial." Whatever else the term covers, it applies at a minimum to prior testimony at a preliminary hearing, before a grand jury, or at a former trial; and to police interrogations. These are the modern practices with closest kinship to the abuses at which the Confrontation Clause was directed.

In this case, the State admitted Sylvia's testimonial statement against petitioner, despite the fact that he had no opportunity to cross-examine her. That alone is sufficient to make out a violation of the Sixth Amendment. *Roberts* notwithstanding, we decline to mine the record in search of indicia of reliability. Where testimonial statements are at issue, the only indicium of reliability sufficient to satisfy constitutional demands is the one the Constitution actually prescribes: confrontation.

The judgment of the Washington Supreme Court is reversed, and the case is remanded for further proceedings not inconsistent with this opinion.

FURTHER CASE LAW, REFLECTIONS, AND QUESTIONS

1. Note that the Confrontation Clause is not implicated if a statement is non-testimonial. Accordingly, in considering whether an out-of-court statement (hearsay) may be used against a defendant in a criminal trial, you should first consider whether the statement is testimonial. In *Crawford*, the Court did not explicitly define what makes a statement testimonial. Instead, it stated that formal statements made for the purpose of proving a fact and which are likely to be used by the prosecution at trial are testimonial. Several years after *Crawford*, the Court clarified what differentiates testimonial and non-testimonial statements.

   > "Statements are nontestimonial when made in the course of police interrogation under circumstances objectively indicating that the primary purpose of the interrogation is to enable police assistance to meet an ongoing emergency. They are testimonial when the circumstances objectively indicate that there is no such ongoing emergency, and that the primary purpose of the interrogation is to establish or prove past events potentially relevant to later criminal prosecution." *Davis v. Washington*, 547 U.S. 813, 822 (2006).

Under the above definition, a 911 call made during the commission of an assault or an ongoing emergency is not testimonial, while responses to questions posed by the police or other government officials after the emergency has subsided are testimonial and subject to the Crawford restrictions. The analysis outlined in *Davis* was reaffirmed by the Court in *Michigan v. Bryant*, 562 U.S. 344 (2011).

2. While *Crawford* and *Davis* involved verbal statements made by a witness in response to questioning, testimonial evidence may also consist of written reports prepared by forensic scientists as part of a criminal investigation. In *Melendez-Diaz v. Massachusetts*, 557 U.S. 305 (2009), the Supreme Court held that forensic science reports, such as those prepared as part of the testing of substances, particularly narcotics, are part of the "core class of testimonial statements." Accordingly, for such reports to be admissible at trial, the person who conducts the forensic tests and prepares the report must appear in court and be subjected to cross-examination by the defense. Before *Crawford,* such reports were routinely admitted into evidence without the testimony of the forensic analyst because they fit under a recognized hearsay exception and were deemed reliable as required by *Ohio v. Roberts*. It was widely feared that requiring the individual analyst who conducted the tests to appear at trial and be available to be cross-examined for dozens of trials a year would have profound impacts on the criminal court system.

3. In June 2011, the Court expounded on the requirements announced in *Melendez-Diaz v. Massachusetts. Bullcoming v. New Mexico*, 564 U.S. 647 (2011), involved a prosecution for aggravated driving while intoxicated. At trial, the prosecution submitted into evidence the certified blood analysis report that indicated the defendant was drunk. Rather than have the crime analyst who conducted the blood-alcohol analysis and prepared the report testify, the prosecution had the analyst's supervisor authenticate the report. The evidence was admitted and Bullcoming was convicted.

   The Supreme Court reversed the conviction. The Court held that Bullcoming's confrontation right had been violated because prosecutors were allowed to offer a crime lab report analyzing Bullcoming's blood sample, without having the lab analyst who did the tests and prepared the report testify. The Court held that producing such a substitute, or "surrogate," witness is insufficient to satisfy the Sixth Amendment confrontation right.

4. Even when a prior statement is undoubtedly testimonial in nature, it might still be used against a defendant if the unavailability of the witness is due to the defendant's acts of intimidation or violence directed at a witness to prevent the witness from testifying. In such cases, it is said that the defendant forfeits his right to cross-examine the witness. In *Giles v. California,* 544 U.S 353, (2008), the Supreme Court considered the limits of the forfeiture doctrine and whether a defendant who kills a witness who had made prior statements that could be used

against the defendant at trial has the right to raise a Confrontation Clause claim to keep the witnesses hearsay statement from being admitted at trial.

Dwayne Giles was prosecuted for shooting and killing his girlfriend. At trial, Giles claimed self-defense. To rebut this claim, the prosecution introduced evidence that several weeks before her death, she had called the police to report an incident of domestic violence. Evidence was presented that the victim, "who was crying when she spoke, told the officer that Giles had accused her of having an affair and that after the two began to argue, Giles grabbed her by the shirt, lifted her off the floor, and began to choke her." *Giles* at 357. She also told the police that Giles punched her, pulled a knife on her, and threatened to kill her. Generally, the victim's statements to the police would be inadmissible as out-of-court hearsay, but the statements were admitted due to an exception to the hearsay rule, which allows the admission of out-of-court statements by a witness when the defendant has made that witness unavailable to testify at trial. The jury rejected the defendant's claim of self-defense and found him guilty of murder.

Giles appealed, arguing that the admission of the victim's statements, which were testimonial hearsay, violated his right to confrontation since he did not have the chance to cross-examine her. The government argued that the statements were properly admitted into evidence under the forfeiture doctrine. Since Giles had made the victim unavailable by killing her, under the doctrine of forfeiture, he could not now claim his confrontation rights were violated by having her prior statements presented to the jury.

The United States Supreme Court held that for the forfeiture doctrine to apply, in performing an act that made a witness unavailable to testify, the defendant must have acted with the specific intent to prevent the witness from testifying. The Court found that while Giles may have acted with the intent to harm the victim, this was not done to prevent her from testifying. Accordingly, since he had not had the opportunity to cross-examine the victim, under the rule established in *Crawford*, the victim's statements to the police about the prior domestic violence should not have been admitted at trial, and their admission violated Giles' rights under the Confrontation Clause.

The Defendant's Right to Be Present During the Trial

The Confrontation Clause of the Sixth Amendment implicitly guarantees a defendant's right to be present at his or her trial. As with most constitutional rights, the right to be present at trial is not absolute. If it were, a defendant could not be placed on trial if she refused to go to court or disrupted the proceedings to such a degree that they could not go forward. An Illinois trial court faced such a situation during William Allen's trial for armed robbery.

Illinois v. Allen

397 U.S. 337 (1970)

MR. JUSTICE BLACK delivered the opinion of the Court.

The Confrontation Clause of the Sixth Amendment to the United States Constitution provides that: "In all criminal prosecutions, the accused shall enjoy the right to be confronted with the witnesses against him." One of the most basic of the rights guaranteed by the Confrontation Clause is the accused's right to be present in the courtroom at every stage of his trial. The question presented in this case is whether an accused can claim the benefit of this constitutional right to remain in the courtroom while at the same time he engages in speech and conduct which is so noisy, disorderly, and disruptive that it is exceedingly difficult or wholly impossible to carry on the trial.

[Allen was charged with and convicted of armed robbery. At his trial, he insisted on acting as his own attorney. During the jury selection process, Allen repeatedly disrupted the proceedings, doing such things as threatening the judge, refusing to follow the court's instructions, and tearing his advisory counsel's file apart and throwing its remains across the courtroom. The judge had Allen removed from the courtroom until such time as he could behave properly.

[After the lunch break, the judge allowed Allen to reappear in court. As before, Allen was very disruptive. He repeatedly yelled, "There is going to be no proceeding." Allen was once again removed from the courtroom.

[After this second removal, Allen remained out of the courtroom during the presentation of the State's **case-in-chief**, except that he was brought in on several occasions for purposes of identification. During one of these latter appearances, Allen responded to one of the judge's questions with vile and abusive language. After the prosecution's case had been presented, the trial judge reiterated his promise to Allen that he could return to the courtroom whenever he agreed to conduct himself properly. Allen gave some assurances of proper conduct and was permitted to be present through the remainder of the trial, principally his defense, which was conducted by his appointed counsel.

[Allen was convicted and sentenced to serve 10 to 30 years in prison. His conviction was affirmed by the Supreme Court of Illinois. Upon considering the denial of Allen's Petition for Habeas Corpus, the 7th Circuit Court of Appeals reversed, holding that a defendant has an absolute right to be present at his trial.]

The Court of Appeals [held] that the Supreme Court of Illinois was wrong in ruling that Allen had by his conduct relinquished his constitutional right to be present, declaring that:

> No conditions may be imposed on the absolute right of a criminal defendant to be present at all stages of the proceeding. The insistence of a de-

> fendant that he exercise this right under unreasonable conditions does not amount to a waiver. Such conditions, if insisted upon, should and must be dealt with in a manner that does not compel the relinquishment of his right.

The Court of Appeals felt that the defendant's Sixth Amendment right to be present at his own trial was so "absolute" that, no matter how unruly or disruptive the defendant's conduct might be, he could never be held to have lost that right so long as he continued to insist upon it, as Allen clearly did. Therefore the Court of Appeals concluded that a trial judge could never expel a defendant from his own trial and that the judge's ultimate remedy when faced with an obstreperous defendant like Allen who determines to make his trial impossible is to bind and gag him.

We cannot agree that the Sixth Amendment, the cases upon which the Court of Appeals relied, or any other cases of this Court so handicap a trial judge in conducting a criminal trial. We accept instead the statement of Mr. Justice Cardozo who, speaking for the Court in *Snyder v. Massachusetts*, 291 U.S. 97, 106 (1934), said: "No doubt the privilege (of personally confronting witnesses) may be lost by consent or at times even by misconduct." Although mindful that courts must indulge every reasonable presumption against the loss of constitutional rights, we explicitly hold today that a defendant can lose his right to be present at trial if, after he has been warned by the judge that he will be removed if he continues his disruptive behavior, he nevertheless insists on conducting himself in a manner so disorderly, disruptive, and disrespectful of the court that his trial cannot be carried on with him in the courtroom. Once lost, the right to be present can, of course, be reclaimed as soon as the defendant is willing to conduct himself consistently with the decorum and respect inherent in the concept of courts and judicial proceedings.

It is essential to the proper administration of criminal justice that dignity, order, and decorum be the hallmarks of all court proceedings in our country. The flagrant disregard in the courtroom of elementary standards of proper conduct should not and cannot be tolerated. We believe trial judges confronted with disruptive, contumacious, stubbornly defiant defendants must be given sufficient discretion to meet the circumstances of each case. No one formula for maintaining the appropriate courtroom atmosphere will be best in all situations. We think there are at least three constitutionally permissible ways for a trial judge to handle an obstreperous defendant like Allen: (1) bind and gag him, thereby keeping him present; (2) cite him for contempt; (3) take him out of the courtroom until he promises to conduct himself properly.

I

Trying a defendant for a crime while he sits bound and gagged before the judge and jury would to an extent comply with that part of the Sixth Amendment's purposes that accords the defendant an opportunity to confront the witnesses at the trial. But even to contemplate such a technique, much less see it, arouses a feeling that no person should be tried while shackled and gagged except as a last resort. Not only is it possible that the sight of shackles and gags might have a significant effect on the jury's feelings about the defendant, but the use of this technique is itself something of an affront to the very dignity and decorum of judicial proceedings that the judge is seeking to uphold. Moreover, one of the defendant's primary advantages of being present at the trial, his ability to communicate with his counsel, is greatly reduced when the defendant is in a condition of total physical restraint. It is in part because of these inherent disadvantages and limitations in this method of dealing with disorderly defendants that we decline to hold with the Court of Appeals that a defendant cannot under any possible circumstances be deprived of his right to be present at trial. However, in some situations which we need not attempt to foresee, binding and gagging might possibly be the fairest and most reasonable way to handle a defendant who acts as Allen did here.

II

In a footnote the Court of Appeals suggested the possible availability of contempt of court as a remedy to make Allen behave in his robbery trial. Of course, if the defendant is determined to prevent any trial, then a court in attempting to try the defendant for contempt is still confronted with the identical dilemma that the Illinois court faced in this case. And criminal contempt has obvious limitations as a sanction when the defendant is charged with a crime so serious that a very severe sentence such as death or life imprisonment is likely to be imposed. In such a case the defendant might not be affected by a mere contempt sentence when he ultimately faces a far more serious sanction. Nevertheless, the contempt remedy should be borne in mind by a judge in the circumstances of this case.

III

The trial court in this case decided under the circumstances to remove the defendant from the courtroom and to continue his trial in his absence until and unless he promised to conduct himself in a manner befitting an American courtroom. As we said earlier, we find nothing unconstitutional about this procedure. Allen's behavior was clearly of such an extreme and aggravated nature as to justify either his removal from the courtroom or his total physical restraint. Prior to his removal he was repeatedly warned by the trial judge that he would be removed from the courtroom if he persisted in his unruly conduct, and, as Judge Hastings observed in his dissenting opinion, the record demonstrates that Allen would not have been at all dissuaded by the trial judge's use of his criminal contempt powers. Allen was constantly informed that he could return to the trial when he would agree to conduct himself in an orderly manner. Under these circumstances we hold that Allen lost his right guaranteed by the Sixth and Fourteenth Amendments to be present throughout his trial.

IV

If our courts are to remain what the Founders intended, the citadels of justice, their proceedings cannot and must not be infected with the sort of scurrilous, abusive language and conduct paraded before the Illinois trial judge in this case. The record shows that the Illinois judge at all times conducted himself with that dignity, decorum, and patience that befit a judge. We do not hold that removing this defendant from his own trial was the only way the Illinois judge could have constitutionally solved the problem he had. We do hold, however, that there is nothing whatever in this record to show that the judge did not act completely within his discretion. Deplorable as it is to remove a man from his own trial, even for a short time, we hold that the judge did not commit legal error in doing what he did.

The judgment of the Court of Appeals is reversed.

FURTHER CASE LAW, REFLECTIONS, AND QUESTIONS

1. If a defendant is so disruptive that he must be removed from the courtroom, does the state have an obligation to provide him with access to the proceedings via closed-circuit television? Must he be given a telephone to speak with his attorney outside the courtroom? In other words, how far must the state go to protect a defendant's right to be present at trial when the accused will not behave well enough to remain in the courtroom?

2. In a situation like *Allen*, would it make a difference if the defendant was behaving improperly as a result of a mental illness beyond his control?

3. Does the confrontation clause guarantee a defendant the right to be present at all proceedings connected with his trial? *Kentucky v. Stincer*, 482 U.S. 730 (1987) involved the prosecution of a man charged with molesting three young children. Shortly after his trial began, the judge conducted an examination in his chambers of two of the children, ages eight and seven, to determine whether they were competent to testify. No substantive issues were dealt with during the examination, but only matters relating to the children's ability to distinguish the truth from lies and to recall and describe the facts of the case. Stincer was not permitted to attend this examination. The judge subsequently found the children competent to testify, and Stincer was convicted on the strength of their testimony and other evidence. Stincer appealed his conviction, asserting a Sixth Amendment right to be present in the judge's chambers during the competency hearing. The Supreme Court held that the Confrontation Clause does not guarantee a criminal defendant the right to be present at such a proceeding. The justices ruled that

since defense counsel was present and was allowed to cross-examine the children, Stincer's right to confrontation was not violated.

4. If a defendant voluntarily decides not to appear (or refuses to appear) at trial, does the trial court have to wait to begin or continue the proceedings until the defendant is present in court? The answer is no. It has consistently been found that a defendant who knowingly and voluntarily opts not to be present at trial waives his or her right to be present. In such a case the court may decide to proceed *in absentia* (in the absence.) "In deciding whether to try a defendant in absentia, the district court must make factual findings to determine whether a defendant's absence is knowing and voluntary and, if so, whether the public interest in proceeding with trial clearly outweighs the interests of the voluntarily absent defendant in attending his trial." *United States v. St. James*, 415 F.3d 800, 804 (8th Cir. 2005). What public interests are involved in proceeding without a defendant who has chosen not to be present?

Box 12.6 You Be the Judge

At the sentencing phase of Deck's capital murder trial, Deck was required to wear shackles in the courtroom. Deck's attorney objected on the grounds that it would make Deck seem dangerous to the jury. The prosecutor argued that the shackles were necessary for security and safety reasons, and since Deck had already been found guilty of murder, any additional impact on the jury would be minimal.

Were Deck's rights violated in the above scenario? What additional information might be helpful in answering this question?

See *Deck v. Missouri*, 544 U.S. 622 (2005)

Conclusion

"Trial by jury in criminal cases is fundamental to the American scheme of justice." This statement by Justice White in *Duncan v. Louisiana*, 391 U.S. 145, 149 (1968) reflects the importance of trial by jury possessed in the minds of the Founding Fathers. Although only a small percentage of prosecutions end with a jury trial, the very nature of the trial and its associated rights given to a person accused of a crime make it the hallmark of the American justice system. The fact-finding function of the trial, designed to be achieved through adversarial proceedings, aims to ferret out the truth, achieve justice, and protect an individual's liberty unless the government can prove guilt beyond a reasonable doubt.

Key to the trial process are the rights provided under the Fifth and Sixth Amendments. These rights help level the playing field and prevent wrongful convictions based on the might of the government versus the helplessness of an individual defendant. As William Blackstone famously stated, "it is better that ten guilty persons escape than that one innocent suffer." Whether or not one agrees with the specifics of "Blackstone's Ratio," it is undeniable that trial by jury limits the government's ability to impose arbitrary justice on suspected criminals.

In this chapter, we examined not only when a criminal defendant is entitled to a jury, but also what such a jury would look like. In addition to the right to a trial by a jury, we explored other valuable rights provided by the Fifth and Sixth Amendments related to jury trials. These amendments allow a defendant to be present at their trial, to have the help of an attorney, to present evidence and have witnesses (willing or unwilling) to testify on their behalf, to confront and cross-examine government witnesses, and to stand silent and require the government to present proof of guilt beyond a reasonable doubt. People may differ on which of these rights is most important, but most would agree that all are necessary for the outcome of a criminal trial to be trusted by society.

KEY TERMS

case-in-chief	jury panel
challenge for cause	jury pool
compulsory process clause	mistrial
confrontation clause	peremptory challenge
closing argument	petit jury
cross-examination	speedy trial
fair cross-section of the community	venire
hearsay	venue
hung jury	vicinage
jury instructions	voir dire
jury nullification	

REVIEW QUESTIONS

1. What is the essential function of a criminal trial?
2. What are the four factors used to determine if the right to a speedy trial has been violated? What is the remedy if a court concludes the right to a speedy trial has been violated?
3. When is a defendant entitled to a trial by jury?

4. What does it mean that a jury must represent a fair cross-section of the community? What groups cannot be systematically excluded?
5. What are the three distinct phases of the jury selection process? What is the main goal at each stage?
6. What is the difference between a challenge for cause and a peremptory challenge?
7. What is a Batson violation? How is this proven?
8. What rights fall under the umbrella of compulsory process?
9. Why is hearsay generally not allowed as evidence?
10. Under what circumstances may a trial proceed without the defendant's presence?

APPLYING THE LAW

Below are five hypothetical fact scenarios. To practice your understanding of the law that you learned in this chapter and your ability to apply it, answer each question posed by applying that law to the hypothetical scenarios. Your answers should be supported by relevant caselaw and judicially created rules and tests.

1. Washington state passed a law that for a full-time college student to be eligible for jury service, they must file a statement with the county clerk that they want to serve on a jury. Harmon, a student at Washington State University, was arrested and charged with robbery. After she was convicted at a jury trial, she appealed that the Washington law violated the fair cross-section of the community requirement of the 6th and 14th Amendments. Should Harmon's appeal be successful?

2. Jose, a Latino man, was called to serve on a jury for a trial involving Pedro, a Latino male charged with aggravated assault. During jury selection, Jose tells the court (1) he was a victim of an aggravated assault, and (2) he lives across the street from the defense attorney. When asked by the judge if he could be fair and impartial despite these items, Jose said, "Yes, I believe I can."

   Should Jose be excluded from the jury for cause?

3. Ann was charged with murder. She invoked her Miranda rights and chose not to testify at trial. During the closing argument, her attorney argued that the government had unfairly deprived her of the opportunity to tell her side of the story. In response, the prosecutor argued to the jury that Ann had several opportunities to explain her actions, including the opportunity to testify at trial, but chose to remain silent. Ann was found guilty. On appeal, she argued that the prosecutor's comments about her remaining silent violated her Fifth Amendment privilege against compulsory self-incrimination.

   Were Ann's rights violated?

4. Fred and Pete were arrested and charged with murder in 2005. The state chose to try Pete first and then use Pete as a witness against Fred. The state encountered many obstacles in trying Pete, finally obtaining a conviction after four years. During those four years, Fred and the state agreed to 11 continuances of Fred's trial. When the state requested a twelfth continuance, Fred objected and filed a motion to dismiss on speedy trial grounds. The motion was denied. After several more continuances, half of which were objected to by Fred, Fred went to trial in 2010, five years after his arrest. Fred was found guilty and given a life sentence.

   Fred appealed his conviction on speedy trial grounds. Based on the case law, what information should the appellate court obtain and consider before making a decision? How should the court rule?

5. Bill was a greyhound trainer. In January, he had a heart attack and was in the hospital for two weeks. While in the hospital, Bill's 55 greyhounds were not cared for. Ten dogs died, and the rest were seriously malnourished. Bill was arrested and charged with fifty-five counts of misdemeanor cruelty to animals. Each count carries a maximum sentence of four months in jail. After he is arraigned, Bill files a demand for a jury trial. Is Bill entitled to a jury trial?

ORAL ARGUMENTS

Baldwin v. New York: www.oyez.org/cases/1969/188
Barker v. Wingo: www.oyez.org/cases/1970-1979/1971/1971_71_5255/argument
Batson v. Kentucky: www.oyez.org/cases/1980-1989/1985/1985_84_6263/argument
Crawford v. Washington: www.oyez.org/cases/2003/02-9410
Davis v. Alaska: www.oyez.org/cases/1970-1979/1973/1973_72_5794/argument
Deck v. Missouri: www.oyez.org/cases/2004/04-5293
Doggett v. United States: www.oyez.org/cases/1991/90-857
Duncan v. Louisiana: www.oyez.org/cases/1967/410
Duren v. Missouri: www.oyez.org/cases/1978/77-6067
Griffin v. California: www.oyez.org/cases/1964/202
Holmes v. South Carolina: www.oyez.org/cases/2005/04-1327
Illinois v. Allen: www.oyez.org/cases/1969/606
Maryland v. Craig: www.oyez.org/cases/1980-1989/1989/1989_89_478/argument
Ramos v. Louisiana: www.oyez.org/cases/2019/18-5924
Rock v. Arkansas: www.oyez.org/cases/1980-1989/1986/1986_86_130/argument
Taylor v. Louisiana: www.oyez.org/cases/1970-1979/1974/1974_73_5744/argument
United States v. Martinez-Salazar: www.oyez.org/cases/1999/98-1255
Washington v. Texas: www.oyez.org/cases/1966/649
Williams v. Florida: www.oyez.org/cases/1969/927

REFERENCES

Lewis, A. (1964). *Gideon's trumpet.* Random House.

Scheflin, A., & Van Dyke, J. (1980). Jury nullification: The contours of a controversy. *Law and Contemporary Problems, 43*(4), 52–115.

Glossary

abandoned property: Personal property of which the owner intentionally relinquishes all rights to its control.

accuracy: Reliable fact-finding to ensure the guilty are punished, and the innocent remain free.

administrative searches: Searches conducted by government officials designed to determine whether there are violations of a large range of administrative regulations.

affiant: A person who signs an affidavit and swears to its truth before a notary public or some person authorized to take oaths

affidavit: A written statement voluntarily made under an oath or affirmation which is administered by a person who is authorized to do so by law.

Aguilar-Spinelli test: Test of probable cause that requires a search warrant affidavit detail an informant's credibility and basis of knowledge.

anonymous tip: Information provided to law enforcement from an unknown person.

anticipatory warrant: A warrant based upon an affidavit showing probable cause that at some future time specific evidence of a crime will be located at a particular place.

apparent authority: A person who police reasonably believe has authority to give consent to search.

appeal: The process by which a party may seek to obtain review and reversal by an appellate court of a lower court's decision based on an error in the application or interpretation of the law.

arraignment: An appearance before a court of law for the purpose of entering a plea to a criminal charge.

arrest: The act of taking an individual into custody for the purpose of charging the arrestee with a criminal offense.

arrest warrant: A document, based on a judicial finding that there is probable cause to believe a person committed a crime, authorizing police to arrest an individual for a criminal offense.

articulable suspicion: Suspicion that is capable of being expressed and explained.

attenuated: If the causal link or connection between the illegal conduct of the police and obtaining illegal evidence is weak enough the evidence may not be used against the defendant to prove guilt. Associated with fruit of the poisonous tree doctrine.

automobile exception: An exception to the warrant requirement that allows the police to conduct a warrantless search, based on probable cause, of a vehicle because of their inherent mobility and reduced expectation of privacy.

bail: A set amount of money or security given to a court by or on behalf of one accused of committing a crime to obtain release from incarceration and to ensure he or she appears for their court date.

Bail Reform Act of 1984: Federal law that authorized federal courts to detain defendants before trial based on the risk they posed to the community or the safety of others, even if they could afford bail.

basis of knowledge: Underlying circumstances from which one concludes a crime was committed.

Bill of Rights: The first ten amendments to the United States Constitution.

booking: The process of registering charges against an alleged offender by a police officer. This usually includes the recording of the suspect's name and address, the offense they were arrested for, the date and time of the booking, as well as fingerprinting and photographing the suspect.

Brady rule: The prosecution must turn over all exculpatory evidence to the defendant in a criminal case.

break in custody rule: A break in custody that is of sufficient length dissipates any coercive effects of an interrogation.

case brief: A simple and structured summary of a case decision.

case-in-chief: The portion of a trial where the party with the burden of proof in the case presents its evidence. In a criminal trial this is typically the prosecution.

caselaw: Body of law developed from judicial opinions or decisions over time.

certiorari: A court's decision to hear an appeal.

challenge for cause: A request that a prospective juror be dismissed because there is reason to believe the person cannot be fair, unbiased, or capable of serving as a juror.

closely regulated business: A type of business in which regulation is pervasive and long-standing.

collateral proceedings: Hearings not directly related to a defendant's trial.

complaint: A brief statement of the charges against the alleged offender.

compulsory process clause: Sixth Amendment right to compel the appearance of witnesses.

concurring opinion: An appellate opinion of one or more justices or judges which supports the result reached in a case for reasons not stated in the majority opinion.

confession: A statement made by the accused by which they acknowledge they are guilty of a crime.

confrontation clause: The Sixth Amendment right of a defendant to confront their accusers. Includes the right to cross-examine witnesses in court.

consent search: The voluntary agreement by someone of age and mentally capable to permit police to conduct a search.

corporeal lineup: Identification procedure where the suspect is physically present.

court of general jurisdiction Court that hears serious criminal and civil cases.

crime control perspective: One perspective developed by Packer that focuses on the efficient processing of offenders through the criminal justice system.

criminal procedure law: Comprises the legal rules and principles that regulate the administration of criminal procedure.

critical stage: A point during a criminal process where the actions may impact the rights or defenses of the accused, leading to the activation of their Sixth Amendment right to have a lawyer.

cross-examination: The questioning of an opponent's witness at a trial or at a hearing following the witness's direct examination.

curtilage: The area immediately surrounding a house where intimate activities take place. Considered to be part of the home.

custodial interrogation: Questioning by law enforcement officers after a suspect is taken into custody or deprived of freedom of action in any significant way.

deliberately elicit: When law enforcement officers purposefully and knowingly extract information from the subject through questioning or other actions. Such acts are the equivalent to interrogations.

derivative evidence: Evidence obtained as a direct or indirect result of illegally obtained evidence.

discovery: The process by which each party to a case learns of the evidence that the opposition plans to present. Exculpatory material evidence in possession of the prosecution must be turned over to the defense.

dissenting opinion: A written statement by a judge or justice expressing disagreement with the majority opinion of a court in a case and explaining the dissenting judge's reasoning for disagreeing with the majority's decision.

drug courier profile: A set of characteristics found to be typical of persons transporting illegal drugs. Law enforcement officers often rely on such profiles to justify stopping and question citizens as to if they are carrying illegal drugs.

due process clause: Clause in the Fourteenth Amendment that states no "No State [shall] deprive any person of life, liberty, or property, without due process of law."

due process perspective: One perspective developed by Packer that emphasizes the rights of criminal defendants as they are adjudicated through the criminal justice system.

emergency aid doctrine: An exception to the warrant requirement that allows the police to enter a home without a warrant to provide emergency assistance.

en banc: A court session in which a case is heard before all the judges of a court (before the entire bench) rather than by one judge or a three-member panel.

exclusionary rule: A judicially created prophylactic rule designed to safeguard the Fourth Amendment and other rights and ensures evidence obtained in violation of the Constitution is inadmissible at trial to prove guilt.

exigent circumstances: Exigent circumstances are urgent situations that necessitate immediate action, allowing law enforcement to bypass the need for a warrant when it would otherwise be required.

expert testimony: A witness who has specialized knowledge and training, who is permitted to testify to a jury about their opinions concerning a matter outside the knowledge of the average juror.

express waiver: When a suspect affirmatively relinquishes the right to counsel and the right to remain silent and agrees to speak with the police.

eyewitness: Someone present during an event who is often called upon to testify at a trial or identify parties involved in a crime.

eyewitness identification: The process where a witness identifies a suspect from a lineup, photo array, or show up, or testifies in court about a crime they witnessed, aiming to identify the perpetrator.

facts: In a case brief, the "facts" section provides a concise summary of the key events and circumstances that led to the legal dispute and the court's decision. It focuses on the legally relevant details, outlining the "who, when, what, where, and why" of the case. The facts section aims to capture the essential story of the case, highlighting the events that the court considered important in reaching its judgment.

fair cross-section of the community: The requirement that a jury must be selected from a group of individuals that fairly represents the community.

federalism: The division of power between states and a national government.

felony: More serious class of crimes, such as arson, murder, rape, robbery, etc., that are punishable by imprisonment in excess of one year.

fleeing felon rule: Common law rule that allowed officers to use deadly force against any fleeing suspect who was believed to have committed a felony.

fruit of the poisonous tree: Secondary or derivative evidence obtained from an illegal search or interrogation is generally excluded from trial.

functional equivalent of questioning: In considering if an interrogation has occurred court will consider if any words or actions on the part of the police that the police should know are reasonably likely to elicit an incriminating response. Announced in *Rhode Island v. Innis.*

fundamental fairness doctrine: A rule that applies the principles of due process to a judicial proceeding. Fundamental-Fairness is considered synonymous with due process.

good-faith exception: An exception to the exclusionary rule that allows illegally seized evidence to be admissible in court if police officers reasonably relied on a valid search warrant or statute that was later found to be defective or unconstitutional.

grabbing area: The area police may search without a warrant when arresting a suspect.

grand jury: A selection of citizens whose purpose is to determine whether or not there is probable cause to believe the accused committed the crime alleged. There can be up to 23 people who operate in secrecy, listening only to witnesses and evidence presented by the prosecution.

hearsay: A witness's testimony about what someone else said that is introduced to prove a matter asserted.

holding: In a case brief, the answer to the question posed in the issue.

hot pursuit: An exception to the warrant requirement that provides that police, when in pursuit of a suspect, may enter a premises without a warrant to prevent the escape or effectuate the arrest of someone suspected of committing or having committed a crime.

hung jury: When a jury in a trial cannot reach a unanimous or required supermajority verdict after deliberation. A hung jury leads to a mistrial.

impeachment: The process of challenging the testimony and credibility of a witness with conflicting evidence or testimony

impeachment exception: Illegally obtained evidence may be used in court to discredit a witness's testimony, even if that evidence would otherwise be inadmissible under the exclusionary rule.

implied waiver: Words or actions from a suspect that suggest and can be interpreted that they waive their right to remain silent, their right to counsel, and voluntarily agree to speak with the police.

incorporation: A legal principle that extends the protections of the Bill of Rights to state governments through the Fourteenth Amendment's Due Process Clause.

independent source doctrine: An exception to the fruit of the poisonous tree doctrine that states evidence seized as part of an unconstitutional search or interrogation is admissible at trial if the government can prove it would have been discovered by lawful means that are completely independent of the illegal police activity.

indictment: A formal written statement prepared by a prosecuting authority charging a person with a crime and returned by a grand jury.

indigent: Someone who cannot afford legal counsel for a criminal trial and is entitled to the appointment of counsel at public cost.

ineffective assistance of counsel: Counsel that is rendered ineffective because the performance was below the range of professionally competent assistance, and there was a reasonable probability that, but for counsel's unprofessional errors, the result of the proceeding would have been different.

inevitable discovery rule: An exception to the fruit of the poisonous tree doctrine that states evidence seized as part of an unconstitutional search or interrogation is admissible at trial if the government can prove that the evidence would have been inevitably discovered by lawful means regardless of the illegal police actions.

information: A formal written accusation signed by a prosecutor charging an individual with a crime.

initial appearance: A brief, non-adversarial process where a judge or magistrate informs the offender of the charges made in the complaint, determines if the police had probable cause to arrest the offender, and sets conditions for release.

interrogation: Questioning of a suspect or witness by police officers that includes any words or actions they know are reasonably likely to elicit an incriminating response.

inventory search: A warrantless search conducted when law enforcement takes custody of a vehicle or personal belongings, typically during an arrest or seizure. The primary purpose is not to search for evidence of a crime, but rather to document and safeguard property in the vehicle to prevent claims of theft or damage.

involuntary confession: A statement given during police questioning that is made under coercion or duress, where the suspect's will is overborne.

issue: The legal matter(s) that the court must make a decision regarding. The issue is often thought of as the matter in controversy and is always framed as a question.

jurisdiction: The authority of a court or legal entity to hear and decide a case.

jury: A body of people (typically twelve in number) sworn to give a verdict in a legal case on the basis of evidence submitted to them in court.

jury instructions: Directions given by a judge to a jury, explaining the relevant legal principles and standards they must apply to the facts of the case to reach a verdict.

jury nullification: A jury's refusal to follow the law and finds the defendant not guilty.

jury pool: The group of individuals summoned for jury duty.

knock and announce: The requirement that the police knock and announce their presence prior to executing a search warrant.

lineup: An investigative process where police arrange a suspect and other individuals in a row for a witness to identify or not identify the suspect.

magistrate: A civil or judicial official vested with limited judicial powers. In criminal cases typically decides preliminary matters.

majority opinion: A judicial opinion that is joined by more than half the judges deciding a case. Typically explains the basis for decision. Majority opinions frequently become precedent.

Miranda warnings: A requirement set by the U.S. Supreme Court in *Miranda v. Arizona* that prior to a custodial interrogation a person suspected of a crime must be informed that she or he has "the right to remain silent, the right to legal counsel, and the right to be told that anything she or he says can be used in court against" him or her.

misdemeanor: An offense that is less serious than a felony and can be punishable by fine, penalty, forfeiture, or short-term jail time of up to one year.

mistrial: The termination of a trial before its normal conclusion.

motor vehicle checkpoint: A special needs search where the police stop vehicles at a fixed point without articulable suspicion.

non-routine border search: A search at a border or its functional equivalent that goes beyond a limited intrusion. These searches can include more invasive methods, like strip searches, searches of electronics, or prolonged detentions, and may require a reasonable suspicion of unlawful activity.

non-testimonial evidence: Evidence that doesn't rely on someone speaking or writing about an event. Noncommunicative in nature.

objective expectation of privacy: An individual's belief that a specific location or item is private, and that belief is one that society is prepared to recognize as reasonable and legitimate.

open fields doctrine: The Fourth Amendment protection of privacy does not extend to areas distant from the home.

particularity requirement: A Fourth Amendment requirement that states a warrant must be specific in terms of the objects to be seized and the place to be searched.

per curiam: A per curiam decision is a court opinion issued in the name of the Court rather than a specific judge.

peremptory challenges: A method of dismissing a potential trial juror without having to cite a reason for the dismissal.

petit jury: A trial jury.

petitioner: The party who presents a petition to the court. On appeal, the petitioner is usually the party who lost in the lower court.

photographic lineup: An identification procedure in which photographs of a suspect and individuals who look similar to the suspect are presented to witnesses of a crime to determine whether the suspect committed the crime.

plain touch doctrine: Allows police officers to seize any contraband they clearly and instantly identify on the basis of touch during a legally conducted pat-down. To seize the contraband, it must be immediately apparent.

plain view doctrine: An exception to the warrant requirement that allows police officers to seize an item absent a warrant when they view the illegal item from a lawful vantage point, and it is immediately apparent the item is contraband or evidence of a crime.

plea bargain: An agreement between a defendant and a prosecutor where the defendant agrees to plead guilty or no contest to charges in return for a lessening in the severity or dismissal of some of the charges or some other benefit.

plurality opinion: An appellate decision where no single opinion receives a majority vote, but one opinion has the most votes of any other opinion. It has no precedential value.

precedent: A decision by an appellate court that serves as binding authority on the issue in question.

preliminary hearing: Adversarial hearing where the prosecution presents evidence to a judge seeking to establish probable cause to believe the accused committed the crime alleged. If the judge finds probable cause, which they often do, the accused is bound over for trial.

pretextual arrest: An arrest of a person for a minor offense for the opportunity to investigate the person's involvement in a more serious offense for which there is no lawful grounds to make an arrest.

pretrial motion: A request for a ruling or an order before the commencement of trial. Examples include motion to suppress, discovery, and continuance.

probable cause: Facts and circumstances that would lead a reasonably intelligent and prudent person to believe that a crime has been committed by an individual.

protective sweep: A quick and limited search of premises incident to an arrest, and conducted to protect the safety of police officers or others.

public safety exception: Confessions obtained without Miranda warnings are admissible in court if the circumstances in which the confession was obtained created a clear and present danger to public or officer safety and if the officers reasonably believe that the information given by the confession will quell the situation.

rationale: In a case brief, a summary of the legal reasons given by the court in support of its decision.

reasonable suspicion: An objective factual basis to believe a fact to be true. Less than probable cause but more than a hunch. The legal standard of proof required to conduct a stop and a frisk.

reasonableness clause: The first portion of the Fourth Amendment, which states: "The right of the people to be secure in secure in their persons, houses, papers, and effects, against unreasonable searches and seizures, shall not be violated..."

respondent: The person with whom an appeal has been taken and who defends the appeal. Typically, the party who won in the lower court.

routine border search: Unintrusive search at the border or its functional equivalent that may be performed without any suspicion.

scrupulously honored: The police may question an individual who has invoked their right to silence about a crime different in nature, time, and place after waiting a significant period of time and giving a fresh set of Miranda warnings.

search: A governmental examination of a person or person's premises, papers, and effects, when they have a reasonable expectation of privacy, to find evidence of criminal activity.

search incident to arrest: An exception to the warrant requirement that states the police can always search a suspect and the area within their immediate control when done contemporaneously to arrest.

search warrant: An official order based on probable cause and authorized by a neutral and detached magistrate allowing law enforcement to search someone's home or other location for specific persons or items to be seized.

seizure: The taking of property allegedly used in connection with criminal activity by a law enforcement officer with the interest in retaining that property in custody.

selective incorporation: Only selected provisions in the Bill of Rights should be incorporated and made applicable to state court proceedings via the Due Process Clause in the Fourteenth Amendment.

selective prosecution: A prosecutorial decision to single out certain defendants for constitutionally impermissible reasons outside the criminal justice system, such as race, class, gender, etc.

self-incrimination: Giving evidence of something, by word or action, that could subject a person to criminal prosecution.

self-representation: A choice by a defendant to represent himself or herself in a court of law. This is typically discouraged by the courts but is a constitutionally guaranteed right.

sentencing hearing: A hearing held by a trial court before a sentence is pronounced.

show up: An identification procedure in which the police present a. single suspect to an eyewitness and then ask the eyewitness whether the. suspect is the perpetrator.

special needs searches: Searches conducted absent probable cause or reasonable suspicion that do not serve the normal needs of law enforcement.

speedy trial: The defendant is tried for their alleged crimes within a reasonable time period. Guaranteed by the Sixth Amendment.

stale: A warrant becomes invalid if not executed after a specific time period.

standing: The right to assert a constitutional violation. A person must be able to show that they were personally aggrieved because of illegal or unconstitutional activity.

Star Chamber: A former court of inquisitorial and criminal jurisdiction in England that sat without a jury and that became noted for its arbitrary methods and severe punishments. Abolished in 1641.

stare decisis: The doctrine of precedent whereby judgments made by previous courts guide the decisions of other courts in similar cases.

state supreme court: Typically, the highest level of state appellate courts.

stop: A type of seizure where the police temporarily detain someone based on at least reasonable suspicion.

stop and frisk: A police practice where officers can temporarily detain a person, ask them questions, and conduct a limited search (frisk) of their outer clothing for weapons if they have a reasonable suspicion of criminal activity.

subjective expectation of privacy: An individual's opinion that a certain location or situation is private which varies greatly from person to person.

suggestive identification procedure: Identifications that influence the result of an identification procedure by highlighting one of the participants.

supremacy clause: Clause in the U.S. Constitution that federal law takes precedence over any conflicting state law.

testimonial evidence: Statements or declarations made by a witness under oath or affirmation, presented as proof in a legal setting.

total incorporation: The entire Bill of Rights should be made applicable to states via the Due Process Clause of the Fourteenth Amendment.

trespass doctrine: The practice used by the Court prior to *Katz*, which required a physical intrusion by a government actor for a Fourth Amendment search to take place.

true bill: A formal indictment by a grand jury based on probable cause and a finding of sufficient evidence to warrant a criminal charge.

venire: Panel of individuals from which a jury will be chosen.

venue: Judicial district where the crime occurred and trial is presumptively held.

vicinage: The district in which a crime takes place and from which the accused is entitled to have an impartial jury selected as required by the Sixth Amendment.

vindictive prosecution: A decision by a prosecutor to retaliate against a defendant for exercising his or her constitutional right.

voir dire: The questioning of potential jurors by both the prosecution and defense attorneys to determine their qualifications and suitability to serve on a jury to ensure a nonbiased and fair jury.

Wade-Gilbert rule: A suspect has the right to have an attorney present at a post-indictment lineup. If an attorney is not present at the lineup, testimony regarding the lineup is not admissible at trial. An in-court identification of a suspect following an illegal lineup is permitted if the prosecution can prove by clear and convincing evidence that the in-court identification was made independent of the lineup.

writ of certiorari: A request made by either the defendant or the state for a higher court review a case previously decided by a lower appellate court.

Table of Cases

Primary cases and page references are found in **bold**.

Index